MACRO/MICRO

A BRIEF INTRODUCTION TO SOCIOLOGY

Second Edition

Lorne Tepperman

UNIVERSITY OF TORONTO

Michael Rosenberg

DAWSON COLLEGE

WITH THE ASSISTANCE OF ANDREW TEPPERMAN

PRENTICE HALL CANADA INC., SCARBOROUGH, ONTARIO

Canadian Cataloguing in Publication Data

Tepperman, Lorne, 1943–
      Macro/micro : a brief introduction to sociology

2nd ed.
ISBN 0-13-065392-6

1. Sociology.   I. Rosenberg, M. Michael.
II. Title

HM51.T47 1995   301   C94-931342-4

Prentice-Hall, Inc., Englewood Cliffs, New Jersey
Prentice-Hall International (UK) Limited, London
Prentice-Hall of Australia, Pty. Limited, Sydney
Prentice-Hall Hispanoamericana, S.A., Mexico City
Prentice-Hall of India Private Limited, New Delhi
Prentice-Hall of Japan, Inc., Tokyo
Simon & Schuster Asia Private Limited, Singapore
Editora Prentice-Hall do Brasil, Ltda., Rio de Janeiro

ISBN 0-13-065392-6

Acquisitions Editor: Marjorie Munroe
Developmental Editor: Linda Gorman
Copy Editor: Agatha Cinader
Production Editor: Valerie Adams
Production Coordinator: Deborah Starks
Permissions/Photo Research: Karen Taylor
Cover Design: Julie Fletcher
Cover Image: Diana Ong/Superstock
Page Layout: Jerry Langton
Indexer: Andrew Tepperman

   3 4 5   CC   99 98 97 96

Printed and bound in the United States of America.

Every reasonable effort has been made to obtain permissions for
all articles and data used in this edition. If errors or omissions
have occurred, they will be corrected in future editions provided
written notification has been received by the publisher.

 This book is printed on recycled paper.

TABLE OF CONTENTS

3 SOCIALIZATION 62

6 ETHNIC AND RACE RELATIONS

9 WORK AND THE ECONOMIC ORDER...................250

10 POPULATION AND ENVIRONMENT

PREFACE

Readers liked the first edition of MACRO/MICRO. That meant that, in revising the book for a second edition, we faced a hard choice: should the book stay the same, with a few minor changes, or not? Staying the same would be easy for us and, we think, okay with our readers. But that is not what we ended up doing. You can tell that from the change in the book's size. The second edition is about 100 pages longer than the first edition.

Why did we take the not-so-easy path? The reason is, since the first edition came out, we have changed, Canadian sociology has changed, and the world has changed. The second edition of MACRO/MICRO reflects these changes. Without going into detail, here are some of the changes you will notice:

(1) a new chapter on gender relations (Chapter 7), and new treatments of politics (in Chapter 11) and the environment (in Chapter 10);
(2) a much more international flavour, with insights and examples drawn from around the world;
(3) a large number of up-to-date references which make this edition useful as a starting point for term papers;
(4) an even stronger focus on world events, including a switch from extracts of academic work to textual inserts by journalists.

In writing the first edition, we assumed that it is possible to explain anything sociological to anyone who wants to understand it. The book's popularity proved us right. In writing the second edition, we have continued to make this assumption. The result is an even richer, more provocative conversation about sociology than before — but a book that is still reader-friendly.

There are certain features of the new edition that bear special mention. First, this edition is marked by an international outlook. The only way for students to learn about the various influences on, and forms of, social life that exist in a modern world, and the kinds of institutional arrangements that support them is by studying society from an international perspective. So in this textbook Canadian society is examined against a backdrop of societies around the world and society as a whole.

A second feature of the book is its historical perspective. Some factors affecting social life today have been developing for decades, if not centuries. They include the spread of capitalistic values and modern technology, the collapse of communism and the equality movements for women and racial minorities. To understand social life today, students must know about these historic forces and trends.

A third feature of the book is its future orientation. A future-looking approach is, and always has been, key in social science. We believe a future orientation is important for two main reasons. First, students—in fact, people in general—are increasingly anxious about their futures, whether personal, societal or as part of the human species. Second, trying to predict the future forces us to evaluate our social theories more rigorously than we do when we are trying to explain the past or present.

A fourth feature of the book is the provision of learning aids. You will note that each chapter begins with an overview and ends with a summary. Whenever we introduce a concept in the text, we identify it in boldfaced type; a glossary at the end of the book defines each term clearly and concisely. Also at the end of the book you will find a list of suggested readings. Finally, for each chapter, we have provided discussion questions and exercises to help the student understand and review the topic.

Like the first edition, the second edition examines the main paradigms of sociology. But this second edition examines not three but four paradigms: now, the feminist paradigm is included too, along with structural functionalism, the conflict approach and symbolic interactionism. Most important, the book explains the relationship between macro- and micro-sociological processes. For it is our belief that, in social life, the personal is political (and vise versa), and just as C. Wright Mills said, public issues are usually the flip side of personal troubles.

We think we got it right. Tell us what *you* think and, most important, enjoy!

ACKNOWLEDGEMENTS

This revision began in the fall of 1992, when we solicited the comments of people who used, and didn't use, the first edition of MACRO/MICRO in their classroom teaching. These comments were central to our plans for the second edition.

Work began in earnest in the spring of 1993. The single most important helper was Andrew Tepperman, who organized, wrote up and inserted chunks of material from outside Canada. At 23 already an excellent scholar and writer, Andrew proved to be the perfect research assistant. Thanks, Andrew.

As always, our work benefitted considerably from the comments of known and anonymous readers. But this time, it benefitted more than usual from our own students.

At the University of Toronto, Professor Tepperman recruited readers from among his introductory sociology students. They included Ada Aizenberg, Steven Beg, Dana Zedner, Allene Huber, Jo-Anne Kennedy, Steve Unger and Anita Winter. A few teaching assistants also provided valuable, and in some cases, detailed criticism; they were Tracey Aaron, Slobodan Drakulic, Chris Kevill and Danita Mushkat. Colleagues at the University of Toronto — notably Ed Thompson, Nancy Howell and Rosemary Gartner — also provided detailed suggestions for improvement. Thanks to all of you for your enthusiastic, thoughtful and critical comments.

Outside the University of Toronto, we benefitted from the comments of anonymous reviews at several stages in the proceedings. We later learned that they included Jim Jackson (Humber College), Dave Dwyer (Fanshawe College) and Jean Ballard-Kent (University College of the Fraser Valley). Far less anonymous was our good friend Jim Curtis, at the University of Waterloo. Near the end of the project, he offered "big picture" suggestions about how to smooth and streamline the text. Thanks, Jim, you're the best.

In this edition, almost all of the textual inserts are drawn from Toronto's *Globe and Mail* newspaper. What we like about the *Globe* is that it is always well-written and it opens up a window on the world outside Canada.

We have particularly benefitted from the excellent journalism of foreign correspondents John Stackhouse in India, Isabel Vincent in South America and Jan Wong in China. (Tepperman takes an unreasonable pride in the fact that Vincent was once his student in Introductory Sociology.) Thank you, *Globe and Mail* (especially Amanda Blake) for letting us use your material, and thank you, journalists, for being (often) such good sociologists.

The discussions of nurses and nursing in Chapter 7 are adapted from a module on sociology for nurses, co-authored by Tom Callaghan and Lorne Tepperman (1993). The reference for this source is Callaghan, T.J. and L. Tepperman (1993) *Sociology and Nursing Practice*. Scarborough: Prentice Hall Canada. Thanks, Tom, for letting me use this material.

At Prentice Hall Canada, the process of book-making went as smoothly as it always does. Mike Bickerstaff, the Acquisitions Editor, got the ball rolling. Lisa Penttila, our first Developmental Editor, provided advice and encouragement. Ed O'Connor, our second Developmental Editor, provided more of the same. The ball was then passed to Valerie Adams, the Production Editor, Agatha Cinader, the Copy Editor, and Andrew Tepperman, the Indexer. They were all great, but we want to single out Agatha for praise. She did an enormous amount of work to smooth the writing and still managed to keep a cheerful disposition all the while. Amazing! If you like the photos — and we do — you have Karen Taylor to thank for them. In fact, everyone at Prentice Hall is great to work with — totally professional and good-humoured. Thanks guys.

This book is dedicated to our students — the ones at the University of Toronto and at Dawson College on whom we crash-tested our material, and students elsewhere who are reading this book. We hope they find the ideas interesting and provocative.

C H A P T E R

1

All sociologists watch everyday life. The more closely we watch it, the more complex the patterns of relationships we can see.

Dick Hemingway

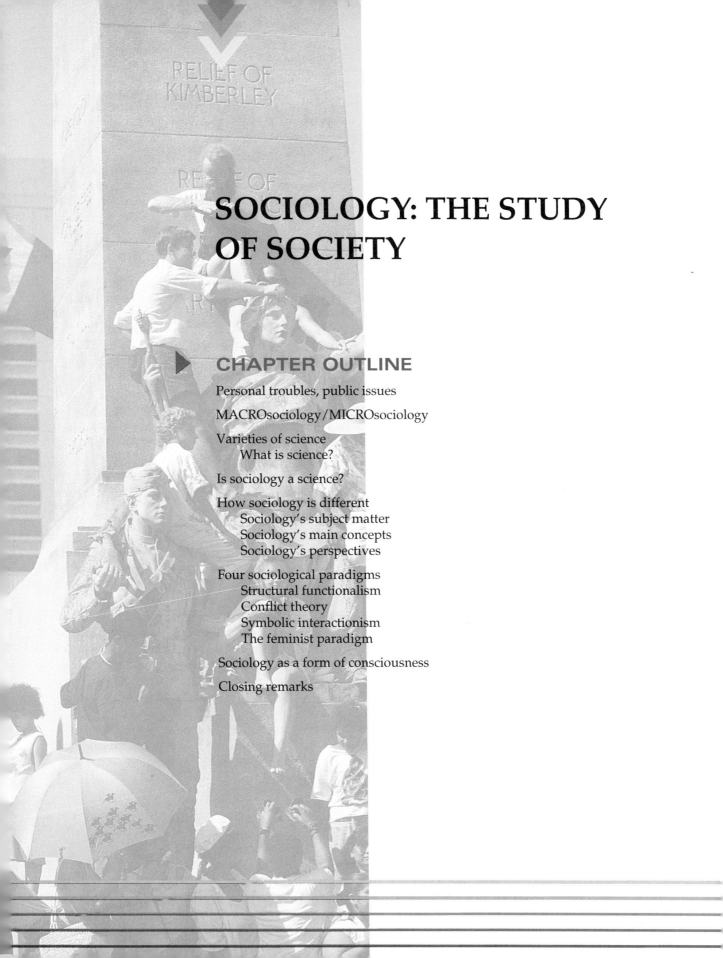

SOCIOLOGY: THE STUDY OF SOCIETY

▶ **CHAPTER OUTLINE**

PERSONAL TROUBLES, PUBLIC ISSUES

No one is born with plans to become a sociologist. Young children know that they will have a job when they grow up, but probably they think of becoming fire fighters, police officers, teachers, doctors, nurses, or rock stars — not sociologists.

Yet all of us are sociologists of a kind by the time we grow up: not by engaging in formal scientific teaching or research, but by trying to understand our own lives and the lives of people around us. That kind of understanding — usually called common sense — gives us explanations about people's behaviour and the society we live in. Most of the time, for most of what we do, this common-sense sociological knowledge is good enough.

We will consider the strengths and weaknesses of common-sense knowledge later in this chapter, but you may already realize that there are many questions that common sense cannot answer adequately: Why are some people rich and others poor? Why is the divorce rate so high? Why is the murder rate in the United States much higher than it is in Canada? Why do the native peoples have such a high suicide rate? Why do many people get upset about the arrival of a few illegal immigrants? and so on.

Some of these questions may interest you, others may not. But even when it comes to your personal life there will be many questions for which common sense has no answer: Why should I keep going to school? When am I going to learn something that will help me get a job? Why do I have to put up with so many rules wherever I go? Why are my parents always saying that television and rock music are junk? Where did that kid Frank's father get so much money?

Like other people, sociologists have thought about all of these questions, and many more. Sociologists, however, want to replace common-sense understanding with scientific explanation. They study lives and relationships in an attempt to understand how people are affected by the society in which they live. That means that sociologists are fascinated by big "public issues" such as poverty, race, and the impact of technology. But they recognize that there is another side to these public issues, a personal side. They know that your "personal" problems are similar to many other people's problems. Often, these are problems our society ought to try to solve, because individuals cannot solve them. In that sense, many of our problems are really the personal side of public issues.

Sociologists know that understanding and finding solutions to both public issues and personal problems requires clear thinking and careful research. Common sense and personal experience are just not enough to help you understand how the world works and how your own life fits in. Instead of depending on common sense, sociologists have developed a variety of concepts, theories and scientific research methods, many of which we will discuss in this book.

Our starting point is the connection sociologists make between personal problems and public issues. In terms of concepts and research, it is a connection between what sociologists call macrosociology and microsociology. (And that, incidentally, is why we titled this book *MACRO/MICRO*!)

MACROsociology/ MICROsociology

Now it is time for a formal definition of sociology. Scholars have defined it in a great many ways, but most sociologists think of sociology as the scientific study of human society and social behaviour.

Humans are "social" beings in the sense that most of the things we do are done together with other people. That's why sociologists take as their subject matter the social groups we create when we join together with others. They range from small groups — as few as two people — to large corporations and even whole societies. When looking at social groups, sociologists study the various ways in which group membership affects the behaviour and experiences of individuals.

As you can imagine, this is an enormous area of study. However, most of what sociologists look at falls into one of two related but distinct subfields: macrosociology and microsociology.

Macrosociology is the study of social institutions (for example, the Roman Catholic Church, the Canadian economy, or the government of Britain) and large social groups (for example, ethnic minorities or college students.) It also includes the study of social processes and patterns that characterize whole societies (for example, social control, social change), and the system of social arrangements that makes up a society. Macrosociology, then, studies the large patterns that large groups of people form over long periods of time.

The other side of sociology is microsociology. It looks at social institutions and social groups from a different point of view. Microsociology examines the processes and patterns of face-to-face interaction that take place among people within groups. Generally, then, microsociology is the analysis of small groups (for example, a rock band, a street gang, your classroom, your best friend's family). It studies the interactions, negotiations and daily struggles for power which, together, produce the stable and enduring patterns macrosociologists like to study.

The contrast with macrosociology is obvious. Where macrosociology takes a broad view of society and a long view of social change — often in terms of decades, centuries or even millennia — microsociology studies what may happen in the course of a conversation, a party, a classroom lecture or a love affair.

The differences in perspective show up in a variety of ways. Macrosociologists are likely to emphasize how slowly things change and how remarkably persistent a social pattern is as it imprints itself on one generation after another. By contrast, microsociologists are likely to emphasize how rapidly and subtly things change. They see people constantly creating and refining their relationships and in this way, creating and refining the social order.

To the new student of sociology, these differences may seem like impossible barriers between the two subfields, but they are not. Helped by what the great American sociologist C. Wright Mills called the sociological imagination, we can see that these two approaches to sociology are merely different pictures of the social world that are equally real. The trick is to understand how the large and the small, the macro and micro, fit together. Indeed, that is the purpose of this book.

Combining macro and micro approaches can improve our understanding of the world. Consider a common social phenomenon: racial discrimination in the workplace. From the macro perspective, racial discrimination is a large-scale social process affecting millions of people. Yet, from the micro perspective, it only occurs because (some) people make certain assumptions about skin colour. They think of other racial groups as superior or inferior to their own, as more or less intelligent, lazier or more diligent, and so on. Thus, individual people who assign values to physical features are at the bottom of the discrimination problem.

For this reason, microsociologists might study why and how certain physical features came to have those meanings. Or they might study how people act out those meanings by engaging in discrimination in a particular workplace. However, discrimination is not *only* an individual issue. It is perpetuated because discrimination benefits certain groups economically. That's why macrosociologists might study *how* face-to-face discrimination provides ongoing economic advantages for the racial majority.

C. Wright Mills (1959) wrote that the **sociological imagination** is the ability to see connections between large and small, changing and unchanging, portions of social life. It requires an awareness of the relation between individuals and the wider society. It helps us to look at our own personal experiences in a different, more objective way. It forces us to ask how our lives are shaped by the larger social context in which we live. Finally, the sociological imagination helps us to see society as the result of millions of people working out their own personal lives.

Imagine sociology as the study of a complex woven tapestry we call "society." Each strand is a single human life. Sociology studies the laws by which these strands combine and come apart, to come together again in a new, never-to-be-repeated pattern. It is sociology's concern with discovering the laws of social life that, ultimately, makes sociology a science.

VARIETIES OF SCIENCE

What is "science"?

We have mentioned several times now that sociology is a science. Before going on, we had better clarify what we mean by "science" and in what sense we can consider sociology a science.

All of us are able to remember our experiences and draw lessons from them. Jack tells us, "Last week, the veal at Smith's supermarket was great but the vegetables were terrible, so tomorrow I will get the hamburger I need at Smith's store and buy my tomatoes at Sally's corner grocery." We do not need scientific study to make these kinds of ordinary, everyday decisions. As we noted earlier, experience and common sense are usually just fine for our daily needs.

In fact, common sense and remembered experience build up over a long time into something people call folk wisdom. This folk wisdom contains many "rules of thumb" — rules of behaviour that people have found useful over the course of time. Rules of thumb often become pieces of popular advice; for example, "Don't go swimming right after eating a heavy meal." Here are a few more examples from a collection by Tom Parker (1983) called *Rules of Thumb*:

- Thinly cut cheese tastes more flavourful than thickly cut cheese.
- Expect to lose one sock each time you do the laundry.
- In editing something you have written, when in doubt, cross it out.

We would not consider any of these to be scientific statements, even if they make sense to us and seem true. Why not? The difference between common sense and science is that common sense is *not* carefully tested with data; scientific knowledge is.

The danger in relying on common sense to understand society is clear when we examine some of the "common-sense" ideas expressed in Exhibit 1.1. This excerpt comes from an Ann Landers newspaper column, which is known for its common-sense approach to people's problems. In this excerpt, not only do many of the ideas expressed sound ordinary and familiar; they sound

EXHIBIT 1.1   *One person's guide to being human*

Dear Ann Landers:

Your advice reaches millions of readers daily. I ran across these rules for being human and have been passing them along whenever I get the chance. . . . M.M., Ashland, ORE.

The Rules for Being Human

You will receive a body. You may like it or hate it, but it will be yours for as long as you live. How you take care of it or fail to take care of it can make an enormous difference in the quality of your life.

You will learn lessons. You are enrolled in a full-time, informal school called Life. Each day, you will be presented with opportunities to learn what you need to know. The lessons presented are often completely different from those you *think* you need.

There are no mistakes, only lessons. Growth is a process of trial, error and experimentation. You can learn as much from failure as you can from success. Maybe more.

A lesson is repeated until it is learned. A lesson will be presented to you in various forms until you have learned it. When you have learned it (as evidenced by a change in your attitude and ultimately your behavior), then you can go on to the next lesson.

Learning lessons does not end. There is no stage of life that does not contain some lessons.

As long as you live there will be something more to learn.

"There" is no better than "Here." When your "there" has become a "here," you will simply discover another "there" that will again look better than your "here." Don't be fooled by believing that the unattainable is better than what you have.

Others are merely mirrors of you. You cannot love or hate something about another person unless it reflects something you love or hate about yourself. When tempted to criticize others, ask yourself why you feel so strongly.

What you make of your life is up to you. You have all the tools and resources you need. What you create with those tools and resources is up to you. Remember that through desire, goal setting and unflagging effort you can have anything you want. Persistence is the key to success.

The answers lie inside you. The solutions to all of life's problems lie within your grasp. All you need to do is ask, look, listen and trust.

You will forget all this. Unless you consistently stay focused on the goals you have set for yourself, everything you've just read won't mean a thing. . . .

Source: Ann Landers, "One person's guide to being human" *The Boston Globe*, Saturday, June 26, 1993, p. 39

believable and encouraging. You feel good after reading Ann Landers: as if, now, you can put your life in order and everything will be okay. That's what common sense advice is *supposed* to do for you.

Unfortunately, sociological research would lead us to disagree with most of the advice offered in this excerpt. (It's unfortunate because you may end up feeling worried or sad after reading some sociology. On the other hand, sociology is organized to tell the truth, not make you feel good!)

The advice offered in this excerpt is based on what sociologists have called a "voluntaristic" view of life, meaning that it focuses attention on people's desire or *will* (from the Latin word, *voluntas*, meaning "will") to live in certain ways.

According to this view, people's lives reflect what they *want* them to reflect: their ideas, attitudes and values. People with good ideas, attitudes and values will have good lives; people with bad ideas, attitudes and values will have bad lives. That is why this excerpt urges us to think of life as an ongoing lesson we must learn from. It says explicitly "What you make of your life is up to you" and "The answers [to life's questions] lie within your grasp."

Is that really true? Most sociologists would disagree with such voluntaristic common sense, pointing to examples like the following:

(1) certain kinds of people (e.g., people who are poor) get sick more often and die at younger ages than other kinds of people (e.g., people who are rich);

(2) certain kinds of people (e.g., people who are black) are less likely to get hired for a job than other kinds of people (e.g., people who are white);

(3) certain kinds of people (e.g., married women, even those who work outside the home) end up doing more housework than other kinds of people (e.g., married men).

Do you really think that poor people *want* to die younger? or black people *want* to be unemployed? or married women *want* to do more housework? or that these people lack the right attitudes and values, as the common-sense argument seems to say? That, if only they changed their ways of thinking, they would live longer, get better jobs, and do less housework? Or, on the other hand, do they experience problems because the circumstances within which they live cause, or force, these people to experience things they would prefer to avoid?

This question is at the heart of sociology — indeed, all social science. It raises additional questions like: What do we mean by "free will"? What do we mean by "cause and effect"? Where do the ideas contained in "common sense" come from? Does "common sense" work better for some groups in society (e.g., rich, white men) than for other people (e.g., poor, black women)?

By the end of this book, you will have a beginner's answer to all of these questions. But for the time being understand that, because of their biases, common-sense explanations are more likely to be wrong than right. Sociologists would like to achieve a higher batting average. That's why they take a scientific, instead of common-sense, approach to understanding everyday life.

Science is the discovery, explanation, and prediction of events in the world we experience, and of the relations between these events. Science requires *research*, while common sense does not. By research, we mean the application of logical, systematic methods to verifiable evidence. The **scientific method** requires us to follow a systematic, organized series of steps that ensures as much objectivity as possible in researching a problem. The process forces us to construct theories, collect evidence, test predictions against careful observations, and accurately record our findings. If our predictions fail, we must change or reject our original theory.

To give a better idea of the difference between science and non-science (or common sense), let's consider an issue about which most people have an opinion: namely, the ways men and women drive automobiles. Insurance companies have long known that young men have more automobile accidents than young women do, but there are two competing explanations: (1) in a given year, young men drive more often, and longer distances, than young women do; or (2) young men drive more dangerously (for example, they are more likely to speed, or to drive while intoxicated) than young women do.

It is worth knowing which answer is more correct and which cause of accidents is more important. If we know the right answer we can take steps to reduce traffic accidents and fatalities. But we cannot know the answer without collecting data.

For example, we can collect data on how many kilometres people drive, and how many accidents they have, per year. With these data, we can calculate an annual accident rate: the number of accidents per 10,000 kilometres driven. If the annual accident rate is the same for young men and young women, then there is no difference in the "dangerousness" of male and female driving. In other words, explanation (1) is valid and there is no support for (2).

On the other hand, if the annual accident rate is *not* the same for young men and women, then explanation (1) is not valid and there may be support for explanation (2). If so, we now have to collect data on the *ways* that men and women drive cars: how often they drink and drive, how quickly they drive, whether they obey the traffic rules, and so on.

Researchers of driving behaviour have done this work and found that, in all of these respects, young men drive more recklessly than young women. A scientist then wants to ask *why* they do that. Is it genetic, something to do with the hormone levels in young men? Is it a universal feature of men growing up, one of the ways young men grow into adulthood, a *rite of passage* that involves risk-taking, danger and luck? Or is it a feature of our own society's view of adolescence, masculinity and the relationship between people and machinery?

These are the questions that go through a scientist's mind after someone has asked an interesting question. This brief example has suggested some of the special features of scientific method and thinking.

First, science tries to be objective, not subjective. *Objectivity* is a way of interpreting events, or the relations among them, by using reason and the best evidence possible. To do this means avoiding personal bias, prejudice or preconception. The opposite, *subjectivity* is a tendency to interpret reality from a viewpoint shaped by our own experiences, emotions, opinion, values, and beliefs.

Scientists recognize that, in their own everyday lives, subjectivity is bound to creep in. As human beings, we all run the risk of jumping to conclusions without enough regard for evidence or reason. Being scientific in all aspects of our daily life is impossible. What's more, it denies the part of us that is, and ought to be, intuitive and emotional. Nevertheless, if science is to be more than a collection of personal prejudices and anecdotes, the scientist must strive to be as objective as possible.

The difference between objectivity and subjectivity can be clarified by an example. Dutch sociologist Ruut Veenhoven (1984) has noted that many people criticize life in modern societies. Often they say that life is less satisfying today than it was when they were younger, or in pioneer days, or perhaps even than it is for people living in small pre-industrial villages scattered around the globe. This view of modern society is subjective because it states a personal opinion, shaped by personal experience. It does not use data collected in reliable ways to make a careful comparison of our own society with other ones.

For his part, Veenhoven uses data from hundreds of studies carried out around the world to show that the average person's satisfaction with life is just as high in our own society as it is in any society surveyed. As well, measures of health care, life expectancy, and standard of living suggest that our society may also be better than most. On these objective grounds, we cannot conclude that life is better or more satisfying in another kind of society.

This is not to say that Veenhoven is right, that life really *is* better in our own society than anywhere else. However, it means that if we are going to debate this issue objectively, we must carefully define what we mean by "better" and collect relevant information to defend our position.

This illustrates a second characteristic of science: its concern with developing and testing theories. A *theory* is an explanation of the causal relationship between various phenomena or events. An effective theory will not only have explanatory power; it will also enable the scientist to predict future events. In that sense, explanation and prediction are two sides of the same coin.

A well-reasoned theory provides *hypotheses* that allow us to test the theory. A hypothesis formulates a research problem in such a way that we may test a theory empirically, with data. It takes the form of a proposition or prediction about the relation between two or more events. When we make hypotheses, we predict the future. When we collect data to test our predictions, we find out if the data support our theory. If the data do not show what we predicted, our theoretical explanation is thrown into doubt: we need to revise the theory.

Let's see how this works in our previous example by looking at two of the possible explanations for the high rate of male auto accidents. One possibility is that the behaviour is genetic: young men just can't avoid stomping on the accelerator pedal. Another is that it is cultural: in our culture, young men feel their manhood is in doubt unless they risk their lives while driving. They *choose* to stomp on the accelerator pedal.

Now, if the second (or cultural) explanation is valid, we should be able to prove it in any number of different ways. For example, we should be able to find cultures where people have conceptions of masculinity that do not involve fast driving. In those cultures, young men and women will have the same accident rates. We would do this research by collecting data from a variety of different societies. This is called *comparative (or cross-national) research.*

Likewise, if the cultural explanation is valid, we should be able to distinguish among young men in our own culture and predict their respective driving records. According to our theory, young men who feel secure about their manhood won't feel they have to prove their bravery to anyone. As a result, they will have a lower accident rate than young men who feel unsure about their manhood. We would do this research by carrying out a *survey* of young men, using questionnaires or interviews to find out their attitudes and self-images.

Finally, if the cultural theory is valid, we should be able to change people's driving behaviour with a new kind of driving school. In this school, we would try to change people's attitudes about cars, driving and masculinity. We would predict that young men who graduated from this driving school would have a lower accident rate than young men who graduated from a traditional driving school that emphasized "the rules of the road." (Young women would have the same accident rate, regardless of the school they graduated from.) An *experiment* would tell us whether the theory was valid or not.

We will discuss all of these research methods at length in Chapter 12. For the time being, we want to emphasize that sociology is concerned with testing theories, and all theories can be tested in a number of different ways.

IS SOCIOLOGY A SCIENCE?

Perhaps you are wondering if sociology really can be scientific. After all, the popular image we have of science is based on physics and chemistry. When we hear the word "science" we often imagine people wearing white coats in a laboratory, surrounded by expensive equipment. Maybe we imagine rows of computers churning out columns of figures and interesting diagrams with Greek symbols on them. Or the chemistry lab's usual smell of rotten eggs. In fact, what we are imagining is not science, but the artifacts of a particular science at a particular time and place. (*Artifacts* are elements of material culture created by human workers.)

Sociology doesn't involve these kinds of artifacts, but it *does* take a scientific approach to problem solving. Sociological research, like any scientific research, works by the collection, organization, and interpretation of data, for the purposes of testing a hypothesis, or discovering new relations among phenomena. Often, however, sociologists are more limited than researchers in the physical sciences in the methods they can use in their research. For example, it is often difficult for sociologists to carry out the kinds of experiments they would like to, such as the driving school experiments we discussed earlier. That is because public institutions (like high schools) are often unwilling to cooperate. Their motives are humane, if not scientific: they believe you shouldn't set up a new educational program (like a driving school) if you don't know the likely outcome. If you know the program will *harm* people, you definitely shouldn't do it. If you know it will *help* people, then everyone should be permitted to take part; there should be no excluded comparison (or what experimenters call "control") group.

Other research questions pose other difficulties. Suppose we wanted to explain why, unlike many South American countries, Canada has never been ruled by a military dictator. As sociologists, we can think about this question in objective ways and even formulate theories, but there is no experiment we can perform that will tell us the answer. What's more, Canadian history will never repeat itself, so an experiment would be irrelevant to predicting the future even if it helped us understand the past.

Fortunately, the scientific method does not require experimentation: there are other scientific ways to carry out research. Some fields that study human behaviour — for example, psychology — use experiments almost exclusively. Other fields that study human behaviour — for example, history, economics, and anthropology — use no experiments at all. We shall have a great deal more to say about how sociologists go about doing research in Chapter 12.

There remains a second major problem facing sociology as a science: the problem of objectivity. Physicists, chemists and astronomers study phenomena which are important but have little impact on most peoples' daily lives. In contrast, sociologists often study problems they know about at first hand and which may have an impact on their own lives. For example, a sociologist studying divorce may be going through a divorce.

As human beings, sociologists are bound to be prejudiced, emotional, and irrational at times. A science of social behaviour is possible only if sociologists do their best to ensure that their work is *value free*.

That does not mean value-*less* — lacking in either morality or human concern. Consider the appeal mysticism has for people, especially the appeal of Madame Zelda, "Psychic Extraordinaire" (see Exhibit 1.2). The advertisement guarantees help in matters of "life, marriage, business, love affairs, alcoholism, and drug addiction." We would all love guaranteed help with important per-

EXHIBIT 1.2   *A non-sociological approach to life*

FIRST TIME IN THIS AREA!

She is not like any other reader that you might have seen. All her readings are GUARANTEED. Madame Zelda can help you in matters of: Life, Marriage, Business, Love Affairs, Alcoholism, and Drug Addiction.

She can join loved ones closer together and remove evil influences, calling them by name. Before you call Zelda ask yourself the following questions, and see if you fit under one of these categories.

1. Is your loved one unfaithful to you?
2. Are you in love with a married man?
3. Are you always going around in circles, but can't get a grip on life?
4. Are you lonely?
5. Are you tired of replacing what you already had?
6. Are you sick?
7. Do you feel like you are unlucky?
8. Do you feel like life is weighing you down?
9. Is your business going down?

If you fit under ANY of these categories, don't fail to call Zelda today and be rid of your problems tomorrow.

MADAME ZELDA

555-1721

All readings are strictly confidential. Please don't litter. Thank you!

sonal problems: the question is, how to achieve it. Would card reading, a crystal ball, or tea leaves help? Scientists don't think so. In fact, they think the first thing to do, in solving a problem, is to back away from it and try to see it from a fresh, impersonal perspective.

Value-free research is research that excludes all ideological or unscientific assumptions, as well as all personal judgments or biases. Obviously, this is not easy to do. The problem of achieving value freedom faces all of the social sciences. That is because the things that we study often include subjects of political debate, religious teaching, or personal commitment. We have to avoid setting up the research problem in a way that protects our own political, religious, or personal beliefs.

Let's consider an important example of this. Our society is dominated by men, so men define what is valuable and "important." As a result, until about twenty years ago, no one had done any serious research on housework. Yet housework is a job that has historically occupied more people than any other. Why had it been ignored? The answer is that, until recently, most sociologists were men and men rarely do housework. Not surprisingly, women sociologists have led the way in doing research on this activity (Oakley, 1974).

But even in other areas of research, there are many cases where sociologists have formulated a research problem inadequately because of a narrow way of seeing the world. This is why some sociologists argue that you need female researchers to give a female perspective on society. Similarly, people belonging to racial minorities, or growing up in poverty, have claimed there is a need for members of their own groups to study society from their own perspectives.

If sociology has fallen far short of value-free research in the past, this does not prove that we should give up the goal of value-free research. Value freedom in sociology may be *nearly* impossible, but it is — and should be — the continuing goal of all sociologists.

This view has implications for sociology students as well as for professional sociologists. It means that when you study sociology, you must be alert to the hidden assumptions that are shaping an argument. Value-freedom is even more important to good research than carefully collected facts and powerful statistical techniques.

The need for value freedom is most important when you are applying social research to public issues. Such research can play a part in making policies to deal with child abuse, racial discrimination, or school reform, for example. Good science is always possible, but the personal limitations of the researcher and the preconceptions of those who are funding the research always threaten value freedom.

We will see this point illustrated throughout the book; but perhaps nowhere is it clearer than in the area of gender relations. As you will learn in Chapter 7, for most of its history, male-dominated sociology has ignored or misunderstood women's lives. Today, large numbers of women sociologists are helping to solve this problem; but even so, many difficulties remain.

For example, there is still a great deal of controversy about three issues we shall discuss later: the extent and causes of (1) domestic inequality (i.e., who does what around the home); (2) workplace inequality (i.e., the hiring, pay, promotion and treatment of men and women on the job); and (3) violence between intimates, both inside and outside marriage. As you can imagine, these are all complex, emotionally charged topics in which sociologists of both sexes must struggle to find out the truth despite their personal limitations and anxieties.

To repeat, sociology is a science, like physics or biology; but as a science, sociology is more like the other fields called *social sciences* than it is like the physical or natural sciences.

The social sciences are a related group of disciplines that study some aspect of human behaviour. These disciplines include psychology, anthropology, political science, and economics. Historically, researchers in each of these fields have learned from, and referred to, work done in other social sciences. Sociology has been particularly likely to borrow from the other social sciences, a tendency that is natural and healthy.

HOW SOCIOLOGY IS DIFFERENT

So far we have taken great pains to argue that sociology is just as scientific as the other sciences. In particular, sociology is a lot like the other nonexperimental social sciences — especially anthropology, political science, and economics — from which it also borrows a great deal. Yet sociology is also distinct from other disciplines, even from the other social sciences.

Sociology is characterized as a distinctive discipline by: (1) its subject matter, (2) its basic concepts, and (3) the way it approaches its subject matter.

Sociology's subject matter

The biggest difference between sociology and the other social sciences is its subject matter, which is usually described as the relation between individual and society; between social structure and the socialized member of society.

Social structure is any enduring, predictable pattern of social relations among elements of society. These elements may be people, roles, groups or whole institutions. The key words here are "enduring," "predictable," "pattern," and "people."

Like sociologists, astronomers study enduring, predictable patterns of relations — but these are relations among stars and planets. Like sociologists, psychologists study enduring, predictable patterns of relations — the relations among attitudes, behaviours, and personality traits *within* individuals. Sociologists study enduring patterns of behaviour that cut across individuals because these behaviours grow out of relationships between people.

In the abstract, these ideas may sound difficult, but in practice they are familiar and simple. Consider a common example — the relationship between a doctor and a patient — that was the topic of a classic analysis by the sociologist Talcott Parsons (1951).

When you visit a doctor for a check-up, you take along very specific expectations. Even if you have never visited that doctor before, you expect him or her to act in a serious, concerned, and knowledgeable manner. The doctor also expects certain behaviours from you as a patient. He or she expects you to show concern for your health, pay attention to the diagnosis, and follow the professional advice you receive.

How do we know that people really have such expectations and that these expectations are enduring and predictable? If we violate them, both participants — the doctor and patient alike — will feel uncomfortable, even upset or disoriented. If the doctor comes in dressed like a rock star or starts talking to you like an intimate friend, this will confuse and disturb you. If you laugh at the news of a serious health problem, deny the doctor's expertise, or refuse to take the medicine prescribed, the doctor will be puzzled. The interaction will stop flowing smoothly. Both doctor and patient will start wondering what to say and do next.

There are many reasons that social relationships, from the (two-person) **dyad** all the way up through a complete society, are enduring and stable. We learn to value stable relationships. Often, we lack the knowledge or courage to change relationships. Sometimes we develop a strong investment in the way things are and stand to lose something if they change. People with the most to gain urge us to meet other people's expectations. These reasons, and many others we shall discuss, help to maintain the social relationships of the society in which we live.

Sociologists have found that what we learn about one social relationship — for example, the doctor-patient relationship — can help us understand other, quite different social relationships. Sociology is fascinated by the similarities and differences between relationships. It is also fascinated by the structures they form when fitted together. In the end, sociology is the study of many social structures — the doctor-patient relationship, the business enterprise, a marriage, a political campaign, or a total society. Sociologists can readily apply sociological concepts across a wide range of different relationships because these relationships are similar and interconnected. The willingness to generalize is one of sociology's most distinctive features.

Sociology's main concepts

People who have spent a lot of time being students or teaching students know that *concepts* are the key to understanding any field. Concepts are the tools of thought and argument: they make the work of study and research easier. You could make a pretty good guess at the nature of roadbuilding by studying a jackhammer, dump truck, grader, tar truck, and steamroller. In the same way, you can understand sociology more easily by learning the conceptual tools that sociologists actually use.

The terms *social structure* and *social relationships* refer to two basic sociological concepts used by most sociologists. We have used them repeatedly in this chapter. Social structure, as we noted earlier, refers to any enduring, predictable pattern of social relationships among people. "Society" in this sense is the largest social structure: the basic large-scale human group. Members of a society interact with one another and share a common geographic territory. To some degree, they also share a common culture and sense of collective existence and they take part in social institutions together.

A *social institution* is one kind of social structure, made up of a number of relationships. Typically, institutions achieve intended goals for people, as schools do for students, for example, or hospitals do for patients. People within a social institution are thus part of one or more social relationships, stable patterns of meaningful orientations to one another, such as the connections between teacher and student, doctor and patient, or parent and child.

The five main sets of institutions in a society are: (1) the cultural, concerned with religious, scientific and artistic activities (see Chapter 2); (2) stratification, which determine the distribution of life chances (see Chapters 5, 6 and 7); (3) kinship, which deal with marriage and the family (see Chapter 8); (4) economic, which produce and distribute goods and services (see Chapter 9); and (5) political institutions, which regulate the use of and access to power and authority (see Chapter 11).

Being a parent or a student or a doctor defines one's status in an institution. Statuses are socially defined positions that determine how the individual should relate to other people (that is, the rights and responsibilities of office) and with whom the individual will interact. *Roles* are actual patterns of interaction with others. Thus, being a doctor is a status, while acting like a doctor is a role performance. *Role expectations* are shared ideas about how people — any people — should carry out the duties attached to a particular status, regardless of the personal characteristics of those people.

These three scholars were among sociology's most sophisticated people-watchers. In his own way, each set the stage for the work all sociologists do today. Pictured from left to right are Max Weber, Emile Durkheim, and Karl Marx.

Another way to say this is that status refers to what a person is, while role refers to the behaviours we expect (and usually get) from people in that status. "Status" could be likened to a job title and "role" to a job description.

The concept of social relationship is the meeting point of the macro and the micro. Each of us participates in social life in terms of the statuses and roles we have adopted or have been assigned. Being a "student," for example, carries with it a lot of learned behaviour patterns, expectations, and motives. We all learn to be students — a painful process for many of us — in elementary school. Once that role is learned, we carry around with us expectations of what it means to be a student and how to do whatever it is that students do. We also carry around with us expectations about teachers and how and why teachers do whatever it is that they do.

For an individual, however, being a student does not mean carrying out some impersonal set of duties, obligations, or expectations. We each have our own reasons for doing things, our own sense of capacity, self-worth, and achievement. We may have a learning disability that makes studying for tests a kind of torture. Or we may have financial difficulties, which mean that we have to drop out of school and get a job if we do not get a scholarship. Or we may be taking a particular course because we hope to get a chance to date one of the other students.

We are all individuals, and we experience and act out our roles and statuses in our own particular ways. Yet, despite this, classroom behaviour is still largely predictable. Sociologically speaking, one class of students is pretty much like another, whether it is located in Montreal, Regina, Halifax or Yellowknife; whether the topic is sociology, physics, or ancient religion; and whether the year is 1995, 1975 or even 1955. It is remarkable how slowly social structures change and how little they vary from one place to another, as we shall see repeatedly in this book.

Sociology's perspectives

Sociology developed as a scientific discipline in the late 19th and early 20th centuries, as European thinkers tried to understand the dramatic changes that accompanied industrialization. For most of human history, change was slow and few people wondered much about their society. Things were as they always had been (or so it seemed), and people who wondered why were most likely to look to God, to fate or to the supernatural for an explanation.

This attitude began to shift in the face of technological, political, and religious changes within the last two centuries. People began to try to understand their society and to ask if these dramatic changes could be predicted and controlled. Chief among them, three individuals are credited with founding sociology as a scientific discipline: they are Karl Marx, Emile Durkheim, and Max Weber.

Karl Marx (1818–1883) was not, strictly speaking, a sociologist. Nevertheless, sociology derived many of its key concepts — such as the term *class*, — from his work. The questions Marx asked and the answers he provided remain important in contemporary sociological thought.

In his writings, Marx (1936, 1969; and Engels, 1955) developed a theory of society and of social change that does not fall within the boundaries of any one modern social science discipline. But Marx assumed that economic processes — what he called *modes of production* — are the most fundamental ones in society and explain a great deal about how society is organized.

A mode of production such as hunting will produce a different set of social relationships among people than will industrial production. In a hunting society, there will be no private property because the animals which are hunted do not belong to anyone. They are outside the boundaries of the society and are hunted for the benefit of all. In contrast, a factory may have an owner and this puts owners and workers in different social categories or *classes*.

Consider another difference. People all benefit equally in a hunting society. For this reason, there will be little social (or group) conflict among people. But in an industrial society, owners and workers will have different interests and will not benefit equally and this will result, inevitably, in class conflict. However much an owner and a worker admire one another as individuals, owners and workers as groups are bound to conflict with each other.

Marx's work was noteworthy for a number of reasons. He made the first attempt to uncover objective, scientific laws with which to understand society. He also made the first significant attempt to use history to predict the future course of economic and social change. Marx's questions about how society works remain relevant today, even for scholars who reject his answers.

One of those who rejected Marx's answers was the French sociologist Emile Durkheim (1858–1917). In fact, Durkheim rejected any explanation of society — whether economic, biological, psychological, or philosophical — that he did not deem sufficiently sociological. Durkheim was one of the first European academics to describe himself as a sociologist, and he devoted much of his career to establishing sociology as a distinct and respected social science.

The starting point of Durkheim's sociology was the predominance of society over the individual. Society, Durkheim insisted, creates, constrains and transforms the individual. All of our values, beliefs, and attitudes — even our ways of thinking — are derived from society. As an illustration, Durkheim (1951) took the case of suicide. He showed that suicide is not only an individual act, it is also a social act: suicide rates change in accordance with social factors such as place of residence, religion, marital status, age, and gender. As evidence of this sociological approach, see Exhibit 1.3 (on suicide).

Equally, Durkheim recognized that suicide is not only an indication of personal problems, it is also a sign of social problems. Because of the rapid pace of social change, modern society is characterized by anomie. In this condition, society no longer effectively regulates people's desires and aspirations. People in this condition become profoundly depressed and more likely to kill themselves; but the depression is social, not individual in origin.

EXHIBIT 1.3   *Why can't we reduce our suicide rate?*

Young people between the ages of 15 and 24 in this country, a nation with one of the highest standards of living in the world, are killing themselves at a rate twice that of Britain or Japan, five times that of Italy. Only Australia and Norway have worse records. Of every 100,000 young Canadians, 16 will end their own lives — about 615 a year. . . .

Canada's record is doubly cursed, because our high national rate, for young people in particular, masks a native component that is unconscionably worse.

Comparable records are hard to come by; Statistics Canada does not like to keep figures based on ethnicity. But the federal Department of Health and Welfare has statistics for registered Indians — which show a suicide rate for 20-year-olds of more than four times (68 per 100,000) the national average. . . .

But even the native statistics, sad as they are, do not tell the full story. Factor them out and the Canadian rate for young people (it would drop to about 14 per 100,000) is still higher than that of almost every other major industrialized country, including the United States. . . .

There are plans to ameliorate suicidal tendencies. We don't have to just accept it. Menno Boldt, an Alberta academic, chaired a provincial inquiry a decade ago that advocated an educational and community-response system which was at least partly implemented. Its basic premise was that suicide prevention should not be farmed out to just one group; it had to be a factor in the thinking of all major community organizations. Alberta rates moderated in the mid-eighties, but perhaps that was also because the economic situation improved a bit.

Some countries — Sweden, the former West Germany, Japan — have seen the suicide rates among their young people actually decline over the past two decades, according to the Unicef study. Japan's has been cut almost in half. What are their secrets?

In this country, despite some hard times, we have kept bad things such as the murder rate from growing. Why can we not do that with suicide?

Source: "Why can't we reduce our suicide rate?" The Globe and Mail, Tues., Sept. 28, 1993, p. A27

In Durkheim's analysis, suicidal depression — a personal problem — is shown to be the outcome of broader social forces. Durkheim's consistent ability to link such phenomena as crime, suicide, and religion to broader social processes has served as a source of inspiration to later generations of sociologists. Sociologists have also admired Durkheim's (1938) attempts to develop rigorous and consistent sociological research methods, such as his use of suicide *rates* to uncover the link between suicide and social factors. Though some of Durkheim's assumptions and findings are rejected today, his image of sociology continues to inspire sociologists.

Like Durkheim, Max Weber (1864–1920) rejected much of Marx's approach, but he did so for different reasons. In particular, Weber rejected the idea that any one factor or set of factors determines either society or the individual. Weber saw society as an extraordinarily complex set of social relationships. In his view, society can never be completely explained and its course never completely predicted. All we can do is try to understand the more important factors and identify the impact these factors have had on history.

For this reason Weber looks not only to economic factors to explain society but to such other factors as religion, the growth of cities, changes in the law, science and technology, and different types of political organization (Weber, 1961).

To a large extent, Weber's sociology focuses on domination and power. In that respect, Weber is typical of German thinkers at the turn of the century. Where he stands out is in his remarkable historical and technical knowledge, and in his ability to link together vastly different social processes. Like Durkheim, Weber had a flair for the non-obvious, uncommon insight.

For example, Weber (1974) linked the rise of capitalism to religious doctrine, especially the so-called *Protestant ethic* of hard work (see Chapter 2 for a fuller discussion). He also linked the rise of capitalism to other factors: for example, the tendency of European monarchs during the Middle Ages to ally themselves with large cities in order to gain control over the independent feudal nobility. In return for their support, monarchs granted the cities many rights which freed them from feudal obligations. This allowed their "citizens" (i.e., "city-dwellers") to experiment with new forms of production (such as factories), commerce (such as banking and insurance) and government (such as elected rulers).

Weber's impact upon modern sociology is immense. Many key areas of sociological research, such as stratification and bureaucratic organization, are heavily indebted to his pioneering work (Weber, 1958a). Perhaps the most enduring legacy, however, is his lesson to sociologists never to be satisfied with an easy answer and to avoid all forms of determinism (Weber, 1958b).

Today, sociologists still differ in what they consider to be the most fruitful approach to the study of society. Some prefer to follow Marx, others Durkheim and still others Weber. In fact, most sociologists fall into one of several main groups which embrace different sociological "paradigms." A **paradigm** is a general way of seeing the world. It embodies broad assumptions about the nature of society and social behaviour. A paradigm suggests which questions to ask, and how to interpret the answers obtained by research. To some degree, different paradigms are associated with different founding figures of sociology.

FOUR SOCIOLOGICAL PARADIGMS

Structural functionalism

One of these paradigms is **structural functionalism**, often just called *functionalism*. Inspired partly by Emile Durkheim, structural functionalism looks at society as a social system — a set of components or structures that are organized in an orderly way and integrated to form a whole. The term *whole* is important here and, as you can probably guess, functionalists are typically concerned with macrosociological issues. The main assumptions of structural functionalism are as follows:

- Each social system has certain basic needs that must be met if it is going to continue to survive.
- The various interdependent structures in a social system exist in order to fulfil one or more of these needs.
- Under normal conditions, the social system has a tendency to be in "equilibrium," a state of balance, stability, harmony, and consensus.
- Because all the structures are interrelated and integrated, changes in one will provoke changes in others, so that a new equilibrium is reached.
- Among all the members of society, there is widespread agreement or consensus on what values should be upheld, on what is functional and dysfunctional in society, and on the preference for stability over change.

Structural functionalists depict society as orderly and stable — an "organism" that works to meet the needs of the social system as a whole. In doing so, it also meets many of the personal, irrational, or subjective needs of its members.

Because the existing social system is generally beneficial, change is more likely to disrupt society than to provide benefits. That's why functionalists emphasize order over change. Confronted with a social event or relationship, functionalists ask one basic question: How does this event or relationship help to maintain the social system? Generally, they argue that the event or relationship occurs because it helps to maintain the social order. In other words, it contributes to preserving the social system.

To illustrate these complex ideas, let us return to the doctor-patient relationship discussed earlier. Suppose we want to justify doctors' rights to bill extra fees over and above what public health insurance permits. A structural functionalist (or a doctor) might justify extra billing in the following way:

Extra billing helps society survive by helping to ensure good health. It encourages doctors to give their patients better service. It also discourages frivolous visits and encourages patients to take their doctors' advice more seriously, since they are paying for it directly. People in our society value good health highly: that is why doctors are so highly respected and highly paid. If doctors could not bill their patients extra, this would disturb a traditional part of the doctor-patient relationship. The doctor would become like any other public servant, paid directly from the public purse. It would be more difficult to maintain the rest of the doctor-patient relationship, which calls for trust, discretion, and mutual respect. Once patients lost their respect for the relationship, they would stop taking the good advice doctors offered them.

Yet life in the real world is rarely as sensible as this argument suggests. One solution developed by structural functionalists to explain the seeming senselessness of much social behaviour is to distinguish between *manifest* and *latent* functions (Merton, 1957a). To uncover the functions of a given structure or behaviour, sociologists look at its actual *consequences*, not at what the behaviour is popularly supposed to do. When we do this, we often discover that any social event or relationship may have consequences other than those that were intended.

Manifest functions are functions that are obvious and intended. For example, the manifest functions of a school system are to educate the young and teach them to be responsible citizens. By contrast, *latent functions* are unintended and often unrecognized but have significant social effects nonetheless. For example, the latent function of schooling may be: to provide free baby-sitting services, which helps working parents; to teach obedience and conformity to rules, which helps future employers when the students join the work force; and to supply employers with credentials identifying which students were adequate. It may be that schools survive in their present form *not* because of their manifest functions (which are generally *not* met) but because of their latent functions (which *are* met).

As we can see from Exhibit 1.4, formal education is playing an ever more important role in peoples' careers. But what sociologists want to find out, through research, is *why* education is important. We cannot assume it is because schools do what they say they do.

EXHIBIT 1.4   *Why it pays to stay in school*

Education has become the most obvious dividing line in the Canadian job market. Those who can flash a piece of paper that says they've attained some degree of skill get the jobs; those who can't, don't. . . .

Take a look at the statistical breakdown for the three-year period from 1990 to 1993, when total employment had fallen by 189,000 jobs from the peak before the recession:

♦ 308,000 more jobs (up 17 per cent from 1990) for the university graduates.

♦ 170,000 more jobs (up 5 per cent) for those who completed other forms of post-secondary education or training.

♦ 16,000 fewer jobs (down 0.4 per cent) for high-school graduates.

♦ A staggering 651,000 fewer jobs (down 19 per cent) for those who dropped out before finishing high school. . . .

[There is] clear evidence that the Canadian labour market is being buffeted by forces far more profound than a recession and slow recovery. Employers are clearing out the uneducated and untrained, but continue to find room for those whose skills can be vouched for with formal diplomas and degrees.

In effect, the job market has been undergoing a revolution of rising skills. . . .

For all the advantages it confers, the precious piece of paper earned at educational institutions is not a guarantee of a job. Despite the growth in employment, the jobless rate for those with better education and training rose to 8 per cent in 1992 and 1993 from 5.4 per cent in 1990. That's because more people with degrees and diplomas went looking for work than there were jobs available.

But for those with less education, the jobless rate was 13.7 per cent in each of the past two years, compared with 9.9 per cent in 1990.

The 1993 data reinforce the conclusions reached in a study by Philip Cross of Statistics Canada: "Education, not experience, increasingly determines one's ability to compete in today's labour market."

Source: Bruce Little, "Why it pays to stay in school," *The Globe and Mail*, Mon., Jan. 17, 1994, p. A9

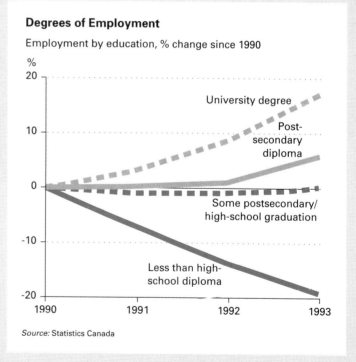

Degrees of Employment

Employment by education, % change since 1990

Source: Statistics Canada

Since society is a system of interrelated structures, changes in one part of society always produce changes — often unintended — in another part. Society is always reacting and readjusting to new inputs, even when people do not intend the changes that occur.

This fact is important for sociology and also for social planning. Unless we are aware of the likely consequences of a planned change — the latent as well as the manifest functions, and the dysfunctions as well as the functions — we are likely to end up with changes we did not want. One sociologist (Sieber, 1981) has coined the term "fatal remedies" to describe attempts at social planning that fail to think through the consequences. In the end, they do more (unintended) harm than they do (intended) good. Why? Because society is a social system whose workings remain largely unknown to us, despite more than a century of sociological research.

Conflict theory

Many sociologists find the structural-functional emphasis on order, harmony, and stability one-sided and misleading. How, for example, would structural functionalists explain domestic violence? Or physicians' abuse of their patients, which research tells us is not uncommon? In these, and many other instances, the functionalist tendency to justify the existing order is intolerable. More important, it offers a distorted picture of how society actually works. An alternate approach many adopt is conflict theory.

Conflict theory is a paradigm that emphasizes conflict and change as basic features of social life. For conflict theorists, change is the only constant in society. Conflict and change are inevitable because society is composed of groups which differ in their power, status, and influence. These groups are always trying to maintain or improve their respective positions.

For a conflict theorist, there is one basic sociological question: Who benefits from the existing social order and who suffers? Like structural functionalists, conflict theorists pay attention to the consequences of behaviours or relationships. However, the conflict theorist does not suppose that any behaviour or relationship will benefit the whole society, and does not look for such a benefit. Instead, the conflict theorist looks for particular groups that will benefit most and have the power to seize this benefit.

They reject the functionalist emphasis on the social "whole." The conflict approach does not assume that people are antagonistic by nature, or that conflict takes place only between individuals. Instead, conflict theorists explain that different groups in society come into conflict because the things that people value highly and desire — wealth, prestige, and power — are scarce.

To gain control of these valued things means denying them to others. Conflict develops between groups whose goals differ or even oppose each other — for example, the rich and the poor, men and women, workers and management. These categories of opposing people differ in at least one social characteristic: respectively, the amount of wealth they have, their gender, or their relationship to power at work. In each case, it is the key difference that sets the conflict in motion.

Conflict also arise out of different conceptions of what is valuable, desirable, or good. Groups often struggle with one another over the right to define good and bad, valuable and worthless. Conflicts over the legalization of marijuana or the abolition of the death penalty reflect such differing conceptions of good and bad.

Conflict theorists do not consider conflict to be a destructive force; instead, they believe it focuses attention on social problems and brings people together to solve these problems. Indeed, conflict is the source of social movements like the women's movement, civil rights movements, and trade unionism. As a result, conflict serves as the vehicle of positive social change.

This outlook on social life focuses attention away from shared values and towards ideologies. An **ideology** is a coherent set of interrelated beliefs about the nature of the world and of people. It guides a person's interpretation of, and reaction to, external events.

For example, many people in our society believe they are responsible for their own success or failure. They think, "I am free to choose the path I will take; if my choice turns out badly, I have only myself to blame." This thinking is part of what is called the "liberal ideology." (Perhaps you can see how this is related to the Ann Landers' column we looked at earlier.)

Liberal ideology affects the way people behave in a wide variety of situations. On the macrosociological side, it influences which political party they will vote for and whether they will support welfare benefits for the poor, or capital gains taxes for the rich. On the microsociological side, it influences how they will react if they are thrown out of work, battered by a spouse, or mistreated by the government. In all cases, this ideology encourages people to "blame the victim" and support the status quo.

In conflict theory, the *dominant ideology* is the ideology of the dominant group, justifying its power and wealth. The rest of us do not rebel because we have come to believe in the dominant ideology. Young people are taught this ideology in the schools, churches and media; we hear it repeated throughout life. However passively, we learn to live with the *status quo*.

Marxist theorists embrace a particular version of conflict theory. They claim that the dominant ideology promotes "false consciousness," a perception of the world that is not in accord with objective reality. We see this when people blame the shortcomings of other people, and not the way society is organized, for causing widespread problems. For example, they may think,"Women who wear revealing clothes are to blame if they get raped," or "Young people who don't get a college diploma are to blame if they can't find work," or "Widows who rely on the old age pension are to blame if they run short of money." These are all views that hold the victims responsible for their misfortunes. They all illustrate what conflict theorists consider "false consciousness."

Often, even victims of the system blame themselves. For example, the chronically unemployed display this false consciousness and subscribe to the dominant ideology (see Schlozman and Verba, 1979).

Conflict theorists vary in what they consider to be the central conflicts in society. Some believe that there are many possible sources of conflict. These may include, for example, differences in wealth, gender, position at work, ethnicity, race and religion. Others, especially Marxian theorists, see these conflicts as secondary to, and connected with, one central conflict in capitalist society: class conflict.

In Marxist terms, a **class** is a set of people with the same relation to the means of production. People who control the means of production — the organizations that hire workers and own the capital that finances these organizations — control the lives of everyone else. These capitalists are the ruling class, and their view about how the world works serves to justify their position. They also influence huge social institutions that perpetuate the capitalists' position at the expense of others.

Class, then, is important because it gives rise to different "life chances" — chances of gaining wealth, prestige, and power, or even good health and

Boundaries between the bourgeoisie (or capitalist class) and proletariat (or working class) were easier to define in the 19th century, when Marx was writing.

a steady job. It does so because one class — the capitalists — controls everyone else.

The influence of Marx and his work is evident in conflict theory. However the work of Weber also inspired sociologists who follow the conflict paradigm. Weber (1958a) argued that conflict arises as much over such intangibles as values, status, and a sense of personal honour as over tangibles such as money or good health. From Weber's point of view, even modern corporations with no identifiable "owner" experience conflict. The bureaucratic managers of the corporation come to think of themselves as a status group and act to further their own group interests. That is why, Weberian theorists argue, conflict can be found in *any* society, not only in capitalist societies.

We shall have more to say about all of these issues in Chapter 5 (on class and status relations) and Chapter 11 (on politics, protest and change.)

Symbolic interactionism

A little while ago, we considered how a structural functionalist would interpret the relationship between a doctor and patient, and the question of extra billing. A conflict theorist would view the same relationship in terms of competing interests (Friedson, 1975; Johnson, 1972). He or she would argue that doctors have a monopoly on medical knowledge and the right to apply it. They use their advantage to gain the largest payment and as much deference as possible while helping the patient. The patient's goal, by contrast, is to gain as much help as possible for the least money and deference.

Both views of the doctor-patient relationship — structural functionalist and conflict theorist — may be partly right. However, each misses the subtlety of the interaction between patient and doctor. Structural functionalism and conflict theory are primarily macrosociological approaches. Neither explains *how* the doctor lays a claim to expertise or threatens an uncooperative patient, for example. We must turn to **symbolic interactionism**, a third paradigm in sociology, for a detailed account of the ways in which people work out, or negotiate, an interaction and its outcome.

Symbolic interactionism is a theoretical paradigm that sees society as a product of continuous face-to-face interaction among individuals in different settings. To understand this approach, let us consider the words that make up its name: "symbol" and "interaction."

In simple terms, a *symbol* is something that meaningfully represents something else. It can be a written or spoken word, a gesture, or a sign (such as a raised fist). *Interaction* refers to the ways two or more people respond to one another. Most interaction among human beings is symbolic, in the sense that words and actions all have meanings beyond themselves. A frown, a kiss, a smile, a word of greeting — all have meanings which are learned, shared, and changed through interaction. Some even have hidden meanings and double meanings.

Symbolic interactionism focuses on the processes by which people interpret and respond to the actions of others. It studies the way social structures, as patterns of behaviour, arise out of these processes. In some ways this is like studying the way that waves create a beach, by bringing new grains of sand and taking old ones away.

The main assumption of this approach is that people do not respond to the world directly. They respond to *interpretations* of the world. These interpretations rest on meanings that people attach to the various events, gestures, words, and actions around them. The meanings are social because people create them when interacting, share them, learn them, and often pass them down from one generation to the next.

Unlike macrosociologists, symbolic interactionists do not focus on the major institutions of society, such as the economy or government. Instead, they study personal daily life in close detail. They believe that major institutions only come into being through day-to-day processes of change and renewal — just like a beach.

However, in important ways society is *not* like a beach and social relations are *not* like grains of sand deposited on the beach. Unlike grains of sand, people have consciousness and will. To a large degree, ordinary people make the waves that build up the beach we call social structure. So, to understand social structures we have to understand what is in the minds of the people — powerful and less powerful — who make these social waves.

The German sociologist Max Weber said that sociologists must practice *verstehen*, a German word meaning "understanding" or "insight." In sociology, we take this to mean that sociologists must understand the emotions, thoughts, beliefs, and attitudes of all acting individuals. We must know their intentions — their reasons for the behaviour we observe. *Verstehen* consists of placing ourselves in the position of the actors and seeing the world from their point of view; it is empathetic understanding.

According to Weber, it is not enough for sociologists to explain a social phenomenon only by referring to large social forces, as Durkheim did with suicide, for example. We must try to link this explanation with what is happening in people's minds. We must interpret the situation as they do.

The need to understand an actor's point of view is captured in another important concept, the *definition of the situation*. We must understand an actor's definition of the situation, because people will act meaningfully in relation to *their* definition of reality, not ours. Take a simple illustration: self-destructive behaviour. At one time or another, we have all seen an intelligent, attractive person act in an obnoxious way; call this one Bruce. We may know Bruce wants to have friends, but his obnoxious behaviour is causing other people to stay away in droves. We begin to wonder if Bruce is crazy to act in such a self-defeating way.

Our view may change once we get inside Bruce's mind. He feels ugly and undesirable as a friend. He avoids interactions that might end in rejection. Obnoxious behaviour poses a difficult test for anyone who wants to be Bruce's friend, so someone surviving this "ordeal by obnoxiousness" would surely be a friend worth having. Once we understand Bruce's reasons, the obnoxious, self-destructive behaviour makes perfect sense and does not seem irrational at all.

Now, you will recall that Durkheim studied self-destructive behaviour (namely, suicide) and he thought it was unnecessary to know what was in people's minds. One only needed to know the "social facts." For certain kinds of self-destructive behaviour and certain kinds of understanding — especially, for purposes of predicting behaviour — this may be true. However you can see that Durkheim's insight may not help us in many other situations. At the very least, it would not help us counsel someone who had attempted suicide or was contemplating it.

To this day, sociologists disagree on which is the right approach: ignoring the actor's thoughts or understanding them fully. That is why some follow Durkheim and others, Weber.

Note one other feature of the scenario we just sketched out: it is that behaviour — whether obnoxious or nice — often produces the very reaction that is expected or feared. A person who expects a rejection often gets rejected — indeed, often causes rejection. A person expecting friendship, on the other hand, often gets friendship. This led sociologists (Thomas and Thomas, 1928) to conclude that "a situation that is believed to be real is [often] real in its consequences." This simple theorem applies in a wide variety of situations.

In short, social interactions produce relationships that reflect the beliefs and expectations people bring to them. But how can social order emerge from two (or sometimes many more) different beliefs, expectations, and definitions of the same situation? The answer is, through *negotiation*.

According to symbolic interactionists, social arrangements require continuous negotiation, dialogue, bargaining and compromise among the people present. Negotiation takes place in the House of Commons when a law is being changed or a new law is being voted into effect. It also takes place when people are deciding what movie to see on a Friday night.

As you might imagine, negotiation requires a great many social skills, and we all learn these skills in interaction, throughout our entire lives. We learn them the same way we learn language, through trial and error. With practice, we all become good at *verstehen*, at understanding other people's definition of the situation, because we have to. To reach agreements with people, we have to see the world the way they do, however imperfectly. Reaching agreement is often easiest if we can lead people to redefine the situation: to see the interaction in our way, and as a chance for cooperation, not conflict.

Women continue to lead lives that are, in many ways, different from men's. This gives women a different view of society.

Progressive Conservative Party

The feminist paradigm

A fourth, and relatively new paradigm which is having a major impact upon sociology is the *feminist paradigm*. Like other sociological approaches, the feminist approach is composed of a wide variety of different points of view and diverse, sometimes conflicting, theories. Nevertheless, there are a number of common themes and concerns which can be identified in the work of feminists.

First of all, note that feminism *is not* something new. Then note that, despite the bad press given feminism by many extremists, it *is not* a blanket condemnation of men nor a rejection of heterosexuality. Feminism *is not* a brand of hate literature, nor is it a political strategy to put women above men at work or in the family. Rather, feminism *is* a paradigm that goes back at least two centuries, to the English philosopher Mary Wollstonecraft, and its most general goal is equality between the sexes. It seeks to promote political, social and psychological changes by calling attention to facts and issues many have neglected.

The application of feminism in sociology illustrates all of these concerns. Most particularly, it calls attention to the androcentric (or male-dominated) history of sociological thinking. To remedy this, feminist sociologists emphasize the experiences of women, "because there can be no sociological generalizations about human beings as long as a large number of such beings are systematically excluded or ignored" (Sydie, 1987: 360).

Sydie (ibid.) also points out that feminist sociology is political because "it reveals the manner in which past sociologists have provided intellectual justifications for the persistence of gender inequalities." So, for example, male sociologists were quick to defend gender inequalities in the family by creating theories — the so-called "functional theories" we shall discuss in Chapter 8 — that made gender inequality seem not only inevitable but desirable.

As we have noted, feminism is not only an academic outlook. It is also a form of political activism that attempts to change the circumstances within which men and women live their lives. Feminists emphasize that our notions of what it means to be male or female and our dealings with one another as male or female are a result of the social arrangements prevalent in our society. No one is ever "just" male or female because gender is neither biological nor "natural."

To be a female in our society is to act out a role that is defined for us by others and by the expectations we carry around with us. To be a female is also to participate in a set of social relations which defines for us our status vis-a-vis others.

This is true for males too, but with this difference: the "feminine" role in our society places women in a subservient role to men, in which they are sometimes degraded or victimized. Feminism, then, has an emancipatory goal. If gender relations always reflect the larger pattern of social relations in a society, then changing gender relations requires changing those social relations as well.

There is no denying that there are many differences among the major paradigms of sociology. Students planning to continue their studies of sociology should take note of these differences. There are also national differences in the ways sociologists from different countries study and explain reality (on this topic, see Smelser, 1989).

In general, American sociology has been more "voluntaristic," empirical and concerned with social problem-solving than European sociology. It has also focused more on consensus than on conflict. By contrast, French Canadian sociology has drawn a great deal from French sociology, which tends to be philosophical and abstract. For its part, English Canadian sociology is a unique mixture of American voluntarism, British class analysis, and Canadian history and political economy.

However, this book is going to blur the differences between nations and paradigms and stress the similarities. We are going to walk down the main street of sociology, not the side streets. We do this for two main reasons: because many differences are more apparent than real, and because the similarities are more numerous and important than the differences.

There is no simple relationship between the four main paradigms (functionalist, conflict, symbolic interactionist, and feminist) and the two levels of analysis (macrosociological and microsociological). True, symbolic interactionism tends to specialize in microsociological analysis and functionalism and conflict theory in macrosociological analysis. Yet each paradigm has valuable insights to contribute at both levels of analysis. Certainly this is true of the feminist approach. And this is not surprising since, as we have argued, the two levels of analysis are merely different ways of looking at the same thing.

All four paradigms have explanations for both order and change, consensus and conflict. In one situation, the structural functionalist or feminist explanation may be best. In another, the conflict paradigm or symbolic interactionist paradigm may be best. No conclusive evidence proves that one paradigm is always or never appropriate, or that combining paradigms is misleading and fruitless.

On the contrary, many sociological researchers — especially sociologists working on applied questions with a practical significance — use all four paradigms interchangeably. They would gain nothing by ignoring other paradigms. Fortunately, the connections among paradigms are clear enough that switching among them is easy.

Here's an exercise: look at the story in Exhibit 1.5 and see how it would be possible — and useful — to re-examine the problem from *each* of the four sociological paradigms. What would you learn by doing this?

EXHIBIT 1.5 *Scrambling for cover as the violence spreads*

To walk through the halls of education these days is more and more like an excursion into the roughest neighbourhood in town.

And the violence stalking the schools is no longer restricted to the inner cities of the United States, or even the major cities of Canada. Consider these incidents recently listed by a report from Canadian Press:

◆ In a small Northern Ontario town of Atikokan a 15-year-old student held a teacher at gunpoint after someone was sprayed with mustard.

◆ In Ste-Anne-Des-Monts, Que., unruly behavior by students, including the beating of a security guard, forced the closure of a local school for several days.

◆ In Winnipeg, three 14-year-olds opened fire in a school hallway with a pellet gun, sending students scrambling for cover. One student was shot in the neck.

◆ Nineteen students were expelled from the Edmonton school board last year for assaults causing harm or the possession of weapons.

◆ In Calgary, a Grade 7 student was stabbed to death in a schoolyard.

Across the country, the statistics concerning violence in schools are frightening. A survey by the Manitoba Teachers Society found that one in 10 teachers reported being physically attacked by a student. In Ontario, an Ontario Teachers' Federation survey found assaults on students,

teachers and staff had risen 150 per cent in the past three years.

What is even more depressing is the increasingly young age of the offenders. It is now common for elementary school students to witness; or be a victim of, assaults by their peers.

Central Toronto Youth Services, a children's mental health centre, surveyed 845 students. The centre learned that between 66 per cent and 75 per cent of Grade 6 to Grade 9 students had committed, or knew someone who had committed, an act of violence in the past nine months. . . .

In Canada, authorities are just starting to deal seriously with the problem of violence. The solutions range from a "zero-tolerance" policy adopted by the Scarborough Board of Education, which calls for lifetime suspensions for students who use or threaten to use weapons, to a simple communications strategy favoured by the Winnipeg School Division.

In more and more communities, the police are being counted on to help solve the problem. . . .

Detective John Muise of the Metro Toronto Police Department told the Globe and Mail that police believe more than 80 per cent of the violent crimes in Toronto schools go unreported. This has to change, he said, or students' education will suffer because soon they'll be more concerned with protecting themselves than studying. . . .

Source: David Shoalts, "Scrambling for cover as the violence spreads," *The Globe and Mail*, Thurs., Nov. 25, 1993, p. C8

SOCIOLOGY AS A FORM OF CONSCIOUSNESS

One thing all the paradigms have in common is a tendency to question the existing order.

As the case of the feminist paradigm makes particularly clear, sociology is not only a science. Feminism's emancipatory goals lead feminist sociologists to try to change society in certain ways. This is true for many conflict sociologists as well. These sociologists want to remind us that there are other, probably better, ways our society could operate: more humane, fair and efficient ways. We can only make such changes if we understand the flaws in our current way of doing things.

Some have argued that this makes sociology not only a science but an outlook, or form of consciousness. This outlook has several characteristics, among them cosmopolitanism, a sense of irony, a disregard for disciplinary boundaries, a tendency to question the basic assumptions of daily life, and a desire to use our knowledge to improve the social world.

All sociologists, whatever their perspective and whether they seek to change society or simply to understand it, refuse to take the "facts" of ordinary, daily life for granted.

Instead sociologists continually question our everyday assumptions. For a sociologist these common-sense "facts" are part of our subject matter. Understanding the assumptions of daily life — without being subjected to them — is an essential part of sociological analysis. This makes sociology inherently critical and contentious. For just as sociologists refuse to take the received wisdom of everyday life at face value, they refuse to accept the received wisdom of sociology itself at face value.

Sociology's multiple perspectives and multiple theories are a result of this critical tendency. It makes sociology less unified (and dignified) than other sciences, but it also generates the energy and excitement we enjoy in good sociology.

Closely related to sociology's critical tendency is a sense of irony, usually found in good sociology. As the dictionary will tell you, *irony* is an incongruity — a bad fit — between what people expect and what actually happens. In the case of sociology, irony is a bad fit between what we intend and what actually happens, and between what we believe and what is really so. Because sociological research is directed at what people are really doing, not what they claim to be doing, sociologists know that life is full of ironies.

To study sociology is to look at everyday life with an eye to its ironies and contradictions. It is to explore how different we really are from the roles we play; and how, and why, the actions we take not only fail to produce the outcomes we expected; often —perhaps, usually — they produce the exact opposite.

One reason our actions produce unintended results is the extraordinary complexity of social life. To study social life, sociologists often find they must take into account history, geography, economics, politics and so on. We cannot understand family life without studying economic life: the two systems continually influence each other. Families provide the economy with workers and consumers. The economy provides families with jobs and goods. Likewise, we cannot understand crime and deviance without understanding the political system. We cannot understand people's sex lives without studying the mass media; and vice versa. Nor can we begin to make sense of cities or workplaces without understanding modern technology.

This means that sociology is inherently cross-disciplinary. There are many different factors which must be taken into account when trying to understand any aspect of social life. For this reason sociologists may find any social phenomenon relevant, regardless of the specific discipline which lays claim to it. Whether it be the Industrial Revolution in 18th century England, ethnic relations in the Balkans, or the ritual processes underlying a handshake, sociologists feel free to examine *any* kind of evidence that seems promising.

Again, this makes sociology less orderly than the other social sciences. But this very freedom to question and consider diverse phenomena is what feeds the "sociological imagination" we spoke of earlier.

As to making use of what we find out, not all sociologists are as committed to promoting social change as feminists or conflict theorists. Yet almost all sociologists see sociology as having a practical benefit, even if this benefit is only that of allowing people to better understand the circumstances of their own lives. Knowledge is power and a better understanding of our lives empowers all of us.

CLOSING REMARKS

As you can see, sociologists are involved in a wide variety of research activities, many having great practical significance to people's lives. If you think about it, you will probably realize that there are many good reasons to study sociology. In general, sociology will help you gain a broad perspective on the social world. There are careers in sociology for people who become interested in continuing their studies. As well, sociology — as a science — will help you see that things are not always what they seem to be.

By helping you understand the social world better, sociology will provide you with useful life skills. After studying sociology, you will be able to put your own problems in a broader context. That will help you understand the groups you are part of — your family, friends, school classes, work groups, and so on. Sociology will give you tools that allow you to collect and analyze data about the social world. Finally, sociology will help you think about the world and its problems more objectively.

It is now time to examine one of the most important and basic topics in all of sociology: culture.

CHAPTER 2

John McNeill

North Americans are strangely fascinated with dinosaurs—especially with the killers, like tyrannosaurus rex. Is this because our culture has a secret attraction to violence?

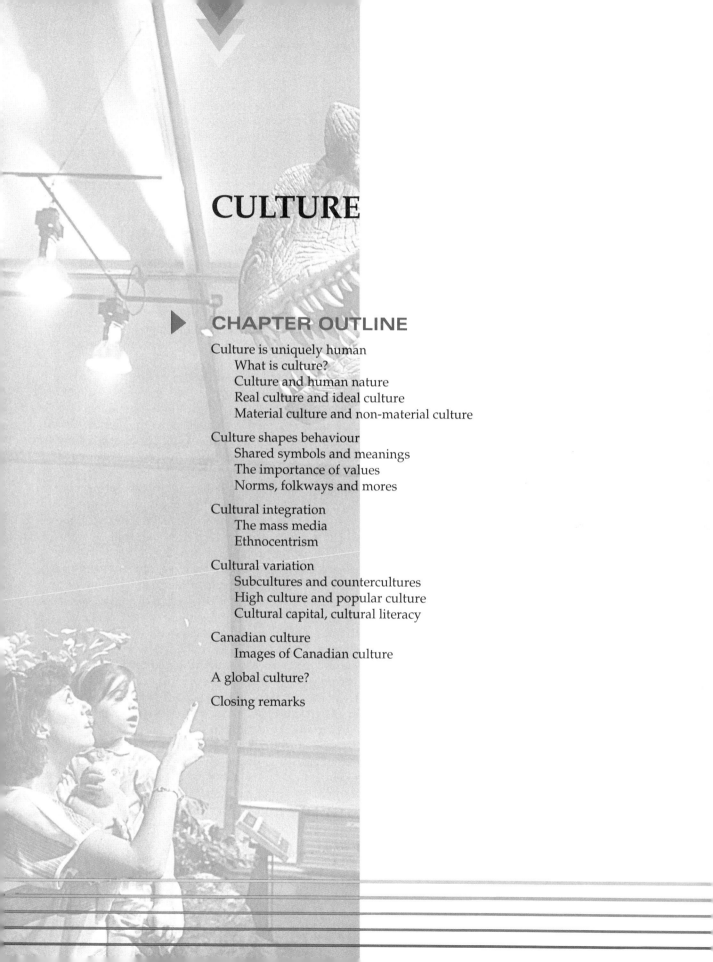

CULTURE

▶ CHAPTER OUTLINE

CULTURE IS UNIQUELY HUMAN

What is culture?

As human beings, we live in a world that differs dramatically from the world other species inhabit. For the most part, animals live in a *natural* environment to which they must adapt. Even domesticated animals respond to their environment as if it were a natural one. But humans live in a *social* environment which is gradually coming to dominate the natural environment. For the most part, we adapt it to us. This humanly created environment in which we live is **culture**

Of course, people also live in a natural environment which constrains us. Like the other creatures with whom we share this planet, we breathe the air, enjoy seeing the grass and trees, swim in lakes, and run for shelter from the rain. Without air or food or water, we too will die. Like other animals, we humans catch diseases, put on weight, and grow feeble with age.

Nevertheless, if you look around, almost everything you see is the product of human activity: buildings, roads, cars — even the grass and trees in our parks and lawns are laid out as they are because people planted them that way. Some grasses and trees are even human-made! Culture is our uniquely human environment.

In its broadest sense, *culture* includes all of the objects, artifacts, institutions, organizations, ideas and beliefs that make up the social environment of human life. This social environment is also "symbolic," in the sense that every human group produces "meanings" locked in symbols or words that remain in a society's memory. From this standpoint, culture — symbolized in a society's literature, arts and sciences — is the group's memory. As memory, it supports the cultural identity of that group or society (Ferrarotti, 1991).

Culture is a shared symbolic environment and the people who share a culture are bound to be similar in certain ways. Culture structures a person's perception of the world and shapes his or her behaviour. People who share a common culture experience the world in a similar way. As a result, a common culture helps to hold a society together. On the other hand, people brought up in *different* cultures perceive the world in *different* ways. They have different memories, traditions, values, attitudes, and beliefs. Concretely, they eat different foods, wear different clothes and speak different languages. Even two nations as similar as Canada and the United States differ culturally in important ways.

If we are to understand a society and the people who live in it, understanding its culture is essential. That's why anthropologists, who study small-scale societies, focus on culture to get a sense of the whole society. Sociologists, who deal with large and complex societies, look at culture somewhat differently. We sociologists are interested in the kinds of social differences — class, gender, ethnic, and so on — that exist *within* a society and we analyze the role of culture in creating or preserving these differences.

People know most about other cultures that are similar to their own. That's why our daily experience suggests that people are all pretty much the same. Despite variations in speech and dress, the people you meet on the streets of Canada are a lot like one another. Even in the cities of Europe, Asia, Africa and Latin America, you meet people like yourself. Their food, clothes and television programs are similar to our own. You will see music videos on television in Paris, roller blades in Rio de Janeiro, skyscrapers in Delhi, Hong Kong, and Lagos.

Cultural differences are more striking once we set foot in the rural parts of the "underdeveloped" nations. In rural regions of Asia, Africa and Latin America, we see poorer versions of our own society mixed with remnants of older, possibly unfamiliar cultures. In fact, we find a puzzling mix and clash of many lifestyles, few of which are seen in North America. But even this degree of difference from our own culture does not capture the full range of human possibility.

Only the study of history and anthropology makes us aware of how widely cultures have varied over the ages. This variation tells us that people are able to create a huge variety of social relationships and forms of social organization.

Culture and human nature

Before we examine the different aspects of culture in detail, let us look more closely at the distinction between culture and nature. We tend to take culture for granted because most of us assume that our behaviour is a result of "human nature." We like to think that our own ways of seeing the world and behaving in it are natural. Sometimes we even think that our goals, motives, attitudes, and beliefs are the only sensible ones. Everyone else would share them with us if their cultures did not get in the way.

Yet nothing could be further from the truth. We are born with few predispositions to any particular forms of social behaviour or organization. Usually, our ways of thinking and acting are neither "natural" nor genetic, as they are with many animals (although much animal behaviour is not inborn either).

Of course, people and animals have a lot in common — not surprisingly, since people *are* animals. Like people, other animals have patterned ways of thinking and behaving. They also have stable relationships with one another, such as parental or dominance patterns. Some even have a division of labour, or **specialization**, within which different individuals gather food, reproduce, and defend the colony or group. Sometimes the work is divided along age and gender lines; for example, among bees we find a queen bee, worker bees, and drones.

And like people, most animals live with other animals. One need only consider sea creatures — schools of fish, banks of coral, and communities of Portuguese men-of-war — to see that isolation is rare among living creatures. The most complex and highly evolved animals are even able to communicate information about the location of food and enemies.

But animal behaviour is largely genetic or inborn. That is why it does not vary much within the species. Nor does it change within a generation, or even scores of generations. And so far, researchers have found little ability among higher animals to learn what people can learn.

Like people, animals have a microsociology of their own; members of most species cooperate and communicate. They even have a macrosociology — a division of labour and a ranking system, among other things. But among most animals, both the small "interpersonal" processes and larger social arrangements are, for the most part, genetically programmed. Neither is open to a great deal of choice or voluntary change.

We know little about the genetic bases of human social behaviour. But despite our similarities to animals, we people are far ahead of other animals in our ability to change our environment, learn from our experiences, and pass on what we have learned to our children. More than any other animals, we people adjust our behaviours to meet new challenges. Our abilities to think, plan, remember and communicate ideas give us a decided edge in creating complex social structures.

Among people, *both* the micro- and macro-structures are open to change. Indeed, the human ability to change micro-structures — to imagine, plan and set about creating new futures — is precisely what allows us to change our larger social structures.

Is there anything that *does* limit how widely human cultures can vary; and if so, what is it? The search for an answer to this question has led generations of sociologists and anthropologists to look for cultural universals. *Cultural universals* are, in the simplest terms, practices that are found in every known human culture. Anthropologist George Murdock (1945: 124) listed many cultural universals, including the following general attributes:

- athletic sports
- bodily adornment
- cooking
- dancing
- funeral ceremonies
- gift giving
- language

- laws
- music
- numerals and counting
- personal names
- religion
- sexual restrictions
- toolmaking

Other researchers have identified additional universals, such as the human ability to use fire (Goudsblom, 1987). This ability to use fire serves as a good example of how people have historically sought to control nature — in effect, to transform nature into culture. Not content with merely *using* fire, people possess the ability to make fire as well, something no other animals can do. By making fire we control it, ensure that it serves our purposes, and make it part of our cultural bag of tricks.

If certain cultural activities are universal, we must allow for the possibility that they meet universal human needs, whether physical, emotional, intellectual, or spiritual. Yet, however "natural" these needs might be, people meet them in a great variety of ways.

Take religion: it includes all of the thoughts and practices that put people in touch with the "supernatural." The followers of some religions believe the supernatural lives in natural objects like the ocean and natural forces like the wind. Others think of distinct supernatural creatures — gods, goddesses, nymphs, devils, and so on. Some religions have many gods, others have only one, while some — like Buddhism — have none. Some believe in an afterlife or in reincarnation, while others do not. Differences in ideas of good and evil, and in ritual practices, also distinguish the religions of the world.

To say that all human cultures contain religion is to point to something that unites human beings and (so far as we know) separates us from other animals. Yet religions vary enormously. The same is true of all the other cultural universals which have been found. The processes people use to meet a common need differ widely among cultures.

The only real universal is culture itself: the central role culture plays in tying people to their society. That is because culture is connected to both social structure and personality. ("Personality" is a relatively stable combination of traits that make up the way a particular person views the world and interacts with others.) As a result, the concept of culture is an important link between the macro and micro perspectives on society we discussed in the first chapter.

People who grow up in different cultures often adopt very different approaches to the same problems. This point is made humorously in Exhibit 2.1. It contains a variety of jokes about Canadians and the ways they are different from other people. It appears that culture has made Canadians cautious, modest and prudent (compared with Americans, for example).

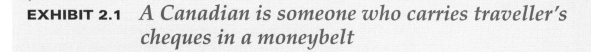

EXHIBIT 2.1   *A Canadian is someone who carries traveller's cheques in a moneybelt*

The challenge was to define a Canadian. The winner is Edward Barrett of Montreal:

A Canadian is someone who thinks an income-tax refund is a gift from the government.

Other True North traits:
A Canadian is someone who. . .

On seeing a light at the end of tunnel, assumes it is a train. When given a compliment, always looks behind to see for whom it is intended. (R.W. Crosby, Toronto)

Knows the difference between the Northern Lights and a Northern Lite. (Victoria Napier, Kingston, Ont.)

Doesn't know anyone who owns a flag. Finds Kentucky Fried Chicken "a bit too spicy." (David Linklater, Edmonton)

Holds the world's record for telephone use, probably listening to: "Don't hang up. Your call is important to us. . . " (Ken Purvis, Toronto)

Is constantly pulling himself up by the roots to see whether he is still growing. (Robert C. Hamilton, Calgary)

Will drive to an unemployment protest meeting — in his Toyota. (Al Lever, Renfrew, Ont.)

Thinks he speaks English without an accent. (Alanna Little, Toronto)

Is convinced that democracy involves keeping your opinions to yourself. (Al Wilkinson, Barrie, Ont.)

In a restaurant, apologizes for not being ready to order at the waiter's convenience. (Ian D. Brown, Toronto)

Will travel across the border to buy cigarettes and return home for subsidized cancer therapy. (Alexander Menard, Lethbridge, Alta.)

Says "sorry" when you accidentally bump into him. (Eusebio L. Koh, Regina)

Waits for the light to change before crossing a deserted intersection at 3 a.m. (Robert Davis, Toronto)

Takes as a signal for a standing ovation any two people who happen to be leaving during curtain calls. Believes the Free Trade Agreement is an agreement about free trade. (Jim Parr, Toronto)

Says "no big deal" to a sidewalk cyclist who's just knocked him down. (Erick Adams, Toronto)

Considers turning up the thermostat an integral part of foreplay. (Carolyn Germain Smith, Surrey, B.C.)

Says "excuse me" when he burps, even if he's alone. (Georgina L. Clark, Saskatoon)

Says "no thanks" to a telemarketing tape. Never sits in someone else's seat, even if the ticket-holder doesn't show. Says hello to anyone walking a dog. (Marg Gillies, Oshawa, Ont.)

Spends an inordinate amount of time trying to define exactly what a Canadian is. (Edward Baxter, Stratford, Ont.)

Goes to hot-tub parties where people wear bathing suits. Finds himself thinking about sending off to *Hinterland Who's Who* for "further information on the loon." (Christopher Gudgeon, Toronto)

Carries travellers cheques in a moneybelt. Dwayne W. Rowe, Sidney, B.C.)

Heartily proclaims, "Sure it's 38 below, but it's a dry cold." (Mariam Bernstein, Winnipeg)

When he musters enough courage to buy a Rolex watch, wears it hidden under a long-sleeve shirt and an Eaton's suit. (Byron Bellows, Toronto)

Source. Warren Clements, "A Canadian is someone who carries traveller's cheques in a moneybelt," *The Globe and Mail*, Sat., July 17, 1993, p. D4

At the macro level, the dominant **values** of a culture — the socially shared conceptions of what a group or society considers good, right, and desirable — are expressed in its social institutions. But culture works at the micro level to shape personalities through socialization, a process which we will discuss in the next chapter. However, as we also noted in the last chapter, we live in societies where things are not always what they seem. In fact, we live in two cultural settings at once: one is real and the other is ideal.

Real culture and ideal culture

Ideal culture is that aspect of culture that lives only in people's minds. It is the set of values people claim to believe in, not the culture they express in their actual behaviour. People express their ideal culture in many forms: in holy books, laws, social institutions, novels, and television programs, for example. In principle, they adhere to this ideal culture and try to build social relationships around it.

On the other hand, people express their **real culture** in real behaviour — how they dress, talk, act, relate, and think. What they actually do may differ markedly from the values and **norms** — the expectations serving as guidelines for appropriate and normal kinds of behaviour — they claim to believe in. Christians, for example, claim to follow values and norms spelled out in the New Testament, yet how many Christians really turn the other cheek or love their neighbour as they love themselves? Not many. In fact, Christians are no less selfish and no more compassionate or loving than Jews, Muslims or Hindus.

This split between real and ideal culture causes *real* problems, whether we recognize them or not. For example, where families are concerned, we pay lip service to an ideal of the family that hardly exists any more in real life. That ideal family includes a man and woman, married for the first time, and two or more children born to that couple, all of whom are living together. The man is the family bread-winner and the woman is a housewife who earns no income. Television programs, popular novels, and social movements like REAL Women and Pro-Life continue to promote this ideal family. Social welfare policies view single mothers with distrust and treat them with contempt, as though the ideal version of the family were a common reality.

Yet, in fact, a large proportion of Canadian adults are single, separated, or divorced. Many live together without marrying, others are married for a second time. A great many married couples have no children or only one child, are raising the children of another marriage, or have borne children who have since left home. In a majority of Canadian families of all kinds, adult women earn a weekly income: they too are bread-winners. The traditional, "ideal" family is now a rarity in Canadian life.

This split between ideal and actual culture leaves many people feeling abnormal, guilty, or disadvantaged. A feeling that life is not what it should be results from this lack of cultural integration. *Cultural integration* is the ability of parts of a culture to fit together and complement one another. The failure of social policies — laws, regulations, and welfare practices — to catch up to social changes that have already occurred in family life, reflects a lack of cultural integration with respect to family life. Similar problems are found throughout society: our ideal culture (often expressed in law and religion) is always far behind our real culture.

Compared to modern societies, small-scale, traditional societies in the past were more culturally integrated than our own, because most people's lives had little variety and held out few possibilities. As a result, there was little distinction between what people expected and what they experienced. People's lives and thoughts were similar. Changes in any element of the culture, though rare, brought changes in all the other elements of culture.

In these respects, modern societies are different. The specialization of activities, the isolation of different groups, and the rapid pace of change prevent a high level of integration. Technology and the marketplace are always changing North American culture. New goods and services are continually entering and changing people's lives, even if they do not square with the ideal culture. The result is a wide variation in people's real lives (by region, ethnic group, social class, and otherwise) and vast differences between what people say they want — their expressed values — and what they really do (and buy).

Material culture and non-material culture

We learn a great deal about people's real lives by studying their **material culture** — the physical and technological aspects of their lives. Material culture includes all the physical objects that members of a culture create and use. It has an important and somewhat unpredictable relationship with non-material culture.

Like ideal culture, *non-material culture* is a part of the culture that goes on in people's minds. It includes values, beliefs, philosophies, and patterns of government: in short, all the aspects of a culture that do not have a physical existence. So, for example, the material culture of Christianity includes churches, hymn books, crucifixes, statues and art objects depicting Jesus, his family and his followers. The non-material culture of Christianity consists of a body of ideas about Christ's mission on earth and the relationship between God and humanity.

Non-material culture is important; but in a culture as committed to a high standard of living and consumer goods as ours is, we often learn more from the physical objects that surround us. That is because these objects are as much our cultural masters as they are our servants. Material goods even shape our social interactions. The cellular telephone, the fax machine, and the computer bulletin board have each had a major impact, in a short time, on how we communicate with each other. The "Walkman" has had an equally significant effect on preventing or inhibiting communication.

Imagine Grok, a future sociologist who is trying to understand our culture by examining its physical objects, or artifacts. Grok would be able to learn a lot about our central values by studying a teenager's room. First, Grok would notice the information-saving and information-transmitting devices: books, magazines, televisions, records, tapes, radios, telephones, VCRs, videotapes, computers. From these, Grok might conclude that teenagers in our society depend on information for their education, recreation, social life, and livelihood.

Second, Grok would notice a variety of time-keeping devices: clocks, wristwatches, calendars, schedules and datebooks, among others. From these, Grok might conclude that teenagers in our society use time efficiently, or at least precisely; and that they value hard work and reliability.

Third, Grok would notice many objects of adornment: clothing for different occasions, jewellery, cosmetics, and false body parts (wigs, braces, false eyelashes and nails, contact lenses). From these, Grok might conclude that teenagers in our society have to look good if they want to hold on to their friendships and romances — also, that Canadian teenagers value friendship, being loved, and success.

On the other hand, Grok would be unlikely to find material clues that Canadian teenagers value freedom, which they do. After all, there is no one-to-one fit between material and non-material culture — no physical object that corresponds to each and every cultural value.

Even in China, the distinctive Coca-Cola bottle shape, and the lettering of its name, signifies the Western lifestyle which many non-Westerners find attractive.

Source: UPI/BETTMANN

Still, objects of material culture tell us a great deal about what people *really* value. That is because people have to spend valued time and money to acquire these objects. This is equally true in non-Western societies, where social ranking may depend on buying Western items. For example, Congolese teens use European clothing as a way of showing their social status (Friedman, 1990).

By now, there are few parts of the world where you won't find *someone* wearing fake Levi jeans, fake Nike shoes and a fake Harvard sweatshirt. These are all cultural signs of membership in a Westernized world. In general, then, consumption is a cultural strategy for defining oneself, either in agreement with or in opposition to the consumption patterns of other well-defined groups. That's why material culture is likely to tell us something important about non-material culture.

CULTURE SHAPES BEHAVIOUR

Shared symbols and meanings

Another good way to understand a culture is by studying its signs and symbols. Signs are things — gestures, artifacts, or words — that signify, express, or meaningfully represent something else. A "stop sign" stands for the legal command "Stop!" just as the word "woman" stands for a human female. A **symbol** is a sign whose relationship with something else expresses a value or evokes an emotion. A picture of a dove, for example, not only stands for a particular species of bird but also for the idea of peace. A flag not only identifies a country but embodies the sense of pride and identification its citizens feel.

To the dismay of travellers, cultures use different symbols to mean the same things and assign different meanings to the same symbols. What one person considers a simple design or pattern might mean a great deal to the member of another culture. For example, Muslims in Tongi, Bangladesh, ransacked a Canadian-owned Bata shoe store to protest the sale of sandals bearing a logo they considered blasphemous. The logo resembled the Arabic word for *Allah*, or God. Police had to fire tear gas and rifles to disperse the angry crowd. One person was killed and 50 were injured in this upset over a design Bata Shoes had never expected to have any symbolic meaning.

Closer to home, a Quebec law requires that all public signs in the province must be written in French. If the same information is provided in English, the French words must be dominant. The conflict here is symbolic, not practical. Legislators wrote this law to signify the dominance of French- over English-Canadian culture in Quebec. The passage of this law followed a great deal of emotional display and political argument.

Such examples show that artifacts, words and actions carry important cultural meanings. Their meanings can stir people to action, even to risking their lives. People's willingness to pay so high a price also indicates the strength of a symbol's meaning. In people's eyes, protecting and honouring these symbols is the same as protecting and honouring their own group. Actively opposing hated signs (for example, a swastika) also honours a person's own group and strengthens group solidarity.

Because people endow simple objects with powerful meanings and emotions, learning to participate in another culture is a slow, often difficult process. People only learn the meanings of signs and symbols through observation, trial and error, by immersing themselves in a culture.

The importance of values

As we have seen, people use signs and symbols to express, or challenge, the values of a society. Once internalized — that is, learned and endowed with emotion and meaning — values influence peoples' behaviour. They also serve as standards for evaluating the actions of others.

Surprisingly, values from one realm of life also influence behaviours in another realm of life. In his classic study of the rise of capitalism, the German sociologist Max Weber (1974) argued that the *economic behaviour* we associate with modern life in the West would have been impossible without a major shift in the *religious values* of medieval Europe.

Today we have a hard time believing that people once thought life on earth was less important than life after death, or that people considered hard work, thrift, and saving to be wicked or inconsequential. Yet, in the medieval, Catholic societies of Europe, people thought a concern with worldly activities, wealth, and making a profit through the investment of money at interest *was* immoral or base. Weber linked the rise of capitalism — a new style of economic thinking — with the rise of Protestantism, a new form of Christianity. In particular, he tied it to Calvinism, a form of Protestantism that developed in western Europe in the 16th century.

What Weber called the *Protestant ethic* is a doctrine formulated by Protestant reformer Martin Luther, who believed that everyone should work very hard for the glory of God. Later Protestants, called Calvinists, took this doctrine of Luther's, combined it with a belief in predestination, and unwittingly helped to create a new economic system: capitalism. Weber explained as follows: Calvinists believed that all people are predestined to go to either Heaven or Hell. Precisely who is going to Heaven and who is going to Hell is already decided. Nothing people do will change the outcome, and (strangely) this is what makes people free. As a result, Calvinist religion strongly emphasizes the freedom of the individual, and reduces people's dependence on the Church, priesthood, and ritual.

Such autonomy and independence played a key role in the historic rise of capitalism. Just as important to the emergence of capitalism, was the development of new attitudes toward economic success among Calvinists, and their compulsion to make as much money as possible, which they would then re-invest in business. Weber suggested that, because they believed salvation was predestined, Calvinists searched for a sign from God that they were among the elect. Since they believed they were working for God, it made sense to see success at work as a sign of their good standing with God.

The "Protestant ethic" argument has been successfully attacked on many grounds (see, for example, Collins, 1982). At best, it stands today as a theory that is only partly valid; but it remains a good illustration of Weber's approach to studying culture. His demonstration of a link between the rise of Protestantism and capitalism shows how changes in one cultural element (here, religion) un-expectedly bring about changes in another cultural element (here, the economy).

This linkage is important for several reasons. First, it shows that social and economic development demands cultural change. Second, it proves that every society is a complex whole, or *system*, in which the change of one part generates unexpected changes in another part. Finally, it reminds us that culture is not static, nor always a hindrance to change. Cultures change too; and as they do, they cushion the psychological hardships of social change (Dube, 1988).

Do Protestant values still guide people's lives? When Bibby and Posterski (1985) surveyed Canadian teenagers and asked them what they were looking for in life, over 80% cited friendship, being loved, and freedom as goals. Other values popular among the teenagers were success, a comfortable life, and privacy. By contrast, few of the teenagers cared much for popularity, fame (or recognition), or acceptance by God.

In some ways, Canadian teenagers are similar to the Calvinists of four centuries ago, in that they value individual freedom and material success. It's true that Calvinism does *not* seem to live on in teenagers' *life goals*. Particularly, teenagers today consider God much *less* important than Calvinists did and they consider love, privacy, and freedom much *more* important. But some of these attitudes will change as the teenagers age. In time, these young Canadians will become more like their parents and put a higher value on family life and economic security.

More important, when asked how they thought people ought to live, two teenagers in three voted for cleanliness, hard work, reliability, and forgiveness. Sixteenth century Calvinists would have approved. And like today's teenagers, the Calvinists would have considered imagination, politeness, and intelligence fairly unimportant.

Isn't it remarkable — this strong commitment of teenagers to values developed over 400 years ago in another part of the world? It shows us that cultural continuity is at least as common as cultural change. And, as we shall see in the next chapter, people start learning their culture's traditional values at a young age and never stop.

Another dramatic example of cultural continuity is something we shall discuss at length in Chapter 8, which deals with the family. All of us are accustomed to hearing about changes in "the family" and, even, about "the death of the family." Certainly, there are many ways in which the family today is different from families a decade, a generation, or a century ago. But from another standpoint what is even more impressive is how *similar* family life is today to family life in the past.

So, for example, the neolocal **nuclear family** with which we are all acquainted — a small family that sets up its own household after marriage — has been typical in England and other parts of Western Europe for at least 500 years. The same is true of monogamy and romantic love: they have also been around for a long time. So we must resist the urge to imagine that family life in the "old days" was completely different from family life today. On the other hand, some aspects of culture change more often, and more quickly, than others: this is particularly true of social norms.

Norms, folkways and mores

Few of our everyday activities are directed by fundamental goals and values. Sociologists use the concept of norms to refer to the less abstract goals which guide our behaviour in daily life. As we have defined them, norms are expectations which serve as common guidelines; they tell us what kinds of behaviour are appropriate or inappropriate, normal or abnormal.

There are many types of norms. **Folkways**, a term Graham Sumner (1906) invented, refers to the popular habits, traditions, and ordinary usages and conventions of everyday life. People expect others to conform to folkways, but do not punish their violation formally. They do not view the violators of folkways as immoral, so they punish them with exclusion and stares of contempt — nothing worse.

In some societies, we find a close connection between norms and values, indicating a strong degree of cultural integration. For example, advertisements in magazines that people read in the Persian Gulf region follow a narrowly prescribed pattern. They rely on traditional Arab rhetoric, use evaluative (versus factual) content, and reflect Islamic social values and attitudes — both in their language and the images that accompany it. As a result, Middle Eastern advertising is different from North American advertising. It is also very similar from one Islamic country to another and, within countries, from one market segment to another. Said another way, in the Middle East advertisers use the same sales strategies whether they are selling to men or women, old people or young, rich people or poor, and so on (Kavoossi and Frank, 1990).

In our own society, the connection between values and norms is much looser. Consider teenagers' reactions to "nerds," portrayed in many movies of the last decade. The nerds do not violate teenage values. After all, nerds are just as committed to privacy, freedom, and friendship, to honesty, cleanliness, and hard work as anyone else. (In fact, they may be too serious about these goals!)

Where they differ from other teenagers is in the way they dress, talk, and look. Nerds devote too little attention to their appearance, to taking part in teenager activities, or winning popularity. In these ways, nerds stand guilty of deviating from the folkways of teen culture. Other teenagers may punish them with exclusion, ridicule, and contempt.

Too bad for North American nerds! The Mandenka people of Eastern Senegal (in Africa) have a much more sophisticated and inclusive idea about interaction than North American teenagers do. They view conflict as no more than a stage in the development of friendship and believe in the importance of differences, and spaces, between people. To forget the naturalness of differences between people, they believe, is to invite hostility and trouble.

In fact, the Mandenka have invented a practice they call *sannakunnya* that serves as a safety valve for social hostility. They pair up groups or individuals and expect them to exchange insults with one another on a daily basis — a kind of "buddy system" for name-calling. Partners in this game do not have the right to get mad at each other or fight. The myth underlying this institution says that insults addressed to one's partner are, at bottom, addressed to oneself (Camara, 1976). When we discuss "taking the role of the other" in the next chapter, you'll see how sensible this really is.

Mores, another term attributed to Sumner, are norms that do carry moral significance. People believe that mores contribute to the general welfare and continuity of the group. That is why their violation is considered a serious matter and people punish it severely. Indeed, mores are often written into law. We will have more to say about rules and laws in Chapter 4, on deviance and control.

Even where mores are not written into laws, they are treated with deadly seriousness. Consider the problem short people face in China, described in Exhibit 2.2. The Chinese culture justifies discrimination against the "height deprived" because they are violating an unwritten tallness norm. Worst of all, this causes problems of low self-esteem for the hundreds of millions of Chinese people who are shorter than their own rule requires.

In any culture, some behaviour is strongly disapproved and the prohibitions are strongly enforced. These prohibitions, or **taboos**, are powerful social beliefs that a particular act, food, place (and so on) is totally repulsive. Violation of the taboo is supposed to result in immediate punishment by the social group or even by God. An example of such a powerful taboo in our society would be cannibalism, the eating of human flesh.

Researchers once considered incest — sexual relations between two close relatives (for example, father and daughter, brother and sister, or first cousins) — to be the subject of a universal taboo and, in that sense, a cultural universal. And evidence shows that just about every society does forbid certain kin from marrying each other, in the belief that these unions are immoral. However, societies differ markedly in *which* kin they forbid marrying for this reason. Moreover, incestuous behaviour appears to be just as universal as the taboo itself. Certainly, the data suggest incest does occur in Canada, though it is illegal and considered child abuse when one of the participants is a minor (Canada, Government of, 1984).

As with other sociological topics, culture is understood differently by sociologists who follow different paradigms. Because culture orders behaviour, the sociologists who emphasize order —structural functionalists — typically look to culture to explain consensus and stability. For example, they note that societies where people hold certain values and express personal satisfaction with life, trust in others, and support for the existing order tend to have more stable democratic governments than other societies (Inglehart and Garcia-Pardo, 1988). They conclude that a "civic culture" is functional to the survival of democracy. Said another way, you can't have democracy without a civic culture.

Conflict theorists, as always, focus on group differences in power and belief. For example, they would point out that strongly stated values — which suggest value consensus — often indicate a conflict between two groups within the society. One approves of the action and the other strongly opposes it. The

EXHIBIT 2.2 *Getting short end of stick just part of life in China*

In this nation of height-disadvantaged people, shorter citizens face blatant discrimination. Many schools and jobs require above-average height. Short people are considered an unattractive sub-species. And Chinese often discourage intermarriage for fear the union will result in short children — who will in turn endure life-long prejudice. . . .

Being tall here is disproportionately important. Heightism is so bad that people often fib about their height, the way Westerners might lie about their age. One magazine in the western city of Xian runs an advice column especially for short people. High heels are popular not just with women but also with men. Wannabe-tall types send for mail-order "height-increasing machines" that purport to stretch limbs. And anxious parents dose their children with "height-increasing medicine.". . .

At a recent showing of a Hong Kong hit film in Beijing, the audience tittered when a short actress, playing the role of a secretary, appeared on the screen. "Look how short she is," someone yelled.

Chinese aren't used to seeing short people in the movies, or short secretaries in real life. Acting classes at the Beijing Film Academy, for instance, enroll only those of above-average height. And many offices hire secretaries for their looks, which invariably includes above-average height. . . .

According to a recent national survey, the average 15-year-old Chinese urban male is 5 foot 5, slightly taller than his Japanese counterpart and only an inch or two shorter than the average adult North American male, according to insurance-company statistics. The average 15-year-old urban Chinese female is 5 foot 2.

A better diet means that Chinese have been growing taller during the past few decades. The average for a 15-year-old male, for example, is three-quarters of an inch taller than five years earlier, according to the ministry of health, which sponsored the survey.

But dreams keep outpacing reality. Ask a Chinese the ideal height, and the answer invariably is 5 foot 7 for a male and 5 foot 5 for a female. And for no apparent reason, China recently issued what is called "standard weights and measurements" for Chinese people. For males the standard height is 5 foot 7; for females 5 foot 3. . . .

Like racism or sexism, heightism seems an absurd waste of talent. Last year, 17-year-old Zhang Jinxia committed suicide by drinking insecticide after a college in Jiangsu province barred her because of her height. Ms. Zhang had scored top marks in the entrance exam, but her letter of acceptance was annulled when she showed up on registration day and officials realized she was 4 foot 7. Her death and other cases of discrimination have led to the first calls for laws protecting short people in China. . . .

Source: Jan Wong, "Getting short end of stick just part of life in China," *The Globe and Mail*, Thurs., Feb. 3, 1994, pp. A1, A11

ongoing public debate and disagreement over abortion is a good illustration of this. Remember that cultural values, norms and taboos do not always tell us what is *really* going on. Often, formal disapproval of an action, such as incest, proves that the behaviour is far more common than people would like to admit.

For their part, symbolic interactionists emphasize how people make creative use of values and norms in the course of everyday interaction. Two of you may share the same cultural values and norms about love and intimacy, but you have to work out the *details* of your relationship. This can be a thrilling process or a painful one — often it is both — but it is never exactly the same twice. Human beings are complex and creative, so symbolic interactionists caution us against thinking of values or norms as commands which people are programmed to follow in the same ways.

Finally, the feminist paradigm draws our attention to the way in which culture — through language — shapes our perception of men and women. For feminist sociologists, androcentric or sexist language not only illustrates gender inequality in our society, it helps to perpetuate the problem.

Language is one component of culture to which Canadians are particularly sensitive. As a multicultural nation made up of people from many different ethnic, religious, and linguistic backgrounds, the issues surrounding culture and language hold a central place in Canadian society. We will consider these issues in Chapter 6, when discussing ethnic identities.

At the most basic level, language is an abstract system of sounds (speech), signs (written characters), and gestures (non-verbal communication) by which members of a society express their thoughts, feelings, ideas, and desires. This means that language, whether spoken or written, verbal or non-verbal, is the means by which the achievements of one generation are passed on to the next.

Like other signs and symbols, words carry both intended and unintended meanings. We learn both kinds of meanings as active members of a culture, as much through observation and through trial and error as by formal instruction.

According to anthropologists Sapir and Whorf (Sapir, 1929), language expresses our thoughts but also structures them. Language is the most important means we use to communicate. Therefore, the way in which a language is structured has immense significance for the way we experience the world. Different languages provide people with different conceptual tools to organize and interpret reality.

Colour is one such conceptual tool. You see one object as "red," another as "green," still another as "blue" because our culture assigns objects to these categories. Other cultures assign colours differently. In many cultures, what you would see as two distinct colours, "blue" and "green," are seen as two shades of a single colour, in the same way that we see two shades of red as being "pink" and "scarlet."

When children learn to speak the language of their culture, they learn the assumptions that pervade their language. Cultures make words to describe, and thereby teach members of a society to see, what the society cares about. For example the Slave, a native group of the Northwest Territories and Alberta, have a culture that traditionally involved travelling and fishing on ice. Accordingly, they developed a complex vocabulary related to describing ice conditions, one that included separate terms for ice that is thin, thick, brittle, muddy, wet, hollow, slippery, blue, black, white, seamed, cracked, or floating.

Other Inuit categories of snow include: the first snowfall of autumn, very hard compressed and frozen snow, snow covered by bad weather, snow with a hard crust that gives way under footsteps, snow roughened by rain or frost, compact damp snow, melting snow, wet falling snow, half-melted snow, drifting snow, crystalline snow that breaks down and separates like salt, and snow whose surface has frozen after a light spring thaw.

Without such finely graded language, people might still be able to sense differences in the types of snow if they were told to look for them. But without these language categories, people would be *unlikely* to look for such gradations and would have a hard time talking about them even if they found them.

By the same token, the English language has dozens and possibly hundreds of words that describe machines of various kinds. Inuit and other pre-industrial languages have few such words, and often adopt words from English to refer to these items. This makes English a natural choice for discussing modern industrial themes (for example, manufacturing processes).

Most of the assumptions embodied in language are hidden —known but implicit or, even, unrecognized. These tacit assumptions lurk everywhere in our language. A good example, as we mentioned earlier, is the use of androcentric language in English. We are all accustomed to using the words "*man*kind," "police*man*," "chair*man*," and other words that include the word "man." Historically, many of these words have aptly described the role in question; in the past, most police*men* and chair*men* really were men, not women.

The view that people should switch to gender-neutral terms such as "police officer" and "chair person" is more than a quibble. If the Sapir-Whorf hypothesis is valid, our continued use of the masculine words implies that women are still absent from these roles, and perhaps should be. If we continue to see women who fill these roles as being deviant, we end up discouraging women from seeking them. When we use masculine terms, we affirm the traditional exclusion and subordination of women.

Differences in the ways members of different cultures discuss things makes communication across cultures difficult. For example, Chinese people in conversation often speak in proverbs when they discuss their norms and values. This way of thinking and talking about social life is traditionally viewed as a sign of refinement: good breeding and education. It has survived culturally for thousands of years, from classical Chinese writings down to the present. Yet the practice often surprises members of other cultures (Gunther, 1991). These outsiders may think that the Chinese people are speaking in vague or roundabout ways when, in fact, they are stating strong views.

Can you name all the "personal hygiene" equipment in this picture? Congratulations if you can! That proves you are part of modern Western culture.

Similarly, Australian Aborigines have a distinct notion of time which they use in conversation. In particular, the way they talk about their future plans appears mysterious to speakers of other languages. For example, it may be unclear whether a stated intention — to meet on January 22nd — is a hard and fast plan, a wished-for possibility, or one of many equally binding obligations. And it may be difficult for Aborigines to reach even *that* degree of specificity in discussing the future. Since it is hard to get this way of thinking across to non-Aborigines, misunderstandings and hard feelings often result (Eades, 1984).

Finally, misunderstandings have occurred between Ethiopian refugees and Israeli border authorities due to differences in language. Israeli officials have often failed to understand Ethiopian refugees because they lack knowledge about the ways Ethiopians view the world and expect others to behave (Ben-Ezer, 1985). For example, Israeli authorities interpret Ethiopian deference, politeness and indirectness as an indication that the refugees have something to hide, when, in fact, the Ethiopians are simply showing respect as they have learned to do.

Given these differences in the ways we think and communicate about the world, what social institutions are able to draw us together? The answer is, first of all, an increasingly globalized mass media.

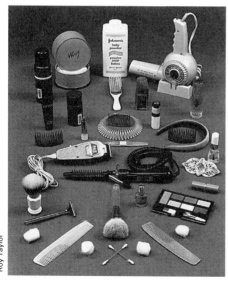

Roy Taylor

CULTURAL INTEGRATION

The mass media

The *mass media* are important sources of cultural integration in the modern world. As our imaginary sociologist, Grok, would have noticed, we consume mass media to a degree that no one would have imagined a century ago. Mass media are forms of communication which impart information to, and influence the opinions of, large audiences, without any personal contact between the senders and receivers of the information. The mass media include television, movies, newspapers, and radio.

Gutenberg's invention of the printing press in the 1430s had many social consequences. By making possible the mass distribution of printed books, it started a revolution in communications. One long-term effect was the spread of literacy, a growth in the number of people who could read and interpret information for themselves. People no longer needed to rely on the village priest to teach them what the Bible said; they could do it for themselves. This change undermined the power of priests and supported the breakaway of Protestants from the Catholic church in 16th-century Europe.

The spread of printed information through newspapers, handbills, and manifestos also helped people to mobilize for political action. Information, and the sense of power it gave people, helped to support the French and American revolutions of the 18th century, and other revolutions ever since.

In the 20th century we have technology — the camera, radio, telephone, and television — that conveys information through sound and image. This technology tells us anything we want to know about problems and opportunities, conflicts and peace settlements around the globe. By listening to a simple transistor radio, even people who are illiterate and live in remote parts of the world know what is going on.

This explosion of information technology has made cultural integration and political rebellion equally possible. People have even claimed that the dramatic changes which swept through Eastern Europe in 1989 were a result of information technology freely crossing national borders. We have yet to see what impact the next generation of information technology will have.

The media's potential both for maintaining and overthrowing order has made its control a central concern in the 20th century. In the Third World, many countries are going through the same steps of national unification that Europe and North America went through centuries earlier. This has made the mass media central to their economic and political development too.

Many governments of developing countries are becoming concerned about the possibility that the mass media will undermine their cultural identity. The electronic mass media tend to convey American ideals and values to a global audience (Tenbruck, 1990). We will say more about this in Chapter 11.

In the Philippines, the government has tried using the media to shape popular values. It has even produced radio dramas on development themes, with a soap opera format (Hartmann, 1979). Their goal has been to fight the passive, defeatist and "counter-developmental" attitudes found in most popular shows. However this pro-development use of the media seems to have met with little viewer acceptance.

Canadian thinker Marshall McLuhan (1965) has written that "the medium is the message." By this he means that the type of medium — whether written word or visual image — will determine the cultural impact and interpretation of a message. New technologies have started a second revolution in mass communications by conveying new kinds of messages in far more powerful ways than books could do in the past. (Just think of the effect a pornographic movie, violent video game or martial arts movie would have on your younger brother or sister!)

Economist and historian Harold Innis (1972) goes even further than McLuhan, claiming that the medium of communication — whether verbal or written — will determine the form a society takes. An oral tradition supports a rich and flexible civilization, based on custom. In contrast, a written tradition supports standardization, discipline, and political unification, says Innis. Writing on paper, not stone, is the means of communication leaders need to use if they want to build empires. It remains to be seen what kind of empire will emerge from information stored on floppy disks.

Ethnocentrism

Though one language fits a given situation better than another, most people would agree that no language is necessarily better than any other. Yet we would have a hard time persuading people that no particular values are better than any others. People are so emotionally involved with their culture that often they do not see that their own values, like other cultural traits, are merely one approach to human life. Their **ethnocentrism** leads them to view everything from the point of view of their own culture.

Ethnocentrism is a tendency to use one's own culture as a basis for evaluating other cultures. One's own culture is taken to be the norm and considered superior to all other cultures which deviate from that norm. Ethnocentrism is natural enough, especially for people who have had little exposure to other cultures. But natural or not, ethnocentrism poses problems in a world filled with different values, languages and perceptions.

Accepting cultural variation as a fact of life and avoiding ethnocentrism are not easy matters. After all, ethnocentrism is not merely cultural shortsightedness; it is rooted in people's upbringing. Consider a stereotype some North Americans hold of Asian students, as passive and overly methodical. Teachers may see these students as poor communicators, but the difference is mainly cultural — the result of a different style of communicating. More often than not, the problem lies on the side of the teacher, not the student (Bannai and Cohen, 1985).

Exhibit 2.3 shows that ethnocentrism also has a humorous side. As travellers, we bump up against other people's ideas of proper behaviour. When this happens, we are forced to re-examine our own rules and ask whether there is any good reason for obeying them.

If there is to be a global society, it will require more than the spread of Western values and practices. To achieve a global society, all cultures will have to cross-pollinate and share their views of the world. Like everyone else, Westerners will benefit by learning some cultural concepts of other societies, with their different ideas of ownership, work, wealth, family, health, community and even self. We need new and better ideas about many of these things if we are to protect human life in the 21st century.

Yet, so far, people in the West have tended to corrupt or denigrate non-Western cultures. For example, the steel drum music of black Trinidadians has a history that reflects oppression and resistance to white people's domination. In this way, it represents black culture and identity. Imagine, then, hearing that music played in Switzerland by small groups of white, middle-class musicians who have converted it into a banal and syrupy pop music. Worse still, imagine

EXHIBIT 2.3 *Cultural mistakes*

The challenge was to devise misleading advice for tourists. The winner is W.P. Kinsella of White Rock, B.C.:

Be sure to take along an adequate supply of raw meat and honey to hand-feed the lovable grizzly bears in Canada's national parks.

If a customs or immigration officer asks you a question you consider too personal, don't be afraid to say, "I don't think that's any of your business."

Other untoward tips:

If you want a good table in a Las Vegas nightclub, don't bribe the maitre d'. It's first come, first served. (Ruth Brown, Toronto)...

Georgia state troopers believe in the principle that you are innocent until proven guilty, and therefore welcome an argument. (Linda Lumsden, Peterborough, Ont.)...

Malaysia, in contrast to its neighbours in the region, is well-known for its relaxed and tolerant attitude toward the use of recreational drugs. Western tourists are encouraged to bring adequate supplies for themselves, their hosts and as gifts for officials. (Alexander J. Baldwin, Halifax)...

During guided tours of the Plains of Abraham, it is customary to sing *Rule Britannia.* (Jim Parr, Toronto)

When visiting very hot countries such as Egypt and Saudi Arabia, men and women should pack plenty of cool clothing such as shorts and tank tops.

Fun-loving airport personnel all over the world enjoy a good laugh, so have lots of drug and bomb jokes ready when you are having your luggage scanned (Helen McCusker, Mississauga, Ont.)...

The Scots, Welsh and Irish all love to be called "English." (Al Wilkinson, Barrie, Ont.)

Quebeckers love to practice their English on visitors but they tend to be shy, so, even if you speak French, insist that they speak English. (Helen and Peter Marucci, Fergus, Ont.)

The best restaurants in France always reserve a bottle of ketchup for their more discriminating guests, so be sure to ask. (Ken Purvis, Toronto)

Source: Warren Clements "Terrible travel advice: Always take lots of recreational drugs to Malaysia," *The Globe and Mail,* Sat., Oct. 23, 1993, p. D4

---

that Westernized music exported to Caribbean tourist resorts. No wonder blacks fear that this "degenerate" form of music, along with white Trinidadians' rejection of black music, will threaten the survival of genuine black music in the Islands (Lotmar, 1987).

Or, consider the problem of rap music — a black art form that is deeply rooted in African music styles like call-and-response. While most rappers are black, much of their audience is white. The call-and-response format, which is part of traditional African culture, requires that rappers accommodate the feedback of their audience, no matter what their race or ethnic background. In the end, rap music requires the emergence of a cultural community which is not defined along colour lines (Stephens, 1991).

Even within societies, powerful groups have corrupted and "commodified" the cultures of minority groups or the poor. This happened with jazz in America, for example. In Brazil, the dominant class and the mass media have likewise adopted popular cultural practices — especially, the Brazilian carnival — and changed them to fit into a consumer-oriented economic system (von Simson, 1983).

If we choose to, we can learn a lot by respecting traditional cultures. In traditional Nigerian society, for example, sport has an intrinsic value, as an expression of culture and a type of enjoyment. The Yorubas dance, canoe, and throw fishing nets and spears at targets. These sports activities help to preserve tribal culture, identify communities and facilitate socialization (Akindutire, 1992). In this context, sport is also a ritual. The exercise of skills and standards, competition and cooperation, and the application of rules, all have a moral meaning.

How different this is from sport for mass consumption in the West, where the viewers are nothing but consumers and the athletes, merely employees. Under these conditions, sport loses its moral power and becomes just a spectacle. Violence, entertainment, and celebrity are central to the event. At its best, Western sport is exciting, but it has no moral or social meaning (Alt, 1983).

Sport, music and many other cultural forms probably do not get any better when they are Westernized. We are likely to see a proliferation of subcultures in the future and we all need to become much more tolerant in preparing for this. At the very least, we have to avoid that knee-jerk reaction of applying our own cultural rules to someone else's culture.

CULTURAL VARIATION

Subcultures and countercultures

As we have seen, there is tremendous cultural variety *across* societies. But even *within* a given society there are many **subcultures** which develop because of generational, class, occupational or other differences.

A subculture is a group that shares the cultural elements of the larger society, but also has its own distinctive values, beliefs, norms, style of dress, and behaviour patterns. In the case of ethnic groups, a subculture may even have its own language. However, people who belong to these distinctive cultural groups still share a great deal with other Canadians.

Among the many cultures and subcultures existing in our society are what social scientists call *organizational cultures*. All organizations have their own culture-in-miniature, complete with norms and values. In formal organizations, culture is what emerges when a group tries to solve the problems of external adaptation and internal integration. In short, organizational culture is the way an organization has learned to deal with its environment. Like every culture, it contains tacit and unconscious assumptions (about nature, truth, humanity and relationships) that underlie all group values and actions (Schein, 1984).

Organizational cultures are particularly important in societies like ours where organizations — especially work organizations — have become more important than most other institutions (Gutknecht, 1982). They provide their members with solidarity, community, social relationships and emotional satisfaction — all of which help to control their behaviour and influence their minds. At the same time, the ways people behave in organizations is influenced by the surrounding national culture. Different national cultures have different ideas about uncertainty, organization and control. Often, these differences surface in multinational corporations and affect the ways different parts of the organization scan, select, interpret and use information (Schneider, 1989).

Like other norms, organizational norms can be violated. Traditionally, people working in industry have pursued their own advancement through seniority or patronage. But in rapidly changing industrial societies, employees have become more aggressive. Actively seeking advancement, they may violate traditional organizational norms. One sign is the demand for participatory ownership and management schemes to satisfy their aspirations for advancement (Sainsaulieu, 1983).

People from different national cultures often hold different organizational values. In one Japanese-owned organization, for example, American and Japanese workers must work side by side, and clear national differences emerge. The American workers are less willing to defer to authority and group norms. They feel stifled by too much group activity. Americans are concerned with equality and see the organization as hindering their growth and liberty.

By contrast, Japanese workers believe that they grow individually *within* the boundaries of the group. The Japanese respect hierarchies and believe that self-development occurs alongside, and even *through*, the development of the organization (Parks, 1982).

Organizational culture is only one type of subculture. Generally, a subculture emerges whenever a particular segment of society faces unique problems or enjoys unique privileges. Members of a subculture often share a common age, religion, ethnic heritage, belief system, occupation, interest, or hobby. Or, like prison inmates or mental patients, they share exclusion from the larger society.

A **counterculture** is a subculture that rejects conventional norms and values and adopts alternative ones. Such a culture is fundamentally at odds with the culture of the larger society. It is often found among younger and less advantaged members of a society. A counterculture develops among people with little reason to conform to the main culture. Such people are unlikely to get rewarded with praise, good jobs, or high incomes even if they value what other people value and conform to other people's rules.

A counterculture helps people cope with their problems by rejecting the majority values and putting substitute values in their place. In effect, a counterculture rejects conventional morality and makes deviance the new standard of behaviour. Keep in mind, though, that members of a counterculture do not reject conformity to everything, only conformity to some of the primary values of the majority.

Like a subculture, a counterculture has its own beliefs, material culture, and problems of cultural integration. Even members of the Hell's Angels have their loyalties; even anarchists follow their own rules. Delinquents, punk rockers, and skinheads have their ideals too. Like any culture, a counterculture contains contradictions between what its members say and what they do.

The distinction between subcultures and countercultures is often a subtle one. For example, gay and lesbian subculture is *not* a counterculture. It provides homosexual people with social supports for living the lifestyle they prefer but it is not, in principle, opposed to the "straight" lifestyle of heterosexuals. It is simply indifferent to the "straight" life.

And, like many subcultures, this one has problems fitting into the larger culture. Consider Almaguer's (1991) study of gays in Latin America. These men must reconcile their gay identity with the androcentric, *macho* culture of their homeland. By rejecting heterosexuality they also reject the sexual outlook of their native culture. By contrast, American and western European cultures provide more room for a gay male identity, though homophobia is still very prevalent. These cultures are less macho, but they are far from the Hispanic tradition in other respects as well. This forces the Hispanic gay male to make a clear choice of host cultures.

Often, we have trouble distinguishing a subculture from a counterculture. Is the often-studied delinquent or gang subculture merely designed to support the delinquent lifestyle of its members? Or is it a purposeful rejection of the values of the mainstream society? Sociologists disagree about this. There is less disagreement that religious cults like the Branch Davidians of Waco, Texas, or politically militant groups such as the white supremacist neo-Nazis, are countercultures and not merely subcultures.

High culture and popular culture

Not all subcultures serve the disadvantaged or the victimized. At the upper end of the social scale, we find people with quite different subcultures. These are not countercultures but neither are they part of the cultural mainstream.

Even though they benefit most from the way society is organized, high status people do not necessarily conform to the culture of the majority. People in the middle class, not the upper class, stand to gain most by conforming to the rules of a culture. If they conform, they are eligible to move up the social ladder; if they do not, they risk sliding down it. People at the bottom of the social scale stand to gain least from conformity. They also have the least to lose from nonconformity: that is why they can risk forming countercultures.

As for people at the top of the social scale, they run little risk of losing their power, wealth and position, and they stand to gain nothing by conforming to ordinary standards of behaviour. So, many members of the upper class participate in a subculture that is just as outlandish as a delinquent or bohemian counterculture. They love doing what the French call *épater les bourgeois*, infuriating the middle-class by their outlandish behaviour. This gives rise to the lavish, grotesque "lifestyles of the rich and famous" we associate with people like Michael Jackson and Donald Trump.

Other upper class people take part in what is called "high culture." **High culture** refers to the set of preferences, habits, tastes, values, and norms that are characteristic of, or supported by, high status groups in society. They include the fine arts, classical music, ballet, and other "highbrow" concerns. Of course, wealthy people are not the only ones who attend symphony concerts, read poetry, or visit art galleries. *Many* people use these cultural organizations to announce to others that they, too, are "cultured"; in this way they improve their own social status (Fine and Ross, 1984). Nevertheless, upper-class philanthropy provides much of the operating budget for these activities. Typically, wealthy and educated people sit on the boards of directors of such cultural organizations. It is to their cultural taste that these activities are directed.

That is one reason why these activities are called "high culture." Another is that these activities require a higher intellectual level than, say, bowling or reading *TV Guide*.

"High culture" has historically glorified the rich. The high culture that painters, poets, and composers created for wealthy patrons before the 20th century dignified the aristocracy's image of itself. According to art historian John Berger (1972), classic works of art

 supplied the higher strata of the ruling class with a system of references for the forms of their own idealized behaviour. They showed how the heightened moments of life — to be found in heroic action, the dignified exercise of power, passion, courageous death, the noble pursuit of pleasure — should be lived, or, at least, should be seen to be lived (Berger, 1972: 101).

Reuters/BETTMAN

Does your social circle include people who dress like this? Neither does ours. The model pictured here presents an idealized version of wealth, glamour, and leisure.

Perhaps intentionally, high culture excludes many more people than it includes. By conveying exotic images and ignoring ordinary lives, high culture has traditionally cut ordinary people off from their own history. No wonder middle- and working-class people develop and make use of a popular culture of their own! **Popular (or mass) culture** is the culture of the masses, and includes those objects, preferences, and tastes that are widespread in a society.

Popular culture is a blanket term for any element of culture that is distinct from the culture of high-status groups. One must be careful to define it as culture for the largest number, and avoid placing an elitist judgement of "poor quality" on it (Gofman, 1990). It includes both high and folk art products, so long as they maintain the individual character of the creator. For example, the comedy of Howie Mandel (or Ren and Stimpy) would be considered part of "popular culture" because it is widely popular, yet distinct from the comedy of, say, Jerry Seinfeld.

Like all forms of culture, popular culture is fragmented along age, sex, and social-class lines. We see this fragmentation in market surveys that identify the viewers of different kinds of television programs: educational television *versus* soap operas *versus* sports. We find just as much fragmentation in people's tastes for leisure, dress, eating, and even living-room decoration. Market research shows us there are many lifestyle types (at least forty, by one count) in North American society.

At the same time, popular culture reflects the influence of high culture. We even see this influence in mass advertising — the lowest common denominator in our culture. Berger has identified many images that advertising has borrowed from classical oil painting. They include the poses used to denote stereotypes of women: serene mother, free-wheeling secretary, perfect hostess, and sex-object. There are also physical stances which are used to convey the wealth and power of men.

The mass media and popular culture have developed hand in hand. They both reflect the rise of enormous new audiences with a great deal of money to spend. But trends in high culture reflect the growth of new audiences too. The fine arts began to change as early as the 19th century with the rise of middle classes who were eager to establish their social worth by buying pictures (White and White, 1965).

As the middle classes adopt the cultural taste and practices of the upper classes, the upper classes seek out new practices in an attempt to maintain their cultural distance. Eventually, the middle classes catch on to the new practices and the process repeats itself. This is one of the dynamics of cultural change, and it has been going on at least since theorist Thorstein Veblen wrote about the "conspicuous waste" of the "leisure class" a century ago.

Cultural capital, cultural literacy

French sociologist Pierre Bourdieu agrees, arguing that culture reflects and supports the stratification system in a society by allowing powerful people to use culture to their own advantage.

One of many important advantages is control over the ideologies which characterize a society. We will discuss the social role of ideology in Chapter 11. Here we discuss two other phenomena which are unequally distributed in society, **cultural capital** and **cultural literacy**.

Bourdieu (1977) coined the term *cultural capital*. It refers to a body of knowledge and interpersonal skills that helps people to get ahead socially. Familiarity with high culture is one form of cultural capital. This familiarity helps in establishing good social relations with wealthy and powerful people.

Young people with more cultural capital — more familiarity with good books, opera, and art, and also a tendency to identify themselves as "cultured" — do better in life than similar young people with less cultural capital (Dimaggio and Mohr, 1985). Cultural capital affects their educational attainment, college attendance, college completion, graduate-school attendance — even their choice of marriage partners.

Cultural capital includes a wide variety of skills that enhance social relationships. These include knowing how to speak interestingly, what topics to discuss, how to order and eat graciously, what beverages to drink, how to dress stylishly but tastefully, how to play a variety of games and sports that others want to play (for example, tennis, sailing, bridge, chess, polo), how to compare scotches or wines or race-horses or hotels in different European cities, and so on. (In Canada, according to research by Erickson (1991), cultural capital also includes the ability to speak confidently and persuasively about the business world.)

Few people learn these things in school. To learn them requires a wide variety of personal experiences, indulgent and knowledgable parents, devoted teachers, and time and money to spare. Cultural capital helps people get ahead because it marks them out from the rest of the field. They end up with more advantages because they start out with more.

Middle-class parents often try to provide their children with experiences that will give them cultural capital: ballet lessons, private schooling, trips abroad, instructional summer camps, and so on. Working-class parents, however, are rarely able to do the same. As a result, working-class children are less likely to get ahead socially than middle-class children.

Occasionally, the value of a particular skill, as cultural capital, is uncertain. Consider the ability to speak French: among European-origin Israelis, that ability has long been a form of cultural capital. For them, as for most Europeans during the last two or three centuries, familiarity with the French language has been a sign of cultural refinement. But among Israelis of North African origin, a knowledge of French is basic, not a refinement at all. And because these French-speaking North African Jews are poor and relatively uneducated, in Israel the ability to speak French is starting to lose its cultural *cachet* (Ben-Rafael, Herzlich and Freund, 1990).

Among the poorer members of society, cultural literacy, not cultural capital, is often the issue. Unlike cultural capital, which is a luxury, cultural literacy is an absolute necessity. Cultural literacy is a solid knowledge of the traditional culture, which contains the building blocks of all communication and learning. To be culturally literate is to have enough general knowledge about the world to be able to communicate effectively with any adult member of society.

Historian E.D. Hirsch (1988) argues that schools ought to provide their students with such a store of cultural knowledge, instead of abstract thinking skills. He cites research to show that effective learning does not depend on general intelligence, creativity, or an ability to solve problems. It depends on an ability to understand words and concepts and to quickly recognize common patterns of meaning.

EXHIBIT 2.4   *Relentless pursuit of fundamental math*

. . . The Kumon method, devised by a Japanese teacher for his son back in the fifties, brought to Canada by Japanese immigrants, takes a decidedly low-tech approach to developing math skills. When I went to take a look at a Kumon centre in Toronto — there are about 170 across Canada — I found myself in a sober-looking, unembellished church basement. There were no computers or other expensive gadgets on display. The teachers were enthusiastic amateurs. The tools of learning were stripped right down to the basics: pencils, paper and a roomful of eager minds.

Kumon isn't expensive — $55 a month, plus a $30 enrollment fee — but that doesn't make it a cut-rate form of learning. The program pares its costs in the most creative way, by placing the responsibility for acquiring knowledge squarely on the child. The bulk of the work is done at home, at a rate of 15 to 20 minutes a day. Twice a week, children check in at the Kumon centre, where they hand in their homework and take a test timed by a prominently placed digital clock.

Speed is of the essence. A child is expected to complete a workbook of 200 questions in — wait till you hear this — 10 minutes. The work is marked, grades and times are recorded in a score book, and a sticker of approval is placed on the plastic workcase that carries away the next week's work. . . .

Relentless repetition is fundamental to the Kumon program, compensating for the classroom tendency to avoid the tedious mechanics of learning. "It's not magic," says Gwen Cheng, a bank manager who runs a Kumon centre. "The Kumon method stresses work habits. You have to practice every day."

Schools, she says, teach math in a spiral: everything is presented over the year, but not in depth. Then the same material returns the next year, and the next until the information sinks in.

At Kumon they act like they're in more of a hurry. They cram numbers into young minds, thinking nothing of subjecting a 7-year-old to hundreds of questions, stressing mental arithmetic and calculating abilities so that children know the answer the moment they see the question. Accuracy is paramount. Students start below their grade level and are not allowed to move up until they can score 100 per cent. . . .

Source: John Allemang, "Relentless pursuit of fundamental math," *The Globe and Mail*, Thurs. Nov. 25, 1993, p. C4

This means that knowledge is more important than creativity, experience more important than "ability." A chess grandmaster, Hirsch claims, is much better than anyone else at identifying traditional game strategies and responding to them. But outside a chess game — say, in fixing a car, filling out an income-tax form, or preparing a meal — the grandmaster is no more capable than you or I. Likewise, the experienced chef is extraordinarily creative in the kitchen, but no more creative than anyone else outside it. So creativity and problem-solving abilities depend on concrete knowledge.

This suggests that, before people can learn anything else, they need to master a body of information. What's more, the body of information they need for everyday life is easy to identify. In North America, it is a storehouse of common knowledge — a few thousand names, dates, concepts, and expressions to which most people refer in their thinking and communication. The vast majority of items in this storehouse date back 50 years or more.

The storehouse of common knowledge is not only useful and slow to change: it is also widely known. Cultural items in this storehouse are used by literate people from every ethnic and racial group, region, and social class. All of us know (or ought to know) what is meant by an "Achilles heel," for example, an expression which refers to a hero in a Greek myth which dates back well over 3000 years.

Many educators, along with Hirsch, feel that schools today ignore cultural literacy. An indication of this concern, and the debate between contending educational researchers, comes through in Exhibit 2.4 (above). Implicitly, the newspaper column favours Hirsch's position. However repetitiously attained, a firm grasp of facts is central to all knowledge, it argues.

Now that we have discussed cultures and cultural processes in many parts of the world, we must finally deal with the most contentious issue of all among Canadian students: does *Canada* have a distinctive culture? If so, what are its characteristics?

CANADIAN CULTURE

Images of Canadian culture

Francophone Quebecers feel they have a distinctive culture. But what about Canada as a whole? Is there a Canadian culture which distinguishes us from, for example, Americans? American sociologist Seymour Martin Lipset (1990) believes that there is. His work presents an image of Canadian culture as elitist, traditional, and focused on the group instead of the individual.

Lipset's vision of Canadian culture is one that many observers of Canada would accept. However, support for this view comes largely from outside Canadian sociology: from novelists (like Margaret Atwood), journalists (like Richard Gwyn, Pierre Berton, and Andrew Malcolm), literary critics (like Northrop Frye and George Woodcock) and historians (like Ramsey Cook). There is evidence, however, that Canadian distinctiveness has lost ground in the last two decades. Recent survey data find little support for Lipset's argument.

Where researchers do find cultural differences between Canadians and Americans, they run in the opposite direction, with Canadians being less traditional and elitist. Both in our social policies, such as medicare, and in our attitudes towards the disadvantaged, Canadians are much more egalitarian than Americans (Baer, Grabb, and Johnston, 1990). Canada's multicultural policy also suggests a greater tolerance and appreciation for ethnic group differences than that found in the United States, even though much of the political and constitutional conflict in Canada in recent years has involved conflict among ethnic groups.

Still other observers argue that Canadian culture does not exist at all, and if it does, it is no more than a collection of regional cultures: a Newfoundland culture, a Maritime culture, a Quebec culture, a central Canadian anglophone culture, a Prairie culture, and a British Columbian culture. Some believe that Canadian culture is precisely the cultural mosaic provided us by Canada's different regions, ethnic and linguistic groups: no more and no less!

Books by George Woodcock (1970), a western literary critic, and Joel Garreau (1981), an American journalist, have supported this idea. They claim that the true vitality in North American culture is found within, not across, its regions. Each region has its own history, environment, economy, and traditional concerns. The people of each region have their own values and way of life. Trying to prove these distinct regions make up a unified Canadian culture is an impossible and fanciful task. Survey data support this view with evidence of strong variations in attitudes across Canada's regions (Blishen and Atkinson, 1982).

When native warriors stood eye to eye against Quebec provincial police and Canadian Forces at Oka, cultural (and political) integrity—for First Nations, for Quebec, and for Canada—was in question.

Canapress

The most persuasive recent evidence on this question is provided in research which analyzed the ways North Americans in all the regions of Canada and the United States answered several dozen survey questions. The findings (Baer, Grabb and Johnston, 1993) gave just about everyone *some* ammunition. First, they provided (slight) evidence of Canadian-American differences, as Lipset would have predicted. Second, they provided (slight) evidence of geographic or regional differences, as Woodcock, Garreau, Blishen and Atkinson would have predicted. Most of all, they found evidence of three main "culture areas" in North America: Quebec, Dixie, and the rest.

On a variety of topics, respondents in Quebec consistently showed the most "progressive" or liberal attitudes. Respondents in the American south consistently showed the most conservative attitudes. The remaining North American respondents were indistinguishable, whether they lived in Toronto or Toledo, Winnipeg or Washington, Vancouver or Vermont. More research is needed to confirm this finding with an even wider variety of questions. At this point, there is good reason to doubt both the "nationalist" and "regionalist" theories.

Whether a unified Canadian culture exists and, indeed, whether there should be one, are important questions. Nationalists argue that without a unified Canadian culture it will be impossible to escape economic, cultural, and political assimilation by the United States. Others, like S.M. Lipset, say that Canadian culture is already strong enough to resist that possibility. Regionalists, like George Woodcock and the Quebec nationalists, would argue that cultural unification can only come at the expense of lively ethnic and regional cultures that people really care about.

These disagreements point to the fact that culture in a modern industrial society does not allow for easy generalizations. As a nation created through the political union of two different groups, then settled by large numbers of immigrants from many different countries, Canada's culture is difficult to study. Moreover, what we learn about Canada helps us to understand the complex nature of ethnic and cultural relations throughout the world.

A GLOBAL CULTURE?

As we look around the world today, we see ethnic fragmentation, the increasing importance of culturally based political movements and a lack of faith in such 19th century cultural ideals as "progress" or "civilization." All this signifies a global struggle between traditional *national* (or subnational) cultures and contemporary *transnational* cultures (Friedman, 1989).

Even national cultures are in question. Touraine (1990a) notes that in the last half century, France has virtually ceased to exist as a national society, with its economy and culture becoming European and international. This has been accompanied by a decline in the state's power, and growth in the autonomy of private life.

A world culture, if it is ever to form, will have to overcome two obstacles. One is the idea that "development" means the gradual elimination of differences in favour of mass participation in *one*, and only one, type of culture. The other is the idea that participation in one particular culture, or nation, should limit communication with others. Neither idea is feasible and neither will survive. The trick is to find a kind of global organization that encourages both cultural development and intercultural communication (Touraine, 1988).

In important ways, all people and all cultures are the same. (This is something we learn the more we study and compare a wide range of societies, and a reason why *this* book is so resolutely international in its outlook.) People differ mainly in the importance they attach to certain cultural concerns over others. The emphasis is always changing, especially through interaction with other cultures. So the creation of a uniform global culture may never come about, though it is always coming closer.

That is made obvious by the information in Exhibit 2.5, which shows us how avidly people in India have adopted western television styles and adapted them to programs which are similar yet uniquely local.

Here is our best bet for the future. Ethnic divisions, local concerns, cultural competition, and a lack of shared experiences will forever prevent the formation of a single global culture (Smith, 1990). Nevertheless, families of cultures will develop through the global use of languages such as English or Swahili, and through the rise of huge blocs such as the European, Islamic, East Asian, Latino, and Pan-African communities.

CLOSING REMARKS

The sociological study of culture offers a prime example of the connection between macro- and micro- perspectives. On the one hand, culture is a macro phenomenon. It exists outside and "above" individual people, in their language, institutions and material artifacts. In this sense, culture is all-encompassing and slow changing: like a huge glacier. The main elements of a culture outlast individuals and even generations of individuals. On the other hand, culture is inside all of us and, as the symbolic interactionists remind

EXHIBIT 2.5   *Television in India: a variety of surprises*

. . . You can flick on the state channel, Doordarshan, and see some of the most brilliant, creative programming anywhere. Or you can flick it on again and see just how hard some Indians try to mimic the West. Or you can flick it on again and see rigid state propaganda that even the Chinese would zap in a flash. . . .

[T]he most engaging show must be the public-service skits shown just before prime time. One evening, the sketch featured an office manager who sends his peon to buy — with government money — school supplies for his children. The peon loads up with enough supplies for his own children, too. Later, the manager sends the department car to take his wife shopping, while an office clerk sits casually at his desk, making personal long distance calls. At the end, a sonorous voice delivers the moral: "This is national property and we should not destroy it. We should not abuse office stationery or office petrol or office phones. We have to get together and save the country's economy."

It's a mild antidote to an evening of raucous entertainment, which begins with 10 to 15 minutes of commercials, each of them as entertaining as the programs they precede. . . .

Then, it's Doordarshan's hottest soap opera, *Phir Wahi Talaash* (Same Search Again). The saga is about a poor village boy who goes to college and falls in love with a rich city girl. When her parents disapprove of the match, the couple tries to elope, but the girl's father catches them and hauls her back home, where she is forced to marry his industrialist friend's son.

"She has the right to decide," a neighbour says, scolding her father.

"The question is not whether she has the right, but whether it's the right decision," the father replies.

"That's why you've lost your daughter," the neighbour concludes. Your daughter doesn't love you any more. You've lost."

Indians love their sagas so much that when the Hindu epic, *Ramayana*, was aired as a television serial, virtually every town and village in the country shut down. In fact, when a power cut affected the northern city of Jammu during one episode, hordes of young men ransacked the local power station. . . .

Source: John Stackhouse, "Now you see it, now you don't," *The Globe and Mail*, Sat., June 19, 1993, pp. C1, C7

us, something we all change or reproduce every day. Culturally accepted patterns change over time because dozens, then thousands, then millions of us change our way of doing things.

At the beginning of this chapter we said that culture can best be understood as a symbolic environment within which we live. As we looked more closely at this environment, however, we discovered that it differs radically from one group to another. The culture of poor people is very different from that of rich people (we will say more of this in the chapter on social classes). The world of an atheist is different from that of the adherent to Hare Krishna. The world of the Italian Canadian is, in many important ways, different from the world of the Inuit. All of us, living together in the same country, are living in different cultures. Understanding these cultures, and how and why they *are* different, is an important task for sociologists.

This issue of people's similarities and differences becomes ever more pressing in a rapidly changing world. We shall have a lot more to say about social and cultural change in the midst of "globalization" in the second-to-last chapter of this book. In particular, we will consider the various factors — social, economic, political and technological — which change our culture and change our lives. But before we do that, we need to understand how people become members of their culture and society. The ways people are socialized to live in their respective worlds is the topic of the next chapter.

C H A P T E R 3

If you grew up in North America, you probably know the rules to this game.
They include (1) no girls are allowed, (2) the youngest child takes the orders, and
(3) people can come back to life an infinite number of times.

Dick Hemingway

SOCIALIZATION

CHAPTER OUTLINE

SOCIALIZATION IS A LIFELONG PROCESS

The last chapter described culture as the socially constructed environment that we live in. It showed that most of the objects around us — whether real or ideal, material or non-material — are cultural objects. People, too, are cultural objects, not only in how we display ourselves to others, but as socialized members of our society.

All of us are, to a large extent, products of our society. Society determines the ways we think and act, the things we say, and the values and norms we live by. But as human beings, we are also free in important ways to create ourselves. Much of who we are and what we do is a result of our own activity. As we shall see, both of these tendencies — freedom and determinism — are central features of socialization.

Socialization is often defined as the social learning process a person goes through to become a capable member of society. The process is "social" because it is through interaction with others that people acquire the culture — the language, perspective and skills, the likes and dislikes, the cluster of norms, values and beliefs — that characterizes the group to which they belong.

Primary socialization is learning that takes place in the early years of a person's life. It is extremely important in forming an individual's personality and charting the course of future development. Almost always, primary socialization takes place within the context of a family. Here, a young child learns many of the social skills needed to participate in a wide variety of social institutions.

Because primary socialization is a fundamental social process both for individuals and for society as a whole, it interests both macrosociologists and microsociologists. Among the former, structural functionalists see primary socialization as the means by which people are integrated into society, coming to take their allotted role and learning to fulfil socially necessary functions. In their eyes, human babies are a "blank slate" waiting to be imprinted with socially meaningful information. It is through this effective social imprinting — for example, the teaching and learning of language — that society manages to survive.

Conflict theorists, by contrast, emphasize the ways in which socialization perpetuates domination. They see socialization as teaching people their "place" in society and convincing them that this "place" is inevitable. Poor people learn to blame themselves for failure and praise the rich for their success. In this way, socialization contributes to the survival of dominant groups. We will have much more to say about this "legitimation" of power in Chapter 5, on class and status inequality.

As microsociologists, symbolic interactionists study the processes by which people are actually socialized, particularly those that lead to the development of a social "self." Through these processes people come to see themselves as others do. They come to think of themselves as good or bad, competent or incompetent, normal or deviant, and so on. We will discuss the interactionist view of the "self" later in this chapter.

Feminist sociologists combine the interests of conflict theorists and symbolic interactionists with a particular focus on gender issues. In respect to socialization, they are particularly interested in the learning of gender identities (or gendered selves) and gendered patterns of domination and submission.

Though this chapter has a lot to say about children, socialization does not end with childhood. It is a lifelong process because we continually undergo new experiences and change in reaction to these experiences. We take on new roles, participate in new institutions, adjust to and identify with new stages of life. The socialization that occurs after childhood is called secondary socialization. It is much more limited than primary socialization and mainly involves the learning of specific roles, norms, attitudes, or beliefs. Secondary socialization has less effect on self-image or sense of competence than primary socialization does, but we should not underestimate its importance.

We all differ in the ways we respond to other people's efforts to socialize us. Yet all of us, at least in our early years, possess an almost endless ability to change and adjust to change.

BECOMING SOCIAL: NATURE VERSUS NURTURE

Where does this human adaptability come from? How much of it is due to our genetic makeup, unique among animals? How much is due to the training we receive that helps us learn and re-learn as we pass through life? What, ultimately, makes each of us the kind of person we are?

These centuries-old questions are at the heart of what is called the "nature *versus* nurture" debate. People holding to the "nature" position believe that human behaviour is genetically determined. Such *biological determinists* argue that the diversity found among individuals and cultures exists because nature has selected for diversity, in the same way it has selected for our enlarged brains and upright walk.

Consider the sociological approach called *sociobiology*. Sociobiology looks for the explanation of human behaviour in animal behaviour, on the assumption that much of our behaviour traces back to our animal origins. So, for example, sociobiologists might look for the explanation of human warfare or interpersonal violence in the animal instincts of aggression or territoriality. Equally, they might look for the explanation of human mating rituals in animal mating and reproductive strategies.

Rather than focusing on symbolism and cognitive processing —as the symbolic interactionists do — sociobiologists would focus on inborn, probably genetic practices. For example, in discussing human inequality, we will spend some time on the ways people symbolize their relations of dominance and submission. Like most sociologists we will argue that ideologies serve to legitimate and stabilize unequal relationships. However, sociobiologists would point out that other animals — for example, chickens — also have stable hierarchies of dominance (you've heard of "pecking orders" among birds, haven't you), yet they don't seem to need ideologies to achieve this.

This simple example shows that sociobiology looks for a different *kind* of explanation. In the realm of socialization, sociobiologists would likely relate stages in the development of human children to stages in the development of other, similar creatures (monkeys, chimpanzees, warthogs and the like). But most sociologists reject or ignore the sociobiological approach for a variety of reasons: some don't know much about it, others think the approach doesn't work for most human behaviour since humans are different from other animals, and still others believe that sociobiology has failed to produce evidence that supports their theories.

The central problem is that sociobiology ignores history, ignores social, economic, and political forces and, just as important, ignores the motivation, character, and reasoning of the individual. Any advocate of the "nurture" position would take an opposite approach and attribute all character traits, and all the diversity among people of different cultures, to learning.

According to this point of view — called (social (or cultural) determinism — infants are born without any significant genetic predispositions, drives, or instincts and no innate personality. As children, they learn the *"dos* and *don'ts"* of their culture, which they then act out. Culture, not genes, determines their later behaviour) There is a great deal to be said in favour of cultural determinism, and if sociologists were forced to pick a side, the vast majority would choose this side, not **biological determinism**. So in this chapter, we are going to favour the dominant social or cultural determinist approach.

Yet there are problems with this approach too. For example, it gives us no help in explaining why members of the same culture, and even members of the same family are often different. If only culture and not biology were involved, and people were subjected to the same cultural influences, we would expect them to develop identical personalities. But, in practice, they don't!

In the end, this debate is impossible to resolve and most social scientists have put it aside. They recognize that both factors — nature and nurture — have an effect. Nature and nurture interact and have an interactive or "emergent" effect that could not be guessed from either of the factors individually. Members of a group are bound to share genetic characteristics because, over a long time, they live and reproduce together. This makes it likely that genes will differ from one group to another and even influence personality; but this influence is limited to forming a behavioural potential. The extent to which people realize this potential will depend on the social setting within which they live and learn.

Consider language as a case in point. The capacity to use language is genetic in origin. Human beings have the vocal cords necessary to produce the sounds out of which words are formed. The human brain is able to differentiate those sounds and identify their appropriate meanings. But while the ability to use language is genetic in origin, language itself is not.

As we saw in the last chapter, language is a product of culture which is learned. If language *were* genetic in origin — that is, if the sounds used and their appropriate meanings were innate — everyone on earth would use the same language in the same way. Yet there are hundreds of different languages and everyone uses language in a different way. Moreover, languages are constantly changing as new words get added, meanings get altered, and old words are dropped.

This illustration is particularly important because, as we saw in the last chapter, language is the means by which we communicate our experience of the world. It is the also the way we learn from others and the way we teach others. Not least, it is the key to primary socialization and, in this way, to adult competence.

Perhaps nothing illustrates the importance of language and primary socialization as well as the case of feral children. These are children who have grown up lacking contact with other people. They have not undergone the typical experiences of socialization, and, in crucial ways, they never become full-fledged members of society.

Feral children

History has recorded many tales and anecdotes about ("feral" children — children supposedly raised outside society, unaffected by human relationships and values) One of the best documented cases is the "Wild Boy of Aveyron" — well documented because of a Doctor Itard, who studied him closely and recorded what he found. The boy, called Victor, emerged from the woods in southern France on a winter morning in the year 1800. He had been caught digging for vegetables in a terraced garden. Though 11 or 12 years old, Victor, who was almost naked, showed no modesty and was not housebroken. He would relieve himself wherever he wanted, squatting to defecate and standing to urinate. He could not speak and made strange, meaningless cries.

Three or four months after Doctor Itard took over his training, the boy became responsive. Victor could pay attention, understand and follow verbal instructions, play games, care for himself, and even invent things with familiar objects. He wore clothes and used a chamber pot to relieve himself, but still felt no shame or modesty. He kept up many of his earlier habits, continuing to avoid other people and escaping company whenever he could. His old, "wild" reactions to nature — to wind, the moon, and snow — never disappeared. In Doctor Itard's hands, the boy's training was, at best, a superficial success. Still, Victor showed affection to the people who protected him and did what they expected.

After spending five years with Itard, Victor lived another 22 years with a devoted woman named Madame Guerin in a little house near an institute for deafmutes. In this period, no one — not even Itard — tried to train Victor further and no one followed his progress closely. By 1816, his civilization had largely eroded. Victor was once again fearful and half-wild, and still could not speak. He had few links to the rest of the community. A state pension kept Victor alive until he finally died, unnoticed.

What does the story of the Wild Boy teach? An obvious lesson is the importance of primary socialization. Despite the attempts Dr. Itard made to teach him, Victor never learned to speak and never adjusted to civilization. There is no way of knowing now what Victor's abilities were, but we suspect that by missing the crucial years of childhood socialization he was never able to achieve his human potential. He had grown up as an animal and could not, after childhood, be socialized as a human.

Was Victor better off after his capture than before it? Perhaps not, but as a wild, naked creature digging for vegetables Victor was much less than a full human being. That is the most important lesson Victor's case teaches us. We are social beings who only fulfil our potential and achieve our goals as members of society. Socialization imposes society's rules on us, it is true; but that is not all. By providing us with knowledge and skills, society also gives us the tools and resources we need to think independently, act creatively, and take advantage of our opportunities.

This does not mean, however, that people need their own Dr. Itard — a person who will take full and everlasting responsibility for their development. After infancy, all of us take an active part in our own socialization and are socialized by a broad range of people and circumstances. Nursery school children display this fact readily. We can see them discussing, at length, aspects of adult culture which they do not understand, in an effort to slowly take personal ownership of that culture (Corsaro and Rizzo, 1988).

In this sense, socialization is a collective process: people socialize one another. Families, schools and workplaces merely provide times and places where this learning can occur.

Where young children are concerned, socialization also depends on who is minding the children. Not *all* childhood learning is from other children. Caregivers also play a role in making them into the kinds of people they will be when they are adults. Exhibit 3.1 shows how very important non-family mem-

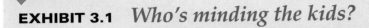

EXHIBIT 3.1   *Who's minding the kids?*

More than half (57 per cent) of all Canadian children under 13 are left in the care of someone other than their parents at least once a week. Here is what happens.

- Infants (up to 17 months): 17.7 per cent go to a relative's home, 15.9 per cent to unlicenced home care and 3.2 per cent to licenced day care.
- Toddlers (18 to 35 months): 19.4 per cent go to an unlicenced home, 16.1 per cent to a relative, 11.7 per cent to licenced day care.

- 3 to 5: 30 per cent go to kindergarten, 19.4 per cent to nursery school, 20.1 per cent stay with family members, 17.6 per cent to an unlicenced home, 13.8 per cent to a relative.
- 6 to 9: When not in school, 29.2 per cent are with family members, 12.8 per cent in unlicenced care, 8.8 per cent at a relative's, 8.8 per cent at home with a baby-sitter.

Source: Canadian National Child Care Study in "Who's Minding the Kids?" *The Globe and Mail*, Wed., April 7, 1993, p. A6.

bers have become in the socialization of Canadian children. To a large degree, "strangers" are responsible for passing social knowledge along to the next generation of Canadians. The average parent probably knows little about the way his or her children are being socialized.

ACQUIRING SOCIAL KNOWLEDGE

Learning and behaviour

Socialization is a form of learning, so understanding how socialization works requires that we understand how people learn.

To start, learning is a natural human process. It is natural in the sense that we all have the ability and the will to learn. Researchers have found that a newborn baby reacts differently to its mother's voice than to that of a nurse or doctor. The infant has learned to recognize that voice even before birth, while still in the womb. This shows that *what* we learn is not determined, but the *desire* to learn is present at least from birth. All of us learn without anyone forcing us to do so.

In fact, we learn best when we learn freely. As you know from school, things we are forced to study are not really learned at all. If they have been memorized, they are only remembered until the next test, then quickly forgotten. By contrast, we will learn something that is meaningful for *us* or useful to us. When we *really* learn, we are gaining knowledge or skills we can use. (This has an implication for teaching too: to be a good teacher, you have to show the student why something to be learned is meaningful or useful!)

Learning can occur in many different ways. We learn by observation, by experiment, and by imitation. We learn from friends, from parents, relatives, and passers-by. We learn from television, radio, books, and billboards. As you can see, little of our lifetime learning takes place in schools.

Through most of human history, few people had any formal education and almost *all* learning occurred informally, through other people. This kind of informal learning can still be seen in the Pueblo native culture of the southwestern United States. Pueblo children spend long hours watching their elders at work farming or producing crafts. This kind of observational learning is less common in our own society, where children learn more through exploration and social dialogue (John-Steiner, 1984).

Like the Pueblo culture, traditional Hawaiian culture puts a great deal of emphasis on the informal, apprenticeship transfer of knowledge and skills. Hawaiian adults feel comfortable about teaching their children household skills, because they perform them routinely and expertly and because housework is cooperative. School learning is a different matter. Not only is it hard to teach literacy through observation, but school learning tends to benefit the individual over the group and does not fit into the helping framework which is congenial to Hawaiian culture (Levin, 1990).

Finally, Inuit learning is also informal and different from our own in important ways. Among the Inuit, various forms of play are important, especially, dramas in which children act out real-life dangers and decide how to deal with them. By doing this, they learn how to solve adult problems in an independent manner. More than that, these children come to see the world as problematic and they develop skills for experimenting in different situations (Briggs, 1991).

The Inuit example illustrates how childhood experiences are a good preparation for the development of adult skills. Let's consider the developmental approach to socialization more fully, focusing particularly on cognitive development.

Cognitive development

(A *developmental approach* to learning examines both the inner workings of a person's mind and his or her observable behaviour.) As people go through the socialization process, they are active participants in learning. They do not merely respond to rewards and punishments, like dogs or trained seals. They respond on the basis of their interpretations of situations. Learning is more than a matter of knowing what to do, how to do it, and when; learning also involves understanding *why* we do, or avoid doing, certain things.

Observation, drama, exploration and dialogue are all ways of learning, thinking and communicating symbolically. As sociologists, we need an approach to socialization that takes this into account. That is why theories of **cognitive development** are valuable. (The term *cognitive* refers to intellectual capacities such as thought, belief, memory, perception, and the ability to reason) (Cognitive development, then, refers to the development of these various abilities.)

The Russian psychologist Pavlov and his colleagues knew a lot about how dogs learn, but little of this knowledge applies to humans. People are much more complicated.

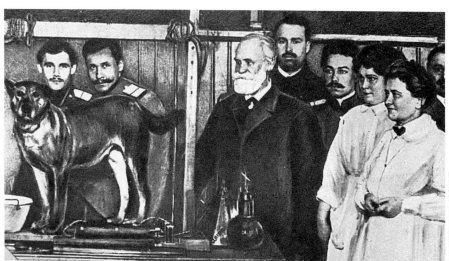

THE BETTMANN ARCHIVE

Most of us can avoid violating norms because we have figured out the rules and know what happens when we violate them. We are able to generalize from past experience, and to apply our generalizations to new situations. This learned ability to generalize is a key part of human socialization.

Learning a language falls into this category. It is unlikely a child ever heard an adult say "he runned" or "it's the goodest" or "my foots hurt." Children make such mistakes because they detect and apply rules in our language, and make up words according to those rules. They do *not* simply copy what they hear others saying: they generalize, apply rules and use language in a creative way. In short, mistakes do not occur because children are failing to follow rules: it's because the rules of the English language are not consistent. It's *easy* to make mistakes in English, because of the great number of idiomatic uses that we learn only from many years of practice.

Idioms — cultural and linguistic practices which do not conform to obvious rules — are the hardest things to learn. Take idiomatic thinking about death. Everyone thinks about death at one time or another, yet no one has been taught *how* to think about it. For that reason, it is surprising to find cultural differences. Death, research reveals, conjures up different images in different cultures: images of violence in American children and images of religious ritual in Swedish children. And in both countries, older children have more complicated ideas about death than younger children do. This indicates a growth in complexity that is a normal part of cognitive development (Wenestam and Wass, 1987).

Consider another, more familiar example: knowing how to pay someone a visit. On occasion, you have probably visited the home of a person you want to impress: a teacher, a boss, or the parents of a girlfriend or boyfriend, for example. Then you have become painfully aware of your ignorance of the relevant norms. You wondered how to dress for the visit. Should you bring a gift, and if so, what? Should you arrive on time, or early, and if early, how early? If offered alcoholic beverages, how many should you accept? Most troubling of all, since you do not want to offend the hosts by leaving too soon or bore them by staying too long, how will you know when it is the right time to leave?

If you can think through questions like these and come up with answers — and you do, each day, in one situation after another —then you have achieved a high level of cognitive development. (After all, Victor the feral boy could *never* have done this!) More likely than not, you have also learned — however unconsciously —the idiomatic rules that govern visiting behaviour in our society.

Moral development

It has been difficult, in such a limited space, to describe the acquisition of social manners and language. Just think how much *more* difficult it is to describe the learning of moral behaviour.

Swiss psychologist Jean Piaget was a pioneer in studying the development of morality. Piaget (1932) researched the way children think about social norms by asking them to discuss a game of marbles. He studied their moral thinking by telling them stories and asking them for comments. From these simple methods, Piaget drew powerful conclusions.

Among children aged about four- to eight-years-old, Piaget found what he called *heteronomous* morality — a respect for adult authority. Young children conceive of right and wrong in very specific and objective terms. A behaviour is "wrong" if the children have seen adults punish or threaten to punish it. Young children consider adult rules and moral values absolute and unchangeable. As a result, they favour punishing rule-breakers severely. Finally, they show little interest in the motivations of wrong-doers: why they did what they did.

However, all this changes as children get older. Among older children Piaget found that *autonomous* morality prevailed. Older children had already begun to think about and follow their own rules of conduct. They saw rules as products of group agreement that promote cooperation within the group. From this viewpoint, justice is a matter of mutual rights and obligations. Often, justice is served best by repairing the harm done, not punishing the wrong-doer. Finally, in their eyes, moral ideas are relative, not absolute. They change as the group wishes them to change.

These changes in moral thinking are a result of interactions between the child, its parents and peers. As well, some social conditions promote moral development more readily than others. For example, a study shows Norwegian children and teenagers are much more knowledgeable about politics than North American children. The reason for this is Norway's social democratic culture, which encourages young people to develop political ideas and identities at an early age (Barthelemy, 1990).

Generally, children in highly politicized communities — in Northern Ireland, South Africa, or Gaza, for example — become politicized themselves very early in life. While North American youth are spending their time on dates, after-school jobs and Nintendo games, these other children are engaged in political acts. This fact also suggests an earlier moral development in societies where children are encouraged or forced to consider adult issues.

An Israeli comparison of children raised in the city and children raised on *kibbutzim* (collective farms) found strong differences in moral reasoning. In general, the kibbutz children were more concerned with justice and humaneness. The city children were more pleasure-seeking and practical — you might even say, "street wise." The evidence showed that between grades 3 and 6, a concern with justice increased much more among the kibbutz children than among the city children (Eisenberg, Hertz-Lazarowitz and Fuchs, 1990).

Why? Because the kibbutz is a social institution with a particular philosophy of life. It is very concerned with justice, equality and sharing. No wonder the kibbutz children developed in the way they did. By contrast, few North American families — parents *or* children — have a philosophy of life. Many parents seem to give little thought to how they are raising their children and whether their acts are having the desired effect.

Take the matter of discipline. The kind of discipline parents use on their children reflects their moral judgment and shapes the moral development of their children. But there is a lack of consensus among Canadian parents about the appropriateness of physical punishment and whether it has beneficial effects. Most social scientists would say that physical punishment is likely to backfire. It teaches a child aggressive behaviour and injures his or her sense of self, instead of helping that sense of self to develop.

Other theories argue that parental absence, not physical abuse, is the problem behind much youth violence today (see Exhibit 3.2) This view rests on certain assumptions about human nature and human development. Can you identify these assumptions?

EXHIBIT 3.2 *Growing up angry*

Two 11-year-olds, identified as Child A and Child B, went on trial in Britain for murder yesterday. The prosecutor said in his opening statement that they knew they were doing evil when they stoned and beat a two-year-old boy to death.

The killing has touched off a major debate in the country over increasing incidents of youth violence. . . .

Schools across the U.S. are rapidly implementing violence-prevention and conflict-resolution programs.

In Canadian schools, too, the need for conflict-resolution programs is pandemic. Increasingly, our children are turning up in the classroom with an impaired ability to resolve their conflicts, frustrations and psychological turmoil through other than aggressive means. . . .

Let's begin to look at what might be behind this. Dr. Paul Steinhauer, senior staff psychiatrist at Toronto's Hospital for Sick Children, has written a paper called, "Youth in the Eighties and Nineties—A 15-Year Trend."

Dr. Steinhauer says children have two crucial biological and social drives which are often not met. The first is the need for a satisfactory and continuous attachment to a parental figure. The second is the universal need to learn to tame and diffuse our inherent aggression. . . .

The development of a sense of right and wrong and the ability to contain and discharge aggression in a controlled manner — both of which are fuelled by a successful attachment to, and consistent structure and reinforcement from, the parents — are important in helping children learn to deal successfully with aggression, and contribute to their behaving in a socially acceptable manner.

An inadequate attachment to a parent can result from parental lack of interest, neglect or abuse. It can result from "lack of continuity of parental figures" (through separations, and especially multiple separations, including repeated changes of caregivers — e.g. nannies — which tear children away from those to whom they are attached.)

Dr. Steinhauer writes: "Children experiencing an unsuccessful attachment or multiple separations frequently have their level of biologically derived aggression greatly increased by the excessive rage resulting from the frustration of their attachment needs. . . .

So let us all read this and think about what we are doing to family life —how many of our kids we have relegated to single-parent families, how many of our kids we think of as interruptions to our work life, how much we are relying on outside caregivers whom we know little about, and how many problems we are loading onto the schools.

Source: Michael Valpy, "Youth in the 1990s: growing up angry," *The Globe and Mail*, Mon., Nov. 2, 1993, p.A2.

DEVELOPMENT OF THE SELF

All sociologists view socialization as a social process, but symbolic interactionists are most concerned with understanding *how* socialization actually works. How do people come to take on the norms, values, attitudes, beliefs, and behaviour patterns of the people around them? How do they, in technical terms, internalize their culture? And how do they do so while maintaining their own personal identity and sense of worth? Many sociologists believe that the key to answering these questions can be found in the concept of the self.

Everyone has a sense of self. By *self*, we mean a person's experience and awareness of having a distinct personal identity that is separate from that of other people. Sociologists believe that the process by which people develop this sense of self is the same as the process by which they internalize their culture.

A child is not born with a sense of self, any more than he or she is born speaking English or knowing how to play baseball. As Piaget showed in his research, young children are *egocentric*; they have no sense of self distinct from other people. They assume that everything happens because of them, that everyone is interested only in them, and that whatever they experience is all that there is. Above all, egocentric children are unable to think about themselves objectively, or consider how others think about them.

Children only become aware of themselves as they become aware that other people (such as their parents or siblings) are distinct from them. It is necessary to learn that these other people have expectations about them, and that they are required to adapt to these expectations.

This means that the self is a social product. It emerges as people interact with others, even with people they hate or admire from afar (such as movie stars or heroic ancestors). The person's experiences in life, the groups to which he or she belongs, and the socio-historical setting of those groups all shape a person's sense of self.

Because the self is a social product, it changes throughout life. Adolescence, in particular, is a critical period for the development of self. As a Hong Kong study shows, during adolescence people become more concerned with their appearance and this makes them feel vulnerable and shy. These changes appear to be especially marked among girls, around the sixth and seventh grades (Lau, 1990).

People's experiences and self-conceptions change throughout life, due to secondary socialization. Though we are emphasizing childhood socialization in this chapter, we should not underestimate the role of adult experiences in continuing to change a person's values, norms and perceptions. In this respect, the workplace — which we discuss in Chapter 9 below — is particularly important. It is a place where we learn and exercise our skills, defer to authority and (occasionally) exert authority, participate in a work group and work culture and, not least, earn an income.

Perhaps just as important, in the workplace we, as adults, continue to develop our conception of "self" — who and what we are. Increasingly, we become what we do for a living and become like the people we do it with. Social theorists differ in their accounts of the emergence of the self, but on one thing they agree: social interaction is central to the growth of the self.

The looking-glass self

American sociologist Charles Cooley (1902) was the first to emphasize the importance of the self in the process of socialization. Cooley developed the notion of the looking-glass self, which emphasizes the role of the social environment in the development of a self-concept. According to Cooley, people form concepts of themselves as they see how other people react to them.

Research suggests that people live up, or down, to the expectations others (such as parents or friends) have of them. They come to see themselves as they believe these significant others do. For example, a little girl will traditionally be told to "act like a lady." After awhile, she will come to see certain activities, such as playing baseball, climbing trees, or boxing with other children as inappropriate or beyond her capacities.

The looking-glass self is the name Cooley gives to a phenomenon we all know intuitively: the process of seeing ourselves through the eyes of others, as others see us. The way we think and feel about ourselves reflects the way we believe others think and feel about us. We behave in ways designed to gain a favourable response from the people who matter most to us. We do this because we rely on others to provide us with a positive self-image.

However, the notion of a looking-glass self is problematic. There are limits to what we will do for approval. We are not mere puppets obeying the wishes of others, no matter how significant they are. Parents know that few of their wishes for their children will come true. As children grow up, they rebel against many of their parents' expectations. This rebellion is not limited to adolescence; for example, child-care experts refer to a two-year-old child as being in the midst of a stage they call "the terrible twos," a stage also known as *negativism*. Parents of children at other ages have their own horror stories to tell, and pet names for other stages.

In the end, Cooley's views illustrate what sociologists have called an *over-socialized* view of the individual (Wrong, 1961). It fails to account for the spontaneity, creativity and independence of real human beings. Moreover, if a looking-glass does exist, then it must be transparent. That's because parents, the supposed socializers, are also socialized by their children. In short, socialization is a two-way process.

Mead on internalization

A more complete approach to socialization can be found in the work of the American social philosopher George Herbert Mead (1934). Mead's particular interest was in the process of internalization. How, he wondered, are the rules, norms, and values which others impose on a child internalized so that the child becomes committed to them and feels guilt or shame when violating them?

The road to guilt and shame is a long one: Mead suggests a child goes through a number of phases as he or she learns to internalize social expectations. The first is called the *preliminary phase* because internalization has not really begun yet: the child does not have the capacity to engage in true social behaviour. During this phase — the first year or so of life — a child's social behaviour is largely limited to imitation. Infants imitate their parents, their siblings, even themselves, repeating gestures or sounds they made at first by chance. A game such as peek-a-boo illustrates the repetitive and imitative nature of an infant's social interaction.

We see a higher level of social behaviour in the *play phase*, when the child engages in solitary play. This stage is roughly equivalent to the egocentric stage described by Piaget. Both Mead and Piaget emphasize that, even if children are playing in each others' presence, play is solitary because it involves no real interaction. Two three-year-old girls playing with their dolls are each in a world of their own. Each talks to her own doll, feeds her own doll, scolds her own doll. These girls are incapable of having one be the "mother" and the other the "child." Said another way, there is no "division of labour" between the children. That is why Piaget referred to conversations among children at this stage as collective monologue.

The next phase, the *game phase*, involves a still higher level of social behaviour, for it means coordinating social roles. Games differ from play because play is largely spontaneous but games have rules that people must follow. Moreover, games always involve other people, so each participant has a role to act out in relation to other players.

A good illustration of an early game is hide and seek. Here children learn to take on one of two roles, those who hide or the one who is "it." There are rules to follow: the person who is "it" (1) must count to ten, (2) must say "ready or not, here I come," and (3) must find another player before returning to "base." The process is not as complicated as putting a spaceship on the moon, perhaps, but it does mean coordinating one's own actions with those of others. In this sense, there is a "division of labour," which is the essence of all grown-up social life.

Since the 1950s, school classrooms have changed dramatically. Which kind did you experience? How does the form of a classroom communicate and structure the classroom culture?

UPI/Bettmann

William Chan

Mead called the process of taking others into account *taking the role of the other*. It is the prerequisite for competent social interaction. During interactions, we all take the role of the other in two senses. First, we orient our actions toward others so that we can be understood. Before teachers stand in front of a class, for example, they ask themselves how they can get the lesson across so that students will understand it. Then, while lecturing, they monitor the students' faces, body language and questions to see if they *do* understand what is being said.

A second sense of taking the role of the other is essential to the development of the self. It is a process of coming to see yourself as others see you and think about yourself in terms of your relationship to other people.

George Herbert Mead coined the term **generalized other** to refer to a person's general idea of society's attitudes and perspectives — of how the larger social group expects him or her to act.

Having a concept of the generalized other is possible because there is a rough consensus among members of the society or subculture to which we belong. Why, for example, do Chinese school children display lower levels of aggression than children from other countries? The answer is, because they have learned their culture. In China, aggressive behaviour violates cultural norms and is shunned much more strongly than it is in the West (Ekblad, 1986).

It is in relation to this sense of the generalized other that we develop conceptions of ourselves: how we are similar to, and different from other people. When we take the role of the generalized other it is no longer Mommy who gets upset when we spill soup; now *we* are the ones who get upset. We feel ashamed or even guilty.

But there is more to us than the socialized player of these internalized roles. Mead tried to incorporate this "something more" by distinguishing between the **I and the Me**. All of us have an aspect of the self that Mead calls the *I*. The *I* is spontaneous, impulsive and self-interested. All of us also have a *Me*, a part of the self that is the result of socialization and is therefore conscious of social norms, values, and expectations. The *Me* is the socialized player of social roles and, unlike the *I*, it is cautious, proper and sociable.

Mead and Cooley's symbolic interactionist theories continue to dominate the study of socialization. Structural functionalists also use Mead's theory to explain how people learn to accept the values, goals, and norms of the society around them. However, Mead's theory does not really mesh well with structural functionalism, because it views people as active participants in their own socialization. This point of view, which is essential to symbolic interactionism, is foreign to functionalism.

Socialization as an active process

We noted earlier the importance of avoiding an oversocialized image of people, for people are neither puppets nor robots. Socializing a person is not the same as programming a computer. Humans act in terms of personal and group interests, and they evaluate their interests themselves.

People do not simply follow the norms or rules of society, for these are merely guidelines — general goals — and not explicit instructions. In practice, people develop their own strategies for achieving goals and obeying the rules.

Take being a student. As students you are aware of the many factors that affect your chances to perform well in school. There is a program of study which specifies the courses you may take. But the course you want is already full or conflicts with a part-time job that forces you to take a course or a teacher you really didn't want to take. In theory, "school" means studying things you want and need to learn. In practice, it may be very different. Real life is like that.

Even such factors as family size and birth order can affect what you study and how well you perform, and then there are things like social class background, family problems, or pressures from peers. Finally, there are the many norms and rules which define how students are supposed to behave in class, in the library, even in the cafeteria.

Under constraints like these, people all develop their own strategies for dealing with teachers, making friends, doing homework, getting to school on time, juggling school work and part-time job, and so on. The ability to make decisions for ourselves and develop effective strategies demonstrates an active and creative response to socialization. Consider how much more complicated schooling is in developing countries, where there are even *more* constraints on schools and students (see Exhibit 3.3.)

Or consider the creative ways children learn to struggle against their parents. No matter how affectionate and considerate parents may be, they have ideas of what they want and expect from their child. Luckily for all concerned, children usually don't conform to these expectations. Imagine how boring a child would be who came out exactly as their parents wished. The child would lack character, imagination, independence and initiative. Generally, creating and enforcing rules creates resentment and fosters conflict. Certainly that seems to be the case with children, who resist socialization. They fight back against parental pressure, often literally kicking and screaming, to get what they want instead of what the parents want.

This conflict is difficult for parents, but it is essential for the child. We noted earlier that children seem to go though a stage known as "negativism" at about the age of two. During this stage they purposely challenge the rules, become obstinate about little things, and insist on having things their own way. They even seem to go around saying "no" all the time, which is why the stage is called "negativism."

Why is such a difficult stage — for both parents and children — necessary for the child's development? Because it is at about this age that the child begins to develop a sense of self and to differentiate itself from others. Negativism helps in this process by teaching the child what it can get away with and what it can't. By testing the rules repeatedly, children find out when parents really mean what they are saying and when they are willing to give in. These are important lessons, not only in learning to get along with parents, but in learning to get along with other people in later life.

When you think about it, the term "negativism is adult-centred. Taking the child's point of view, we can see that he or she is developing strategies for dealing with others: when to manipulate, when to resist, and when to give in graciously as circumstances demand. All of these lessons are essential to becoming an effective participant in social life.

Finally, remember that parents are also being socialized by this process. They, too, are learning what *they* can get away with and what kind of demands they can make on the child. In the end, parents do not get the child they expected, but they usually end up liking the child they get.

EXHIBIT 3.3 *Ten ways to develop better schools*

. . . [D]eveloping countries must solve 10 basic problems that serve as barriers to good schooling:

1. **Not enough staff.** Although governments spend most of their education money on teacher salaries, they still do not have enough teachers. The Central African Republic's pupil-to-teacher ratio is 90 to 1. . . .

2. **Not enough qualified staff.** To meet soaring school populations in the 1970s and 1980s, many countries hired graduates in huge numbers and then forgot to train them. "Most teachers do not know the techniques for the teaching of reading," said a recent study by the Paris-based International Institute for Education Planning. . . .

3. **Not enough female staff.** In South Asia, sub-Saharan African and the Arab states, Unesco estimates two-thirds of all women lack basic literacy skills, leaving few qualified women to teach. And in almost all countries, fewer female teachers means fewer female students.

4. **Not enough choice.** Rarely do textbooks, school hours and vacations vary to meet the differences of region, culture or economy. And the rote learning of words and numbers often means little to a rural girl's future. . . .

5. **Not enough community control.** With local education levies, communities in China pay for 38 per cent of their school budgets. Indian communities, on the other hand, pay directly for only 2 per cent of costs—and in many cases have a lack of control equal to their contribution.

6. **Excessive expenses.** In Tanzania, a typical family with three children in school spends 58 per cent of its household income on educational expenses such as uniforms, books and tutorial fees. In a country that successfully launched a mass literacy program in the 1960s, primary enrolment today is a mere 47 per cent.

7. **Incomplete schools.** One in every five primary schools in the world does not offer a full complement of classes. . . .

8. **Children starting school too late—or too early.** A recent study found that in most of Africa, South Asia and Latin America, barely half of all first grade students started school at the official age. . . .

9. **Children failing early grades.** In sub-Saharan Africa, 21 per cent of children repeat Grade 1, often because no one had prepared them for school. . . .

10. **Lack of teaching aids.** Developing countries spend a mere 1.4 per cent of their combined education budgets on textbooks and teaching guides. Some 83 per cent goes to teachers and another 10 per cent to administration. . . .In Paraguay and Peru, a recent World Bank study found two thirds of primary-school students had no books.

Source: "Ten ways to develop better schools," *The Globe and Mail*, Thurs., Dec. 16, 1993, p. A17

GENDER SOCIALIZATION

Sociologists pay a great deal of attention to primary socialization. It is during this early phase of your life that you learn all the fundamental roles of our society — especially, how to think and act like a competent member of society. In the first few years of life, we also learn such basic facts about ourselves as whether we are male or female and what that means about *who* or *what* we are. In this sense, gender socialization stands as an example of all primary socialization. As we noted earlier, it is a process of special interest to feminist sociologists, since it sets the groundwork for — or "reproduces" — the structures of gendered inequality that we will discuss at length in Chapter 7.

Masculine and feminine ideals

Gender roles are the socially defined expectations people have of appropriate behaviour for individuals of each sex. What we mean by gender socialization is simply socialization into gender roles. It is the process of learning the attitudes, thoughts, and behaviour patterns that a culture considers to be appropriate for members of each sex.

When people are asked what makes males and females different, they usually refer to physiological characteristics such as genitals. But physiology only partly explains the differences between males and females.

In everyday life we almost never make use of physiology to decide who is male or female because there are few people whose genitals are visible to us. We decide who is male or female on the basis of appearance, which is a matter of social convention. As for personality differences, such as the greater aggressiveness of males, the differences between males and females in our society are primarily social constructions — little dramas we put on for one another. We know this because gender roles change over time and vary considerably from one culture to another. They are *not* permanent and inevitable.

People learn gender roles early in life. Infants are identified as male or female at birth. By the age of three, little boys and girls are playing separately, at different kinds of games. Already, they have learned to want different toys, enjoy different games, and avoid fraternizing openly with the opposite sex. Children who violate this last rule are ridiculed. In our own society, the masculine ideal has traditionally included toughness, reason, and action. Conversely, the feminine ideal has traditionally included softness, emotion (or intuition), and passivity.

In many countries, traditional gender roles have gone largely unchanged. In Islamic Iran, the fundamentalist (i.e., religiously orthodox) government has had an enormous effect on gender roles and socialization. Since the Revolution of 1979, it has stressed segregation of the sexes. School textbooks discuss women less often than they discuss men. Women, when discussed at all, are shown within the family context, not doing paid work. This is a change from the more egalitarian portrayals of women before 1979, when a secular (non-religious) government ruled Iran (Higgins and Shoar-Ghaffari, 1991).

But Iran is no exception. Throughout the world, fundamentalist governments have struggled to maintain traditional gender roles and socialization. By contrast, in transitional societies like Singapore, traditional gender roles have started to break down, though school books continue to present men and women as if they were still playing these roles. For example, they show women in the home, never in the workplace (Quah, 1980). But in North America, masculine and feminine ideals, and male and female gender roles, have blurred dramatically.

The blurring of gender roles

The blurring of gender roles takes a variety of forms. First, few women today — with the possible exception of members of fringe groups like REAL Women —are modelling themselves on the traditional image of femininity. Likewise, few men today are modelling themselves on the traditional image of masculinity. The male ideal mainly persists among boys in the five- to fifteen-year-old range. They are the ones who watch WWF wrestling, read violent comic books, and buy fighting video war games, military clothing, and miniature soldier figures.

Second, men and women are sharing more duties and activities than in the past. More women work for pay in jobs that, in the past, only men were allowed to hold. In their work settings, women prove as able as men to be tough, rational, and active. Men, at the same time, are assuming a greater responsibility for child care and housework than they did in the past. At home, they are learning to master softness, emotionality, and, if not passivity, then at least greater tranquility.

The gender roles are also blurring, slowly, in schools. In North America this is far advanced; in other parts of the world, as we have already noted, there is a long way to go, but the process has started. For example, an Italian study finds that girls in junior high school now aspire to the same educational levels as their male peers. Few want to be housewives and most plan on having middle-level jobs that can fit in with the domestic role. Despite exceptionally low birth rates — a factor that generally decreases the domestic burden, and so, the pressure for rigid gender stratification — the family still exerts a great deal of pressure on girls to take on traditional domestic roles. Nevertheless, social practices are gradually changing (Capozza and Tajoli, 1992).

In Holland, many observers are conflicted about gender socialization: whether it is a problem and, if it *is* a problem, what to do about it. On the one hand, a majority of Dutch school teachers still stereotype girls as more "obedient" or "vulnerable" than boys and approve of training them for traditional gender roles. Some do not consider scholastic underachievement by girls to be a problem. Yet the vast majority of teachers express a concern that sex-role differences in Dutch society are too extreme and rigid (Jungbluth, 1984).

Around the world, an increasing number of roles are gender-blind, in the sense that we do not *automatically* associate a particular gender with the role. (Quick: is a pharmacist male or female? How about a comedian? a real estate agent? a public school teacher? a housepainter?)

What's more, Western societies often bring other societies a respect for gender equality. Sometimes, they simply reinforce a traditional respect for equality that has been lost. For example, when the Philippines were under Malayan control, males and females were roughly equal. Filipinos felt there were roughly equal psychological and economic benefits in having a son *or* a daughter. This changed several centuries ago with the coming of Spaniards, who had a strong preference for boys over girls, and viewed men as superior to women. The American arrival a century ago drove out Spanish influence and Filipinos returned to their earlier, egalitarian sentiments towards boys and girls (Bautista-Foley, 1988). Here, Westernization simply restored the equality of the sexes. (In Chapter 7, however, we will look at an African example in which Western colonialism was associated with a decrease in women's status.)

So far, we have ignored the nuts and bolts of socialization —the ways in which people learn to adopt the values and roles that will be important to them. We now turn to a closer consideration of these processes by focussing on the crucially important *agents of socialization*.

AGENTS OF SOCIALIZATION

Agents of socialization are the social institutions and structured relationships within which socialization takes place. The most important of these are the family, school, peer group, and mass media. In modern industrialized societies, these institutions socialize almost everyone. However, religious groups, work groups, and voluntary associations also play a significant role. Often, the effects of various agents of socialization are complementary, or reinforcing. Yet conflicts among them — say, between the family and the peer group — are common too. That is why we must consider these agents one at a time.

Families

Most of us are born into families and have an idea of what "family life" means. As we shall see later in this book, there is a great deal of variation among Canadian families and families are changing rapidly. Nonetheless, a child's first emotional ties are usually to family members. They begin to teach the child the language, norms and values of the culture in a variety of ways.

Some families, for example, are stricter than others. In fact, some societies are stricter than others. In societies which value conformity highly, parents are more likely to use physical punishment to discipline their children. They are also more likely to lecture their children and maintain close overall control than parents in the North American culture, which values self-reliance (Ellis and Petersen, 1992).

Yet, little of what a family transmits through socialization is transmitted directly. For example, in India children are taught to be passive through a passive speech pattern called "causing to be overheard." In this pattern, one person is addressed in speech, though another person — in this case the child — is the intended addressee. For example, the mother may say (loudly enough for her child to hear) "Daddy, Alexander was very naughty today and did not drink up all of his milk. Whatever will we do? And what will become of poor, naughty Alexander?"

As well, children are taught the rules of the community in miniature when mothers repeat traditional stories, poems and word games to their children (Das, 1989). This gentle and roundabout way of teaching rules is quite different from, say, the 19th century European way of teaching children by means of frightening fairy tales (which the Grimm Brothers gathered together) or even scarier morality lessons as in *Struwwelpeter*.

It's hard today, amid concerns about child abuse, to laugh at this well-known 19th century cartoon from the German book Struwwelpeter. *Was it a* **humourous** *attempt to discourage thumbsucking?*

Blackie & Sons Ltd., 1903

Much of family socialization is unspoken. We first learn the meaning of "woman," "wife," and "mother" by watching our own mother. Later, after an opportunity to observe other versions of "woman," "wife," and "mother" in friends' homes or on television, we begin to generalize — to learn which elements are shared among people playing these roles and which ones are not. Once generalizing begins, conscious choice becomes possible and the self can develop more rapidly and uniquely.

Of course, different kinds of socialization take place in different kinds of families, with different effects on the children. For example, living with both your parents is different from living with only one of your parents, or with a stepparent. In a study that was controlled for socioeconomic status, Australian children in "stepfamilies" where one parent has remarried, tend to score lower on reading ability, self control and self-esteem than children in two-parent or single-parent families (Amato and Ochiltree, 1987). This suggests there are parent-child interactions which are *not* a problem in single-parent families but are a disadvantage to children who live in "reconstituted" families.

Social class also shapes the course of family socialization. For example, in urban Indian families, middle-class children have stronger ties to their parents than children from the upper or lower classes (Srivastava, 1985). These middle-class children say they receive more emotional support from their parents and identify more with their parents than other children do. There seems to be no difference in the degree to which Indian parents of different classes discipline their children.

Parents' willingness to give their children some freedom also has an important effect. In North America, teenagers who see their parents as accepting and warm, and as less controlling, tend to have higher self-esteem than other children (Litovsky and Dusek, 1985). In turn, parents with higher self-esteem are more likely to give their child freedom and acceptance, and to have better communication with the child as a result (Small, 1988).

These are only a few of the factors that influence family interaction and socialization. Much more can be said and the importance of the family's influence cannot be overestimated. So, for example, people who were exposed to family violence as children are more likely than other people to end up abusing their own spouse and children. In this respect, childhood experiences can have a very negative influence on adult behaviour (Seltzer and Kalmuss, 1988).

Similarly, children who have been punished by beating grow up to be aggressive towards other family members. A particularly explosive recipe is infrequent reasoning and frequent spanking by the parent. Treating children this way dramatically increases their potential for violence as teenagers (Larzelere, 1986).

Sometimes family socialization is interrupted by war or other troubles, often with long-lasting effects. Consider the experience of children who are refugees, grieving the loss of loved ones, home and country. We are only starting to understand the full effects of "disrupted development" and the problems that are likely to emerge after resettlement (Eisenbruch, 1988).

However, even at the best of times, parents are not in complete control of the socialization process: as we noted earlier, children also socialize their parents. For example, a study of Canadian university students shows that, when the topic turns to sports, leisure, sexuality, drug use, and attitudes towards minorities, adolescents teach their parents a great deal (Peters, 1985).

Schools

Schools are also important agents of socialization. Of course, they provide us with information. More important, they help us understand ourselves and others, and give us skills to function effectively as citizens and workers. They also open the door to a strange new social world. Unlike the family, schools are populated by strangers.

Some of these strangers — the teachers — hold positions of authority. They expect obedience and punish deviation (even if not as firmly today as in the past). Unlike parents, teachers exert control without delivering affection. They expect compliance without exception and will not make special deals of the kind that children usually make with their parents. This is part of treating each student equally, as one of many. In these respects, teachers are the first truly impartial rule-enforcers children are likely to have met. The school is a child's first exposure to the "rule of law."

The school also offers a child his or her first exposure to political life. The classroom is a structure of unequal power, over which the teacher presides. At least in theory, this power is not shared, nor is it up for negotiation. In practice, social order within the classroom is constantly negotiated between teachers and their students. Exposure to this is good training for the way power actually operates in adult political systems.

Primary schools are particularly effective socializers when they are reinforcing ideas the children have brought with them from home. For example, an Indian study shows that schools are successful in reinforcing ideas about obedience to elders, gender differentiation, and social inequality that the student has heard at home. Other ideas, like nationalism and democracy, which the student hears at school but *not* at home, are less likely to be internalized (Khullar, 1989).

The school is also a child's first experience of economic life. Like any economy, the school distributes scarce resources. Some children will get more of the teacher's time and attention than others. Some children will get high marks and special honours; other children will consistently do poorly and end up in a slow learning track. Students are fully aware of this unequal allocation of rewards and punishments. They know who the "teacher's pet" is and who is the "class victim," as Wilfred Martin (1984) found in a study of Newfoundland schoolchildren. What's more, they have strong views about the way the teacher hands out rewards and may rebel if they feel an injustice has been done.

Despite the chance for negotiation between teachers and their students, children enjoy relatively little control over a school's rules and practices. This powerlessness at school provides real-life training for the adult workplace, but it also undoes some of the good that socialization accomplished in the family home. There, children began to develop a sense of control over their environment. The school setting typically reduces opportunities for control and makes children feel *less* competent. This is especially troublesome for children who enter school with fewer than average skills. Their feelings of incompetence will continue throughout school and even into the workplace, affecting later relations with their own children (Tudge, 1982).

At least in the first years of schooling, the academic curriculum — reading, writing, social studies, arithmetic — is far less important than this "hidden" curriculum. What's more, the hidden curriculum varies from one country to another, reflecting the major elements of a society's culture. So, for example, children in Florence — arguably, the historic cultural centre of Italy — are schooled in values that originated in the Renaissance. These include an emphasis on the beauty of public spaces; a strong, highly verbal presentation of the self; and the integration of academic and artistic goals, as is clear from their ornately illustrated notebooks (Garner, 1991).

In North America, as in Italy, the school contributes to the formation of a character and way of behaving that is considered functional in modern industrial society. It offers children a world that more or less predictably rewards middle-class ideas of conformity, good behaviour, and hard work.

Some children learn the new, unfamiliar behaviour and profit from it. Other children — often, working class children (Willis, 1977) — challenge the school with truancy, disruption and other forms of counter-culture: they will not willingly follow a middle-class conception of conformity and upward mobility. Their rebellion against authority is socialization too: a kind of preparation for working class jobs.

Not all of the learning at school takes place within the classroom. In the schoolyard, many children have their first exposure to bullies, team games, much older and younger children, and same-age children of the opposite sex. The school population provides experiences that are unlikely within the family (for example, team games). The variety of students — their peers —forces children to re-assess the rules and roles they learned in infancy.

Peers

Peers too are important agents of socialization and are particularly influential from late childhood through adolescence and early adulthood. The **peer group** is a group of interacting companions who usually share similar social characteristics (age, gender, social class, and religion among others), interests, tastes, and values.

Members of a peer group treat one another as individuals. This means that they are able to get to know one another in terms of interests, activities, and tastes, which become the foundation for close friendships (as well as strong enmities). The friendships of youth are particularly intense because children and adolescents spend so much of the day together, usually in school, engaged in identical or similar activities.

Like parents and teachers, peers are also part of our *reference group*, people to whom we mentally refer when evaluating our own thoughts and behaviour. A reference group provides the standards against which people and behaviour are evaluated. All reference groups act as agents of socialization by giving us clear illustrations of how to behave and, occasionally, by rewarding us for behaving that way.

Consider the attempts young children make to dress like their peers, their older siblings and parents, even the people they see on television. Their sense of what or who is "cool," "beautiful," or "radical" comes from these sources and sometimes their excessive efforts at imitation are laughable. Sometimes, as when we see a ten-year old smoking cigarettes, the imitation is depressing. Laughable or not, by dressing and acting like "the big guys," these children are declaring a desire to *be* like the big guys: indeed, to be accepted by them, and also to be viewed as one of them by others.

There is a huge literature, both fictional and sociological, on peer groups and how they affect young people as they grow up. These groups can be very nurturing or very cruel, and sometimes both. By studying peer groups, we learn about the basic social processes of interpersonal attraction and repulsion, expressed in cliques, friendships and mating patterns. We also see displayed the best and worst features of a society. So, for example, the fatalistic and violent activity of "train surfing" (see Exhibit 3.4) tells us more about contemporary Brazil than a dozen closely argued scholarly studies.

Peers start to be an important reference group as soon as a child starts school, and they become more important through adolescence and early adulthood. The importance of peers as a reference group does not depend on school, however. For example, gangs of train surfers or delinquents provide each other with emotional support and aid by providing a positive sense of self when schools or parents cannot. Why are street gangs so numerous, large and significant in certain parts of the world? It's precisely because they give their members certain kinds of experiences, and opportunities for a positive self-image that no other social groups do (Vigil, 1988).

Peers are even *more* important to street children who have few other people to rely on. Amazingly, these street children are in good mental health, de-

EXHIBIT 3.4 *For Brazil's young people, life is a train trip to nowhere*

Train-surfing is a popular sport among the teenage boys who live in *favelas* (shantytowns) in this city's industrial northern zone. The lanky boys, some of whom are over 20, climb on top of the commuter trains . . . and "surf" while the train is in motion. Every once in a while, a few get electrocuted and die when their bodies come into contact with a live wire or over-hanging cable. But the risk is part of the thrill, they say.

Train-surfing has become a grim metaphor for Brazilian youth in an inflationary, corruption-riddled society. In a country where the currency loses about 1 per cent of its value per day and role models elicit nothing but scorn, the future is in jeopardy. . . .

The country's youth, the majority of the population of 150 million, seem doomed.

What's it like to grow up in Brazil? If you're young in an inflationary economy, it's hard to save money and your job prospects are extremely limited. Middle-class professionals such as doctors and teachers make on average $150 (U.S.) a month—hardly enough to survive in urban centres where the cost of living is, in many ways, equivalent to that in large U.S. cities. Indeed, most middle-class kids rarely dream about working hard to build a career in Brazil. They dream of going to Miami.

Although Brazil's constitution guarantees every child's right to a free education, nearly five million children never go to school. There are excellent free universities, but because entrance requirements are so rigid only those whose parents can afford to send them to private high schools have that opportunity to attend. Kids from the teeming favela neighbourhoods don't really have a fighting chance to get good schooling, largely because the federal government spends a pittance on public education at the primary and secondary levels. . . .

[I]n Brazil, where the older generations have racked up a huge foreign debt, violated democratic principles and left the country morally bankrupt, there seems little hope. For young people, it's becoming harder and harder to have faith in Brazil's democratic institutions or exercise their responsibilities of citizenship.

Gilson, 19, who can be found most days "surfing" at the Central do Brasil station, recently summed up the predicament of youth in his country: "We surf because it's fun. What else do we have to do?"

Source: Isabel Vincent, "For Brazil's young people, life is a train trip to nowhere," *The Globe and Mail*, Mon., Nov. 29, 1993, p. A14

spite the hardships they face. Tests reveal that male street children in Colombia, aged 7 to 16 are generally healthy, intelligent and emotionally stable — not delinquents as many seem to think (Aptekar, 1989a). They owe much of their well-being to close friendships with other street children. Some is also due to frequent contact with their mothers and help they receive from benevolent adults (see also Aptekar, 1989b).

There are many issues about which members of a reference group disagree. As most of you will have long since discovered, parents and peers *often* disagree. Though both parents and peers belong to the same reference group, a child takes their respective opinions into account on different occasions or in relation to different issues. In specific situations, children and parents may be able to find a compromise among competing views (including those of peers).

Consider the conflict between Indian immigrant parents and their children in Canada over issues such as personal freedom and dating behaviour. The teenagers adapt easily to new attitudes, so parents worry that their children are losing their cultural identity. Though immigrant parents are less authoritarian than parents in India, conflicts with their children about personal freedom and double standards for boys and girls remain common (Kurian, 1986).

Mass media

The last chapter noted the importance of mass media in shaping and transmitting culture. So it stands to reason the media play an important role in socialization. Socialization by mass media is a major type of secondary socialization and it influences people's behaviour through modelling and imitation.

In their survey, Bibby and Posterski (1985) found that 90% of Canadian teenagers "very often" listen to music and 57% watch television. By contrast, fewer than 40% "very often" play team sports, work out, read a book, spend time on a hobby, or take part in a youth group. Because so many consume media messages, it is likely that song lyrics, television stories, and plot lines of music videos will have a significant influence on teenagers' behaviour.

But *how* the mass media influence behaviour, and *whether* this influence is good or bad, are hotly debated issues. Much has been written about the way news reporting distorts reality, creating fears that are unwarranted and support for certain policies or political candidates. The effect of violent and pornographic movies and videos on interpersonal relationships has also been studied. The prevailing view is that they probably have a harmful effect but that this has not been conclusively proven.

Other research on the effects of mass media has to do with the way advertising secretly manipulates our desires. Products are advertised in ways that appeal to people's longing for social acceptance or status. Sex is also a powerful attention-grabber; advertisers even imply that their product — whether jeans, beer or even soft drinks — will improve a consumer's sex life.

One television advertisement for a soft drink became notorious for its use of sexual display. It showed a parade of young people marching, singing and dancing down the street with the product in hand. At one point, an attractive young cheerleader did a cartwheel toward the camera. This was the dramatic high point of the advertisement, though it was hard to say why. It became obvious when network censors slowed the ad down to reveal that the young cheerleader had no underpants on.

However enjoyable in its own right, such advertising discourages us from thinking rationally about the merits of the advertised product. Rationally, we should buy Beer X because it tastes better or is cheaper than Beer Y, not because the ad turns us on. By encouraging us to behave irrationally, the mass media undo much of what our other agents of socialization — especially parents and schools — try to accomplish.

The effect of such advertising on prosperous North America is bad enough; it has worse effects where people are less prosperous. Teenagers in the Third World country of Belize have also been socialized by the media and peers to have a materialistic outlook. Though not particularly "political," these teenagers are keenly aware of their position in the world economic system as consumers. This awareness makes them feel inadequate because they have fewer material goods than teenagers in other parts of the world and less opportunity to participate in the world economy (Lundgren, 1988). What do you suppose are the effects of this feeling of inadequacy?

Other agents

There are many other agents of socialization in our society. Because modern societies have so many different social institutions, secondary socialization — particularly within professional schools and work groups — is especially important. Here the socialization process centres more on specific goals and activities than it does in a peer group, family, or primary school.

These agencies prepare people for a coming change of roles. As such they provide anticipatory socialization. **Anticipatory socialization** prepares people for roles they will eventually perform by helping them to understand these roles. Most adult socialization is of this character.

In one sense, all socialization — from birth onward — is anticipatory socialization. For example, in childhood when two children play house (practising parenting roles in advance of actually playing the role), or pretend to be storekeepers or teachers, they are engaging in anticipatory socialization.

Therefore, not all anticipatory socialization is *secondary* socialization, nor is it all *adult* socialization. However, most adult socialization, and most secondary socialization is anticipatory socialization. That is because, in adulthood, we all have a much fuller idea of the roles we are preparing to enter, and much more choice in whether to enter them or not. In adulthood, people are much more likely to choose and pursue the socialization they want to get.

Both job training and professional education are types of anticipatory socialization that prepare people for the work they will do after graduating. Equally important, these programs teach the attitudes, values, and beliefs associated with a future activity. A law school education, for example, teaches students the values of the legal profession and shows them how to think about legal problems. It also teaches students how to speak, dress, and deal with clients in an appropriate professional manner.

Medicine, too, requires professional socialization. A medical education teaches students the parts of the body, types of diseases, the medical language, diagnoses, and possible cures. As well, students learn the ethics of medical practice and ways to give the patient a reassuring show of competence in every situation (Haas and Shaffir, 1977).

During anticipatory socialization, students push themselves to learn new values and skills. Often anticipatory socialization is self-training because, as we have

These three people-in-suits learned how to dress, talk, joke and (generally) get along on the job through workplace socialization.

© Dave Starrett

noted, the students have freely chosen to enter this educational stream. This makes professional education very different from lower levels of education which students have not chosen voluntarily and where they are often socialized against their will.

Workplace socialization, also largely voluntary, is the process of learning what is and what is not acceptable behaviour within a workplace. It includes the process of adopting the values, goals, and perspectives of those with whom a person interacts at work. Workplace socialization also includes learning the specialized language (or argot) of the people at work. This helps give the new worker a sense of belonging and of loyalty to the group.

Much of this learning is imitative and unconscious. For example, junior executives often pay close attention to the way senior executives dress, speak and act, and model their actions after them. A person who prepares for career advancement in this way is more likely to advance than one who does not. A few are also lucky enough to have *mentors* who provide them with advice and support. Mentors can help by giving ambitious young workers more opportunity, contacts, advancement, recognition and work satisfaction than they would have otherwise had (Fagenson, 1989).

SOCIALIZATION OVER THE LIFE CYCLE

As you can see, there are many socialization experiences in a lifetime. In fact, the development of the self and the learning of social behaviour are lifelong processes. Personal change is the only constant in life. And we have noted that current theories of socialization see development occurring in many phases or stages. The notion of developmental stages implies that people's lives follow a pattern as they age and pass through typical social roles. Sociologists call this pattern the life cycle.

What is the life cycle?

The **life cycle** is a socially recognized, predictable sequence of stages through which people pass during the course of their lives. Each stage is characterized by a set of socially defined rights, responsibilities, and expected behaviour patterns.

The recognized sequence in North American society includes infancy, childhood, adolescence, maturity, and old age. Remember, though, that stages of the life cycle are socially and not biologically defined. Adolescence, for example, is not a biological fact, it is a social invention. Adolescence as we know it today did not exist before the 19th century. Two hundred years ago, fifteen-year-olds spent their time in the same ways as people who were 25 or 35: in adult work. If unmarried, they were all equally subject to domination by the head of the household.

Likewise, old age is not a biological reality so much as a social and psychological one (Dychtwald and Flower, 1990). Today, few people of 50, 60 and even 70 years of age think of themselves as old, or do the things old people used to do. People of these ages are much more physically active, travel more, and enter new roles more readily than people of the same age did 50 years ago. They divorce and remarry, have sex, go on exotic vacations if they can afford it, keep working if they are permitted, and so on. It is the behaviour of eighty- and ninety-year-olds today that is similar to the behaviour of sixty-year-olds a century ago. (Indeed, they even constitute(d) similar percentages of the population.)

Because the life cycle is socially defined, life cycles vary across cultures and over history. Different cultures identify different life stages and expect them to last different lengths of time. Our own society has recently recognized a distinct stage between adolescence and mature adulthood: people are calling it the "youth stage," or "young, single, and independent stage."

This new stage has emerged because fewer young people are moving out of their parents' homes to marry and form new families. Some remain in their parents' home, while others move out and live on their own or with a roommate. Many delay marriage while they "find themselves," learn to be independent, or simply have fun.

Even this modified picture of the life cycle is too simple. It leaves the impression that people pass through life in only one way and doing otherwise is wrong or abnormal. In fact, the life cycle is just a statistical summary of what people are doing, not a social law. People vary around the average enormously and they are varying more all the time.

Sociologist Denis Hogan (1981) analyzed data on American men over the past half century and found a growing tendency to deviate from the average life cycle. Fifty years ago, the typical man finished his formal education, got a job, then married. The proportion of men who took another path — for example, married, finished school, then got a job — was extremely small. Since then, the proportion of men following these other patterns has increased dramatically.

As a result of the fact that these other patterns are more common today, they are no longer considered deviant. It is much easier today than it once was to marry while still in school. In fact, two incomes make finishing school easier, not harder, for people who do not live with their parents And people are increasingly moving between work and education over the life course. People no longer feel that when you have started working for pay, your education is over for all time. Women are particularly likely to keep moving between school, part-time work and full-time work in this way (Jones, Marsden, and Tepperman, 1990).

Is there anyone you cannot be?

Throughout life we change our goals and values. In some cases we are even resocialized, which means we change fundamental parts of our personalities, not merely our attitudes or skills. **Resocialization** causes the person to hold a new outlook on the world and a new sense of self. Such basic changes come about through the learning of radically different values, norms, and role expectations from those learned earlier.

Resocialization can be voluntary or involuntary. For example, resocialization is becoming more necessary for people who want to get jobs in a tight economy. Other people, who seek psychological counselling, may also want to be resocialized — to have their personalities "remade." In both cases, resocialization is voluntary. In other cases resocialization is involuntary, as it is for people who live in total institutions.

A *total institution*, as described by sociologist Erving Goffman (1961), is an organization which is set apart physically or socially from the rest of society. Included in this category are prisons, mental hospitals, boarding schools, concentration camps, military barracks, and convents. Inmates in these institutions have little, if any, contact with the outside world. Here, they learn new modes of thought and behaviour that the people in charge deem appropriate.

People do change fundamentally when they are in fundamentally different settings, especially if they have entered them freely. But does this mean there are no limits on how much you or anyone else can change? Does it mean there are conditions under which a gentle person might willingly become a killer, for example? Or a loyal person, a traitor?

The answer to this question is often "yes." Warfare, for example, commonly teaches people to kill. As a total institution, the military programs people to kill enthusiastically and efficiently. And during wartime, the mass media and political leaders whip up even ordinary citizens into blood-lust, under the guise of patriotism and self-defense. In such circumstances, most people find ways to justify their change of attitude and behaviour. They may even find reasons to betray their own family and friends: it has happened many times, in many places.

However, it is appropriate, at the end of this chapter, to remember something that we said at the beginning. That is, early socialization is, in many respects, more critical than later socialization. If we get the early parts wrong, it will be much harder — perhaps, impossible — to make certain changes later on. For example, Exhibit 3.5 shows that inadequate education for girls around the world not only stunts their intellectual growth — it also ensures their continued

Former Prime Minister Pierre Trudeau: Over the life cycle, certain features remain constant, but other features of manner, self-presentation, and self-awareness may change dramatically.

National Archives of Canada

National Archives of Canada

John McNeill

EXHIBIT 3.5 *World lags in education of girls*

...In a report to be released today, the Washington-based Population Action International estimates that, globally, 85 million more boys than girls go to primary or secondary school, a chasm that may reach 179 million by 2005 if nothing is done in the next few years....

The report ranks Canada second only to France in a female-education ranking of 116 countries. Canada scored 99.4 on a scale of 100.

The index measured such criteria as average years of schooling for girls, the ratio of boys to girls in primary and secondary schools and gross enrolment rates for girls.

The survey found that Canadian girls stay in school longer — 11.9 years on average — than girls in any other country except the United States.

It also found, however, that only 93 Canadian girls attend primary school for every 100 boys, lowest among all leading industrialized countries.

The study, *Closing the Gender Gap: Educating Girls*, found a much greater disparity between boys' and girls' education in developing countries. In India, only 71 girls attend primary school for every 100 boys. In neighbouring Nepal, the number was only 47.

The report warns that the lack of girls' education may thwart efforts to stabilize the world's population....

No country with a female education score of less than 60 points had a national fertility rate lower than 4.0 children per woman. Canada's fertility rate was only 1.7 in 1990, the year when PAI collected its data. Italy had the lowest with 1.3.

Educated girls tend to marry later and understand family planning better. Their social status is raised and they tend to respond more effectively to their children's health needs, leading to lower rates of infant mortality.

In less-developed countries where there is no education gap, such as Cuba and Sri Lanka, fertility rates are on par with wealthier countries: 1.9 in Cuba and 2.4 in Sri Lanka....

While the worst records can be found in developing countries, national income is not always a barrier to education....

On average, however, the disparity between the number of girls and boys attending school was widest in southern Asia and the Middle East, and basic female education levels were lowest in sub-Saharan Africa, where girls average less than one year of formal schooling....

Source: John Stackhouse, "World lags in education of girls, study says," *The Globe and Mail*, Mon., Jan. 31, 1994, p. A7

dependence on men and increases the world's fertility level. These conditions are hard to unmake once a woman has reached middle age.

CLOSING REMARKS

Like the sociological study of culture, the study of socialization demonstrates the important connection between macro-and micro- perspectives.

On the one hand, socialization is a macro- phenomenon: something imposed on people (especially infants and children) by more powerful agents of socialization. In this sense, socialization is a top-down process that moulds us in society's image. On the other hand, socialization is a process that we often willingly take part in and even initiate. As the symbolic interactionists remind us, we all have the desire to learn, speak, and interact with other people. From this standpoint, socialization merely gives us the tools to do what we are already programmed to want.

As long as we continue to interact with others and meet new people, we will continue to discover new things about others and ourselves. Good sociology never loses sight of the broad social processes which affect all of us, or the intricate circumstances which are unique to each of us. That's why good sociology avoids determinism and leaves some room for "free will."

As we shall see in succeeding chapters, social determinism causes more problems than it solves. How can we explain social change if we assume that all people are programmed to value only the existing social order? Equally, how can we explain deviance if we assume that all people are socialized to conform to society's norms and values? Some have claimed that deviance results from incomplete or imperfect socialization. Others claim that deviance is conformity to the expectations of an unusual subculture.

By now, it should be clear that what we call "deviant acts" are a normal part of social life: acts that people practice and give up as they pass through life. We explore these issues further in the next chapter.

Canada Wide

By his bodily adornment, this young man is communicating a point of view about rules and conformity, deviance and control. What is the "message"?

DEVIANCE AND CONTROL

SOCIAL ORDER AND RULES

The concept of "society" suggests an enduring, predictable pattern of social relationships. Given this view of society, many sociologists paint a picture of daily life that is highly structured, stable and orderly — a life in which well-socialized people routinely become well-integrated members of their community. Yet all of us know people who do *not* follow the rules: who engage in behaviour that others find reprehensible, dangerous or merely foolish.

At times, all of us have done things we should not have, things that have made us ashamed, anxious, or which gave us a secret thrill. We may even admire people — say, political rebels or environmental activists — who knowingly break the law and risk serious penalties in order to act on their principles.

How do sociologists account for this common tendency to break the rules or flout the laws? How, in other words, do sociologists account for deviance? By now you know enough about sociology to realize that what is most likely to interest a sociologist is not the deviant behaviour itself, but how deviance and conformity are related to each other. Deviance, as we shall see, is another aspect of social order (*society creates deviance* by expecting, insisting upon, and enforcing social order). This is what we mean by the "social construction of deviance," a main theme of this chapter.

Think about it! If you keep all your books on a shelf in no particular order, then no book is out of order when you put it back on the shelf. But if you keep your books in one particular order — let's say, alphabetically by author — then a book must be put back in one and only one location or it is out of place. Creating order is what creates the possibility of deviance (Deviance, then, is not a special topic of study but a measure of how tightly society is organized.)

Every area of social life provides opportunities for deviance. Most of us think of **crime** when we think of deviance and, more specifically, the major crimes such as murder, armed robbery or rape. Yet there is deviance in all the tiny interactions of daily life. Even when we lie, cheat, seduce, disgust or simply irritate one another, we are deviating from *someone's norms*.

On the other side of the topic are deviant organizations such as organized crime and those "legitimate" organizations which engage in criminal acts by bribing officials, cheating customers or selling hazardous and defective products. There are also many subcultural groups, such as juvenile gangs; most people view them as deviant and, often, they are also harmful. Finally, there is also deviance by public officials — police officers who entrap criminals, and Cabinet ministers who violate conflict of interest guidelines, for example.

As you might gather from this list, the study of deviance is the study of everyone — the entire society — seen from one particular angle. This is why the sociology of deviance contains *all* of the controversies that sociologists, and sociology students, are ever likely to encounter.

DEFINING DEVIANCE AND SOCIAL CONTROL

The study of deviance has long been one of sociology's most exciting and contentious areas of research. Disagreement has arisen because different groups hold different conceptions of what behaviour is deviant.

What all behaviours termed "deviant" have in common, however, is that members of one group or another feel their cherished values, or security, are threatened. To sociologists, then, (**deviance** is a general term referring to behaviour of any sort that leads to a negative reaction or response by one group or part of a community.) This includes crimes such as robbery or vandalism;

forms of behaviour involving mental illness or juvenile delinquency; and the violation of institutional rules, such as cheating on an exam or smoking in a non-smoking area. It also includes behaviour that simply does not conform to social norms, such as dressing in a peculiar manner or only taking a shower once every two weeks.

Obviously, deviance is a broad category of social acts. But deviant behaviour always poses a threat to someone. When no one feels threatened by an uncommon behaviour — for example, by the wearing of a polka-dot bow tie — people are likely to see it as simply an expression of individuality. Such behaviour is considered eccentric or idiosyncratic, not deviant. There is a lot of room in North American popular culture for the acceptance, even admiration, of people who are eccentric (like Mother Theresa) or rebel in fashionable ways (like k.d. lang).

This means that reactions to uncommon behaviour depend largely on how the behaviour is perceived. Still, perception by itself is not enough; for an act to be deviant, a perception must be turned into action. How much weight that action carries will depend on how much power people have to *enforce* their own definitions of acceptable behaviour.

Enforcement at the microsociological level translates into agencies of social control at the macrosociological level. (*Social control* refers to the institutions and procedures that make sure members of society conform to rules of expected and approved behaviour.) The operation of social control is most obvious when it is *formal*, especially when laws are enforced through the courts and the police.

(**Formal social control** is institutionalized control which gives specific people (such as police officers) the job of enforcing specific rules or laws, while following specific control procedures.) This type of social control varies widely across countries. Even policing varies, from the localized police system of the United States to the centralized system of France (Hunter, 1990).

The American system is a localized and democratic form of control, with election of some local law enforcement officials, but it tends to be inefficient and open to corruption. By contrast, the French system of policing is more centralized, efficient and less corrupt, but it is also more likely to violate civil liberties. The British system, finally, is more integrated than the American and less centralized than the French system. It strikes a balance between local and national concerns, crime control and the protection of civil liberties. The Canadian system is most like the British one.

Few people have much contact with the police or other agencies which exercise formal social control. Our knowledge of formal control usually comes through the media, not through personal experience. But we do have first-hand knowledge of another kind of social control. We see it whenever ordinary people exercise **informal social control** through gossip, praise or blame. In small-scale, pre-modern societies informal social controls are the main way of maintaining social order. Yet informal controls are not only effective in a village or small town.

Japan is a good example. Though a highly industrialized and urbanized society, it continues to have a low crime rate. In Japan, the importance of family, group membership and community harmony all support the informal control of deviant behaviour. So do local debating societies, neighbourhood newspapers, and conferences of special interest groups (Becker, 1988).

Informal control works in many societies because people tend to seek the approval of others for a feeling of self-worth. Informal controls teach us to obey the rules and gently prod us in the direction of conformity when we show signs of backsliding.

Along with the threat of legal sanctions (e.g., fines or imprisonment), feelings of guilt can be important means of social control, where crimes like tax cheating, petty theft, and drunk driving are concerned. But social embarrassment is not very effective in our own society (Grasmick and Bursik, 1990). It works best in societies like Japan, where people consider "saving face" to be very important.

Because there are different forms of deviance, there are different reasons for deviant behaviour and different theories about it. Each of the major theoretical paradigms — functionalism, conflict theory, symbolic interactionism, and feminism — has its own approach and favourite theories.

THEORIES OF DEVIANCE

Early sociological theories of deviance developed out of what we call a social pathology perspective. *Social pathologists* claimed some societies — especially modern, industrial societies — are more prone to deviance than others. Since deviance varies by the type of society, social pathologists proposed that one should look to society, not to the individual, for an explanation of deviant behaviour.

As their use of the term "pathology" suggests, these social theorists emphasized that in some ways modern society is "sick." They assumed that the industrialization, urbanization, and immigration that accompanied modernization was leading to a "breakdown" of society's traditional order. This in turn caused the spread of social ills, crime and "vice," especially among the working class and the poor. It was their goal to re-establish traditional order, to reform society, and thereby cure it.

This view may have made some sense a century ago, when people were first struggling to come to terms with city life, large-scale immigration, mass production, mass literacy and the rise of the working class. But today we can see that the social pathologists were neither objective nor scientific in their assumptions and methods of research. Their sociology was infused with a moralistic approach which took for granted that deviance was always abhorrent and immoral. We reject these assumptions today.

Contemporary sociologists think about deviance in much the same way as the average police officer. What the police see, day after day, is very ordinary rule-breaking — for example, speeding or dangerous driving (see Exhibit 4.1). Occasionally, deviance gets out of hand and results in accidents, injuries, even deaths. But this is neither "sick" nor "abnormal" behaviour. The police officer would hardly conclude that society was "getting sicker" if the accident rate went up or even if convictions for speeding increased. What is needed is a vision of deviance that emphasizes its "normality," not its pathology.

Durkheim's theory of deviance

The French sociologist, Emile Durkheim, was the first to provide that vision by breaking with the moralistic critique of modern society. Durkheim (1938) argued that, since deviance can be found in every society and every social group, it must be a normal, inevitable, even necessary aspect of society. In fact, it must even be functional for, or beneficial to, society.

There are a number of ways, Durkheim suggested, in which deviance benefits us. For example, deviant behaviour calls attention to flaws in the social system that need mending. It may suggest new ways of getting things done, or

EXHIBIT 4.1 *Drivers showing short tempers on busy highways*

"Nice people turn into monsters when they get out there," says Staff Sergeant Robin McElary-Downer, with a nod in the direction of the busy highway that runs past the busiest traffic enforcement detachment of the Ontario Provincial Police.

The nice people she is referring to are drivers.

She is not sure why it happens, although she thinks the frustrations and strains caused by the recession may have something to do with it, but "these nice people don't seem to realize that they are driving with a loaded shotgun with a hair trigger when they get behind the wheel of a car. These nice people allow somebody to upset them and they become silly and dangerous." . . .

"There just seems to be a mind-set with people on the highway, hurrying to go here, hurrying to go there," she said in a recent interview. "Their tempers are short. We're seeing more and more assaults, where somebody cuts somebody else off, stops on the highway, has a verbal exchange and then gets into a fist fight.

"People aren't working, incomes aren't coming in, someone cuts you off and that just sort of breaks the camel's back." . . .

"We do the best we can, but we get frustrated, particularly with the public's attitude," Staff Sgt.

McElary-Downer said. "The general response is: 'Why aren't you out catching real criminals and the real murderers?' And my response is, 'It's the nice people like you we pick up off the highway when you're speeding and not belted in and you're thrown from the car.' . . .

Source: Peter Moon, "Drivers showing short tempers on busy highways," *The Globe and Mail*, Tues. Aug. 3, 1993, p. A10

Traffic Deaths and Injuries Versus Homicides
Canadians killed or injured by automobiles and homicides

	Homicides*	Vehicles**	
		Persons killed	Persons injured
1982	668	4169	225 717
1983	682	4216	224 297
1984	667	4120	237 455
1985	704	4364	259 189
1986	569	4068	264 481
1987	642	4286	280 575
1988	576	4153	278 618
1989	657	4250	284 937
1990	660	3960	262 604
1991	753	3684	248 626
Total	**6578**	**41 270**	**2 566 499**

Source: *Federal Department of Justice. **Federal Department of Transport

better ways of adapting to changes in the social environment. Minor forms of deviance serve as safety valves, allowing people to let loose in socially acceptable ways (for example, getting drunk at a weekend party). In all these respects, Durkheim believed, both deviance and social control help society to survive and change (for more on this, see also Cohen, 1966).

Durkheim also suggested that deviants provide us with vivid demonstrations of how *not* to act. A society needs deviance to define the boundaries between good and evil, right and wrong, and what is or is not acceptable. People who are identified as deviants serve as scapegoats for social ills — as targets for repressed anger and tension. Having a common enemy helps to unite the group. The exercise of social control increases social cohesion and group solidarity. Said another way, the enforcement of rules ties the group more tightly together. To the degree that deviance both calls forth and justifies punishment, then, deviance is "good" for society.

Durkheim's discussion of the functions of deviance and social control gave sociologists a new way of thinking about deviance, one that remains important today. It contradicts the common-sense bias that deviant behaviour is intrinsically "wrong," "bad," or "evil." Instead, it directs our attention to the social processes that produce deviance. But unlike the social pathology approach, it helps us understand why certain forms of behaviour continue *despite* being considered both immoral and illegal.

There are, however, a number of flaws in Durkheim's functionalist approach and the most glaring have to do with the issue of "benefits." Who exactly benefits from deviance? Compare the benefits with the harms and, often, it is not so certain that deviance and social control are "functional." Why did Nazi Germany decide on Jews as scapegoats for the country's problems instead of the many Polish agricultural workers living in Germany? Was this "functional" for the Jews? or for German society in the long run?

And how can we argue that society "benefits" from rape, child molesting, or murder? Punishing the deviant may strengthen the moral boundaries of society, but is this benefit worth a human life? Durkheim's perspective failed to deal effectively with these kinds of questions. It is simplistic to say that "society" benefits from any deviant act. After all, it is always specific people who benefit while other specific people are harmed. We will return to this issue shortly, when we discuss the conflict approach.

The functionalist approach

The modern functionalist approach to deviance was strongly influenced by Emile Durkheim's view of deviance. To functionalists, deviance serves as an ironic reminder of how social order underlies and is buttressed by even the most bizarre, senseless, or irrational of social acts. Yet functionalist theory is more subtle than Durkheim's approach.

The main functionalist theory of deviance is anomie theory which was developed by American sociologist Robert Merton. According to Merton (1957b), the cause of deviance does not lie in the individual but in society's unequal opportunity structure. In Merton's theory, like Durkheim's, deviance is normal (not pathological), societal (not individual) in origin, and contributes to the survival of the existing order. But in Merton's theory, unlike Durkheim's, deviance is driven by a basic conflict or paradox: a discrepancy between culturally defined goals and socially approved means for attaining those goals.

Merton used American society as his example. Merton argues that one of the primary goals of American society is success, especially in obtaining money, material goods, and "the good life." Most people have been socialized to value success. Yet social inequality ensures that most people will not be successful because they will not have access to the legitimate means and resources that allow them to attain success. Therefore, they are forced to find other means of reaching their goal.

(Merton called this discrepancy between goals and means *anomie*.)This state of anomie allows a variety of solutions, which Merton called *adaptations*. They include *ritualism*, *retreatism*, *rebellion*, and *innovation*. People try one or more of these solutions to deal with the discrepancy between goals and means.

Most people, of course, recognize that they will never really "make it" and simply live out their lives as best they can. To the degree that they never give up hope and continue to admire those who are successful, however, they continue to conform to the values and norms of the society. The long lines of people waiting patiently to buy lottery tickets when there is a big prize expected are an indication of how widespread this type of conformity is.

Others seem to conform, but they are just "going through the motions"; they have given up all hope of personal success. Merton called this adaptation *ritualism*. Such people, Merton suggested, are too well socialized to give up, but they no longer have any expectations for themselves.

Other people, recognizing that they will never achieve their goals, just give up. They become *retreatists* — alcoholics, drug addicts, or suicides, among other things. Today, many people in Eastern Europe are exhibiting such apathy in the face of widespread social change which has left them confused and frightened (Kolarska-Bobinska, 1990). Related to this is learned helplessness and a reliance on public institutions.

Still others *rebel* against inequality and reject the norms and values upon which it is based. They may try to change the political order. Youths in India have, largely, taken this approach to anomie (Basu, 1990). There, crowding, poverty, hunger and noise all generate cynicism and nihilism. For young people from poor backgrounds, education proves alienating because it reveals the extent of social unfairness. Community youth organizers, often from a middle-class background, are committed to wiping out poverty. But they are suspicious of politicians and big business; they realize they will have to bring about changes on their own.

A final adaptation to anomie is *innovation*. As Merton described it, innovation occurs when a person has internalized the cultural goals but has not internalized a commitment to the institutional norms — the legitimate "ways and means" of attaining these goals.

In its simplest form, innovation is crime; the use of illegitimate means to attain wealth and success. In a capitalist society, the many pressures on people to obtain success often make other norms seem trivial. The "Robber Barons" who grabbed corporate power and wealth in the United States towards the end of the 19th century believed that they had to lie, cheat and steal in order to succeed. Their great and visible success not only validated these beliefs: it encouraged everyone else to follow the low road.

Part of the problem is that many social norms are neither clear nor universally accepted; often people disagree about the legitimacy or validity of particular rules. As well, American society differs from other societies in that the cultural values of wealth, success, and ambition are widely diffused among all social classes. Yet Merton claims that innovation — crime — is the form of adaptation most likely to be found among the lower class. While all classes share the same goals, Merton sees the lower class as most lacking in access to the approved means necessary for achieving these goals.

That's why, according to Daniel Bell (1960), crime is as American as apple pie. (Now, with the breakdown of its economy, crime is also as Russian as beet *borscht*.)

It is a tried and true method of upward mobility in a society where people's hopes are high but opportunities are scant. To repeat, explanations of deviance based on anomie are macrosociological and functionalist. Merton insists that it is a combination of cultural and structural factors which produces deviance. By itself, a rigid social structure that limits access to opportunities does *not* generate deviance. Only when such a structure is combined with cultural goals that urge people to strive for success do we get an increase in deviance.

Since his argument is functionalist, Merton does not see innovation as posing a threat to social order. Criminals may endanger other people, but they neither challenge the goals of society nor try to change them. Instead, their adaptation strengthens cultural goals. The criminal exemplifies success and proves that anyone can "make it" in American society. By their flashy display of wealth and power, criminals advertise the pleasures of success among the lower class and keep the American dream alive.

Like the love affair we have with dinosaurs, noted in Chapter 2, North American culture has had a long fascination with gangsters, including the "Godfather" and his sons pictured here. We are really of two minds about crime.

Like Durkheim's theory, Merton's theory fails to specify who benefits from any given adaptation to anomie. Crime reinforces the existing social order by reinforcing cultural goals, but it does so at a serious cost. Like other functionalist explanations of deviance, anomie theory often seems to ignore the violence, fear, degradation and abuse which fills the lives of criminals and their victims. It shows how macrosociological theories that are divorced from microsociological research provide a superficial and distorted picture of social life.

Equally serious, the functionalist theory promotes the myth that crime is just a lower class activity — a stereotype that the mass media and the powerful seem content to perpetuate. As we shall see later, there is more to crime than lower-class "innovation."

The interactionist approach

Unlike the functionalist approach, the interactionist approach to deviance is microsociological. It examines the ordinary social processes that generate deviance. More important, it examines the impact social control has on the experience and self-identity of people who are considered deviant.

The most significant attempt to understand deviance which emerged out of this interactionist approach is called *labelling theory*. **Labelling theory** developed in the 1950s and '60s. It differed from earlier perspectives on deviance in the kinds of questions it asked and the kinds of questions it *didn't* ask.

Earlier perspectives assumed that the crucial issue was understanding *why* a person engages in deviant behaviour. Labelling theorists, however, are not interested in why people first engage in deviance, because they see all people as being deviant some of the time. They assume most people conform to most norms most of the time and everyone violates norms occasionally. The question is not why some people violate norms but how some people get locked into a pattern of repeated norm violation.

EXHIBIT 4.2   *Cheating has its rewards*

. . . A national survey says that, five years after Ben Johnson was at the centre of the biggest doping scandal in Olympic history, 14 per cent of Canadian adolescents share the values and beliefs of athletes who use banned drugs.

And almost one in four Canadian teens in the survey who were advised in a gym to try steroids went on to use the drugs.

"What they're seeing is that winning is rewarded, and it's enforced by the media and the corporate sector," said Paul Melia, director of education for the Canadian Centre for Drug-Free Sport.

There are broad rationalizations used by youngsters who find steroid use feasible in sport. For them, winning is paramount; using performance enhancing drugs isn't really cheating if others are doing it; Olympic athletes who use drugs should be able to compete.

A previous study also showed that steroids are a big magnet for teens who like the cosmetic effect of big muscles.

The school study found that the age for the onset of sport steroid use in male teens is 14 years old. The pattern is less clear for females.

However, it was apparent that children as young as 11 have a positive, idealistic attitude toward sport, but that it erodes steadily with age and exposure to demands for performance.

"Once they start working out in gyms, they're very much exposed to pressures [to start drugs], to coaches who put an emphasis on winning," said Melia. "There's a belief that those who are winning at the international level may be using drugs to win. The spirit of sport gets pushed aside by these external things." . . .

The survey of more than 16,000 adolescents in the sixth grade and higher in 101 schools across Canada...placed 14 per cent of students in the "high" and "very high" risk groups for steroid use, and another 41 per cent at "moderate" risk. Many of them already are using steroids. The balance was rated "low" to "very low" risk.

An interim report of the survey, released in early June, estimated as many as 83,000 youths had used anabolic steroids in the previous 12 months.

The survey also suggested students who were members of fitness clubs, were on a provincial sports team or on a weight-training program, were under much greater pressure to try steroids.

Source: James Christie, "Cheating has its rewards," *The Globe and Mail*, Thurs. Aug. 5, 1993, p. E8

For example, many people feel justified in cheating the "system" by using forbidden drugs to enhance their sports performance in competitions (see Exhibit 4.2). From the athletes' standpoint, winning is everything; *how* you win is not important, so long as you don't get caught. These rule-breakers are simply reflecting the values of the larger society which, as Merton pointed out, has admiration for winners and contempt for losers. For them, the issue is labelling, not "right and wrong." Sooner or later, these athletes will probably stop cheating.

Because labelling theorists reject a moral stance on deviant behaviour, they do not try to explain what they call *primary deviation* — why a person engages in such deviant behaviour in the first place. Instead they focus on secondary deviation — what happens to people after they have been identified or labelled deviant.

Another point made by labelling theorists is the relativity of deviance. They believe that no behaviour is inherently deviant; deviance is always socially defined and created. So, for example, many people in our society consider having tattoos on one's body to be deviant. Some people even believe that tattoos are a symptom of a pathological need to deface or mutilate one's body. Characteristically, we find tattoos in *macho* subcultures, such as prison, the armed services or delinquent gangs. They signify male bonding, a rejection of mainstream culture, and a tolerance for pain, since the process of tattooing is painful.

Yet, among the Maori of New Zealand, tattoos are normal. They are the symbols of full membership in society. There, tattoos mean something quite different from what they mean here and, accordingly, require different explanations.

This relativity of deviance is particularly important for research on deviant subcultures. A **deviant subculture** is made up of people who conform to certain norms and hold certain beliefs which the larger society considers deviant. Members of a subculture often dress, behave and speak in a way that emphasizes the differences between that group and other groups (for example, rival gangs) or "straight" society.

The discovery of deviant subcultures was an important achievement in sociology. Up through the 1930s, when social pathology theories were still in vogue, researchers assumed that normal people would not engage in deviant acts and deviant people would not act "normally". However research on gangs showed sociologists this was not true. First, the study of gang behaviour by Thrasher (1937) showed that, in most respects, gang members were far from abnormal. They conformed very well to their own gang's rules. Later research on gangs has suggested that gang members even recognize the dominant values as desirable, but these values are not relevant for their own lives, given their lack of opportunities.

Research reported by William Foote Whyte (1961) in his classic *Street Corner Society* showed that gangs were an important part of the social organization found within a slum community. Gang activities linked young people to both organized crime and neighbourhood politics and allowed members to carry out important criminal and political work for well-established organizations. From this angle, gang life was a form of professional socialization and an entry into paid work. Earlier researchers had not only misunderstood gangs, they had misunderstood the slum-dweller's way of life. Such findings remind us that gang behaviour, like all subcultural behaviour, is open to interpretation.

As Earl Rubington and Martin Weinberg (1968: v) point out, "... deviance is in the eyes of the beholder ... [it] is defined by what people say and do about persons, situations, acts, or events." This process of defining and treating others as deviant is what sociologists refer to as "labelling."

Labelling can be an extremely damaging social process. In Chapter 10, on population, we discuss the AIDS epidemic. It is worth noting at this point that AIDS victims have suffered almost as much from the ways other people have labelled them as they have from the disease itself.

In general, diseases that can be handled effectively by the medical community tend to be viewed in a more positive light than diseases like AIDS (and even cancer) that respond poorly to medical treatment and require better preventive measures than we are taking at present. Once a condition has been "medicalized" — taken over by the medical community — it no longer attaches any blame or responsibility to the victim.

One effect of the application of a deviant label is stigmatization. A *stigma* is a social attribute that acts as a mark of shame or social disgrace, and discredits an individual or group. The stigma of being labelled a deviant reminds others of what happens to people who violate social norms.

Consider a remote Australian mining town, where whites force aborigines to drink in only one bar in one hotel and in the adjoining park and river bank area. Aboriginal drunkenness, when it occurs, is highly visible to the community and more open to police prosecution than any other drunkenness. In the end, this labelling by the white community, and the arrests it produces, leads to a negative self-image for, and even more drinking by, the aborigines (Healy, Turpin and Hamilton, 1985).

Likewise, newspapers create a stigma by the ways they report on race in crime stories. Just by reporting on the race of an arrested person, the newspaper is implying that race is salient, an important part of explaining why the person committed the criminal act.

So, for example, reporting that a criminal is black is likely to reinforce stereotypes of black people as being inclined towards crime. Reporting that a criminal is white (a fact which is rarely reported) is unlikely to have the opposite, positive effect on perceptions of blacks. Therefore, divulging the race of a criminal does not break down stereotypes and even reinforces them by labelling certain groups as more likely to commit crimes (Winkel, 1990).

A person labelled as deviant by others may come to see himself or herself as such. Ironically, the person is then more likely to engage in deviant behaviour, because that fits in with his or her new self-image.

Of course, there is nothing inevitable about this. For example, a study of alcoholics indicates that the number of times a person had been labelled "alcoholic" by family and friends had little bearing on his or her subsequent drinking behaviour. Often, alcoholism is related to other problems, of which labelling is one of the least important (Combs-Orme, Helzer, and Miller, 1988). That's why we are not able to cure an alcoholic by simply saying "Now you are no longer an alcoholic!" nor turn an abstainer into an alcoholic by saying "You have a serious drinking problem." There must be an interaction between (1) the possibility of a problem (for example, excessive drinking), (2) the person's own perception or fear that there may be a problem, and (3) other people's confirmation, through labelling, that there really is a problem.

Members of the Hell's Angels share a highly developed subculture which includes group rituals and special ways of dressing.

Labelling theory has been criticized from a number of angles. As we have already noted, there are many instances in which labelling is *not* an important influence on people's behaviour. Some people continue their deviant acts even though they have never been labelled. Others give up their deviant acts even though they *have* been labelled. As well, labelling theory can be criticized generally for promoting an image of the deviant as a victim of society. Sometimes this is an appropriate view, but often it is not.

Nonetheless, labelling theory points researchers in some useful directions. It leads them to ask, "Are some people more likely to be singled out and accused of deviance than others?" For example, many people are only too willing to believe that ethnic or racial minorities commit a larger-than-average share of crime. Yet when socioeconomic status is taken into account, this excess disappears. The crime problem usually has more to do with social and economic inequality than it does with race or cultural values (Albrecht, 1987). But this fact does not prevent people from holding prejudiced views and stigmatizing minorities, and the effect can be long-lasting.

Why do they do this? Why, generally, do the law, the press and public opinion tend to stigmatize and punish powerless people? That question interests sociologists who use the conflict paradigm.

Conflict theories of deviance

From the conflict point of view, both deviance and social control are the result of conflicting interests among competing groups. The conflict paradigm takes as its starting point the recognition that creating and enforcing rules leads to people being defined as deviant. Deviance only comes into existence when we apply rules to behaviour. Understanding how, why, and by whom rules are created, then, is the key to understanding deviance.

This view has several interesting implications. The first is the possibility that societies seemingly plagued by rampant deviance actually suffer from too many rules. If we lived with fewer rules and less rule-enforcement — if we adopted a live-and-let-live attitude — we would have less deviance to worry about. By trying to enforce a multitude of laws, the law-makers and police create more problems than they solve.

The argument for the legalization of marijuana makes this important point clearly. Keeping marijuana illegal profits an enormous criminal drug industry which does more harm than the drug itself. Or, to take another commonplace example, the rapid growth of sales and excise taxes in Canada resulted in cigarette smuggling becoming a multimillion dollar industry here. As a result, the federal government was forced to rescind the taxes, as a way of combatting black market sales. Beyond that, more and more people have taken to paying cash for *all* goods and services in order to avoid paying the unpopular Goods and Services Tax (GST).

A second point conflict theorists often make is that social control extends social inequality into the realm of law. In all societies, some people have more power than others. The powerful use their power to protect their own interests and possessions. This means seeing that the government makes, and the police enforce, laws that protect these interests. The powerful also make sure that crimes *they* commit are treated as less serious than crimes the powerless commit.

As a result, we have little in the way of law enforcement against large environmental polluters. A corporation dumping toxic waste into a river that serves as the water supply for millions of people will be treated less severely than a disturbed person who poisons a product on a grocery shelf. In the last decade especially, governments supposedly cracking down on crime have been lenient with corporate crime. This reflects the pro-business attitude of North American governments throughout the 1980s, despite a "get tough" policy in relation to the sentencing and imprisonment of lower-class street criminals (Caringella-MacDonald, 1990).

If we included white collar and corporate crimes (which, dollar-for-dollar, are far more costly to society than lower-class street crimes) in the "Official Statistics," then the popular image of the typical criminal would become older, whiter, more middle and upper class than it is today.

From the conflict standpoint, the study of deviance and control is the study of law-making: why governments make certain laws at certain times, and whom these laws favour. By this reasoning, neither deviance nor control is functional to society. Instead, social control serves one group in society — the powerful — at the expense of everyone else. Deviants are the main victims of this inequality.

Like the functionalist and interactionist approaches, the conflict approach helps us to understand a lot about deviance. Yet, when we look at the controversies and conflicts of interest surrounding deviance, it is hard to interpret many of them as involving the "powerful." Some are conflicts based on religious beliefs, as is conflict over abortion. Others reflect concerns about personal security, such as the demand by police that the death penalty be re-introduced for the killing of police officers.

As for criminals being victimized by the law, most people feel that the real victims are poor, young and powerless people who are the most likely to be robbed, murdered, or raped. In an abstract sense, crimes may be rebellions against the social order and, as even the functionalists would agree, a result of social inequality. Yet this is no justification for crime nor is it a demonstration that all laws repress the poor in order to protect the rich.

The feminist paradigm

Like the conflict theorists and, especially, the critical criminologists, feminist sociologists criticize both society and the discipline of sociology itself. When directed against criminology, the feminist approach asserts that scholarly research has failed to pay enough attention to women, whether as criminals or as the victims of crime.

Some feminist sociologists argue that the lack of attention paid to women as criminals results from a bias among male criminologists. These male researchers have seen women as constitutionally incapable of certain forms of deviance (for example, violent crimes) and constitutionally inclined towards other forms of deviance, such as prostitution or sexual deviance (Smart, 1977). Following this logic, female crime seemed to need no special explanation or research since it was the outcome of supposedly innate "feminine" characteristics or tendencies. In this respect, the study of female deviance progressed little from the time of the social pathologists until the emergence of feminist criminology in the late 1970s.

Some feminists have argued that women have become more likely to commit crimes and be labelled as criminals, as they have become more emancipated and the controls on women have decreased. However, there is research that suggests that this is not the case. While the number of female offenders has been increasing, the rate of increase is lower than that for male offenders. This means that the ratio of female to male offenders is *decreasing*.

In recent years, a number of studies have examined female crime or the female criminal (Adler, 1975; Campbell, 1984; Schur, 1984). They open up what has been, to date, a neglected area of research but they contribute little to a specifically feminist approach. Simply noting that women, too, can be deviant tells us little about how women experience crime, deviance or social control.

On the other hand, feminists have made important contributions to the study of deviance by de-romanticizing the image of the criminal that characterizes both labelling theorists and critical criminologists. They have done this by turning their attention to the study of victims: who gets hurt, why are some kinds of people more likely to get hurt than others, and what can be done about it?

Gartner (1992), for one, looks at violence against women and children — criminal acts which are usually, though not always, committed within the home, or between intimates. Unlike other types of crime and deviance, here we find little ambiguity about the victims, the crimes, or the perpetrators of harm: the key question really is "Why did they do it?" Or, asked in a sociological, not a psychological way, "What are the social conditions under which people are more likely to do that kind of thing?"

So, for example, Gartner finds, across a wide range of societies, social patterns that predict higher and lower risks of violence. Among other things, these "risk factors" include women's education and participation in the paid work force — in short, women's independence from and equality with men. Violence against women tends to increase in those societies in which women are in the midst of becoming legally, economically and socially more independent. In societies where women have achieved greater independence, the rate of violence declines.

Feminists are at the forefront of attempts to change the laws that cover crimes against women. One area in which there has been much publicized progress is in reforming the law against sexual assault. Canada now has one of the strongest laws against rape and other forms of sexual assault. Yet many questions remain about how effective the new laws really are and whether they meet the needs of Canadian women.

Feminists have focused on rape and other forms of sexual assault for a number of reasons. First and foremost, rape is a terrifying, violent and humiliating experience which many women undergo and almost all women fear. Changing the laws related to rape, providing help and other services to women who have been raped, and finding ways to prevent rape are therefore important tasks facing society.

Some feminists assert that rape symbolizes and reflects the pattern of gender relations in our society. While few men are rapists, most men take advantage — wittingly or unwittingly — of the domination over women our society permits them. Fear and dependence, feminists argue, mark womens' social relations with men at work, on dates and in the home, and women can never be equal to men as long as fear and dependence continue.

Rape has been a rallying issue for feminists — a crime which most women would agree is of urgent and personal concern. For this reason, rape has served to sensitize both women and men to the goals of the feminist movement. The media have helped by making people more aware of crimes against women. People are more aware of victimization and victims today than they were a decade or a generation ago, thanks largely to the media.

THE RELATIVITY OF DEVIANCE

This chapter has argued that "deviance" and "conformity" are always being defined and redefined — in short, always being negotiated — in groups and societies. Yet Skovron et al. (1987) find great similarities in the ways people view different types of deviance, especially crimes.

A set of surveys carried out in the United States, India and Kuwait finds respondents scoring penalties for deviance (i.e., fine, jail, torture, and so on) in similar ways. They also evaluate the deviant acts similarly. Whatever country they come from, most people will give a severe penalty for murder and a light penalty for shoplifting, for example.

There is, however, one important difference in the rank-orderings: that is the severity with which (Islamic) Kuwaiti respondents treat offences against morals. Kuwaitis consider these offences, which include adultery, atheism and homosexuality among others, to be just as serious as armed robbery and manslaughter, and they propose to penalize them seriously to reflect this seriousness. This tendency shows the effect of Islamic religious teaching in Kuwait (indeed, in much of the Islamic world) and the reluctance of Muslims to distinguish between sacred and secular, or church and state, concerns.

But, except for major crimes, we find little consensus about what should be considered deviance in North America. In a survey conducted in 1965, American sociologist J. L. Simmons asked 180 people what they considered deviant. They responded with a total of 252 different forms of behaviour. The answers ranged from homosexuality to atheism to divorce (Thio, 1983: 3). This broad range of answers — in many ways similar to the Kuwaiti concerns —suggests there is (or, at least in 1965, *was*) little consensus about what is deviant and, also, what are the norms or rules of their society.

This evidence allows at least two interpretations, each of which has some support. On the one hand, it suggests that in North America people hold widely different, often ambivalent views about a wide variety of acts. They may even change their own views often; certainly, conventional North American views on homosexuality, atheism and divorce have changed since 1965. On the other hand, North American views on deviance are polarized. As in Kuwait, where fundamentalism of an Islamic variety prevails, in rural parts of North America, where Christian fundamentalism prevails, we find a continuing hostility towards atheism, divorce and homosexuality. This contrasts sharply with the moral views that prevail in more highly educated, urban neighbourhoods.

As well, there may be conflict between the official and unofficial norms. Consider the 14-day prison sentence handed out to a woman in a Montreal suburb who failed to pay her library fine for overdue books. Although she returned the books to the library, she did so after the date when the library would still accept her payment. The matter had already been referred to the courts and the library refused to cancel proceedings. Eventually, the court found her guilty and ordered her imprisoned.

Reuters/BETTMANN

Kuwaitis would likely react strongly against the way these young women are "presenting themselves." In North America, opinions would probably range from strong approval to mild disapproval.

The result, as you might imagine, was a huge public outcry. First, people criticized the arbitrary manner in which administrative procedures were transformed into judicial proceedings. Second, people showed they disagreed with this use of the courts and the prison system. Is prison the way we should deal with library fines? they asked. Most people thought it *wasn't*.

Keeping a book overdue is not a serious crime compared to, say, assault with a deadly weapon. Yet even for behaviours which seem clearly deviant, we find a lot of disagreement. For example, a series of surveys in the United States asked people, "Are there any situations that you can imagine in which you would approve of a man punching an adult male stranger?" Between 1968 and 1988, the proportion of people indicating they approved of assault under *some* conditions rose from 51% to 63% (Niemi, Muller and Smith, 1989).

But the survey evidence also points to differing views about the acceptability of assault under a variety of circumstances. Mainly it suggests a growing public acceptance of assault as a way of settling disputes. In many instances, people would even approve of what the courts would consider criminal assault. In other words, there is widespread *dis*agreement with the written law.

This is due to the social and cultural relativity of deviance. As the labelling theorists have shown, deviance is always relative to the group which defines the behaviour. Cannibalism is decidedly deviant in our society, but among the Iroquois and Pawnee it was sacred — an accepted means of seeking revenge. (Then, presumably, refusing to snack on human flesh would appear anti-social.) *Socio-cultural relativity* means that sociologists cannot treat deviance as if it were an intrinsic property of an act, the way physicists can treat atomic bonding as an intrinsic property of matter.

Sociologists must always view deviance as socially constructed and socially defined. For example, many people would regard gambling as deviant. Yet a survey done in Nevada, where gambling provides a main source of income, shows that people there regard it as perfectly normal (Smith, 1986). In this social context, gambling — also, prostitution, and quick marriage and divorce — is a way of life. On the other hand, Nevada has strict laws against marijuana use, from which the state receives no revenue.

Another form of relativity is *situational relativity* (Goode, 1978: 35). Take the example of cannibalism just mentioned, then think of different circumstances in which people in our society would define cannibalism as acceptable. If one were stranded far from civilization with no food, would cannibalism be acceptable? Probably, it would be. A decade ago, survivors of a plane crash were reduced to eating the flesh of their colleagues. They did so with reluctance, but had little choice.

Many people might say "yes" to cannibalism then, with the proviso that the only people to be eaten were already dead and had not been killed for use as food. In this situation, it is unlikely the police would make any effort to reveal and punish cannibalism. This proves that, as the context changes, so too do the socially constructed definitions of the act as deviant or as normal (or at least, necessary). In other words, deviance is not only culturally relative, it is also "situationally relative."

Given these variations in culture and situation, it is not surprising that there is widespread disagreement about deviance and even sociologists will disagree over what should be considered "deviant." But remember, it is not the sociologist's job to decide what deviance really is, much less to pass judgment on "right" and "wrong." What sociologists do is look at how deviance is understood in society and what social processes lead some people to define and treat others as deviant.

KINDS OF DEVIANT BEHAVIOUR

Deviance, as we have seen, includes a variety of behaviours that range in frequency and seriousness from crimes down through what sociologists call norm violations and social diversions. We shall now look briefly at each of these categories of deviance.

Crime

Crime is usually considered the most serious form of deviance. A *crime* is any act formally prohibited by law, specifically by the Criminal Code of Canada. Defining certain acts as crimes gives the state the authority to punish offenders, and the Criminal Code specifies an appropriate range of punishments for each crime.

Within the Criminal Code, we find many different kinds of crime. Some are crimes considered extremely harmful by most people, such as murder, armed robbery, extortion, arson, sexual assault, and kidnapping. In general, there is widespread consensus in Canadian society, and in most other societies, that these forms of behaviour are unacceptable and should be severely punished.

In contrast, there are crimes over which people disagree so much that the law has, in effect, lost jurisdiction. The best example, at the time of this writing, is abortion. A series of court decisions have struck down Canada's abortion law. Yet the issue remains so contentious that the federal government is unable to draft legislation on abortion to either clearly criminalize or clearly legalize it.

Then there are the more standard crimes. Most people consider them wrong but do not wish to debate or increase the severity of punishment. These include offences against property like breaking and entering, automobile theft, and shoplifting; minor assaults and drunken driving; and "white-collar" offences like embezzlement and fraud.

All of these offences have a victim or (as in the case of drunken driving) run a serious risk of victimizing someone. In each case, a victim has pressed charges against the offender or the police have done so, especially where public order was being violated.

Another category includes **victimless crimes**. No one suffers directly from these acts, except perhaps the people engaged in the behaviour and their families. Such victimless crimes include gambling, prostitution, and illicit drug use. They are all crimes because the Criminal Code defines them as crimes, making their perpetrators subject to legal action.

Like other forms of deviance, victimless crimes serve as a focus for small subcultures, with their own rules, rituals and group boundaries. As we can see from Exhibit 4.3, these subcultural practices can be just as dangerous as the victimless crimes themselves. For example, the subculture of drug addicts is more dangerous because it spreads the AIDS virus than because it promotes continued drug addiction.

In practice, the police do not enforce laws against victimless crimes consistently or energetically, nor is the Crown likely to prosecute. Courts, for their part, levy penalties for these crimes that range from a light prison sentence to probation, a fine, or a community-service order.

EXHIBIT 4.3 *Sharing of drug needles a valued ritual*

In the AIDS-haunted world of drug addiction, sharing needles to shoot up is often a communal and sexual ritual that addicts won't part with, a new study shows.

That is just one of the alarming findings of two University of Alberta researchers who have spent the past four years investigating factors leading to the spread of AIDS among intravenous drugs users, believed to be North America's fastest-increasing infected population and the major reason the disease is spreading to heterosexuals and children.

Louis and Ann Marie Pagliaro also were told by about one-third of intravenous drug users they interviewed in Alberta that they would not use free needle-exchange programs intended to keep addicts from sharing needles and spreading AIDS and other diseases.

That sobering news is especially troubling for natives, identified as one of the groups most at risk because of the deadly spiral of poverty and intravenous drug use identified as a major problem for inner-city natives. . . .

In a survey of 47 natives in jails or treatment centres who are or were users of injected drugs — two-thirds of whom were women — 68 per cent said they shared needles during drug use. Sharing needles is considered one of the primary ways of spreading the human immunodeficiency virus, precursor of AIDS. . . .

Addicts who took part in the study told the Pagliaros they sometimes shared needles because they could not wait even 15 minutes for a needle to be delivered. Some also disliked disinfecting with bleach, felt too intoxicated to bother with new needles or were too "lazy" to worry about it.

Others simply felt fatalistically that they were going to die anyway, Ms. Pagliaro said. . . .

Source: Miro Cernetig, "Sharing of drug needles a valued ritual, study finds" *The Globe and Mail*, Wed., July 15, 1992, p. A7

We know a great deal about the prevalence of certain crimes like murder, robbery and kidnapping. That's because occurrences of these crime are usually reported to the police and recorded as official data. Of these reported crimes, a high percentage result in arrests and convictions. But people are much less willing to report other crimes. Sexual assaults are an example: many women —the majority of victims — fear the psychological, legal, and public humiliations that have often accompanied such reporting.

Furthermore, of the sexual assaults reported, only a small percentage result in convictions. Judges and juries are often reluctant to believe the victim, and convictions often result in less than the maximum sentence. The victim may also fear retribution by the criminal upon his release from prison.

Another category of crimes that are likely to go unreported are those committed for gain by professional criminals; they include robbery, arson, selling drugs, and assault with a deadly weapon. Victims are often afraid to report attempts at extortion —demands for money coupled with a threat of physical violence —because they fear revenge by the criminal or his colleagues.

Still, criminologists know enough about crime to permit several generalizations. First, on the issue of crime *trends*, there is evidence of some increase in crimes against property over the last twenty years, though very little change in the rates of homicide and other crimes of violence. Second, crimes of violence, which are usually not committed for gain, often result from disputes between spouses or friends. This is particularly true when women are victimized; men are more likely to be victimized by acquaintances or even strangers. Third, crimes that *are* committed for gain — for example, drug peddling, prostitution, illegal gambling, and extortion — are often connected to **organized crime**.

Because they are so common, easily investigated, and inexpensively prosecuted, a small number of crimes make up the bulk of our criminal statistics at any given time. This suggests that recorded rates of crime most closely reflect the reporting and prosecution of particular crimes. Changes in the crime rate therefore reflect changes in the victims' willingness to report crimes and the willingness of police to investigate them.

Of course, the development of police technology, especially in the area of surveillance, could affect the way criminals are caught. With this technology probing ever deeper into our lives, areas which were once thought beyond the reach of the authorities now are accessible.

It has become common on television, for example, for the police to show videotapes of crimes being committed in the hope that viewers will recognize the criminal and tip off the police. Some television programs even re-enact crimes to encourage members of the public to come forward and provide the police with information. We will have to wait and see how this and other new technology will affect social control (Marx, 1985).

Norm violations

Norm violations are not defined as crimes in the Criminal Code; nonetheless, people view them as significant and serious forms of deviance.

Take begging: In 1861, Henry Mayhew finished cataloguing all the varieties of "street people" to be seen in his native city. The result was a four-volume classic, *London Labour and the London Poor*. There, Mayhew devoted space to discussing street pedlars, petty criminals, prostitutes, homeless people, tramps, juvenile delinquents and beggars. His goal was to distinguish among the many varieties of poor people: to say which ones can work but won't, which ones work at "reputable" but poor-paying jobs, and which ones do disreputable and even criminal work.

A recent work by Igbinovia (1991), on begging in Nigeria, is much shorter than Mayhew's but has a similar flavour and a similar goal. It aims to explain why there are so many beggars in Nigeria's cities, to distinguish which ones could live by more respectable trades if they chose to, and to advise the government on ways to prevent a "scourge" of begging.

In Nigeria's cities today, as in London over a century ago, many people simply cannot survive without state assistance unless they beg in the streets. The same is true in North American cities beset by a scourge of angry poor, and in major Third World cities surrounded by shantytowns and filled with street children. Always, the question is "Who is to blame?" Is it the deviant individual, a heartless state, the sluggish economy, or a combination of all these elements?

In the past, many forms of deviance — like begging — were treated as crimes. Authorities would round up the beggars, vagrants, and homeless and put them in jail or drive them out of town. Today, we tend to view such norm violations as signs that people need help.

Still, the courts have felt little need to limit the state's powers over the socially deviant, the way they do when dealing with criminals. They see the state's role as primarily parental and benevolent. This means that the court can put a person defined as mentally ill in a hospital indefinitely against his or her will. One consequence is that psychiatrists, psychologists, and social workers have played an important role in dealing with deviants. It is only recently that patients have been guaranteed legal representation and due process in proceedings that affect their lives.

Changes in the legal rights of norm violators mean changes in their official (recorded) treatment. This, in turn, means changes in the official statistics sociologists use to monitor deviance. In large part, recorded changes in the frequency of deviant acts reflect changes in the procedures for defining, detecting, and processing deviants. So, if we discovered that the reported rates of mental illness were twice as high this year as ten years ago, we could not fairly conclude that mental illness is twice as common. Possibly, all that had changed was the official definition of mental illness and the procedures used for its detection.

This has two important implications. First, it reminds us that "deviance" is a social construct whose boundary is always shifting. Second, it argues that making accurate judgements about trends in order and disorder, deviance and conformity is always difficult. Not only is reality changing all the time: so are the rules that we use to categorize and describe reality.

Social diversions

There is the most uncertainty surrounding a third category of deviant acts we call social diversions. A *social diversion* is an unusual or rare behaviour that few people would regard as violating norms and fewer still would consider a serious violation. The Criminal Code does not forbid these social diversions, nor do formal institutions — the courts, hospitals, or health professionals — try to control them. Social diversions are mainly activities whose main purpose is recreation, stimulation and subcultural integration (Hagan, 1984: 19).

There are many sexual behaviours which one would list as deviant social diversions. Many people would consider them "odd," "weird," or "sick" but a significant number of people enjoy them nonetheless. Homosexuality is an obvious example: today it is the most visible and most accepted form of alternative sexuality. Other examples would include sadomasochism, fetishism, and cross-dressing. Similarly, oral and anal sex are more commonly accepted now than they were a generation ago.

When Prime Minister Trudeau came to office in the late 1960s, he declared that the Canadian government had no business in the bedrooms of the nation. He meant that official efforts to control homosexuality, non-marital and marital sex were going to end; and they have. Today, condom use is publicly promoted to combat AIDS, birth control is available to everyone, and gay rights are protected in the Human Rights Code of Ontario and, possibly, by the Canadian Charter of Rights.

Informal controls on these behaviours have also diminished since the 1960s. Yet sexual variations remain deviations and the less common forms still raise eyebrows among many Canadians.

Other social diversions include styles of dress, speech, and behaviour that are uncommon among middle-aged, middle-class people. Take, as an example, multiple earrings and nose studs. Such fashions are more common among young people than among the old. Eccentric clothes and speech often signify membership in a group holding values and norms that are uncommon and offend other people. As we noted above, such groups are called deviant subcultures.

▼ EXHIBIT 4.4   *The surprisingly civil shantytowns of Rio*

I bought my first house a few months ago. It's a small, three-room dwelling. . . perched on a mountain overlooking one of Rio de Janeiro's exclusive neighbourhoods. . . .

The house is located at the highest point of Rocinha, a *favela* [shantytown] of 250,000 inhabitants that has one of the worst records in Brazil for drug trafficking and violent crimes related to drugs. It also has the reputation of being one of the most secure and safe places for a person to live, if they keep their nose out of other people's business. . . .

For instance, there is virtually no crime against property or individuals in the *favela*.

While there are shootings nearly every night in the shantytowns — most of Rio's 4,000 murders last year occurred in the *favelas* — the victims are almost always members of the tiny minority involved in the drug trade. Mr. Batista and other residents say they sleep with their doors unlocked at night and have no fear of assault, something unheard of in Rio.

Protecting them are the self-same drug traffickers involved in nightly altercations with police. . . .

The gangs, who have made Rio an important corridor for the export of cocaine from Colombia's Cali cartel to Europe and North America, pour thousands of dollars every year into improvement projects to win the support of the *favelas*. They throw community-wide Christmas parties, provide the poorest people with food and bus passes, and finance day-care centres.

They even "help" local youth by allowing them to work as "airplanes," which is Brazilian slang for drug couriers. . . .

The other side of gang generosity is the iron-fisted control they wield over their *favela* domains, which one Rio newspaper recently described as "republics of white powder." Residents are prohibited on pain of death from telling police about drug activities and many are forced to store arms and drugs, and even hide gang members during police raids. In some cases, hugely popular evangelical Protestant churches in the favelas have been used as bunkers by gangs.

In using their power, the traffickers operate a "justice system" far swifter and harsher than the government's. Informal tribunals dispense penalties of biblical proportion to residents who commit crimes against neighbours or disrupt the drug trade. Rape and robbery are often punished by expulsion or death. Stoning, burning (with a flaming tire "*neclace*"), decapitation or being tossed from a cliff are not uncommon penalties. If a *favela* dweller is involved in a particularly heinous crime, he is sometimes lynched on the spot by neighbours.

Favela citizens fear the traffickers but many are more afraid of Rio's corrupt military and civil police forces, who regularly harass them during searches for arms and gang members. In many *favelas*, gangs pay police officers a monthly bribe, known as a "tax," to look the other way. . . .

"When *favela* residents are forced to choose between a bad situation by siding with the traffickers or a worse situation by siding with the police, most of them prefer the bad situation," says Francisco Alves Filho, a journalist with Brazil's *Isto E* newsmagazine.

Source: Isabel Vincent, "The republics of white powder," *The Globe and Mail*, Sat. Dec. 18, 1993, p. D5

Not everyone who is a member of a deviant subculture breaks rules all the time. In fact, as Exhibit 4.4 shows, communities which are very deviant from one perspective are very safe and rule-abiding from another.

Deviant behaviour, as we see, takes many forms, and all of us at one time or another engage in behaviour which some people would consider deviant. Still, most of us neither commit crimes nor engage in other forms of serious deviance on a regular basis. Who does?

PARTICIPATION IN DEVIANT ACTIVITIES

Who commits crimes? ▶▶

In the case of serious crimes, the most common offenders by far are young, single men.

A recent review of the literature by John Hagan (1994: 28, 29) indicates that, by a wide margin, men continue to exceed women in crimes against the person. Similarly, recent Canadian evidence (Doige, 1990: 12) shows that boys are far more likely than girls to appear in youth courts. Likewise, Johnson (1987: 4) notes that:

> The majority of homicide suspects are young men. In 1986, 57% of all homicide suspects were men, aged 29 or under. Overall, men made up 85% of homicide suspects that year. The age and sex profile of homicide suspects remained relatively constant over the last decade.

Why are criminals so often young, unmarried men? Many believe the reason is that young men lead unstructured lives and are more likely than women to be accustomed to expressing physical aggression. Additionally, in poor communities a high proportion of young men are unemployed and feel very frustrated. This makes them more likely to feel and express aggression. It also makes them more willing to take risks with their own, and other people's, lives.

In fact, men appear to have completely different attitudes toward risk-taking than women. A Toronto study, for example, shows that contact with the police deters teenage girls from marijuana smoking, but it has the opposite effect on boys, making them *more* likely to repeat the act (Keane, Gillis, and Hagan, 1989).

Also, social inequality and a lack of opportunity frustrate young men, who are eager to prove themselves. No wonder researchers have found that social inequality is among the best predictors of a country's homicide rate, in 52 nations studied by Conklin and Simpson (1985).

A rising crime rate, then, reflects the growth of a social and economic underclass. Research in Britain shows a correlation between violent crime, illegitimacy, and dropping out of the work force by young, healthy men. All three are on the rise and serve as warning signs, as they did for the United States. And once an underclass exists, it is hard to solve the problem with social reforms (Murray, 1990).

In addition, ethnic and racial inequality are very important predictors of homicide rates in a community, even after taking poverty, general economic inequality and other factors into account (Balkwell, 1990). Inequality and subordination — whether economic or racial — especially increase the frequency of violence. Not only are the perpetrators of violence typically poor young men: so are the victims — usually students and the unemployed. These young men are most likely to be out in public places and engaged in evening activities outside the home, the circumstances often associated with assault and robbery.

Delinquency

The theories we have examined suggest that despair, born of social and economic inequality, are at the root of crime. To a degree this is true of juvenile delinquents too; but often delinquency reflects no more than a desire for adventure, thrills, and the respect of peers. Many delinquents also use drugs and alcohol, which loosen their inhibitions against socially disapproved activities.

Delinquent activities by teenage boys and young men often display a tough, active, unemotional masculine image. They also display characteristics associated with the culture of poverty discussed in the next chapter: a belief in fate, danger, luck, and taking risks. As research on Japanese motorcycle gangs has shown, such deviant acts can be seen as a kind of rough "play" (Sato, 1982). Behaviour is regulated by a playful definition of the situation, not a desire for gain or revenge. Similar attitudes have been found among teenaged soccer "hooligans" in Britain (Marsh, Rosser and Harre, 1978).

Generally, delinquent activities range in seriousness from vandalism, petty theft (such as shoplifting), breaking and entering, illegal alcohol and drug use, auto theft and dangerous driving, up through drug dealing, robbery, and gang fighting.

Some of these acts are aimed at making money but most are intended to gain or defend status, protect gang turf, or demonstrate manliness. Their symbolic value lies precisely in their danger to life and liberty and lack of practical pay-off. What's more, these same delinquents are extremely loyal to people close to them, which is interesting given their lack of respect for social order. In fact, delinquents' loyalty to people who are close to them — for example, their willingness to defend a victimized buddy — is more intense and more focused than that of other juveniles (Gillis and Hagan, 1990).

Few juvenile delinquents become career criminals; but once police have recorded a contact with a juvenile, the probability of another recorded contact is high. It may be that police only make records for juveniles they think are likely to get into more trouble. A recorded contact may lead the police to keep a closer watch on a particular juvenile. With closer observation, the police will probably detect more deviance. Yet, for all this, most delinquents stop breaking the law when they get older.

A small group we might call *violent predators* do not stop. They continue to commit serious crimes: among them, robberies, assaults, and drug deals. These offenders are, on average, below age 25 when they are first imprisoned. By their mid-20s they have been committing violent crimes for six years or more. Evidence suggests they are less socially stable than other offenders — for example, less likely to hold a steady job or be married. Drug use is also common among violent predators.

Together, violent predators and juvenile delinquents dominate the public's image of the deviant. In part, this is because the legal system focuses its main attention on *street crimes*, which range from public violence down through theft and auto offences to victimless crimes. In part, it is because the media tend to focus on young people in general and, among deviants, on gangs in particular.

White-collar crimes

However, there are many other kinds of criminals whose actions are at least as harmful to the public good. They commit the domestic crimes and white-collar crimes (or *suite* crimes). Compared to its way of handling street crimes, the legal system is less pro-active in dealing with domestic crimes and white-collar crimes.

White collar crimes are committed by high-status members of the community, often in the course of their work. This category includes fraud, forgery, tax evasion, price-fixing, work safety violations, and the embezzlement of funds.

Generally, the difference in types of crimes people commit is related to a difference in their opportunity to commit them. It is easier for an accountant or auditor to embezzle money than it is for a sociologist, clerk-typist, or bartender. Lawyers are in a particularly good position to swindle people and the law societies of Canadian provinces often have to decide whether to disbar lawyers who have used clients' funds for personal gain.

Such white collar crimes, like domestic crimes, are hard to detect and almost impossible to prevent. They are also hard to punish. For one thing, the business and legal communities close ranks to prevent the criminalization of acts that should be considered serious crimes (Goff and Reasons, 1978). Yet acts of corporate deviance, such as dumping toxic waste, bribery of officials, and violating work safety rules, have many victims. They deserve prosecution and punishment more than many acts we routinely consider crimes worth punishing.

Still, in many countries the law has simply never treated corporate crime as a genuine problem. This can have serious consequences: tax evasion by corporations, for example, can lead to a loss of tax revenues and uneven economic development. Yet, for a long time, tax evasion was more or less universally accepted in Italy (Savona, 1981). It is only in the last few years that progress has been made towards stopping political corruption and organized crime (the two are closely related in Italy).

Like most forms of deviance, white-collar or business-oriented crime varies along sociocultural lines. In Japan, corporations have a group mentality that discourages corporate crime for personal gain (a common practice in the United States). But when a white-collar crime benefits the group, the Japanese are more willing to commit it, and the act is deemed more acceptable by peers (Kerbo and Inoue, 1990). Since, in Japan, a white-collar crime is often considered acceptable because it is "socially responsible" to the group, it is easier to hide it.

Female criminals

As we noted earlier, women are less likely than men to commit crimes. Evidence shows some increase in female criminality and this reflects more social and economic activity outside the home than in past generations. But in general, female crime has *not* increased relative to male crime except for (1) teens and young women, where the gender gap has closed somewhat in many crime categories; (2) minor forms of property crime, such as property theft, shoplifting and welfare fraud; and (3) some forms of white collar crime, like embezzlement. For the most part, women continue to stay away from men's traditional crimes — crimes of violence and major property crimes.

The most accepted interpretation is that, with the feminization of poverty (which we will discuss in later chapters), women have turned to minor forms of property crime. This is particularly true in cities, where property crime is relatively easy to commit. Even in developing countries, as women gain opportunities to commit property crimes, their rate of criminal activity goes up (Steffensmeier, Allan, and Streifel, 1989). With economic modernization, there are simply more consumer items to steal.

The rise in women's crime also reflects a greater willingness among police to arrest and lay criminal charges against female offenders, especially teenaged girls. In the past, these women would have benefitted from a popular belief that they were "the gentler sex," and therefore unlikely to commit crimes. Earlier in this century, female offenders were also more likely to be thought mentally ill — hence, blameless — than criminal. Boys were defined and treated as delinquent whereas girls were, at worst, considered "wayward."

Leaving crime

Efforts to break people of their criminal tendencies have had notoriously little success. The violent predators, in particular, resist all attempts at change through treatment. Indeed, each day the prison subculture undoes any efforts at reform. Nor do professional criminals have any desire to change; in fact they have good reason *not* to. But others, especially the amateurs who make up the vast majority of criminals, gradually draw away from law-breaking.

The reasons are simple. Unless they are professionals, people have less time and opportunity for crime as they get older. For example, they have less time to spend with friends in public places because they're spending more time at home with their families. Also, as they get older, people have less physical energy for crime: it is too demanding and the "high" a person gets from engaging in risky acts isn't there any more.

As they age, all people — deviants included — develop a larger *stake in conformity*, a stronger motivation to stay out of trouble. They have a family they want to support, a mortgage to pay, a job they like, or income they need. Many feel less conflict with society at age 35 than they did at 15. Certainly, they have more to lose. So people obey the rules more consistently, whether they believe in them or not.

In the end, most law-breakers stop breaking the laws. But that is not, generally, because of punishment they have received or fear receiving. Usually, prevention is much more effective than punishment where crime is concerned. Research findings support the view that attempts to reduce crime must focus on social development: especially, *higher* rates of early childhood education, high school graduation, college attendance, employment and self-support, and *lower* rates of teen pregnancy and welfare utilization (Weikart, 1989). Getting people off to a good start in life means giving them a bigger stake in conformity from the beginning. That, not laws and police, is what produces conformity.

There is no doubt that criminals who get caught are more likely to be *poor* than rich. Giving people more opportunities helps keep them from being motivated to commit crimes in the first place and gives them a stake in conformity. Still, the fact that most of the people who get caught are poor only means that poor criminals are less able to avoid detection for the crimes they commit.

What is the relationship between crime and social class? Is crime primarily a lower-class adaptation to inequality, as Merton thought? Are lower-class youths the most likely to be socialized into criminal subcultures? Or are sociologists biased in the ways they think about crime and social class?

CLASS AND JUVENILE DELINQUENCY

As in many other areas of deviance, research in juvenile delinquency was hampered for a long time by the assumption that delinquency is mainly a lower-class problem. Much of the effort given to policing and preventing delinquency has, therefore, focused on lower-class youth. A prime example was the costly program the United States' government mounted in the 1960s to prevent delinquency, by offering delinquents opportunities for advancement through legitimate means: in a word, a job-creation program.

The program did not work. Perhaps the lower-class youths did not really want to conform to socially accepted norms, even if doing so brought them a weekly paycheque. Perhaps the inducement offered them — a dead-end job at low pay — was too small to lure young people into a law-abiding life. Perhaps they had learned delinquent skills and values which they were unable to give up. Or perhaps the program ended too soon for us to know whether it might have worked.

Whatever the reason, juvenile delinquency remains a problem in large cities throughout the world. An Israeli study concludes that a certain minimum number of juveniles must be in an area to provide the necessary group dynamic. Delinquency is, in part, a consequence of this urban dynamic (Rahav, 1981). In general, our understanding of delinquency is greater than it once was. We now have better measures of how much unreported delinquency occurs. We also have theories that help us see how similar delinquent culture is to the dominant culture.

More and more criminologists have been using self-report surveys to measure delinquent behaviour among young people of different social classes. Obviously, some respondents misreport their behaviour in this kind of survey, as in any other. Some under-report their past misdeeds, to appear more virtuous than they really are; others exaggerate them to appear more rebellious.

Like most studies of deviance using non-official statistics, the self-report studies show a weaker relationship between social class and delinquency than studies based on official records. In that sense, official records overstate the connection between social class and rates of deviant behaviour, yet:

> Evidence reviewed indicates that forms of deviance considered serious and treated as such are unequally distributed through the class structure, with the lower class experiencing more than its fair share of serious crime and delinquency, hard drug use, problems of alcohol abuse, and mental illness (Hagan, 1984: 79).

Of course, which forms of deviance are considered "serious" is liable to change. As certain types of deviance — for example, recreational drug use — become more common in the middle and upper classes, people consider them less serious and treat them as such. Once behaviour comes to be more acceptable as part of the dominant culture, it is less likely to be defined as delinquent. Class differences in deviant behaviour remain important as do class differences in the societal response.

BIASES IN THE SELECTION PROCESS

The perceived seriousness of a deviant act and the number of prior convictions in an offender's past record often influence the type and severity of societal response. So does the offender's social class. An important part is played by what we call *social resources*.

Middle- and upper-class people have more of these social resources — more knowledge of the law, self-confidence, money for lawyers, social connections, a more respectable appearance and successful demeanour. In short, social resources are cultural capital that can be used in a legal setting. As we know from Chapter 2, our society distributes cultural capital unequally among the members of different social classes.

Because they are of a higher class, perpetrators of corporate crime are treated leniently by employers. In fact, people from higher classes are less likely to even lose their job over such infractions. This reveals the inconsistent attitude many employers show towards white-collar crime. What's more, people who commit large-scale offences are even less likely to suffer the loss of their job than those who commit small-scale crimes (Benson, 1989).

Social resources help people avoid labelling and punishment by the police and courts. For example, in assault or property-damage cases, the police and courts try to interpret behaviour and assess blame before taking any action. They are less likely to label people with more resources as "criminal" or "delinquent" and more likely to label them "alcoholic" or "mentally ill" for a criminal act. For middle- and upper-class people, being labelled "sick" may be embarrassing, but it is far less harmful than being labelled "criminal."

Erving Goffman (1964) calls the use of such social resources to avoid stigmatization **impression management**. Impression management can be defined as the control of personal information flow to manipulate how other people see and treat you. Everyone practises impression management, and people with more social resources and cultural capital are better at it.

In giving preferential treatment to people who are better at impression management, police and judges are simply inferring moral worth from visible class position — from manner of dress, demeanour, and management of impressions. As members of our culture, police and judges are no more or less likely to do this than anyone else. Even primary school children do it (Baldus and Tribe, 1978). There is no hard evidence that officials prefer people with more social resources because of bribery, threats, or conscious discrimination.

The process we are describing is a circular one: some have called it a self-fulfilling prophesy, others a revolving door. Official rule-enforcers (including police and judges, but also social workers, psychiatrists, and the whole correctional and treatment establishment) define as serious the deviant acts in which poor people engage. On the other hand, they tend to "define away" the deviant acts of rich people as signs of illness, not crime. They are more likely to consider those actions morally blameless.

No wonder, then, that criminals and delinquents are people who start out and end up without social resources. The act of labelling them criminal completes the circle and creates a secondary problem, **recidivism**, the tendency to repeat criminal behaviours and get into more trouble with the law.

CLOSING REMARKS

Deviance is one of those topics that are popular with students. As with all human differences, there is something exotic about deviance. Few of us view ourselves as deviant, so we tend to find the underside of the social order fascinating.

The sociological study of deviance offers another good example of the connection between macro- and micro- perspectives. On the one hand, deviance is a macro- phenomenon. It is something that exists outside and "above" individual people — a result of what Durkheim called "social facts" like poverty, social integration (versus isolation) and social regulation (versus anomie). In this sense, deviance is an indication of social inequality, social change and new social strains. It has, seemingly, little to do with particular people and their unique motives and opportunities.

On the other hand, the potential for deviance is inside all of us. We all deviate and conform. As the symbolic interactionists remind us, conformity to the social order is something we negotiate every day. There is no rule, no belief, no taboo so sacred that it is not violated hundreds of times every day; and in every instance, we have to get inside the mind of the deviant actor through that process Weber called *verstehen*, to understand what the particular act of deviance "means." For without such understanding, we can scarcely hope to make effective theories that explain or predict deviant behaviour.

Understanding deviance and control, as we have seen in this chapter, requires understanding how inequality is organized in our society. Despite crime's normality, the fear of crime is often used by the powerful to whip up support for the *status quo*. The more people fear crime, the more power and money they will put in the hands of the powerful (see Exhibit 4.5). But what they are ignoring is the correlation between crime and inequality. If in-

EXHIBIT 4.5   *Contrary to public opininion, murders are not on the increase*

. . . Rosemary Gartner, a sociologist at the University of Toronto, says that what underlies the burgeoning crime statistics is "not just people's willingness to report. It is also the police and justice system's willingness to take these reports more seriously."

This is a healthy trend, she believes, but it can be dangerous. "There's a tendency to think that because we're paying more attention to violence, it's happening more."

A chronic problem with the exact measurement of crime is that statistics are a function of social norms and values. It is these factors that determine which acts are reported, investigated and prosecuted.

From a statistical point of view, crimes such as homicide are better indicators. . . .

By these standards, Canadians are not becoming more homicidal, though they may be more larcenous. While the murder rate in Canada has barely changed over two decades and remains about a third that of the United States, the rate of vehicle theft has shown a marked upward trend since 1988. . . .

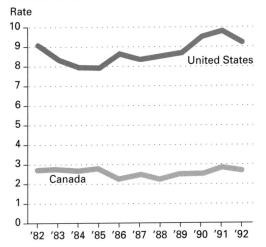

Homicide Rates

Comparative homicide rates*, Canada and the United States

* Rates are calculated on the basis of homicides per 100 000 population

Source: Homicide survey, Policing Services Program, Canadian Centre for Justice Statistics

Continued

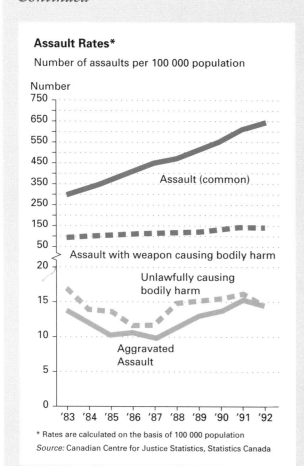

Assault Rates*

Number of assaults per 100 000 population

* Rates are calculated on the basis of 100 000 population
Source: Canadian Centre for Justice Statistics, Statistics Canada

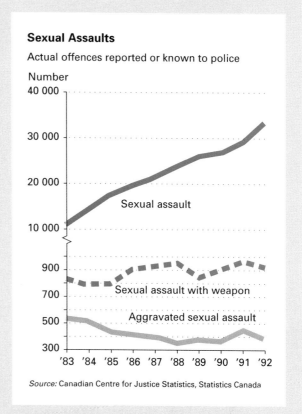

Sexual Assaults

Actual offences reported or known to police

Source: Canadian Centre for Justice Statistics, Statistics Canada

Source: "Shedding light on Canadian crime," *The Globe and Mail*, Mon. Sept. 27, 1993, p. A13

equality causes crime, and stronger crime control increases inequality, then support for the *status quo* simply escalates the crime problem and the need to protect against it. We create a "vicious circle," with no end to crime and no end to control.

However, the organization of inequality in our society is an issue whose significance goes far beyond the issues of crime and deviance, as we shall see in the next chapter.

C H A P T E R 5

Food banks, like the one pictured here, are becoming a sad fact of Canadian life.
So are astronomical salaries and bonuses for corporate elites.

Marko Shark

CLASS AND STATUS INEQUALITY

▶ **CHAPTER OUTLINE**

INEQUALITY AS A FACT OF LIFE

Inequality is a fact of life for all of us. Sociologists use the term *life chances* to describe the effects of inequality, and few terms do as well in capturing the link between large macrosociological processes and private lives. What we mean by the term are the chances a person has of sharing in the economic (or material) and cultural (or symbolic) goods of a society. People who belong to different class or status levels of society have different access to these material and symbolic goods. This chapter is about the reasons why this is so, and the consequences of unequal life chances.

When you pass a homeless "street person" huddled among old newspapers while taking shelter from the weather, you probably realize that such a person's life chances are bleak and few in number. Where will these people be in ten years? If they are not still on the street, then they are likely to be dead. Think, too, of all the poor in Canada. What chances do they have to improve the quality of their lives? You can be sure that they are not spending much time deciding which restaurant to eat in, what movie to see, or where to go on vacation.

As for the rich, life is not so much a matter of chances as of choices. Being rich means you have the choice to live your life pretty much the way you want, with few of the limitations other people must take into account.

Now think of yourself. Even though few of you are rich — most students are members of the middle class — chances are, your life still holds many choices. Because you are not rich, whether you have the sort of life you want will depend mainly on the choices you make and the actions you undertake now. Yet even the best choices you make today will not give you everything you want later.

Canadians are not in the habit of thinking much about inequality. We live in one of the wealthiest and freest countries in the world. One result of this is that Canadians are more likely than people in other nations to attach either praise or blame to the individual, instead of to society, for success or failure in life.

Nevertheless, people in Canada do not all have equal life chances. Large numbers of homeless and jobless people prove that. In Canada and elsewhere, inequality is largely a consequence of what sociologists call the **stratification system**. Learning to recognize inequality as a built-in feature of social organization, not a result of fate, hard work or good character, is an important part of learning sociology.

Social inequality includes all the differences among people that arise out of social characteristics and relationships. It includes differential access to social rewards like wealth, prestige, and influence. The factors influencing inequality are social because they are a result of how a society is organized and the kinds of social relationships which affect people's life chances. These social relationships have meanings attached to them that members of a group share and transmit to future generations. These meanings are the basis on which people act towards one another.

In this chapter and the two that follow, we discuss three important causes of, or risk factors associated with, inequality: namely, class, racial (or ethnic) origin, and gender. Each significantly affects your well-being and the chances you will improve your well-being. In *this* chapter we focus on social class and status, and the inequalities that result from having low rather than high status and belonging to a lower rather than a higher class.

Inequality of wealth is one aspect of social inequality. It arises out of unequal access to wealth (or unequal opportunities to acquire wealth) and it is closely related to class and status.

It is easy to see inequality of wealth as a form of social inequality if we contrast it with inequality in athletic ability, which is, in large part, probably genetically based. Remember, though, that the prestige our society accords to superior athletes can be used to gain wealth, so that athletic ability, too, becomes part of a system of social inequality. This means that there is a social meaning attached to athletic ability, which people share and transmit culturally. Yet, as we shall see, social inequalities (such as unequal wealth) have many more important social consequences, and many more social determinants, than athletic ability.

Sociologists think of inequality as the unequal distribution of resources. There are three interrelated but different systems of inequality: *property*, based on the distribution of material resources; *status*, based on the distribution of symbolic resources; and *domination*, based on the way in which authority is distributed. As we have just noted, social differences, such as class, race and ethnicity, and gender influence property, status, and domination. Together, they form an integrated system of inequality called a stratification system.

In this chapter and the next two, we examine all three forms of inequality. Let's begin with "domination," the ability to control the actions of other people.

PATTERNS OF SUBMISSION AND DOMINATION

Whether you know it or not, almost all of the social relationships in which you take part are unequal. In childhood, your parents were usually able to control your behaviour and, within limits, to get you to do what they wanted. The same was true in school when teachers told you where to sit, when to speak, what to say, and what to do. But these experiences were not unusual. In most social relationships, one person or set of persons dominates the others.

In that sense, domination is a universal feature of social life, found in all societies. What is more, patterns of domination persist over decades, generations, and even centuries.

By **domination**, we mean the exercise of control over a person or group of people. Put in simple terms, domination is the ability to get other people to do what you want them to do. The flip side is **submission**, the act of yielding to the control of another, or doing what others tell you to do. "Submission" often takes the form of acts that symbolize a subordinate status and acceptance of the other's domination. The military salute is one example of such submission.

There are different ways of getting people to do what we want them to do, so there are different forms of domination. But power and authority are the two most common forms of domination in modern industrial societies, and we will focus our discussion on these. **Power** is the capacity to exercise one's will despite resistance —to alter the behaviour of an individual or group with force, if necessary. In the case of power, we submit to the force or the threat of force, not to the people who exercise that force. This means that power is impersonal. When a bank robber, for example, demands money from a teller, it is the gun that compels the teller to submit, not the personal charm or social standing of the robber.

On the other hand, authority means a willing submission to domination. By **authority**, we mean the ability of a person or group to issue commands and have them obeyed because people see this exercise of control as *legitimate*; that is, as justified and fair. Legitimate authority is a general and unquestioned belief that the exercise of control by government — the police and courts included — is justified. It is also a belief that people in positions of authority have a right to be there — a right to rule — and citizens have a duty to obey the rules that are set out for them.

A familiar illustration is the authority of a classroom teacher. The relationship between teacher and student is no more equal in adulthood than it was in childhood. Students still become quiet when a teacher enters; a teacher rarely stops talking when a student enters the classroom. Teachers feel free to call students by their first names; students rarely feel free to call teachers by their first names. When a student meets a teacher, each knows roughly how to behave and who is dominant. The teacher tells you what to do and, if you are a student, chances are you will do it, for two reasons. First, you have been taught the teacher has the right to do this. Second, you believe that the teacher's commands are ultimately in your best interest.

Like power, authority is an impersonal form of domination. The authority of the teacher is a consequence of his or her position, not personality, character, or individual abilities. We obey a teacher, police officer, judge, or boss because of their position. Most of us feel that the people who dominate us — teachers, bosses, and so on — have the right to do so.

Make no mistake, though; authority is as much a form of domination as is coercion. Indeed, Weber argued that this "rational" domination is the most highly developed, effective and efficient form of domination found in any society. It culminates in a type of organization, the bureaucracy, we discuss in Chapter 9. The good bureaucrat is perfectly submissive, a good organizational "citizen" who never questions orders and gives little thought to the results of his or her actions (Weber, 1964).

One sign that domination plays an important role in our society is the frequency with which we see the symbols of domination. Many social roles require particular clothing (often uniforms) and a particular manner to demonstrate dominance and submission. The military is an obvious example in which the uniform indicates each person's rank. Another is the hospital, in which the outfits worn by doctors, nurses, orderlies, and patients are all different and readily recognizable. They denote rank too.

Even where there are no uniforms, symbols of status denote rank. The executive office, embossed business card, expensive German car or in-ground swimming pool are all accepted symbols of high status in our society. Workers with low social standing typically wear jeans or sturdy work clothes every day. People with more authority wear tailored business suits. You can often tell the rankings of the players by the way they dress.

Inequality, then, is far more pervasive in daily life than most Canadians are willing to admit. While we realize that some people are wealthier than others, most of us assume that people who have more money deserve it because they have earned it. We also assume that everyone is better off thanks to people who have the intelligence, energy, creativity and drive to become successful.

So, for example, some people even believe that sports stars deserve the enormous salaries they earn (see Exhibit 5.1). Some of these stars make most of their income not from sports but from advertising endorsements. That's (presumably) because a great many people admire them and want to be like them, even to the point of drinking the same cola or wearing the same shoes. ("Wear Nike Shoes and Be Michael Jordan!") At the time of writing, it is unclear whether Jordan's career will justify the millions of dollars paid for commercial endorsements.

EXHIBIT 5.1 *Jordan's value: up in the air*

Pitchman Michael Jordan's salary as a basketball star was small change compared to his endorsements. Now that he's retired, companies that depend on his fame may decide to cut him loose....

The money Mr. Jordan made playing basketball was clearly small change compared to the cash he could earn from such endorsements, touting everything from Nike's Air Jordans to Hanes underwear and representing such blue-chip corporations as McDonald's Corp., Quaker Oates Co. and Coca-Cola Co.

His dominance on the court was surpassed only by his dominance of the television airwaves, where the dialogue in his commercials for Nike athletic shoes become part of the vernacular of North American youth.

He quit just as the Bulls were preparing to open their training camp for the new season, in the prime of his two careers—his team had won three straight championships and he was raking in more than $30-million (U.S.) a year in endorsement money....

Does his retirement from basketball mean the end of the endorsements that fed off his athletic success?...

Nike, which has had Mr. Jordan under contract since he entered the NBA in 1984, seems to be in the most precarious position. Its stock fell slightly in New York yesterday as investors worried that Nike's share of the intensely competitive sneaker market may slip now that its chief pitchman has retired....

Nike's stable of basketball stars includes clean-cut David Robinson and antihero Charles Barkley, but neither is even close to the celebrity status of Mr. Jordan, who has become the world's most recognizable athlete since Muhammad Ali....

Another company left in a curious position is Quaker Oats Co. It was only two years ago that Mr. Jordan bolted from Coca-Cola to sign a 10-year, $18-million deal to promote Quaker Oats' Gatorade soft drink.

Then Gatorade advertising campaign revolves around Mr. Jordan playing basketball and features the tag line "Be Like Mike." It is uncertain whether Quaker Oats still wants to urge others to be like Mike—namely, to pack it in at the peak of their career....

As a pitchman, Mr. Jordan has proved to be smooth and successful. He has improved the fortunes of almost every product he has touched. He is largely responsible for resurrecting Nike from its malaise of the early eighties.

And the public continues to perceive him as an all-American type despite allegations that he is a heavy gambler and that he hangs around with shady characters....

Source: Scott Feschuck, "Jordan's value: up in the air," *The Globe and Mail*, Thurs., Oct. 7, 1993, p. A21

Still, these sports stars must have more talent, intelligence, energy, creativity and drive to be successful than the rest of us. Or do they? Does this line of thinking really explain inequality? Consider the theory of stratification developed by functionalists to explain why some people are more highly "rewarded" than others.

THEORIES OF SOCIAL STRATIFICATION

Sociologists Kingsley Davis and Wilbert Moore (1945) are credited with developing an explanation of inequality sociologists call the *functional theory of social stratification*. It says social stratification is inevitable and, even, desirable.

The argument goes like this: There are certain positions in a society that are functionally more important than others. Performing adequately in these

The functionalist approach

positions requires special skills, but few people invest enough time and money to acquire these skills. Only through a system of special rewards and privileges is society able to motivate people to get the skills needed to fill important positions. These special rewards include wealth, prestige, and power.

Now let's take an example that shows off the theory in its best light. Consider brain surgery. If you are going to have surgery done on your brain, you want it done by someone who is *very* competent. You want to know that this person has a steady hand, a complete knowledge of the human body, and an up-to-date familiarity with surgical techniques. You would not be surprised to learn that such preparation had required ten or more years of post-secondary education.

Each year would have been filled with hard work: lots of reading, time in the laboratory, time in the clinic, late nights preparing for exams or working on the emergency ward, and so on. While other people their age were off at the beach partying, these future brain surgeons were memorizing the names of nerves and practicing how to tie a knot with one hand.

So if someone told you that brain surgeons earn a lot of money, this would not seem unfair. Obviously, they possess a rare, important and exacting skill which costs a great deal of time and money to develop. Without the possibility of large rewards, few people would be willing to ever *become* brain surgeons.

However, few cases are as clearcut as that of the brain surgeon. For example, we can all agree that brain surgery is important, but is it possible to rank *all* occupations objectively, according to their importance to society? Beyond that, are even the contributions made by brain surgeons all that important to society? Using the term "rewards" implies, perhaps wrongly, that people "deserve" what they receive. (If we called the rewards "plunder" or "booty" or "treasure" we might think about the system differently!)

Even if we could agree that brain surgeons are more important to society than truck drivers, and therefore should be better paid, we would have trouble applying the same logic to explaining the salaries earned in organized crime, professional sports, and popular entertainment. (There, perhaps, "plunder" and "booty" are precisely the words we are looking for.)

Even if we could get past *that* hurdle, we would have trouble using the functional theory to account for *non*-occupational inequalities: why men dominate women, whites dominate non-whites, rich nations dominate poor nations, and so on. Inequality is too complex and, usually, too unfair for the functional theory to handle. Generally, most sociologists today tend to explain stratification using a variety of the conflict approach. In particular, they make use of either the class theory of Karl Marx or the modifications to Marx's theory made by Weber — both versions of the conflict approach we have discussed throughout the book.

Class theory

The theory of social class was first developed by Marx as part of his theory of society and social change. This theory of class is often described as a form of *economic determinism*. Marx saw the stratification system as *determined* by the means of production to be found in a society. The means of production are the tools, objects, techniques, or skills that are used in the production process.

Marx (1936; also Marx and Engels, 1955) described our kind of society as "capitalist" because of the important role capital plays in production. Capital includes money and other forms of wealth which are invested in a business to increase production and profits. In Canada, the means of production are technology, labour, and capital. People's position in the **class system** of social inequality depends on their relationship to the means of production.

In Marx's theory a small group of people, the **bourgeoisie**, own the capital and control the labour of everyone else. As owners, they are able to create and destroy jobs, hire and fire people, and extract "surplus value," or profits, from other people's work. This profit becomes capital when it is re-invested. A second group, the petty (or petite) bourgeoisie, includes small-business owners who have a few employees and work alongside them. Like the bourgeoisie, they own the means of production. Unlike the bourgeoisie, they extract few profits from other people's labour.

Most people belong to a third group, the **proletariat**, and work for the bourgeoisie. They own none of the capital and sell their own labour power to bourgeois employers for a wage.

People in the same social class share the same relationship to the means of production. Consequently, they have similar wealth, authority and power; and as a result of *that*, they have similar lifestyles and life chances. All members of the proletariat, or working class, are vulnerable to the power of the bourgeoisie. They all — construction workers, sales staff, secretaries, and professors alike — sell their labour for wages. All could be thrown out of work, find themselves without an income, and have to rely on savings, welfare, or charity to survive.

As a result, class affects the ways people think of the future. Middle-class people are more committed to values like self-development, achievement and activism than people in the working class (Grabb, 1981). For their part, poor, powerless people tend to think less about the future than people with more wealth and power (Koenig, Swanson and Harter, 1981). They are defending themselves psychologically against the knowledge that they lack the ability to do much about their problems. Instead of organizing themselves *as a social class* to demand changes in society, they often retreat into silent self-blame.

For British royalty, who are at the uppermost end of the social stratification scale, prestige is part of the job.

The Toronto Sun

Generally, societies which are less economically developed have stronger class patterns. For example, people in India identify with their social class more strongly than Canadians do. What's more, there is a wider consensus about the characteristics of each class (Driver, 1981). People agree on the attributes shared by a particular class: for instance, in terms of income and property holdings, occupation, lifestyle and attitude to wealth. What's more, members of all classes tend to hold generally negative images of the lower class and generally positive images of the middle and upper classes. Paradoxically, this makes it easier for the poor to mobilize for political action.

Problems arise when we try to apply class analysis, as Marx originally stated it, to North America today. First, many people in the proletariat do not *think* of themselves as "workers" and identify instead with the "middle class" or even the bourgeoisie. They model their attitudes, goals, and lifestyles on middle-class, not working-class, ideals.

The class consciousness of blue collar workers depends on many factors outside work itself. For example, union membership plays a part in forming a person's identity as a member of the working class, but many working-class people do not belong to unions. Furthermore, the effect of union membership is limited. On the other hand, marrying a woman with a middle-class background increases the chance that a worker will develop a middle-class identity and support non-socialist political parties (Keddie, 1980).

In Australia too, people fail to identify with their real social class. As in Canada, the concept of class is not a part of the "self" we discussed in Chapter 3; it has little significance for Australian people's sense of identity (Emmison and Western, 1990). That is why most workers do not vote for working-class political parties. In fact, so weak are people's class identities that a survey of international voting data has led Clark, Lipset and Rempel (1993) to conclude that social class is no longer useful for predicting political behaviour.

A second problem with Marx's theory is that, in modern capitalism, ownership and control are largely separate. Millions of small stockholders — often through their pension funds — own a great many large business organizations. But effectively, senior management and elected directors, not stockholders, *control* these organizations. This separation of ownership from control is not something Marx had envisioned.

Third, the differences between wage-earning people may be more "real" and more consequential than Marx had imagined. Not all wage-earning people share the same market position: they may receive dramatically different material rewards and life chances, in terms of pay, security, and opportunity for promotion. And not all share the same work situation, i.e., work tasks and production technology, or amount of supervision on the job. Some wage-earners have both better market rewards and better working conditions than others.

Finally, in a society with relatively high rates of social mobility (which we discuss shortly), class lines are blurred, making people even less likely to identify with their social class (Clark and Lipset, 1991). For all these reasons, we need another approach to studying social inequality, and that approach is provided by Weber.

Weber's approach

In categorizing classes in modern society, Weber (1958a) added to Marx's list. He included the propertied class (Marx's bourgeoisie); the traditional petty bourgeois class of small business people, shopkeepers, and farmers; and the working class (Marx's proletariat). As well, he identified a wage-earning intellectual, administrative, and managerial class. Within each of these four classes we find the similarity (and awareness of similar interests) that Marx expected to find.

Both Marx and Weber believed that changing historical conditions would produce new structures of domination and submission. For Marx, the crucial changes were those in the means of production. New means of production create new classes which come into conflict with the old ones. History, to Marx, was the record of class conflict and revolutions in which new classes overthrow old ruling classes.

For Weber, many more factors could change the structures of domination and submission; these include changes in cultural and religious values. More important, Weber was the first to emphasize the independent role of authority. Though class has a huge impact, electoral politics and government bureaucracies also give the state a central role in people's lives.

And unlike Marx, Weber believed that social (or "status") groups are able to control markets too. Like social classes, ethnic, racial, religious, professional, and national groups all have the power to do this. Said another way, all societies use gender, ethnicity and race, as well as class, to distribute wealth, power and *prestige* (or social honour). But unlike other groups (for example, ethnic groups) classes *rarely* organize politically in industrial societies. We have already noted the lack of political action among working class people. As a result, there is no inevitable transition from a shared economic position to shared political interests, as Marx expected.

As for status, Weber claimed that most of the important forms of stratification in the past, such as **caste systems** and slavery, were based on cultural and religious values, not class. He was not entirely right: the Indian caste system is remarkably complicated, and any full treatment of it needs to incorporate class as well. Though the Indian government has officially disbanded the caste system, traditional practices like "untouchability" continue to shape social relations in Indian villages (Sharma, 1986). But caste *and* class are at work at the same time (Sharma, 1984), with the result that Indian society is even more hierarchical than Canadian society.

In fact, as Weber pointed out, all systems of inequality are complex and multi-dimensional. They are not based only on class, or values, or politics: they are based on all of the above and many more factors. That means that any useful theory of stratification has to examine all of these dimensions.

Combining Marx and Weber

Many of the newer theories of stratification are referred to as neo-Marxist or neo-Weberian because they modify the older theories by combining key elements.

The need to do this will become clearer in Chapter 11, which deals with politics, protest and change. In large part, we need to do this because the world has changed drastically since Marx and Weber's time. To understand the kinds of inequality we face today, it is necessary to take into account the kinds of social and economic organization that confront people, at work and at home. A first step in this process, which is far from complete, is to bring together the insights of Marx and Weber.

Erik Olin Wright (1985), among others, has modified the Marxian scheme of class analysis to incorporate Weber's views, especially the emphasis Weber places on domination. In Wright's scheme, as in Marx's and Weber's, there are capitalists and petty bourgeoisie. However, in this typology there are four types of wage-earners. Some exercise workplace control over other wage-earners and others do not. At the same time, some wage-earners are controlled in the workplace and others are not.

The wage-earners who are controlled but control no one else — call them *workers* — are closest to Marx's proletariat. Similar in many respects are wage-earners called *supervisors*, who are controlled at work but also control other workers.

Two other wage-earning groups differ from the supervisors and workers in their social origins, educational attainment, pay level, and workplace autonomy. One is the group of *managers and technocrats* that controls other workers but enjoys a lot of freedom from control on the job. Another is the group of workers — academics, salaried professionals, and technical personnel — who enjoy a lot of freedom on the job and have no control over other workers. Call them *semi-autonomous employees*.

This last type of worker, comprising mainly salaried professionals, has grown in the 20th century and poses a particular problem for Marxist analysis. Consider, as an example, Supreme Court judges. They enjoy high salaries, high job security and a great deal of prestige. They also have a lot of power over the way Canadian society works: their decisions determine all law-making and law-enforcement. Once appointed, they are free to act as they wish; but they don't own any capital or exercise any direct control over other workers.

It's hard to know how to categorize these "workers" and harder still to account for their apparent preference for the rich and powerful (see Exhibit 5.2).

Objectively, salaried professionals like the Supreme Court judges are workers. As workers they lack control over their own work lives and do not control the labour process: what they produce, how they produce it and who gains a profit from that work. But subjectively, they are *not* workers: they think of themselves as independent and, in some respects, they are.

For this reason, Macy (1989) finds that two class-related attributes — opportunity for self-directed work and income — determine people's class identification and their attitudes towards business and labour. Typically, people who earn high salaries and have a lot of freedom at work (whether self-employed or not) tend to be more sympathetic to business than they are to labour. Though they lack power, they increasingly come to think like "bosses" and reject concerns with power and class conflict (Derber, 1983).

Let's put some numbers on these groups we've been discussing. Data from a 1981 Canadian study found that only 2.8% of all employed people were members of the capitalist class. The petite bourgeoisie made up 11.8% of all employed people. Managers and technocrats comprised 7.0%, supervisors 10.9%, semi-autonomous employees 8.1%, and workers the vast majority at 55.9% of the employed population (Ornstein, 1988: 194).

The same study found that capitalists averaged the highest rate of pay, twice that of all wage-earners and nearly three times that of workers. This difference reflected the fact that capitalists had attained a higher level of education, were older, and included proportionately more men than the wage-earning population. However, even controlling for, or equalizing, education, age, and gender, the average capitalist earned nearly twice as much as the average wage-earner and more than twice as much as the average worker.

EXHIBIT 5.2 *Study of Supreme Court decisions says underdogs tend to lose*

Government and big businesses tend to win their cases at Canada's highest court, while unions and individuals lose more often than they win, an Alberta political scientist has found in a ground-breaking study.

Peter McCormick, who studied nearly 4,000 decisions of the Supreme Court of Canada from 1949 to 1992, found substantial differences in the success rates of different groups in society.

"There's no suggestion that the underdog always loses—it's just that they tend to lose, on balance, over the long run," Professor McCormick, a political science professor at the University of Lethbridge, said in an interview....

The top winning percentage belonged to the Crown, followed by the federal government and big businesses. In the middle rank were provincial governments, municipal governments and other businesses. In the back of the pack were unions and individuals.

For example, the Crown won 57 per cent of cases it appealed and 70 per cent of cases when it was responding to appeals of its lower-court victories; individuals won just 40 per cent on appeal and 50 per cent when responding to appeals. Large business organizations—such as railways, airlines, banks, utilities, and major oil, insurance and manufacturing companies—won 50 per cent of their appeals and 65 per cent when responding to appeals. Unions won 41 per cent of their appeals and 51 per cent when responding.

The broad conclusion is that the courts, rather than acting as a check on the rich and powerful, in fact have what Prof. McCormick describes as "privilege-reinforcing tendencies."...

"The Supreme Court is not to blame for these patterns, any more than the basketball referee is to blame when the taller team grabs more of the rebounds; nor should the Supreme Court 'do something' to level the playing field any more than the referee should help the shorter team by not calling fouls against them," he wrote in the *Canadian Journal of Political Science*, which published his study.

One reason some groups do better than others is their status as "repeat players." They are often before the courts and have the financial resources, expertise and opportunity to pick the best cases and develop a comprehensive strategy, he wrote.

Another reason, he said, is that the law tends to favour certain groups—business over unions, for example. The judges themselves tend to be drawn from the more privileged ranks of society.

Source: Sean Fine, "Scales of justice tilt toward power," *The Globe and Mail*, Sat., Nov. 6, 1993, pp. A1, A4

Neo-Marxism argues that every type of society (whether feudal, capitalist or otherwise) has a characteristic form of exploitation. This is why it is important to study groups of similarly exploited people, with similar amounts of control over their lives: for purposes of continuity, we will continue to call them social "classes." However, it is no longer possible to do a class analysis of a society without examining how economic position combines with gender, ethnicity, religion and other social factors (Clement, 1991).

Neo-Weberian theory sees the North American middle class arising from a capitalist investment in worker discipline (i.e., supervision and "management"). Comparative research shows that the Swedes and Finns differ from North Americans where domination is concerned. They give their workers more autonomy, spend less money supervising and disciplining their workers, and are less afraid of new technologies in the workplace. It is obvious how this analysis uses Weberian notions of domination to extend the traditional Marxist outlook (and vice versa).

Feminist approaches

According to feminist theorists, it is necessary to consider gendered patterns of domination both at home and in the workplace. One must try to understand how the subjugation of women at home contributes to the subjugation of women at work. Like the neo-Marxists and neo-Weberians, feminist sociologists have tended to emphasize the interaction between class, gender and racial inequalities. We will see that developed in detail in Chapter 7, on gender relations.

However, it is worth noting at this point that one cannot study class and status inequalities without recognizing the importance of gender differences. For example, in studying Canadian workers Ornstein (1988) found large differences in background, pay and working conditions between manual and non-manual workers: namely, manual workers

◆ are more likely to be men than women;
◆ have less education (on average) than nonmanual workers;
◆ report a much less settled work history than nonmanual workers; and
◆ are more closely supervised than nonmanual workers.

In short, manual workers have less autonomy and job stability than non-manual workers. On the other hand, the typically "pink collar" (female, non-manual) workers earn about 20% less than their "blue collar" (male, manual worker) counterparts. Clearly, a person's place in the stratification system is not just a result of the relations of production. Women doing the same jobs as men are sometimes paid less than men, even substantially less. Also, women doing the same work as men usually have less chance for promotion than do men.

Beyond that, women typically have a different work history than men (on this, see Jones, Marsden and Tepperman, 1990). For example, they are more likely than men to voluntarily take on part-time work, and they are more likely to interrupt their work lives for familial or educational reasons. This reflects women's heavier family responsibilities, which some sociologists have called working women's "double day." It also reflects the way "women's work" evolved, as part of North America's administrative revolution in the early part of this century (Lowe, 1986).

The administrative revolution, between 1911 and 1931, included a huge increase in the clerical sector of the work force, a dramatic shift in the sex ratio (toward female clerks) and the rationalization of office work by scientifically oriented office managers. At the forefront of this expansion of white-collar work was an increase in the total number of clerks, who today constitute more than 15 per cent of the labour force. With feminization, clerical jobs became fragmented and routinized. The spread of the dictation machine and the typing pool signified the rationalization of office work. It also had the effect of reducing the status and skill level of secretarial work.

The development of large central offices reflects the parallel advance of industrialization and capitalism. The main purpose of modern management was to regulate labour and reduce class conflict; here it was accomplished in an office, not a factory, and the main objects of control were women.

As our society has moved away from a manufacturing economy towards a service economy, women have entered poor-paying, insecure and low status jobs in large numbers. For example, women — along with teenagers and recent immigrants — are disproportionately numerous in the fast food industry, flipping burgers or taking change at Burger King (Reiter, 1986). As in the highly controlled offices we just described, their work is specialized but lacks challenge or creativity.

Interactionist approaches

Symbolic interactionists have done little work on class and other forms of inequality. A micro-sociological perspective is unsuitable for developing a full-fledged theory of inequality. However, interactionists and other microsociologists have made important contributions to our understanding of the symbolic and interactional aspects of domination, status, and class differences. For example, Stone (1970) has studied the ways we use appearance, such as clothing, to establish and display a person's social status.

Interactionists have also shown an interest in what is sometimes called *micropolitics* (about which more will be said in Chapter 11 of this book). Micropolitics is concerned with interpersonal struggles for advantage or control in face-to-face groups. This concern is illustrated in Goffman's (1961) study of a mental hospital, in which he examined what he called a "total institution." In this institution, an "underlife" develops as a way of "working the system"; the study provides a good example of the way dominated people avoid submitting to authority. Beyond that, interactionists have been particularly sensitive to the use and meaning of "status symbols."

STATUS AND SYMBOLIC RESOURCES

There is no denying that income and material well-being are important aspects of inequality, but they are not everything. Everywhere, status is a distinct aspect of stratification and it is very important to people.

The term "status" has two related meanings in sociology. One is *status* as a position in a social system — the status of daughter, parent, or professor — that embodies a cluster of rights, responsibilities, and role expectations. A status of this kind shapes role relationships and social interactions among people. The second meaning, derived from the work of Weber, is of status as a measure of social worth or honour.

This second meaning of status directs our study of inequality in two important directions. First, status is *relative*: one person's worth or honour is always determined by comparison with another person's. This makes status harder to measure than material wealth. As well, our desire for status has no limit. Just as celebrities often use their status to get rich (for example, through product endorsements like those of Michael Jordan), so wealthy people spend vast sums of money in ways that (they hope) will gain them higher status (for example, through charitable work or fundraising for the arts).

Second, status is *symbolic*. This means that status can be seen as the unequal distribution of symbolic resources. Some of these resources, like cultural capital, allow a person to acquire more status; others, like the symbols of wealth and conspicuous consumption, allow people to display their status.

Our society has a multi-dimensional stratification system. That means people can simultaneously occupy positions conferring *different* amounts of social status. One result is, often, *status inconsistency*. For example, a person who is highly educated yet works in a low-paying job, belongs to a racial minority, or has a criminal record, can expect to experience status inconsistency.

However, major inconsistencies are rare and people tend to rank similarly on income, job prestige, authority at work, and educational attainment. People who rank similarly on clusters of different dimensions are said to belong to the same social stratum. Within each stratum, people share similar life chances and outlooks on life. Across strata, we find striking differences in life chances and outlook.

Sociologists use the term socio-economic status (or SES) to refer to a social ranking which combines various dimensions of stratification: particularly prestige and wealth. It takes into account a number of factors that determine a person's social status: income, type of occupation, level of education attained, and place of residence, among others.

Criteria for determining who is worthy of status, prestige or respect vary across cultures. For example, in Japan, one element contributing to status is the size of the firm for which a person works. In general, the larger the firm, the higher a person's status; this applies even among people of the same class (Ishidi, 1989). At the extremes of the class structure — that is, among the very poor and the very rich — status is unambiguously defined by people's relations to the means of production. In the middle class, where most people have to sell their labour power, status is determined by the size (and importance) of the organization for which they work.

Similarly, in China, people gain status from the political and administrative power their job provides (Li, Yang and Wang, 1991). Other things being equal, people who work in organizations that control a lot of resources and authority enjoy higher status than people who work in smaller, less important organizations. And, in a society where the state owns most of the means of production, social stratification is based *primarily* on status, not class.

For people at the top and bottom of the stratification system, class and SES coincide, and people's statuses—income, occupation, education, place of residence—are fairly consistent.

Dick Hemingway

In North America, there is much more respect for independent professionals and private entrepreneurs. Here wealth, power, intelligence, athletic competence, and physical attractiveness are all highly valued and all sources of prestige. **Prestige is social honour.** As such, it is a way of measuring social status and how much respect will be shown a person. In our society, a person's job is his or her main source of income, authority, and prestige.

Being the president of a large corporation is a prestigious position and provides a person with great authority. However winning an Olympic gold medal is also prestigious. So, both the president of a corporation and an Olympic athlete enjoy high status, though different amounts of authority.

Research has found that a good way of estimating a person's SES is by measuring his or her occupational prestige. The most prestigious jobs are typically those which pay best and are filled by highly educated people. That's why we can predict how much prestige a person will receive from a job by knowing what the job pays and how much education the job requires. In fact, with that formula and a few assumptions, we could predict the prestige of jobs that don't even exist yet: for example, gender technician, animal spiritualist, robot trainer, or alien life-form translator.

With few exceptions, occupational prestige rankings are remarkably similar from one industrial society to another. The gaps in prestige between medical doctor, door-to-door salesman, machinist, and unskilled construction worker are similar whether we are considering Austria, Finland, West Germany, the Netherlands, Switzerland or the United States (Bornschier, 1986). (An interesting exception is the job of professor, which is worse paid but better regarded in Poland than in North America; on this, see Sawinski and Domanski, 1991.) What's more, with few exceptions — for example, the steadily falling prestige of ministers of religion — prestige rankings were similar in 1990 to what they were in 1970 and 1950.

Status and authority

A good illustration of the importance of status to people is provided in sociologist Joseph Gusfield's (1963) study of the symbolic crusade that led to Prohibition in the United States. Prohibition consisted of a ban, from 1920 to 1933, on the sale and public consumption of alcohol in the United States. Gusfield (1963) argues that the successful lobbying effort organized by the American Temperance Movement which led to Prohibition was an example of what he calls "status politics."

Status politics demonstrate "a struggle between groups for prestige and social position." Defending their position in the status order is as important to people as protecting or expanding their economic power; indeed, the two are often related.

The clash between drinkers and abstainers dramatized a profound conflict in American society. Between 1880 and 1920 the United States changed from a rural, small-town society to an urban, industrial power. During that time, enormous numbers of immigrants poured into American cities. They shifted economic and political control of American society away from the native-born, white Protestant, small-town middle class, which had run the United States up through the 19th century. The new immigrants were foreign-born, mostly Catholic, city dwellers who, because of their numbers and differentness, many native-born Americans found menacing.

American Protestants had made a virtue of "temperance," but the new immigrants saw nothing immoral in the use of alcohol. For this reason, small-town, middle-class Americans came to associate immigrants with the consumption, manufacture, and distribution of alcohol: the Italians with wine, the Germans with beer, the Irish with whisky, and the Poles with vodka.

Symbolically, the attempt to impose temperance through Prohibition was an attempt to turn the clock back to a time when the United States was a homogeneous society dominated by middle-class Protestants. Its goal, however unconscious, was to show the immigrants *who* ran the country. But by the time the Amendment was repealed in 1933, it had proved unenforceable and almost universally unpopular. Rural small-towners had lost the battle and, with that, their symbolic status.

UNEQUAL CONDITIONS AND OPPORTUNITIES

We have stressed that there are many different types of social inequality but also that there are many connections between them. Indeed, social inequalities often overlap and reinforce one another so that some people enjoy a great many advantages and others, a great many disadvantages. How would we go about equalizing the advantages and disadvantages? Our answer depends, first, on what we mean by equality.

Many people favour **equality of condition** — equal portions of wealth, prestige and power for all members of society. (Cuba is one society where people live under largely equal conditions.) Other people favour **equality of opportunity** — equal access to those things valued by society. Equal opportunity means that all positions in society are equally open to all people, regardless of age, race, gender, religion, or class of origin. In principle, recruitment is done according to merit or on the basis of personal talent. Inequalities of opportunity are differences in the chance that people (or their children) will get to enjoy an improved social condition: more wealth, authority, and prestige; better health; more happiness.

However, in no society do we find complete equality of either kind. Instead, we find inequalities of wealth, authority, and prestige. At their worst, these translate into differences in food, shelter, physical security, health, and education. In India, for example, children from poor families have significantly poorer nutrition (and, as a result, weigh less and are shorter) and lower social maturity (as measured by a standard Social Maturity Scale) than wealthier children (Luthra, 1983). Indirectly, social differences also translate into differences of mental health and happiness.

Inequalities of condition and opportunity are not scattered randomly among members of a society. Instead, they vary from one social stratum to another. People in the same social stratum live in similar conditions and have similar chances to change those conditions. People in higher strata have both better conditions and better chances for improving them further. What is more, their children also have better chances than the children born into lower strata.

Take health as a case in point: research has shown time and again that people from higher social strata enjoy a higher level of overall health. That's because they have better housing, fewer financial problems, and better nutrition. What's more, there is no evidence that this relationship between social class and good health (or longevity) is diminishing: class is just as important as it always was. Indeed, recent American research suggests the class differential for longevity is widening (Pappas et al., 1993; see also Guralnik et al., 1993), partly because of the lack of universal health insurance in the United States.

In most studies, education proves to be the single best indicator of class or socio-economic status, as well as the best predictor of health status. Probably, gaining more education helps people improve their class position *and* makes them more sensitive to the need for good health practices.

Better conditions and better opportunities for improving those conditions go together. People cannot have much opportunity to get what they want if they start out with little wealth, power, and respect. This means a society cannot equalize opportunities without greatly reducing the range of unequal starting points. Only if people were all born with the same social position, social connections, and amount of money, would they all have an equal opportunity to improve their condition.

SOCIAL MOBILITY: MOVEMENT WITHIN STRATIFICATION

Despite unequal opportunities, most people fight to "get ahead." They consider upward **social mobility** to be a realistic goal and devote much of their time and energy to improving their position in the social hierarchy. It is this ideal that has kept enrollments at colleges and universities increasing while the actual number of traditionally school-aged persons has declined. Education is seen as a means of social mobility in our society. But how realistic is this goal of "getting ahead," given the context of unequal conditions we have discussed? The answer is that it depends on where you start from and how far you want to get.

Social mobility is the movement of people among different levels of the social hierarchy. Usually these levels are defined occupationally. *Vertical social mobility* is the change from one occupational status to another that is higher or lower in rank: from lawyer to bartender, nurse to doctor, or short-order cook to architect.

Some vertical mobility is upward, to a higher stratum than the person (or person's parents) held before, and some is downward. Typically, sociologists who want to discover the pattern of social mobility in a society will measure the relative amounts of upward and downward mobility: whether more people move up than down, for example.

In studying a stratification system, sociologists routinely find out what fraction of upward mobility is structural and what fraction is exchange mobility. Research has shown that most upward mobility is *structural mobility*, which results from a growth in the number of "good" jobs available in the economy. Only a small amount of upward mobility is exchange mobility, which requires that one person move down for every person who moves up.

Professional baseball can illustrate both types of mobility. Expansion of the league generates structural mobility for all players. More athletes can play major league baseball if there is an increase in the number of teams. As well, during periods of expansion there is usually more movement from one team to another. But *without* expansion, all mobility is exchange mobility. Each team can only have a limited number of players. For one player to be added to the team, another player must be subtracted (through death, retirement, trade to another team or demotion to the minor league).

Finally, social mobility may be intergenerational or intragenerational. *Intergenerational social mobility* refers to the difference between the rank a person currently occupies, and the rank his or her parents occupied at the same age.

Intragenerational social mobility, also called "career mobility," refers to a person's movement between various positions over the course of a lifetime.

The most commonly studied are patterns of vertical, intergenerational mobility among males. (We will discuss female patterns in Chapter 7.) Researchers find similar patterns in all industrial societies (Ishida, Goldthorpe, and Erikson, 1991). Despite differences between countries (e.g., Japan compared with Western European nations) in the *absolute* amounts of mobility (that is, in how many people move up how many levels), the *relative* amounts of mobility are remarkably similar.

As Lipset and Bendix (1959) pointed out in thier classic work *Social Mobility in Industrial Society*, we find the same pattern of mobility in countries with very different cultures. So, despite the historic importance of the Protestant ethic in Western economic development, there is no less social mobility in industrial Catholic, Jewish, Buddhist, Islamic or Confucian societies. What is critical is *industrial growth*, a topic we will discuss in Chapter 9.

Who is most and least mobile?

Within the broad band of people — the middle 80% — who are neither desperately poor nor fabulously rich, the most mobile are those people who are well-educated.

Repeated studies of social mobility in Canada have confirmed the results obtained elsewhere. They show that formal education is the single most important factor in overcoming the disadvantages of low class position. Even in a country as culturally different from Canada as Chile, education is the most important means of upward social mobility (Farrell and Schiefelbein, 1985). As in Canada, in Chile a large part of the population (just under half) is upwardly mobile, thanks to education and a growth in jobs due to industrialization. The better education a person obtains, the more likely that person is to get ahead.

Evidence of the social effects of free trade, though incomplete, suggests that (as workers had feared) the results include job loss, unemployment, and massive downward mobility.

Canada Wide

So-called "status attainment" studies show that people with equal amounts of formal education tend to get jobs of roughly equal prestige, whatever their class of origin. This is because the best paying, most prestigious and secure jobs require education. Higher education provides skills and credentials for getting a good job, and also cultural capital which is useful in advancing a career. In this respect, post-secondary education is better than a secondary education and a professional degree is best of all (we will have more to say about the professions in Chapter 9).

Rural people are less likely to get a higher education than urban people, and women are still slightly less likely to get a higher education than men. Most important of all, people born into lower-class positions are less likely than those born into higher class positions to get a higher education. For these people, the psychic and financial costs of remaining in school are much heavier than for a middle- or upper-class student. In bad economic times, it becomes harder for poor people to stay in school. For example, in the United States, the rates of college attendance by low-income men have declined since the 1970s. This reflects an increase in social inequality over the 1980s (Alexander et al., 1987). However, it is not known whether there has also been a reduction in the college and university attendance levels of low-income Canadian men.

Given the importance of higher education, the most upwardly mobile Canadian is likely to be a professionally educated male born into a middle-

EXHIBIT 5.3 *Welfare profile moves upscale: Applicants better trained, educated*

People applying for welfare today have more education and better work histories than ever before, and once added to the welfare rolls, they are staying there longer, a study by Metro Toronto shows.

In a survey of general trends in the welfare caseload, Metro staff have found that as the number of people receiving welfare from Metro has soared—from a monthly caseload of 36,000 in 1988 to 119,000 this October—the nature of those who need social assistance has also changed.

The number of people who have never applied for welfare before is up 10 per cent over last year, to about 1,200 a month out of about 13,000 new applicants. And the number of first-time applicants who have at least some post-secondary education is up 16.5 per cent over last year, to 627 a month.

Many of those first-time applicants held their last jobs for more than two years, showing them to have the "workplace attachment" that in the past would have made them unlikely candidates for social assistance.

"It indicates to me that welfare is reaching groups of people that it never did before," said Metro's commissioner of social services, Don Richmond. "This is staggering stuff."

Mr. Richmond said the depth of the current recession has meant that more and more educated and experienced workers who lose their jobs and cannot find new ones exhaust their unemployment-insurance benefits and are forced onto welfare.

"UI isn't adequate any more, and we are catching that group," he said.

The study also showed that the length of time people stay on welfare has increased substantially since 1988.

Source: Jane Coutts, "Welfare profile moves upscale: Applicants better trained, educated," *The Globe and Mail*, Tues., Nov. 23, 1993, p. A1

class family. The least upwardly mobile person is likely to have a high-school education or less. He or she will live in a small town or city where educational and job opportunities are limited. We shall discuss women's mobility, and the mobility of ethnic and racial minorities, in the next two chapters.

Education aside, the overwhelming fact about social mobility is the most obvious one: economic growth is key. During an economic recession, almost no one gets ahead, regardless of education, hard work or good values. Since most upward mobility is structural mobility, if there is no economic growth, then no one will get ahead except through the deaths and retirements of others. Given our current economic troubles, it is no wonder people fear the "death of the middle class" and a coming generation of children who are downwardly mobile, compared to their parents (see Exhibit 5.3 on p. 143).

ELITES

Until the last decade, social mobility was common in Canadian society — common enough for people to dream big dreams. For that reason, few people thought about how *un*common mobility into the top ranks of the stratification system really is. These top ranks are often referred to as the elite.

An **elite** is a small group of people with power or influence over many others. The top, or dominant, few percent in a society, organization, political party, or other collection of people is that group's elite. Typically, the elite make decisions that affect society at large and set the trends everyone else follows.

Elite domination

Elites from different sectors of society struggle to promote the goals of their own groups. Each has some power in this struggle but, usually, none has *enough* power to prevail over all the others. Consequently, elites must cooperate to achieve their goals. Appropriately, this process is called "elite accommodation."

In the long run, elite accommodation furthers the interests of all the groups they represent. So whatever their source of power, the elites are basically committed to keeping things as they are. They want to avoid upsetting a social order that works to their advantage. As well, they often share a common set of values. In part, that is because they interact with one another very often. Many elites are acquaintances, friends, or members of the same social class, with similar school backgrounds. Occasionally, elite members are even related by birth or marriage.

On the other hand, though they are tied together socially, politically and culturally, elites fight to further their *own* organizations' interests. There is an inevitable conflict between governing and nongoverning elites, for example. This is what makes democracy such a precarious form of government. And it is through clashes of interest between elites that social changes come about (Etzioni-Halevy, 1989).

In Canada, John Porter's work, *The Vertical Mosaic* (1965), has given the most sustained attention to this idea of accommodating elites. The book concludes that continuity and change in Canadian society are the product of acts, or failures to act, by Canadian elites. According to Porter, Canada is ruled by five collaborating elite groups. These elite groups consist of people in the top positions of five broad areas of Canadian society: the major economic corporations, political organizations, government bureaucracies, labour organizations, and ideological (that is, church, educational and media) organizations.

Of the five elite subgroups, two are more powerful than the rest. In first place, the economic (or "corporate") elite has been most successful of all in ensuring that its interests are served. Canada's *corporate elite*, the top executives of major Canadian corporations, is Canada's dominant elite. In second place is the *bureaucratic elite*, made up of high-ranking civil servants — the so-called "mandarins" of government. Federal bureaucrats are the most powerful civil servants, followed closely by high-ranking personnel of the largest provincial bureaucracies.

The corporate and bureaucratic elites are powerful because of the enormous economic resources each commands and the fact that they employ large fractions of the Canadian working population. Both sectors also provide elites with better-paying and more stable careers than politicians and labour leaders typically enjoy. This enables the corporate and bureaucratic sectors to recruit many talented people for membership.

Despite occasional conflict, these elites tend to cooperate with one another. This is made easier by a common set of values and interests. Each of the elites has many members who subscribe to the idea that corporate capitalism is "for the common good," and they share in the "Western" values of democracy, nationalism and Christianity. They come to these common views from similar social backgrounds and through similar social experiences: training in upper-class schools, interaction on boards of directors, memberships in men's clubs, and so on. These connections resemble the "web of kinship and lineage which provides cohesion to primitive life" (Porter, 1965: 304).

Class versus elite analysis

Some sociologists disagree with Porter's analysis. They note (see, for example Clement, 1975, 1977) that the dominant economic elite is filled by people from the hereditary upper class and by a few "new" capitalists. The elite structure of society duplicates the capitalist class structure. Thus we need to analyse classes, not elites, to understand how power is used in Canadian society.

By this reasoning, what *appears* to be elite accommodation is actually cooperation among capitalists and their agents. Class interests overrule state, family, community, and other interests. In the end, the economy dominates all other social institutions, and the upper class dominates the economy (Dugger, 1988).

Class theorists argue that: (1) the state and its offshoots (such as the courts and legislatures) serve the interests of the capitalist class; (2) schools, media and churches serve to "legitimate" (or justify) unequal economic power and give the interests of capitalism moral authority; and (3) decision-making in our society is closed and hierarchical (anti-democratic), though it is designed to appear open and democratic.

These theorists have particularly criticized Porter's treatment of the role of social class in the distribution of power. Many insist that the Canadian capitalist class exercises enormous control through the corporate elite and the state. In this theory, the other elites are forced to cooperate or lose out.

Often, the corporate elite of a country is tightly tied into the corporate elite of other countries, especially the United States. It is necessary, therefore, to distinguish between **comprador** elites and *indigenous elites* within the Canadian corporate elite. "Comprador elites" work for foreign-owned companies in Canada. They run these organizations as "branch plants," with most major policies originating in the foreign-based parent firm. By contrast, "indigenous elites" are people who control firms that are Canadian-owned.

Porter, for his part, stopped short of concluding that there is a dominant capitalist class. He rejected this possibility because he found the Marxist theory of the state, in which "the economic ... system is the master" (1965: 206), too simplistic. The paramount strength of the corporate elite, and the shared, entrenched values of the elite group suggest otherwise. So Porter remained impressed by the "counteracting power" of the other elites (1965: 522-23)

Whichever view we adopt, there is little doubt that elites play an important, if largely invisible, role in Canadian life. Elites are able to dominate because they are more unified and less confused about their interests than other groups in Canadian society.

Can you get into the elite?

Societies vary in the extent to which their various elites (political, intellectual, economic, and so on) form a cohesive ruling group. Where such a group exists, the ruling elite makes decisions affecting everyone else. In most societies, the children of people who are elite members have the best chance to enter the elite themselves.

Ruling elites differ in the extent to which they are open to entry from outside — that is, by children of non-elite parents. Heath (1981) found that, in Britain, elites recruit new members mainly from within their own ranks; and research in other countries supports this finding. Yet, even in a country as rigid in its class and caste structures as India, there is movement into the elite. Since colonial times, the higher Indian castes have been weakening and, increasingly, highly educated people are moving up today. This change is aided by a modernization of job structures. The stratum of professionals and intellectuals now forms part of the new elite, leading a trend towards achievement-based vertical mobility, as in the West (Pande, 1982).

Certain general findings about elites hold for Canada as well as for India, Britain and other Western countries. However, there are also unique features that make it necessary for us to examine the Canadian elites more closely. In fact, there has been fine Canadian research on this topic. Canada is different from Britain (and indeed many other Western countries) in the following ways:

(1)   there has never been a landed aristocracy in Canada;
(2)   a significant portion of the Canadian economy is controlled by foreign-owned (especially American-owned) multi-national corporations;
(3)   the state has always played a particularly vigorous part in Canada's social and economic development;
(4)   Canada has always had a high rate of immigration; and
(5)   the Canadian population and economy have grown rapidly and unevenly since the Second World War.

The fact that there has never been a landed aristocracy in Canada has probably made it much easier for people to move into elite positions. In Canada, as in the United States, great wealth and power are enough to gain a person entry into most social circles. Converting money into social acceptance has always been harder and slower in Europe, where family lineage has counted for more.

Clement (1975) has found much more upward mobility into comprador elite positions than into indigenous elite positions. Most likely, this proves that (Canadian-owned) financial institutions recruit more conservatively than (American-owned) industrial organizations.

As well, the important role of the state in Canada's economy has meant that government (especially civil service) elites are as important as corporate elites. So mobility into corporate elite positions has to resemble mobility into government elite positions. Indeed, Porter (1965) found many similarities in the backgrounds of corporate and civil-service elite groups, including an over-representation of upper-class people in both.

In recent years there has been a great deal of concern with employment equity in hiring and promotion. Unlike affirmative action, an American process which has implied quotas and has been largely unsuccessful, employment equity uses goals and timetables. It has aimed at increasing the proportion of francophones, women, visible minorities, and other disadvantaged people in positions of power.

The corporate elite has had to follow the government's lead in order to keep up good relations with the federal bureaucracy and a good public image. Today, the proportion of francophones, women, and visible minorities in the corporate elite is still small, but it has grown since Porter first described the elite 30 years ago.

The Canadian elite has been changing, and so has the opportunity for upward mobility into the elite. Although Clement argues that this opportunity has shrunk since Porter's research 20 years earlier, little evidence supports that view. On the contrary, evidence suggests that new players have entered the elite in the last 30 years and this number may continue to grow (see, for example, Peter Newman's *The New Acquisitors* (1981)).

Still, rags-to-riches mobility remains extremely rare. It is unrealistic to set your heart on entering the corporate elite. Unless you are the child of a member of this elite, your chances of entering it are tiny. The fact that a few people do enter the elite from below does not prove that Canada is a *meritocracy* — a system in which leaders are selected on the basis of talent and achievement. No one has yet demonstrated that members of elites are more talented than other people. The key to gaining elite status is still financial capital, cultural capital, good luck, and choosing the right parents.

In hard economic times, the rich continue to get richer but the poor do not; in fact, they get poorer. As a result, economic inequality has been increasing over the last few decades — in Canada as well as the United States and elsewhere. While governments talked about little else but deficit reduction and responsible spending, more money was funnelled into the hands of the rich. And since the economy was not growing, as the rich got richer, the poor got poorer.

We turn now from the powerful and wealthy to the powerless and poor. Everywhere, the recession has meant an increase in the numbers of working poor, unemployed poor, homeless people and beggars. As Exhibit 5.4 shows, poverty and economic inequality are far worse in Mexico — our new trade partner — than they are in Canada. But many fear that, for most Canadian workers, free trade will mean levelling *down* to the Mexican standard of living rather than bringing Mexicans up to ours. And economically, many Canadians are already in deep trouble.

EXHIBIT 5.4 *Economic inequality widespread*

The inequality of living standards that was at the heart of the peasant uprising in the state of Chiapas is a characteristic of all of Mexico. . . .

"It is a common pattern in poorer countries," said economic analyst Sergio Sarmiento. "The elite is pretty concentrated in most Latin American countries and it is no different in Mexico."

Mexico's national statistics institute (INEGI), for example, has found that the percentage of total income earned by the wealthiest 10 per cent of families has fluctuated between 33 and 42 per cent since 1963 — with the rate at the moment thought to fall about midway between.

That is an extreme concentration of wealth compared with Mexico's free-trade partners. In Canada, the top 20 per cent of wage earners make about 40 per cent of national income while in the United States the figure is about 45 per cent.

Still, the INEGI studies may underestimate income inequality, according to recent tabulations by the American Chamber of Commerce of Mexico. . . .

A recent study by the United Nations concluded that the number of Mexicans living in extreme poverty declined to 13.6 million in 1992 from 14.9 million in 1989. The decline was concentrated in urban areas as the number of rural Mexicans living in extreme poverty—defined as being unable to afford subsistence-level food and shelter—increased marginally.

The number of people with incomes at least twice the poverty line increased to 47.1 million in 1992 from 41.3 million in 1989. . . .

But while the economic recovery of recent years has helped almost everyone, the degree of benefit has fluctuated with income.

The American Chamber of Commerce of Mexico recently concluded, for example, that wages for skilled manufacturing workers have risen 24 per cent in recent years after accounting for inflation. Managers' salaries have risen more.

But. . . the earnings of workers in industries in the *maquiladora* zone (in which non-Mexican factories operate duty-free) along Mexico's northern border still have not returned to the levels of 15 years ago.

In 1980, average low-skilled *maquiladora* employees received wages and benefits worth $3.45 (U.S.) an hour, as expressed in 1993 dollars.

But last year it was back up to only $3.02 after sliding drastically throughout the eighties. . . .

Source: Drew Fagan, "Economic inequality widespread," *The Globe and Mail*, Mon., Jan. 24, 1994, p. B9

POVERTY

Defining and measuring poverty

In studying the topic, sociologists distinguish between relative and absolute poverty.

We speak of **absolute poverty** when people do not have enough of the basic necessities — food and shelter — for their physical survival. So, for example, in Meherchandi (Bangladesh), poor households spend only 3% of their household income on health, medicine, recreation and social responsibility (charity). The rest, 97%, goes for food and shelter (Sadeque, 1986). They are surviving, but just barely. Amazingly, in view of this, the majority has neither given up hope nor stopped trying to escape poverty.

In contrast, researchers define **relative poverty** by reference to the general living standards of the society or social group. Since not all societies or groups within a society are equally wealthy, what people consider "poor" varies too. In industrial societies, we consider people to be "poor" if they have much less than the average income. To measure this, statisticians have established a Low Income Cut-off (LICO) Point.

The LICO Point is the income level below which a person (or family) is judged to be living in poverty. Judgments of what constitutes "poverty" vary over time and from one region (or social group) to another. They also vary with family size and the size of the community in which a family lives. Larger families who live in larger communities require more income to live at the same level as smaller families in smaller communities. The guiding principle is that a low-income person or family spends 58.5% or more of its income on food, shelter, and clothing.

Each year statisticians update the specific dollar cut-off lines using the Consumer Price Index, to account for yearly changes in the cost of living. By some reports, poverty is decreasing in Canada (Health and Welfare Canada, 1989b: 35). But whether we can believe that this trend is real depends on whether we agree with the way in which government statisticians measure low-income.

Criticizing this mode of analysis, Methot (1987: 7) says that LICO fails to take into account other factors such as accumulated wealth, non-monetary income, and future earnings potential. These, Methot notes, are also important in determining the economic well-being of families and individuals.

The exact placement of the "poverty line" was a political football under Brian Mulroney's Conservative government. Even today, some believe that the line ought to be set much higher, with the result that a great many more people are shown to be "in poverty." Such a finding would suggest government has mismanaged the economy. On the other side, government supporters argue in favour of *lowering* the poverty line, to suggest that there are fewer poor than we had believed.

In the end, what we mean by "poverty" and how we choose to measure it is a result of our ideology and political agenda. But, for now, we have no better measure of poverty than the LICO point. At least this method allows us to compare groups *within* Canadian society and see which are doing worst.

Who are the poor?

Health and Welfare Canada reports that among families, the incidence of low income is *lowest* in families without children, with multiple income-earners, or headed by an elderly male. It is *highest* among elderly widows, in families with three or more children, and in families headed by mothers (usually, single parents). In 1991, nearly two-thirds (61%) of all families headed by single mothers had low incomes and this percentage had increased since 1981. Indeed, families headed by lone female parents make up about one-third of all low-income families.

This growing problem is what people have called the **feminization of poverty**. The incidence of low incomes among families headed by lone male parents is also growing. Yet it remains about half as high as for families headed by female lone parents. What's more, families headed by a lone parent are far more likely to have a female than a male family head. After divorce or separation, women usually take custody of the children. So the female-headed family is likely to remain poor unless the state takes strong measures to change things.

Causes of poverty

We have not yet mentioned the group that is likeliest of all Canadians to live in poverty and that gives us the most insight into the causes of poverty. The group we mean is *children*. By 1991, over one-quarter of the 4.2 million Canadian poor — 1.2 million of them — were children under the age of 18. Nearly one Canadian child in five was living in a low-income family — a fraction that had increased from just over one child in seven in 1981 (see Exhibit 5.5).

EXHIBIT 5.5 *Child poverty rising in Canada*

More than 1.2 million Canadian children were living in poverty in 1991, a 30-per-cent increase in two years in the number of people under 18 whose families can scarcely afford the essentials of life. . . .

"If we continue to increase at this rate, child poverty is going to double by the year 2000. It's not going to be eliminated. . . .

The members of Campaign 2000, predominantly anti-poverty groups and public-health organizations, pin the blame on the massive loss of jobs during four years of recession.

They accuse Ottawa of making a bad situation worse by failing to adopt a strategy to create jobs, backing away from a pledge to introduce national child care, and reigning over an unfair taxation policy that has widened the gap between rich and poor in recent years.

Based on an analysis of Statscan figures, the coalition also found:

♦ More than 800,000 children had a parent who was collecting unemployment insurance for at least six months in 1991—a 41-per cent increase from 1989.

♦ More than one million children in Canada lived in families collecting social assistance in March, 1992—50 per cent more than three years earlier.

♦ There were 436 food banks registered in Canada this past February, a jump of 100 from the previous August.

♦ In 1992, an estimated 900,000 children relied on provisions from a food bank at least once, up from 700,000 using food banks in 1991.

♦ The richest 20 per cent of Canadians garnered 40 per cent of pretax income in Canada in 1991, compared with 6 per cent collected by the poorest fifth of the population.

"The time has come for us to seriously examine the question of income distribution," said Lynne Toupin, executive director of the National Anti-Poverty Organization.

"Can we continue to allow rich people to have access to RRSPs at very high limits when you've got kids who are lining up at food banks and kids who are sleeping in shelters?". . .

It [the Coalition] said that even in Canada, where public-health standards rank among the

---

The numbers are similar for children in the United States. Children living in single-parent families are at the highest risk of living in poverty, and many proposals have been made to remedy the situation (Bane and Ellwood, 1989). In particular, there is a need to increase support from absent fathers, improve job training for single mothers, and increase supports other than welfare (such as high quality, low cost daycare).

Children are clearly not to blame for their poverty. Child poverty demonstrates the general error in thinking that poor people have only themselves to blame. The poverty of children does not result from bad values or bad behaviour but from forces beyond their control. About 40 per cent of poor children live with a mother who is divorced, separated or single, for example. They suffer from their parents' inability to find work or stable partners and from the insufficiency of social supports (like free daycare) which would permit them to work.

Since 1981, the greatest increase in numbers of poor children has been among children with two parents (aged 25-44) at home. Their poverty problem is not due to marital breakdown. Like the female lone parents, these parents cannot find work or, if they work, are not paid above the low-income level.

Continued

best in the world, children in poor families start out life with almost twice the chance of dying before their first birthday than the children of wealthier parents.

Later in life, they are more than twice as likely to drop out of school before the age of 18, perpetuating the cycle of disadvantage handed down by their parents that could well be passed along to their own children, the coalition said. . . .

"It's the human deficit we're creating by not addressing the poverty issue."

"You cannot expect children who go to school hungry to learn, to stay in school and to be productive citizens who will fulfill their potential and bring prosperity to Canada. We're not taking care of the generation of the future."

Source: Margaret Philp, "Child poverty rising in Canada, coalition says," *The Globe and Mail,* Thurs., Nov. 25, 1993, p. A8

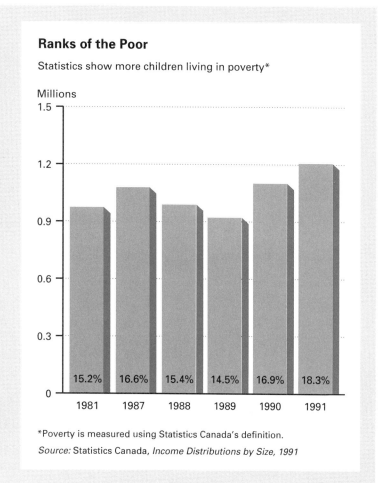

Ranks of the Poor

Statistics show more children living in poverty*

Millions

Year	Percent
1981	15.2%
1987	16.6%
1988	15.4%
1989	14.5%
1990	16.9%
1991	18.3%

*Poverty is measured using Statistics Canada's definition.

Source: Statistics Canada, *Income Distributions by Size, 1991*

Another group making up a significant fraction of the poor in many countries is the homeless. Not only are they poor, this group is unhealthy and suffers from malnutrition and a high incidence of infectious diseases (such as tuberculosis).

The reasons why so many people are homeless in industrial countries have been widely debated. Regrettably, outsiders have little understanding of the lifestyle of the homeless and the poor. Though some groups of people are homeless by choice — for example, Irish tinkers travelling in trailer caravans and New Age gypsies — a larger share of the homeless drifting poor are mentally ill (Kerridge, 1985). Jobless and without income, they squat in vacant or condemned apartments, move from hostel to hostel, or wait without hope in run-down rooming houses.

Observers have suggested that, in the United Kingdom, homelessness is mainly the result of an insufficient housing supply which caused housing costs to skyrocket (Drake, 1989). By definition, if more good, cheap housing were available, fewer people would end up homeless. Yet this misses the main issue, which is the gap between the cost of available housing and the amount of income certain kinds of people can spend on housing.

In undeveloped nations, the causes of homelessness are even more complicated. There, for many people, insufficient food, not homelessness is the most critical problem. In the poorer countries of Latin America live an estimated 25 million street children. Their lives are marked by violence, drug abuse, and prostitution. A variety of solutions have been considered but so far the problem remains unsolved (Lusk, 1989).

In a few developing countries, though, measures are being taken to provide housing which draws on the resources of homeless people themselves. These self-help programs are proving cost-effective and, from them, industrial countries like Canada and the United States could learn better ways of fighting homelessness (Burns, 1988).

Canada and Britain have developed complex social welfare systems, but many homeless people have trouble getting help from them. The United States does even worse, with mainly stopgap measures, such as emergency shelters, which are not intended to solve the problem (Daly, 1989). Comprehensive and, perhaps, long-term services will be needed to deal with the growing numbers of homeless poor.

The culture of poverty

In many cases, the poor are lacking in more than money, jobs and housing. They also lack the skills and cultural capital that are, increasingly, needed in our economy. But people without access to cultural capital and deprived of cultural literacy often have their own distinctive pattern of values, ideas, and behaviours. Anthropologist Oscar Lewis (1961) carried out extensive field research on poor people living in slum communities of Mexico and other less developed countries and found what he called a culture of poverty.

This culture of poverty is the "structure, rationale, and defence mechanisms" of people "who are at the very bottom of the socio-economic scale, the poorest peasants, plantation labourers, and that large heterogeneous mass of small artisans usually referred to as the lumpen proletariat" (Lewis, 1961: xxiv, xxv).

Compared to other cultures, the culture of poverty lacks cultural integration. Perhaps more than any other form of culture we have discussed, it patches together traditional and modern, rural and urban traits. Old beliefs and new practices, ancient superstitions and modern street smarts make up the culture. The people who live in the culture of poverty lack the resources they would need to develop a set of institutions (such as, for example, schools, and community organizations) that would preserve and communicate their culture. (There will be more on this in Chapter 6.) Yet some features of the culture of poverty — like reggae and rap music — catch on with people higher up in the social order.

The culture of poverty reflects the experience of these people as victims of inequality and social change. Important cultural elements include a belief in luck, magic, and destiny. Males learn to show off and take careless risks with their lives. They rarely plan and prepare for the future, and seek excitement and bravado in a life that is otherwise filled with drudgery and deprivation.

The culture of poverty is full of defeats and self-defeating actions. Unfortunately, it steers people away from cultural literacy and a mainstream lifestyle. In this way, it perpetuates victimization and lets the rest of us feel blameless and virtuous in our enjoyment of prosperity.

McAuley and Kremer (1990) describe a poor community in Belfast, Northern Ireland, whose members are out of the mainstream of society. They suffer great poverty and frequent civil disturbance. Consequently, they have constructed a distinctive culture of their own, but this only draws them farther away from the majority of people in the surrounding society. This is typical of a culture of poverty.

Inhabitants of the slums of Rio de Janeiro, Brazil provide another illustration of the same behaviour. They are so far outside the mainstream culture that their relation to others in the neighbourhood is the only social status that matters (Gobbi, 1988). The more people are integrated into their own *favela* (or shantytown), the more isolated they are — socially, culturally and economically — from the urban society they were hoping to enter.

In our own society, the culture of poverty is found among poor urban immigrants, native peoples on reserves, and impoverished groups who have migrated to cities from northern Canada and the Maritimes.

Public attitudes to poverty

These children do not have much cultural capital or cultural literacy. So what will they have to work with as adults?

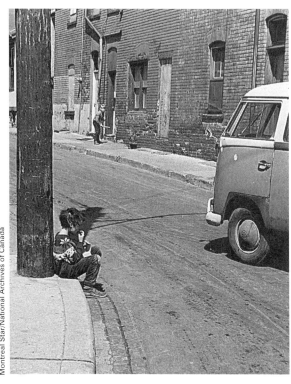

Montreal Star/National Archives of Canada

Public attitudes to inequality are mixed and confused, and so are public attitudes to poverty. People occasionally see themselves as victims of forces beyond their control. They are then willing to believe that poverty resulting from unemployment, old age, or ill health deserves assistance. At other times people see themselves as masters of their own fate. They then hold the poor responsible for their own poverty and feel that these people do not deserve public assistance.

The amount of assistance a province makes available to poor people varies with the perceived causes of poverty. The elderly and the physically disabled receive the most help, since people tend to consider them the blameless "deserving poor." They often consider single mothers and chronically unemployed people the "undeserving poor." As a result, these two groups receive less generous and secure assistance. Social assistance payments to this latter group fail to meet actual living expenses — especially for people who live in large cities like Toronto and Vancouver, where rents are high.

People in countries with undeveloped social security systems have even greater problems. In India, for example, there are estimated to be over one million beggars in the major cities (Pande, 1982). Large-scale migration from the countryside to the city, and a lack of social security for people who cannot find work once they reach the city, contribute to the share of urban poor.

According to Igbinovia (1991), there are three million beggars in Nigeria. There, economic conditions may "precipitate begging," but they are not alone in causing it. Other factors that encourage begging include religious traditions that legitimate the activity and honour people who give money to beggars. Still, the main problems facing Nigerian beggars are poverty, unemployment and a lack of proper training.

In Canada, there are fewer beggars and the problems of poverty, unemployment and worker training are more manageable. Yet many believe that, if social assistance payments exceeded the minimum wage level, unemployed people would be reluctant to get off welfare and take a job, though hundreds of thousands cannot find a job. Throughout the 1980s, the unemployment rate hovered around 10%. In some regions and for some groups the rate has been much higher. Certain groups, such as female lone parents of small children, cannot afford to pay the daycare costs that would allow them to take a job. Others, such as the physically disabled, cannot find a job that fits their abilities.

CLOSING REMARKS

The sociological study of class and status offers another good example of the connection between macro- and micro- perspectives. On the one hand, a class and status (or stratification) system is a macro- phenomenon. Especially for the poor and powerless, it is a world they never made or agreed to, something outside and "above" their control. In this sense, stratification — like culture — is all-encompassing and slow changing: like a huge glacier. By means of laws, dominant ideologies and property rights, stratification systems outlast individuals and even generations of individuals. They press down on the poor and powerless, depriving them of a sense of worth and dignity.

On the other hand, social stratification — like every other element of culture — is a human product. We are all changing or reproducing stratification every day. Practices of social inequality change over time because dozens, then thousands, then millions of us change our way of doing things. In the most dramatic cases, change occurs by means of a revolution — the overthrow of one stratification system and its replacement with another. In less dramatic cases, change occurs through social mobility, protest, and legislative reform.

We began this chapter by noting that, although inequality is a fact of life for all of us, few Canadians are in the habit of thinking much about it. Most just assume that some people are better off financially because they work harder, plan better and stay out of trouble. Poor people, they assume, do the opposite and that's why they're poor. The idea that there is a "stratification system" — a set of impersonal forces beyond our immediate control that shape our life chances — is foreign to most Canadians.

But, however unfamiliar, this idea is basic to understanding Canadian society and the way our own lives fit into the society. Most sociologists would see our place in the stratification system as the most crucial component in our life chances. And as we have seen, the stratification system is much influenced by the economic order, which we discuss separately in Chapter 9.

As for status, we noted earlier the significance gender and ethnicity have for inequality in Canada. Much of the political life of Canada is ethnic politics, and ethnic origins have an impact on both people's status and their economic opportunities. Understanding how ethnicity pervades the structure of Canadian society is the topic of the next chapter.

At Toronto's annual Caribana festival, hundreds of thousands gather to celebrate the warm weather and cultural distinctiveness.

Canada Wide

ETHNIC AND RACE RELATIONS

WORLDWIDE CONFLICT

If you have been watching the news lately, you will know that ethnic and race relations are a major concern around the world. They have become such a major issue that some people argue that ethnic relations are even more contentious than class relations today.

Ethnic or racial conflicts have erupted in nations which, just a few years ago, seemed to have overcome "tribal" divisions. Despite years of "Russification," ethnic conflict played a large part in the death of the Soviet Union. Ethnic conflicts also smoulder in other parts of eastern Europe. They are a life-and-death problem in the former Yugoslavia (where conflicts involve the Serbs, Croats and Muslims) and in Romania (where conflicts involve the Hungarian minority).

Like the former USSR, these countries once had socialist governments that did not accept ethnic loyalties as a legitimate expression of people's identity and feelings. Today, with the current emphasis on democracy and self-determination, many ethnic groups are fighting to define themselves as independent nation-states. And with the release of nationalist sentiments, old conflicts come to the surface once again. No longer contained by force or communist ideology, these conflicts have flared up all over Central and Eastern Europe (Devetak, 1991).

As for racial conflict, despite the recent elimination of its racist system of *apartheid*, South Africa will take a long time to recover from the racial oppression and violence it has created. While the formerly white-controlled state seems to have given blacks equal political rights, many white Afrikaaners oppose ending the traditional racist policies. It is even likely that they have secretly supported the (black) Zulus who have continued to shed African blood.

Other places exploding with ethnic conflict include Ethiopia, India (involving the Sikhs and the Moslem minority), and Sri Lanka (involving the Tamils). The conflict in Sri Lanka illustrates the danger and volatility of ethnic sentiment. It began as a rivalry between elites, then expanded. By appealing to ethnic loyalty, the elites generated intense feeling in the public at large and blew up the conflict into a civil war (Perera, 1990). There are no signs the war will end soon.

These conflicts around the world remind us of how hard it is to establish a peaceful, democratic state, composed of a variety of linguistic, cultural and religious factions. They also suggest the need, in many countries, to explore political arrangements which respect the validity of ethnic differences.

Like everything else in this book, ethnic and race relations can be explored from both a macro- and micro-perspective. Minority people who suffer political and economic discrimination often react by organizing themselves *as groups*. In doing so, they hope to gain political power, change the laws, or gain an economic advantage.

Macrosociologists have made many efforts to construct "models" that explain why ethnic groups mobilize or conflicts occur. They specify the conditions — such as competition, discrimination, and perception of threat — under which an ethnic conflict is likely to explode (Turner, 1986). These models provide a useful starting point for studying contemporary or historical cases of ethnic conflict.

Another aspect of ethnic and race relations is micro-sociological and has to do with the personal experience of minority status. This side is harder to see but no less important.

Taking a micro-approach to race and ethnicity, we ask questions like: What impact does a negative ethnic stereotype have on a person's sense of self? How, for example, will a young Sikh boy respond when classmates ridicule his ceremonial turban and dagger? Or, how does a black (or Chinese or native) person feel about the shortage of role models on television or in politics?

As usual, the major sociological paradigms differ in their approaches to ethnic and race relations. Because of their emphasis on common values, functionalists expected ethnic differences to disappear through assimilation. Today, ethnicity remains important but functionalists argue that its importance is essentially "symbolic" (Parsons, 1975). Ethnic identity is a source of pride, they say, but it has little impact on how we lead our lives.

For their part, symbolic interactionists have emphasized the links between ethnicity and identity. They have also made valuable contributions to our understanding of the way ethnic communities maintain their boundaries (Shaffir, 1974). Feminist sociologists have contributed too, by focusing on the relationships between ethnicity, class and gender. We will touch briefly on their contribution later in this chapter and say more about it in Chapter 7.

But for the most part, Canadian sociologists who have studied ethnicity have emphasized the links between ethnicity and social inequality. They have made primary use of a conflict perspective, so most of this chapter presents ideas and research that take this approach.

THE CONCEPTS OF ETHNICITY AND RACE

The term **ethnicity** refers to characteristics that, taken together, give a group a sense of collective identity and shared history. Such an ethnic identity is likely to develop among people with a distinctive culture, language, religion, or national origin. Thus, an *ethnic group* is a socially defined group. Members feel they are culturally and socially united, and that is also how others regard them. In some cases they may also consider themselves to be biologically united on the basis of a presumed common origin. In other cases they may accept diverse origins but see themselves as culturally united.

In Canada, we measure ethnicity in a variety of ways. When studying ethnicity, researchers usually ask people where their ancestors lived before coming to Canada, what ethnic group they think they belong to, and what language they learned as children or regularly speak at home.

In contrast to "ethnicity," people define a **race** as a group whose members share the same physical characteristics. A race may include members of many social backgrounds and is defined in terms of shared appearance rather than shared history.

Many researchers have used racial categories to divide the human species into distinct physical types. There are from three to over one hundred racial categories based on physical characteristics, depending on who is making the classification. However, these categories are arbitrary. A researcher creates them and, in that way, shapes his or her "findings" with assumptions about the human species.

Interethnic and interracial contacts, including sexual contacts, have been occurring for thousands of years. As a result, racial groups are not genetically pure and racial categories do not reflect genetic realities. In fact, we are all a mixture of races and racial traits. That is why researchers find a wide range of subtly varied racial features among human beings. Skin tones, for example, range through many shades of pale "white" skin into a wider range of dark "white" skin, then into the lighter "brown," "red," and "yellow" skin colours of other "non-white" races. All racial features — shape of head, size of nose, hair texture, and so on — vary continuously in that way.

In the end, a continuum of human types more accurately describes the human species than a categorization of races. In other words, race is a social or cultural reality, not a biological one.

But even though they are not biologically meaningful, group markers carry social meanings and people respond to these markers. If people see themselves, and others see them, as members of an identifiable biological category, then in practice they form a race. Race is real in the sense that its consequences are real. Often people choose their friends and spouses, places of work and residence, even hire employees and elect officials, on the basis of race.

PLURALISM AND THE VERTICAL MOSAIC

Canada has always been a *pluralist* society made up of diverse groups. Some ethnic groups have been eager to keep their distinctive cultural traits, preserve their identity, and remain conscious of who they are and where they came from. Others have been more willing to assimilate. For the most part, Canadian minorities have kept their heritage alive while living among members of the dominant group and members of other ethnic groups. This pluralism grows out of a founding fact of Canadian history: the federation of two distinct cultures, French and English.

Pluralism exists in various forms all around the world. For example, in a small part of southwest China's Szechuan province, there are no fewer than four major ethnic groups. Each defines its identity in relation to neighbouring groups and the state. The groups all see themselves as belonging to the Yi "nationality." However they vary in the ways they express their ethnic heritage and the degree to which they have assimilated with their ethnically dominant Han neighbours (Harrell, 1990).

Increasingly, Canadians have found it useful to distinguish between traditional (or liberal) pluralism and multiculturalism. Traditional pluralism protects the rights of minority individuals through provincial human rights codes and other legislation. By contrast, the new multiculturalism sees each of us as a member of an ethnic or racial group — a representative of the groups we belong to. In this case, it is the group — not the individual —that is to be protected by law.

The difference between these two kinds of pluralism is important. By its nature, traditional pluralism is concerned with civil liberties. But where traditional pluralism would protect individual job-seekers against discrimination, the new multiculturalism would support blanket preferences — employment equity — in the hiring of traditionally discriminated-against groups. Likewise, traditional pluralism would forbid the publication of certain pre-trial information in criminal cases if it threatened the right of the accused to a fair trial. By contrast, the new multiculturalism would categorically oppose the collection or publication of statistics on the ethnic or racial origins of criminals.

In the following discussion we will examine both kinds of pluralism. We will also distinguish among four major categories of ethnic group, each with a distinctive place in Canadian society. These four categories are the native peoples, Charter groups, European ethnics, and visible minorities. Let's briefly consider each one in turn.

The native peoples

Canada's native peoples come from a variety of geographic locales and cultural backgrounds. There are many variations among the groups that make up this population. Perhaps because they have different languages and cultural practices, they have historically thought of themselves as belonging to different ethnic groups.

The variations are partly a result of living in different physical environments: forests *versus* plains *versus* coastal regions, for example. As well, **band** and **reserve** sizes differ greatly from one group to another, and from one region to another. The average reserve (or settlement) in Ontario is about ten times the size of a reserve in British Columbia. Geographic distance and language differences have reinforced the cultural differences between groups. Historically, political, economic, and military conflicts — even wars — have increased the differences even more.

Today we can divide Canada's native peoples into three main groups: Indians, Eskimos, and Métis. Each of these groups includes several subgroups.

The first main group are *registered* or *status* Indians, who belong to bands. They fall under the jurisdiction of the Indian Act. If they lack band membership, they are registered with the Department of Indian Affairs and Northern Development. About 70% of Canada's roughly 500,000 status Indians live on one of nearly 2,300 reserves. Most of the remaining 30% have migrated to cities, in hopes of better economic opportunities.

A subgroup of native people, *non-status* Indians, lost their Indian status through marriage to non-Indians or as the children of such marriages. There were fewer than 100,000 such Indians in the Canadian Census of 1991 and many do not live on reserves. Bill C-31, passed in 1985 by the federal government, allows some non-status Indians to regain their status. So far, about 70,000 have done so.

A second main group, the Eskimo people, include the Inuvialuit of the western Arctic and the Inuit of the eastern Arctic and Labrador. Most of these approximately 15,000 still live in their native communities. Unlike the Indian peoples, they have not moved to large cities in significant numbers.

As Exhibit 6.1 suggests, the Inuit people have a cultural system unlike that of most Canadians. Even their system of reading and writing differs from the dominant Canadian system. At the least, this difference makes it hard for people to communicate across the native- non-native divide.

A third main group, the "Métis," are descendants of the native-French couples who never received registered Indian status. The 1991 Census counted fewer than 100,000 Métis. Most live in small rural communities or among the non-native population of larger communities. Though few live in ethnically separate settlements, the Métis maintain an identity that is distinct from that of Indians and Eskimos.

All three types of native people experience problems we typically associate with Third World conditions. For example, they receive little schooling, and few get a post-secondary education (on barriers to their educational advancement, see Frideres, 1988; Wotherspoon, 1991). They are much more likely than white Canadians to live in poverty and their urban unemployment rates are higher than average. On reserves, many of their homes fail to meet national health and safety standards. Overcrowding is common, so infectious diseases spread in the population. Given these conditions, rates of mortality are much higher than the national average and life expectancy at birth is much lower.

EXHIBIT 6.1   *Most Canadian Inuit still use the syllabics introduced last century by missionaries*

When Andrew Tagak spells his name, he writes a long, graceful row of geometric symbols and squiggles that seem baffling to someone trained in the ABCs.

INUIT SYLLABIC SYMBOLS AND THEIR ENGLISH PHONETIC EQUIVALENTS

△ i	▷ u	◁ a	
Λ pi	⋗ pu	⋖ pa	‹ p
∩ ti	⊃ tu	⊂ ta	⊂+
P ki	d ku	b ka	b k
Γ gi	J gu	L ga	L g
Γ mi	⌐ mu	L ma	L m
σ ni	ᴐ nu	ᴑ na	n
⌐ si	⌐ su	⌐ sa	s
⌐ li	ᴐ lu	⌐ la	l
⌐ ji	⊲ ju	⌐ ja	j
⊿ vi	⊋ vu	⊲ va	v
∩ ri	P ru	⊃ ra	r
⊲P qi	⊲d qu	⊲b qa	⊲b q
⌐ ngi	ᴐ ngu	∟ nga	ng

⌐ ↓i	⌐ ↓u	⌐ ↓a

SOME MODERN ADDITIONS TO INUKTITUT
(in roman orthography)

English	Inuktitut	Meaning literally
computer	qaritaujaq	like a brain
satellite	qangatatitausimajuq	an item raised to the heavens
fax	sukatunik titraut	fast letters
ozone layer	sikajuap igalavja	covering for the Earth
HIV	anamaijautiqarunituq	No longer having any good warriors in the body to fight bad infection

Like his Inuit forebears, he writes in syllabics, a system introduced to the treeless shores of Baffin Island by Anglican missionary James Peck in 1876. Missionaries before him devised it as a quick way to teach Canada's Inuit to read the Bible. To this day, syllabics, and not the Roman orthography used for the English alphabet, remain the most popular way to transcribe Inuktitut, the language of the Inuit. . . .

There is no question that Inuktitut is thriving in the Eastern and Central Arctic. New words are added to the language each year and most Inuit children are conversant in it.

But [Inuit leader] Mr. Amagoalik points out that the Inuit in Greenland, Alaska and Labrador use Roman orthography. As a result, he says, the syllabics system isolates Inuit in the Northwest Territories and complicates the task of creating an Inuit culture that transcends national boundaries.

Inuit children must learn both the English alphabet and syllabics to get through school. Mr. Amagoalik believes this is a needless and intellectually taxing complication for younger generations of Inuit, whose success in graduating from Grade 12 is well below the national average.

Since a system already exists for writing Inuktitut using the letters of Roman orthography, Mr. Amagoalik says, it should be used. This, he believes, will simplify the process of building the linguistic bridge between the English and Inuit worlds. . . .

Mary Wilman, an Inuk who is a senior administrator for the Northwest Territories government. . . believes that the syllabics are now an integral part of the modern Inuit culture. The system must be retained, she says, to preserve pronunciation and retain contact with elders who can only read the writing system the missionaries gave them a century before. . . .

Source: Miro Cernetig, "The Inuit script their future," *The Globe and Mail*, Wed., Aug. 4, 1993, p. A9

Because they are less likely to survive into old age, native peoples are much more likely than average to die of infectious (especially respiratory and gastro-intestinal) diseases, or from accidents, poisoning and violence. They are less likely than other Canadians to die of chronic diseases, cancer or stroke. Native peoples also have the highest alcoholism, suicide, and crime rates in Canada.

Federal and provincial authorities have tried to deal with the problems facing native people. For example, the federal government provides a range of services at almost no cost to the native peoples. But, for the most part, these efforts have not been successful. In return for the "handouts" they get, the native peoples pay a high social cost: especially, little respect from the dominant society and little control over their own lives. As well, they encounter barriers that others do not. For example, because they don't own property on the reserves, they don't pay property taxes. But they also cannot obtain mortgages and business loans.

Many natives believe that Canadian governments have little commitment to solving their problems, and little idea of how to go about doing so. This is one reason that many native people are set on pursuing self-government. The blockades Mohawk Warriors built at Oka, Quebec, in the summer of 1990, dramatized this sentiment. Many native peoples feel they must take charge of their own lives if they are to improve their life chances. Despite the apparent benevolence of governments, native peoples cannot forget a long record of conquest, trickery, and betrayal. By the active role they have played in recent constitutional discussions, native people have shown that they will not remain the victims of paternalism and neglect.

The Charter Groups: English and French Canadians

The term **Charter Groups** denotes the important status British and French groups have in Canadian society. It is a status that makes them politically, economically, and socially dominant over everyone else. The source of this status is historical: *Charter Groups* are groups which initially conquer and colonize a land. They set up the institutions and rules which serve as a framework for the new society. Conquered groups, like the native people, and those who immigrate after the period of conquest is ended, are expected to go along with these arrangements.

Both British and French Charter Groups shaped Canada's institutions during the country's first century of nationhood. However, their influence over Canadian society has declined as their numbers have dropped. Since 1871, the fraction claiming British (that is, English, Scottish, Welsh, or Irish) origin has dropped continuously, from about 60% to less than 40% today. The fraction claiming French origin has remained almost constant at 30%. This means that about one-third of Canada's current population has ethnic origins that are *neither* French nor British.

Though they now represent a smaller fraction of the population, Charter Group members remain dominant for several reasons. One is that Canada's other ethnic groups have spread themselves unevenly (and sometimes thinly) throughout the nation. By contrast, most of the French Canadian population is in Quebec, where they make up over 80% of the population. In Quebec, the numerical majority has given French Canadians control over the provincial government and allowed them to take steps to ensure their political, economic, and cultural domination.

Quebec's motto of *Je me souviens* ("I remember") reflects both French Canada's history and its social agenda. What Canadians of French descent

French- and English-Canadian views of what happened on the Plains of Abraham—the historical significance of a battle over 200 years ago—continue to haunt Canadian Confederation. (Above: The Death of General Wolfe by Benjamin West; below: Mort de Montcalm, engraving by Maret, based on the design by Resfontaines.)

Public Archives of Canada

Public Archives of Canada

remember is that, in their opinion, almost all of Canada was once theirs. Today, many French Canadians feel threatened by a decrease in their numbers. They want to ensure that they win the political and cultural rights to which they feel entitled: thus, the continued strength of sovereigntist movements in Quebec.

Like native peoples and British Canadians, French Canadians do not really consider themselves an ethnic group so much as a national group. Many feel Quebec is their country. A large minority does *not* want to remain a part of Canada. But if they are to remain, Quebecers believe that it must be as equal partners in a state uniting two nations, one of them French Canadian.

Other countries have pluralistic arrangements that are like Canada's. Many of these, like Belgium and Sri Lanka, suffer from ethnic conflict. Others, like Guyana, Malaysia and Fiji suffer from less ethnic conflict. Milne (1988) argues that ethnic groups get along peacefully in these latter societies because, although one group is always dominant, the other groups are represented. More important, perhaps, the groups are geographically dispersed, so there are no territorial bases for separation.

Even so, the situation in Fiji and Malaysia may not be as rosy as Milne suggests. Most of the natives want to undo the European colonization which has caused an ethnic crisis. Because of inequalities between the native and immigrant populations, enforced pluralism has not worked. In the end, Fijian and Malay natives lack much interest in creating an ethnically plural society. Efforts to force it on them have backfired, fueling policies aimed at undermining immigrants (Chappell, 1990). So maybe Canada's ethnic conflict is not so unusual after all!

In Canada, British and French Canadians have diligently tried to avoid conflict for 200 years by leading separate lives. Hugh MacLennan dramatized this separation in his aptly named novel *Two Solitudes*.

In Quebec, the contact between British and French Canadians was, for a long time, limited to politics and work (Guindon, 1968). When non-British immigrants began to arrive in Canada after Confederation, this pattern of quiet isolation continued with the new arrivals. To a degree, it still typifies ethnic group relations in Canada.

European ethnics

The settlement of Canada has always reflected the country's changing need for labour power. In periods when the country needed more farmers or workers, the Canadian government made more vigorous efforts to attract immigrants.

Over the last two and a half decades, Canada has accepted immigrants who are unlike the Charter Groups in important ways. In doing so, it was following a "points system" that was guided by economic concerns. However, in the country's early years, there was a preference for people much like the English and French: first for northern (Protestant) Europeans and second for eastern and southern (Catholic) Europeans.

After Confederation, the national government committed itself to strengthening the state against threats of an American invasion. It did this by building a railroad from coast to coast and bringing settlers to the sparsely populated Prairies. In the first decade of this century, about one-and-a-half million immigrants came to Canada. The people Canada gained through immigration more than made up for the number it had lost in the previous four decades, when more people left Canada for the United States than entered it from all sources.

By 1911, large numbers of immigrants from Austria-Hungary, Germany, Russia (including Poland and the Ukraine), and Scandinavia were already living in Canada. A majority had come to Ontario and the Prairies. Most of them lived on farms or in small towns, but even by 1911, over one-third had chosen to live in cities of more than 25,000 people. The lure of city-life would grow throughout the 20th century.

Immigration to Canada slowed between 1914 and 1945 because of two world wars, the Depression of the 1930s, and a decline in the demand for labour. But after the Second World War, immigration entered a new phase. As before, large numbers came from Britain, northern and eastern Europe. As well, throughout the 1950s, '60s, and '70s, vastly increased numbers came from southern Europe: first Italy, then other Mediterranean countries (Greece, Portugal, and Spain). Most of them settled in the rapidly growing cities of central Canada.

Visible minorities

Anxiety about culturally and racially different immigrants had long been a central feature of Canadian life. Nowhere is this clearer than in the head tax imposed on Chinese immigrants in 1885, a tax increased to a forbidding $500 in 1903. An even more explicitly restrictive Chinese Immigration Act was passed in 1923. Until 1947, this Act excluded virtually all new Chinese immigrants.

Today, people of Chinese ancestry have lived in Canada for over a century. Some came from China to work on the Canadian railways and then settled in the West. Because of this, in the first half of this century nearly every small town on the Prairies had a Chinese laundry and a Chinese restaurant (Li, 1982). But it was not until after the Second World War that a repressive immigration act was repealed and the Chinese were made welcome in the country.

Treatment of the Chinese was symptomatic of a general dislike of visible minorities, whether from China, India, Africa, the Pacific islands or the Caribbean. But in the 1970s and '80s non-white immigrants began to pour into Canada. Many Chinese came from Hong Kong, since the 19th century a British colony beside China. As well, for the first time many Asians came from other parts of the British Commonwealth, especially India and Pakistan. By 1980, the numbers of immigrants from Latin America, the Caribbean, and southeast Asia had also increased dramatically.

Many of these people were fleeing poverty, desperate postwar strife or political upheaval. Yet entry into Canada has never been open to all. Canada's policies currently use a "point system" to grade applicants for immigration. Canada has usually put the needs of business and industry first and immigrants have had to bring skills that fit current economic needs. Some immigrants have also brought large amounts of capital, which has earned them a high priority with officials. Only recently have refugees, who are exempt from the point system, entered Canada in larger numbers than other immigrants.

Business needs the skills, hard work and capital of city-dwelling visible minorities. It is this need that has changed Canada's historic preference for white northern Europeans. It seems likely that, in the future, labour requirements will continue to shape Canada's policies. Consequently, immigration will continue to change Canada's ethnic and racial make-up and the country's economic wellbeing will continue to shape immigration policies.

There are few areas of social research which could benefit more from careful, unbiased investigation than the topic of migration. Many people are challenging the wisdom of current policies, some demanding far higher rates of immigration and others, far lower rates. We need reliable research on the consequences of immigration. What happens to immigrants once they come to Canada? Who benefits from high rates and who loses? Also, how have immigrants historically helped the economy? the culture? the country's social life? Uncertainty about the answers to these questions is causing conflict in our race and ethnic relations and a lack of clear official policy.

PATTERNS OF ETHNIC AND RACE RELATIONS

How do the members of different ethnic groups get along with one another in a pluralist society? What rights and duties are given to some and denied to others? Is there a dominant culture? If so, how are the various ethnic groups integrated into that culture?

In a broad sense, we can say that ethnic relations in a society take the form of either assimilation or segregation. Assimilation is a process by which the members of an ethnic group abandon their own social patterns and adopt the dominant patterns. Doing so often results in a growing similarity between the life chances of the minority and those of the dominant group. Thus, the economic and professional characteristics of the two groups become similar. In time, the minority loses itself within the dominant group.

There are various forms of assimilation. *Acculturation* is the process of becoming a member of a new culture — usually the dominant culture. People accomplish this by learning the behaviour, language, customs, values, norms, and roles of that culture. This is only possible if minorities are willing to interact with members of the dominant culture, and vice versa. Acculturation is usually necessary for assimilation to be complete.

Today, the mass media play an important role in this. Television and radio weaken ethnic and cultural identities, by exposing people to similar kinds of external influences. The result is an interesting paradox: as many groups are starting to assert their cultural uniqueness in militant ways, they are becoming more alike than ever before in history. The question is how to satisfy people's needs for cultural distinctiveness while recognizing that, worldwide, people's cultures *are* becoming more similar (Fitzgerald, 1991).

Amalgamation is the process by which different racial or ethnic groups blend in a new cultural mix, with all groups contributing equally. For example, the United States is the product of such an amalgamation. It sees itself as a *melting pot*, where people from many ethnic backgrounds learn to think of themselves as individuals (not members of ethnic groups) and Americans. This illustrates the way the process is supposed to work, though in practice, ethnic identities are as strong in the United States as they are in Canada (Reitz and Breton, 1994)

The opposite process is segregation. Segregation separates two or more groups of people within the same territory. It may be social separation, as when one group avoids interacting with another. Or it may be involuntary physical separation. Here the groups live in separate and distinct geographic areas, whether in ghettoes or in separate but equal neighbourhoods. *Apartheid* in South Africa was an extreme and horrible form of involuntary segregation.

Assimilation and segregation are not the only forms of ethnic group relations. An extreme alternative is genocide, the attempted murder of an entire people. Methods of genocide have included slaughter with bombs, chemical weapons, starvation and gas chambers. In modern history, societies have committed genocide against the Jews, Armenians, Kurds, and Gypsies (Romany), to name a few groups. In the former Yugoslavia, Bosnian Muslims are the recent victims of genocide by the Serbs. So are the Croats, although Serbs see this as revenge for genocide committed against them during the Second World War.

Historically, native peoples of North and South America have also died in large numbers from infectious diseases and mass starvation. But it is unclear whether mass murder was intended.

What we mainly see in Canada is *self-segregation* — separation chosen and practised voluntarily by the members of a given ethnic group. Neither the larger society nor the dominant group imposes it. Groups that separate themselves from the mainstream of society — such as the Hutterites, a rural religious group in western Canada, or the Amish in Ontario — illustrate the process. Many other ethnic groups in Canada practise a less extreme form of self-segregation, too. They participate in the mainstream of Canadian life but also keep their own institutions and culture alive.

As we mentioned earlier, the model for this process has been French Canada. The data in Exhibit 6.2 show that, despite efforts at bilingualism, Quebec and the rest of Canada are becoming more distinct linguistically and culturally. But as the French-English split becomes more blatant and extreme, other cultural and language groups have found a way of combining economic and social assimilation with communal vitality.

EXHIBIT 6.2 *Drifting toward a more French Quebec and a more English rest-of-Canada*

The next time Canadians search for the hot button of language policy, they should desist and remember the lessons of this week's Statistics Canada report on the nation's languages.

Friends who fear that French is taking over outside Quebec, or that French is being shoved down our throats, should take a Valium. About one-third of francophones outside Quebec speak English at home; less than 1 per cent of anglophones speak French at home. This is hardly a harbinger of a French takeover.

Nation-wide, French is slipping slightly, down from 24.7 per cent in 1981 to 23.3 per cent in 1991. Those who fear French outside Quebec take heart: Your enemy is disappearing, albeit slowly.

Quebec friends who go on about the impending doom of French in that province should remember and repeat often one number: 83 per cent. In 1900, 83 per cent of the population of Quebec spoke French; in 1986, 83.1 per cent of the population spoke French; in 1991, 83 per cent of the population spoke French. Menace? Doom? Gloom?

French in Quebec remains robust despite one of the Western world's lowest birth rates. Unilingual anglophones have departed. Only 280,000 of them remain, compared with 432,375 who are bilingual.

The English are learning more French in Quebec. Immigrants, too, are learning somewhat more French. About 37 per cent of them now learn French as their first official language, compared with 28 per cent a decade ago.

If this pattern continues, half the immigrants to Quebec will be learning French before English by the year 2000. The figure may rise even higher if Quebec's policy of encouraging immigration from French-speaking countries pays off. . . .

That 35 per cent of francophones outside Quebec speak French in the home discourages those who had hoped for more French vibrancy outside Quebec. It also confirms Quebec nationalists in their view that French-speaking minorities outside the province are *une cause perdue.*

A fairer interpretation, one previously articulated by demographer Richard Joy, is that slowly, very slowly, Canada is drifting toward a more French Quebec and a more English rest-of-Canada.

Inevitably, if that demographic drift persists, more voices will be raised questioning the application of existing federal language policy, and perhaps fewer voices of impeding doom will be raised in Quebec about the status of French. . . .

Source: "Drifting toward a more French Quebec and a more English rest-of-Canada," *The Globe and Mail*, Thurs., Jan. 14, 1993, p. A18

Elements of ethnic self-segregation

We noted earlier that Canada's ethnic groups are spread unequally throughout the country. For example, many Ukrainian Canadians but few Chinese Canadians live in rural Manitoba. On the other hand, many Chinese Canadians but few Ukrainian Canadians live in downtown Toronto.

This reflects different histories of immigration — what jobs immigrants could find, and where they could find those jobs when they arrived in Canada. It also reflects *chain migration*, the process by which people come to areas where similar, often related, people are already living. Segregation also reflects longstanding preferences. For example, certain groups favour urban over rural life. In Canada, this is the case for visible minorities (excluding native peoples), Jews, Italians, and Greeks. This preference feeds on itself: visible minorities like to live in neighbourhoods made up of people like themselves, so they continue living in cities.

Residential segregation and ethnic identity

Ethnic segregation is as highly developed in Canadian cities as it is in American ones (Balakrishnan, 1976, 1982). Indeed, we can see it all over the world. So the segregation of ethnic and racial groups is not uniquely Canadian. Nor is it recent; sociologists have studied it for generations now. But, in Canada, the extent of ethnic residential segregation — that is, who you live near to and, as a result, who you interact with, befriend and marry (among other things) — is very high in major cities.

Further, it has an enormous impact on people's lives and identities. Consider the results of a study of Toronto's ethnic groups (Breton et al., 1991). Usually, segregation decreases with each passing generation. Groups also segregate themselves less as their social status and schooling increase. But the Toronto Jews are a rarity in both respects: over generations, they have continued to segregate themselves, despite rises in social status.

Residential segregation influences who you get to know. After all, you have to meet someone before you can become a friend or acquaintance. If

It's easy to tell, from signs on doors and windows, what ethnic group predominates in a particular neighbourhood— even, what is the extent of institutional completeness.

Dick Hemingway

you are mainly meeting people of your own ethnic group, these are the people who are likely to become your friends. For similar reasons, segregated people are likely to marry within their own group. Consequently, Toronto Jews are very endogamous (that is, in-marrying). This tendency to marry within the group also persists across generations and it is the factor most important in maintaining the difference between Jewish-, Ukrainian-, Italian- and German-Torontonians.

People who segregate themselves also remain familiar with their ethnic language. In fact, large numbers of Ukrainian-Canadians, Italian-Canadians and Jewish-Canadians keep up their ancestral language. They not only know and use the language, they also encourage their children to learn it. German-Canadians, by contrast, are much less likely to retain their ancestral language.

The economic factors at work in maintaining ethnic identity are important too. When the Jews first settled in Toronto, they suffered from anti-Semitism. Discrimination was as severe as that facing nonwhite immigrants today.

The Jews dealt with this in several ways. First, they entered professions or created businesses which would let them be their own bosses. Even today, many Jews are self-employed. Second, they drummed up business within their own ethnic group, so they wouldn't have to rely on members of other groups. As a result, even today Toronto Jews are much more likely than other people to report that their customers belong to their own ethnic group.

To judge from these data, an ethnic identity flourishes when people surround themselves with others of the same ethnic group, marry them, befriend them, sell to them and buy from them. Under these conditions, it is easy to keep up the traditional ethnic language and customs. And this process reproduces itself. Strong ethnic identities increase the likelihood of continued segregation. It continues to be most typical among recent immigrants, especially in groups characterized by a high degree of what sociologist Raymond Breton (1964) has called institutional completeness.

Institutional completeness

Institutional completeness is a measure of the degree to which an ethnic group provides its members with the services they require through their own institutions. These institutions include churches, schools, banks, and media that are separate from those of the larger society. In a group with strong institutional (or community) completeness, members do not need to depend on "outsiders."

Full community completeness is rare, however. Whether an ethnic group can develop a complete range of institutions depends on many factors. These include the size of the ethnic group, its prosperity, and the ties of friendship, family, and work among group members. Ethnic solidarity and identity are also critical. Not least, community completeness depends on the range of jobs that are available in or near the ethnic community.

In turn, a community's degree of completeness influences the number of members who conduct most of their activities within the ethnic group. Ethnic organizations — schools, daycare centres, camps, churches, business groups, social clubs, mutual aid societies, and credit unions — all give people a chance to meet other group members. They also make people more conscious of their ethnicity and promote group interests.

The kinds of problems immigrants face on arrival in Canada influence the degree of completeness a group develops. Immigrants may be unable to speak English or French. They may be unaccustomed to city life or lack marketable skills and job contacts outside their own community. On the positive side, they may have brought social contacts from their homeland that they can use to develop business and friendship ties here. So new immigrants create a community that plays to their strengths and hides their weaknesses.

This is very important for groups that face serious prejudice in Canada. Living in a community with institutional completeness can protect immigrants from a hostile social environment.

Jews and Chinese in Canada, both victims of prejudice in the past, have historically practised this self-protective strategy. The same is true of East Indian people in South Africa. Over time, many Indians have flourished and become elite businesspeople there (Jithoo, 1985). Like many Canadian Jews and Chinese, they have used family businesses and a strong ethnic community to concentrate their capital. Often, they have put some of their profits back into the community.

Such ethnic groups keep to themselves in separate communities even after the discrimination has diminished or disappeared. The group continues to defend its members against discrimination and pressures to assimilate. It also maintains group cohesion by creating institutions, gaining control of resources, and providing a variety of cultural and social services. The community is self-perpetuating; institutions formed within it create a demand for the services they provide. For example, ethnic schools foster the belief that they provide a better or richer education for their students; they also keep children in contact with others of their own group.

Thus, the mere survival of an ethnic community does not prove that discrimination is occurring. Neither does the absence of an ethnic community prove it is *not* occurring. Some groups which suffer from discrimination have little chance to protect their own interests, despite good reasons to do so. For example, Canadian blacks lack the community completeness that would help them prosper. Because they come from many birthplaces and cultural backgrounds, blacks have been unable to unite to develop common institutions.

Canada's pattern of ethnic pluralism and self-segregation has led sociologists to describe Canada as a "mosaic." And because of the connection between ethnicity and life chances, sociologists have made a close study of Canada's system of ethnic stratification. As we mentioned earlier, the conflict paradigm has played a central role in the ways Canadian sociologists have studied ethnic relations.

ETHNIC STRATIFICATION

Ethnic stratification is a social ranking of people based on ethnicity. In a society that is ethnically stratified, each ethnic group occupies a well-defined status. At the top of the ranking system are people with the power to define which characteristics are most socially desirable. These characteristics are usually their own. Other groups are judged on their similarity to the top group.

Ethnic stratification only occurs in a society whose members attach cultural meanings to physical and ancestral characteristics — to skin colour, hair colour, shape of nose or cheekbones, birthplace or preferred foods and clothing. There is nothing about the characteristics themselves that naturally signals "good" or "bad," "smart" or "dumb," "hardworking" or "lazy." Ethnic stratification exists because people attach meanings to these characteristics and base their behaviour on them.

In Canadian sociology, the study of ethnic stratification took centre-stage when John Porter published his classic work *The Vertical Mosaic* (1965). This view of Canadian society emphasized the historic connection between class inequality and ethnicity.

The discovery that ethnicity and race are part of Canada's stratification system led Porter to describe Canada as a **vertical mosaic**. Since then, that description has become a part of our national identity. A *mosaic* is a pattern made of small, distinct pieces. Sociologically, a mosaic is a society in which members of different ethnic groups are encouraged to retain their distinct identities and cultures.

Porter called Canada a "vertical" mosaic because he found that people's ethnic backgrounds decide their place in the system of inequality. Not all groups have equal access to all sectors of the economy, let alone to the economic and political elites. Porter claimed that Canadian society is stratified along racial and ethnic lines, with the English and French Canadian Charter Groups at the top of the social ladder. Other ethnic groups are ranked according to how closely they resemble Anglo-Saxons, who form the dominant group.

Because of this, Porter argued that you could predict a person's education, income, and job prestige just by knowing his or her ethnic origin. People's life chances were largely determined by their ethnic origins.

As we have already seen, this correlation between ethnicity and social status arose from Canada's pattern of immigration. Certain groups had come to do certain kinds of work: the Ukrainians to farm the Prairies, the Italians to build Canada's cities, and so on. Over time, they and their descendants had remained at the same economic level, even in the same industry. The reason, Porter believed, was discrimination and a lack of educational opportunity.

Though Porter focused on Canada, the same processes have operated in many other countries. For example, we find them in Germany, a country which has received many southern European immigrants over the past few decades. Studies show these immigrants are stratified, with those from southern Europe at the bottom of the social ladder. German companies prefer to hire native German workers, thus keeping immigrants from integrating into the German economy (Kurthen, 1991).

According to Porter, the United States, unlike Canada, has never been a vertical mosaic. It has always sought to be a *melting pot* which would achieve near-total assimilation of its members. There, people considered themselves Americans first and ethnic minorities second, if at all. America has always fought to create a new national identity, not a combination of old identities.

In support of this view, there have been criticisms of the recent American trend toward multicultural education. Critics of the new multiculturalism believe that public education should unify Americans of all cultural backgrounds, not protect and perpetuate ethnic identities (Schlesinger, 1991). People on the other side of the issue attack Eurocentric education and see multilingual and multicultural education as ways of increasing black and Hispanic pride.

For their part, Canadians have always been less certain of their national identity than Americans. By default, ethnic and regional identities have always been important in Canada (see, for example, Bibby, 1992). Yet Porter believed that a modern society should break down ethnic identities by increasing chances for postsecondary education and encouraging minorities to get this education. This is largely why Porter strongly supported the growth of Canada's university and college systems.

In the 1950s and 1960s, most sociologists expected that as educational inequalities diminished, economic inequalities would diminish too. As economic inequalities diminished, ethnic identification would weaken. However, data from many countries cast doubt on this theory.

For example, in Malaysia, educational reformers tried to weaken the link between ethnicity and social status. As in Canada, they hoped that educational expansion would lead to educational equality, and in turn, to more equal incomes. Instead, an expanded educational system *widened* the income gap between native Malays and other groups. This sharpened ethnic tensions — not the result expected, but a common result nonetheless (Selvaratnam, 1988). Typically, economic inequalities *increase* with the spread of higher education. The reason is that educational credentials go mainly to middle-class people. They serve to justify inequalities that already exist in the society.

As well, a higher education is no guarantee that people will give up their ethnic identity. Many upwardly mobile people keep a strong ethnic identity *despite* their higher education and prosperity (Mucha, 1987). The Toronto Jews are an example of a group that does this (Breton et al., 1990). So it is hard to argue that the retention of ethnic identity is temporary. And there is no evidence that more schools will solve the problems of social inequality.

Though ethnic stratification works differently in different countries, most multi-ethnic societies are vertical mosaics, at least for a time. For example, Israel is a multi-ethnic society made up largely of immigrants. Research shows that *within* the Jewish population of that country, the "Charter Group" — Jews who were living in the area before 1948, the time of statehood — are more advantaged than other Jews. The groups arriving in Israel more recently — from Asia, Northern Africa and Eastern Europe — are worse off. Not only are they poorer and less educated, but their investments in higher education do not pay off as well as equal investments by the Charter Group (Tyree, Semyonov and Kraus, 1987).

Some multi-ethnic societies like Nigeria manage to achieve a balance between the dominant group and other groups. They interact strategically to avoid conflict and help ensure economic success. People from the subordinate ethnic groups rarely challenge the dominant Hausa group, even when that means swallowing their own ethnic pride (Ogunnika, 1988).

We may have passed this stage in Canada, with the breakdown of ethnic exclusiveness. Continuing research on the topic has cast serious doubt on Porter's idea that Canada is, from the ethnic standpoint, a "vertical mosaic" (see Exhibit 6.3).

More recent research on ethnic and race relations has gone in one of two directions. Some has focused on racism and racial discrimination, of which we will say more shortly. The rest has focused on the survival of ethnic communities and, within this context, on the role of ethnic identities and politics.

EXHIBIT 6.3   *Is Canada a vertical mosaic?*

Since Porter released his findings on the vertical mosaic in 1965, sociologists have researched every corner of this question. They have done so with better data and more powerful techniques of analysis than Porter had available. As a result, they have drawn different conclusions, summarized by Brym and Fox (1989: 107):

◆ Ethnicity is not a particularly good predictor of either socio-economic status or of mobility.

◆ Ethnic inequality seems to be decreasing over time.

◆ The members of many ethnic groups do experience considerable "net" upward mobility.

◆ The effect of ethnicity on "status attainment" becomes weaker as immigrants become more "acculturated."

Brym and Fox concede that "these generalizations do not hold as strongly for members of some groups — especially some racial minorities — as they do overall." Canada remains a vertical mosaic along racial, if not ethnic lines, then.

Considering how much Canadian society has changed since 1965, we cannot now know if Porter was simply wrong in his analysis of Canadian society or if his analysis was right for the period of time in which it was produced.

ETHNIC COHESION AND SURVIVAL

Language and culture

Why do some ethnic communities survive longer and "better" than others? In a study of ethnic communities in Canada, sociologist Jeffrey Reitz (1980) surveyed ten groups in five Canadian cities. He wanted to discover which factors influence some groups to remain cohesive and others to disappear through the assimilation of their members into mainstream society.

Reitz measured many aspects of people's attachment to their ethnic group. He found that, if you want to know how well an ethnic group is maintaining its community and culture, you must look at patterns of interaction and patterns of language use. These patterns are closely correlated and, what's more, they are both important ways of staying involved in one's ethnic group. They even increase a person's chances of marrying within the group.

Living in an ethnic neighbourhood, although important, is a weaker way of staying involved if you do not speak the ethnic language. That's because people can remain strongly involved even if they move far away from the ethnic community, *if* they keep up their ethnic language use. On the other hand, living near other members increases the chance of using the language and staying involved with other group members, as we saw earlier in this chapter.

Knowing and using the language, then, is key to ethnic cultural survival. So it makes sense that language would play a key part in maintaining the ethnic community. First, the use of a minority language includes only community members and excludes everyone else. In that way, it forms an invisible boundary around the group. This influences patterns of social interaction: who is friends with whom, and how often people interact outside their group. Second, in Canada the opportunity to speak one's native language lessens the pressure on immigrants to assimilate — to learn and use English or French.

Third, as we recall from the chapter on culture, language is a way of viewing the world. Use of the ethnic language maintains ethnic traditions of thinking and acting, and traditional values. It also symbolizes identification with, and loyalty to, those cultural values and ways of thinking. Ancestral language thus helps to define the "self."

A sign of the role that language plays in cultural maintenance is the importance francophones in Quebec attach to the use of French. They are not alone in this concern. Far away, in Mauritius (Africa), groups are quarrelling over the use of Kreol — a dialect that is rarely written — in schools and as the national language. The conflict has mobilized ethnic sentiments and caused problems for ethnic cooperation in this multi-ethnic society (Eriksen, 1990). In both Quebec and Mauritius, we find concerns expressed over the practical and symbolic importance of language.

Not only does language use increase people's ethnic identification. Ethnic identification also increases people's language use, according to a study of Welsh-speaking bilinguals in Wales (Giles and Johnson, 1987). People who feel strongly about their ethnic identity make a point of speaking their ethnic language, as much for symbolic as for practical reasons.

In the United States, rap music provides another interesting example of cultural maintenance through language. Though rap grows out of African traditions and most rappers are black, audiences are often white. This has led to debates over rap as cultural or ethnic property; who "owns" rap, who has a right to "use" it, should it be monopolized by blacks? and so on. As a language, rap is able to cross over ethnic lines, but even as it does so it retains many of its traditional African aspects (Stephens, 1991).

Distinctive symbols and concerns

Language use is only one part — however conspicuous — of a community's effort to maintain a distinctive identity and tradition. Ethnic religion often plays the same role.

Like language use, church attendance is a good predictor of ethnic attachment. A person who attends the ethnic church regularly is likely to live in an ethnic neighbourhood, interact regularly with other members of the group, and use the ethnic language. Like language, religion encodes a system of cultural assumptions about life, the world, and the supernatural. Moreover, attending one church means not attending another: like language use, church attendance draws an invisible boundary around the group.

Involvement in an ethnic religion also shapes people's values and aspirations, thus limiting their assimilation. By limiting their assimilation it contributes to the survival of the ethnic group.

This influence is greatest where ethnic religion is in control of the group's ethnic education, as it is in parochial schools. For example, before the Quiet Revolution of the 1960s, Quebec's Catholic school system played an important part in maintaining a traditional humanistic (not scientific or business-oriented) outlook on life. One result of this was to steer Quebec francophones away from scientific or business careers by limiting their opportunities to do otherwise.

Many other cases show how religion affects ethnic practices. For example, congregations of Filipino, Indonesian and Malaysian Christians in Canada have their own churches, although church authorities are ambivalent about the idea. These separate churches discourage the mixing of ethnic groups, and in this way help to maintain segregation. In the end, the flowering of separate ethnic congregations reflects the ethnic ranking of the wider society and perpetuates inequalities between groups (Nagata, 1987). Contrary to the religion's professed beliefs, being Christian does not significantly encourage social equality, at least not in Canada.

In the former Soviet Union, the government tried to limit ethnic identification to strengthen loyalty to the nation-state. Similarly, it discouraged religious identification and practice. But over the past few decades, religion has crept back into Russian life, promoting a resurgence of ethnic nationalism. In turn, this ethnic and religious nationalism encouraged demands for national self-determination and the overthrow of communism (Warhola, 1991).

So at the least, revived religiosity has strengthened ethnic identity in a significant portion of Russian society and thus helped to overthrow the antireligious communist regime.

Ethnic politics

Many different factors — including religion, language, residential segregation, and in-marriage — help people to retain their ethnic identity and form a boundary around the group. When such factors overlap with political divisions, ethnic groups are likely to compete for control over state institutions and entitlements. Sociologists call this ethnic competition for control "ethnic politics."

In Canada, the existence of Quebec as a mainly-French province has stimulated the practice of ethnic politics throughout the country. However, ethnic politics are not limited to Canada. For example, in Italy's Aosto Valley, ethnic politics are highly developed. There, we find pockets of French, German and Slovene speakers, as well as Italians. These groups differ in their ethnic cohesion and in their degree of political activism.

German-speakers are the most cohesive and active, while French-speakers are least so. The politically active German-speakers of the Italian town of Bolzano have succeeded in getting a law passed that requires everyone to declare their ethnic origin. In turn, these data control people's access to jobs, low-rent housing, and public services. The respective groups receive no more or less than their proper share of the resources. Some would view this as progressive and fair. But researchers Canestrini and Basso (1989) believe it denies respect for the individual and puts too much emphasis on the rights of the group.

In Canada, we find similar sentiments: groups are very protective of their rights. Beyond that, ethnic groups with strong community completeness, like the Hutterites we spoke of earlier, are almost self-sufficient. Often, members of such groups interact with members of other groups only through their communal leaders. Even groups that are less self-sufficient often delegate to leaders the responsibility for *political* contact with other ethnic groups. This can lead to problems.

Think about it for a moment. Just imagine a society in which there were (say) three of everything: three primary school systems, three college and university systems, three public broadcasting systems, three banking systems, three public service unions, three charitable organizations like the United Way, three Boy Scouts organizations, and so on. If you have been able to imagine this, you are coming close to imagining Holland, with its three parallel structures (for Catholics, Protestants and nonbelievers). In fact, Holland is more complex than that (Goudsblom, 1967). So is Canada.

In Canada, not only do we find parallel systems based on religion. We also find parallel systems based on ethnicity; for example, different sets of institutions for Irish, Portuguese, Italian, and Chinese Catholics. Cross-cutting this, we find

Like other Canadian groups that have been oppressed, native peoples have sometimes taken their grievances to the streets.

David Smiley

provincial and federal institutions which increase the separation of these sub-communities.

The degree of parallelism also influences what kinds of matters will become public issues in ethnic communities and what social bargaining will take place. These problems arise because groups often think they are in a *zero-sum* situation, with one ethnic group gaining power only at the expense of another. The greater the parallelism, the more likely it is that ethnic communities will want access to the same resources and rewards, and the greater the threat one community will represent to another. As well, the greater the parallelism, the more conflicts are likely to arise over jurisdiction and the more effort each group will make to capture control of the larger political system.

Sound complicated? It is. The question sociologists ask is, What connects all these parallel structures together into a single country? The answer is ethnic leadership, which plays a central role in Canada's social life. The political process requires that group leaders reach agreements with other leaders. In a society like Canada, made up of many parallel social structures, politics is based on competing ethnic groups and cooperating leaders — what we called in the last chapter "accommodating elites."

In the end, ethnicity has more influence on Canadian politics than class does. People are far more likely to vote for a candidate of their own ethnic group than for a candidate of their income or occupational category. As a result, ethnic leaders can more consistently get community members to vote as a bloc than even union leaders can. This gives ethnic leaders tremendous power. In the struggle for organizational power, people use the networks they have at their disposal.

Community leaders are the main beneficiaries of ethnic parallelism, but they are not the only ones. Members also benefit from belonging to highly organized and powerful ethnic groups.

These comments on ethnic politics apply most to French Canadians in Quebec but, increasingly, they also apply to other well-organized ethnic groups like Italian Canadians, Ukrainian Canadians, Jewish Canadians and, more recently, Chinese Canadians. As their numbers, capital, and community completeness grow, these ethnic groups will become more potent forces in Canadian politics. The political party most skilled at getting the support of ethnic elites has the best chance of winning elections in Canada today.

In many countries besides Canada, politicians have to seek votes across ethnic lines, and often interethnic relations benefit from this need. The process demands political compromises and avoids making any one ethnic group feel left out. So, for example, Malaysia (like Canada) has a potentially volatile ethnic situation. Yet, because of the need to form political alliances across ethnic groups, there is little actual conflict.

At the other extreme is Sri Lanka, where no such compromise occurs and ethnic conflict is widespread (Horowitz, 1989). This could be a valuable lesson for the developing Pacific Island nations we mentioned earlier. Some, like Fiji, have the added problem of trying to reconcile the ideas of Western democracy with the traditional customs and group rights of native people (Hassall, 1991). An effort at political compromise might defuse the situation.

It is easy to see the social, cultural and political benefits groups can gain through self-segregation. However, the flip side of inclusion is exclusion. What one person considers a mere preference for "people like myself" seems like discrimination or even racism to someone else.

PREJUDICE AND DISCRIMINATION

Although many people confuse the two terms, social scientists treat prejudice and discrimination as distinct phenomena. **Prejudice** is a negative, hostile social attitude toward members of another group. All members of the group are assumed to have undesirable qualities because of their group membership. **Discrimination** refers to actions carried out against another person or group because of his or her group membership. In particular, it is the denial of opportunities that people would grant to equally qualified members of their own group.

An important element in prejudice is the use of stereotypes — fixed mental images that prejudiced people believe typify members of a given group. When we make use of stereotypes, we categorize people without regard to their unique characteristics.

For example, one study (Rainville and McCormick, 1977) compared the ways American sportscasters report the achievements of white and black football players. It found that white television announcers criticize black NFL players more and praise them less than they do white players with similar abilities, playing the same positions. The commentators also describe black players more often as targets of aggression and white players as initiators. Finally, they portray the white players as more intelligent than the black players. By inference, the choices and tactics of black players are determined by instinct or luck, for which they deserve no credit.

These findings may be outdated by now; we certainly hope so. But note the salient features of these findings, for they are found in all cases of racial prejudice. Typically, prejudiced views are negative views based on *hidden assumptions* about the way race is related to intelligence, morality or other valued qualities. Sometimes these views are even worded like praise, as in "Jewish accountants *really* know how to juggle the books" or "Black boxers *really* can take a lot of punishment" or "French Canadian women are *really* hot."

Most stereotypes *are* both prejudiced and prejudicial. They legitimate our prejudices against racial and ethnic minorities, giving them shape and order. In doing so they justify prejudice. There is no clearer evidence of the harmfulness of prejudice than the effect of Naziism's anti-Semitic policies on Germany itself. In the 1930s and 1940s, German society made huge sacrifices to carry out its racist policies. Leaving aside the moral issue, this was money, time, and effort that would have been better spent improving the lives of average Germans.

Racist prejudice destroyed the German universities, fine arts, professional, scientific and engineering capabilities, and even Germany's business community and civil service. This was all part of the effort to keep non-Aryans out of public life. Germany and the Germans had to pay a heavy price for their prejudice, and most Germans have learned the folly of racism from that experience. Unfortunately, a violent minority continues to threaten and harm visible minorities (such as Turkish "guest-workers" and Asian refugees).

Social distance

Stereotypes aside, prejudice is also likely to express itself in **social distance**. This is a reserve placed on interactions between people who belong to groups ranked as superior and inferior in status. The differences in status that create a social distance may be based on class, race or ethnicity, or on one of many authority relationships (doctor-patient or teacher-student, for example).

All socially "distant" relationships are unequal. They are governed by norms and expectations about the way superiors and inferiors should relate to one another. So, if such relations do become intimate, they still oblige participants to keep their "proper place."

In race and ethnic relations, fear, suspicion, and hostility often accompany social distance. E.S. Bogardus (1959) developed the most commonly used measure of social distance. It asks people to say to which steps on the following scale of intimacy they would admit members of various ethnic and racial groups:

(1) to close kinship by marriage
(2) to my club as personal chums
(3) to my street as neighbours
(4) to employment in my occupation
(5) to citizenship in my country
(6) as visitors only to my country
(7) would exclude from my country

Research using this procedure has found that people of different income, regional, educational, occupational, and even ethnic groups show similar patterns of preference in rating other groups. In the United States, the most acceptable groups — those granted the least distance on average, or considered equals — are most like the dominant white, Anglo-Saxon group; namely, the (white) English and (white) Canadians. Most people would accept them as citizens, neighbours, even family members. At the other extreme, white respondents have put Hindus, Turks, and blacks at the greatest distance, on average.

In a similar Canadian study (Mackie, 1974), Albertans put "Canadians," (meaning WASPs), British, and Americans at the least social distance. Northern Europeans and French Canadians followed closely, then eastern Europeans. At the bottom of the ranking were visible minorities — in descending order, Chinese, Japanese, West Indians, Eskimos, East Indians, native Indians, and Métis. On average, respondents wanted twice as much social distance from the visible minorities as they did from "Canadians."

The results vary depending on who is doing the rating. People will typically rate members of their own group higher on the list, according them less social distance, than people outside the group would do. For a minority group to conform to dominant views does not mean a rejection of its own ethnic group (Mackie, 1974: 125.)

Yet conformity to dominant views proves the power of socialization to impose similar values and perceptions on all of us, whatever our ethnic or racial background. As a result, measures of social distance confirm other measures of prejudice and stereotyping. We prefer being close to others who possess the qualities we idealize (if not possess).

They also reflect past experiences of intimacy: we prefer to be close to people we have been close to before. Conversely, we avoid people we have had little contact with in the past. For example, Australians show the largest social distance to ethnic groups which immigrated most recently; notably, the Vietnamese. They show the least social distance from ethnic groups which immigrated longest ago; that is, Europeans. Asians, Indians and Middle Eastern peoples score between these extremes on the distance measure (McAllister and Moore, 1991).

So people we have not been with — people we scarcely know — are not people we want to imagine being close to. Because of this association between social distance and familiarity, many believe that we can reduce social distance and stereotypes by getting people to learn more about other ethnic groups. It is hard to hold fanciful ideas when you have good information about the ways people actually behave (Hagendoorn and Kleinpenning, 1991). In support of this view, a study of black Ethiopian immigrants to Israel showed that the more contact a person had with the newcomers, the less social distance that person wanted from them. Therefore, ignorance *is* a factor in distance ratings (Goldberg and Kirschenbaum, 1989).

However, ignorance is not the only factor influencing social distance. Social distance is also affected by economic elements such as social class. For example, research in Egypt using the Bogardus scale showed that upper-class students want less social distance from (high-status) Westerners and more distance from (lower-status) Arabs. By contrast, lower-class Egyptian students are averse to outsiders and want less social distance from Arabs (Sell, 1990). In many cases, creating ethnic boundaries and keeping another group socially distant is part of an effort to protect against other (possibly hostile) groups and to counteract assimilation.

In North America, there is considerable tolerance for cultural and social diversity. The good news is that, in the last 65 years or so, research has found a (roughly) 50% reduction in the average social distance that people say they want to maintain. Everyone is getting closer to everyone else and even the distance between whites and visible minorities is much less than it once was.

Discrimination

Prejudice is the outcome of many different factors and it may be inevitable. What's more, prejudice may even be tolerable if it does not become discrimination. As human beings, we all like some people and dislike others. We feel drawn to some people and repulsed by others, often with no good reason. This happens even among our neighbours, school friends and relatives.

So, for example, there has historically been a subtle stereotyping of blondes in our society. On the one hand there is the idea that blondes have more fun (and *are* more fun)! Alongside this, there is the notion of the female "dumb blonde." She is either unintelligent or keeps her intelligence from showing, in the interests of good relations with men. Exhibit 6.4 shows that, in some societies where natural blondes are particularly rare, these ideas may be taken to extremes that are both racist and sexist.

A problem only arises when we transform our feelings and attitudes into action, as for example, when a teacher gives a student he or she does not like an unwarranted lower grade. That is discrimination.

Discrimination takes a variety of forms: job segregation, unequal pay for equal work, or denial of promotion. It is hard to measure the direct effects of discrimination, as they are often subtle. However, we can usually show that the members of some ethnic and racial groups have advantages over the members of others. When people with the same qualifications receive different rewards for doing the same work, we can claim that, logically, discrimination exists.

Nazism destroyed Germany and much of the rest of the world in this century. Neo-nazism is now, once again, threatening the peace and security of minority peoples.

Reuters/Bettmann

EXHIBIT 6.4   *Success-seeking women are dyeing to be blonde*

Regininha Sousa used to consider herself underprivileged because she was born a brunette in Brazil.

But last year the 23-year-old go-go dancer and model took charge of her life. She changed her name and, more important, her hair colour.

"Ever since I became a blonde, I feel like a more complete woman. I feel more sensual, more Sharon Stone," she says, toying with her fake blond tresses and sipping mineral water in a trendy Ipanema bar. . . .

"Below the equator blondes gain a fascinating quality that they would never have in Europe or North America. They become a symbol of purity and paradise," says Fausto Fawcett, a Rio writer and professional bohemian who hosts a late-night television show called *Basic Instinct*.

Mr. Fawcett's program is popular in Brazil because it features several scantily clad blond women dancing and posing while the host recites his poetry about — what else? — blondes. . . .

Despite the popularity of *Basic Instinct* and Xuxa [an entertainer], many in Brazil say the fixation with blond women is sexist and even racist. Black activist Cristina Rodrigues goes so far as to say that the country's fascination with light-skinned blondes is a major symptom of racism. . . .

"People want to be blond and white in Brazil because it is a symbol of power and wealth," says Ms. Rodrigues, a member of the black cultural and social activist group Olodum. . . .

"In Brazil, nobody wants to be black because the mass media equates black with poor and stupid," says Ms. Rodrigues, adding that among the black population there are 53 different words for black. Depending on the shade of their skin, many black or mixed-race Brazilians will classify themselves as "chocolate" or "bon-bon" or "coffee with milk" rather than call themselves black, she says. During the last census in 1991, the federal government launched a nation-wide campaign to encourage black Brazilians to take pride in their roots and count themselves black in the census. . . .

"In a *mestizo* society, the darker people are always stigmatized. The higher you get in Brazilian society, the whiter it is. Ever since the last Brazilian emperor married a blond Austrian woman, the aristocracy has always been very white and very blond," Brazilian anthropologist Roberto Damatta says.

For one of Rio's top hair stylists, Eduardo Meckelburg, the Brazilian fascination with blondes is good for business. At his tony salon in Ipanema, Mr. Meckelburg, known as Dudu to his clients, says that more than 40 per cent of his customers are blond. Of that number only 5 per cent are authentic blondes; the others come in to colour their hair on a regular basis, he says.

"Many women I know became blondes because of my show," says Ms. Sousa, still toying with her fake blond tresses. . . .

Source: Isabel Vincent, "Success-seeking women are dyeing to be blonde," *The Globe and Mail*, Mon., Feb. 7, 1994, pp. A1, A2

It took field experiments by Henry and Ginzberg (1985) to show the *true* extent of job discrimination. In one set of experiments, they sent two job applicants matched with respect to age, sex, education, experience, style of dress, and personality to apply for the same advertised job. The applicants differed in only one respect: race. One was white and the other black. In all, teams of applicants sought a total of 201 jobs in this way.

Some applicants were young male or female students applying for semiskilled or unskilled jobs — waitress, gas station attendant, bus boy, or store clerk — that people might expect them to seek. Other applicants were middle-aged professional actors. Armed with fake résumés, they applied for positions in retail management, sales jobs in prestigious stores, and waiting and hosting jobs in fancy restaurants.

In a second set of experiments, researchers called 237 telephone numbers published in the classified job section of the newspaper and presented themselves as applicants. The jobs they were seeking ranged widely from unskilled up to highly skilled, well-paying jobs. Henry and Ginzberg report that callers phoned each number four times, using different voices. One voice had no discernible accent (it sounded like a white-majority Canadian), the second had a Slavic or Italian accent, the third had a Jamaican-accent, and the fourth had a Pakistani accent (Henry and Ginzberg, 1990: 307.)

Men who did the calling (no women took part in this study) presented themselves as having the same characteristics: same age, education, years of job experience, and so on. As before, the applicants were suited in age and (imaginary) experience for the jobs they were seeking.

With data collected in this way, the researchers created an Index of Discrimination that combined the results of in-person and telephone testing. They found that, in 20 calls, black applicants would be offered 13 interviews yielding one job. By contrast, in 20 calls, white applicants would be offered 17 interviews yielding three jobs. Henry and Ginzberg conclude that *"The overall Index of Discrimination is therefore three to one.* Whites have three job prospects to every one that blacks have" (*ibid*: 308).

This study and others like it prove that discrimination is not the result of a few bigoted employers. There is a general bias against hiring nonwhites.

No less serious than this blatant and intentional discrimination is what people have called **systemic**, *community*, or *constructive* **discrimination**. This is unintended discrimination that is so deeply embedded in a society's institutions and customs that it is hard to recognize. It shows itself in practices whose legitimacy and "naturalness" we take for granted, and whose underlying assumptions we forget to question.

One example is the height requirement for police officers and fire fighters. Because northern racial and ethnic groups are often taller than southern ones, this rule will unintentionally discriminate against the latter. Taking a height requirement for granted is part of the problem. Once people realize that such a rule is unnecessary — that shorter people can do just as good a job as taller people — the basis for racial discrimination disappears.

Similar problems have arisen with respect to work scheduling. Christians will want to have Sunday off, but orthodox Jews will want Saturday off, and Moslems Friday. A rigid rule that Sunday is the only acceptable Sabbath will eliminate all non-Christian applicants for the job. But often there is no reason for the rule. Once the rule goes, unintended religious discrimination goes too.

Discrimination is harmful in many ways — not least, that it encourages reverse discrimination. Until all institutions are kept from practising discrimination against minorities, minority groups will discriminate in their own favour. As in the past, their best strategy is to rely on community completeness and the formation of subeconomies. But so far, some racial minorities, like the blacks, still have trouble doing this. They continue to lack the wealth, connections, education and community completeness of the Canadians of Jewish, Chinese, Italian, Greek, and Ukrainian bacgrounds.

Like social distance, the problem of discrimination is starting to change for the better. With provincial human rights codes and the federal Charter of Rights in place, the last decade has seen one victory over discrimination after another. Not only ethnic and racial minorities, but women, the elderly, the physically disabled, and homosexuals have all called for protection against direct and systemic discrimination. Almost without exception, the courts have decided in their favour.

RACISM

What is racism?

As we saw in Chapter 2, *ethnocentrism* is a tendency to view the world from the perspective of one's own culture; in effect, to use one's own culture as a measuring stick. Racism is ethnocentrism carried to an extreme — a belief that one's own biological group or race is superior to all the others.

Over the course of human history, there have been many motives for racism. Most often, however, racism has served to justify inequality, whether the inequality is economic, political, or symbolic.

It would comfort us to think that people always have a reason, such as political or economic domination, for their racism. But the case of Nazi Germany showed that racism can be a manifestation of nothing more than irrational, sadistic, violent emotions. There, the claims to be furthering political and economic domination serve as *excuses*, not causes of the racism.

However, conflict theorists argue that unequal racial and ethnic relations are mainly a consequence of economic inequality. As we saw in the last chapter, people have different amounts of money and different access to opportunities for more wealth and power. Because money is a scarce resource, people can only have it by denying it to others. People with the most wealth, prestige, and power — the dominant group — maintain their position through exploitation. To do this in large numbers, some ethnic or racial groups exploit other groups.

But the beneficiaries and exploiters have to justify this inequality so they can feel good about themselves. Enter racism. Racism develops out of a group's need to justify the exploitation of another group. Members of the dominant group ease their consciences by blaming the victim. They blame the misfortunes of the subordinate group on an inferior genetic constitution (laziness, stupidity, aggressiveness, and so on), bad cultural values, or both.

Competition for scarce resources often surfaces as interethnic (or racial) conflict. We can see this in an Australian study of 180 Greek-born people wrongly arrested for welfare fraud. Officials justified their actions by charging the welfare recipients with dishonesty. They claimed dishonesty was natural to Greeks (Kondos, 1992).

People with the most intensely racist feelings are not always the ones to gain most from a system of inequality. Often, they are people who feel they have the most to *lose* should the targets of their racism gain equal status. Swaan (1989) calls this "downward jealousy." Economic competition from minorities poses the greatest threat to low-status members of the dominant cultural group —"white trash" in the southern United States or Afrikaaner farmers in the Transvaal, for example.

Consider the experience of Japanese Canadians on Canada's west coast. In 1941, most Japanese Canadians were taken from coastal British Columbia to isolated interior camps and settlements. Officials gave the excuse that Japanese Canadians, of whom three-quarters had been born in Canada, posed a national security threat during Canada's war with Japan.

Yet there had been ample evidence of hostility towards Japanese Canadians even before the war. Most of the hostility came from people lower down the social scale. Social distance and stereotyping were evident on the west coast even before the First World War. Among the victims were Japanese, Chinese, and East Indian Canadians. The success of Japanese Canadians in fishing, farming, and lumbering threatened the ordinary Canadians they competed with. Anti-Japanese feelings culminated in the Vancouver Race Riots of 1907 (Ujimoto, 1983).

Concerns that the Japanese would take away their jobs led the white Anglo-Saxon majority to press for an agreement with Japan that would limit further immigration to Canada (Baar, 1978). It's against this historic backdrop of competition and dislike that we must understand anti-Japanese actions during the Second World War.

Even where racism does not grow into genocide, recessions produce an insecure economic climate in which domestic workers may think that immigrants are taking jobs away from them. As we have said, racism develops out of a need to justify the exploitation of another group. Unfortunately, it does not disappear after the conditions that produced it disappear. This is because racism's underlying economic rationale is usually hidden. People think social inequality reflects real differences in people's moral values or moral worth. They therefore have trouble thinking differently about the group whose oppression they used to consider natural. For people to turn their backs on racism, they have to deal with guilt about their own past acts of discrimination against other, supposedly inferior groups.

Exhibit 6.5 shows that, in British Columbia, there is evidence that the legal system and the police have historically mistreated native peoples. A recent report calls for a massive overhaul of the system of justice, to ensure that this does not continue. In some instances, this mistreatment has been a result of conscious discrimination. Far more often, it has been a result of unconscious but no less harmful racism.

Ethnic and racial conflict, even serious conflict that includes riots, can have a positive effect. That's because such conflicts finally focus public attention on group relations. In turn, this forces politicians to take action. In the long-term, there are likely to be gains, as happened with race relations in Great Britain (Cashmore, 1990).

Canadians pride themselves on having avoided large-scale race riots of the kind that have occurred in the United States, Britain and other countries. This success, along with the country's formal commitment to multiculturalism, has led many Canadians to assume there is no "race problem" in Canada.

But sociologist Jeffrey Reitz (1988) draws a different conclusion. He argues that, in fact, there *is* a race problem in Canada that is no different, and no less, than that which exists in Britain. This is proven by the identical results obtained in job discrimination research done in the two countries: the data argue that there is no less discrimination against black people in Canada than there is in the United Kingdom.

Reitz cites four factors which are controlling racial conflict today but may disappear in the future, leaving Canada to play out Britain's racial conflicts of several decades earlier. We may be facing the creation of a black underclass of the kind found in the United States (Wilson, 1984). What should we do if Reitz is right? At the very least, we should stop being smug and complacent. We also need to take steps to overcome racial discrimination in the workplace and elsewhere; this may avert the disaster Reitz is projecting. And even if Reitz is wrong, the country has lost nothing by opposing racism: it has simply made good on the promise of multiculturalism.

EXHIBIT 6.5 *Law mistreats natives, judge finds*

A report on the legal system's treatment of natives in the Cariboo-Chilcotin region of British Columbia calls for a far-reaching overhaul of legal institutions.

Written by retired Provincial Court judge Anthony Sarich, the report begins by urging posthumous pardons for five Chilcotin chiefs hanged in 1864 after the massacre of 13 whites in what has become known as the Chilcotin War.

It also issues a detailed prescription for the renovation of a justice system that, from the start, has been foreign to and distrusted by natives.

The report was written after Mr. Sarich heard more than 179 complaints from residents attending hearings of a provincial inquiry that travelled to reserves in the area. Most frequently, the complaints concerned the RCMP, who police the area from six scattered detachments.

Released yesterday by B.C. Attorney-General Colin Gabelmann at the Toosey Reserve outside Williams Lake, the report calls for the creation of native police forces on those reserves that desire them; the selection and training of native peacekeepers in tiny, remote communities that are far from RCMP detachments; and more careful selection and training of RCMP officers for those native communities wishing to retain RCMP services. . . .

Mr. Sarich's report describes members of the 15 Indian bands surrounding the small cities of Williams Lake and Quesnel as "a once proud and independent people" reduced to complete de-pendency, anger and confusion. He blamed a combination of government assimilation policies, bureaucratic interference and segregation on reserves.

He praised the efforts of some RCMP officers but noted that "there emerged a pattern of conduct by some police officers toward native people that ranged from indifference through arrogance and disrespect, to bordering on contempt." . . .

Two historic events underscored the frustrations and distrust among area natives, he said. A simmering resentment still survives among Chilcotin Indians over the hanging of the five chiefs in 1864. Later, Mr. Sarich said, native traditions and family ties were destroyed through children's forced attendance at the St. Joseph's Mission residential school near Williams Lake.

Mr. Sarich said the natives are also confronted by pervasive attitudes based on the Indian Act's premise that native people are incapable of managing their own lives. That premise is ingrained in the non-native community, and among white police officers and reflected in officers' readiness to unquestioningly accept allegations made against natives while keeping a closed mind to anything they raise in answer," Mr. Sarich wrote. "It tends to explain the apparent disrespect for any rights of native people and the aggression and arrogance to which they are often subjected."

Source: Deborah Wilson, "Law mistreats natives, judge finds," *The Globe and Mail*, Fri. Oct. 29, 1993, p. A8

CLOSING REMARKS

Like other topics we have discussed so far, the study of ethnic and race relations offers a good example of the connection between macro- and micro- perspectives. On the one hand, ethnic (and racial) groups are macro-phenomena: large categories of people that exist outside and "above" individuals, in their language, institutions and material artifacts. National identities and customs are slow to change; indeed many civilizations have lasted for thousands of years. Generation after generation is steeped in the traditional wisdom and taught what it means to be a Quebecer, a Jew, a Buddhist, or a black person in a white country.

On the other hand, notions of ethnicity and race are held by all of us. Every day, we reproduce these categories, these ways of thinking and behaving. At all times, we can change or even reject the ideas we have learned about race and ethnicity. As a result, accepted ways of thinking, speaking and behaving change over time. People marry out of their group, change religions, ignore the traditional ways. Slowly the traditions bend and change because dozens, then thousands, then millions of us have re-thought our way of doing things.

As we have seen in this chapter, Canada is a society built on differences. The British and French of North America built the country to preserve their cultures in the face of American influence. From the beginning, ethnicity, language and religion were central to the creation of Canada and to the ways Canadians think about themselves and others. Therefore, it is not surprising that ethnicity became tied into the politics and stratification of the country. The result was a vertical mosaic.

In the next chapter, we look at the third in our trio of major inequalities: gender inequality, and relations between men and women. Increasingly, sociologists believe that we need to see how these various inequalities *combine* to influence people's lives. So, in the next chapter, we shall see how each form of inequality complicates the problems that arise from other forms of inequality.

Dave Starrett

Until recently, life has been a different experience for men and women — whether as husbands and wives, fathers and mothers, sons and daughters, or brothers and sisters.

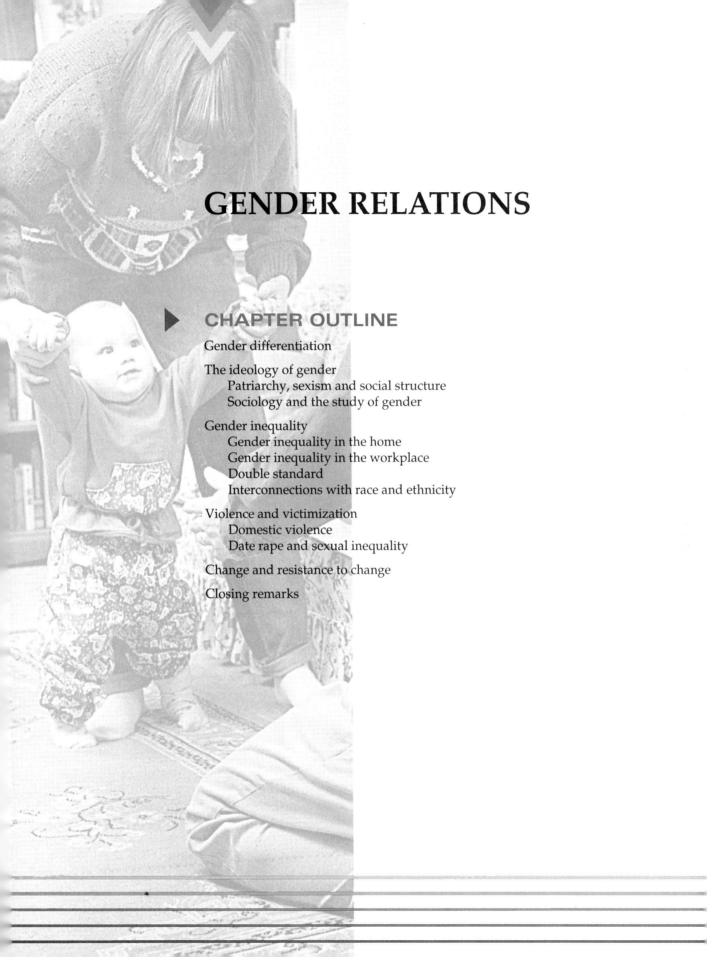

GENDER RELATIONS

GENDER DIFFERENTIATION

As we have seen, Canadian society is split into different class, ethnic and racial groupings. The two previous chapters have shown that the social distinctions which exist among people, whether they are based on class, ethnicity, or race, often have significant effects on their lives. Racial distinctions, for example, can shade over into prejudice and discrimination in the workplace, and may be a factor in determining who are considered suitable friends, dates and marriage partners.

Like class and ethnic distinctions, gender distinctions, too, constitute a system of social differences. Our society is split into gender groupings of males and females. Many of us may feel this distinction is as relevant as, or more relevant than, class, race or ethnicity. At their most trivial, gender differences are pleasant and enjoyable. As the French say, *Vive la différence!*, meaning "How wonderful it is that men and women are different in such delightful ways." But many differences are neither trivial, delightful *nor* funny.

You may not have thought of gender differences as part of a system of inequality. Yet, just as class or ethnic differences set up distinctions which disadvantage some and advantage others, so too do gender differences. Indeed, we can go farther and note that in Canadian society class and ethnic differences are often intertwined with gender differences. For example, women are more likely to be poor than men. This means that failing to take gender sufficiently into account prevents us from getting a complete and accurate picture of poverty in Canada.

This chapter is concerned with the forms gender inequality and gender conflict take in society, and the ways they affect our social relations. But before we get into the substance of this discussion, we need to define some important terms, starting with sex and gender.

Sex is a biological concept. People are male or female from the moment of conception, with biological differences between the sexes that are anatomic, genetic and hormonal. As far as we know, these differences have few (if any) inevitable effects on modern-day social life. Men and women have different reproductive functions, but there is no scientific evidence that there are biologically based psychological differences (such as, for example, a "maternal instinct") between human males and females.

In contrast to biological sex, gender refers to culturally learned notions of masculinity and femininity. Gender roles are learned patterns of behaviour that a society expects of men or women, and they are a pervasive aspect of social life. By masculinity, then, we mean that package of traits that people in our society expect to find in a typical man. By femininity we mean that package of traits people expect to find in a typical woman.

Since gender is learned, gender roles vary from one culture to another. According to Hansen (1986), for example, it was men who dominated domestic service in colonial Zambia. This fact challenges Western views that housework is always low in status and always implies subordination of women. It shows that housework is not everywhere, nor at all times, a woman's activity, nor is housework inherently demeaning. There are historic and cultural reasons why women are at times excluded from domestic service, as they were in colonial Zambia. At other times and places, domestic service comes to be seen as "women's work" — again, for historical and cultural reasons.

In short, beliefs about what males and females are like and how they should behave are not linked to sex in the same way in all societies. Gender is a cultural phenomenon which varies historically and across societies.

Gender roles can also vary within a given society, from one period to another and from one group to another. In our own society, for example, traditional assumptions and beliefs about gender — what we can call the ideology of gender — have never been shared by all segments of society. Before we examine these differences, however, it would be useful to examine the ideology of gender. It has tended to shape traditional views of masculinity and femininity even to this day.

THE IDEOLOGY OF GENDER

A degree of **patriarchy** exists in every society. By patriarchy we mean male dominance over women that has been legitimated, or justified, in the society's system of values. All known societies are patriarchal to some extent. However, the degree and character of inequality between the sexes varies considerably from one society to another. So too does the legitimation of gender inequality. In many societies, legitimation is sacred (based on religious texts and teachings) and in other cases, secular.

In our own culture's gender relations, domination and submission are symbolized in ways that make existing inequalities seem appropriate, even desirable. Men are expected to have more dominant personalities and to play more important economic roles than women. Women are expected to be obedient, nurturing and cooperative, even if this means they will advance more slowly in paid work.

As a result, most people expect women in our culture to be submissive. Even religious teachings put forward this idea. For a woman to behave otherwise is for her to risk being labelled unfeminine or a "bitch." Conversely, people expect men to be dominant. For them to act in a submissive manner is to risk being called a "sissy" or a "wimp."

Common ways of expressing gender inequality are also the least tangible. One way of expressing domination is to assume decision-making powers in a relationship. In a marriage, one spouse may control the way money is spent. In a dating couple, one person may decide how to spend an evening or whether there will be sexual intercourse. In conversation, one person — typically a male — will cut off or break in on the speech of another.

As we saw in an earlier chapter, people learn their gender-based habits of behaviour through *gender socialization*. The socialization process links gender to personal identity — in the form of **gender identity** — and to distinctive activities — in the form of **gender roles**. The major agents of socialization we discussed in Chapter 3 — family, peer groups, schools, and the mass media — all serve to reinforce cultural definitions of masculinity and femininity.

What do we mean by "masculinity" and "femininity"? Consider the very obvious difference between men's and women's interest in football. Men are more likely to play football and watch football games than women, but the difference doesn't end there. Men also use football playing and football watching as an occasion for male-bonding (see Exhibit 7.1). Televised football games model a certain style of male talk and behaviour that one does not see in relation to other popular sports (e.g., baseball, basketball or even hockey). In the end, football is almost the practical definition of *macho* behaviour in our society.

We see a paler version of male-female difference in styles of verbal and non-verbal communication. In conversation, men learn to be more dominant, and to see themselves as more dominant, than women (Gudykunst and Lim,

EXHIBIT 7.1 *Men watching football are a lot like adolescents*

. . . I have just finished reading a fascinating and mind-boggling new book entitled *Why Men Watch Football*, written by a Florida journalist named Bob Andelman. . . .

Andelman interviewed dozens of psychologists, psychiatrists, sociologists, journalists and fans before compiling his 156-page explanation of why men are downright obsessed with watching football.

And Andelman's message is blunt—that football appeals to males largely because it gives them a chance to be separate from females. . . .

[F]ootball provides to a lot of men in this day and age "a place where they are clearly superior and different from women—whereas in all other aspects of our lives there are women moving into positions of power and authority."

Andelman writes: "Men watching games with other men—and without women—creates a masculine space, not unlike an adolescent's tree house."

Of course, the author supplies readers with a boatload of other explanations for why men watch football, such as:

◆ The sheer beauty of the game. . . .
"Baseball is too slow. Basketball is too fast. Hockey and soccer are too confusing. But football stops just enough so we can analyze it and think about it."

◆ Football portrays men the way they are.
"Aggressive, action-oriented, controlling," Andelman writes. "Baseball, on the other hand, portrays men the way we think we once were or that we would like to be: thoughtful, deliberate, patient."

◆ Football has military appeal for men. . . .
"Military games have a lot of appeal to many

men. They involve strategy and calculation; the manipulation of varied components to accomplish a common goal, outsmarting, outwitting, outplaying and outfighting an opponent. . . . Football is a military game with military correlates. It appeals to men on that basis.

◆ Football gives men something to talk about.
"Were it not for football," Andelman writes, "many men would have nothing to talk about.
"Psychologists have observed that women tend to communicate more freely over a vast range of topics, including emotions. Men tend to be more limited in their communication. Sports, particularly football, gives men something to talk about."

◆ Football means great gambling.
"You're never certain of the outcome until the game is well under way," Andelman writes. "The suspense turns men on and makes it easy for sports to be linked to gambling. . . .

◆ Football has a pleasurable kinesthetic stimulation for men. . . .
[M]en who know the game well have this ability to relate to the performers, and as a result, when they are spectating they are likely to have this pleasurable kinesthetic stimulation.". . .
"Fewer females obviously play this game when they are little girls, and that is one factor that explains why men have more interest."

And Andelman has a message for women whose men watch football:
Leave them alone.

Source: Marty York, "Men watching football are a lot like adolescents," *The Globe and Mail*, Thurs., Dec. 23, 1993, p. C8

1985). This gender-based difference extends into all areas of life. For example, male and female doctors exhibit different attitudes towards their patients, and this shows up in the way they communicate. Female doctors are more interested in their relationship with the patient. Male doctors are mainly interested in getting and giving specific information (Hein and Wodak, 1987).

Learned gender differences in communication also show up in our intimate relations. For example, women saw their responses following a miscarriage as different from those of their spouses, and they adopted coping strategies that reflected these differences (Black, 1991). Likewise, the distinct ways men and women behave in a marital conflict are due to a difference in gender roles (Fitzpatrick, 1991). Women often try to talk about the issues that concern them while men prefer to avoid discussing them.

In short, learned patterns of communication create and maintain gender distinctions and reinforce social arrangements between the sexes. Often, they complicate our understanding of what is going on between the sexes. It is as though men and women are speaking two different languages. However, such differences in communication between the sexes are socially created. They need not remain as they are for all time (Epstein, 1986).

Often these differences are maintained by the different positions men and women hold in the occupational structure. For example, research shows that men and women resolve conflicts differently at home and at work, both using more competitive styles at work and more accommodating styles at home. But at work, at any given managerial level, men and women resolve conflicts in the same way (Chusmir and Mills, 1989). They do it the "male way," because that is the only way in which women have been able to achieve promotion in male-dominated workplaces. There are indications that in female-dominated workplaces, women use a more consensual, less hierarchical model (Arliss, 1989-90).

As we have said, several agents of socialization ensure that the sexes learn proper gender characteristics. The most important of these agents are the family, schools, and mass media; each reinforces existing patterns. Gender socialization begins as soon as an infant is born and continues in pre-school and primary school. Young children learn gender identities when they experiment with hair and clothing styles, role-playing games and body decoration, and also by ob-

"Rah, rah! We're the best!" Is that point of view common to all sporting groups, or peculiar to men, whether in sports, business, or war?

Canada Wide

serving others at nursery school or daycare. Their imitative efforts all reflect enormous pressures to conform to assigned gender identities (Cahill, 1989).

Research indicates that men, older people and poor people are the most likely to hold, and teach their children, traditional, gendered attitudes to housework (Lackey, 1989). Other studies routinely show that parents assign more household tasks to daughters than to sons (Sanik and Stafford, 1985). As a result, fathers raising teenage daughters receive more help from their children than fathers who are raising teenage sons (Greif, 1985). The tasks people assign to their sons are more usually "handyman" tasks, not cleaning, childcare or meal preparation (Burns and Homel, 1989). Not surprisingly, children form traditional, gender-based attitudes towards housework before the end of high school (Hansen and Darling, 1985). In this way, they perpetuate age-old stereotypes without being aware of doing so.

Even parents who believe they treat their children equally often treat boys and girls differently. And even the children of parents who reject traditional gender roles are affected by the stereotypes around them. For example, where gender identity, role, and sexual orientation are concerned, the adult daughters of lesbian mothers do not differ from those of heterosexual mothers (Gottman, 1989). Children in these "nontraditional" families learn essentially the same gender attitudes as their peers.

The mass media reinforce traditional gender stereotypes through fictional portrayals of men and women and the use of gender role stereotypes to sell products. So, for example, Fox (1990) analysed 962 advertisements for household appliances appearing in *Ladies Home Journal*. She found that, between 1909 and 1980, advertisers continued to urge women to "serve" their families. Their ads glorified household products by suggesting they would make housework easier or less boring. They also raised the status of housework, in this way motivating women to engage in housework.

Media images of gender roles still influence children, who end up holding stereotyped ideas of male and female behaviour. So, for example, when asked to write stories on any topic, students aged 9 to 16 show strong evidence of media influenced sex-role stereotyping. They depict men in a variety of occupations, using violent means to resolve conflict. Women are portrayed in more traditional female roles, are less active, and use less violence (Peirce and Edwards, 1988).

Patriarchy, sexism, and social structure

We typically think of patriarchy as belonging to social structures of the past. But, even today, some governments participate in prolonging patriarchy. Iran and Pakistan, for example, both have patriarchal family systems supported by the state. These countries provide examples of instances where partial modernization has worsened women's position. Members of traditional groups, fearing that development may cause them to lose their cultural identity, call for the restoration of women to their "proper place" and press for a return to patriarchy. Men in much of the Islamic world support traditional family and marital laws because these laws strengthen their own power (Moghadam, 1992).

There were many other examples of state support for patriarchy in the past. During the early part of this century, British colonial rulers in Zimbabwe (then Rhodesia) adopted measures which liberated women to some degree. They limited bridewealth and prohibited child marriage and the marriage of women without their consent. But these laws undermined the traditional structures of authority. A resulting crisis of authority in the rural areas forced state officials to reconsider their actions.

By the 1920s, a backlash against women's emancipation was underway. Colonial state administrators and African patriarchs worked together to re-assert control over African women. As it happens, they failed. It proved impossible to keep women from escaping to European mission stations, farming and mining compounds and African urban areas (Schmidt, 1990). In Zimbabwe, as elsewhere, it has proved less and less possible to force women back into traditional subordination.

What is particularly interesting about gender relations in developing countries is that there is often a conflict between longstanding traditions and the dynamics of a newly modernizing society. Some aspects of women's status change rapidly while others change slowly or not at all. For example, in Iran, development is improving women's access to education and health care but not their opportunities to earn an income. A social status like gender is multi-dimensional and development affects different dimensions at different rates (Aghajanian, 1991). Gender role differences continue to exist in North America, and they are expressed both in learned personality traits and in the division of labour. The socio-economic conditions which supported patriarchy have largely disappeared from industrial societies. However male dominance continues to be defended by sexism, just as racial dominance is defended by racism. "Sexism," like other ideologies, is a belief system that upholds the status quo, yet it carries important costs and consequences. For example, traditional sex roles prevent part of the population from playing an effective part in the economy. They also have undesirable social and psychological effects on both men and women.

Many women, as well as men, believe sexual inequalities are rooted in biology. In this respect, some women contribute to their own subordination. Like men, women are socialized to accept sexist ideologies. As we grow up, we learn to play our social roles reasonably effectively. The process of socialization teaches us how and why to conform to cultural values and social norms. But socialization also teaches us how *not* to function in our social roles.

Gender socialization has the effect of controlling access to rewards and opportunities by discouraging women from competing for the rewards everyone desires. As a result, many women don't think of themselves as able to compete.

This may explain the small proportion of Canadian women who enter engineering, a traditionally male field of work. In fact, women's chances of getting an engineering degree, compared to men's, are six times greater in Belgium than in Canada (see Exhibit 7.2).

Nevertheless, it would be incorrect to say that all women have accepted the traditional ideology of gender found in our society. The traditional belief that a woman should stay home to look after her children has never been shared by everyone.

In fact, hundreds of thousands of immigrant women in Canada and the United States worked long hours in sweatshops and basement factories in order to support themselves and their families (Glenn, 1989).They did so out of necessity, but without any sense of guilt about violating the ideology. Many others have worked as domestics. In their case, neither the homes they have worked in nor the children they have looked after were their own. As for the notion

EXHIBIT 7.2 *Still male-dominated*

The low number of women engineering graduates in Canada is the subject of considerable debate. Some say it is because the engineers' culture is hopelessly macho. Others blame it on socialization and schooling.

Most countries face the same dilemma—although many to a lesser degree than Canada. The chart displays the five major industrialized countries with the largest proportion of university graduates awarded engineering degrees. Percentages are expressed in terms of gender, and compared with Canada's numbers. Throughout the industrial world, an average of 3.5 per cent of female university graduates are engineers, compared with 20.4 per cent of male graduates.

Canada's overall performance in graduating engineers is quite low. But we do relatively well getting students into post-secondary education—30 per cent of the working-age population has some such training. Students here have a greater access to liberal arts programs than in many places.

Source: "Still male-dominated," The Globe and Mail, Tues., Oct. 12, 1993, p. B18, Canadian Social Trends (Statistics Canada).

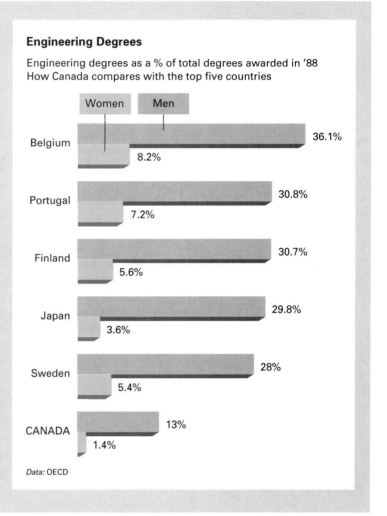

Engineering Degrees

Engineering degrees as a % of total degrees awarded in '88
How Canada compares with the top five countries

Women   Men

Belgium   36.1%
8.2%

Portugal   30.8%
7.2%

Finland   30.7%
5.6%

Japan   29.8%
3.6%

Sweden   28%
5.4%

CANADA   13%
1.4%

Data: OECD

that women should be passive and subservient, this has been rejected by many, too. We can point to the important role women played in organizing unions and struggling to obtain basic rights and decent working conditions (Glen, 1990). In all of these instances, the traditional views of womanhood lost their hold when women organized to oppose them.

Since they are cultural in origin, traditional ideas about the value of males versus females can change. An example is parents' preferences for male children. Whereas parents at one time preferred to have male children, research (Chen and Balakrishnan, 1990) suggests that, today, most Canadian parents care little whether their children are boys or girls. In fact, they prefer a mixture of boys and girls, a sign that males and females are equally valued. This is not true everywhere. Americans, for example, continue to express a stronger preference for boys.

In our own society, traditional notions of masculinity and femininity do seem to be breaking down. In addition, consciously designed social or state policies have altered gender roles in many other societies. As a result, women today are, in many respects, acting in ways people would have considered "unfeminine" a mere generation or two ago.

Consider just two examples of this. Forty years ago, few women supervised men at work. Those women who did supervise men ran a two-sided risk. If they were less assertive than male supervisors — that is, "ladylike" by traditional standards — their subordinates might ignore or ridicule them. If they were just as assertive as male supervisors, they risked being labelled unfeminine. People assumed they were hostile to men or would use their authority in unfair and cruel ways. Women supervisors in such a situation faced problems male supervisors did not and had to decide, very carefully, how to handle these problems.

Likewise, forty years ago, few women were sexually active much before they were engaged or married. Men were much more sexually active before marriage. A "double standard" existed, about which we will say more later. Here too, unmarried women ran a two-sided risk. If they resisted male sexual advances too vigorously, they might be labelled "frigid" and not be asked out on dates. If they did not resist male sexual advances vigorously enough, or even made sexual advances of their own, they might be labelled "easy" or a "tramp." They would be asked out on dates, but not seriously considered for marriage. Again, this was a situation in which women were at a disadvantage compared to men.

Traditional notions of masculinity and femininity are changing almost everywhere to some degree, but such traditional notions remain entrenched in some regions of the world. Parental preference for boys, for example, is still strong in many parts of the world such as India, China and the rest of southeast Asia (Arnold and Zhaoxiang, 1986). In India, parents display their bias by bringing daughters for their first immunization at a significantly later age than sons. They seem to give less thought to the health and well-being of their daughters. Girls also have poorer nutrition than boys, indicating that parents do not feed them as well (Sharma and Sharma, 1991).

Hull (1990) estimates that, every year in China, there are about 500,000 fewer recorded births of girls than we would expect to find, given the Chinese birth rate. A possible reason for this is the one-child policy. It has the unintended consequence of encouraging parents, particularly in rural areas, to abort, murder or conceal girl children so they can legally proceed to bear sons. Sons are preferred because they are considered to be better able to take care of their parents in their old age. As you can see, the combination of government policy and traditional notions about gender pose a danger to the safety of girls and women in China.

There is some evidence of growing equality for women in China. Today, for example, many women aspire to higher education, and they are more active in their communities than were their mothers and grandmothers. But Chinese society still shows a strong preference for sons, and the costs of marriage for women are growing. Rural areas will have to develop socially and economically before these traditional Confucian ideas disappear and women enjoy the same treatment as men (Dai, 1991).

Throughout much of the world, men and women are treated *unequally*. Gender roles — like class, status, race and ethnic roles — are part of the stratification system of a society. That is, in most known societies gender differences give rise to gender inequalities. With few exceptions, men are the advantaged gender and women, the disadvantaged one.

Sociology and the study of gender

Considering how central a role gender plays in society, it may surprise you to learn that sociologists did not pay much attention to gender issues until recently. In part, this was because most sociologists shared the traditional assumptions and stereotypes about gender that characterized Western society. A second reason is that most sociologists, until recently, were males (Ritzer, 1988). As such, they paid less attention to issues related to gender and were less sensitive to the problems women faced.

It is not that male sociologists ignored gender — only that their views of gender roles took for granted the traditional assumptions about gender. Furthermore, the various branches of sociology also made assumptions about the "naturalness" of gender relations, so male sociologists lacked both the interest and detachment needed to address gender issues effectively.

Functionalists, as we have seen, are concerned with how society and its institutions are integrated. As a result, they have tended to ignore gender differences which do not support or contribute to the integration of society. They have seen the different roles assigned to men and women as fulfilling both personal needs for emotional support and social needs for reproduction and child rearing.

This led functionalists such as Talcott Parsons to consider the family as a social institution that was essential to the survival of a society. But from the functionalist point of view, everyone benefits from maintaining a gendered division of labour — a view that few North Americans hold today.

Marxists have tended to consider gender differences in society as less significant than class differences. In that respect, Marxists believe that a male and female worker have more interests in common than a male worker has with a male employer or a female worker with a female employer. Indeed, Marxists see gender differences as largely a consequence of class and property differences.

Friedrich Engels (1962), for example, linked gender stratification to the development of private property. He claimed that capitalism increased male dominance by devaluing women as homemakers working for no pay. In this view, traditional sex roles reflect a conflict of interest between men and women. They will change as women gain more economic power. If, as we shall see, women are more likely than men to be poor, this is because of the capitalist nature of Canadian society. It takes advantage of and exploits those workers who are most vulnerable.

While there is much to be said in favour of this argument, the fact remains that men and women experience the same class positions in different ways. What's more, there is no evidence that class awareness and solidarity lead to greater cooperation between male and female members of the same class. Historically, for example, the Canadian labour union movement has ignored women's concerns and focused on the well-being of men. (This has not occurred everywhere; in Finland, for example, women's interests and union interests went hand-in-hand.)

The other major influence on conflict theory, the work of Max Weber, also shows little interest in or understanding of gender issues. This is particularly surprising because Weber's wife, Marianne Weber, also a sociologist, was *very* interested in gender issues. Perhaps it shows the degree to which male sociologists of the past were unable to free themselves from the fundamental biases about gender that characterized men in their society.

Male interactionists, too, have had difficulty "taking the role" of the female other. One of the most influential of the early interactionists, W. I. Thomas, wrote a book entitled *The Unadjusted Girl* to examine the effects of rapid social change and the breakdown of traditional norms on young women. Notice that Thomas saw these as having negative effects upon women in particular. Girls became "unadjusted" because they no longer had standards to guide them.

Like other sociologists of the period, Thomas saw the family as having a central role in preventing criminal or disorderly behaviour. "In general," Thomas (1967: 150) wrote, "it is true . . . that if you have a good family you do not have a bad individual." There is much to be said about (and in favour of) the family and we say some of it in the next chapter. However, Thomas was wrong to suppose that people's problems — especially, women's problems — could be reduced to family issues.

There have always been *some* women sociologists, such as Harriet Martineau (Hoecker-Drysdale, 1992), who emphasized the significance of gender relations in society. But, until recently, they were few in number and marginal to the mainstream of sociological work. The number of female sociologists began to increase rapidly in the 1970s. This was accompanied by the rise of feminist sociology which, more than any other sociological perspective, is grounded in women's experience of inequality in everyday life. These developments have also meant a greater awareness of the role of gender in society on the part of all sociologists, whether male or female.

In Canada and the rest of the world, the feminist Women's Movement has also been an important force for change. A first and crucial step of the movement was to draw public and academic attention to issues of sexual inequality. Working within formal political organizations and in grass-roots community groups, women have effectively challenged the roots of gendered inequality. But because gender is a foundation of every society, feminism has met with strong resistance everywhere. For example, two-thirds of Americans expressed support for the Equal Rights Amendment. Yet this legislation — first proposed in 1923 — has yet to become part of the U.S. Constitution.

A second wave of feminism, which began in the 1970s, has initiated more thoroughgoing reforms. They include new educational and employment opportunities, protection for women's right to reproductive choice, and freedom from abuse. The 1960s and '70s were a time when many new perspectives and theories were being developed in sociology. Many of these have now either disappeared or been absorbed by the major perspectives. Not so feminism. It remains a vital and developing perspective in sociology because the experience upon which it was founded, gender inequality, remains a reality for most women.

GENDER INEQUALITY

As we have seen throughout this book, other cultures are unlike our own in many respects. However, all societies treat their members unequally — not just differently — according to their sex. What's more, almost all cultures show evidence of men's dominance and women's subordination. Everywhere, men tend to have more access than women to property, prestige and power. Even in the most industrialized countries, women remain under-represented in positions of power and influence.

Gender stratification disadvantages women in a number of ways. For example, most Canadian women are now in the paid labour force. The dramatic increase in women's labour force participation has signalled a major change in gender roles. Yet women still tend to do "women's work." These are jobs that pay less, have lower prestige, and require longer hours of work than jobs in which most workers are men. This is part of what sociologists call a **gendered division of labour**.

A gendered division of labour and inequality in relations between men and women are not necessarily caused by the attitudes held by the particular people involved. Instead, a gendered division of labour is structural. That means it is patterned or built into the expectations and obligations attached to the different roles found in a particular institution.

The example of the work relationship between nurses and doctors may help to make this point clearer. Historically, men have tended to demand and receive more authority than women. This inequality is evident in the ways doctors and nurses relate to one another. By tradition, the nurse has been the "handmaid" of the doctor. The doctor is viewed as the professional who possesses the training, expert knowledge, authority and prestige. The nurse's role is to carry out the doctor's wishes with competence, an attitude of obedience, selflessness, loyalty and total dedication to caring for patients. In short, the nurse serves as an "instrument" or "tool" of the doctor — not as the doctor's co-worker.

Kerr and MacPhail (1991: 21) point out that "sex stereotyped views of nursing emphasize subservience, lack of assertiveness and domination of nurses who are primarily female, by physicians, who are primarily male." From a feminist perspective, nurses form a minority group who are kept powerless by doctors and hospital administrators. The domination of (usually female) nurses by (usually male) doctors and administrators is only one form of a general domination of women in our society.

As we would expect, the occupational domination of women also has economic consequences. For example, a registered nurse makes only about a third as much money as a doctor and half as much as a hospital administrator. Most people do not consider the work of nurses to be as valuable as that of (male) physicians and hospital administrators. Perhaps because most nurses are women, and women are expected to be nurturing, nurses are also expected to settle for low pay and high emotional satisfaction for a job well done. Also, because most of them are women, nurses are often assumed to be working to supplement a husband's income, not working to earn an income in their own right. Because these false ideas about women's work and women's worth persist, women's concerns, financial and otherwise, are viewed by some people as less serious than those of men. And it is not only in the health field that women continue to earn less than men.

As we see, the patterns of gender inequality in the relationship between doctors and nurses are structural. They have nothing to do with the virtues or weaknesses of particular doctors or particular nurses. Rather, they are built into how particular types of organizations "work," how different tasks are valued, and how roles are assigned. An individual doctor may be male or female, sympathetic to the concerns of women or indifferent to those concerns. Nevertheless, hospitals and the practice of medicine are arranged in such a way that nurses are subordinate to doctors. (Some changes do seem to be taking place in the relations between doctors and nurses, an issue we will address a little later on in this chapter.)

Since gender inequality is structured into many sectors of our society, the experience of inequality is common among women. We find the macrosociological patterns of gender relations to be most relevant to people's own microsociological experiences of dealing with one another in two particular areas of everyday life: the family and the workplace. Here, gender inequality takes on special significance.

Moreover, family and work are linked for many women. Whether they work for pay outside the home or not, the home is also a work setting for most women. Additionally, work and the family are often intertwined. A woman's family obligations may affect her ability to work for pay, while work obligations may affect her family relations. We will look at both settings, the family and the workplace, in turn.

Gender inequality in the home

The structure and organization of family life have changed dramatically in the second half of the 20th century. As we noted earlier, family changes and changes in the organization of paid work have had more impact on women than on men. Women have entered the labour force in large numbers. However, many men have not made the parallel shift to assuming an equal responsibility for domestic work. One result is that wives typically have less free time than their husbands and feel overburdened.

Within the household, we usually find a gendered division of labour. Some jobs are done exclusively by women, other jobs exclusively by men, and some jobs are shared or rotated between them. However, studies of domestic labour have found that husbands get more say in financial matters, and take less responsibility for the children and household than their wives. Also, spouses who earn more have more say at home than spouses who earn less, and wives are often the spouses who earn less (Steil and Weltman, 1991).

For the last few decades, most women in the paid labour force have suffered from a double load, double day, second shift, or "social penalty" (e.g., Sinopoloulos, 1990). Names like the "double day" or the "second shift" remind us that, despite a job outside the home, women continue to do (or organize) the largest share of housework and childcare. In the late 1980s, one researcher concluded that 76% of American wives who were employed full time still did most of the housework (Ross, 1987). The situation is even worse in traditional societies. There, avoiding conflict between spouses over the wife's employment status depends on the wife's willingness to accept full responsibility for the housework (Aghajanian, 1988).

There is no doubt that such conditions of domestic inequality continue to prevail in many parts of the world, even in many parts of Canada. However, things are starting to change. For example, Ferree (1991) reports that, in two-earner American couples, husbands and wives are spending equal amounts of time on productive work, though this work is gender-specialized. Whoever does less paid work does more housework, and gendered expectations of the husband and wife determine *who* performs *which* household tasks.

Recent Canadian data (Harvey, Marshall and Frederick, 1991: 27, 32 et passim) lead to a similar conclusion, and another Canadian study (Devereaux, 1993: 14) reports that, in the early 1990s, working women were doing only

12 minutes more of housework than their husbands. This is different from the conditions that held ten years ago. Inequality in domestic work is becoming a thing of the past for many women, to judge from these data. However, another Canadian study (see Exhibit 7.3) shows that women continue to have the main responsibility for most domestic tasks, even though their husbands help out.

Part of the increase in men's housework "is due to the fact that divorced and never-married men are a growing share of all men, and these men are responsible for all their own housework. Husbands and fathers are also spending more time on overall housework. But these increases are primarily in the areas of child care and shopping. . . . Household cleaning has yet to become trendy among married men" (Crispell, 1992: 40).

Trendy or not, men are starting to do a little more around the house. For example, time budget data from the 1960s, 1970s and 1980s reveal an increase in

EXHIBIT 7.3   *Wife still chief cook, bottle washer*

Men may be spending more time doing housework, but women still plan most of it and perform the lion's share of chores in the home, says a Statistics Canada report.

In asking how the responsibility for housework is divided in families with single and dual wage earners, the agency found that housework is shared more equitably as the wife's education and earning power increase, but this does not hold as the number of children increases. The more children in the family, the more the woman takes care of the housework, regardless of her working status.

In the average Canadian family, the woman still prepares the meals, cleans up afterward, and does the cleaning and laundry. Men still perform almost all house maintenance and outside work, such as gardening, but statisticians are quick to point out that these maintenance jobs are largely discretionary and can be delayed, unlike meals and laundry. . . .

The study focused on meal preparation and cleanup, household cleaning, laundry and maintenance because they were the top four labour-intensive jobs. . . .

The survey found that at meal-time, more than 86 per cent of women who either work part-time or not at all do all the preparation, and that more than 72 per cent clean up afterward.

But the numbers drop a little when the woman is a full-time worker. About 72 per cent of women with full-time jobs prepare all the meals, and 59 per cent clean up afterward. . . .

The dual responsibilities for paid work and unpaid housework continue into the area of cleaning and laundry, in which 74 per cent of women with full-time jobs assume most of the work, while 86 per cent of women with part-time or no jobs do all the work. . . .

The major factors that affect how couples share the housework are age, marital status and education. Younger couples — those under 35 — are more likely to share work equally, as are those couples living in common-law arrangements.

Women with higher education were less likely to assume all responsibility for housework, and men with higher educations were most likely to share responsibility for those chores.

Smaller families are more likely to share the work more equitably, the survey found.

In families with only one child, 44 per cent of wives with full-time or part-time jobs had sole responsibility for the housework. That number increased to 50 per cent for families with two children, to 63 per cent with three children, and to 83 per cent with four or more children.

Source: Jack Kapica, "Wife still chief cook, bottle washer," *The Globe and Mail*, Wed., Dec. 22, 1993. pp. A1, A2

Increasingly, men are learning to do the household tasks historically associated with women.

Kathleen Belleisles

men's unpaid housework in the United Kingdom (Gershuny et al., 1986). Time budget data from 1971 and 1981 also reveal a change in men's housework and child care activities in Canada (Douthitt, 1989). In fact, fathers in dual-earner Canadian families appear to be moving from a traditional fatherhood role in which their main responsibility was economic to one in which they contribute to homemaking and caregiving, as well as providing economic support (Lupri, 1988).

We should not be surprised to see such changes. In Western countries spouses depend on each other in making purchasing decisions and in other personal matters. In more patriarchal societies, such as India or Turkey, spouses are not as interdependent. There is far more role segregation and husbands exercise more autonomy in making decisions about certain household expenditures. This contrast provides evidence of progress in our own society (Wagner, Kirchler and Clack, 1990).

Not all husbands or other family members are willing to do their share of domestic work. Some men see housework as women's work and refuse to help out. Wives can try to compel their spouses and children to cooperate more, but that works only up to a point. They can also risk their mental and physical health by working harder. Or they can opt for part-time instead of full-time paid work — especially while their children are young. Many rely increasingly on paid domestic and child-care services (daycare, fast food, house cleaners, and so on). And many others set their aspirations and expectations low and think of what they are doing for pay as a job, not a career.

Evidence suggests that in traditionally male-dominated careers, where women would have the greatest difficulty lowering their aspirations and expectations, women's domestic lives are at risk. Compared with women in traditionally female careers, women in traditionally male careers are less likely to marry. If married, they are less likely to remain married, or, if they remain married, they are less likely to bear children (Marshall, 1987).

It is difficult to have a serious career *and* a serious marriage if you are a woman, since you are expected to carry a full load in both activities. Many women are succeeding at doing just that, but our society provides women with few of the tools — such as universal day care — needed to ease their burden. Men, by contrast, have not been expected to invest as much of themselves in their marriages, at the expense of their careers.

Women who carry a heavy domestic responsibility find it hard to compete effectively with men at work. Moreover, employers expect women to be carrying this domestic responsibility and, therefore, see women as less valuable — since less available — employees. This means that continued gender inequality at home will almost ensure continued gender inequality in the workplace.

Gender inequality in the workplace

At one time, people expected that women would have the primary responsibility of caring for young children and looking after a home. These responsibilities made working women more likely than men to quit paid work and stay home to raise their children. They typically did so during those years when most workers are promoted to positions of authority and build up their salaries through seniority. As a result, many women failed to develop their careers the way men of the same age were able to.

Today, few women quit their work when they have children, though many interrupt it for a maternity leave. Fully 63% of mothers of preschoolers and 70% of mothers of school-age children are employed. Nevertheless, many women find that the old expectations have not disappeared and that their status and needs in the workplace are not treated as seriously as are those of men.

Worldwide, it is hard to determine precise rates of labour force participation by women. That is because much of women's work is done in the informal economy and so it is not officially counted. In 1990, the highest rates of paid economic activity by women were in the former USSR (60%), eastern Asia (59%) and North America (50%). Lowest participation rates were found in Latin America and the Caribbean (32%), southern and western Asia (24% and 21%) and northern Africa (16%) (United Nations, 1991: 84). In Canada, 58% of all Canadian women are in the labour force and they make up 46% of the Canadian paid labour force.

Like the domestic division of labour, occupational segregation is universal. In western societies, women typically work in clerical, service and sales jobs. In Africa and Asia, women typically work in agriculture. It is no accident that these "women's jobs" all have low status and are poorly paid.

Does a "double standard" exist in North America when it comes to hiring, promoting and paying women? Do bosses treat women differently from men? Are women *discriminated* against, becoming victims of a "double standard" in the workplace? These are hard questions to answer.

The average wage of women (across all occupations) is about 68 per cent of what men receive. True, the wage differences are most marked among men and women over the age of 50. For younger men and women with equal years of education and work experience in the same occupation, there is little if any wage difference. What difference remains can be largely ascribed to marital status. Married women suffer a wage disability (in relation to married men) that single women do not (see Exhibit 7.4).

Still, a difference in male and female wages continues to exist in Canada as elsewhere, for a number of reasons. First, more women than men in paid employment are in part-time, not full-time jobs. Second, most women work in sectors of the economy which contain mainly insecure, poorly paying jobs requiring skills that are easy to acquire.

Third, in Canada as in many parts of the world, women are saddled with most of the responsibility for housework and childcare. Data for developing regions is sparse, but analysts (United Nations, 1991: 82) note that "women everywhere have nearly total responsibility for housework. [In fact] men in developing regions generally do even fewer household chores than men in the developed regions."

To see the effect of marriage and housework on women's wages, we need only look at the data on men's and women's incomes in Canada's ten best-paying jobs. They include jobs like judge, physician, lawyer, dentist, senior manager, and university professor. The data show that women working fulltime

EXHIBIT 7.4 *Sex, statistics and wages*

. . . The subject is the much ballyhooed "wage gap" between men and women, documented annually by Statistics Canada. . .

It was reported that women's wages rose to 69.6 per cent of men's in 1991, from 67.6 per cent the year before. But what does that mean? For starters, it does *not* mean . . . that women are being paid nearly one-third less to do the same jobs. . . .

. . . Women with a university degree earned more, not less, than men with lower levels of education. When one considers that a majority of those enrolled in Canadian universities are female (55.3 per cent of full- and part-time university students are women) it's hard to imagine a future in which the wage difference will not continue to narrow.

. . . There is already almost no wage gap between single men and single women. In 1991, single women's average earnings were 91.1 per cent of those of their male counterparts. For some women, there was even less of a difference. Data compiled by Statistics Canada at The Globe and Mail's request show that the income of single women age 35 to 44 was 94.5 per cent of that earned by men of the same age. And looking only

at the most educated members of that age group — single females with a university degree — women actually made six per cent more money than single, 35 to 44 year-old, university-educated men. (In fairness, the margin of error in Statscan's survey is large, so these last two percentages could be off by several points.)

All of these numbers refer, of course, to full-time workers. But not all full-time workers work the same number of hours. On average, men work more than women: 40.4 hours vs. 35.2 hours a week. In other words, the average man works 12.9 per cent longer, explaining a large part of the wage gap.

But the biggest factor is marriage. The earnings of single women, single men and married women working full-time are roughly comparable. But the earnings of the average married man rise above those of everyone else. That is the only real "wage-gap.". . . Its existence suggests that, as one would expect, married men and women choose certain career and life paths, different from those chosen by singles. . . .

Source: "Sex, statistics and wages," *The Globe and Mail*, Thurs., Jan. 21, 1993

at these jobs in 1990 earned about 60-70% of what men earned working full-time in the same jobs, during the same year. Even among dentists, who are mainly self-employed (and don't discriminate against themselves!), there is a roughly 30% income gap between men and women.

Again, let's consider possible explanations. First, some women who work "full-time" do in fact work fewer hours per week, or fewer weeks per year, than men who work "full-time." This is because they take more time off work to attend to family business (e.g., taking sick children to the doctor). That might account for their lower income.

Second, women in a particular occupation may have less experience and seniority than men in the same occupation. Since income is often a function of age, experience and seniority, women will earn lower incomes than men on average, until they get more seniority.

Third, women may hold jobs in worse-paying organizations or geographic locales than men. So, for example, a doctor or dentist in a small town is likely to earn less than a doctor or dentist in Montreal, Toronto or Vancouver. Likewise, a manager in a small company is likely to earn less than a manager in a large company and women may be more likely than men to get work in small towns or small companies. If so, they will have lower incomes than men, on average.

Women are also at a disadvantage in the work world because few have received the kind of education that would win them well-paid, highly-skilled jobs. Historically, women were excluded from higher education; now women form a slight majority of all college students and receive half of the master's degrees awarded. Most doctorates and professional degrees still go to men. However, as women continue gradually to improve their educational credentials, they will continue to improve their position in the work world.

All of these are plausible explanations of income inequality between men and women. All would result in women having lower incomes than men even *without* there being prejudice or discrimination against women employees. A study done by the Bank of Montreal asked employees why women were not in more senior positions and gave the explanations just noted. Yet the data on employees showed that women in the bank had more years of experience and more education than the men. These data suggest that between five and twenty per cent of the wage gap *cannot* be explained by anything but discrimination.

Other recent research shows that differences in *current* salary reflect differences in *starting* salary. In turn, a sizeable percentage (in the United States, over 40%) of the difference between male and female starting salaries is due to differences in the college major of the employee (Gerhart, 1990). In other words, men and women specialize in different fields; men tend to specialize in the better paying fields.

For example, there is evidence that mathematical fields (e.g., physics, engineering, computing) are still dominated by men. Though this pattern is changing, the process is slow because gender-differentiated aspirations are formed in high school, if not before (Wilson and Boldizar, 1990). We are often left wondering how much of the wage inequality is due to acceptable factors like

As secretaries and administrative assistants, women in the paid work force have put their learned interpersonal skills—as cooperative team players and excellent listeners—to good use. Unfortunately, these essential jobs pay poorly and have a low status in most organizations.

Prentice Hall Canada

occupational choice and how much is due to discrimination — a double standard in the work world. One study, based on American data which appears to take both of these factors into account, claims that between 40% and 60% of the gender wage gap in professional occupations is due to discrimination (Kemp, 1990).

In the West, the consequences of gender inequality are most dramatic for women caught between domestic and wage-earning responsibilities. For example, the single mothers of young children often cannot earn enough to both maintain a decent standard of living and cover their child-care costs. Welfare payments are below the poverty line and people are penalized for earning over a minimum amount. Not surprisingly, single mothers face a higher risk of poverty than any other group and make up a high percentage of Canada's poor.

Elderly women are another group of women at particular risk for poverty. Since few of them had paying careers when they were younger, few have incomes from job-based pensions when they get older (Ginn and Arber, 1991). We will have more to say about this topic in Chapter 8, on the family.

Because of their experiences of inequality, all women can be considered members of a "minority group." This is not meant to suggest that they are a small segment of the population — in fact, they are a numerical majority — but, instead, to note their distinctive identity and socially disadvantaged position. And like other victimized "minority groups," women suffer from oppression because of ideologies which justify gender inequality.

Double standard

Men and women are treated differently in our society. Likewise, men and women draw unequal rewards, whether we measure these as income, prestige, authority, power or otherwise. But does inequality prove the existence of prejudice and discrimination against women? Remember from the last chapter that researchers (Henry and Ginsberg, 1990) needed to run experimental field trials to gain compelling proof that there was racial discrimination against blacks. Mere inequality was not proof enough.

One kind of evidence of prejudice and discrimination is a so-called **double standard** of the kind we mentioned earlier. The basic idea behind a "double standard" is that two groups are judged against different standards of conduct — a patently unfair thing to do. Imagine, for example, that you are writing an examination in this course and the teacher tells you that men and women will be graded in different ways. Women's exam papers will be graded only for content: i.e., how many right answers they give. Men's exam papers will also be graded for prose style, quality of handwriting, imaginativeness and neatness.

Under these conditions, women will end up with higher average grades than men: after all, they were graded according to an easier standard. The men will, rightly, feel they have been discriminated against. Well, that's the sort of thing that happens to women in many areas of life, most especially where sex is concerned.

Let's look at comparative data from China and the United States. The data in Exhibit 7.5 show that women in both countries oppose non-marital sex more than men do. Second, Chinese people are more opposed to pre-marital sex than American people are.

EXHIBIT 7.5 *Attitudes towards non-marital sex: China* and U.S.A., 1988*

Per Cent Against Pre-marital Sex			Per Cent Against Extra-marital Sex		
	China	USA		China	USA
Men	50	31	Men	84	87
Women	62	41	Women	92	94

* Urban China only, ages 24-60 (M), 20-55 (F); US sample, all ages 18 and over, rural and urban

Sources: (China) Z. Bo and G. Wenxiu, "Sexuality in Urban China," *Australian Journal of Chinese Affairs*, July, 1992: 10, 12; (USA) Niemi, Muller and Smith, *Trends in Public Opinion, 1989*; 193, 194.

Why are the Chinese so much more opposed to pre-marital sex than Americans? The answer is that the Chinese place a higher value on female virginity than Americans do. Bo and Wenxiu (1991) report that, in China, 73% of male and 78% of female respondents say virginity is a girl's most valuable possession. This suggests a double standard for men and women in China. Women are expected to be virgins at marriage though men are not.

North America is different in this respect; here, attitudes have changed radically in the last 30 years. Darling et al. (1984) report that until the late 1940s or early 1950s there *was* a double standard in the United States: non-marital sex was permitted for men and prohibited for women. From about 1950 to 1970, there was a period of "permissiveness with affection," during which pre-marital intercourse was acceptable so long as it occurred in a love relationship that was expected to lead to marriage.

Since about 1970, there has been a general acceptance — certainly among young people — that sexual intercourse is a natural and expected part of a relationship for both men and women, whether or not that relationship is expected to lead to marriage (McLaughlin et al., 1988). Physical or emotional exploitation of the sexual partner is still considered unacceptable.

So, in North America today, people put little value on female virginity at marriage. At the same time, even in China there is a conflict between what we would call ideal culture and real culture. Female virginity at marriage is part of the ideal culture. In reality, a large fraction of Chinese men and women are having sex before marriage. It would appear that the Chinese are endorsing an ideal norm like the one North Americans held before 1950, but are following an actual norm like the one that North Americans held between 1950 and 1970.

The continued attachment to virginity in China, and in North America up to about 1970, tells us that in the past, women were regarded as the sexual property of their husbands. Without their virginity they were considered *used* property; therefore, of lower value than virgins.

With changes in the status of women, this kind of double standard in China will diminish. Yet there is often what sociologists call *culture lag* — a tendency for cultural ideas to change more slowly than technology or real behaviour. Despite the increased equality of women in modern China, there is still a strong attachment to a pre-modern, non-egalitarian idea: namely, virginity.

Interconnections with race and ethnicity

We noted earlier that gender differences are not only interconnected with class differences, but with racial and ethnic differences as well.

Take the case of native women in Canada. Until Bill C-31 was passed in 1985, native women suffered from discriminatory legislation. A native woman who married a non-native man, for example, lost all rights for herself and her children under the Indian Act and even her legal status as a native. In effect, native women who married non-native men were not only thereby cut off from their rights and property but even from their own identity. Native men who married non-native women suffered from no such discrimination; in fact, their non-native wives became status Indians, entitled to Indian benefits.

We should not underestimate the impact this discrimination has had upon the native peoples, both male and female. Entire generations of natives were cut off from their society as a result of this type of legislation. Indeed, when the right to native status was restored in 1985, hundreds of thousands of people applied for and received renewed native status.

This shift of women out of and back into native society has also disrupted the role of women in native society. That native women can no longer trust traditional social relations and values to protect them became evident in the debate over aboriginal self-government which was a part of the failed constitutional referendum of 1992. Many native women argued *against* Aboriginal self-government which did not include specific guarantees to protect the rights of women.

Immigrant women are another group which is disadvantaged in Canadian society. Stasiulis (1990: 287) points to the symbolic images which underlie the treatment of immigrant women in Canadian society:

 Images of sturdy, asexual, and subservient Black domestics and of exotic, sexually dextrous, and compliant Asian women are pervasive in Western popular culture and mass-media advertising . . . Such racially and culturally specific notions of femininity play an important role in elevating women of different "races" and ethnicities to specific occupations, in barring them from entry into others, and in conditioning managerial strategies of control.

Immigrant women are often relegated to the lowest paying, lowest status, and most tedious occupations — as domestics or in manufacturing. Immigrant women are far more susceptible to exploitation in these circumstances because they are often unfamiliar with Canada's laws or the agencies designed to protect their rights. As well, they often lack any kind of social network to look after them should they lose their jobs. As a result, they fear unemployment more than discrimination in the workplace. This makes it difficult to unionize immigrant women in many industries.

At home, too, immigrant women face major disadvantages. Married women often have to work long hours at low pay, then are still expected by their husbands to perform the household tasks which, traditionally, they would have been expected to do in their country of origin. They are still expected to do all of the cleaning, cooking and child care activities. Immigrant men often find that they, too, are working long hours for low pay at jobs much lower in status than their skills or education would lead them to expect. As a result they are often frustrated and sometimes become aggressive and violent towards their wives and children.

VIOLENCE AND VICTIMIZATION

In our society, violence against women runs a gamut from verbal and psychological harassment to physical assault, sexual assault, and homicide. Horrible as this is, some societies have even failed to stamp out the killing of baby girls (see Exhibit 7.6). This is the most extreme version of violence against and victimization of females and it is a worldwide problem.

Domestic violence

In our own society, relations between men and women are often violent. Unfortunately, we have no reliable figures on *all* the violence that takes place. Domestic violence and rape appear to be much more common than the official statistics reveal. Likewise, **sexual harassment** directly affects a large but undetermined number of Canadian women.

Research on criminal victimization in Canada (Sacco and Johnson, 1990: 21) shows that "rates of personal victimization are highest among males, the young, urban dwellers, those who are single or unemployed . . . Risk of personal victimization is also greater among Canadians who frequently engage in evening activities outside the home and among heavier consumers of alcohol." Most recorded victimization is male victimization in public; but this is not the *female* experience of crime or victimization.

This issue of "experience" is important. It puts into focus the concerns and fears with which women in our society must deal and men, for the most part, ignore. Women, for example, fear to go out to a park at night, or even to take a stroll in their own neighbourhood. Women at universities in Montreal and Toronto have arranged for escorts to accompany them after late classes to the subway station or wait with them at a bus stop. They are always conscious of the potential danger of male attack which men less often have to take into account.

Without ever taking a sociology course, young women soon learn the truth of what we noted in Chapter 4 on deviance; that is, the most dangerous, crime-prone (including violence-prone) people in Canadian society are young, single men. Yet the danger to women is *least* likely to come from strangers outside the home. More often than not, it comes from intimates: from spouses, dates, male acquaintances and workmates. In particular, family life has the potential for both physical and mental abuse since stronger family members have the power to take out their frustrations on weaker ones.

The data tell us that most domestic violence is physical and is carried out by men upon women. Expert estimates (see, for example, MacLeod, 1987; Lupri, 1989, 1991) range from at least one woman in ten to one in four having been beaten by her partner. Repeated severe violence is believed to occur in one in every 14 marriages. People who work in shelters for battered women believe that (approximately) nine times out of ten it is men who abuse their partners or their children.

For a variety of reasons, the data on domestic violence are somewhat uncertain. For example, research done by York University's Institute for Social Research (1992) shows that women's reporting of sexual abuse on a survey is sig-

EXHIBIT 7.6 *Killing unwanted baby girls continues in pockets of India*

It has been more than a year since Rani killed her six-month-old daughter by pouring poisonous oleander berries ground in oil down her throat. "There is no money in our family," says Rani, 37, her knot of hair shining in the moonlight. "I just could not keep her." The baby was Rani's second daughter.

She wouldn't consider adoption. Who knows, the new parents might beat the child, or sell her into prostitution. The baby girl, Rani says resolutely, was *kuzhipappa*—"the child that was meant for the burial pit."

Despite repeated government attempts to stop female infanticide, it continues to thrive in pockets of rural India. There are no large factories in Usilampatti, and therefore female children are of less use than they are in the plains, the heartland of the child-labour belt. . . .

In a survey of 1,250 families last year by the Community Services Guild in Tamil Nadu's Salem district, one-third admitted killing at least one female baby. . . .

In one village after another, people talk openly about the methods employed: oleander berries, tobacco paste, boiling liquids, pesticides, suffocation.

In the Community Services Guild study, two-thirds of the families, most of whom owned property, said they considered girls an asset. But the costs of a girl child, built up by centuries of tradition, can be prohibitive even for the wealthy.

In the Gounder tribe, parents are required to throw elaborate celebrations at virtually every turn in a girl's life: when they name the girl, when she reaches puberty, when she is married, when she sets up a home, when her first child is born,

and, if the parents are still alive, when she reaches menopause. And if their daughter has a daughter, they must give the paternal grandparents up to 10,000 rupees ($450). . . .

What disturbs researchers is that infanticide may be increasing, as some tribes open up to other cultures, resulting in the adoption of customs such as dowry and divorce, which turn parents against daughters. "Modernization, I would say, has accelerated the practice, not reduced it," says K. Bose, principal of Usilampatti's PMT College.

To halt the practice, the state government last year began arresting couples, including a Salem forestry official, although prosecution is difficult in a land where infant mortality already is high.

The state has also set up a 2,000-rupee trust for new-born girls that matures to 10,000 rupees by the time they reach marrying age. . . .

Another group, the Women's Emancipation and Development (WED) Trust, offers women loans for sewing machines, dairy cows and basket-making, and has trained 58 women in tailoring. The loan money comes from women's savings co-operatives that WED organized in the villages. So far, 415 women have saved about 40,000 rupees ($1,800).

One of the savings co-operatives this year attracted a new member: Rani. She has managed to put away 200 rupees and hopes to buy a cow.

More important, say WED officials, is that Rani this year gave birth to twins, both girls, and she says she will let them live.

Source: "Killing unwanted baby girls continues in pockets of India," *The Globe and Mail*, Sat., Nov. 20, 1993, p. D3

nificantly affected by (1) whether another person is present at the time of the interview, and (2) whether the respondent likes or does not like the interviewer. This evidence of an "interviewer effect" on the reporting of abuse should alert us to the fact that *all* data are gathered in a social environment. All data are "social facts" in more than one sense. Therefore, they are always open to debate and re-analysis.

Generally, research on abuse shows that violence often occurs at the same time as alcohol abuse, a spillover of work stress, and a loss of control over anger. The state's attitude towards violence against women significantly affects domestic conditions women have to face everyday. Often, for example, police are reluctant to intervene when the neighbours call to complain of a noisy family dispute, or even if the wife herself complains. Many people, police included, still believe that people who are members of the same family should be allowed to work things out for themselves. Police and social workers, they believe, should stay out of the picture until there are overwhelming grounds for outside involvement.

As a result, within affluent groups, violence may be hidden. The affluent rarely use shelters and legal clinics, even though they may suffer from just as much domestic violence as other women.

According to the National Survey of Families and Households (Burch, 1985), in much of the reported violence between married partners, *both* partners are perpetrators. In other words, women as well as men commit violent acts in married couples. However, the NSFH data indicate that the probabilities of injury for male and female respondents differ significantly. As one might expect, since men are usually stronger than women, wives are more often injured than are husbands, even when both partners are acting violently.

One survey of self-reported domestic violence in Canada (Lupri, 1993) concludes that wives are even more violent towards their spouses than husbands are. This unexpected result suggests that men are under-reporting the extent and severity of their own actions.

However, other results of this study confirm findings of previous studies (see also Lupri et al., forthcoming). They show that (1) younger people are more violent than older people; (2) unemployed people are more violent than employed people; but (3) lower income and less-educated people are no more violent than higher income, highly-educated people.

The most revealing and significant finding in this study is that high rates of domestic violence are associated with high levels of domestic stress. Concretely, the more stressful events a person reports experiencing in the previous year, the more violence will have taken place within the household.

These stressful events include the following: unemployment for more than a month, personal bankruptcy, a drop in wage or salary, taking an additional job to make ends meet, working more overtime than desired to make ends meet, new child support or alimony payments to make, a move to less expensive accommodations, taking in a boarder to make ends meet, one or more demotions at work, loss of income due to going back to university, another important career setback, or some other important setback in economic well-being.

Reading through this list of "events," it is easy to imagine how they might cause intense frustration and, in this way, violence. And not surprisingly, since we have been living through a period of economic recession, rates of spousal assault appear to be rising dramatically. For example, Ontario's Solicitor General reports that in 1991 (as compared with 1990), total spousal assaults were up 18%. Charges laid by police were up by 23%; and assaults in which weapons were used were up 51% (*The Globe and Mail*, November 15, 1992: A9).

Economic conditions aside, there is a relationship between a belief in patriarchy and wife battering. Husbands who believe men ought to rule women are more likely than other husbands to beat their wives. In turn, a belief in patriarchy appears to depend on educational and occupational level. Specifically, the belief appeals to lower status, less educated men (Smith, M. D., 1990).

Still, if stress and frustrations give rise to violence, they do not excuse it. The real problem underlying violence is not stress or frustration but the fact that some men find it acceptable to channel their frustrations into violence towards family members. A marriage licence is not a licence to batter. As long as our society tolerates and even condones family violence, it will continue.

Date rape and sexual inequality

Another current concern is "date rape." A survey was conducted on 44 college and university campuses across Canada by sociologists Walter Dekeseredy and Katharine Kelly. It found four women in five claiming they had been subjected to abuse by a dating partner. Overall, nearly as many men admitted having acted abusively towards their dates (*The Globe and Mail*, February 8, 1993: A1, A2).

Unfortunately, the validity of the study was attacked because the study listed such a wide range of behaviours under the heading of "abuse." These behaviours included insults, swearing, accusations of flirting with others or acting spitefully, as well as violent and grotesque acts such as using or threatening to use a gun or knife, beating, kicking or biting the dating partner. So it is best to separate out the violent from the less violent abuses before we attempt to analyze the results.

When we do this, certain patterns fall into place. First, where *violent* abuses are concerned, women are more than twice as likely as men to acknowledge their occurrence. Where less violent abuses are concerned, men and women acknowledge them equally often.

For example, 65% of women report being insulted or sworn at by a date, and 63.6% of men report having done that to a date. On the other hand, 11.1% of women report being slapped by a date, yet only 4.5% of men report slapping a date. Likewise, 8.1% of women report being kicked, bitten or hit with a fist, yet only 2.4% of men report having done any of those things (*The Globe and Mail*, February 8, 1993: A11).

This consistent discrepancy leads to one of three possible conclusions. Either (1) violent and abusive men date a lot more women than gentle, non-abusive men, (2) women tell a lot of lies about their dates, or (3) many men are ashamed to admit the things they have done to their dates.

The data also show that violent abuses on dates are not only physical, they are also sexual. For example, one woman in three reports having been forced by psychological means into unwanted sexplay. One woman in five reports having been forced by psychological means into unwanted sexual intercourse. One woman in seven reports being sexually abused (i.e., mounted without intercourse or mounted *with* intercourse) when she was too drunk or high on drugs to fight off her date. One woman in 11 reports physical force being used to compel sex play or attempted intercourse. And finally, one woman in 16 reports actually being raped on a date: that is, giving in to physical force aimed at compelling sexual intercourse.

As before, male respondents are only about one-half or one-third as likely to report doing these things as women are to report having them done.

Bear in mind that most instances of forced sexual activity occur between people who know each other. Unfortunately, the result is, too often, that women blame themselves for the experience. Because they know the assailant, they react passively to the sexual assault. Because they react passively, they blame themselves for not reacting more forcefully. A few even continue the dating relationship (Murnan et al., 1989).

Sexual harassment is another form of sexual assault, and is especially prevalent in the workplace. Research shows that perceptions of sexual harassment vary by gender. College-aged men are much less likely to label behaviour "harassment" than their female peers. After exposure to the workforce, men's awareness grows and they, too, come to see certain behaviour as harassment. Overall, women label more behaviours as harassing than men do, but this discrepancy decreases with experience in the workforce, as women become accustomed to "the norm" (Booth-Butterfield, 1989).

CHANGE AND RESISTANCE TO CHANGE

That's an introduction to the nature of the "battle of the sexes" in Canada today. But things are changing rapidly. The main force changing gender relations is **feminism**, an ideology that holds that men and women should be treated equally. Feminism supports the social equality of the sexes and opposes patriarchy and sexism. Challenging the cultural division of humanity into masculine and feminine worlds, it seeks to eliminate the social disadvantages women have historically faced.

Feminist thought has become an important influence on contemporary social science, as we have seen in other chapters of this book. But does the acceptance of feminist ideology and attitudes reduce gender inequality in ordinary, everyday social relationships? The evidence says it does — somewhat. For example, newlyweds in New Zealand who said that they accepted feminist ideas expected to allocate household tasks on a more equal basis than those who said they did not accept feminism (Koopman-Boyden and Abbott, 1985). However, backsliding occurs. Behaviour changes in a more traditional, less egalitarian direction after marriage.

Likewise, the acceptance by a couple of egalitarian sex-role attitudes predicts greater participation by the father in child care (Fishbein, 1990). A combination of egalitarian sex-role attitudes and wives working outside the home brings about a change in the household division of labour (Hardesty and Bokemeier, 1989). A combination of egalitarian sex-role attitudes and wives working outside the home also brings about a change in the father's involvement in childcare (Barnett and Baruch, 1987). Finally, changes to less traditional gender attitudes play an important part in changing the domestic division of labour among immigrant families (Haddadd and Lam, 1988).

Yet the goal of equality remains elusive and the present world recession, which is creating a climate of anti-feminist sentiment, is another obstacle to achieving that equality. People's patriarchal attitudes about men and women resist change, despite legislative attempts to limit systemic discrimination. Our assumptions about what it means to be male or female are among the most fundamental to our sense of self and our perception of others.

According to research in the United States, Britain, Germany and Austria, women are more supportive of efforts to combat gender inequality than are men. One study finds women with employed husbands and well-educated people less supportive of such efforts than less well-educated people. (Davis and Robinson, 1991). What this research shows is that the pressure and ability to change vary from one country to another and from one group to another. In general, changing such a crucial part of our own identity and our way of dealing with one another does not come easily.

Among Western countries, Sweden is the forerunner in legislative efforts to ensure that women have reproductive control, and equality in the workplace, and that both spouses participate equally in family duties. But even in Sweden, occupational segregation and a gendered division of domestic labour persist. There, most women still work in "women's" jobs, where they receive lower salaries. At home, domestic work and childcare still remain largely women's work (Spakes, 1992). Still, the percentage of women in male-dominated careers is greater and the wage gap is smaller than in Canada.

North American sex roles are changing rapidly and, in the future, both men and women will be able to choose from a wider range of acceptable options. In large part, this is because there is a significant increase in the amount of formal education women are receiving.

Women have recently begun to graduate in greater numbers from programs such as medicine and the law, and they have been elected in increasing numbers to public office. However, women still have less control than do men of resources such as property, prestige and power. Likewise, the number of women in politics has increased sharply in recent decades, yet the vast majority of national officials are men.

Until recently, women's job histories were very different from those of men. A generation ago most women spent little of their lives in the paid work force. Many worked for pay only before having children or after all their children were in school full-time. Even then, they fitted their work lives around their family responsibilities and avoided careers requiring too much time away from home.

As a result, the majority had jobs, not careers. As well, women suffered discrimination in the labour force. This made it harder for women to get good jobs, promotions when they competed with men, or even equal pay for equal work.

As professional rocket scientists, women in the paid work force will win higher wages and more respect than in the past. But can they rely on their husbands to get the children to the dentist or put dinner on the table by 6:30?

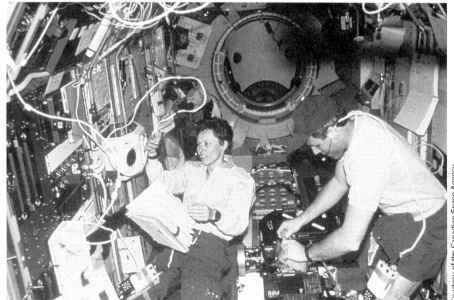

Courtesy of the Canadian Space Agency

Under these circumstances, most married women held the social rank their husband, the "breadwinner," had been able to attain. As a result, women would gain their greatest social mobility by marrying and supporting their husbands' efforts. Some women married up while others married down. Not so long ago, British data analyzed by Heath (1981: 114) showed that "a woman's class fate is more loosely linked to her social origins than is a man's," and conversely, more tightly linked to her spouse's fortunes.

Until recently, women's fates in the job market have also been more "loosely linked to social origins" than men's fates. In enormous numbers, women have filled a small variety of low-to-medium-prestige jobs. These jobs have been chiefly in sales, clerical work, service, and light manufacturing, while some have been in professional work (like nursing and school-teaching). To women from working-class backgrounds, these jobs have often meant upward mobility. To women from middle- or upper-middle-class backgrounds, these jobs have meant downward mobility. Again, fewer women than men have inherited their parent's class position.

In the United States, most women's occupations are confined to the lower 66% of the prestige scale (Stevens and Hoisington, 1987). This reflects the traditionally male-dominated job market. These patterns have begun to change as women are attaining higher levels of education, having fewer children, spending more years in the labour force, and experiencing less discrimination. Increasingly, women's patterns of social mobility grow more similar to those of men. Yet the patterns are far from identical or equal.

The problem is similar, though of varying magnitude, in most industrial societies. For example, since the fall of communism in Poland, women have been facing job discrimination that is much worse than in Canada and is leading to high rates of unemployment. It appears that Polish employers feel free to express their hiring preferences in advertisements: male or female, married or single, and so on. This anti-woman initiative is supported by Roman Catholic politicians and nationalists, who are promoting a "traditional Polish family." As well, with women out of the workforce, the official unemployment rates are lower.

Such sentiments as these find a sympathetic response from *some* Canadians, but *most* Canadians would consider them backward, sexist and unacceptable. As a result, discrimination against women in Canadian workplaces is hidden and hard to measure.

As we saw earlier, even today family obligations limit the social mobility of women in ways they do not limit men. On the other hand, the results of a study of female engineers by Jagacinski, LeBold, and Linden (1987) challenge popular explanations for the gender differences in career advancement, though it leaves the actual causes unknown. The study finds that gender differences in the career advancement of engineers *cannot* be explained by differences in education level, grades, self-perceptions of ability, or career interruptions (to care for children). Many female engineers — expecting career problems due to role conflict — have remained single and/or childless to avoid such problems. In light of this study, they gain nothing by doing so.

We spoke earlier about traditional relations between doctors and nurses. Even these relations are starting to change, illustrating the general process of change that is taking place in gender relations. We are finding a more collaborative relationship between nurses and doctors, men and women. In this newer relationship, the doctor and nurse are professional co-workers who form a team and cooperate in the design and application of a treatment plan.

The physician is still responsible for diagnosing the illness but the nurses play a more important part in planning and providing the treatment. There is less tendency in this kind of relationship to see nursing care as trivial. Here, the doctor and nurse work hand-in-hand, not as "hand" and "maid." The nurse is no longer the traditional "maid" or "technician," but a professional giver of health care.

This is not the final stage in the process of change. A third kind of relationship is evolving in some places. Especially in the United States, the nursing role is developing into that of "independent practitioner" or "nurse therapist." In this situation, the nurse takes on "sole" responsibility for patient *care*. A doctor continues to be responsible for diagnosis and prognosis. The independent nurse practitioner plans, carries out, and evaluates all parts of the treatment plan.

This nursing approach has many advantages over the other two. It gives the nurse more autonomy, more money and higher status as a caregiver, but nurses are not the only beneficiaries. The change also leads to more specialization of nursing activities; for example, to specialization in obstetrics, emergency, chronic care, and so on. In community clinics, many nurses work as specialists in family practice nursing. (On the other hand, many nurses resist this change. They feel they are becoming second-class doctors instead of first-class nurses.)

In short, the doctor-nurse relationship appears to be changing from one based on a paternalistic model, through a model based on collaboration, to a model in which the nurse works as an independent practitioner. Still, the dominant model continues to be paternalistic, especially in Canada; most nurses remain subordinate to doctors.

What is particularly insidious about the gendered division of labour is not only that women are restricted to work which is subordinate to, and lower in status than that of men, but that jobs often lose their status and authority as more women enter them. For example, nursing, teaching and secretarial work were largely male occupations in the 19th century. The movement of women into these occupations coincided with a dramatic decline in status and authority in each of these positions.

Or take a more contemporary example: doctors. Once the symbol of the autonomous, high status professional, doctors are more and more being transformed into employees of the state. This change has structural causes and affects the status of all physicians, not just women. But it does indicate that women are always playing "catch-up." They often succeed in moving into a previously restricted occupation or role only to find that many of the benefits to be gained from the occupation have moved on as well.

Traditional gender roles have both positive and negative consequences. The negative consequences for women of traditional gender roles have been the basis of efforts by the feminist movement and others to press for change. North American women have indeed gained. However, unless these legal rights are enforced, women and men will still not have equal access to social rewards. Gender stratification will continue to be an important aspect of society.

Men and women may never have identical lives, but it is critical that, one day, they enjoy equally fulfilling, equally free lives. Discrimination has advantages for men, and for employers, who pass along the consequences — such

Perhaps violence against women will be less tolerated as women increasingly come to make, interpret, and enforce the laws of the country.

as female poverty — to the taxpaying public. It is not so advantageous for women, nor is it just. On the other hand, it is hard to devise a way of measuring "comparable worth" so that we can give each kind of work the rewards it deserves.

In reality we all — men and women alike — lose from the persistence of gender inequality. Justice and fairness aside, we are not using the talents of our population effectively, not taking advantage of the knowledge, enterprise and skills possessed by both men and women.

The movement of large numbers of women into the labour force means that many issues, such as inadequate daycare facilities for children, now affect both husbands and wives. The failure of our society to provide supports for the new problems husbands and wives are facing contributes to high divorce rates and increased gender conflict.

CLOSING REMARKS

What is important to remember in closing is that gender relations offer us the best example yet of C. Wright Mills' view that public issues are really the other side of personal troubles (and vice versa). But as a public issue, gender relations are in a confused state indeed!

On the one hand, people experience the recent shifts in gender relations as personal troubles. As Luxton (1983) found on returning to Flin Flon (a mining town in northern Manitoba), traditional work patterns are eroding and new ones are emerging. More women are working for pay, and as they begin to do so, their views on how labour should be divided by spouses at home are changing. This leads to personal struggles with their husbands. Seeing change in terms of personal conflicts, rather than as a public issue or sociological trend, increases the tension between men and women.

On the other hand, we can all see major changes in women's lives during the 20th century. Consider, for example, the influx of women into wage labour, which merged the market and domestic economies in a new way. Now, as Glucksmann (1990) says, market and domestic economies — paid and unpaid labour (formerly, men's work and women's work) — must be viewed as two poles in a larger framework of production. And, as Gershuny (1987) points out, the growing importance of unpaid, home or informal work has an enormous impact on the formal economy. We buy more goods instead of services, for example.

What we all need now is time to catch up with, and reflect upon, the wide-ranging changes that have already taken place in every area of our private lives. Most important, we need the knowledge and patience to apply our macrosociological understanding of the "war between the sexes" to our personal lives. Nowhere is this need to re-think personal relations in the light of large structural trends more important than in the realm of family life. That is what we discuss in the next chapter.

C H A P T E R 8

UPI/Bettman Newsphotos

Nikki Abraham

"Family" conveys a set of meanings to all of us: ideally, it means intimacy, familiarity, support and dependency—even love. Unfortunately, not all families achieve this ideal.

THE FAMILY

THE FAMILY AS A MAJOR INSTITUTION

The family is the only social institution we will be examining in detail. There is a good reason for paying such close attention to the family, for it may be the most basic social institution of all. It is in the family that most people come to be socialized, learn who they are, what others expect of them, and what they can reasonably expect of others. It is in the family that we learn to get along with people, to love and occasionally to hate, to express our innermost feelings and also to lie, to resent being subject to other people's authority, and to manipulate others to get what we want.

Family life illustrates the relationship between our macro and micro social worlds. After all, our most intimate moments are lived within the "family" or "household" setting and, not surprisingly, some people have called the family a "haven in a heartless world."

Yet what happens in the family is affected by what happens outside it. Family inequality mirrors inequality in the larger society. Those who are more powerful *outside* the family tend to hold more power *inside* the family. Those who suffer the most degradation *outside* the family may try to degrade and humiliate others *inside* the family. You may have seen the cartoon where the boss bawls out the dad, dad comes home and bawls out the mom, mom bawls out the big kids, big kids bawl out the little kids, and little kids bawl out the pets. We *do* take out our workplace frustrations on the people who are closest to us, whether they deserve it or not.

At the same time, our public lives *outside* the home are also affected by what is happening *inside* the home. Family conflict, separation, divorce, and other domestic stresses all influence how we perform at school and on the job. Because of this, employers are beginning to take family responsibilities into account, by providing on-the-job child care, greater flexibility in work hours, assistance in career planning, and even programs to assist employees who are having problems at home. Employers are no longer able to ignore their employees' personal troubles if they want the highest level of productivity.

For the first few years of our lives, the family is a microcosm of the larger society in which we will one day participate. By learning to be a family member, we are learning how to be members of society. Then, after we leave the shelter (or oppression) of our family, most of us marry and begin our own adult families. The new roles we take on — as spouse, and parent — become a crucial part of our identity. New intense relationships with others give us satisfaction and self-esteem but also limit what we can do or hope to do.

For better or worse, the family is the context within which most of us live out our private lives. It is in our family relationships that we can expect to find many of our greatest joys and greatest sorrows.

Defining the family

Before we examine the diverse forms a family can take, let us develop a definition of the family that gives us a common starting point for analysis. We can say that a family consists of a group of people who are related to one another through marriage, descent, or legal adoption. Family members have institutionalized roles that define what they can expect from one another and what obligations they owe each other.

In Canada, as elsewhere, the nature of these rights and responsibilities is determined by cultural values. In turn, they are influenced by economic realities and backed-up by the laws of the state.

Adult family members have a legal responsibility to take care of their dependent children. This means tending to their basic survival needs, like food and shelter. Ideally, it includes providing love, comfort, and a sense of security. Good families also teach their children the language, customs, beliefs, norms, skills, and values they will need to fit into their society. To a degree, all families do all of these things. Yet real families fall short of the ideal in many ways, and this can cause problems. Just like the society at large that it mirrors, the family can display selfishness and cruelty, inequality and violence.

A family is an economic, as well as emotional, unit. In many cultures, and for most of human history, this economic unit both produced and consumed goods and services collectively. But families are no longer the central economic unit of production, and few Canadians today work as members of a family. Nevertheless, family members still tend to consume goods and services together.

Much of the data we have about family life in Canada comes from information gathered by Statistics Canada. For several reasons, these data cannot be taken directly from the Statistics Canada information. One of these reasons has to do with the diversity of ways in which people define family membership. Because the family is a fundamental social institution, membership is not limited to a particular time or place. If you move to Winnipeg and the rest of your family stays in Vancouver, you still consider yourself to be a family member. You also consider your grandparents, uncles, aunts, and cousins, none of whom may live with you, to be members.

Gathering statistical data on the family, however, requires having a clearly defined unit which can be measured and compared. Because the family can take on so many forms and can change so dramatically over time, this unit cannot be based on either the "legal" or the "ideal" model of the family. For these reasons, Statistics Canada uses the concept of a *family household* as the basis for its analyses.

A family household is a group that includes an adult who shares a dwelling and maintains a household with at least *one* other relative, whether a spouse, child, parent, or other kin (for example, cousin). The members of a family household may be related by blood ties, marriage, or adoption. This definition differs from the sociologists' definition given above, because, for the sociologist, the family is not limited to the walls of the dwelling. That is, family members need not live together in order to be a family.

Unlike Statistics Canada, which needs a uniform measurement standard, sociologists and anthropologists are interested in examining the many different forms a family can take. By looking at the differences, we hope to recognize the fundamentals that stay the same. Also, by uncovering what social, economic, and cultural factors gave rise to these differences, we can better predict how the family will change in the future and understand why.

To accomplish this, sociologists focus on two basic activities — marriage and parenthood — which are found in one form or another in all family systems. We will soon discuss each of these in some detail. First, a few words are needed about the differences in sociological approach.

PERSPECTIVES ON THE FAMILY

Because the family is such a fundamental institution, it has been a central focus for research by sociologists working within all of the major sociological perspectives. One result is that the family is yet another topic about which there is extensive debate and controversy. Yet the family is such a diverse social institution that each of the four perspectives described below can tell us different and valuable things.

The functionalist perspective

As you might expect, the functionalist perspective emphasizes the various functions performed by the family as a social unit.

Functionalists note that the family's role as a key social institution grows out of our long period of dependence on others for survival. The human infant's physical dependence requires that others feed, care for, and *teach* it. In order to function well as adults, human infants rely more than infants of any other species on social contacts and teaching. This combination of biological and social factors makes the family a particularly important social institution for the survival both of the individual and society.

Marriage, too, emerges from a combination of biological and social factors. In all societies, women have the primary responsibility for child care, at least during infancy. That women bear, suckle, and generally care for infants means that they are, at least temporarily, limited in their ability to protect and economically support themselves. The dependence of infants on women and of women on men may have given rise to the universal practice of marriage. However, the form marriage takes and the set of relationships and attachments that develop among family members are socially, not biologically, determined.

Functionalists identify a number of specific functions carried out by the typical family. These are, the "socialization of children, sexual regulation, reproduction, economic cooperation, affection, intimacy, emotional support and status placement" (Mandell, 1987: 151). By carrying out these functions, the family ensures survival of the society and of the individual. It provides a setting within which the personality of the individual is moulded, and ensures people's integration into the culture and society.

Given its central role, the family — in one form or another — is found in every society. In the same way, marriage is a cultural universal and, like every cultural universal, its form varies from one culture to another.

Although functionalists emphasize the universal functions of the family, they recognize that the family has changed radically in the last few centuries. Talcott Parsons (Parsons and Bales, 1955), for example, argued that the family's major functions in the past were economic. A peasant family, for instance, served as an economic and productive unit. Everyone worked together to produce what the family needed to survive. This means that it was also within the family that most children learned the work they would do as adults, such as the tasks of a farmer, housewife, warrior, merchant, and so on.

In this way, the family was responsible for both economic production and occupational socialization. These two major functions, Parsons said, have both been removed from the contemporary family. Few people today work at home and most occupational socialization has been turned over to schools and the workplace. Even primary socialization has shifted to daycare centres, peer groups, and television.

This change means that the family has lost its functions at the macrosociological level. Its new functions are largely microsociological. The family is still important for integrating people into society, and it remains the setting in which people lead their private lives and maintain intimate relationships.

The conflict perspective

Both conflict and interactionist critics of the functionalist approach have argued that the family described by the functionalists is an ideal model, not a real family.

Instead of focusing on the functions of the family, followers of the conflict approach have focused on the social relationships out of which the family is composed. Marxists, for example, suggest that the family remains an economic unit in our society even if it is no longer a unit of production. Relationships between men and women within the family reflect the economic conditions and forces found in society.

Consider, first, the distinction between *nuclear* and *extended* families. In an *extended* family, people live in large household units of several generations, among parents, aunts and uncles, brothers and sisters and their spouses and children. Such families were, and to some extent still are, common in agricultural societies. The modern nuclear family, by contrast, is much smaller: it contains just one set of spouses with or without children. Marxists suggest this type of family is a product of capitalism and serves to perpetuate the capitalist economic system.

They argue that once industrial capitalism took away the family's ability to function as a self-contained productive unit, family members became dependent upon the wage earned by the husband and often by the wife. The *nuclear* family, by eliminating the economic supports of the *extended* family, increased everyone's dependence: the worker's dependence on the capitalist, the wife's dependence on her husband, and the child's dependence on his or her parents.

The interactionist perspective

Interactionists have typically focused on the family as the context within which primary socialization occurs. For this reason, they have focused their research largely on the microsociological processes of interaction among family members which lead to the emergence of identity and the "self" (see Chapter 3). Recently, however, interactionists have begun to pay more attention to the family as a specific social institution. For example, Mandell (1987: 153) notes that interactionists have used qualitative interviews to discover "the strains and conflicts women encounter in juggling their multiple responsibilities of domestic and wage labour."

One symbolic interactionist (Vaughan, 1987) has written a book titled *Uncoupling*, which describes the process by which marriages come apart and end in separation or divorce. The author is interested in the typical stages of dissolution and the reasons why reconciliation proves impossible in certain cases. As a result of her research, Vaughan argues against secrecy in marriage and in favour of couples airing their grievances as they arise. The longer problems go unspoken, the more likely it is they will lead to marriage breakdown.

The feminist perspective

Feminist contributions to the study of family life are fundamental and wide-ranging. We have already discussed issues like patriarchy and the household division of labour in the previous chapter on gender relations. Both of these concerns have been heavily influenced by researchers working with this paradigm.

Feminists emphasize the family's role as a microcosm of the broader patterns of male domination in society. In this respect, the family becomes a political unit within which this domination is acted out on a daily basis. The family teaches and justifies the subordination of women through the roles and values assigned on the basis of gender and passed on to the next generation.

In Chapter 10 on population and the environment, we will have occasion to discuss international changes in childbearing behaviour. We cannot understand why a worldwide fertility decline began around 1870 and has continued ever since unless we know something about the changes in men's and women's power within families and the relative advantages of low fertility for men and women. This, too, has been a topic of interest to sociologists working in the feminist paradigm.

MATING AND MARRIAGE

As we noted, two social relationships are central to the family. The first is *marriage*, the relationship between spouses (usually, a husband and wife). The second is *kinship*, the relationship between parent and child. Variations in family life, then, will include variations in the relationships between (1) spouses and (2) parents and children.

Types of marriage

Broadly defined, marriage is a socially approved sexual and economic union between two or more people that is expected to last for a long time. People often enter this union with public formalities or a ceremony, such as a wedding.

In Canada, traditional marriage is going through a period of declining popularity (see Exhibit 8.1). In order to understand what this means, and what it predicts for the future, we need to take a larger view of the institution of marriage and the many ways societies provide "marriage-like" arrangements between people.

After all, societies *do* vary in their patterns of marriage, family, and kinship. For example, they vary in the range of choice given to would-be marriage partners; their reasons for marrying; the rules about premarital and extramarital intimacies; and, whether the same rules apply to both men and women. Even the desired age at marriage and the desired age difference between spouses varies from one society to another.

In some societies, people wed more than one mate at a time. Polygamy is the generic name for this arrangement. Within this general category, polyandry is the marriage of one woman to more than one man, and polygyny the marriage of one man to more than one woman. Polygamy was common in most preindustrial societies and is still permitted in a few. In Nigeria, for example, half of all marriages were polygynous as recently as 1975. But polygyny is banned in all industrial societies.

Polyandry, on the other hand, has always been a rare form of marriage. It occurs in societies like Nepal, where living conditions are harsh and few men are able to support a wife and children on their own. A woman is therefore "shared" by a group of men — usually, brothers — and she is a wife to all of them. Female infanticide is practiced, with the justification that the number of women "needed" in such a society is much less than the number of men.

Monogamy — marriage between only one woman and one man — is the marriage form that is most familiar in Canada. However, variations on monogamy, too, are becoming more and more common. One of these which is increasing in incidence is cohabitation in a marriage-like fashion between two people of the same sex. Another is what sociologists have called serial (or sequential) monogamy. Serial monogamy is the marriage of a person over the life course to a series (or sequence) of spouses, though only one at a time. In a society with high rates of divorce and remarriage such as ours, a growing number of people practice serial monogamy.

EXHIBIT 8.1   *Canadian marriage rates go into dive*

Canada's marriage rate has taken a steep dive, plummeting to a level not seen since the depths of the 1930s depression....

In 1991, there were 6.4 marriages for every 1,000 Canadians, a drop of 9.9 per cent from the 1990 rate. The last time the rate was this low was in the years from 1931 to 1933....

Statscan also reported yesterday that those who marry do so later in life. The average age of women marrying for the first time rose to 26.2 in 1991 from 22.6 in 1971. For men, it rose to 28.2 from 24.9....

Academics said part of the drop in the marriage rate is certainly the result of Canada's prolonged economic recession in the early 1990s. Historically, Canadians have delayed marriage in tough times.

"There is no doubt a relation to economic conditions, as there was in the '30s," said Roderick Phillips, a historian at Carleton University in Ottawa and an expert in the history of marriage.

However, demographers said the new figures are not necessarily a sign that Canada is in a depression-era or wartime-style crisis. . . .

"It doesn't mean people have abandoned life as a couple," said Nicole Marcil-Gratton, a demographer at the University of Montreal. "It means we're evolving into something new, not something worse."

She said that some couples who might have married in earlier eras are now opting to live common-law, and said this is largely responsible for the decline in the marriage rate. In Quebec such unions are no longer just the preludes to marriage they once were, she said. Now couples live together and never marry.

Legally permanent relationships are "not seen any more as something to look forward to," she said.

Ellen Gee, a demographer at Simon Fraser University in Burnaby, B.C., said the marriage rate may also be falling because divorced people, particularly women, no longer feel obliged to remarry. Their financial situations are likely improved, thanks to divorce laws, and society is somewhat more accepting of them. . . .

Some sociologists have begun to declare that the institution of marriage is dying.

But Dr. Phillips disagreed.

"I don't think marriage is going out of style. To say it is is really to take a very narrow view of what marriage is," he said. "Society might well be falling to pieces, but it's not because of the collapse of marriage."

Dr. Gee, who has studied the history of marriage in Canada, agreed that it is unwise to focus on the 1950s and 1960s as the nuptial ideal. She said that era was "tremendously anomalous."

Not only that, but society was much more rigid then, and may not have been best for families, she said, citing the legions of child sexual-abuse cases that happened in that era and are just now coming to light.

"Something was fundamentally wrong," she said. "There was very little room for individual variation."

In earlier times, for example in the late 1800s and early 1900s, couples did not have to follow such a prescribed marital course, she said. Many married in their teens, but many others married much later in life, she found. . . .

Demographers said it is impossible to predict whether marriage rates will continue to decline. In parts of Europe, for example, marriage has become uncommon, replaced by common-law unions.

Source: Alanna Mitchell, "Canadian marriage rates go into dive," *The Globe and Mail*, Thurs., March 4, 1993, pp. A1, A8

In pre-industrial societies, marriage was rarely considered to be the concern of the marriage partners alone. Instead, people saw marriage as the joining together of two kin groups. Each group considered carefully whether the proposed match was good for all its members. This was largely because, upon marriage, family property — land, animals, or other group possessions — would pass from one group to the other. A gift of property would pass from the groom to the bride or her family (as *bride-price*) or from the bride to groom or his family (as *dowry*), or to their eventual offspring, through inheritance.

Another variation found in marriage is the expected place of residence. Anthropologists have found three basic patterns of residence: **patrilocal** (living with the husband's family), **matrilocal** (living with the wife's family), or **neolocal** (living with neither family and, often, at a distance from the spouses' parental families). Place of residence was an important issue in pre-industrial societies because the family was a unit of production. In industrial societies, where the family is not a unit of production, neolocal residence is most common.

As we mentioned, in pre-industrial societies, marriage was a relationship between kin groups, not merely spouses. Usually, the kin groups arranged the marriage and the partners involved had little, if any, choice in the matter. Relationships work differently in our society, where *individuals* get married and their motivations for marriage are considered to be personal.

Romantic love

The tradtional view of marriage — sacred, lifelong and male-dominated—has given way in many cultures to a view that marriage is a residential or lifestyle choice, provisional, and egalitarian.

The Ontario Archives

A central feature of marriage in Canada is commitment to the ideals of romantic love. Love and marriage do not always go together. Yet most people do get married and do so because they believe they love their partner. Nothing feels as natural to us as falling in love. In our culture, we recognize Mr. or Ms. "Right" — the person we want to marry or to be with — by falling in love. Messages such as "If you love her, that's all that matters" and "Love will save the day" are constantly being sent to us in magazines, movies, television, and popular music.

Yet, for all this belief in the inevitability of love, we feel we also have to assist the process. How else to explain the enormous amount of time and money single people spend on personal display ("advertising themselves"), searching for the right mate, and dating candidates for the position of Mr. or Ms. Right!

The ideal of romantic love plays a small role, if any, in mate selection and marriage in many parts of the world. Instead, marriage is usually seen as a practical arrangement, in which love is irrelevant or a matter of luck. What *is* relevant is whether the potential husband will be a good provider, whether the potential wife will be a good homemaker, and whether the union will supply the family and kin group with sons.

In our culture people expect, and are expected, to marry for love. Another way of stating this is that Canadian families are ideally founded on *expressive exchange*, not *instrumental exchange*. The term *exchange* refers to a process of on-going interaction between interdependent spouses. The exchange perspective sees marriage as a give-and-take process, in which each spouse both gives and gets. The stability and well-being of a relationship depends on how well a balance is struck and maintained in this exchange between spouses.

Expressive exchanges in marriage are exchanges of emotional services between spouses. They include hugs and kisses, sexual

Warren Toda, The Toronto Sun

Knight in shining armour? That idea of love and marriage came from the medieval tradition of chivalry.

gratification, companionship, a shoulder to lean on, empathy and understanding. They affirm the affection and love each spouse has for the other. By contrast, *instrumental exchanges* are non-emotional. They maintain a household in practical ways, and include such services as sharing the housework, paying the bills and looking after the children.

As you would expect, every real marriage is a mixture of expressive and instrumental exchanges. As well, every culture values both types of exchange. But cultures differ in the importance they attach to each. In our society, instrumental exchanges have always been important, particularly in families raising children. However, our culture considers expressive exchanges to be more important in marriage than instrumental ones.

In our society, people are urged to marry partners they love, not just people who would help out in practical ways. If Parsons is right and the family has lost most of its practical functions, then the modern family is mainly expressive, directed to satisfying emotional, psychological, and personality needs.

Unlike many other institutions in society, families re-distribute the product of other larger organizations (e.g., paychecks) and do so along expressive, not purely instrumental lines. Both economic and non-economic rules of exchange are present at the same time, which is often what makes family life so hard to understand (Curtis, 1986). For example, it is often hard to know why more couples *don't* break up: whether it is because of hidden but strong emotions or more practical concerns like the welfare of the children, or a shared income.

Mate selection

Historically, people have tended to practise endogamy in choosing a mate. **Endogamy** is the requirement or preference that people marry within their own social group. In a village of several hundred people, the "marriage pool" of eligible mates is larger than an extended family household, but people are tied together by generations of intermarriage. Everyone is related to everyone else at a few removes.

In a larger village or town, a person would probably marry someone not even distantly connected by earlier marriage. However, rules of endogamy would require that person to marry within his or her own social class, caste, religious group, ethnic or racial group, or geographic region. To some degree, kin group advantage was the goal of such a practice. Wherever land or other immovable property might be lost through marriage, the pressure toward endogamy is still strong.

But to a larger degree, endogamy is rooted in feelings of social distance, which we discussed in Chapter 6. People are simply more comfortable marrying "insiders." For that reason, endogamy increases when the group is suffering discrimination by outsiders and has to strengthen its cohesion by emphasizing group boundaries in marriage.

Even today, these factors influence the likelihood someone will marry a person much like themselves — for example, belonging to the same religious or ethnic background. Research on students in Manitoba finds a strong relationship between ethnic identity and the desire to marry within one's ethnic group.

People who prefer to marry members of their own ethnic group usually have a strong ethnic identity (Parsonson, 1987).

Exogamy means marrying *outside* one's social group. Exogamous societies are occasionally small and based on kinship, like the Kung bushmen of the Kalahari desert. Exogamy gives the members of small societies a better chance to survive because it increases the size of the group they can call on in the event of famine, war, or other trouble. It is a good survival strategy where group resources are few and the group does not feel threatened by (all) outside groups.

Exogamy is also practised, increasingly, in our own society. To a large extent, endogamous norms such as ethnic and religious preference, have broken down. People feel less committed to marrying within their own group than they once did.

Naturally, the emphasis on romantic love in marriage has put a great emphasis on careful mate selection and the choice of a spouse who is emotionally compatible (if not socially similar). Yet, despite our avowals of "love at first sight" and our assertion that "love is blind," social scientists have discovered a method to our mating madness. As a general rule, people fall in love with and marry people who are similar to them in important ways.

Homogamy is what sociologists call this tendency for like to marry like — for people to marry others who are similar in their racial, ethnic, national, or religious background. Similarities in age, physical attractiveness and appearance, class and social status, and geographic proximity are also important considerations.

There are several reasons why people tend to be homogamous. First, they are more likely to meet others who are (at least socially) like themselves than to meet people unlike themselves. This is a consequence of the social circles within which people move and interact with others. Second, we usually like people who think the way we do and act the way we expect them to; usually, we feel comfortable in their presence. If we like ourselves, we will probably like people who are similar to us. Third, instrumental and expressive exchanges are easier to balance where like is marrying like. That's because people are bringing similar qualities and resources to the marriage.

The benefits of homogamy show up throughout the research literature on families. For example, an American study has found that couples of the same religious denomination — especially, couples who attend church together — have more successful marriages than other couples (Heaton and Pratt, 1990). Australians also prefer partners of the same religious identification, although members of *some* religious denominations are much more homogamous than others (Hayes, 1991).

Couples also regard educational homogamy as important in choosing their mate. In fact, its importance has been increasing over time, while the importance of social class and other ascriptive (inborn or hard to change) similarities (like religion) has been decreasing (Kalmijn, 1991).

By contrast, **heterogamy** is marriage between people who differ in important respects, whether socially or psychologically. Though heterogamy is more often the exception than the rule, there are many reasons why heterogamy is common and, possibly, increasing.

First, marriageable people are meeting a wider variety of potential mates than they did in the past, especially at college or university. This gives them a larger marriage pool and a wider range of choice, if they want to exercise it. Second, many people want to escape from the groups and communities in which they grew up, and marrying an outsider is a good way to do this. In particular, heterogamous marriage offers the chance for upward mobility. Third, heterogamy offers a larger range of possible exchanges in marriage. It allows a mate to trade off one quality or characteristic for another: for example, youth and beauty for wealth and status.

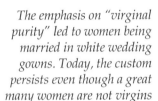

Erotic property

Let's take this notion of "marriage as exchange" to the limit. If we strip away the romantic notions, marriage is like the purchase of a "consumer durable" — a house or recreational vehicle. (We will have more to say about consumer durables later in this chapter.) By marrying, we take ownership of "erotic property," and that means exclusive sexual rights to someone's body. Sociologist Randall Collins makes two main points about this system of erotic property: namely, that (1) marriage is a system of property relations, and (2) every marriage system is unequally structured: men have far more property rights over women than women have over men.

As Collins (1982: 123) notes:

A couple who live together and have sexual intercourse exclusively with each other are for all intents and purposes married. If this goes on for several years, in many places they are considered legally married, as a "common law" marriage. On the other hand, a couple who are legally married but never have sexual intercourse is said not to have "consummated" the marriage. This is grounds for legal annulment, since the implicit terms of the marriage contract are not put into effect. In our society, then, marriage seems to be a contract for exclusive rights to sexual access between two people. Socially speaking, they are exchanging their bodies as sexual property to each other.

The emphasis on "virginal purity" led to women being married in white wedding gowns. Today, the custom persists even though a great many women are not virgins when they marry, and many North Americans no longer care about this issue.

Dick Hemingway

Collins believes that sexual property "is the key to the family structure; it is the hinge on which everything else turns." This can be shown, Collins argues, by our ideas about infidelity. "Traditionally, before the legal reforms of recent decades, the only way one could get divorced was by proving adultery. This has been true up to the present day in conservative, Catholic-dominated countries such as Italy" (*ibid.*). Adultery is considered such a serious infraction because it violates the right to exclusive sexual access.

This also helps to explain why most societies placed a heavy emphasis on the bride being a virgin at marriage but have not usually regarded male virginity at marriage as being equally important, if at all. In almost every case, the property system underlying marriage was one of males owning women's bodies.

These ideas continue to exert a strong hold on people's thinking. A recent survey of sexual attitudes and behaviour reveals that in Quebec, apparently the most liberated province in Canada, 96.4% believe faithfulness between a couple is essential — even more important than a stable relationship or active sex life; however, 22.4% of men and 11.1 per cent of women admit they have cheated on their partner. (*The Globe and Mail*, January 20, 1994: A4).

Arranged marriages versus love marriages

If we put erotic property under kin group control, we get "arranged marriage." In most societies for most of history, marriages have *not* been based on love but on the needs, beliefs or desires of a couple's relatives. Such "arranged marriages" are most common in societies where we find extended families.

There, rights to the land are passed from one generation to the next (usually, from father to son). Since marriage is an arrangement between families — not just between individual mates — it makes sense that marriages are arranged in order to protect family assets. Parents also want to minimize conflict between the families that will be joined together by their children's marriage.

For these reasons, the choice of marriage partners is far too important to be left to the whims of youth. Spouses are chosen because the union is economically advantageous, or because of friendship or kinship obligations. Occasionally, people marry other people they have never met.

In his classic study *World Revolution and Family Patterns*, William Goode (1963) predicted that modernization would do away with extended families, leaving only the nuclear families with which we are all familiar. Yet, for people who live in such societies (i.e., those undergoing modernization), arranged marriage persists because it maintains social traditions. According to Ashraf Ahmed, a Bangladesh sociologist (1986), it (1) helps keep the family traditions and value systems intact, (2) helps consolidate and extend family property, (3) enhances the value of the kinship group, (4) keeps young people from getting into the uncertainty of searching for a mate and (5) strengthens parental power over the children. Less intentionally, the system also maintains social stratification.

As you can see, arranged marriage is much concerned with instrumental, instead of expressive, exchanges. In India, for example, marriage has traditionally been arranged between young children. Usually the couple would not live together until the wife reached sexual maturity. In other cases, young girls were initiated into sexual activity long before they reached adolescence. It is now illegal for children under 15 to marry in India, but reports say the practice still continues.

In the West today, few marriages are "arranged" in the traditional sense. Yet in an article in the University of Toronto's student newspaper *The Varsity* (January 25, 1993: page 7), Aziza Khan reported that

 Most second generation Canadian-Pakistanis grew up expecting and accepting the concept of an arranged marriage — an arranged marriage was inevitable and the social norm. And yet the definition of an arranged marriage today differs from the definition of one 20 years ago... In Toronto today, most individuals actively participate in selecting their partners. The couple meets first with their families. If they are interested in each other, they can speak to each other on the phone and go out with or without a chaperon, depending on the values of the families.

As in the past, the family — not the young people themselves — are in charge. Khan continues

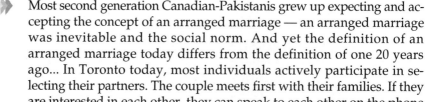 Parents are the major instigators when it comes to an arranged marriage. They try to match up their child with someone from the same socioeconomic and educational background. It's not a relationship be-

tween individuals but rather one between families. It's not an individual decision but a collective [one], involving six family members at least.

As you can see, marriage is a complex relationship involving a wide variety of social factors and influences. Modern marriage has its own complexities and raises a whole host of new problems in the relations between a husband and wife. We will return to this issue after examining another crucial relationship, the one between parent and child.

PARENTS AND CHILDREN

Historically, the relationship between parent and child was the kernel of a broader set of relationships called *kinship relations*. We are related to many more people than our immediate family. The total network of people related by common ancestry or adoption is called a *kin group*.

In our society, relatives of both our parents are considered kin. In many other societies, however, people trace their descent through one line only — either their father's or mother's line. In a *matrilineal* society, a person traces descent (or kinship) through the mother's line only. The father, his parents, brothers and sisters, and their children are not included in that person's kin group.

So, in a matrilineal society, you will only have cousins through your mother's sisters, not through your father's. In a *patrilineal* society, this pattern is exactly reversed. All descent is traced through the father, his brothers and his father.

Our society is neither matrilineal nor patrilineal — it is *bilateral*. This means that relatives of both of our parents are considered kin. We have maternal and paternal aunts, uncles, grandparents, cousins, and so on. Bilateral descent fits well with an equalitarian authority structure where father and mother have a roughly equal say in family matters.

In many societies, what we consider the family is embedded in a much broader web of kinship relations, and a household will encompass numerous kin. In others, such as our own, a household usually consists of parents and their unmarried children. These two main forms of family household are referred to as the *extended family* and the *nuclear family*.

As we noted earlier, the common type of family household in our society is a nuclear family. It consists of one or two generations living together — typically, one or two parents and their children. The nuclear family is a *conjugal family*, in which priority is given to marital ties over blood ties. The fundamental relationship is between spouses, not between one or more spouses and their parents, siblings or more distant kin (like aunts, uncles, and cousins).

An extended family is one in which two or more generations of relatives live together. For example, it may include grandparents and/or grandchildren, and relatives connected by other relations than marriage and parenthood, such as uncles, aunts, and cousins. The extended family is a *consanguine family*, since priority is given to blood ties over marital ties. Consanguine families stress the importance of relationships between parents and their children, among siblings, and with other "blood-related" members of the kin group.

Each of these forms has its advantages and disadvantages. The extended family usually serves as one big productive unit, with all able-bodied members contributing to the family's common good. The members of this unit cooperate in such productive activities as agriculture, craft work, hunting and gathering, building shelters, and other activities related to subsistence.

One benefit of such a family structure is that members of an extended family are able to rely on one another when they need emotional support. For example, children can go to aunts and uncles, cousins and grandparents when they have a problem they feel they cannot talk about with their parents. Spouses can rely on their parents and siblings for comfort and support. This puts less strain on the marital relationship. And, in an extended family, grandparents can be sure they will be taken care of in their old age.

Grandparents also act as supplementary or surrogate parents in their own right. For example, grandmothers still play an important role in many black American families (Pearson et al., 1990). There, they are often surrogate mothers and, in this role, help to control and punish the family's children. Grandparents in white families play a different role: they interact with their grandchildren less often and are more likely to reward, not discipline them.

The nuclear family has some advantages over the extended family. For example, such a family is not obliged to remain in any particular location. Because it is small it can move easily to take advantage of job opportunities in another part of the country, or in another country entirely. In industrial societies, most people must live where they can find employment, and that often forces them to move.

It follows, then, that the emergence of a middle class and industrial society helped shape the development of the nuclear family as a private institution. Britain and the North American colonies were among the first areas to display this form of organization (Johnson, 1989).

However, the nuclear family also has its disadvantages. It offers its members too few people to rely on in times of financial trouble or emotional stress. Family members are liable to expect too much from each other because they have no one else to turn to. This reliance puts a lot of strain on relationships between spouses, or between parents and children.

As family life changes, so do many other aspects of our lives, both major and minor. This change in family composition has important consequences for the many immigrants to North America, who have often left members of their extended family behind. For example, Korean families in North America are moving towards nuclear family structures; as a result, many family traditions, such as filial obligation, may soon disappear (Kim et al., 1991). This change to a nuclear family structure also weakens people's connections with their extended kin in Korea and with Korean culture as well.

Child care and child raising

Most people marry with the idea of having children. What they rarely know or admit is that, for all its pleasures, parenthood imposes a great many burdens. Family instability and conflict often arises out of the trials of parenthood.

The onset of parenthood is a trying time. "Both men and women express more feeling of strain at this stage than at any other period of their married lives" (Campbell, 1980: 1984). Raising small children strains the marriage: disagreements become more common, both husband and wife feel they get less companionship from their mate than they once did, marital satisfaction declines and the enjoyment of parenthood is slight."Two out of five of these mothers of small children go so far as to admit they sometimes wish they could be free of the responsibilities of being a parent, a much larger proportion than is found among mothers of older children" (Campbell, 1980: 188).

A comparison of families (Lupri and Frideres, 1981: 300) shows that, at all ages and marital durations, women without children are more satisfied with marriage than are women *with* children. Whether or not a woman works outside the home also affects the pressures of parenthood. Employed wives reach a lower level of satisfaction with marriage than housewives. Conversely, the husbands of housewives reach a lower level of marital satisfaction than husbands of women who work for pay. In all cases, the lowest point occurs when the children are adolescents.

Parenthood has the greatest impact on employed wives because of their heavy dual responsibilities at work and home. Research (Marshall, 1993) finds that Canadian women aged 15 to 44 with a full-time (paid) job are twice as likely to feel severely "time crunched" as either their husband (at any age) or women over age 45 with a full-time paid job. Presumably the reason is, there are children at home for whom they are primarily responsible.

On the other hand, husbands of housewives are more affected by parenthood than their spouses because their financial burden increases as their children enter adolescence. This greater need for money in middle age, just when a husband's income has started to level off, is often called the "life cycle squeeze" (Lupri and Frideres, *op. cit.*).

The sociological evidence leaves no doubt that parenthood strains the relationship between husbands and wives. This in itself is a good explanation of why many couples are reducing or eliminating childbearing, but not the only one. The decline in parenthood has been going on for over a century, for other reasons. Chiefly, it has become progressively harder to live a comfortable, middle-class urban life with many children. In fact, the financial problems which affect parents and strain the husband-wife relationship can strain parent-child relations as well. Economic hardship can lead parents to provide inconsistent and punitive discipline which, in turn, causes the child emotional distress and other social, emotional and cognitive harm (McLloyd, 1990).

Given the choice between having more children and having more disposable income, most Canadians over the last 100 years have chosen the latter. With the recurring economic recessions of the 1970s, early 1980s and 1990s, the motivation to further limit childbearing grew stronger and, with the development of new contraceptive technology, the wish for a smaller family was easier to fulfil.

Prolonged dependency

For most of you reading this book, parenthood and its problems are still in the future. In your household, you are probably the son or daughter, not the mother or father. It's no picnic being a parent today, but no picnic being a grown-up child either. **Parents and children, like husbands and wives, have different perceptions of the family that reflect structural features of our society, not individual personality differences. These differences of perception are often referred to as the generation gap**

The most significant structural feature that promotes a generation gap is the lengthening of the time that a person is economically and emotionally dependent upon his or her family. In pre-industrial societies, adulthood came soon after the end of childhood, usually around the late teens. At this time a person would get married and be considered a full adult member of society. Age categories such as "adolescence" and "youth," which we have come to take for granted, did not exist.

In many third-world societies, this arrangement still exists. For example, Aptekar (1990) writes of street children from poor families in Colombia who are raised for early independence. Children from wealthier families live within a more rigid family structure, and become independent at a much later age.

Several factors have led to the lengthening of the period of dependency and childhood. As we saw in the chapter on socialization, one factor is modern education. In pre-industrial societies, most people spent their lives doing what their mother or father had done. If a boy's father was a peasant farmer, he too would become a farmer; if a girl's mother looked after the home and the garden, she would do the same. Children learned to perform the work expected of them as adults by performing their tasks from early childhood on at home. By the end of childhood, they were ready for adult responsibilities.

Today, we learn most of what adults need to know — especially, future job skills — outside the home. And because we have so much more to learn in an industrial society, we have to attend school for many years. This means that many people are still students in their early thirties: still dependent financially on their families, often still living at home. As Exhibit 8.2 shows, this period of dependency has been extended, and filled with uncertainty, by a continuing recession.

This financial dependency prolongs the unequal relationship between parents and children past the point where young people willingly accept their parents' authority. It is difficult to attend college or university — where you are expected to act responsibly, think for yourself, and succeed or fail by your own efforts — and then come home to be treated as a child again.

In many cases, the roles are reversed when parents enter old age. But like adolescence, old age with its many characteristic features—such as disengagement from the world—is a social construct, not merely a biological "fact of life."

John McNeill

In pre-industrial societies, becoming an adult usually meant marrying and taking on the responsibility for raising your own children. Today, few couples get married until they are in their twenties. This prolongs the period of *emotional* dependence on parents. Young adults find that their parents' opinion of them continues to be an important part of their sense of self, just at the time when structural factors, such as financial dependence, lack of autonomy, joblessness, and a prolonged skill training period are lowering that opinion. They are still locked into an intense emotional relationship with their parents at an age at which, in another society, they would be independent, responsible adults with a spouse and children of their own.

The result of this lengthened period of dependence is that adulthood is put off. The age categories of adolescence and youth have emerged as a result. They do not reflect a biological fact about age; they are social categories generated by specific structural features of our society. This does not mean that they are not "real," however. In our society, they are as real as ethnicity, race, or gender: that is, they have real social consequences.

EXHIBIT 8.2 *Recession creates lost generation*

The recession has had such a disastrous effect on the job prospects of young Canadians that it may actually have created a lost generation. . . .

- Unprecedented numbers of young Canadians have been wrestled out of the work force;
- Proportionately, more of them lost their jobs than adults;
- It will take years longer for them to gain back jobs than it will for adults. . . .

[I]n 1989, before the recession hit, 62.3 per cent of Canadians aged 15 to 24 were employed. By November of 1992, the number had fallen to 50 per cent. Adult employment, meanwhile, had overtaken the levels it had reached before the recession. . . .

Young Canadians also began losing jobs fully eight months before the beginning of the recession, the Statistics Canada study says. And by November of 1993, 16 per cent of Canadians aged 15 to 24 had never held a job, a sharp increase from the 10 per cent who had not worked in November of 1989. . . .

And while more young Canadians are turning to school to fill their days (Statistics Canada says 56 per cent of young people were in school full time in November of 1993, compared with 49 per cent in November of 1989), this avenue, too, is being barricaded with steep increases in tuition fees and much tougher entrance guidelines.

Not only that, this additional education does not guarantee a good job if the jobs are nowhere to be found, said Lars Osberg, an economist at Dalhousie University. "Going back to school only delays the problem. It doesn't actually solve it." . . .

Dr. [Gordon] Betcherman [director of a labour research group at Queen's University in Kingston] said that this generation of Canadians may not find its niche in the job market until the end of the century, when the oldest batch of baby boomers begins to retire.

The boomers "are sort of jamming up the system," he said.

He said he believes that the government should step forcefully into the issue by devising policies to help young, skilled Canadians into what he called the "good-jobs" sector.

Source: Alanna Mitchell, "Future is bleak for youth, study says," *The Globe and Mail*, Thurs. March 3, 1994, p. A1, A2

Back to the Books

The chart shows a steep rise in the school attendance rate among 20 to 24-year olds

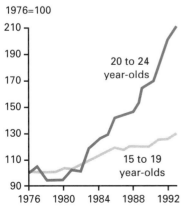

Source: Statistics Canada Labour Force Survey

Young and Dispensable

The number of youths with jobs or looking for work between 15 and 24 fell further in the latest recession than in previous ones.

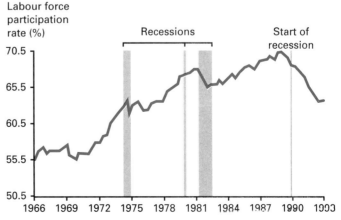

Source: Statistics Canada Labour Force Survey

Economic aspects of family change

Traditional families continue to survive but their numbers are growing slowly while non-traditional families — especially two-income marriages, common-law marriages, and lone-parent households — are increasing rapidly and show no sign of ceasing to grow. These forms of non-traditional family all have consequences for adults' experience of parenthood and, even more, for children's experience of childhood.

In well over half of all married couples, both spouses work for pay. Today, few women stop working when they get married. Of women who stop work to have a baby, most return to work shortly after their child is born. The number of two-earner families will continue to rise as more and more women enter the work force and stay in it for a larger part of their adult lives.

The rise of the two-earner family has caused many changes in the marketplace during the last decade. Since both spouses work, they have less time to spend on such tasks as cleaning, cooking, and taking care of the children. They look to outside services and hired help to do these tasks. Fortunately, two incomes provide these couples with the extra money they need to buy conveniences. Their new demands account for a growth in the sales of frozen foods, restaurant foods, household care and child-care services. Two-earner couples have also contributed to the growth of the appliance industry (which makes items like microwave ovens and dishwashers) and the leisure goods industry (which makes VCRs and sports equipment, among other things).

Childless couples have even more *discretionary income* — money to spend on things other than necessities like food and shelter— than families with children do; and this makes childless couples important consumers. *Two* factors explain their large discretionary income: high earning power and low expenses. Most childless couples earn two incomes and childless couples also make about 20% more money than couples with children. In part, this is related to their higher-than-average education: the more education a woman gets, the more likely she will avoid or delay bearing children.

As a result, highly educated, high-income people spend a large portion of their lives without children, enjoying a large discretionary income.

Without child-care expenses to pay, these childless couples have a lot more money to spend on themselves. Economist Gary Becker (1981) has compared childbearing to the purchase of *consumer durables* — long-lasting, often expensive items like automobiles or dishwashers. This comparison has a lot to recommend it; but actually the lifetime expense of raising children — in energy and emotion, as well as money — far outdistances most consumer durables on the market. (The only durable that demands nearly as much time and money is a house.)

This new family imagery — children as consumer durables, mates as erotic property — resists fuzzy, emotional thinking almost to the point of cynicism. But does it simply take a wiseguy "what-if" approach to matters of the heart? Or does it help us understand the trends in marriage and parenthood?

TRENDS IN FAMILY LIFE

As the data in Exhibit 8.3 indicate, a number of important changes *have* been occurring in the Canadian family. They include an increase in the number of families with both husband and wife working for pay, a decline in childbearing and family size, and — another result of the decline in childbearing — the aging of the Canadian population. Does the "new imagery" help us account for the ways people treat their children and mates; for example, the

EXHIBIT 8.3 *Major Family Trends*

Between 1986 and 1992, the Demographic Review Secretariat, working under Statistics Canada, commissioned more than 200 studies and discussed its findings with more than 30,000 Canadians. The Review examined four major trends in Canadian family life: fertility (birth rates), the relationship between fertility and societal aging, people leaving home as place of work, and the diversification of family patterns. These three graphs display some of the findings and conclusions of the research.

Source: "Four major trends for Canada's families," *Transition*, Sept. 1993, pp. 4-7

The Changing Canadian Family

Source: the Demographic Review

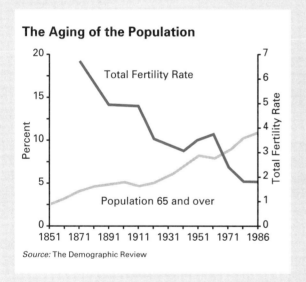

The Aging of the Population

Source: The Demographic Review

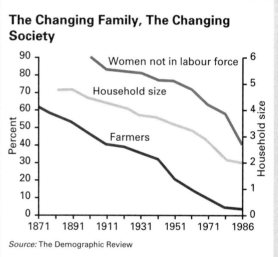

The Changing Family, The Changing Society

Source: The Demographic Review

high rates of divorce, the low rates of childbearing and widespread domestic violence?

It's hard to say. Today, it is impossible to talk about a typical family or typical marriage. The old-style "monolithic family" model (Eichler, 1981) — with a single male breadwinner and stay-at-home wife who looks after two or three children — no longer describes the majority of Canadian adult lives.

In keeping with the new imagery, rates of first marriage have fallen to an all-time low in Canada (Statistics Canada, 1987: 19). This falling national marriage rate has been led by large declines in Quebec which "has not only the lowest rate of all the provinces but one of the lowest rates in the world" (*ibid*). The trend of younger people opting for common-law unions over marriage partly explains this decline. Most people are merely delaying, not rejecting marriage, so the average age at first marriage is increasing.

Catholics are particularly likely to postpone marriage or reject it altogether since, for Catholics, divorce is not widely accepted. Certainly, the Church is reluctant to see people re-marry. Thus, for Catholics, marriage is riskier or comes at a higher "cost" (Ritchey and Dietz, 1990). So both increased common-law cohabitation and delayed marriage reflect a temporary (if not permanent) flight from marriage, and predict lower percentages of people ever marrying. Probably the family will survive as an institution, but not in the form we have grown up idealizing.

Is there a distinct "Canadian" family?

Focusing on the variations outlined above, we can see that the typical Canadian family is nuclear, its residence is neolocal, marriage is monogamous, descent is bilateral, and increasingly the authority structure is equalitarian. The selection of marriage partners is homogamous and usually endogamous, although not as limited as in pre-industrial societies.

In all of these respects, Canadian families are a lot like the families we would find in other industrial countries; in the United States, West Germany, Italy, or Japan, for example. Like families in these other nations, Canadian families are undergoing a great many changes both in terms of norms and in structure. Three recent changes are particularly significant throughout the industrial world: the dramatic rise in the divorce rate, the increase in the number of single-parent families, and the growing acceptance of cohabitation before (or instead of) legal marriage.

Cohabitation

Cohabitation is an arrangement in which an unmarried couple lives together to find out if they are compatible, to cut down on living expenses, or as an alternative to marriage. The major difference between marriage and cohabitation is that the former is an explicit legal commitment and the latter is not.

Even so, the law regards cohabitation that continues for more than three years as a legally binding relationship in certain respects (thus a common-law partnership). Long-term cohabitants owe each other support obligations (though not the sharing of community property) in the event of a breakup. So even here, the difference between marriage and cohabitation has blurred.

New housing patterns make living together easier than ever for unmarried people. Research done in 1984 found that about one adult respondent in six had been in a common-law partnership at one time or another (Burch, 1985: Table 4A). Among young people aged 18 to 29, the proportion was much higher: about one man in five and one woman in four. By 1986, the percentage of people living as couples, who were in cohabiting relationships, had risen from 6.4 in 1981 to 8.3 (Turcotte, 1990). And by Census Day, 1991 one couple in ten was in a cohabiting relationship (*The Globe and Mail*, July 8, 1992: A1).

Often, common-law partnerships are a prelude to marriage. The 1984 Family History Survey revealed that just under half of the people ever in a common-law union ended up marrying their common-law partner. This suggests that common-law unions often serve as trial marriages (Burch, 1985: Table 5), an interpretation supported by evidence (Table 4A) that fewer than 2% of all respondents report having been in more than one such relationship. Indeed, 46% of males and 43% of females who ever cohabited report marrying their common-law partner.

However, cohabiting before marriage does not make the marriage more likely to succeed; in fact, there is evidence to the contrary. Prior cohabitation is found to be positively related to marital disagreement, and an increased probability of divorce. We do not know why this is so. Perhaps people who cohabit are poor marriage risks before they marry. We have no proof that cohabitation itself causes a decline in the quality of a later marriage; but neither is there any proof that cohabitation improves mate selection or trains people for marriage (Booth and Johnson, 1988).

Divorce

A second significant change in North American family life is the increase of divorce. **Divorce** is the legal, formal dissolution of a legal marriage, freeing the spouses to remarry. American research (Glenn, 1989) reports that by the mid-1980s, fewer than one-third of the persons who first married during the mid-1970s were still in their first marriages and were "very happy" with these marriages.

Divorce is increasingly accepted as a valid and appropriate way out of an unhappy marital situation. When children are involved, many people feel that the children are better off with single parents than in a family filled with conflict and, occasionally, violence.

But divorce has its disadvantages too. The increased incidence of child poverty since 1960 has been traced to, among other factors, an increase in divorce and single-parent families. In fact, researchers estimate that child poverty rates in the United States would have been one-third lower if divorce rates had remained at their 1960 level. In particular, the high rate of single-parent black families largely accounts for the different economic experiences of black and white children (Eggebeen and Lichter, 1991).

The Family History Survey (Burch, 1985) shows that about one in ten ever-married males and one in eight ever-married females have ended a marriage in divorce. The situation is changing, though. A larger proportion of people aged 30 to 49 have experienced divorce than those aged 50 to 64. These data help to explain why most demographers project that newly married couples run a roughly 40% risk of future divorce. Their projections assume that rates of divorce will continue to rise, or at least remain high among young and middle-aged people.

Analyses of divorce data show that divorce rates are high among couples who married when they were very young or knew each other for only a short time before marrying. People who marry early are often unprepared for the reality of married life. Today, there is wide and growing recognition of the pitfalls of early marriage:

 The divorce rate among such young marriages is estimated at from two to four times that among persons who marry after 20 years of age. The divorce rate is related to low educational levels, low economic levels, premarital pregnancies, and possibly to personality difficulties (Leslie and Korman, 1985: 396).

Young women who marry or bear children before completing their education run an even higher risk than men. Data from the 1984 Family History Survey (Pool and Moore, 1986: 49) suggest that many female lone parents became parents too soon, before acquiring the education and job skills to make themselves economically independent. The authors continue, "In the longer run, this lack of job-related resources may have limited their power within a marriage or union and, thus, may have predisposed its termination."

Other studies also show that the factors which cause marital instability, such as health problems, lack of social integration, or low income, have the strongest effect on young couples (Booth et al., 1986). To make matters worse, the duration of marriage also affects marital satisfaction, especially for women and blacks. As such, people who marry young are more likely to divorce; but if they do not divorce, they will spend a longer time than other people feeling unhappy in their marriage (Glenn, 1989).

Risks of divorce are also high among people who live in the city, have friends and relatives who did not look favourably on the marriage, or (according to some research) were previously married. Low socio-economic status also increases the likelihood of divorce. Finally, divorce is more likely where the wife is economically independent than where she is not.

What causes marital breakdown, whether it ends in divorce or not? Some researchers believe the causes include too much pressure on the nuclear family. In the event of a crisis, we have few people to rely on for comfort and support. Others suggest couples have unfulfilled expectations of a love that will last forever. People feel their marriage has failed when it loses its romantic lustre. Finally, researchers note that the growing economic independence of women means that more women can leave unhappy marriages today than in the past. Women are exercising more control over their own lives. But research has also revealed some of the factors that contribute to a happy marriage.

Studies have shown that couples who regard each other as good friends are usually happier than average; these couples also work harder than others to maintain a good marriage (Altrocchi, 1988). Research also finds that spouses who are autonomous (or independent) are more likely to enjoy stable marriages with each other. Better able to manage freedom and intimacy than other people, they require less traditional sex-roles. This promotes egalitarianism in the marriage, which research shows is more in line with modern society and also more satisfying to spouses (Vannoy, 1991).

Finally, as we mentioned above, people who share things in common with their partner — for example, family worship, a similar degree of religiosity, and church attendance — tend to be more satisfied with married life (Dudley and Kosinski, 1990). Apparently, it is the *process of sharing* with a spouse, not precisely what is *shared*, that accounts for the higher-than-average degree of marital satisfaction (for more on this, see Tepperman, 1994: cc. 5 and 8).

Single-parent families

As more marriages end in separation or divorce, single-parent families increase in numbers. A **single-parent family** is a family in which only one parent lives with the dependent children; however, child care and child support may be provided by both parents.

The great majority of these families are headed by women. This has caused a debate, as yet largely unresolved, over whether the absence of a male parent has harmful effects on child development, especially at low SES levels. For example, Brownfield (1987) posits that for boys, identifying with a father figure curbs violent behaviour. Yet the physical absence of a father is unrelated to (self-reported) violent behaviour. At the least, children from a single-parent family feel a sense of loss about their absent parent. In contrast, research on single-parent families in India shows that the problems children have are economic more often than psychological (Bharat, 1988).

Recently published research conducted in Nova Scotia (see Exhibit 8.4) suggests that, in Canada too, the main issues are economic. Poverty aside, single mothers and their children seem to have few difficulties with their family lives.

EXHIBIT 8.4 *Unwed mothers vindicated in study*

. . . The first definitive study of unmarried mothers, its results just published, shows that a mother's schooling, not her marital status, determines how well her children turn out. . . .

Poverty, it found, is the big culprit when it comes to the health and welfare of children. . . .

The study shatters a number of myths—most of them imported from the United States—about unmarried mothers and their children. . . .

The study showed that both married and unmarried mothers with high-school diplomas, and therefore the prospect of earning higher wages, were less likely to bring their children up in poverty than women without diplomas. And conversely, mothers without a diploma were more likely to bring their children up in poverty, whether married or not.

The study also found that unmarried mothers do not have scads of children. Those who never married during the 10 years the study was conducted had an average of 1.55 children, compared to the 2.40 children of mothers who were married throughout the period. . . .

The children of unmarried mothers do not live in violence and neglect. Over the 10 years of the study, none of the unmarried mothers was reported to authorities for abusing or neglecting her child. In fact, extensive intelligence and behavioural tests showed that the children of both married and unmarried mothers fell into the normal range. They were generally well cared for.

And while the study showed that many of the mothers—both unmarried and married—drew on social assistance during the decade, it also showed that the unmarried mothers did not get on welfare and stay there. . . .

Just 3 per cent of all the mothers had been on welfare for more than nine years. . . .

In general,. . . the study found that many of the unmarried mothers never caught up with the married mothers when it came to education and income. . . .

. . . 77 per cent of the married mothers had graduated from high school but only 39 per cent of the unmarried ones had.

[As a result] poverty rates among the unmarried mothers were. . . dramatically higher than among married mothers. Fifty-three per cent of unmarried mothers lived in poverty compared to 18 per cent of the married mothers.

It was this poverty — whether it stemmed from unmarried or married mothers — that caused problems for the children, the report concluded. The poor children, who were 10 at the time, scored lower on tests of vocabulary, verbal comprehension, IQ determinants, reading and math. . . .

Source: Alanna Mitchell, "Unwed mothers vindicated in study," *The Globe and Mail*, Mon., March 14, 1994, pp. A1, A2

Single-parent families are becoming common. They also constitute a high proportion of all family, and especially all childhood, experiences of poverty. They are a stark reminder of what sociologists call the **feminization of poverty**: as we noted in Chapter 5, on class and status inequality, the "poor" in Canada are predominantly women and children. The women include single mothers living on welfare, who cannot work because they cannot afford daycare for their children; and elderly women who spent their lives as homemakers and could not contribute to a pension plan that would support them decently in their old age.

Being a single parent is difficult all over the world. In a traditionally patriarchal society like India, single-mothers' problems are compounded by a host of other factors. Divorced and widowed females have low social status, especially since Indian society attaches a stigma to divorce. Given a sex-segregated labour force, single mothers and their children have a hard time surviving in India (Bharat, 1986).

Just as the nuclear family once represented a separation of the tasks of production from reproduction, "the lone-parent family represents the separation of marital and child rearing processes. As the adult adapts to movement between the lone, nuclear and **reconstituted families**, children provide the continuity as they grow through all the developmental stages" (Moore, 1989: 348). For both mother and child, family living is a series of adjustments. The most reliably constant relationship is that between parent and child, and even that will change significantly when the child leaves home.

PROBLEMS OF THE MODERN FAMILY

Spousal inequalities

Across societies, we see wide variations in the extent to which rights and responsibilities are shared equally within families. Families differ in whether they are **equalitarian** (or egalitarian), **patriarchal**, or **matriarchal**.

In the **patriarchal family** the husband/father is the formal household head. He has the final say in all important matters because of his role, not because he has demonstrated more wisdom, or has more skill or more experience. In this type of family, maleness alone confers authority.

In societies where such families are found — for example, throughout the Islamic world and in many parts of Latin America — women have a limited or nonexistent role in public life, and usually their restricted status is sanctioned by fundamentalist religious beliefs. Even in the United States, religious fundamentalism proves to be the best predictor of preference for a patriarchal family.

Patriarchal authority relations characterized family life in many pre-industrial societies, and patriarchal features remain in our own. The extreme alternative to a patriarchal family, a matriarchal family, is rare in human societies. A **matriarchal family** is one in which the woman/mother is formal head of the household. We have many examples of such families in our own society, especially where a marriage breakdown has left the mother head of a *single-parent family*. Sociologists (e.g., Wilson, 1988) report that, at least since the Second World War, this pattern has characterized the black family in America, in a subculture where males have been particularly transient. The result has been a large proportion of children living in mother-dominated, single-parent families. However, we do not know of an entire society in which the matriarchal family was a dominant or idealized family form.

Compared to families in other societies, most families in our society are closer in form to equalitarian than to patriarchal or matriarchal families. In an *equalitarian family*, the wife and husband make important decisions jointly. Their opinions are equally important and mutually respected. Neither has authority over the other in the eyes of the law, and both have a roughly equal say in all family matters.

This does not mean that all families today are equalitarian. It is difficult in a great many households to know if a family is equalitarian or not. Also, although spousal equality has become the ideal, it may not yet have become the practice. Especially in families of middle-aged or less-educated people, there is still a lot of inequality between husbands and wives *in practice*.

The result is a gender-based difference in women's and men's experience of marriage. Sociologist Jesse Bernard (1973) calls this a difference between *his marriage* and *her marriage*. According to Bernard, marriages often contain two very different views of the relationship: the wife's and the husband's. The two perspectives are different enough, and equally distant from the objective reality, to constitute two different marriages.

These differences in marital experience have, if anything, been reinforced by women's large-scale entry into paid work. Now married women inhabit what sociologists Hugh and Pat Armstrong (1978) call a "double ghetto." We find this phenomenon all over the world; for example, a Greek study reports that a quarter of all Greek women work this double load (Sinopoulos, 1990).

As we saw in the last chapter, women's freedom to work for pay, pursue a career, and be economically independent does not mean freedom from domestic work. On the contrary, women continue to be mainly responsible for the household chores, even after they have put in a full day's work outside the home. ("Being responsible" doesn't mean that they *do* all the work; in many cases, husbands share it. But it does mean that, no matter what, women are obliged to make sure the work gets done.)

Though husbands and children are often slow to admit it, the work housewives provide to their families would cost billions of dollars if paid for on the open market. Yet when married women go out to work for pay, their husbands do *not* significantly increase the time they spend on domestic duties, even if young children are present. The result is a worrisome "devaluation of children." Even college students of both sexes expect that, upon starting a family, the wife will play a larger role in the home than the husband (Spade and Reese, 1991). Unfortunately, domestic inequality often mirrors women's subordination on the job. Their workplace experiences of domination reinforce their domestic experiences, and vice versa.

An American study found that husbands and wives identify with work outside the home in more or less the same way, but they relate it to family life in different ways. Wives feel that they should give precedence to their identity within the family, rather than to their work. Husbands, on the other hand, feel no need to make any choice between the two, and strive for a balance of work and family roles (Bielby and Bielby, 1989). This difference is illustrated by the fact that wives are more reluctant than husbands to accept a promotion if it means relocating. This has to do with women still holding traditional beliefs about the primacy of the family (Bielby and Bielby, 1992).

Likewise, a survey in Brazil has shown that most working women define their primary role as maternal, and would put their family before their job (Meleis et al., 1990).

Generally, feminists view the family as a source of female subordination, but black feminists take issue with this: "They argue that ... in racist societies, the family is commonly experienced by Black women as the *least oppressive* institution" (Stasiulis, 1990: 284). People experience many more kinds of marriage than just the *his marriage* and *her marriage* described by Bernard. Unfortunately, this variety of types of marital experience has not yet been adequately researched.

Family violence

Because the family has long been considered the most private institution in our society, until recently few people realized how pervasive violence is as a part of family life. In the past, it was taken for granted that parents had a right to use physical force to discipline their children. Most parents had little hesitation in giving their child a slap in public. Violence between spouses was less acceptable, at least in public, but many men believed that they had as much right to hit their wives as to discipline their children.

Feminists argue that wife-battering and child abuse are two aspects of the same phenomenon: they both stem from gender inequality. What's more, reported incidents of physical abuse against children who receive hospital attention reveal that wife battering is also the most common context for child abuse (Stark and Flitcraft, 1988).

Verbal aggression is another type of family violence and it commonly results from a deficiency in communication skills; that is, people are not able to express their grievances in constructive ways. The worst type of verbal abuse is characterized by attacks on the character of the other person. Evidence shows that character attacks correlate with physical violence more highly than any other kind of verbal aggression (Infante and Sabourin, 1990).

A third form of family violence we are beginning to learn about is elder abuse, mistreatment directed toward the elderly by their children and grandchildren. In Japan, elder abuse often takes place between wives and their mothers-in-law; in this context, verbal abuse is much more common than physical violence or neglect. At the root of such conflicts are personality differences, disagreement over disciplining grandchildren, and difficulties arising from sharing the same kitchen (Kaneko and Yamada, 1990).

In many cultures, family violence is not seen as acceptable at all. For example, in Fiji physical violence occurs occasionally. But it is traditionally unacceptable, particularly within families, since women and children are seen as weak and deserving of protection. As well, such behaviour violates the expectation that family members will cooperate and help one another. To a degree, violence in Fiji is also controlled by fears of ancestral punishment (Aucoin, 1990).

Such cultural brakes on family violence do not exist in North America. Far from being a safe haven in a difficult world, the family has been, for many people, a source of pain, humiliation, and anger. The psychological consequences of living with the terror of family violence are only beginning to be explored. They include shared delusional disorders — that is, similar mental illnesses for all family members — characterized by paranoia and an extreme identification with the aggressor in the family (Wexler, 1992). Social isolation and marginality, and repeated crises, work to promote this family pattern.

The abusiveness in family life is illustrated by the law's failure to recognize marital rape as a crime until 1983. That marital rape was not considered assault tells us both that it was taken for granted that wives should be sexually available at their husband's will and that the use of violence by men was considered acceptable when directed against their wives (Pettifer and Torge, 1987). Conversely, the change in law that made it a crime suggests declining support for the idea of the wife as "erotic property."

Living in a violent household also gives children a predisposition towards violence. As well, the more violent and punitive the parents, the lower a child's self-esteem, emotional well-being, and interpersonal competence (Scott et al., 1991).

Although the laws and people's attitudes have changed slightly, much family violence goes unreported. The Canadian Urban Victimization Survey conducted in 1982 showed that only 44% of cases of wife abuse were reported to the police (Johnson, 1988). Half the wives who did not seek help from the police indicated that they feared revenge by the offender, and about a third indicated that they "wanted to protect the offender" (Johnson, 1988: 19). Altogether, 59% considered the abuse to be "a personal matter and of no concern to the police." An even smaller proportion of cases of child or elder abuse are reported to authorities.

Because of the failure to report family violence, we do not have good statistics on the prevalence of such violence. However, homicide statistics, which are usually quite complete, tell the same tale as surveys of sexual and child abuse. People are at a greater risk of physical injury from a spouse or family member than from a stranger. Johnson and Chisholm (1989: 17) report that 40% of solved homicides between 1985 and 1987 were cases of domestic homicide, and in the vast majority of these cases men killed their wives or common-law partners.

We have no proof that wife battering and child abuse are increasing, only an indication that they are widespread. A national survey conducted in 1986 (Lupri, 1989) found 18% of men admitting to one or more acts of violence against their partners. Younger men (aged 29 or younger) were the most likely to act violently. Men in British Columbia had the highest rate, 26%, while those in Quebec had the lowest, 13%.

More recent analyses (Lupri, 1993) find no correlation between violence and income or education. In other words, violence is found in the richest homes as often as it is in the poorest ones. However, as we noted in Chapter 7, men who have experienced many "stressful" life events, such as unemployment or having to work overtime, are particularly likely to abuse their spouse (Lupri, 1989). This does not mean that stress *caused* the violence. Expressing violence in this way shows that abusers see their wives as acceptable outlets for a husband's frustration.

Finally, Lupri finds a high degree of correlation between different kinds of domestic violence: physical, verbal, psychological and symbolic (that is, violence directed against household objects). It would be wrong to think that frustrated people who release their anger verbally, or by breaking dishes, have reduced the risk of physical abuse. On the contrary, other types of violence are no substitute for physical violence. In fact, they are often a prelude to it. This has several implications. One is that we cannot hope to prevent physical violence by simply re-directing it. Another is that, in a relationship marked by any form of violence, a partner is well-advised to flee.

CLOSING REMARKS

The sociological study of family life offers a good illustration of the connection between macro- and micro- perspectives. On the one hand, family life is a macro- phenomenon. Some aspects of family life — for example, the norm of marital fidelity — are slow to change and the main elements of a culture outlast all of us. The "family" as a cultural ideal exists outside and "above" individual people, in the ways that people of a particular society think about love, marriage, parenthood, the domestic division of labour and so on.

On the other hand, family life is constantly being constructed and every family bears the unique stamp of its members. No two families portray love, marriage, parenthood, or domestic work in precisely the same way. If anything, the study of families makes clear that social life is a process of contin-

EXHIBIT 8.5 *Others enjoy benefits unheard of in Canada*

. . . .The family has reinvented itself over the past few decades—but programs aimed at families have not.

"There is no family policy in Canada," says Malcolm Shookner, executive director of the Ontario Social Development Council.

"There are a number of piecemeal policies that affect families, mostly adversely. Families have been left to fend for themselves. It's a kind of survival of the fittest."

Issues that affect families most obviously include day care, maternity leave and time off work to care for sick children. But there are others: tax breaks for parents, employment legislation giving parents the right to work part-time and pensions for parents who stay out of the work force to look after children. . . .

Simple things such as allowing children to stay at school for lunch, letting parents work flexible hours or having buses make unscheduled stops for senior citizens can make plenty of difference to families. . . .

Programs taken for granted in other countries are unimaginable here. They include maternity leave at close to full pay for all working mothers, plentiful day care, weeks of state-legislated time off work to care for sick children, even an hour or two off work each day for breast-feeding mothers.

Yet even as families require more support, billions of dollars have been stripped from social programs aimed at families over the past several years. . . .

"I don't think the government can continue to abdicate and erode," says sociologist Susan McDaniel of the University of Alberta in Edmonton. "I think at some point there has to be an outbreak of reasonableness."

Critics say advances in Canadian family policy have been crippled by nostalgia for the family as it was in the 1940s, 1950s and 1960s, when Canada's social-program network was built.

Then, most husbands worked while wives stayed at home to take care of the children. Policy-making on family matters was simpler because no one had to take into account a myriad of models. . . .

Universal education and health-care programs continue to provide important security for families, says Robert Glossop, co-ordinator of programs and research at the Vanier Institute. But other policies work on the old assumption that families ought to have one breadwinner.

These include a tax system that treats wives as deductions and pension-plan rules that cut a wife's income in half after her husband dies, while leaving him with full benefits if she dies.

Still other potential programs have failed to materialize, despite women's relentless march into the work force. One is the sort of organized, standardized child-care system that families in many European countries rely on.

Canada's maternity benefits scheme—engineered to replace some of a new mother's lost wages as she cares for a baby—gives significantly less support than those of countries such as France, Germany and Italy. . . .

Source: Mitchell, Alanna, "Others enjoy benefits unheard of in Canada," *The Globe and Mail*, Jan. 24, 1994, pp. A1, A4

ued uncertainty, variety and negotiation. We get the families we struggle for, although some family members have more power in the struggle than others do.

Yet the data we have examined show that families *have* changed dramatically in the last thirty or so years. Accepted ways of thinking, speaking and behaving have changed because dozens, then thousands, then millions of family members have changed their way of doing things.

We should not conclude that we are in the midst of a breakdown of "the family," in which a mate is no more than erotic property, or a child no more than a consumer durable. Most people continue to struggle and sacrifice for their family *as though* they mean a great deal more.

But if family life is to improve, we are going to need to consider some policies that are already in practice elsewhere (see Exhibit 8.5). Otherwise we can look forward to serious disruptions in all parts of our daily lives, not least our work lives which are discussed in the next chapter.

C
H
A
P
T
E
R

9

The modern workplace—for many, the location of our biggest challenges and mightiest achievements; for others, a place of petty status-games and mind-wrenching boredom.

Unisys

WORK AND THE ECONOMIC ORDER

THE ECONOMIC ORDER

Just about everyone works at something. Young people work at going to school, then most move on to work at a job or career. Some people work in the home, keeping house or caring for children; normally, they get no pay for doing this. Others work at home and earn an income by selling a good or service outside the home. Most of them work in large organizations — in factories or offices — to earn a living. Working together in large numbers, they create goods and services, earn a wage, and produce a profit for the company.

The daily work routine is so prevalent that people who break the pattern seem abnormal. No wonder so many unemployed and retired people feel like outsiders to the "real" business of society. For the same reason, many people have trouble relaxing at night, on the weekend or holidays. For some, chronic stress and sleep disorders have become a permanent problem. For many full-time housewives, the problem is boredom and a sense of worthlessness; they look to alcohol or anti-depressants for solace. In short, as work has become more and more central to our society, it has also become a main source of stress in our lives.

We spend a large part of all our waking hours preparing for work, then doing it. In doing it, we create the **economic order** of society: that is, the institutionalized system that produces, distributes, and consumes material resources. Even if few people talk about it by name, they experience the economic order in a variety of ways. They all know there is a connection between the pay they get each week and the health of the economy. They experience the economic order firsthand whenever they shop for groceries, buy or sell a house, lose a job or get transferred to another city, pay taxes or fill the car's tank with gas.

But most of us think of the economic order in terms of a job. It is in the realm of work that we can easily see the problems and opportunities the economic order provides. For most, work life, like family life, is a social context where macrosociological processes meet microsociological experiences.

It is at work that we experience control or freedom from control; social integration or isolation. We form unions or associations to look after our interests; in this way we develop a sense of ourselves as workers, managers, or employers. In the end, our job identity is a key part of our social selves.

THE FOUR MAJOR PARADIGMS

Because work is so central to our daily lives, all of the major sociological paradigms have a great deal to say about it. Yet, as usual, they focus on different issues and study them in different ways.

The functionalists, for example, follow Durkheim's lead and focus on specialization, industrialization and the division of labour. They ask such questions as, Are all industrial societies alike, and if so *how* are they alike? Do all societies become the same when they industrialize? If so, why? And, what are the human costs of too-rapid change? of over-specialization? of unregulated industrial conflict? Is it possible to increase the efficiency of work without over-regulating the economy? For that matter, what is the right balance between too many and too few economic rules? Finally, how do new technologies change the way work (and social life more generally) are organized?

For their part, conflict theorists focus on inequality and power. An example we discuss below is the view of the workplace as a "contested terrain" where managers struggle to find better ways of controlling workers and workers struggle to find better ways of resisting control. The conflict approach to work and the economy grows out of classic writings by Marx (on capitalism) and Weber (on bureaucratic control). As we shall see, other issues of interest to conflict theorists are alienation and de-skilling.

Symbolic interactionists focus on interpersonal processes in and around the workplace. These include workplace socialization (discussed in Chapter 3), professionalization, the content of workplace subcultures, and the ways people negotiate order at work. Given the conflict of interests between workers and managers, how (they ask) does the work actually get done? As well, how do men and women get along at work? or whites and visible minorities? part-time and full-time workers? and so on.

Finally, feminist sociologists contribute to our understanding of job "ghettoes" such as the "pink-collar" world of female office workers. As well, they turn our thoughts to the (gender-based) differences between primary and secondary labour markets (which we discuss later in this chapter). They raise questions about job equity and different jobs of "comparable worth." And they study the reasons women with children are likely to take part-time work rather than full-time work, or choose jobs rather than careers. More generally, as we have seen in earlier chapters, they call our attention to the boundary between domestic life and paid work — a meeting point of critical significance to women with children.

Work, as we shall see, influences even the most intimate and leisurely parts of our lives. Yet the social importance people in our society accord to work is recent. Neither the forms of work which are common in our society, nor the economic order with which we are familiar today even existed before the Industrial Revolution.

THE INDUSTRIAL REVOLUTION

The term **Industrial Revolution** refers to a set of economic and social changes that started in England in the last quarter of the 18th century and later spread to other parts of the world. Before then, people produced most goods at home, on farms, or in small shops with simple tools they owned. The use of new sources of energy, such as water, steam, and later electrical energy, allowed large-scale production to develop. This proved more economical than the old handicraft method. An abundance of inanimate energy made it possible to develop machines for mass production. This increased the size, complexity, and cost of productive technology.

Mass production, as the name implies, is the production of goods in large numbers. It concentrates manufacturing in a large self-contained area such as a factory. The work involved in producing an item is broken into small, specialized steps, each performed by different people or machines in sequence. The use of machinery to perform routine tasks is especially important.

The development of mass production transformed social life. First England, and then other western European societies, were converted from rural, agricultural communities into urban, industrial nation-states. These changes not only dislocated people, they altered the ways in which people experienced society and their place in it. For example, the rise of factories gathered large numbers — hundreds and even thousands of workers — under the same roof. By talking to one another, they began to share ideas and experiences, and to understand their own lives in collective terms. Before the Industrial Revolution, societies had changed slowly and few people thought about *why* society was organized as it was. Their lives were the same as those of their parents and neighbours. Most people assumed that their form of social life was "natural," or that God had so ordained it. No such assumption could be made about the "hellish" working conditions of early industrialism, described so vividly by Charles Dickens and other 19th century English authors. These conditions have largely disappeared from developed countries but continue in developing societies such as India. There, as Exhibit 9.1 indicates, even children are exploited mercilessly for the profit of a few.

In England, conditions improved and the pace of social and economic change increased dramatically. Soon it was obvious to everyone that these changes were a consequence of human acts, not the work of God or nature. A new perspective on society developed. It recognized that society is created by human beings and society changes because of what we choose to do or fail to do.

A new perspective on society

The spread of this new outlook altered the way people understood themselves and their ties to one another. It promoted the development of sociology and the other social sciences. Indeed, heightened concern with understanding the nature of "modernization" — social, economic, and political change — produced many new theories of society.

The new perspective influenced all of the different groups in society. For most workers, the factory was their first experience of power-driven machinery and highly specialized work. That experience created a group awareness of common problems that centred around work and relations with the employer. Workers realized they could solve the problems only by changing these relations. The stage was set for class conflict and, later, for the growth of labour unions.

In this way, the new perspective on society also fostered what Karl Marx called *class consciousness* among the bourgeoisie, or capitalist class. Class consciousness refers to an awareness of class interests and a willingness to act to attain those interests.

Before the Industrial Revolution, a master craftsman and his workers were tied together by mutual responsibilities. Workers were usually apprentices or journeymen entitled to a customary level of pay, often including room and board. Most important, they were entitled to learn the skills of the craftsman.

But with industrialization and the introduction of machinery, cheap, untrained workers replaced craftsmen and their apprentices. The breakdown of customary relations between employers and employees ended all notions of obligation. Unlike the craftspeople who worked alongside their apprentices, bourgeois employers exploited their workers and paid them the lowest wage possible.

The bourgeoisie developed attitudes which legitimized this exploitation. These included a belief in unlimited opportunity and inevitable progress. According to bourgeois ideology no one should put limits on either profits or output. The bourgeoisie saw the whole world as ripe for the picking.

Social theories of the age justified these attitudes. The destruction of religious dogma and traditional belief meant that people could develop explanations of the world, as well as exploit it, more freely. Most social theorists came from a bourgeois background, so it is not surprising that their views of how society "works" suited (and justified) the attitudes of the bourgeoisie.

EXHIBIT 9.1 *The girls of Tamil Nadu*

Six mornings a week, Panjankani walks down the road from her family's one-room house, her two sisters beside her, three brothers behind. It might seem like a normal start to a school day, until the boys veer down one path to Mamsapuram's school and the girls follow another trail to a nearby matchstick factory.

For the next 12 hours, Panjankani and her younger sisters sit on dank, concrete floors in a room heaving with toxic fumes, shuffling matches into a mound of matchboxes before them. They work so quickly that often the matches ignite. "I don't know how many times I've been burned," Panjankani, 14, says, opening palms scarred by four years of match-factory work. "When it happens, I cry, but my mother scolds me and says, 'You must keep working.'" All this, for just 15 rupees (65 cents) a day.

On these drought-stricken plains of Tamil Nadu in Southern India, close to 100,000 children — three-quarters of them girls — go to work every morning in match factories, fireworks plants, rock quarries, tobacco mills, repair shops and tea houses. Together, they make up the single biggest concentration of child labour in the world.

In an age when child labour has disappeared from much of the world, it continues to be rampant in South Asia. The Operations Research Group, a respected Indian organization, has pegged the number of full-time child workers at 44 million in India, with perhaps 10 million more toiling in neighbouring Pakistan, Bangladesh, Nepal and Sri Lanka — a total almost equal to the population of Britain.

But this isn't just child labour. It is predominantly girl labour: Extensive research shows that two of three child workers in the subcontinent are female....A government survey of Tamil Nadu's main districts published this year found 70 per cent of boys attend school while 80 per cent of girls work full-time. "The problem of child labour is also a manifestation of the problem of the girl child," the report concluded....

Most important of all [to eradicate child labour] is education, compulsory if need be. "The theory that it is the poorest of the poor who cannot afford to send their children to school and that until poverty is eliminated, there is nothing educationists can do, is unfounded," concludes a recent Unicef study of Tamil Nadu. "In Kerala and Sri Lanka, poverty is far from eliminated, yet they are very close to achieving universal primary education." The same was true decades ago in Japan and Korea....

The roots of child labour appear to spread far deeper and wider through the soil of Indian society.

The caste system stretches one way. By many counts, three-quarters of the children at work in the Sivakasi matchstick bet are from landless backward castes.

The pressures of drought-prone land stretch another way, as landless labourers find their debts mounting from harvest to harvest. "If the adults got higher wages, then they would not bring their children to work," says R. Vidyasagar, a child-labour researcher at the Madras Institute of Development Studies.

And public apathy stretches a third way. For all the research and legislation on child labour in India, the country's powerful labour unions, teachers groups, religious organizations and political parties rarely speak of the problem....

To get children out of factories, many experts, like Myron Weiner, author of *The Child and the State in India*, believe compulsory education is the biggest step....But he believes efforts fail because India focuses on "amelioration, not abolition" of child labour, and "incentives, not compulsion" for education....

Source: John Stackhouse, "The girls of Tamil Nadu," *The Globe and Mail*, Sat. Nov. 20, 1993, pp., D1, D3

In 1776, the English philosopher Adam Smith published *The Wealth of Nations*, the essential work in what scholars call classical economics. In it, Smith argued in favour of *laissez-faire economies* — markets in which people could

For Canada, geographically vast as it is, railroad construction was a central part of industrialization and the creation of a market economy.

John McNeill

buy and sell anything at an unregulated price. The term **laissez-faire capitalism** refers to an economy that is free from interference (especially by the state). Smith believed that such free markets would allow materials and products to fetch a just price. As a result of this, more people would receive more benefits from the economic order.

Classical economists also promoted a new view of social life. According to this view, everyone was driven by a desire to maximize their own well-being in the marketplace. Ideally, people would cooperate and *everyone* would benefit. Economic exchanges were to be stripped of customs that were not "rational," such as customary obligations, ethnic loyalties or religious beliefs. Social life was to be based only on what Karl Marx later called the "cash nexus."

The idea that people can create the lives they want by choosing wisely in a competitive system is part of an outlook called *liberal democracy*, or the *liberal ideology*. It grows out of this philosophy of laissez-faire capitalism.

Liberal democracy rests on free choice and free competition in a market where people trade labour, goods, and ideas (Macpherson, 1962). We usually find these freedoms in societies with a capitalist economy, universal suffrage, and two or more political parties. But given social inequality — unequal starting points — freedom conflicts with fairness. That is because liberal democracy expects people to protect their own interests. It ignores the fact that some people are less able than others to protect these interests. It also denies that any collective interests — for example, environmental safety and world peace — may be more important than individual interests —for example, the unlimited use of resources or the right to sell weapons.

By destroying the old economic and political order, liberal thinking gave people new opportunities, freedoms, and rights. But it also produced an economic system characterized by insecure jobs, terrible working conditions, and poor pay. In the long run, there were bound to be dramatic clashes between the workers and the capitalists. It was in this climate of conflict that Karl Marx developed his analysis of capitalism.

Corporate capitalism

Karl Marx introduced the term "capitalism" into economic and social theory. Marx defined capitalism as a system in which there is private ownership of the means of production. Workers do not own what they produce and owners of capital reinvest their business profits to earn more capital.

Capitalism enshrines the profit motive and the ideal of free competition motivated by personal gain. It not only permits greed, capitalism encourages it. A capitalist culture sees the acquisition of wealth as a central goal of life. Newspapers, magazines, television, and the other media glorify people who have achieved this goal.

Some people in our society make huge fortunes by helping the economy grow: for example, by developing new technologies that produce goods more cheaply, or by finding new markets overseas. However, this is not usually the case. Most fortunes are made at other people's expense — for example, through currency or stock market gambling, which adds nothing whatever to the output of the economy.

Even allowing for the capitalist's right to a fair return on money invested, workers receive in wages only a small part of the profits made by the company for which they work. The surplus value of their work, or profit (after all costs are deducted), goes to the capitalist.

Marx's writings describe the form of capitalism common during his lifetime (that is, the mid-19th century). Then, an individual entrepreneur typically ran his business himself and made all of the decisions affecting it. But in the past century, the economic order has evolved into corporate capitalism. Under **corporate capitalism**, the key players are not individual owners but managers and corporate groups. They make most of the important decisions that influence the economy. Individuals have influence only as officers in the corporate bodies to which they belong — especially as directors of the business. This means that shareholders, who actually own the business, are separate from the people who run it.

Another important feature of corporate capitalism is the spread of monopolies and oligopolies. When one company controls 100% of the market, as Bell has done with local telephone services in much of Canada, it holds a **monopoly**. And when a company holds a monopoly, the consumer has no choice but to buy its product at the asking price, or do without. Those who control monopolies exercise an enormous amount of control over people who need their goods or services. So, the state tries to regulate monopolies in the interests of consumers. For example, the CRTC recently acted to prevent Bell Telephone from receiving the 40% rate increase it was seeking.

In an *oligopoly*, which is far more common, a few large firms control an entire industry. We find oligopolies in banking, insurance, the oil industry, and (until recently) the auto industry. Oligopolies are common in all industries where competitors have each invested a large amount of money.

In principle, there could be vigorous competition among these firms. In practice, there isn't. Ask yourself when a North American automobile company or cable company voluntarily offered consumers something new or better at a lower price? The answer is, never. Without regulation or competition, there is no search for better ways of doing things, no lowering of prices, and no offer of better goods and services. On the contrary, there is often price-fixing — an illegal activity that the state rarely prosecutes.

Canada has laws aimed at limiting monopolies and oligopolies. For example, the state can prohibit the merger of two companies if the resulting company will control over 50% of the market. In this way, the state tries to achieve the classical ideal of perfect competition.

Yet monopolies and oligopolies remain — for example, in the mass media where a few companies control a majority of newspapers, television, and radio stations. Everyone, including the government, knows the problem this lack of competition creates. So far, though, the state has done little to change things.

As you can see, there are serious problems with liberal ideology. In particular, the belief that people can protect their own interest and no one else needs to do so, is unfounded. Even during the heyday of laissez-faire capitalism (the 19th century), governments regularly protected the interests of business and hereditary wealth (Polanyi, 1944). Eventually, governments came to realize that other interests also needed protecting. Widespread poverty endangered the social order; it was a problem which called for more comprehensive "poor" laws and, eventually, current welfare laws.

Poor laws provided for public relief and support of the poor. Up through the first decades of this century, they were the only public income assistance available to poor people. But poor laws typically required a proof of poverty (what we would call a "means test"), degraded people receiving the assistance, and required them to live and work in harsh circumstances. The punitive nature of English poor laws, whose effects Charles Dickens depicted so well in his novels, showed that middle-class people held the poor responsible for their troubles. Their feelings for the poor were a mixture of fear and contempt.

During the worldwide Depression of the 1930s, states learned to intercede more effectively. British economist John Maynard Keynes argued that capitalism could not survive without more and better state involvement in the economy. Government needed to "prime the pumps" and stabilize earning, spending, and saving.

Today, all industrial economies operate through an extremely complex mechanism of laws and assistance to both business and private citizens. Virtually no sphere of life goes unregulated.

Regulations aside, Marx would have a hard time applying his 19th century understanding of capitalism to today's global enterprises. The big success stories of industrial capitalism now include Walt Disney Company as well as SONY and General Motors. Disney Inc. — a multi-national entertainment giant — has achieved an economic status once reserved for railways, banks and steel companies. Manufacturing (or blue collar) jobs, which dominated in the first half of the 20th century, have been shrinking in number, while the number of clerical, managerial and professional (or white collar) jobs has been surging (see Exhibit 9.2).

Some would say that the type of businesses and societies that exist today are too different from those to which the 19th century term "capitalism" referred to still be called capitalist. As we shall see, there are also large differences among

EXHIBIT 9.2 *Taking the job rate by the collar*

The so-called jobless recovery is a selective affair in Canada. So far, if you're a blue-collar worker, there has been no recovery. But if your occupation lies in the upper reaches of the white-collar labour market, the jobs are growing at a healthy clip. . . .

Blue-collar jobs have been transitory. They appear and disappear as the economy expands and contracts. Last year, there were 3.5-million of them altogether. This represented an increase from 1975 of—are you ready for this?—13,000. That's a whopping 0.4 per cent over 18 years.

Most of those blue-collar jobs are in construction, manufacturing, distribution and primary industries (such as farming, fishing, forestry and mining), a list that reads like a compilation of four years of layoff headlines. . . .

Meanwhile, the number of jobs has expanded for the well-educated, well-trained members of the white-collar set. They include the managers and administrators who clutter every workplace but also take in engineers, teachers, doctors, dentists, nurses, natural and social scientists and people in artistic and literary occupations (even journalists).

There are just over 4 million white-collar workers now. . . .

The top white-collar jobs accounted for 22 per cent of all employment in 1975; in 1993, the figure was 32 per cent.

Between white and blue lies the vast army of clerical, sales and service workers—secretaries and shipping clerks, street vendors and real-estate agents, bartenders and firefighters. Together, they represent the biggest group — almost 4.9-million in 1993.

They are prone to losing jobs during recessions (like blue-collar workers), but the losses are small compared to the jobs they gain in the economy's expansion phase. Their share of the labour market has remained steady at about 40 per cent since 1975.

Within this group, service workers have fared best in recent years. Between 1990 and 1993, total employment in Canada fell 1.5 per cent, but the number of service jobs increased by 3.2 per cent. Sales jobs remained flat, while clerical work declined 7.5 per cent. Compare this with the managerial and professional class, for whom employment rose 6 per cent. . . .

Most of the pain has been felt by the blue-collar crowd. Their unemployment rate last year was 14.7 per cent, up from just under 11 per cent in 1990. . . .

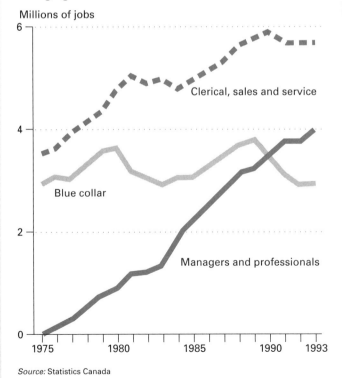

Changing Job Market

Millions of jobs

Source: Statistics Canada

Source: Bruce Little, "Taking the job rate by the collar," *The Globe and Mail*, Mon., Feb. 7, 1994, p. A9

capitalist societies and large similarities among industrial societies which may or may not be "capitalist" in the traditional sense. For this reason, many sociologists believe that our society is now better described as an industrial society.

INDUSTRIAL SOCIETY

The term industrial society refers not only to a society in which industrial (or mass) production prevails, but to a whole packet of features we consider essential to contemporary life. In the transition to an industrial society,

(1) subsistence farming disappears;
(2) the number of people in agriculture declines;
(3) people produce for exchange, not consumption;
(4) workers begin to produce goods in large factories;
(5) large machines increasingly assist production;
(6) jobs and workers become highly specialized;
(7) the number of wage-labourers increases;
(8) more people come to live in large cities;
(9) more people learn how to read and write;
(10) scientific research changes industrial production; and
(11) people are increasingly concerned with efficiency.

In these respects, societies as different as Canada and China, Russia and Argentina, are all industrial societies. Whatever the political system or economic ideology, industrialization leads a society to develop the set of features listed above.

The social background of industrialism

Sociologists have spent a lot of effort identifying the key features of industrial society. The factors which lead societies to industrialize are so many and complex that we can only discuss three main ones:

Cultural factors

In the chapter on culture, we discussed Max Weber's theory of the Protestant ethic and its role in the rise of capitalism. Much research has been done to test and extend Weber's insight that culture influences economic growth.

So, for example, Hargrove (1988) notes the important role played in America's economic growth by cultural factors like the Protestant ethic, the sense of a boundless frontier, and a unifying national ideology (illustrated by the slogan *e pluribus unum*). Half way around the world, Alo (1985) argues the importance of understanding the way Nigerians "make sense" of work and their own role in it: the place of work in life, what makes work worthy or unworthy, and so on. Presumably, how (and how hard) people work is affected by these perceptions.

Rofel (1992) discusses the difficulty in applying Western ideas of scientific management, productivity and discipline in a Chinese silk factory. Because of China's traditional culture, industrialization will not follow the European model exactly, nor is it necessary that it should. But one cannot ignore the importance of cultural factors in helping or hindering economic growth. Take, as an example, the importance a culture attaches to competitiveness.

Exhibit 9.3 shows that most Canadians hold values, such as competitiveness, that are considered essential for modern industrialism. In fact, Canadians are — in many instances — even more competitive than Americans, contrary to stereotypes of Canadian culture we discussed in Chapter 2.

EXHIBIT 9.3   *Competitiveness not new to Canadians*

Canadians, it turns out, are more American than Americans.

Three-quarters of Canadians believe competition leads to excellence, and fully 90 per cent believe they can't get ahead without taking risks, according to a study of Canadian attitudes. More Canadians than Americans feel that the profit motive teaches the value of hard work and that few would strive to do their best if private enterprise were abolished.

The recently released study, commissioned by the federal government, suggests the ideological banners of entrepreneurialism, competitiveness and capitalism usually associated with Americans are waved even more zealously by their Canadian cousins.

"The picture that emerges is of a people who greatly value individual achievement, believe in rewarding merit and believe in the benefits of competition," said the study's author, Joseph Fletcher, political science professor at the University of Toronto. . . .

More Canadians than Americans thought it was "very important" to compete to see how good they are while, surprisingly, Americans seemed more inclined to accept the necessity of government regulation of business than Canadians. Over all, the results show marked similarities between Canadians and Americans. Statistically speaking, the differences in their responses were small. . . .

"The old myths about Canadian and American cultural differences in the value placed upon achievement, merit, competition and free enterprise simply cannot be sustained based upon what we have seen here," Mr. Fletcher says in the study. . . .

Some findings confirmed stereotypical views of Canadians. Seventy-five per cent said compromise and looking for common ground are more important than competition and trying to win.

Nearly half the Canadians said the government should see to it that everyone has a job and a decent standard of living.

Yet 71 per cent said that even if they fail, they would rather be free and stand on their own than depend on government. . . .

Canadians Keen on Competitiveness

	% in agreement with questions	
	Canadians	Americans
In a fair economic system, people with more ability should earn more	71	78
When businesses are allowed to make as much money as they can, everyone gains	35	42
Government regulation of business is necessary to keep industry from being too powerful	35	45
It's very important to compete against each other to show how good you are	18	14
It's very important to be the best at what you do	74	55
Competitiveness, whether at school, work or business, leads to a better performance and a desire for excellence	73	81
The profit system usually teaches the value of hard work	61	54
If the system of private enterprise were abolished, very few would do their best	54	48

Source: Canadian Attitudes Toward Competitiveness and Entrepreneurship

Source: Harvey Enchin, "Competitiveness not new to Canadians," *The Globe and Mail*, Thurs., May 7, 1992, pp. B1, B4

Human capital

A second key feature of industrial society is a concern with improving human capital. Human capital theorists are concerned with improving people's general well-being through better health, education, welfare and public security. After all, they argue, people are central to creating wealth in an industrial order. Money invested in human well-being (that is, in human capital) is money invested in future economic growth.

Still, debates continue about the kinds of investment that will make a difference to the economy. So, for example, Roy (1992) points out that school reform in Saudi Arabia over the past two decades has increased the enrolment of students. However, major problems remain. They include high illiteracy and drop-out rates, political repression in the school system, a tendency for the state to hire and promote unqualified workers, and a reliance on foreign workers in key technical areas. Saudi Arabia will have to solve all of these problems if it wants students to stay in school and human capital to reach industrial standards.

Mexico has had more success in getting large numbers of students into the school system. However, an increased *quantity* of education is not the same thing as increased *quality*. The quality, and not just quantity of schooling affects manufacturing output and even, to a lesser degree, the output of commercial agriculture (Fuller, Edwards and Gorman, 1986).

As these examples show, investment in human capital is expensive and slow in bringing expected payoffs. On the other hand, such investment changes many parts of the economy and society unexpectedly. One such change is the effect on class structure and the class struggle. Generally, an investment in human capital is likely to unsettle the population and mobilize protest.

Class structure

We have already noted one way that the rise of an industrial society changes class relations: the "cash nexus" replaces customary feudal ties of obligation.

Investment in human capital is critical to the process of industrialization. Students cannot learn well if they lack the basic amount of food, shelter and personal security.

UPI/Bettmann

New social classes — especially, the bourgeoisie and proletariat — emerge as a result.

But the class structure changes in other ways too. For example, industrialization pushes and pulls the rural peasantry into cities and factories. In some ways, this is a small matter: part-time farming has coexisted with part-time wage work for a long time. For this reason, the categories of "worker" and "peasant" are fluid. So it is easy to gain cooperation between workers and peasants, as the Chinese have shown in reforming their agriculture (Hsu and Ching, 1991). Often the workers and peasants are, if not the very same people, closely related.

This connection also makes the changeover from agricultural to wage labour inevitable. Conversion of the peasantry to a wage-earning proletariat (as happened on sugar plantations in Southeast Asia before 1940, for example) can be gradual. More and more peasants are forced off the land and into wage labour as landholdings become larger and privatized, producing cash crops rather than subsistence crops.

Likewise, crop changes and improvements to farm production (for example, through better irrigation) may increase crop yields by a large degree, yet also reduce the demand for labour, as they did in Mexico's El Bajio region (Young, 1988).

However, even if the changeover from peasant to worker (and back) is easy, some believe it may not be entirely desirable. The interests of a permanent working class are different from those of part-timers who return to the farm as soon as job opportunities worsen in the cities. Back-and-forth movement weakens the proletariat. In many developing countries (like Thailand, for example) permanent working class members are rare — a kind of labour aristocracy.

Another condition affecting class structure is the evenness of economic growth. Under conditions of *un*even growth, industrialism produces a multi-layered working class, in which the layers have different problems and conflicting interests. In the South African metal industry, for example, several labour processes — and workers with different skills and levels of schooling — exist side by side. Of these, some are being "de-skilled" by the industry while others are being re-skilled (Kraak, 1987).

Convergence

The contrasts between Canada and India, Brazil or Nigeria point up differences between industrial societies (as a group) and nonindustrial or developing societies. Generally, industrial societies have (1) a secular culture focused on efficiency, consumerism and a high standard of living, (2) a highly developed state which provides health, education and welfare benefits to its citizens and (3) a class structure dominated (numerically) by the urban, middle class.

As a result, there are important similarities between industrial societies like Canada and Japan which, a century ago, had almost nothing in common. The growing similarity of industrial societies around the world has produced what sociologists call the *convergence thesis*. Proponents of this thesis argue that as societies industrialize, their social patterns converge or become more similar, despite differences that existed before.

The convergence thesis is an important part of the theory of industrial society. It rests on the idea that industrialization gives rise to changes — like mass literacy, a nuclear family, and respect for the rule of law — that were never intended and are distantly connected to economic life. However, the connections are easy to understand. For example, as people become literate, they become better informed, more politically active, and more eager to demand political liberties. The result is participatory democracy.

Another common feature is the growth of a political rights-seeking middle class which administers large businesses. One emerged in Korea in the 1980s and, another, in Thailand in the 1990s. Canada's administrative revolution began in the first few decades of this century. (We will discuss this revolution later on.) The point is, similar changes seem to occur in *every* industrial society, though not always in the same sequence.

What is remarkable about convergence is the inevitability of the process. If all industrial societies are alike, then capitalism does not determine what form the economy will take: industrialism does. The convergence thesis de-emphasizes capitalism as a crucial feature of economic life and puts industrial society in its place. It argues that what is important in world history is industrialism, not capitalism. And *that* says the theories of Weber and Durkheim — not Marx — are most important, for Marx emphasized the determining role of capitalism while Weber and Durkheim did not.

With exceptions, non-Western experience has provided much support for the convergence thesis. Developing societies differ mainly in whether they incorporate selected "modern" ideas into their existing culture, as Japan has done, or rearrange their cultures around these ideas, as in Singapore. However they do it, industrialization everywhere has certain distinctive features. But it is not clear whether industrial societies converge because they must satisfy the same societal needs (e.g., for literacy) or because social practices spread from more to less prosperous societies. There is evidence to support both views.

In the past, "industrialization" meant "westernization," since economic and social practices used to spread from west to east (and north to south). But now, given the huge impact of Japanese practices on American and European industry, the convergence of work practices is just as likely to mean "easternization."

Industrial organization in Japan

Since the Second World War, Japanese managers have been enormously successful. The Japanese approach to management has been credited with producing high-quality goods at low cost and, thus, with creating a trade surplus for Japan.

Characteristics of the Japanese approach include teamwork (for example, a common discipline, work uniforms, collective social activities, consensual decision-making) and concern for the workers (for example, willingness to seek ideas from employees, a flexible team concept to reduce assembly-line monotony). The result has been efficient production, high quality products, and an absence of conflict in the workplace (Seabrook, 1990).

In Japan, workers and managers communicate openly about industrial or technical problems. Because managers attach importance to workers' knowledge, they ask for and act upon employees' suggestions. Thus Japanese workers participate in industrial engineering; they also push one another to do their best (Wood, 1989). This, and other aspects of company policy, increases both worker loyalty and engineering excellence. It is even possible that Japanese workers are more committed to their employers than American workers, but there is no certain evidence of it. (Granovetter, 1990).

Many experts believe the Japanese approach is a logical successor to the American style of industrial production invented by Henry Ford to manufacture cars. The Japanese approach promotes economic growth in a way that suits the late 20th century service economy very well (Kenney and Florida, 1989).

In the last few years, even the Japanese have suffered economic setbacks. As a result, there has been a move away from the most distinctive features of Japanese organization, such as jobs for life, and a growing use of temporary and subcontracted workers in Japan (Dore, 1989). However, this is not an abandonment of Japanese principles — just a result of labour market changes and global competition. No one expects that Japanese managers will give up their other practices in favour of the less successful, more confrontational American ones.

Can Japanese practices work outside Japan? Or do they rely too heavily on customary Japanese ways of doing things that Americans and other Westerners would have trouble learning? The convergence thesis suggests that Japanese practices will gradually spread.

True, the Japanese have too little concern for workplace democracy to suit Americans. Not that the American workplace itself is democratic, but unions do keep up a struggle for worker representation that is absent in paternalistic Japan. On the other hand, the adoption of Japanese practices in America would lead managers to listen to workers more attentively. Managers might even pay less attention to labour costs than in the past, and more attention to quality. (Hodson, 1990).

We can already see a Japanese influence on American industry, and studies have not reported that problems occur when Americans work in Japanese-owned firms in the United States. In fact, Japanese and Japanese-American workers have more trouble working in these firms than anyone else. In Britain too, Japanese methods are widely accepted. Evidence shows that these methods

Mechanization and specialization were both central to the development of industrial society. But is it any wonder that many workers felt endangered—at the mercy of their machines?

The Bettman Archive

improve engineering skills and increase both shopfloor autonomy and managerial control (Bratton, 1991).

What is particularly interesting to many sociologists about the adoption of Japanese ways is that it seems to go against the main current of Western work history. The Japanese approach is at odds with three processes — specialization, bureaucratization, and professionalization — which, in the West, have played a key part in the industrialization of work. We will discuss each of these in turn.

KEY PROCESSES OF INDUSTRIALIZATION

Specialization and the division of labour

Both Emile Durkheim and Max Weber had theories about specialization and the division of labour. Durkheim (1964) thought that a continuous growth in the division of labour led to specialization and what he called *organic solidarity*. For Weber (1958c; 1961) industrialization meant the increasing rationalization of social and economic behaviour and the spread of impersonal forms of control by the bureaucracy. We will examine each of these accounts in detail and see how well they fit the characteristics of industrial society.

A task undergoes a division of labour when it is broken into many smaller tasks, each carried out by a different person. Then, we say the tasks are "specialized." With specialization, people are limited to performing a single task or step in the work process. This may mean drilling a hole in a strip of wood that will later become part of a coffee table, putting slices of pepperoni on dough that will become a frozen pizza, or sorting letters into appropriate slots for transport to another city.

Specialization is almost inevitable in a large organization. Breaking up a big job into small, easy to perform tasks, and then having people perform each task repeatedly in a chain operation, drastically reduces the time needed to do the job. The factory can now produce more for less money. Consumers benefit because producers sell their goods and services at a lower price, while maintaining a healthy profit margin.

The problem of anomie

But specialization carries costs of its own. Often, it makes jobs repetitive and dull, causing workers to become bored and frustrated. People are not machines, and they feel the effects of too little mental exercise. But not only is specialization dehumanizing; as sociologist Harry Braverman (1974) wrote, it is also "de-skilling." It takes away skills that people once had, making them less able to perform a variety of jobs and more dependent on their employers.

Specialization often turns work — a potentially creative and pride-inspiring activity — into something that is mind-numbing and depressing. We will have more to say about these "alienating" effects of work later in this chapter.

Emile Durkheim was the first sociologist to see that extreme specialization would pose a serious threat to social solidarity. The factories of early capitalism provided people with common experiences, common problems, and a feeling of group membership. But with continued specialization, work fosters differences among people. Our jobs, our experiences, and eventually our identities become different.

Faced with this, Durkheim wondered what would hold a society with a high degree of specialization together. Even if we all had a common religion or morality — which we don't — that would not be enough. He concluded that different groups within society, leading different lives, need different codes of behaviour. Yet they also need a way to be part of the same social order.

In periods of rapid social and economic change, problems of disorganization — or anomie — arise. By anomie, Durkheim meant a state of moral drift. When society fails to regulate people's wants, they are morally and socially "at sea." In Chapter 4, we discussed the relationship between anomie and deviance. In general, specialization, mobility and rapid social change all cut people off from one another. Without ties to others, the anomic person neither feels safe nor acts responsibly.

Anomie leads to unpredictable behaviour and a strong belief in luck (Seeman, 1959). The anomic person is confused about socially approved behaviour and has lost faith that socially approved behaviour will achieve desired goals. Anomie even produces a belief that people will need socially *dis*approved behaviour to achieve their goals. So, a worker will see little connection between his work-life and the rest of his life, nor between the effort that is expended and the rewards obtained. In such a climate of drift and despair, there is also a tendency to deal with conflicts in violent and disorderly ways.

"What could solve these problems?" Durkheim asked himself. To find the answer, Durkheim began by comparing industrial society with earlier — small, homogeneous, pre-industrial — societies that had little division of labour. He concluded that small homogeneous societies are held together by what he called *mechanical solidarity*.

When the division of labour is slight, based mainly on age and gender, most people make a living the same ways. They have roughly the same experiences, share beliefs, and feel like they belong to the same group. Members of the group feel a sense of solidarity based on these common experiences, feelings, values and beliefs. This "mechanical solidarity" proves to be a powerful form of social control.

Now, imagine all these elements gone — the geographic and social stability, shared experiences, long acquaintanceships, interwoven kinship, even the shared social norms and moral beliefs. What can pull together such a varied set of people? Durkheim's answer was organic solidarity.

In a community that has organic solidarity, there is a sense of interdependence with others. The extensive division of labour means no one can live without the contributions made by other people. We all need the farmer and the grocer for food, the logger and carpenter for shelter, the doctor and nurse for health, and so on. We may not know all of the people we depend on, but we need them and we know we do.

In such a society, people learn to cultivate a "live and let live" philosophy. It is almost as though an unwritten contract binds us together. Without this social contract, we cannot trust one another and live together in peace and safety. In an industrial society all social, political, and economic relations rest on what Durkheim called these "non-contractual elements of contract."

The problems of social life associated with industrialism do not solve themselves. People need intimacy, emotional attachments and rules to live by. They also need to find ways of resolving disputes with the people and groups they rely on but do not know well. Thus, the society with organic solidarity must develop new means of pulling people together in a more complex social order.

Depending on the group, it is possible to integrate people in one of several different ways. For example, we face different problems integrating: a multifunctional community like an Israeli kibbutz (which combines work, family and social life); a group that has fewer functions than the kibbutz (such as a school or trade union); and a group that has a single purpose, such as a business firm like IBM (Rosner, 1991).

One way to integrate the group is to seek new ways of reducing group size and decentralizing production (Taplin, 1989). Durkheim probably would have favoured that solution.

At the other end of the continuum, the work group may be integrated forcibly by regimenting members in a large organization called a "bureaucracy." As Weber noted, this was the more common solution in early 20th century industrial societies.

Bureaucracy and control

Max Weber was the first sociologist to study bureaucracy closely. He was not really interested in problems of integration, nor in forms of social organization *per se*, but in the way bureaucracies bring rationality to *legitimate social control* (a topic we touched on in Chapter 5).

What is "bureaucracy?"

A bureaucracy is a hierarchical organization found in all industrial societies. Weber saw the emergence of bureaucracy as important because he believed that bureaucracies promote reasonable and impersonal social relations. Weber believed that the bureaucracy is the most effective means of decision-making precisely because it is impersonal. It does not always make the best decisions, but a bureaucracy usually makes sure that workers carry out the decisions that have been made. For this reason, Weber saw bureaucracy as the main instrument of domination — hence, integration — in industrial societies.

To better describe it, Weber (1958c) constructed what he called an "ideal type" model of bureaucracy. This "ideal" bureaucracy has the following characteristics:

(1) a well-defined division of labour, with tasks distributed as official duties;
(2) hierarchical authority, with well-defined areas of command and responsibility;
(3) a formal body of rules that govern the organization;
(4) administration that is based on written records;
(5) work relations that are impersonal and based on the status of the office-holder(s);
(6) hiring of workers based on ability and technical knowledge — or achieved, not ascribed grounds; and
(7) freedom of employees from arbitrary dismissal.

We often think of bureaucracies as inefficient and mired in "red tape." But bureaucracies are efficient and rational when compared to other forms of organization, most of which are even *less* efficient and rational. To see this, compare bureaucracy with another form of organization Weber called "patrimonialism." In that kind of organization, an autocrat makes all the decisions and a personal staff carries out his decisions without question. In its most benevolent form, this gives rise to what Weber called *kadijustiz*, a system in which the ruler, or his deputy, makes decisions as he sees fit. (King Solomon, in the Old Testament, was a wise and benevolent practitioner of Kadijustiz, for example.)

Throughout the East today, patrimonialism is still a common practice in government and business. Many decisions are based on bribery or a leader's whim. Not only is the system whimsical, it is also intensely personal, creating deep loyalties and hatreds. In Korea, it leads to rivalries between firms which turn into clan-based conflicts — almost vendettas (Biggart, 1990). As you can imagine, this is a less-than-reasonable way of running a business and it hinders a society's industrial growth.

By contrast, a bureaucracy tries to do away with bribery, whim, personal loyalties and strong emotions. It makes decisions slowly, but it makes them impersonally and, for the most part, predictably. This last point is particularly important. An industrial organization requires predictability if it is to make and carry out plans for the future. A bureaucracy meets that requirement.

But bureaucracy is not without its shortcomings. Many problems within a bureaucracy are a result of overspecialization, such that few employees can see what the organization is trying to accomplish. As officeholders bound by rules, bureaucrats come to focus on those rules, not on the intended outcomes. This problem is called goal displacement. Employees may even come to care more about the survival of the group (or their jobs) than about achieving the goals for which the organization was created. The result is the "make-work" project — a specifically bureaucratic form of time-wasting.

As well, an organization has no inherent morality. As structures, bureaucracies are rational; however the behaviour of people within them is *not*. People working in a bureaucracy learn to follow orders without wondering why or thinking about the consequences of their actions. They are expected to follow rules, not apply their own morality to their jobs. In any event, they rarely know enough about the organization's plans to do otherwise.

Bureaucracy is one of a number of "formal organizations" which have similar problems. The most striking fact about them is that they work similarly even when they have very different goals. In the ways they make and carry out decisions, there is more similarity among the Canadian Forces, the Roman Catholic Church, and IBM than there is between any of these and your family.

The critical factor is *size*. With enormous size and complex goals, a group needs to coordinate and control its workers. Whether for good or ill, the bureaucratic way of administering is the most effective way of doing this.

Bureaucracy as control

Bureaucracies are ways of controlling people and they are as good at controlling people who work within them as they are for controlling the people they "serve." Because authority and responsibility belong to the bureaucracy itself, not to the people who happen to work in it, the good bureaucrat never questions orders.

To appreciate just how effectively bureaucracies control people, let's contrast bureaucratic control with other, less effective forms: namely, "simple" and "technical" control.

Gaining control in the workplace often occurs through combat over what Richard Edwards (1979) has called a "contested terrain." The workplace is like any other social arena: all participants fight for a say in how the workplace will be governed. Workers are motivated by their own agendas which include compliance, resistance and creative efforts to re-structure the workplace. In large part, the shift of managers from one kind of control to another reflects changes in the effectiveness of customary means of controlling workers (or in the resistance by the workers.)

Simple control, as its name suggests, uses few formal rules and procedures. A boss tells the workers what they are to do that day and establishes routines. He or she even assigns tasks to particular workers, but detailed management is unnecessary. The boss can see if people are doing their jobs properly and can easily correct any problem that arises. This form of control is often found in small workplaces that lack a complex division of labour, especially if no union is present to limit the boss's authority.

Simple control was common up through the 19th century but we can still see simple control in any small shop or restaurant. The manager tells a waiter to serve tables 8-15 on the patio during lunch, then help serve drinks inside, to tables 40-58, during the evening. The waiter knows what he has to do. If he messes up — gets the customers angry, drops food, breaks dishes, or fails to collect all the money owing — the manager will know it right away, or at least when she tallies the accounts at the end of the day. If the waiter messes up a few days in a row, he gets fired. That's simple control!

Simple control works well where the boss can see most of the workers most of the time. But it does not suit large-scale production, where hundreds of employees work under a single roof, doing many related but different jobs. The boss cannot possibly watch everyone or even know what every worker is supposed to do. She needs another form of control; namely, technical control.

Like simple control, technical control lacks elaborate rules and procedures, at least initially. Here, the productive technology controls the workers. Anyone who has worked in a factory, or seen Charlie Chaplin in the movie *Modern Times*, knows how this operates. Each worker has a narrowly defined task to perform hundreds or thousands of times a day. An assembly line keeps the work rolling. The worker stays in place and does something to the product before it passes to the next worker in line.

The rate at which the line is moving decides the rate at which work is done. Quality checks at various points quickly show how well particular workers have done their job. Parker and Slaughter (1990) have called the system "management by stress." Sometimes, management even turns the stress level up, by having groups compete against one another. Then, competing teams (or even plants) can maintain their positions only through unrelenting effort and close attention.

Technical control has changed in the past 50 years — partly because of new problems that needed new solutions, and partly because unions challenged the working conditions. Its most refined, computerized form is an "Active Badge" (see Exhibit 9.4); but even in this form, technical control is inadequate. It may even reduce productivity, if it robs the workers of loyalty or motivation.

Technical control was *always* inappropriate for some workplaces. It is particularly inappropriate where the boss needs workers to be independent and creative. In such a case, machines can neither do the job nor monitor whether it is being done well, much less force it to be done quickly. Accordingly, some types of workplace need another kind of control: namely, bureaucratic control.

This type of control combines two key elements. One element is a great mass of formal, written rules and procedures. The other is a promise of career rewards for conformity and effective performance. This is to serve as an inter-

EXHIBIT 9.4 *How computer 'eyes' track employees*

... The "Active Badge" produced by the Olivetti company looks very much like a typical employee identification card that many workers now wear at the office. It's about the same size and carries the name and photo of an employee. But it also contains a microchip, a battery, an infrared transmitter and a tiny speaker.

The chip sends a coded electronic signal, unique to that badge, to the infrared transmitter, which emits pulses of infrared light that are picked up by receivers around the building. The badge recycles its message — "I am John Doe," or "I am Jane Doe" — every 10 seconds.

Each sensor, which is about twice the size of the badge and can be easily mounted to a wall or desk top, covers a 120-degree area, extending out about 15 metres.

When the sensors receive an infrared message they send the information back to a central computer, which displays it as a name and a location. The computer also reports how long it has been monitoring a badge at a specific place.

So if the boss wants to know where an employee is, all he or she has to do is ask the computer.

The technology can do more than catch slackers in the cafeteria or discover that Jane and John Doe have been in the supply closet together for 45 minutes, says Olivetti.

The Active Badge's main mission is controlling access to a building and keeping track of people in secure areas. Many companies now require employees to put an ID card with a magnetic strip into a card reader to get into the building, or into secure zones within a building.

Without being put into a card reader, the Active Badge tells the computer whether its wearer is authorized to have access. If so, the door is automatically unlocked. No more need for keys to the executive washroom.

If a building is being evacuated, the computer can quickly tell rescuers whether everyone is out and, if not, where they are, provided the computer is still working.

The badge can also control office equipment. A sensor on top of your computer could recognize your badge and turn on the machine without needing a password. It could also lock users out of computer files or systems they are not authorized to use.

Likewise, it could shut down a computer or blank the screen when unauthorized visitors are walking by. ...

... [S]ince separate technologies to monitor workers' phone calls, computer work and building access already exist, devices such as the Active Badge, which combine them all into one neat package, seem inevitable.

Source: Geoffrey Rowan, "How computer 'eyes' track employees," *The Globe and Mail*, Tues. Nov. 30, 1993, p. A11

---

nalized source of control over behaviour. Looked at another way, career opportunities are the carrot and written rules are the stick. Together, they ensure conformity and control in the hands of the organization.

The type of worker found in a bureaucracy is more highly educated than those in the groups discussed above and, usually, possesses middle-class goals. Such a worker has learned to follow rules, both by formal schooling (at least through secondary school) and (often) by a middle-class upbringing. He or she also wants to get ahead. These goals persuade the worker to trade present conformity for future rewards. When there is no chance to reward conformity with advancement, employers find other rewards — for example, loose supervision, worker autonomy and self-direction. But all of this depends on a careful choice and training of employees (Finlay, 1988).

Bureaucratic control is most common in large offices that manage production, provide services, or manipulate information. The work is too complex and the group too large to respond to simple control. And since machines cannot do the work, technical control is impossible. The best type of control, here, is bureaucratic control.

Organizing work in "professions" is yet another way to solve problems of integration and control. In fact, this was the solution Durkheim favoured in his own time. It remains important today.

Professions and professionalization

In the professions, each person is considered a specialized expert and each has a high degree of control over decision-making. One example is a physician who works in the emergency ward of a hospital. Sometimes, without consulting others, the physician must make quick decisions which have immediate life and death consequences. Worse still, physicians often have to base these decisions on limited knowledge. In the emergency ward, bureaucratic decision-making would be a disaster for everyone. It's just too slow.

In our society, professionalization is the main alternative to bureaucratic control. Whereas a bureaucracy is impersonal and monopolizes all authority for itself, a profession assigns both high status and autonomy to individuals. Professionals do high-status, high-paying, specialized work that typically requires a lot of schooling and permits a lot of freedom.

The growing importance of professionalization is shown by the fact that, increasingly, access to high-paying jobs in industrial societies requires a "credential." This credential, which is usually an educational degree, shows that a person qualifies for the job. Degrees from medical schools are particularly valuable: virtually no doctors are unemployed or poorly paid. Yet the state does not permit anyone without a degree in medicine to practise medicine. This rule protects doctors by giving them a monopoly on medical practice. It also prevents competent nurses, paramedics, and other health professionals from practising medicine. Such a monopoly on what is, in effect, an essential service generates a high income for doctors.

Usually, professional status gives an occupational group more income, control over access to the profession, and social respectability. Therefore, we often see highly-educated groups — for example, social workers and psychologists — trying to professionalize themselves.

We learn most about **professionalization** from the attempts that fail. For example, Mitford (1963) has described the attempts undertakers have made to upgrade their status. Not content with being viewed (and paid) as technicians or businesspeople, undertakers seek greater credibility as professional "funeral directors" or "grief management consultants." So far, their attempts at upgrading have failed to persuade the public.

In most people's thoughts, the "professional" contrasts not only with the "amateur" but also with the person who has a job instead of a "calling." In this sense, physicians, lawyers and the clergy serve as the models of professionals. They all have a "calling" and their own equivalent of a Hippocratic oath, which defines the ethical standards they are supposed to uphold. These standards reflect the fact that professionals provide services of a personal nature to their clients and that they are seen to hold a position of trust.

A profession is more than just a job—it's a "calling." Professions, such as medicine, are bound by rigid ethical standards.

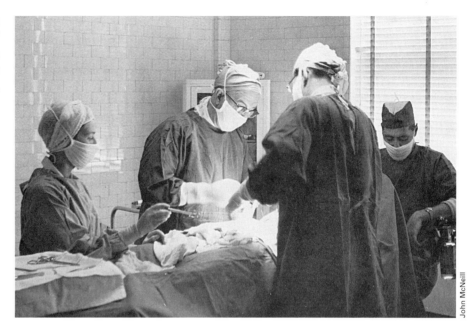

John McNeill

Often "professionals" do precisely what we hope they would. For example, doctors with the strongest desire to serve their patients, most expertise (i.e., certification in a medical specialty), and greatest commitment to excellence are the least likely to complain about their workload (Stevens, et al., 1992). Along similar lines, Finlay et al. (1990) report that when medical residents face long line-ups of patients and limited resources, they work even harder. They enjoy having a direct responsibility for patient care.

However, we should not confuse the ideology of professions with the actuality. Remember, professionals do not *always* uphold the duties of their profession and their colleagues do not always punish them for breaking the rules. So, in actual practice, the crucial, defining feature of a profession is not its ideals, it is the power of a professional association to protect its members.

Professional associations

In many respects, professional associations are like the ethnic groups we discussed in Chapter 6. For example, they have their own group boundaries, membership criteria, rituals, customs and jargon. Like ethnic groups, some professions are more institutionally complete than others. Those which are more complete are more powerful and successful. For both ethnic groups and professions, such completeness insulates members from outside pressures and increases their protection against the hostility and envy of outsiders.

In many respects, professional associations are similar to trade unions: both aim to protect and promote the economic interests of their members. However they differ in two important respects.

First, professional associations help middle-class people protect middle-class incomes, while unions help working-class people protect working-class incomes. That is not how most people view the role of professional associations. Because of the higher social origins of professionals, people more willingly believe their associations really act in the public interest. Yet the champions of public health in North America have *not* been leaders of medical associations. The reduction of illness and mortality has historically owed more to public works, sewage and garbage management, and clean water, than to the work of practising physicians.

Even now, medical bodies show little interest in workplace safety, environmental pollution, addiction, or other major causes of illness and death. Instead, North American medicine increasingly addresses itself to high-tech, high-cost remedies that benefit only the few; for example, the recipients of organ transplants.

The second difference between professional associations and unions is that, as movements, they have used different means to protect their members. Unions threaten or use strikes to increase workers' incomes, employing collective means to pursue collective guarantees for their members. While professional groups sometimes do this, they rely on political lobbying and manipulating public opinion through the mass media to control the public image of their members.

Associations protect their members from political interference and personal liability in dealings with the public. They also help their members earn whatever the market will bear. The professional association may provide the public with some protection, but it is much less than the public may imagine they are getting.

In future, professional organization may be the basis for most personal services, even for some industrial work. Still, there is evidence that some professions are losing their high status. For example, in hospitals the privileged status of doctors is starting to erode. In the United States, where there is an increased supply of doctors, state regulation of medicine and corporate ownership of hospitals, hospital managers are becoming more powerful than doctors (Alexander, Morrissey and Shortell, 1986). We may even see a "proletarianization" of doctors in hospitals, as happened to lawyers in large law firms and engineers in large companies like IBM.

But one aspect of professionalism is not going to change, and that is the continuing importance of expertise based on education. According to Exhibit 9.5, the traditional workplace is vanishing. The post-industrial (or postmodern) economy is marked by uncertainty, low expectations, and a decline in the number of traditional jobs. Faced with these conditions, jobs that require technical expertise will survive better than jobs that require few skills and little expertise.

TYPES OF WORK

Whether they gather in offices, stores, workshops, supermarkets, or factories, all of the people we have been discussing have one thing in common: they do work.

By "work," we don't just mean "paid jobs." School work is as much work as is the part-time job many students take to cover their expenses. And don't forget housework — the most common work in our society. But not all kinds of work are treated equally. So, for example, most people ignore housework when they speak of work: they focus mainly on participation in the labour force. The *labour force* includes all the people over the age of 15 who work for pay, and people who do not currently work for pay but who want to and are looking for paid work.

Payment does not prove the social value of work done, only the ability of the worker to convert his or her effort into money. And even *within* the paid labour force, workers vary in this ability. The same effort expended in one part of the economy or labour market will bring far more money than it will in another. Similarly, the same educational degrees will earn twice as much in one

EXHIBIT 9.5 *The myths about the work we'll do*

In 1986. . . Roy Hanna of the strategic planning division of Employment and Immigration Canada wrote a paper called *The Future of Work*.

Mr. Hanna predicted persistent high unemployment, increasing division of the workplace into well-paying good jobs and poorly paid dead-end jobs, and the destruction of any social consensus about the nature and purpose of work.

To address those concerns, he said, the education system would have to shift its emphasis from schooling the young to a more flexible system of lifelong, recurring education for people of all ages.

Individuals — inevitably faced with greater leisure time and "loss of the job-for-life pattern of employment" — would have to develop greater flexibility in their working lives and "a stronger sense of personal identity, purpose and meaning that does not depend on a specific job or career.". . .

. . . [But] while the truth of his predictions has come at us at the gallop, there has been infinitesimal movement on his prescriptive responses.

That is because we Canadians still believe in the technological quick fix, or, to a lesser degree, the deregulatory quick fix. We think life will be okay if we train young people for all the new-age knowledge jobs and get rid of things like minimum-wage and pay-equity laws. . . .

. . . [However] economic globalization means the new-age knowledge jobs that are created — probably fewer than expected — will more than likely go to someone in New Delhi, Budapest or Singapore who will do the job at a fraction of the cost of a Canadian.

A New Delhi computer programmer comes cheaper than a Vancouver computer programmer. A Budapest accountant weighs in at a much lower fee than a Toronto accountant. A Singapore lawyer, advertising copywriter, management consultant, engineer or biomedical researcher will do the job for a lot less money than his or her counterpart in Montreal.

Economic globalization also means that the medium- to low-skills production jobs that aren't vanishing offshore are disappearing to automation and robotization. . . .

Either we can train young people for jobs they will never get or we can start talking about new definitions of work — like global tourism, like community work with a salary attached. We can work at stitching together fragile family life by putting pressures on employers to develop more family-supportive policies: onsite day care, flexible work hours, work-sharing. We can search for human values that are more important than the efficient production of goods and services.

Why? Because the traditional workplace is vanishing.

Source: "The myths we believe about the work we'll do," *The Globe and Mail*, Wed. Nov. 24, 1993, p. A2

---

part as they will in another. This means we must understand these different parts of the economic order, for they structure people's experiences as workers.

Labour market segments

People compete for their jobs in a *labour market*. If you look in a newspaper you will see that one part — the "Help Wanted" section — advertises jobs in factories, as domestics, or in fast food outlets. Another part — "Careers" — advertises management, accounting, or teaching posts, along with jobs for computer programmers or sales representatives. There is not one big labour market in which every person who is willing to work competes for the same jobs. On the contrary, there are *many* labour markets and segments within each of these. As you can judge from the newspaper ads, some segments contain better-paying and higher-status jobs than others.

According to the so-called "dual labour market" model, national labour markets comprise two (or more) subdivisions: a primary and secondary labour market. These subdivide by geography: by region, province, and size of community.

The **primary labour market** consists of jobs which offer good wages, opportunities for getting ahead, and job security: jobs like lawyer, plumber, and teacher. The **secondary (or marginal) labour market** consists of jobs that pay low wages, offer little chance to get ahead, and guarantee little job security: jobs like taxi driver, secretary, or bank teller.

Typically, people with different social characteristics, backgrounds, and skills are found in different markets. For example, there are far more women and visible minorities in the secondary labour market, and far more white men in the primary labour market than could have occurred by chance. In particular, the more educated and skilled white men find work in the primary market.

The big difference between primary and secondary markets tends to blur smaller but still important differences among jobs in the *same* market. For example, though both are in the primary labour market, few teachers feel they have the sort of advantages and opportunities that doctors do. And, though both are in the secondary labour market, few bank tellers would consider their work to be the same as that of taxi drivers. Still, the distinction between primary and secondary markets gives us a crude indicator of the differences in life chances that they afford.

Another major aspect of any job is the sort of organization in which a person works. As we have seen, managers organize work in different ways, depending on the work being done and prevailing theories about the best way to manage (or control) workers. As a result, schools are different from auto-

Unions played a large part, historically, in ensuring white working men of a place in the primary labour market. They did it through protest and collective action.

mobile factories in the ways they organize work. And schoolwork is organized differently today from the way it was organized 50 years ago.

Even within an organization, different divisions may split up and manage the work differently. For example, the administration of a college is usually much more bureaucratic than the administration of a teaching division within the college. Also, teachers have more freedom in the way they do their work than people who work as administrators. But the administrators will have much more freedom than members of the caretaking staff.

Organizations also contain different labour market segments. Some jobs are well-paying and secure, while others are not. The chance to move across segments within the organization is rare, if possible at all. The promotion from secretary to manager in a business is just as rare as a promotion from private to lieutenant in the military, or nurse to doctor in a hospital.

Increasingly, technological changes are altering the shape of labour markets and work organization. We shall now briefly discuss this issue.

WORK AND THE NEW TECHNOLOGY

Computerization and knowledge work

No one can doubt that we live in a period of constant and sweeping changes in the nature of work. Some of these changes are a result of the tools we use, some are a result of the purposes for which we use them. More and more often, people are doing work which involves the acquisition and use of knowledge.

We noted earlier that in a bureaucracy information goes in one end, gets processed, then comes out the other end as decisions and rules. So knowledge is central to bureaucratic work. It is also central to the professions. Professionals gain *their* status and autonomy through a knowledge of and control over techniques and information. The physician, for example, has the knowledge to diagnose and deal with illness. Generally, we find that collecting, interpreting and controlling information are crucial features of the way we organize work in our society.

Think about the high-tech industries: they include software producers (who make up video games for Nintendo or data analysis packages for IBM), data base producers (who create mailing lists for advertisers, check your credit for banks, or keep up-to-date information on stock market listings), and hardware producers (who create computerized weaponry for the armed forces). All of these jobs manipulate and apply information.

In the fast-changing, high-technology industries, "There is less formality and fewer layers of bureaucracy; financial risks are more often shared with employees" (Von Glinow, 1988: 4.) That is because of the uncertainty in these industries. Causes of uncertainty include a dependence on outside capital, young and inexperienced managers, foreign marketing and competition, a short product life, and the frequent introduction of innovations. To survive this uncertainty, high-technology industries spend a large part of their earnings on research and development. They value knowledge even when the immediate practical benefits are not readily apparent.

In industrial society, knowledge constantly accumulates and alters what we do and how we do it. As a result, we find ourselves undergoing dramatic changes in the work we do over our lifetimes. Some of us will find that our jobs disappear as new tools or skills take over. Secretaries, for example, found in the early 1980s that word processors were replacing typewriters. To keep their jobs, they had to learn how to use the new machines. Yet, by the late 1980s, computers had almost completely replaced word processors, requiring yet more training and the acquisition of new skills. Today a secretary's desk will contain drawers filled with software guides, a booklet on how to fix the copier, and a manual on how to use the fax machine.

Computers also decrease the need for secretaries because they can store "boilerplate," phrases which appear repeatedly in a variety of documents. Now, for example, a lawyer can use a computer to generate a will or a contract — which consists largely of boilerplate — and simply add in whatever specific information he or she needs. Other computer systems can obey spoken commands. Once these systems are perfected, they will further reduce the need for secretaries.

For similar reasons, computers have rendered the work of many supervisors and middle managers redundant. As we saw earlier in Exhibit 9.4, on active badges, computers can easily monitor the work of employees. If necessary, they could provide a single manager with easy-to-understand statistics on scores or even hundreds of workers.

Technology in the workplace

Having said that, the effects of technological change largely depend on the social context within which the change takes place. As a result, it is impossible to make general rules about the effects of technological change.

For example, the effect of automation at an automobile factory is positive for some workers and negative for others. Skilled workers gain more responsibility and job challenge. Semi-skilled workers lose skills and become subordinated to the new equipment. Research on telephone workers also shows automation affects different occupational groups in different ways (Vallas, 1988).

The effect of technological change at a high-technology firm is different for managers and computer professionals, than for computer operators and secretaries. Generally, people higher up in the organization experience more positive effects, and fewer negative effects, than people lower down. Computer operators, specialty professionals and secretaries report being the most controlled by the work process; they are right to expect the fewest chances of advancement (Kaufman et al., 1988).

Everywhere, social factors influence the pace and outcome of technological change. Technology is not class-neutral. In the end, new technologies embody the dreams and plans of the industrially powerful. However, these industrialists have to manipulate actual work practices within particular industrial settings (Webster, 1991). Technologies are never the deciding factors in the way in which work is organized — only tools that can be used in different ways and for different purposes, depending on who is controlling them.

So, whether a technology will degrade or enhance work depends on the organizational milieu in which people use the technology and the economic environment surrounding the organization. The social and economic effects of computer-based technology, for example, are *not* determined by the technology itself. All the actors involved have a say, according to their relative power (Betcherman, 1990). Culture also plays a part, forcing organizations to adapt technologies to local uses, instead of directly copying from other organizations.

Stockmarkets around the world (for example) have quickly adopted similar computerized techniques of collecting, storing and analyzing financial data.

The result is that capital circulates at increasing speed, while labour remains trapped within national borders. Some believe that this tilts the class balance further in favour of capital. But what this illustrates is not the overwhelming importance of technology so much as the overwhelming importance of power wielded by capital. And this, of course, brings us back to Marx.

WORK SATISFACTION AND ALIENATION

Sociologists who follow Marx's approach see current work problems as primarily a result of capitalism. These problems would disappear, or at least improve dramatically, if socialist economic organization replaced capitalism. Those who follow Durkheim's approach see problems as primarily the result of over-specialized labour, large organizations, and rapid change. And those who follow Weber's approach see problems to be the result of rationalization and overly rigid bureaucratization.

These different perspectives are associated with different theories about work satisfaction and alienation: why many people hate working and some people love it.

Work satisfaction: its causes and effects

Many jobs are mindless and boring, yet evidence shows that most North Americans *say* they like their jobs. Four out of five workers are satisfied to some degree, and one in three describe themselves as "completely satisfied" (Campbell, 1980). Three out of four people even say they enjoy their work (Casale and Lerman, 1986: 117).

Yet we have good reason to doubt these findings. Most married people *say* they are satisfied with their marriage, yet roughly four in ten will divorce at least once during their lives. When asked their opinions in surveys, people put a pleasant face on unpleasant situations. What is more, there is widespread evidence of dissatisfaction with work. This evidence includes high rates of absenteeism, indifference to what happens at work, the attitude that life begins when work ends, industrial sabotage, and attempts by workers to increase their control over the production process, through strikes and working to rule.

What causes people to be satisfied or dissatisfied with their job? Most research into causes of job satisfaction has focused on objective job characteristics. Surveying the literature, Locke (1976: 1342) notes that job satisfaction results when work "is varied, allows autonomy, is not physically fatiguing,...is mentally challenging, ...allows the individual to experience success, and... is personally interesting."

Social and organizational aspects of a job play an important part in job satisfaction too. Think about the people who taught you in high school: research shows that their biggest sources of satisfaction are orderly students, encouraging principals, supportive administrators, and cooperative fellow-teachers (Newman et al., 1989).

The social acceptability of a job also makes a difference. Hood (1988) reports a problem that arose among caretakers at an urban university when they were forced to change from the night shift to the day shift. This change put them in contact with the building's higher-status daytime occupants, creating problems in status management. You see, "clean work" done at one time of day (e.g., at night, in isolation) becomes "dirty work" when done at another time. When they looked at themselves through the eyes of professors and students, the caretakers became less satisfied with their job.

So, objective job characteristics are not the only things that matter. Locke finds that even satisfaction with rewards depends on "the fairness or equity with which [rewards] are administered and the degree to which they are congruent with the individual's personal aspirations" (ibid.). Along similar lines, the more central a task is to the organization's normative and technical structure, the more highly workers will rate its intrinsic value (Fuller and Dornbusch, 1988). Said another way, people like to do something important.

Occasionally, people can learn to accept work conditions they don't like and adapt to the frustrations of their job. People are *often* able to commit to, and identify with, new job demands. So, for example, the factory worker promoted to supervisor gradually learns (and tries to adopt) the viewpoint of management. The young academic leaves behind the viewpoint of student for that of teacher. In these and other cases, people learn to change their goals, standards and behaviour.

However, human adaptability has its limits. The high rates of turnover and absenteeism even among well-paid automobile workers make that point. Feelings of work dissatisfaction run deep and their causes are complicated.

The problem of alienation

Marx thought dissatisfaction reflected a problem of unequal social relations in a capitalist society. At the core of his theory is the concept of **alienation**. As Marx describes it, alienation has both objective and subjective dimensions. Work has an enormous power to alienate us because it has an enormous importance in our lives. Marx viewed work as the most important medium we have to express and develop ourselves. It is an activity in which people can express their uniquely human qualities. Both objective and subjective consequences follow from this.

The objective dimension of alienation has several aspects: a separation of workers from the product of their labour, a lack of control by workers over the labour process itself, estrangement of workers from their own humanity, and estrangement of workers from each other (see Rinehart, 1987).

To get a better handle on this, try to imagine living in a small, single-industry town. There's only one factory, and if you want to stay — or *have* to stay, because of your spouse, your aging parents, or children — you have to take a dull job at that factory. You must work to live, and to support your sick mother, so you can't move away to find another job, but you hate this one. Everything about the job — the working conditions, the pay, the way you are supervised — is rotten. You dread going in to work each day and you count the minutes until the work day is over, but you don't have any choice. What's more, the boss knows it.

These are the "objective aspects" of alienation Marx had in mind. They are "objective" in the sense that they are inevitable consequences of social organization (and, in Marxist theory, inevitable consequences of capitalism). They are real, not imaginary, troubles, rooted in real relations of power and production. But as you can see, they also include subjective aspects.

Subjective alienation varies from one person to another. In that respect, alienation looks more like a personal trouble than a public issue. Subjective alienation includes feelings of powerlessness, meaninglessness, and self-estrangement. Workers experience these feelings as a direct result of controlling neither the production process, nor their own labour (Seeman, 1959).

EXHIBIT 9.6 *Hard times cause stress, depression*

Tough economic times seem to be taking a toll on the Canadian psyche.

A study released yesterday suggests that Canadians are suffering disturbingly high levels of stress and depression because of employment and financial pressures associated with the decline in the economy. . . .

Almost half of the 1,500 respondents — 47 per cent — said they feel "really stressed" anywhere from a few times a week to all the time, while one-third said they're "really depressed" at least once a month.

And why do they feel this way? Fifty-eight per cent cited problems related to work and money.

The survey shows that people who make up the backbone of the economy — those between 25 and 54 — are experiencing the highest levels of stress, while young people are most prone to outright depression. About 40 per cent of respondents between 18 and 24 reported feeling "really depressed" once a month or more. . . .

The survey also found marked differences based on income. While 48 per cent of people earning less than $30,000 a year reported frequent depression, a mere 18 per cent of those earning more than $100,000 felt the same.

On the other hand, stress was a problem for 66 per cent in the high-income bracket, compared with 45 per cent of the low-income group. . . .

Men and women reported almost identical levels of both depression and stress, the results show. . . .

The survey. . . put to rest [a] commonly held belief—that stress is higher in large urban areas. The stress levels reported in Manitoba and Saskatchewan (49 per cent) on a daily and weekly basis were almost level with those felt in Toronto (50 per cent).

The findings all point to the same conclusion: "It is essential that we start paying more attention to our mental health," Dr. Gosselin said.

"Left unchecked, stress and mild depression can escalate into more serious or chronic conditions. Our immunological system goes down the drain."

Illnesses such as heart disease, high blood pressure and cancer have been strongly linked to stress, he said.

"We estimate that about 50 per cent of depression goes untreated," he said. "The cost to society for lost productivity and ill health is staggering."

Source: Joan Breckenridge, "Canada suffering bad case of blues," *The Globe and Mail*, Thurs., Oct. 1, 1992, pp. A1, A10.

Exhibit 9.6 shows that, in Canada today, some workers experience alienation in the form of stress, while others experience depression. Stress, often indicated by a feeling that you are late or short of time, certainly suggests an absence of control over the work process. Depression — seen by many as anger turned inward or converted into hopelessness — also suggests a lack of control over the work process, and a feeling of being trapped. Both stress and depression are common among Canadian workers.

Cures for alienation

We get nowhere by treating the symptoms of alienation if we leave the causes unchanged. The only way of curing the illness is by eliminating the causes of powerlessness, meaninglessness, and estrangement. This means giving people a chance — at work and elsewhere — to express their creative selves: to make the work place truly human. Researchers have come up with various ideas for doing this.

One idea involves the re-skilling of workers. In many industries, there is evidence of de-skilling due to technological innovation, as we noted earlier.

However, research also shows that, in some countries, de-skilling tendencies have been short-lived and rare.

In West Germany, for example, employers have pushed for re-skilling that is based on trust and responsible autonomy in the workplace. National programs of vocational education are helping to shape and redesign Germany's work culture (Littek and Heisig, 1991). There and elsewhere, the Quality of Working Life approach to industrial organization has pushed for job enrichment, enlargement and rotation. In this way, not only do workers attain more useful and usable skills, but they also feel more involved in their work and in the workplace.

Businesses have become places of learning as well as of production, providing an urgently needed supply of new skills (Streeck, 1989). New skills are a precondition for economic success, but in order to ensure that workers learn new skills, capitalists and unions must cooperate. In the end, it is an interplay of managerial goals and established shop floor subcultures that decides new skill levels (Taplin, 1992). All de-skilling or re-skilling depends on the struggle for control in that "contested terrain," the workplace.

CLOSING REMARKS

What will happen to the close link in our society between work and identity when people routinely have to change their job or career, possibly several times, during their working lives? Will we see even more people engaged in free-floating "consultancies," working for a variety of employers, with no permanent loyalty to any company or, even, to any line of work?

Japanese research reveals that occupational self-direction has the most powerful effect on work-related attitudes. Self-direction — in effect, being one's own boss — decreases alienation and improves attitudes towards one's own work. So, in the long run, it may be a good thing if workers are less locked into particular organizations.

We will further consider the economic and social changes which are transforming the world in Chapter 11. However, the point is that the rapid and dramatic pace of change initiated by the Industrial Revolution has not abated, but is continuing still.

As we have seen, the Industrial Revolution brought people a new perspective on society — in particular, a willingness to doubt traditional authority and try to control their own work lives. But even as workers became more organized and powerful, so did employers. Unions were developed under traditional bourgeois capitalism. But at the same time as workers were perfecting their unions, bourgeois capitalism was being replaced by globalized corporate capitalism.

Throughout the industrial world we have seen the same kinds of social changes, and this fact has several implications. First, it means that we can predict the ways newly developing nations will change as they industrialize. Second, we can predict an increasing similarity among industrialized nations of the world. Third, we can expect cultural influences to pass from older industrial nations like the United States, to newer ones, like Japan.

Specialization and a detailed division of labour continue to characterize industrial society. So do anomie and alienation. As new efforts are made to solve the problem of the anomie Durkheim described, bureaucracies and professions continue to change form.

For many workers, the most important new developments at work are technological — for example, the adoption of computerized aids to production and decision-making (or expert systems). However, as we have said repeatedly, the structure of power determines how technology will be used. No matter how much the technology changes, little will change in the workplace until power is used differently.

That means, in turn, that people's satisfaction with work will still depend on relations of power — just as it did a century ago. In the next chapter we discuss another changing aspect of the modern world — *population.*

A large fraction of all the people who have ever lived are alive today. Not surprisingly, most of our waking hours are spent with many people—at large workplaces, in large cities, within large nation-states. It is also too soon to know how humans will adapt to living as part of large populations.

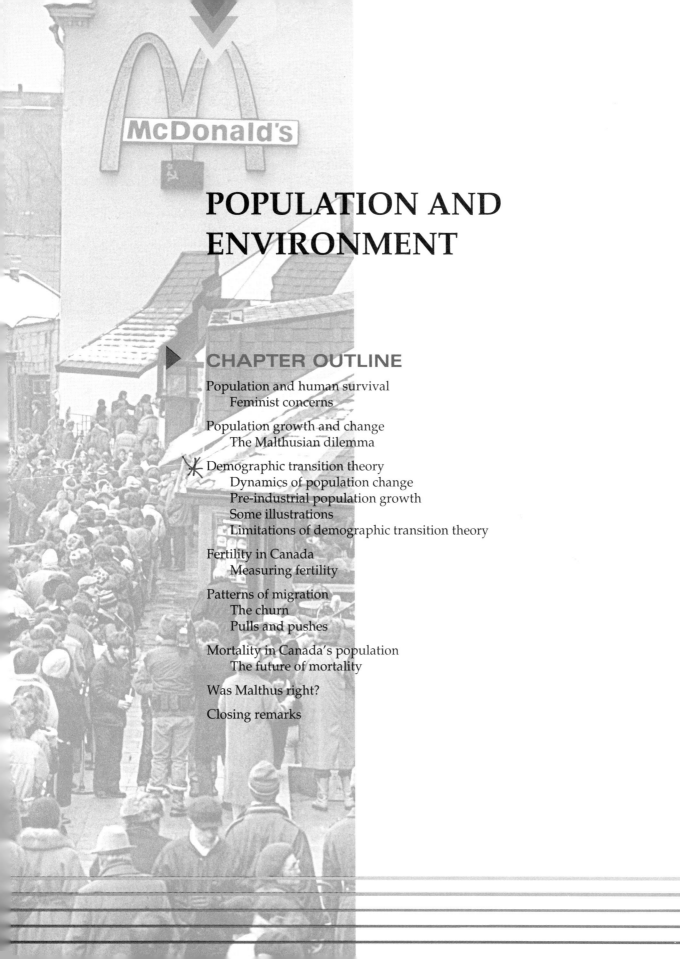

POPULATION AND ENVIRONMENT

POPULATION AND HUMAN SURVIVAL

In Chapter 9 we looked at social upheavals that accompanied the Industrial Revolution and led people to adopt a new outlook on society. After the Industrial Revolution, the social world was no longer seen as a product of natural "forces" or supernatural "design," but as a human creation. The results of this change in thinking were dramatic. People realized that if *we* had made society the way it is, we could also remake it. We could reshape society to fit our needs. New theories about what form society could or should take led to the development of sociology.

Today, we are in the midst of another revolution just as profound. Many of the problems historically connected to industrial development and capitalism — for example, worker health and safety — have been improved, if not solved. New organizations — labour unions, social democratic political parties, feminist movements, and a welfare state — have made important contributions to workers' well-being. And with the ending of the "cold war" — a long-lasting conflict between capitalist and communist states — the chance of world war is less than it has been for decades and the world is safer for everyone.

However, there are new concerns about the future course of world history and many of these have to do with the environment and ecology. There is little doubt that we are dramatically transforming the planet on which we live. We hear that the depletion of the ozone layer and the "greenhouse effect" are making it hazardous just to be out in the sun. The destruction of the Amazon rain forest and the emission of industrial pollutants threaten air quality. Oil spills and the dumping of industrial wastes threaten life in the rivers, lakes, and oceans.

Even ordinary activities and consumer products now seem threatening when we hear, for instance, that the electromagnetic radiation from colour TVs and the nitrites found in hot dogs may cause cancer.

These new social problems face us *all*, regardless of class or political system. The former Soviet Union had its Chernobyl nuclear "mishap," just as the United States had its "accident" at Three Mile Island (although the former cost a great many lives while the latter did not). The Third World suffers as much, and usually more, than the developed world. Indeed, the Union Carbide accident in Bhopal, India showed that industrial technology has placed the whole world at risk.

Closer to home, the Atlantic banks have been emptied of fish through over-fishing (see Exhibit 10.1). Generally, more and more Canadians are concerned about ecology and damage to the environment. Even in the short term, the depletion of natural resources means a loss of jobs and the end of traditional ways of life. In the longer run, it may mean global disaster.

As Chapter 3 on socialization showed, we all change, and learn to change, throughout our lives. The prospect of having to change our ways of living is not threatening to most people. But *how* and *what* should we change, if we are to solve the problems facing us? And can we make the changes soon enough for them to have the desired effect?

Let's begin our discussion of the environment and ecology by looking at population issues. To a large extent the ecological problem is "us," people. Most problems — ecological and otherwise — are aggravated by the sheer number of people in the world.

Research shows it is harder to solve problems of poverty and inequality, intolerance and war, environmental damage and a falling quality of life, when the population is growing rapidly. For ecological and other reasons, we must come to terms with the world's population problem — understand it, then solve it. The social science that provides materials for the study of population is demography.

EXHIBIT 10.1 *Decline of the Maritime Fishery Industry*

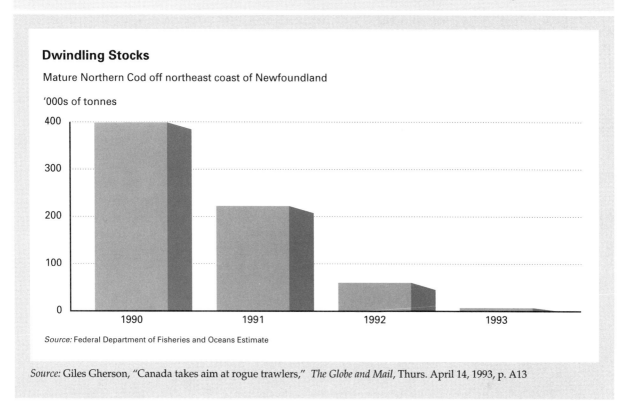

Dwindling Stocks

Mature Northern Cod off northeast coast of Newfoundland

'000s of tonnes

Source: Federal Department of Fisheries and Oceans Estimate

Source: Giles Gherson, "Canada takes aim at rogue trawlers," *The Globe and Mail*, Thurs. April 14, 1993, p. A13

Sociology and demography are two separate disciplines, but they are intimately linked. Demographers are often found as members of university sociology departments and sociologists obtain much of the data with which they work from demographers. **Demography** is the scientific study of the size, structure, distribution, and growth of the world's population. "Social demography," the topic of this chapter, is concerned with the effects of population on the organization of societies.

Demographers play a central role in collecting and analyzing Census data. And sociologists rely on demographers for this information to help us understand population problems. In this chapter we will focus on one central issue: population growth.

The process of population growth illustrates the premise of this book, that macro events and micro events are intertwined. Population analysis is typically macro in scope, because it looks at large numbers of people over long periods of time. Yet the actual patterns it uncovers are a result of millions of couples making personal decisions, such as when to marry and how many children to have. For example, as we shall see, the world's birth rate declined historically because millions of couples decided, quite separately, to have fewer children. The macro-result was a much older and smaller population — something no one had intended.

The combined effect of millions of individual, micro-level decisions yields the pattern we discern when we look at population through a macro lens. Demographers are like astronomers viewing the patterns among millions of stars and planets. Each is moving in its own separate, though interdependent, orbit. Each is part of a large, complex, unintended pattern.

The science of population itself illustrates another premise of this book: namely, that social reality looks different from different theoretical perspectives (or paradigms). Nowhere is this clearer than in the feminist critique of demography.

Feminist concerns

Historically, the field of population studies has been dominated by a male viewpoint. For example, Watkins (1993) notes that demographic research leads us to

 conclude that women are primarily producers of children and of child services; that they produce with little assistance from men; that they are socially isolated from relatives and friends; and that their commitment to the production of children and child services is expected to be rather fragile. (Watkins, 1993: 553)

Beyond that, Watkins writes, "[we] would learn even less about men" from demographic writings than we learn about women. Finally, she concludes that "to a surprising degree, our research draws on what we take for granted about women, men, and the relations between them in order to pose our research questions, to collect our data, and to interpret our results" (*ibid.*)

Some reasons for these problems are easy enough to identify. For one thing, men were instrumental in founding the field of demography. They brought to the discipline a male perspective that is only slowly being modified. Second and probably more important, demography developed with a "hard science" mentality. This is symbolized in a heavy reliance on quantitative data, the use of higher mathematics to develop models, and a style of writing that strives to imitate the physical and natural sciences. (In these respects, demography is more like economics than it is like sociology.)

The implicit notion was that demography would be a science of birth, death and migration that was precise and almost timeless — like astronomy, for example. Achieving this meant oversimplifying our notions about how, for example, people "decide" to have children. This, in turn, meant oversimplifying notions about the way in which power is distributed and decisions are made within a marriage when it comes to questions of sex and conception. And this, in turn, meant oversimplifying notions about what men and women want out of life and marriage, and how they go about getting it.

The founders must have hoped demographic research would be cleansed of messy sociological concerns. They appear to have thought that investigations could be performed as though in isolated, sterile laboratories where men were "males" and women were "females" (and, for that matter, "females" existed only between the ages of 15-50, when they were capable of "reproduction"). The emotionally and conceptually messy facts of everyday life — love, sex, conflict, family violence — were ignored or given more clinical names.

A failure to address these issues — in effect, to wish them away — has led to problems in understanding reality. For example, demographers are still wondering why central theories, like demographic transition theory, which we discuss in more detail later, fail to predict trends in population change adequately. From a feminist standpoint, the answer is plain enough: there are errors in the assumptions on which these theories are built. For example, we will see that demographic transition theory argued industrial conditions and opportunities change people's valuation of children. But whose valuations change? The husband's? The wife's? Both? And in the event of differences, whose ideas prevail? And given changes in contraceptive availability, whose ideas dominate? And how does the intra-marital struggle of values, ideas and behaviours fit into a larger network of friendship and kinship influences?

Beyond values, there are the non-familial influences on people's behaviour. Watkins notes (1993: 559) that demographic research tends to ignore many characteristics that might explain people's behaviour. When it *does* examine a wider variety of characteristics, it often fails to compare women and men, to see whether they are similar or different. Little attention is paid to what constitutes "a separate women's culture" (Watkins, 1993: 560): for example, women's experiences of domestic work, paid work, or community life (e.g., the PTA, volunteer work). As we saw in Chapter 7, women's and men's lives are different in many ways. Yet the differences are rarely reflected in demographic research.

If traditional demographic approaches *were* hugely successful in explaining and predicting population growth, we might be willing to ignore these shortcomings but, in fact, these approaches have failed conspicuously. That means we have to go back and re-think first principles such as: Who has the power over childbearing decisions? How are people influenced to change their values and behaviours? Are men different from women, and if so, in what (demographically relevant) respects?

These are the kinds of questions a feminist approach brings to the study of population processes. They help to re-focus the field and push it to ask new kinds of questions. However, we should not sell demography short: it already has developed some powerful techniques for doing certain kinds of analyses, as we shall see.

POPULATION GROWTH AND CHANGE

One of the traditional concerns of demography is measuring and predicting population growth. Changes in the size and structure of a population have continuing important effects on our personal lives. For example, they influence the demand for, and availability of, housing, education, health care, and employment.

No wonder, then, people were worried by the conclusions stated in Exhibit 10.2: namely, that the Earth's *optimum* population size is one or two billion, but its *expected* population size in 100 years is between 12 and 15 billion. Still, this conclusion is up for debate. It supposes we know what the optimum (or ideal) population is today, or in a century from now. It also implies that we can accurately predict how the world's population will change over the next century. By the end of this chapter, you will have formed some opinions of your own about these issues.

As well, the "population problem" takes a different shape in different parts of the globe. In Canada, the government decided in 1990 to raise the ceiling on

EXHIBIT 10.2 *Earth has too many people, study says*

San Francisco — The number of people on Earth will have to fall to at least one-third the current level by 2100 in order to be sustained in relative prosperity," a study by ecologists concludes.

David Pimentel, a professor of agricultural science at Cornell University, told the annual conference of the American Association for the Advancement of Science yesterday that the population would have to fall substantially to reach an optimum" of between one and two billion people.

The current population is near six billion, and predictions using current growth rates put it at between 12 billion and 15 billion people in 2100.

"We're going to have enormous numbers of people living in misery, poverty, disease and starvation — and they already are," Dr. Pimentel said. "We ought to define an optimum population for the world."

A year-long study by researchers at Cornell's department of ecology and systematics found that the natural resources required to sustain humans, including land, forests, water, energy and biological organisms, will dwindle as the population grows.

The study found that with a population of two billion or fewer by 2100, Earth would provide the 1.2 acres of fertile land per person necessary to provide a diverse, nutritious diet of plant and animal products." Currently, there is only .7 acres of fertile land per person.

A population of two billion people would have an adequate supply of fresh water, albeit half the current consumption of 100 gallons per person a day in the United States, and could have adequate levels of energy from renewable sources such as solar, thermal and wind power.

Dr. Pimentel said that bringing the population to fewer than two billion by 2100 could be accomplished if every couple had only 1.5 children, which represents a population contraction of .5 per cent a year.

He said that at the current growth rate of 1.1 per cent a year in the United States, the population of the country in 2100 could be 1.2 billion people, the current population of China.

Today, each American consumes about 23 times more goods and services than the average person in the Third World and 53 times more than someone in China.

The question is do we want to live like the Chinese?"...

Dr. Pimentel said that reducing the world's population to two billion would pose social, economic and political problems, but continued rapid population growth will result in even more severe social, economic and political conflicts — plus catastrophic public health and environmental problems."

Source: Mary Gooderham, "Earth has too many people, study says," *The Globe and Mail*, Tues., February 22, 1994, p. A5

the number of immigrants allowed into the country. That decision was informed by a prediction based on current demographic trends. These trends suggested that unless we increase the immigration rate, Canada's population by the year 2025 will be *smaller* than it is today. In Africa, by contrast, the population is projected to grow to over 1.3 billion people without any substantial immigration. Nigeria, for example, is expected to grow into the fourth most populous country in the world by 2025 (Tarver and Miller, 1986). Since Nigeria is very poor in comparison with Canada, this growth has the potential to cause serious problems.

Population growth and change take place within a cultural, political, economic, and social context. Elements beyond human control also play a part.

For example, there is evidence that long-term temperature trends influence population. Periods of global cooling may mean lower rates of growth through changes in birth and death rates and, indirectly, through changes in the food supply (Galloway, 1986). Cultural beliefs and practices affect the size and structure of a population too. They include views on preferred family size, the use of birth control, and the killing of female babies, among other things.

Equally, the size and structure of a population affects cultural practices. For example, as the fraction of people who are over age 65 increases, tolerance for older people grows (though esteem may diminish). There is a growing acceptance of aging as a natural, even desirable, part of life. With the aging of the large baby boom generation, we may even see old age glorified.

The idea that population growth constitutes a serious problem for the world is not a new one. It was first put forward 200 years ago, by the economist and population theorist Thomas Malthus.

The Malthusian dilemma

Thomas Malthus (1766-1834) is considered one of the founders of demography. He was the first to take seriously the possibility that the earth would soon be "overpopulated."

Malthus's main contribution was to argue that population growth takes place *exponentially* (or geometrically). A population increasing exponentially at a constant rate is adding more people every year than the year before.

Consider a population of 1000 women and 1000 men. Each woman marries and has four children. If all survive, in the next generation there will be roughly 2000 women and 2000 men. If all of *these* women have four children each, in the next generation there will be roughly 4000 women and 4000 men, and in the generation after *that*, 8000 women and 8000 men. Thus, with a constant pattern of four births per woman, the population doubles every generation (roughly 30 years). In four generations, or about 120 years, it grows from 2000 people to 16 000 people. (In 300 years it would exceed a million people!) This is the power of exponential growth.

Malthus argued that, on the other hand, increases in the food supply are only additive or *arithmetic*. The growth in food supplies is limited by the amount of land available, the soil quality, and the level of technology a society has attained. Malthus believed that there is a real risk of population outgrowing increases in the food supply. This possibility that food supplies will not be sufficient to feed the earth's growing population poses an ongoing threat to the survival of the human species.

Checks (or limits) on population growth are needed to ensure that growth is kept in line with the food supply. Welfare schemes to help the poor are futile, said Malthus. If we feed the hungry, they will simply increase their numbers until they are hungry again. The only sure solutions are positive checks and preventive checks. **Positive checks** prevent overpopulation by increasing the death rate. They include war, famine, pestilence, and disease. **Preventive checks** prevent overpopulation by limiting the number of live births. They include abortion, infanticide, sexual abstinence, delaying marriage and using contraceptives.

As you can see, Malthus painted a grim picture of the world's future. But was he right? "Overpopulation" is a word that is often used but is hard to measure. An area is thought to be overpopulated when inhabitants do not have the means available to support themselves; when there are more mouths to feed than there is food. Yet numbers of people are not all that determines whether an area is overpopulated. What is critical is the *relationship* between a population and the environment in which it is located. Some environments can support more people than others. The type of technology available to exploit this environment, and the system of distribution, are also important.

Despite the views reported in Exhibit 10.2 above, it is hard to put meaningful absolute numbers on the world's **carrying capacity** (that is, the number of people who can be supported by the available resources at a given level of technology). However, it is easy to see when a territory is far beyond its carrying capacity. Then, scarcity starts to show itself in dramatic ways — famines and epidemics, for example — and the conflict over resources increases.

Malthus did not realize that technological advances in agriculture would make it possible to vastly increase the food supply, to the point where most of the people in industrialized countries are able to live off the food produced by

The World Population Explosion

Most of the world's population increase has taken place in the past two centuries. It took hundreds of thousands of years for the human race to reach its 1960 total of about 3 billion people. But in the 30 years that followed, it grew by another 2 billion people, to its present total of over 5 billion.

Source: G.T. Trewartha (1969), *A Geography of Population: World Patterns*, New York: Wiley, p. 29.

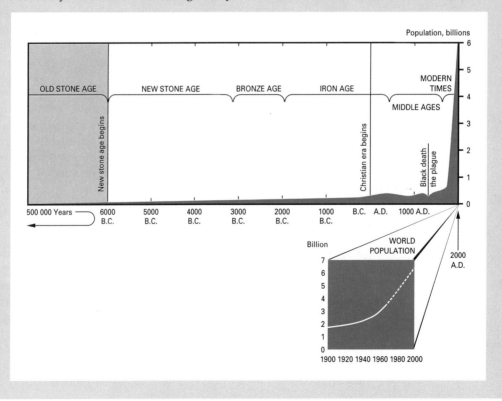

3%-4% of the population. Today, even in less-developed countries, most people have food to eat, though many do not have enough food and others do not eat the right kinds of food for good health.

The famines that have plagued Africa — for example, Ethiopia and Somalia — in recent years are not a result of overpopulation. They are a result of improper land use, civil wars, and other social and political factors, such as low prices set on food goods by the state. For strategic reasons, a government sometimes puts a low priority on shipping food to regions of the country where rebel supporters are most numerous. In this way, it tries to starve the rebels into submission. This procedure of strategic famine has a long history. For example, Britain ignored its starving and troublesome Irish subjects in the 1840s. The Soviet Union withheld or withdrew food from the Ukraine in the 1930s; it held back resources from the Baltic states in the 1980s, as did the USA from Iraq, in 1990.

So we cannot take famines, in themselves, as proof of overpopulation. Indeed, many developed nations pay their farmers not to grow crops, even if this means a shortage somewhere else in the world. Furthermore, demographers have used historical records and computer simulations to study the effects of famine on human history. The results suggest that, contrary to what Malthus argued, famines have *not* played a significant role as "positive checks" on population size (Watkins and Menken, 1985).

Likewise, we *cannot* assume plagues or epidemics are positive checks that result from overpopulation. In fact, they may sometimes indicate economic development (even if *uneven* development) is taking place. For example, one of the reasons plague took such a large toll (12 million deaths) in India in the first quarter of this century was because of "imbalanced modernization" (Klein, 1988).

On the one hand, there were many conditions which allowed the plague to spread throughout India. They included a large railway, a grain trade and considerable human mobility within the country. On the other hand, the country had few of the conditions which could have hindered the spread of disease, such as good nutrition, housing, and sanitation. Because of people's opposition to mandatory health inspection, fumigation, quarantine and hospitalization for those infected, health measures were left voluntary. As a result, the illness spread quickly and over an extensive area.

Some economists believe the reason for world poverty (and the positive checks we have been discussing) is that Third World countries do not have enough resources — for example, arable land or minerals — to exploit, or do not know how to exploit them. Yet this cannot be true. Industrialized countries rely heavily on Third World countries for many resources such as timber and zinc, iron and copper, oil and natural gas, that they cannot get in their own countries. They also rely on the Third World for foods they cannot grow, such as sugar, coffee, tea, and bananas.

The less-developed countries *do* have valuable resources. However, control over these resources is often in the hands of the developed world. What's more, it is in the interest of the developed nations to keep the price of resources low. The small amount paid for resources leaves Third World countries with little money to invest in their own industrial development. This means they cannot develop manufacturing or break free from dependence on the industrial nations for capital or manufactured goods.

In poorer nations, then, the problem is not too many people; it is a shortage of capital and the consequent difficulty of getting industry started. As we have said, the problems of poverty, dependency, plague and famine are compounded by a large, rapidly growing population. Faced with world population concerns, many have come to advocate **zero population growth** (ZPG) as a temporary solution, until a longer-term solution is found. Zero population growth occurs when the factors leading to population growth, especially births, are exactly balanced by the factors leading to population decline, especially deaths. Under conditions of ZPG, births and deaths are equal. Then the size of the population remains constant over time.

Such a goal is realistic if the demographic changes we have seen in the industrial world spread elsewhere. These changes are part of a process of demographic transition which began in Europe about two centuries ago and profoundly altered population growth patterns.

DEMOGRAPHIC TRANSITION THEORY

The term **demographic transition** refers to the change a society undergoes, from *high* birth and death rates to *low* birth and death rates, usually during industrialization (Davis, 1945; Stolnitz, 1964). This type of change has taken place in Europe from the onset of the Industrial Revolution up to the present day. Currently, much of the Third World is in the middle of this transition process.

In its most general form, the transition is brought about by a package of changes, called "modernization," which include, among other things, industrialization, urbanization, and increases in literacy.

As you will gather, the demographic transition theory is a structural functionalist theory. One of its earliest proponents, Kingsley Davis, is also credited with the "functional theory of stratification" we discussed in Chapter 5 (Davis and Moore, 1945). Several features of the demographic transition theory show that it belongs to the functionalist paradigm: the theory

(1) is macrosociological and describes social changes that take a long time to unfold;
(2) views societies as systems of interrelated parts. Change in one part changes other parts, as would happen in an evolving organism;
(3) has nothing to say about social inequality or social conflict;
(4) holds a generally positive, benevolent and optimistic view of social change.

According to the theory, modernization first causes a drop in mortality, then (after a time) a drop in fertility. Why does this happen? To answer this question, we need to back up a bit and consider the dynamics of population change.

Dynamics of population change

There are only a few factors that affect the size of a population. In a "closed" system with no migration in or out — like the world as a whole — only births and deaths will affect the population size.

A population's fertility rate (or total fertility rate) is the average number of children a woman in a given society bears. For a society like ours to replace itself — to stay the same size from one generation to the next — the fertility rate should be about 2.1 children, or 1.05 daughters, per woman.

Each woman who gives birth must reproduce for herself and her mate, and also for the women in her generation who never reproduce (because they die before they reach reproductive age, choose not to have children, or are unable to do so). Note that this is an average. Some must have more than two children to compensate for those who have fewer.

To measure the risks of death in a population, demographers measure a mortality rate for people of each age; paradoxically, this collection of death risks is called a "life table." From this they can calculate life expectancies at each age. The most commonly used indicator is life expectancy at birth. In Canada, a woman's life expectancy at birth is about 80 years. That is, the moment she is born, a woman can expect to live 80 years. A man's life expectancy at birth is seven years less, according to the widely known Population Reference Bureau's *World Population Data Sheet* (1992).

Pre-industrial population growth

In pre-industrial societies, birth and death rates were nearly identical. Before modern medicine and sanitation, death rates were high (as you would expect), and so were birth rates. As a result, the rate of natural increase — the difference between births and deaths, expressed as a ratio of the total population — was nearly zero. That is, there was little change in the population size from year to year. The population was young and constantly "turning over" through births and deaths, and it was not growing larger.

Given the high death rate, women would bear as many children as possible. Then, children were an economic asset, and even today in non-industrial countries, children continue to be an economic asset. In rural areas, they start to work at an early age as farm hands, doing chores in the home, or earning extra wages on other farms or in nearby factories. In parts of the world where old-age security, pension plans, and welfare assistance do not exist, children are the only source of support when parents get old and cannot take care of themselves.

In a pre-industrial society, the more children a couple has, the more chance they will be looked after in their "golden years." Sons are especially important. In rural South Asia, for example, they provide a kind of income insurance for their parents' old age, and the failure to rear a son is often seen as a material loss. These perceptions are supported by hard evidence. Among old people without a surviving son, one finds higher mortality risks and a higher chance of property loss. The consequences are more severe for mothers than they are for fathers. Women have even more reason for wanting many children than do men (Cain, 1986).

In societies with arranged marriages, children allow a family to form economic and social ties to other families for mutual assistance. It is desirable to have many children because the more children one has, the more ties one will have to other families.

The pattern of high birth and death rates described above started to change in Europe in the 18th century when nutrition, sanitation and medical treatment began to improve and the death rate fell dramatically. For awhile, women kept on bearing children at the traditional rate. But with many more children surviving to reproductive age, the population grew rapidly.

Eventually, women began bearing fewer children — only as many as they thought they could support. They no longer had to bear ten children in the hope that four would survive. As well, parents began to *want* fewer children as the burden of social security shifted from the family to the state. Urbanization, extended education, and social and geographic mobility all lowered the economic value of children. At the same time, the cost of raising children went up. More recently still, the changing roles of women — especially, the growing availability of paid work — also made women less willing to bear many children.

In European history, first mortality rates fell, then fertility rates fell. In between, the population grew rapidly. To some degree, non-European societies are repeating this pattern.

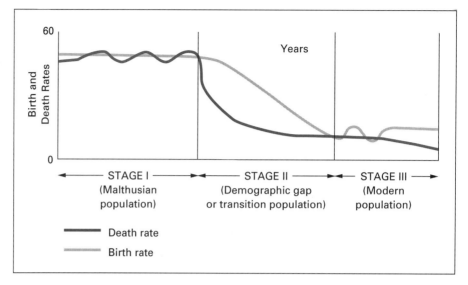

For all these reasons, the birth rate began to fall. In the West, it continued falling until, finally, it was below the death rate. As a result, the population growth rate is negative in most developed societies today.

As the data in Exhibit 10.3 show, there is an enormous difference in the fertility and life expectancy of societies — like Canada and Japan — which have completed the demographic transition, and societies like Ethiopia and Nigeria, which have scarcely begun it. What is equally interesting is the effect this difference will have on global population in the next 30 years. The poor, high fertility, high mortality societies will become a larger and larger segment of the world's population — a change which is sure to have explosive political consequences.

Some illustrations

Mexico provides a fairly recent example of demographic transition theory in action. Before about 1950, Mexico was essentially a pre-industrial society. As the country industrialized, mortality began to fall. Between 1950 and 1985, the population tripled and, in about 1965, fertility started to fall. Since then, the population size has been fairly stable, but because of the decline in fertility, the average age has risen. This has created problems of social planning that Mexico has never had to face before (Partida-Bush, 1990).

Thailand provides another example of the transition and its effects. In rural areas, fertility is at the traditional (high) levels. In newly-settled areas, fertility has declined. The declines are associated with land-saving and labour-saving changes; for example, industrialization and high wage rates. These have made bearing children less necessary than in the past (Hutaserani and Roumasset, 1991).

Limitations of demographic transition theory

Demographic transition theory has great practical as well as theoretical importance. It describes what seems to be a universal process. The theory also makes an important contribution to our understanding of economic development and the way population is tied to development. Today, this theory is the dominant way of thinking about population and it is behind every forecast of world populations.

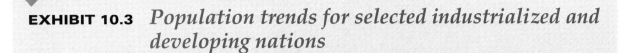

EXHIBIT 10.3 *Population trends for selected industrialized and developing nations*

Earth Watch

Population trends for selected industrialized and developing nations.

	Population (millions)		Average growth rate (%) 1990-95	Life expectancy 1990-95	Fertility rate per woman 1990-95
	1992	2025			
Ethiopia	53	130	3.1	47	7.0
Uganda	18	45	3.0	42	7.3
Egypt	54	93	2.2	62	4.1
Nigeria	115	285	3.1	53	6.4
China	1,188	1,539	1.4	71	2.2
Japan	124	127	0.4	79	1.7
Indonesia	191	283	1.8	63	3.1
India	879	1,393	1.9	60	3.9
Turkey	58	92	2.0	67	3.5
U.K.	57	60	0.2	78	1.4
Italy	57	56	0.1	77	1.3
Spain	39	40	0.2	78	1.4
France	57	60	0.4	77	1.8
Germany	80	83	0.4	76	1.5
Mexico	88	137	2.1	70	3.2
Brazil	154	219	1.6	66	2.7
Canada	27	38	1.4	77	1.8
U.S.	255	322	1.0	76	2.1
WORLD **TOTAL**	**5,479**	**8,472**	**1.7**	**65**	**3.3**

Source: United Nations Population Fund, *Globe and Mail*, Tuesday, March 22, 1994, p. A19

The theory reminds us that a low-mortality/low-fertility population type is critical if people wish to maintain a high standard of living. Yet research over the past 20 years has cast doubt on the theory's validity. Some data (for example, Coale and Watkins, 1987) show that the theory does not apply to European history as well as people once believed. It does even worse with non-European, Third World countries. That is because the theory fails to consider many problems that are common in Third World societies.

One problem is the permanent damage a long-term population explosion can do to a nation's economy or eco-system. An example is Brazil's destruction of the Amazon rain forest — the result of migration, rapid population growth and the Brazilian state's hunger for a growth in national revenues (through the export of meat and lumber). Such damage makes transition to the final stage impossible (or even restores a high-mortality/high-fertility balance).

A second problem is the inability of Third World countries to provide the socio-economic conditions that make fertility reduction attractive. These conditions include social security, education, urbanization, social mobility, and careers for women. Furthermore, in central Africa and the Indian subcontinent, people have little opportunity to improve their lives by reduced childbearing. So they may still have many children even if doing so provides only a slight or temporary economic advantage.

A different way of interpreting the same facts is provided by researchers (for example, Ratcliffe, 1983; Caldwell, 1986) who have studied several societies — among them, Costa Rica, Sri Lanka and Kerala State (India) — that have enjoyed notable success in lowering the birth rate. They conclude that low mortality and fertility rates are the result of a long process that begins with fairer income distribution, better nutrition, more education (especially for women), more autonomy for women, higher rates of political awareness and participation for all, and universal access to health services. In particular, income (or land) redistribution and political involvement give people more sense of involvement in their own lives — hence, more to gain from changing their fertility decisions. This is particularly true of women who, with more education and autonomy, are no longer so reliant on children for social status and income security.

Beyond that, traditional cultural factors encourage the persistence of large families. So, although mortality has fallen in Nigeria, people still put a high value on children. People will not adopt Western family planning techniques unless these values change (Orubuloye, 1991). As well, in many countries there are people with a vested political interest in large families. For example, in Nigeria, members of the dominant ethnic group — the Hausa — prefer large families. Perhaps this is because maintaining a large population helps them remain politically dominant (Adebayo and Adamchak, 1991).

A third problem is the need of Third World countries to choose among competing social investments — to spend money on social security *versus* education *versus* health care *versus* exportable manufactured goods, for example. The theory says little about which factors are most important in the transition process and which should be given top priority.

Often, the result of so many conflicting demands is political tension. For example, many Arab countries have a problem with high fertility because it reduces per capita income. It also creates a young population: in Arab countries, the median age is ten or more years lower than one finds in an industrial Western nation. Nor are women allowed to participate in the labour force. The combination of poverty, youth unemployment and the suppression of women is likely to cause political problems in the future for many Third World countries (Moustafa, 1988).

In China, high fertility poses a different version of this problem. China needs reforms of almost every kind — agricultural, industrial, educational, economic, and so on. Money could be usefully invested in thousands of different activities and choosing among the possibilities, though inevitable, is very difficult. Worse still, every year as many new Chinese babies are born as there are people alive in Canada — about 25 million. To planners, these new citizens represent new demands on the public purse.

This is why China has turned to the "one child" policy. However, this policy poses problems of its own. In rural areas it leaves parents with little security in their old age, for it is difficult for one child to support two aged parents (Goldstein and Goldstein, 1986).

This could be one reason why the policy has been slow to catch on. In China, single-child families are still much rarer than they are in Western countries — only one family in eight — despite a great drop in fertility. In developed countries, people also marry at later ages and the average intervals between births are longer than in China (Poston and Yu, 1986). So dramatic changes in childbearing will require changes in living conditions, not merely in state policy.

By contrast, Hungary, with the world's highest fraction (25%) of single-child families, has a long history of low fertility for reasons that are poorly understood. It is not, apparently, a result of modernization. Rural regions of Hungary have long had a one-child system, perhaps to keep up the tradition of peasant self-sufficiency. In the 20th century, this system came under attack, as many Hungarians feared population decline and national extinction (Vasary, 1989). Yet low fertility has continued.

In the end, demographic transition theory describes Western demographic history in vague generalities. It describes the macrodynamics of contemporary populations, yet it is unable to explain the details of demographic history in any given country. As such, it contributes little to forecasts or social planning. This is especially true in an industrial country like Canada which has had significant immigration.

FERTILITY IN CANADA

As demographic transition theory would have predicted, Canadian *mortality* began to fall in the early 19th century and continued falling through the early 20th century. It declined more slowly in the north, on native reserves, and in isolated parts of the Maritimes, well into the second half of this century. In other parts of the country, mortality rates levelled off around mid-century.

Also, as the theory would have predicted, by the end of the 19th century, *fertility* had already begun to decline. It has continued to decline — with two irregularities — until now. The two irregularities were the Depression of the 1930s (when many fewer children were born than demographers expected) and the 1950s (when many more children were born than expected). Leaving aside these exceptions, the Canadian transition to low fertility has gone much as expected. Since about 1980, the growth rate has levelled off at a level just below zero.

In the past, high fertility played a critical part in Canada's population development. Contrary to what many believe, immigration has *not* played the decisive role in 20th century Canada. In fact, Beaujot (1988: 54) reports, "The net migration of 4.0 million persons from 1901 to 1981 comprised 21.2% of [Canada's] population growth over this period." The other nearly 80% occurred through natural increase. The reason immigration had so little impact was because, often, there were as many people (or more) leaving the country as there were entering it.

The rate of increase of Quebec's French population illustrates the power of local reproduction — a rate of growth that has rarely been equalled in world history. Between 1608 and 1760, a mere 10 000 French colonists came to New

France. By doubling every 25 years until the first years of this century, they produced all of the millions of Francophones in North America.

Last century, this extraordinarily high level of population growth was referred to by francophone nationalists as "the revenge of the cradle." It partly made up for the failure to attract new immigrants from France. More important, it helped prevent the assimilation of most francophones into an overwhelming anglophone majority.

Today, Quebec's fertility is the lowest in Canada and Canadian fertility rates are among the lowest in the world. Continuing low fertility will give variations in mortality and migration more importance than ever in Canada's population picture. We shall discuss these after completing our brief examination of fertility.

Measuring fertility

As noted earlier, the fertility rate is the number of children an average woman of childbearing age bears in a given society. There are patterns in the number of children women bear — for example, religious, traditional-minded women will bear more children than non-religious women. There is also a pattern in the ages at which women will bear their offspring. For example, less-educated women tend to bear children at earlier ages and continue for a longer time. However, in calculating a fertility rate, we ignore these variations.

Age-specific fertility rates are annual fertility rates that we are likely to find among women in specific age groups: ages 15 to 19, 20 to 24, 25 to 29, and so on. A total fertility rate is calculated from these rates. By summing these rates, we can estimate the average number of live births to a woman who lives through the childbearing years of 15 to 49.

Today, women spend much less of their adult lives producing children than they did in the past. For example, the average age at which a woman bears her first child is closer to 30 than it is to 15. And few women continue to have children at the biologically possible maximum. Because more women have career ambitions which take them into educational institutions and the workplace, they have less time available to bear many children.

As well, cultural attitudes make it possible for women to delay having children until they have completed their education and established themselves in a career. They also make it socially acceptable for women to have fewer children overall. Even women who have their first child in their teens — often the result of an unwanted pregnancy — are unlikely to continue bearing children at a biologically maximum rate. Like women who begin their childbearing later, they will want a family that is closer to two or three children in number than to ten or fifteen.

Not only are childbearing norms — people's desired family size — lower today than in the past; so are childbearing realities. Modern contraception allows most women to have the number of children they actually want, when they want to have them. They can also space their childbearing, so that births occur almost exactly when they will be most convenient.

As a result, the age of women when they first give birth has increased sharply since the advent of modern contraception (Ostby, 1989). Changed cohabitation patterns, a changed labour market, and increased educational opportunities have all played a part. It is improved contraception that makes it possible, as never before, for women to have careers the way men do, yet still bear children.

By contrast, the use of contraceptives is often low in developing countries. A survey of young people in Harare, Zimbabwe, indicates that high fertility is not due to a lack of knowledge about contraception so much as it is due to a failure to use contraceptives. Only 14% of unmarried women and 18% of unmarried men used contraceptives at the time of first intercourse. Only 36% of women and 29% of men are currently using them. This results in a high number of unwanted premarital pregnancies. In turn, it also affects school attendance and increases the risk of AIDS (Boohene and Tsodzai, 1991).

Since the Second World War, the biggest population change in Canada, as elsewhere, was caused by the baby boom. This was a sudden and considerable rise in the birth rate in the 1950s and early 1960s. It was a response to the end of restraints on marriage and childbearing caused by the Depression and then the war, as well as the rapid increase in economic prosperity after the war. The birth rate reached its peak, then began to decline again around the end of the 1950s. It has since fallen to its lowest level ever.

However, the social changes caused by this burst of fertility will last well into the next century. Because of more than usually stiff competition for education, jobs, and marriage partners, the baby boomers have had continuing problems with getting ahead (Easterlin, 1980).

At a group level, cohort size is *positively* associated with social advantage. A cohort is a group of people who share similar life experiences at the same point in time. For example, all the people who were born in the same year form a birth cohort. The people who got married in a given year form a marriage cohort. Large birth cohorts, like the baby boomers, control the culture at each stage of their development — hippies in the 1960s and 1970s, yuppies in the 1970s and 1980s, for example. No wonder we have heard so much about "the family" in the last ten years and are starting to hear so much about menopause today. We are hearing about the experiences of one particular cohort, the baby boomers.

However, at an individual level, cohort size is often *negatively* associated with social advantage. Other things being equal, it is scarcity which brings high rewards and the baby boomers will never be scarce. In this sense, whether you were born in a small or large *birth cohort* has a huge impact on your life chances in a competitive society.

Cohorts are interesting because, although the people who make them up do not know one another, they go through many of the same life experiences at the same time, since they face the same constraints and compete for the same opportunities. The larger your birth cohort — that is, the higher the birth rate at the time you were born — the more people with whom you must compete throughout life, and the more likely you personally are to fail, though your cohort as a whole succeeds.

Because they are finding it harder to get jobs than members of previous generations, members of the baby-boom generation are having smaller families. In the 1970s and '80s, Canadian women postponed marriage and childbearing and had fewer children. Dual-earner families are increasingly common, largely because most couples need two incomes to maintain the standard of living they expect in Canadian cities today.

These economic difficulties will not stop when baby boomers reach age 65; baby boomers will have also had more difficulty earning and saving for old age. Younger age groups are too small to be able to support baby boomers through contributions to pension and social security funds. New solutions for supporting the aged will be needed early in the next century; and this is the case around the world. Even in high-fertility African countries, the numbers of people over age 65 are increasing. The number of elderly in sub-Saharan Africa is expected to increase by 93% between 2000 and 2020. Because these countries are poor, finding new ways to help the aged will be even harder (Adamchak, 1989).

This aging of the population is an interesting turn-around in the world's demographic outlook. During earlier periods of history, when birth rates were high, the **dependency ratio** — the ratio of economically unproductive people to income producers — was high because so many infants and children were present. As the birth rate has fallen, so (temporarily) has the dependency ratio. Now the dependency ratio is rising again. The ratio of (old) economically unproductive people to income producers is going to get higher and higher as the baby boomers pass into retirement. This problem of dependency could easily become a central concern of Canadian society in the next century.

In short, this unusual burst of high fertility — the baby boom — has reshaped Canada's society and culture. Unfortunately, members of the baby-boom generation will end up paying most of the social and economic costs of their parents' high fertility. This is a fertility level that does not work well in industrial societies, where standards of living are high.

Normally, the younger siblings and children of the baby boomers — variously called the "baby bust" generation and Generation X — would be benefitting from their small cohort size. That is because they are, demographically, in short supply, and that ought to make them more valuable in the job market. However, this expected advantage has, so far, failed to materialize, due to a worldwide recession which has kept unemployment rates high and wages low, and sent young people back to school for more and different kinds of education. Here is a clear case of economic difficulty that is *not* due to what people have called "overpopulation."

Like the United States, Israel, Australia, and Argentina, Canada has always been a nation of immigrants, with enormous numbers entering (and often leaving) every decade. It is impossible to exaggerate the impact of so much population movement on our national identity.

National Archives Of Canada/PA48697

PATTERNS OF MIGRATION

Another important factor in population growth is **migration**. In and of itself, migration does not increase the world's population, it merely redistributes it. Yet such redistribution can have a profound impact. The large numbers of people moving into ecologically delicate areas, such as, for example, the Amazon jungle in Brazil, threaten to alter the world's environment.

In Canada, migration has played a significant role in national development. Understanding the processes promoting or inhibiting migration is important for understanding Canada's national character. As a country with a short history and much migration, Canada is especially hard to analyze using demographic transition theory.

That is not to say that demographic transition theory fails to apply to Canada. As we have seen, it applies fairly well in its general outline. But the theory has nothing to say about migration and, when we consider Canadian history, immigration (movement into an area), emigration (movement out of an area), and internal migration all play an important part in population trends. As noted earlier, migration will be playing an ever greater role, now that fertility is so low.

The *migration rate* is the number of people who enter or leave the population in a given year (per 1000 inhabitants at mid-year). The **net migration rate** is the number of immigrants, minus the number of emigrants, per year per thousand inhabitants.

Internal migration refers to people moving from one region of a country to another. Internal migration patterns are useful indexes of changing circumstances in various regions. As we shall see, migration out of an area may reflect changes in the job opportunities available around the country, a rising cost of living, a lack of affordable housing, or feared discrimination against a given ethnic group.

International migration refers to the number of people moving from one country to another, and these statistics also serve as useful indexes of changing circumstances in various countries.

All migration is affected by push and pull factors. **Pull factors** in migration are all those factors that encourage people to move to a particular area, or make that particular location desirable. They include better job opportunities, more tolerance for ethnic or religious minorities, and greater freedom. Generally speaking, pull factors are those that promise people a better life. **Push factors** are all those factors that encourage people to leave an area. They include famine, a lack of job opportunities, discrimination, and fear of oppression.

Changes in the size of a given population are caused by variations in the birth rate, the death rate, and the net migration rate. The **growth rate** is the rate at which population size increases each year. (In the case of negative population growth, it is the rate at which population size declines.) The growth rate is calculated by subtracting the number of deaths and out-migrations from the number of births and in-migrations, and expressing the result as a proportion of the mid-year population.

Immigration has always been an important concern in Canada since, like other countries in the Americas, Canada is largely populated by immigrants.

Recently, as Exhibit 10.4 indicates, immigration has become an explosive political issue. Many immigrants inside the country want the chance to bring their relatives over to Canada. Many people outside the country want a chance to get in. But a weak economy makes many native-born Canadians resist the push for an increase in immigrant numbers. Some even want the immigration rate cut back.

EXHIBIT 10.4   *Federal study finds majority think there are too many newcomers*

"Most Canadians believe there are too many immigrants," especially from visible minorities, according to a new survey commissioned for the federal government.

Four in 10 Canadians believe there are too many members of visible minorities, singling out Arabs, blacks and Asians for discrimination.

And in Toronto, where the largest number of immigrants to Canada live, the survey showed a startling rise recently in intolerant attitudes. About 67 per cent of the respondents in Canada's largest city said there were too many immigrants, compared with 46 per cent just two years ago. . . .

Ekos president Frank Graves said yesterday he believes it is the first time a clear majority of Canadians surveyed have said there are too many immigrants. . . .

Mr. Graves said his "disturbing" survey does not mean that Canada has shed its tradition of compassion and embraced intolerance. Indeed, nearly three-quarters of those surveyed agreed that a mix of cultures makes Canada a more attractive place to live.

But Mr. Graves said a variety of factors, including the shift to non-European immigrants in the past three decades, means the open society is under increasing pressure. . . .

He said cultural insecurity — the fear that an ill-defined Canadian way of life is disappearing — ranked ahead of economic stress as a key factor in shaping attitudes. Six of 10 respondents, for example, agreed with the statement that too many

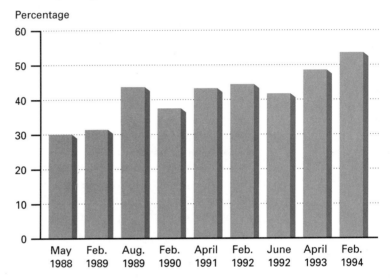

The Rising Intolerance

This bar graph shows that a growing number of Canadians think there are too many immigrants.

Percentage

May 1988 | Feb. 1989 | Aug. 1989 | Feb. 1990 | April 1991 | Feb. 1992 | June 1992 | April 1993 | Feb. 1994

Source: Ekos Research Associates Inc.

immigrants feel no obligation to adapt to Canadian values." . . .

Intolerance was highest among anglophones and was more predominant among older people, and those with a high-school education or less. Concern about immigration varied according to political affiliation, with the Reform Party providing an ideological home for English-speaking Canadians who say there are too many immigrants.

Mr. Graves said only a small percentage of Canadians — about 16 per cent — are hard-core xenophobes. A larger group, representing about one-quarter of the population, is flirting with intolerance because it has seen its economic prospects dimmed by the recession. . . .

Source: Murray Campbell, "Attitudes on immigrants harden," *The Globe and Mail*, Thurs., March 10, 1994, pp. A1, A6

Historically, Canada's population has always shown great fluidity and mobility through migration. Indeed, the large number of comings and goings led sociologist John Porter (1965) to compare the country to a great train station.

Postwar immigrants have been drawn to Canada primarily from southern Europe and the non-Western countries — Asia, Africa, the Caribbean, South America. These types of immigrants are inclined to settle in large metropolitan centres. In this respect, they are following the general trend: more and more Canadians are living near large cities.

In Canada's 25 largest cities, immigrants form a significant and growing proportion of the total population. By 1986, nearly 40% of Toronto's population, 30% of Vancouver's, and 20% of Edmonton's and Calgary's populations were foreign born, to cite a few important examples (Badets, 1989).

The trend towards urban living holds for much of the Third World as well as for Canada, and urban areas in the Third World are growing at a remarkable rate. Unfortunately, in many cases the job prospects for people who have moved to the city from the country are not good. The experience of rural migrants in the West has suggested that, after a period of time (decades and even generations), they significantly improve upon their entry status. However, a study of rural in-migrants in Bangkok, Thailand and Bogota, Columbia indicates little upward mobility has taken place over time (Kallan, 1985). In fact, upward mobility is generally low in these cities, even for those who are native-born.

The churn

Canada's population is mobile, with people often relocating themselves as their plans and opportunities change. Mobility and migration have a number of causes. Every separation and divorce brings someone a change of location — at least a change of households, or even a change of cities or regions. Likewise, most marriages bring the spouses a change of location. Beyond these factors, changes in location often result from increases in family size (through birth), decreases in family size (through death or children leaving home), and changes in family income and new job opportunities.

With so many economic and demographic events taking place, we would expect a large amount of movement, and data from the 1990 General Social Survey (an annual survey co-ordinated by Statistics Canada) bear out this expectation. Nearly two Canadian adults in three have moved in the last ten years, one adult in two has moved in the last five years, and nearly one adult in five has moved in the past year. Some of this is short distance (within-city) movement, while some of it is longer distance — movement *between* cities. Large cities and their surrounding suburbs continue to gain from this inter-city movement.

Historically, the Canadian population has been moving westward since the European immigrants started arriving. The trend, though uneven, has been well established and the patterns witnessed since the 1970s are not new (Foot, 1982: 74). In this respect, Canada's population is not so different from that of the United States. It, too, has moved westward for the past century or so. American westward movement sped up dramatically after the Second World War. Demographers there also project a continuing westward movement rivalled in size only by strong movement southward. In Canada, the population is already concentrated on the southern border, so that further migration southward becomes international.

Today, migrants are being strongly attracted to Ontario once again, especially to the cities. In- and out-migration are nearly balanced in Quebec, and the Atlantic provinces are back to losing more migrants than they take in. The overall trend continues to be westward, but countervailing economic, social, and cultural forces have slowed that movement dramatically. And more international migrants are entering from the west, with Vancouver as the port of entry.

Pulls and pushes

The process of mobility cannot be understood just by focusing on the personal characteristics of movers. Some communities will attract or lose more people than others, depending on the opportunities they offer. Population churning is a joint result of two social processes. One is mobility resulting from changes in the quality of **human capital** — people's more common ability, via higher education, capital, or rare skills, to locate wherever they want to.

A second is the changing attractiveness of different locations within Canada. As the population becomes increasingly concerned with getting a high-quality lifestyle, more and more people are drawn to communities with a pleasant environment and a wide variety of social, cultural, economic, and recreational opportunities.

We discussed changing gender relations in Chapter 7. They have played an important part in changing the pattern of mobility in North American society. On the one hand, women have been getting more education. As a result, they have been getting better jobs and more opportunity for career mobility. In fact, a woman often has as much opportunity as her husband does. This has meant that, when moving, couples need to consider the demands of both partners' careers.

Furthermore, women's growing equality in the workplace and in the home has meant that wives' wishes concerning where and how the family is going to live are gaining more influence. Whereas, previously, relocation was based on (the husband's) job opportunities, now both husbands and wives cast a vote on the issue and it is no longer a certainty that job and career will prevail over all other considerations.

The importance of geographic pushes and pulls is shown in a study by Linda Gerber, who analyzed migration out of Canadian Indian reserves (Gerber, 1984). She reports that involvement in mainstream employment and education "stimulates out-migration" (Gerber, 1984: 158). On the other hand "distance from major urban centres and institutional completeness inhibit migration." Greater distance makes the move off-reserve more costly, by making it harder to stay in touch with the reserve community.

The native person leaving a reserve must leave it behind for long periods, at a heavy psychic cost. Increases in institutional completeness, on the other hand, make out-migration less necessary. Institutional completeness even allows people with more education and skills to continue living and working on the reserve.

The same can be said of ethnic and racial communities in large Canadian cities. People with more education and job skills are more likely to leave these communities for other neighbourhoods and work settings. The greater the *social distance* between an ethnic group and the outside world, the less likely people are to make that "trip." If their own community is institutionally complete, they are much more likely to stay within it.

Possible Future De-Population

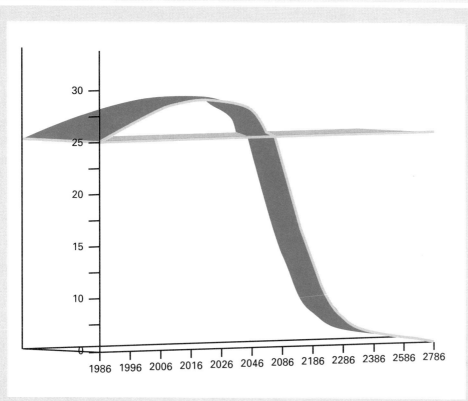

With Canadians bearing fewer children than are needed to replace their parents' generation, a disappearance of the Canadian population is entirely possible. Demographic projections show that, if all immigration were halted tomorrow and present rates of childbearing continued, the vanishing of Canada's population would take about 800 years — precisely until the year 2786.

Source: *Charting Canada's Future: A Report of the Demographic Review* (Supply and Services Catalogue No. H21-105/1-1989) Ottawa: Health and Welfare, 1989, p. 2. Reproduced with the permission of the Minister of Supply and Services, 1994.

MORTALITY IN CANADA'S POPULATION

So far, we have seen how fertility and migration have affected Canada's population growth. A third factor affecting it is mortality. In Canada, mortality rates have been steadily declining, at least since 1921. (For a clearly-written, brief account of changes in mortality and the Canadian life course, see Lavoie and Oderkirk, 1993). However, women continue to enjoy a lower mortality rate than men at every age. This is the case in all industrial countries, including Canada.

There are various reasons for this. Males have much higher mortality rates as infants and this, along with other evidence, suggests that women are biologically hardier than men. Tobacco and alcohol use, more frequent among men, also has an effect. As well, men have typically died in larger numbers as casualties of war, from automobile accidents, and from stress-related illnesses.

Cancer has become an increasingly important cause of death, and here too there are differences between the sexes. In 1900, women had a much higher incidence of cancer than men; now the roles are reversed. A reason for this is that the traditionally "female" cancers of the breast and uterus are today more treatable than in the past. They are also more treatable than traditionally "male" cancers of the digestive system and lung.

As sociologists from the conflict perspective would be quick to point out, socio-economic status is an important factor in mortality risks. What's more, it is a factor whose importance has increased in the last 30 years (Pappas et al., 1993; see also Guralnik et al., 1993). In most countries, people with high socio-economic status have the lowest mortality rates. Lower-status people are more exposed to occupational hazards. They have a generally lower standard of living which includes less and poorer food, and worse sanitation.

The poor also have less access to medical care. That's why there are large class differences in the mortality rates for diseases which are medically treatable. For those illnesses medicine has had little success in curing, there is no class difference in mortality rates. Gender inequality has a similar effect. Where women have much lower status than men, they are much more likely to die early than men. For example, the deaths of women during childbirth and pregnancy are generally preventable, yet an estimated 500 000 per year die worldwide from these causes. The vast majority of these deaths take place in those poor, developing countries where women are less valued than men (Seipel, 1992).

Mortality is evidently related to the level of economic well-being in a country, so there has been a lot of research to find out if mortality is related to the business cycle. The research suggests it is. For example, there is a long-term relationship between unemployment rates and mortality rates (Brenner, 1987). In particular, the incidence of heart disease and heart attacks increases during periods of high unemployment. It remains to be seen whether public health measures can reduce these effects.

Ethnicity and race are other factors affecting mortality risks. For example, Canadian native peoples have a lower life expectancy and higher rates of disability than other Canadians (see Exhibit 10.5): the reasons include poverty and poor health care. Even so, the differences are not as great as in the past (Trovato, 1988).

French Canadians also have higher age-specific mortality rates than English Canadians. Persisting differences in mortality rates between ethnic groups are caused by lower than average income, nutrition, and education among the non-dominant groups. They also reflect regional variations in environmental quality and standards of living.

Groups even differ in their causes of death. For example, French- and British-origin Canadians run high risks of death from cancer and heart disease. Young native men are at a particularly high risk of dying from accidents or as a result of violence.

Mortality rates in the inner cities can also be much higher than the national average. For example, a study of mortality in central Harlem, New York, where 96% of the population is black, showed that men's rates of survival beyond age 40 are lower than one finds in rural Bangladesh, a desperately poor, undeveloped country (McCord and Freeman, 1990). Mortality rates are double those of the general American population, even after adjustments for age difference. One reason for this huge disparity is that black slum dwellers have limited health care.

What these data show is that mortality rates are a reflection of social inequalities. People live longer, healthier lives in rich regions of rich countries. In these regions, the richest, best-educated people live longest of all. Race, eth-

EXHIBIT 10.5 *Disability rate higher for natives, Statscan says*

The disability rate for aboriginal people is more than double that of other Canadians, and in the 15-to-34 age group it is three times the national rate, Statistics Canada said yesterday. . . .

Culled from a 1991 national aboriginal survey, the statistics show that 31 per cent of aboriginal people reported some level of disability, compared with 15 per cent of the Canadian population.

Statscan cited a 10-year-old report by a special parliamentary committee on the disabled to offer an explanation. The committee attributed the problem to poorer living conditions.

Natives suffer on a daily basis from living conditions that other Canadians experience only rarely," the committee said. These adversities — political, economic, social and cultural in nature — greatly increase the probability of being disabled at some point."

The 1991 Statscan survey found that native dwellings were not only more likely to be in poorer shape, but 50 per cent were more crowded" than the rate for Canada as a whole.

Even newer housing does not translate into better-quality housing," Statscan said, noting that while housing on reserves was newer than the Canadian average, 20 per cent of it needed major repairs compared with a Canadian rate of 8 per cent. . . .

Among aboriginal people, Indians on reserves had the highest rate of disability (33 per cent) while the Inuit reported the lowest (29 per cent).

But among Inuit, hearing disabilities were highest with a rate almost twice that of Canada's adult population. Forty-four per cent of Inuit disabilities related to hearing.

Those statistics don't surprise me one bit," said Dr. James Baxter, emeritus professor of otolaryngology at McGill University. I could have told them that a long time ago." . . .

Inuit children have a high rate of chronic otitis media, a middle-ear disease, he said. But adding to the problem for Inuit is noise pollution from the widespread earlier use of noisy snowmobiles, high velocity rifles and loud machinery, Dr. Baxter said. . . .

Dr. Baxter said noise conditions and infection rates have improved among Inuit today, but the past effects are showing up in the adult statistics.

Source: Rudy Platiel, "Disability rate higher for natives, Statscan says," *The Globe and Mail*, Thurs., March 26, 1994, p. A7.

nicity, and religion are important factors insofar as they are associated with class position. They also shape people's lifestyles, the health-related information they get, and the care they are encouraged to take.

Religious practices influence death rates, but these are hard to separate from ethnic influences. As well, religious practices include positive *and* negative health features. For example, Christian Scientists refuse medical aid. Yet their life expectancy is no different than anyone else's, because they also shun smoking and drinking. So do Mormons, who have lower than average death rates (Jarvis and Northcott, 1987).

A great deal of evidence shows that there are health benefits in getting married and staying married. Unmarried people have a higher risk of mortality than married people (Hu, 1987). Research in Japan, Hong Kong, the United States, Britain, Italy, and Greece, as well as Canada has found that marriage contributes to people's well-being. In addition, men gain larger increases in life expectancy by marrying than women do (Trovato and Lauris, 1989).

These differences in mortality risks have policy implications. In the future, people's risks of death will decrease if societies reduce poverty and inequality, diffuse health information, and promote marriage as an institution. On the other hand, any gains from these influences will be lost through unhealthy activities. For example, smoking continues to be the most significant avoidable determinant of mortality rates (Hirdes and Forbes, 1989).

The success that modern medicine has had in treating infectious diseases and identifying the biological bases of diseases has led many to believe that we shall continue to make progress against death without significant social and cultural changes. However, there is no easy road to universal good health and longer lives.

The future of mortality

For a long time, demographers largely ignored mortality patterns. They left the problem to actuaries, who work for insurance companies, calculating risks of death at different ages. Demographers may have had several reasons for ignoring death as a factor in population change.

First, they may have felt that everything that needed to be said about death had already been said. Malthus, for example, had argued that preventive checks on population growth — measures that limited births — would largely avoid the play of positive checks, which increased deaths. Since Malthus, preventive checks have become more common and effective. As predicted, positive checks have become less common or necessary. For its part, demographic transition theory had argued that a declining death rate comes first and a declining birth rate later. We are at the stage of declining or low birth rates now. The era of high death rates is long gone, according to this theory.

Second, demographers may have felt that we have made all the major gains in the fight against mortality. Fewer and fewer people are dying each year from infectious diseases, the traditional killer in high-mortality populations. Instead, more people are dying from endogenous causes such as cancer, or deterioration of the heart or lungs. People's life expectancies have increased throughout the 20th century, but now we appear to have hit a plateau. At birth, Canadians cannot expect to live more than about 80 years, and this fact has changed little for a generation or more.

As familiar infectious diseases have been beaten back by medicine, nutrition, and sanitation, more people in developed countries have been dying from causes that are avoidable and often self-inflicted. Consider the main causes of death among Canadians in the prime years of their lives, ages 10 to 50. They include suicide, homicide, and accidents — especially automobile accidents.

In less-developed countries, there are still a huge number of deaths from disease and malnutrition which need not occur: two-thirds of the world's childhood deaths could be avoided by improving health care, education, and nutrition (Chandler, 1986). This view is supported by evidence from China and Sri Lanka, both of which have rapidly reduced infant mortality levels. What's more, the same strategies could be used in North American cities.

Some research suggests that homicide is more prevalent in underdeveloped societies than it is in developed societies, especially within the family. Gradually, violence decreases as education increases, poverty is reduced, and the state becomes more developed. Prosperity and strong states bring about a civilization of manners (Chesnais, 1992). The United States may be an exception to this rule, owing to the inadequate control of handguns.

These decreases in the mortality rate are heartening. Still, there is considerable progress yet to be made in many parts of the world. And, for the most part, the leading causes of death are still uniquely human. To prevent them means understanding the uniquely human capacity for self-destruction and the destruction of others. So far, we know little about how to reduce these causes of death. For example, we probably know less about homicide and suicide than we know about the ways to prevent death from cancer. Yet many consider cancer to be the most mysterious cause of death today.

We have failed to address these uniquely human killers partly because they have not been claimed as medical problems by the health establishment. These problems call for preventive measures. However, modern medicine generally focuses on curing, not preventing, afflictions. Prevention means restructuring the society, not merely helping the person or persons most immediately at risk.

The health establishment will learn this lesson as it tries to deal with other causes of death which lie closer to its traditional concerns. For example, increasing evidence shows that cancers are caused by genetic mutations triggered by dangerous substances all around us — in our water, our air, the foods we eat, and so on. Humans put many of those dangerous substances there, through auto emissions, factory smokestacks, toxic waste dumping, or badly tested manufacturing. We people, some of us more than others, are responsible for causing this problem and should pay to remedy it. We should be responsible for preventing it in future.

The AIDS epidemic tells a slightly different tale. For some, the epidemic "demonstrates" that drug addicts and sexual "perverts" get punished for their sins. So long as AIDS is limited to the drug-using and gay communities, this definition of the problem, unsound though it is, will have a certain popularity. Yet the conception that AIDS is a geographically limited, homosexual disease was outdated at least five years ago (Heilig and Wills, 1989: 1).

As the information in Exhibit 10.6 indicates, demographers and policy makers expect dramatic increases in the prevalence of AIDS. It will gradually spread through the rest of the population (see also the Royal Society of Canada's 1988 report, *AIDS: A Perspective for Canadians*). Efforts to improve nutrition and reduce drug abuse and the spread of AIDS through education will probably have little effect without improvements in employment and housing conditions.

Sub-Saharan Africa is expected to record the most AIDS-related deaths, as safe sexual practices such as condom use have not increased much since the epidemic began. Yet, the huge and growing number of AIDS deaths has the potential to cause widespread social breakdown by creating as many as 1.2 million orphans in sub-Saharan Africa. Even if these children find shelter in extended family networks, they are still at a higher risk of death than they would be otherwise (Hunter, 1990). This is because of the economic and health stresses they put on their caretakers, who are often elderly people.

Throughout history, new diseases have arisen when old ones were beaten. History shows us the futility of believing in progress towards perfect health. There will always be new health-killers to conquer. Some of them (like suicide and war) are due to avoidable social problems while others (like cancer) are an interaction of new viruses or contaminants and new lifestyles. We have failed to significantly decrease mortality (or increase life expectancy) in the latter half of the 20th century. This indicates too great a focus on high-tech medical cures — which

EXHIBIT 10.6 *AIDS marches through Asia*

AIDS Ahead

Researchers at the Harvard university School of Public Health in Cambridge, Mass., say the number of HIV infections in Asia will double by 1995. Estimates for 1992 are as of Jan. 1.

	Infected with HIV (in thousands)	
Region	All adults (1992 estimate)	All adults (1995 projected)
North America	1 167	1 495
Western Europe	718	1 186
Australia/Oceania	28	40
Latin America	995	1 407
Sub-Saharan Africa	7 803	11 449
Caribbean	310	474
Eastern Europe	27	44
Southeast Mediterranean	35	59
Northeast Asia	41	80
Southeast Asia	675	1 220
WORLD	11 799	17 454

* Bhutan, Cambodia, China, Hong Kong, North Korea, South Korea, Japan, Laos, Macao, Mongolia, Vietnam.
** Bangladesh, Brunei, Burma, India, Indonesia, Malaysia, Maldives, Nepal, Philippines, Singapore, Sri Lanka, Thailand.

Source: Jonathan Mann, Daniel Tarantola and Thomas Netter, *Aids in the World 1992*, Harvard University Press as published in "AIDS marches through Asia," *The Globe and Mail*, Tues. Dec. 1, 1992, p. A4

rely on expensive technology and treat a relatively small, relatively wealthy population — and too little focus on preventive measures, including social research and social reform, which would tackle the world's major health problems, for instance, malnutrition, pollution and infectious diseases.

New health strategies require a dedication to reducing conflict between humans, in order to war more effectively against disease than against one another. They also require a commitment to decreasing poverty and improving health internationally, because these factors affect how long, and how well, people can live. These insights are central to the conflict approach to population studies.

Dealing with the AIDS epidemic will require as yet untapped reserves of optimism and generosity.

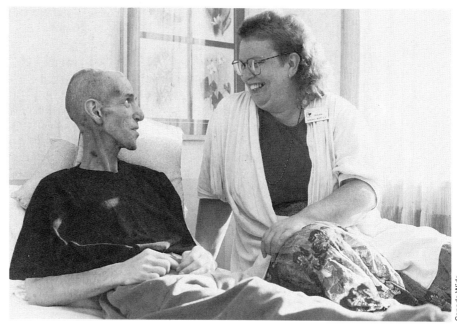

Canada Wide

WAS MALTHUS RIGHT?

Today, few demographers would completely support Malthus's gloomy views. Claims of overpopulation are occasionally used to cloud the issues of powerlessness and social inequality. Mitchell (1991), writing about Egypt, notes that powerful groups want us to think there is too little food and too many people. In fact, the problem may be a distorted agricultural economy. The elites have transformed the economy from one producing staples to one producing luxury items, or from one producing for local consumption to one producing for export.

Similarly, some urban problems of the less developed world (such as scarcity of housing and pollution) are due to a failure to promote rural development. This failure has resulted in a drain of capital, as well as people, from the country to the city (Hyman, 1990). Neglect of the rural areas, not overpopulation, is the problem.

In short, it is not always clear whether problems are caused by overpopulation or by some other factor(s). Still, some observers point pessimistically to swelling population figures, recurring famines in many parts of the world and growing shortages of nonrenewable resources (even shortages of water) in the developed world (Meadows et al., 1972; Higgins, 1980).

What we have seen in Western societies is a dramatic and justifiable growth in concern about the environment within the last ten years. More and more people feel strongly about the need for improvements in water purity and air quality. They want higher waste disposal standards — including improved monitoring of landfills, recycling, packaging, and toxic chemical disposal. People want assurance that consumer products are environmentally safe. More and more, they support the conservation of energy, the reduction of acid rain, and safer use of pesticides.

Environmental concern is as economically significant as it is socially significant. Protecting the environment requires changes in consumer behaviour, and increases the price of consumer products. It also requires more state regulation and higher production costs, which, in turn, creates a higher risk of job losses, since a company that cannot afford to make the changes a state demands may relocate to a place with lower environmental standards.

Yet these costs, risks, and changes are inevitable. In recent decades, humans have dramatically transformed the environment. The entire global ecology is affected, especially the equilibrium of the biosphere and the interdependence between living systems. This raises issues affecting the survival of humanity.

The ultimate source of concern for environmental change is its potential effect on the "livability" of the globe and its ability to support the variety and complexity of on-going human activities. Urban-industrial civilization threatens human self-regulating systems as well as natural ecosystems. For instance, in some cases respiratory and cardiovascular health problems are related to environmental pollution. Continuing high infant mortality rates in high fertility/low income communities are another clue. The future of humanity depends on a better understanding of natural ecosystems and their relation to human populations (Wolanski, 1989).

Throughout the world, international bodies (like UNESCO), governments at every level, and even local movements are responding. They are developing plans for research, education, legislation, and regulation of the environment. The failure to take such preventive and preparatory steps will lead to the positive checks Malthus associated with overpopulation — massive death and dislocation.

Society will have to change dramatically if the Earth is unable to support our current standards of human life. But for a world-wide issue such as global warming, new types of policy-making challenges are in store. To deal with global problems like the greenhouse effect, governments will have to build international consensus, and sacrifices will be needed (Christie, 1992).

After all, there are limits to how many people the Earth can support. Carrying capacity is limited by the resources available, by human technology and by the standard of living people will accept. Given our present level of technology, all the world's people cannot possibly enjoy the level of affluence North Americans enjoy today. This is not a problem of distribution, for there is just not enough wealth to go around. To raise the world average, we must find many more resources (an unlikely event), and improve our technology; and we in the Western industrialized nations must lower our own expectations.

Evidence suggests that technology *will* continue to improve, yet technology also has harmful side effects. In any case, we cannot know beforehand what technology will do for us or to us.

For example, Commoner (1991) asserts that it is technology, not population size, which determines the amount of pollution generated. Likewise, Najafizadeh and Mennerick (1989) blame technology for destroying the ecosystem — also, depleting natural resources, contributing to environmental problems and (even) perpetuating social inequality.

To illustrate these concerns, Ling (1989) notes how irresponsible economic growth in Malaysia exposed female plantation workers to serious dangers. Chemical pesticides and radioactive byproducts of industry poisoned local villagers and destroyed the forests in Sarawak. Or consider the Amazon rain forest in Brazil. There, the national economy is pressing for ecologically insensitive development, since land is cheap and plentiful (Kyle and Cunha, 1992). Future generations will pay the costs of present-day opportunism.

In the end, technology and development, poverty and population are all tied together in a knot. Chowdhry et al. (1989) claim that poverty leads the poor to overuse, and in that way, degrade the land. Results include erosion, pollution, deforestation, the wrongful use of common lands — in short, a "destructive cycle" which worsens the long-term prospects of the rural poor and their children.

The poor also suffer in Third World cities. Environmental problems such as unsafe water, overcrowding, air pollution, and hazardous work conditions all affect the poor more than anyone else. Yet aid agencies and governments pay little attention to urban infrastructure (Hardoy and Satterthwaite, 1991). To get the Third World's cooperation in addressing global problems, the Western world must help it address the environmental problems that affect its poorer citizens.

For O'Connor (1989), the population and environment problem arises because of uneven development. By bringing capital, industry and population to bear on a particular geographic location, the chances are great that industrial wastes will overwhelm the natural recycling processes. Pollution is the inevitable result. The pollution could have been avoided if the process of development had been spread out more evenly over time and space.

Industrial and ecological crises like those at Bhopal (India), Three Mile Island, and Chernobyl are also the result of uneven or unconsidered development (Shrivastava, Miller and Miglani, 1991). A factory or power plant begins operating under conditions of rapid growth and prosperity but, eventually, changes occur. Speeded-up operation, sudden changes in policy, cutbacks in staff, and other uncertainties occur because of political or economic change. The resulting confusion can trigger a crisis which kills people and poisons the earth, air and water for generations to come.

In short, environmental problems result from an interaction of technological, social and economic factors. By itself, population plays only a small part. Nonetheless, population planning can play a part in solving these problems or making them worse. Controlling population helps us protect our future better than a reliance on new technology and new resources. These are far less certain.

This chapter has ended on a sombre note, and that may be appropriate. Yet, many observers are far more optimistic about population and environmental issues than we have indicated. They point out, as data in Exhibit 10.7 show, that — on balance — things are getting better around the world. Fertility is falling, life expectancy is rising. People have more food to eat, they are more literate, and at least some environmental problems — like the lack of control over the world production of chlorofluorocarbons — are improving dramatically. What do you think? Is the glass half empty or half full?

CLOSING REMARKS

The sociological study of population offers another clear illustration of the connection between macro- and micro- perspectives. On the one hand, population is a macro-phenomenon which exists outside and "above" individual people. After all, the size, location, rate of growth, life expectancy, and age composition of the population are all beyond the control of any individual. They are "givens" of life in a society. In this sense, population is all-encompassing and changes slowly, over decades and generations. The main elements of a population are characteristic of a society. They change much more slowly than the people who make up the society (for example, a population "ages" more slowly than a person does).

EXHIBIT 10.7 *Apocalypse deferred: the end isn't nigh*

The latest volley of doomsaying would have us believe we are living in a period of profound instability, on the brink of chaos. But look at the facts. It just isn't so.

Source: Marcus Gee, "Apocalypse deferred," *The Globe and Mail*, Sat. April 9, 1994, pp. D1, D6.

Environment

World production of chloroflourocarbons 1950–92

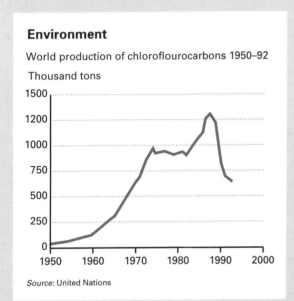

Source: United Nations

Military Expenditures

Billions of 1992 $U.S.

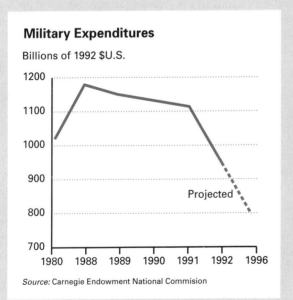

Source: Carnegie Endowment National Commision

Trends in Life Expectancy

1950–1990

Life expectancy at birth

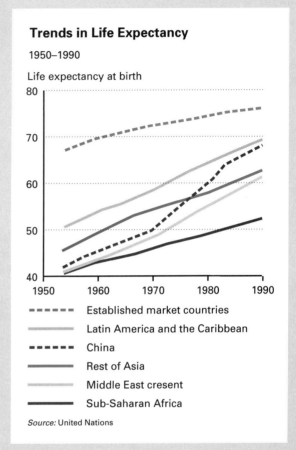

Source: United Nations

World Child Mortality

Deaths per 1000 children under 5

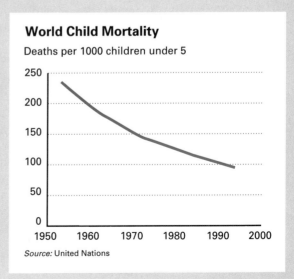

Source: United Nations

Exhibit 10.7 continued

World Crude-oil Reserves

Billions of cubic metres

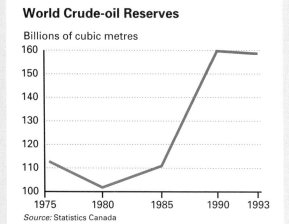

Source: Statistics Canada

Gross World Product

Per person, 1950–92, in 1987 $U.S.

Source: World Bank, International Money Fund

Adult Literacy

% literate

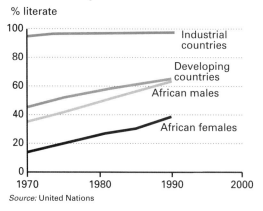

Source: United Nations

Food in Developing Countries

1970–90   1970=100

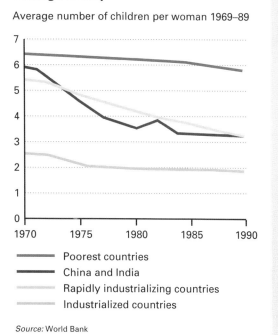

Source: U.S. Department of Agriculture

Falling Fertility

Average number of children per woman 1969–89

Poorest countries
China and India
Rapidly industrializing countries
Industrialized countries

Source: World Bank

On the other hand, *we* together are the population. Without us, there is no population. If we all kill ourselves or emigrate, there's no population left. If we have too few children to replace ourselves, the population gets older, then gradually disappears. We are the people who decide how many children to have, where to live, when (and whether) to marry, whether to live in a healthy, life-extending or unhealthy, life-shortening manner. The population changes over time because millions of individuals change their way of doing things.

We began this chapter by referring to grim prospects facing the world. Perhaps industrial society has reached the limits of its development. Many social scientists are making reference to the notion of post-industrial society. The development of inanimate sources of energy led to the industrial revolution. Today, the development of automation, computers, and robots is causing a new revolution. We need fewer people than in the past.

Are we moving in a direction that promises to change society for the better? If not, how do we go about getting started? The topic of *social change*, to which we now turn, addresses these issues.

C H A P T E R

11

The past decade has seen dramatic social and political upheavals. One of the most surprising of these was the collapse of Soviet Communism as symbolized by the destruction of the Berlin Wall.

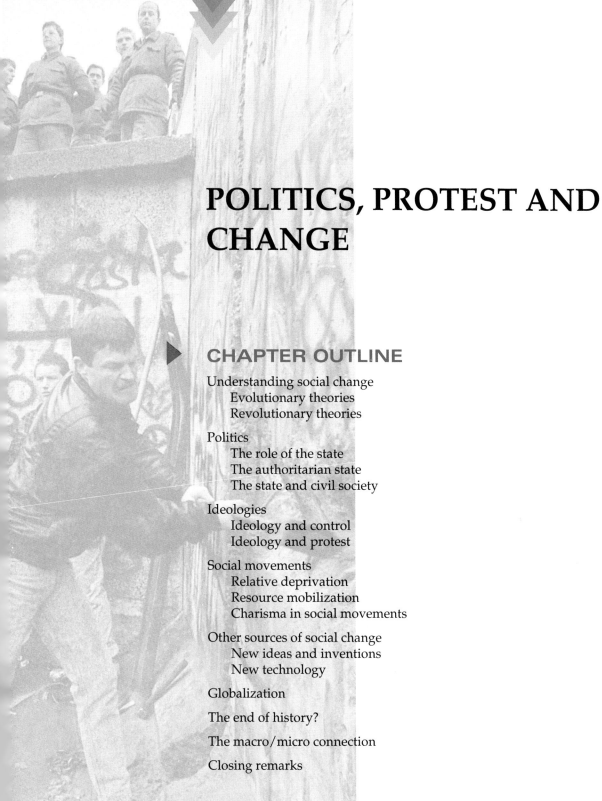

POLITICS, PROTEST AND CHANGE

UNDERSTANDING SOCIAL CHANGE

People have an amazing ability to adjust to change. So it may be hard to convince you just how quickly the world is changing in important ways, because you have already started to take yesterday's changes for granted. But here's something to think about:

For most of human history, life was very quiet. People didn't hear many sounds and most of the sounds they did hear were natural ones: animals, wind, and running water, for example. They didn't see large crowds or large buildings. Nor did people travel long distances very often. That's why they didn't get to know people very different from themselves. They didn't know much about the world outside their own community. There was no reason to spend time thinking about things that didn't affect them directly. People just assumed life would go on forever much as it had in the past.

Do you see how different life is today, at least for those of us in urban, industrial Canada? We live in an age in which change is built into our society. Elections every four years or so, new car models every year, newspapers every day, television news continuously: we devour change and news about change. Whole industries — fashion, luxury goods and the mass media, for example — depend on that taste for change. Often they don't satisfy our desires — they set them afire and keep them burning.

As we shall see, social change may begin at either a macro or micro level; eventually, its effects show up at both levels. Take the growth of high-tech industries. Automated manufacturing is gradually replacing workers with machines and computers. In this way, it is changing the lives of thousands of workers and their families. Or consider people's decisions to delay childbearing, to have no children or only one child. These are micro-level choices that people are making one couple at a time, and their impact builds slowly. Yet taken together, these choices are changing the whole society.

The difference between micro-change and macro-change does not lie in the number of people affected or the importance of the change. It lies in the change's point of origin. But whether a change begins at the macro or micro level, understanding it usually demands a macro level of explanation.

Evolutionary theories

There are two types of macro-theories about change: theories of *evolution* and theories of *revolution*. Evolutionary theories see societies as systems that continually adapt to changes in the environment. Changes are gradual and take place over a long time. Thus, an evolutionary theorist might refer to the Judeo-Christian tradition, or the influence of Greek culture on today's language, arts, and thought.

Behind evolutionary theories of social change, from Durkheim and Spencer onward, is the idea that societies always become more complex. The world comes closer to being what Canadian thinker Marshall McLuhan called a "global village," as distances shrink through faster travel and communication. In the end we are all tied together in a single, complex social order. Sociologists call this general process "globalization," and we will discuss it later.

Within the global context, two main evolutionary processes are at work: **differentiation** and **integration**. Differentiation is the process that splits up tasks previously performed by one person or group, so that different people or groups then perform them.

The division of labour we discussed in Chapter 9 is one form of differentiation. Another good example is the way a modern family operates. In the past, families not only consumed goods: they also produced them and educated children. But in the last century or so, the family's functions have been differentiated. Today, the family is primarily a consuming unit. Almost everyone who works for pay works outside the family home. Schools and other institutions are mainly responsible for educating family members. That leaves the family with much less to do than in the past.

One result is that the family redefines itself. As we saw in Chapter 8, increasingly, marriage is based on love, not economic exchange. Increasingly, parenthood is a lifestyle choice, rather than a way to produce necessary labour power to help support the family.

Integration, a complementary process of social evolution, combines specialized parts or elements of a society to form a unified whole. Integration helps people to cooperate effectively as a group, and to avoid or reduce conflicts.

So, for example, within the "new" family, people search for ways of integrating their very different activities. Spouses need to find time for each other and parents need to find time for their children. All family members need to integrate their domestic work and paid work, their personal goals and family goals, their responsibilities to the nuclear family with their responsibilities to the extended family, and so on. As we noted in our discussion of anomie in Chapter 9, the more specialized people's lives become, the more difficult it is to integrate their activities.

We can see the same process, and problem, of integration on a global scale. In some periods of history, large parts of the world were isolated from one another. As colonialism brought them into contact, some areas industrialized rapidly while others did not. Throughout the 19th century, colonial states directly dominated their colonies. Today, the world is a more complex system. The parts — states and regions — fit together in a way that allows them more freedom and gives them a better chance to resolve their conflicts peacefully.

These are recent examples, but integration is not a recent development. Societies have always had to differentiate and integrate their activities. After all, that is what we mean by the process of social evolution, which has gone on as long as societies have existed.

People who study change from an evolutionary perspective often take a functionalist approach. They focus on **social statics**, processes that keep societies stable. Social institutions that do this include the family, churches, mass media and the educational system — all of which develop and spread the culture of a society. They also include institutions that slow change and resolve conflicts; the legal system is particularly important in this way.

As we said in the first chapter, functionalists see a social system as a set of interrelated structures that, together, form a complete whole. Some parts of a society are tightly integrated with others — for example, the political system with the legal system. Others are more loosely integrated — for example, in our society, the political system with the religious system.

Functionalists argue that in tightly integrated structures, a change in one part will cause changes in the others. A social system continually adjusts to the flow of new, often conflicting demands — political, economic, cultural and so on — from its many subsystems. It does this by continually differentiating and integrating.

Not all evolutionary theories are functionalist, however. Emergent norm theory, for example, looks at the processes which allow people to share an understanding of their situation. Emergent norms differ from one situation to another. By attaching meanings to these situations, people create appropriate norms to which they can commit themselves.

An example of this is the "wave," a relatively new form of fan behaviour at sporting events. Each new "wave" occurs because people at a particular time and place willingly participate. Recently, participation has become a norm at sporting events. Many people enjoy taking part in activities like the "wave" as much as they enjoy the game they are watching. Both the wave (as a norm) and the wave-performance are "emergent," in the sense of being spontaneous and self-creating.

Unlike most of the theories we have been discussing, emergent norm theory is a symbolic interactionist theory of social change. It also explains the development and persistence of **social movements**, of which we will say more later (Turner and Killian, 1987). Like other evolutionary theories, emergent norm theory views social change as the gradual result of thousands — even millions — of actions, interactions and interpretations.

Revolutionary theories

By contrast, according to the other main orientation, social change is revolutionary in character. According to this view, the change from one social order to the next is abrupt and occasionally violent. The new order is different in kind from the old one and breaks with the past profoundly. Because of their interest in qualitative change, revolutionary theorists look for turning points in history — "revolutions" — whether these are political, cultural, technological, or otherwise.

A revolutionary theorist, for example, would emphasize the ways in which our society *differs* from feudal England or slave-holding Athens. He or she would point out basic social changes caused by the printing press, industrialism, the French Revolution, nuclear energy, the population explosion, genetic engineering, and changes in the ozone layer.

The emphasis here is on *social dynamics*, all the factors that promote change and can be seen as turning points in world history. The best known example of a revolutionary theory is Marxism. Marx's theory argued that as a result of changes in the means of production, Western society has undergone a number of revolutionary changes during which almost all social, economic, and political relationships among people have been completely transformed.

According to German sociologist Georg Simmel (see Simmel, Ritter and Whimster, 1991), the invention of money by itself marked a turning point in history. Simmel claims the spread of money had an important social and cultural effect, by creating links between more people than ever before. The social connections it created were new and impersonal. Money lets us do business with a lot of people we care nothing about. What's more, money lets us spend our wealth where and when we want to. Unlike perishable food and live animals, money can be accumulated and stored forever, freely exchanged when convenient, and passed down from one generation to the next. In these ways, money breaks down primary social ties and encourages individualism. Ultimately, having money even becomes an end in itself, since it signifies freedom and success.

You may agree or disagree with these theories. No doubt, other revolutionary sociologists would have other candidates for the key turning points in history. Some focus on the spread of new technologies. As Exhibit 11.1 shows, we have all adopted a large number of new household technologies in the last decade or two. Have they revolutionized our lives? We can debate that question endlessly. The point to make here is that revolutionary theorists look for major

EXHIBIT 11.1   *Gadgets and gismos go gonzo*

When a new product catches the imagination of consumers, its takeover of the home can be swift. A decade ago, only one of 10 Canadian households boasted a microwave oven or a video cassette recorder; today, it's closer to eight of 10. . . .

. . . This year, now that the microwave market is near saturation, the hot items to watch are compact-disc players, computers and camcorders.

CD players are furthest along in their conquest of the home. As the accompanying chart shows, a third of Canadian households already have one, a big increase from the 8 per cent that owned one five years ago.

But CD players have found it harder to win over consumers than the VCR did in the 1980s. In 1988, five years after Statscan started asking Canadians whether or not they owned a VCR, the time-shifter's delight could be found in over half of all Canadian homes. Now, over three-quarters have at least one VCR and 13 per cent have more than one.

VCRs are keeping pace with microwave ovens, which are now to be found in 79 per cent of Canadian homes. . . .

Why do Canadians find these electronic goodies so compelling that they go out and buy more? Beyond their intrinsic appeal, there's one simple reason—price. Typically, products like these cost a lot when first introduced. But prices fall rapidly as more competitors get into the game. The first VCRs cost over $1,000; today, you can get a better one for $200.

And what are the household necessities of the future? This year, Statscan began tracking satellite dishes for the first time; for now, they're to be found in only 3 per cent of Canadian households. Next year, the agency may add modems—the machines that let computers transmit over phone lines—and fax machines.

Source: Bruce Little "Gadgets and gismos go gonzo," *The Globe and Mail*, Mon., Dec. 13, 1993, p. A9.

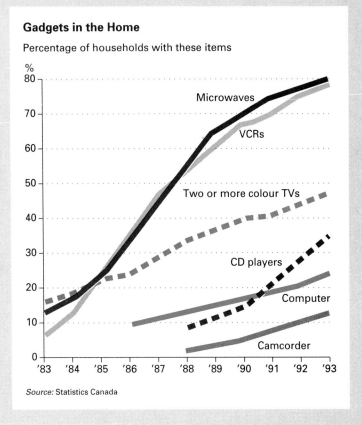

Gadgets in the Home

Percentage of households with these items

Source: Statistics Canada

changes in people's ways of thinking and behaving. The sources of change can be anything.

Unlike 19th-century theorists, few sociologists today try to make a single, general law they can apply to all social change. The ideas of "evolution" and "revolution" which prevailed in the past were based on Western ideas of progress and the natural law that strucured relations between God and humanity, humanity and nature, one class and another, and men and women. Such ideas are no longer useful. Though many use the idea of "globalization" to cover a large variety of economic, cultural and political changes, few believe that these changes necessarily signify "progress" (in the sense of providing better lives for more people).

Most theorists recognize that social change depends on the context within which it takes place. The Western idea of progress is based on the idea that people can remake society by applying reason and political will. But this is not the prevailing ideology in many countries. That is why most sociologists today have more modest goals: they examine changes within a particular society or social institution.

One important focus is on the role politics play in social change. For one thing, all social change has political consequences. And often, social change begins with a political act. So in much of this chapter we will focus on the role played by two political actors — the state and the protest movement — in bringing about social change.

POLITICS

Who makes the decisions that shape people's histories and change their futures? Why does the distribution of power differ from one society to another? What determines how people will share power? Such questions have been central to sociology since its beginnings and are addressed by political sociology.

Sociologists study politics in a different way from political scientists. First, sociologists are interested in the social and cultural factors which lead to changes in the laws, political institutions and voting patterns. This means they study a larger number of variables than political scientists usually do.

Second, sociologists are also more interested in what some call "micro-politics" — the politics of everyday life. Politics is not limited to the state. It is an activity in which people and groups struggle for control over resources, such as wealth, status and power. Schools, businesses, and even families are governed by politics and, within these institutions, people vie for control. One of sociology's goals is to reveal the hidden politics of everyday life and develop political theories that apply to all social institutions.

For example, we may study the growth of feminist goals and ideas within mainstream social institutions such as the military or the Catholic Church. Or, we may observe the processes by which neighbourhoods organize to oppose group homes for the mentally ill. In this way we discover which groups are more likely to mobilize and which are most likely to achieve their goals (Graham and Hogan, 1990).

The role of the state

To repeat, within any social unit — family, school, local community, state, or otherwise — the conflict over resources is a political conflict. But among social units, the state does have a special part to play, for it always controls and monitors the ways groups compete (Panitch, 1977). In Canadian society this is especially true of competition based on ethnicity, language, class, or gender. There, the role of the state is crucial (Stasiulis, 1988).

The *state* is a set of public organizations that makes and enforces decisions. It includes the elected government, civil service, courts, police and military. These state bodies make the decisions that are binding upon every member of a society (Weber, 1946). The right to use violence puts muscle behind these state decisions, and only a member of the police or military has the legitimate "right" to use violence without fear of punishment.

In many societies, politics converts the struggle for state power into a competition for electoral votes. Both the need to gain electoral popularity, and constitutional rules, limit the state's use of raw force. In this way, "civil society" is able to exercise some control over the state which controls it.

By "civil society," we mean all of society except the state. This would include such important institutions as labour unions, churches, business organizations, charities, and interest groups; also people's private (personal, family and work) lives. Sociologists have long studied the relationship between the state and civil society. In fact, the distinction between state and civil society dates back to Thomas Hobbes, an English philosopher who lived three centuries ago. It marks the attempt by liberal thinkers to "define a private sphere independent of the state, thus freeing civil society from political interference" (Held, 1989: 13).

The authoritarian state

At one extreme of political life we find the authoritarian state, which represses civil society and political dissent. For example, throughout Latin America we find states made all-powerful by politically active military and police forces. (Can you imagine the Canadian Forces or the Royal Canadian Mounted Police seizing control of Canada's government? That's the kind of thing that happens in many countries.)

Usually a military dictator rules the authoritarian state. In different historical periods, dictators have drawn support from different sources: wealthy landowners, multinational corporations, crime syndicates, labour unions, or even the uneducated peasantry. Rarely does a dictator need to depend on the middle class, a main source of political power in North American society. This is because, in societies with an authoritarian state, the middle class is undeveloped.

Often the military dictatorship in Latin America also depends on church support to legitimate its rule. In these circumstances, the Roman Catholic Church faces a difficult choice. On the one hand, it receives privileges given to no other institution outside the state. On the other hand, by identifying with an unpopular and repressive regime, the Church risks its own popularity and spiritual mission (Johnston and Figa, 1988). The less legitimate the regime, the more the state needs the Church's *legitimacy* and the more legitimacy the Church stands to lose. In many instances, courageous clergy have turned against the ruling class and promoted the interests of the poor. Still, they are the exception, not the rule.

Authoritarianism usually promotes economic development by uniting some social groups and excluding others (Garcia-Menendez, 1987). It is easy to confuse authoritarianism with militarism and fascism because all three weaken popular or collective social protest. Each creates an all-powerful state which intervenes in the economy and social life. Paraguay is a prime example of an authoritarian government. Brazil, Argentina and Mexico (among others) have also had such governments at one time or another.

An authoritarian state allows no independence to civil society. It penetrates everyday life fully and, compared to the form of government we have in Canada, it is extremely repressive. For example, in Argentina between 1976 and 1980, the state even controlled the dress and hairstyle of ordinary citizens (O'Donnell, 1987). (In Singapore today, chewing gum or dirtying a public place are punishable offences.)

Far more chilling is the way government violently represses opposing political views. By now, most Canadians have heard that, in Latin America, governments often deal with political opponents by kidnaping, torturing, imprisoning and even murdering them. Amnesty International reports that such practices are to be found in many other countries as well.

Brazilian history shows that weak political parties and party systems make it easier for dictators to achieve authoritarian power. So does help from the large financial and agriculture-exporting elites (Cespedes, 1988). In his classic study of political systems, Barrington Moore (1969) argues that fascist governments appear where the middle class is smaller and weaker than the landed aristocracy. As a result, social change typically takes place "from the top down." This describes the Latin American experience well, just as it describes early 20th century Italy, Germany and Japan.

However, one significant change in recent years has been the success of democratic movements in challenging authoritarian regimes throughout the world. Naturally, political sociologists have tried to explain how and why this occurs. Their studies suggest that there are many roads to democracy.

Support for an authoritarian leader may decay because even devoted supporters can see the government isn't working well. For example, an economic crisis in Brazil increased patriotic, anti-government sentiment. In the end, even the military turned against the government (Zirker, 1986; 1991). Something similar happened in Argentina, Chile and Uruguay. There, internal divisions grew among supporters of the regime during the economic recession of the 1980s (Portes and Kincaid, 1988).

In South Korea (Cotton, 1989), support for the dictatorship eroded because there was conflict within the ruling group itself. As well, educated, middle-class Koreans became less willing to follow traditional Confucian ideas about authority and hierarchy.

As you might imagine, the change from an authoritarian to a democratic system is a long, hard process. Usually, it demands changes in both attitudes and political bodies. In Haiti, for example, the struggle for democracy is far from over. It will have to overcome economic and political obstacles left by past dictatorships. Poverty, underdevelopment, and a dual stratification system based on class and race make the change difficult. Lighter-coloured Haitians consider themselves European by origin and still oppress darker-coloured Haitians (Armand, 1989). The Haitian state, seized by violent means, continues to use violence aginst the poor, who oppose it.

In Russia, the change from authoritarianism to democracy has required economic and legal reforms. It has also required symbolic reforms, to deal with the collapse of old myths and promote the acceptance of new ones. In the end, democracy needs its citizens to trust the state and believe the state will devote itself to their welfare.

Making changes of this magnitude is not easy. For example, Exhibit 11.2 describes the violence that exploded in Mexico's Chiapas state in 1993. It is hard to say what caused this outbreak. It seems to go back to issues of inequality that originated in 1910, at the end of the Mexican revolution. But recent events, like the signing of the North American Free Trade Agreement, have brought the conflict to a head.

EXHIBIT 11.2   *The old grievances in Mexico's Chiapas*

. . . Chiapas is one of Mexico's poorest states, with high rates of illiteracy, malnutrition and disease. According to the Fray Bartolome de las Casas Human Rights Centre in Chiapas, the number of deaths from tuberculosis in the state surpasses the total for the rest of the country. . . .

. . . Fifty-six per cent of Chiapas residents live in extreme poverty, and 80 per cent suffer some kind of malnutrition.

Chiapas also has one of Mexico's highest rates of human-rights abuses, no small matter in a country where arbitrary imprisonment, torture and political assassination have been part of political life over decades of rule by the Institutional Revolutionary Party (PRI). Most of the Chiapas abuses result from land disputes, another problem with which the state is well endowed.

The land redistribution that followed the 1910 Mexican revolution, and that was provided for in the country's constitution, never took hold in Chiapas. There, huge landholders still dominate the landscape, as they dominated the country in the last century.

As a result, Indian peasants, who practice subsistence or small-scale farming, find themselves working increasingly small and marginal plots of land. Efforts to extend those plots through the legal means provided for precisely that purpose have, in most cases, produced few results.

That suits the large landholders, most of whom either are influential in the state and local governments or are actual members of them, and who use their power—as well as their control over police forces and freelance armies—to maintain their hold on the state's best real estate. Juan Mendez, executive director of the human-rights group Americas Watch, calls these landowning bosses "the local expression of the PRI."

Recently the national government, headed by President Carlos Salinas de Gortari, passed laws eliminating the constitutional right to be granted land by the government and allowing lands once set aside for communal use to be sold or rented. Those measures threaten Indian peasants' already tenuous hold on the land.

Add to that reality the North American free-trade agreement, and its encouragement of large-scale export-oriented agriculture—rather than the small-scale food production of the peasants—and you get the picture. The new measures will likely improve Mexico's agricultural output, but they threaten the basis of a culture that has existed for centuries.

The Indian rebels of Chiapas are resisting that verdict on their worth, as would any other self-respecting people. The army, in turn, has been dealing with the uprising by strafing and bombing the mountains of Chiapas, putting innocent villagers as well as rebels at risk. . . .

Source: Linda Hossie, "The old grievances in Mexico's Chiapas," *The Globe and Mail*, Fri., Jan. 7, 1994, p. A19.

The state and civil society

The importance of civil society is clearest wherever the state tries to control people's personal lives. For example, the communist states in Eastern Europe controlled civil society for over 40 years. This created problems that persist even today, when people need a strong civil society to help establish democracy and a market economy.

Under communism, people in Poland, for example, learned to be highly dependent on the state. The result was widespread social apathy. Today, both political and social involvement are lacking in Poland (Kolarska-Bobinska, 1990). The needed civil society is developing very slowly.

The distinction between state and civil society can be useful, especially in authoritarian countries. But it tends to confuse our understanding of North

American society. For example, it encourages us to view the state as always repressive and bureaucratic. It also leads us to think of relations between civil society and the state as conflict-ridden (Frankel, 1983). It implies that there is a barrier between the state and the rest of society. Finally, it suggests the state is a unified body with clear interests, goals, and policies.

Many would disagree with these views of the relationship between the state and the rest of society, at least as they apply to Canada. Here, some see the state as an impartial referee which mediates among society's varied interest groups. Others see it responding only to the interests of the dominant capitalist class. Still others, in Canada and elsewhere, see the state as largely autonomous; though it serves the interests of dominant groups or class factions, it does not automatically obey their wishes (Poulantzas, 1973).

The state, as Canadians experience it, is *not* a unified body with a clear, integrated policy. It is a set of separate agencies and agents with whom citizens interact in different ways, at different times, and for different reasons. And in Canada, the state is visibly "fragmented." Constitutional crises have plagued the country in recent years, proving that the federal part of the state must struggle to control the willful provincial governments.

Nothing shows the fragmentation of the Canadian state more clearly than the growth of regional politics in the 1990s. A recent example is the rise of the Reform Party in Western Canada and the Bloc Quebecois in Quebec.

Even procedurally, the state is not an organized whole. It is a "cluster of agencies, departments, tiers and levels, each with its own rules and resources and often with conflicting purposes and objectives" (Held, 1989: 2). So it would be wrong to say that the state is united, even in opposition to civil society. And is the state really opposed to civil society?

In Canada, it is no easy matter to distinguish the state from "civil society." To assume a clear boundary exists between the state and civil society is to underestimate how much the state invades the rest of society. In truth, the state regulates *most* aspects of Canadian life. And because the state is "embedded in our socioeconomic systems," we cannot treat it as distinct from those systems (Held, 1989: 2). The state is a set of institutions or agencies that structures the relationships among all the sectors of society.

Many recent theorists have dropped the distinction between the state and civil society. The state is *not* distinct from society; it is embedded in our social relations. In fact, "politics" pervades all social life, and vice versa.

The educational system, for example, is part of both the state and civil society. After all, a school must follow ministerial rules, and it must also consider the relationships among teachers, students, and parents. No one can understand education in a particular province without referring to the civil *and* state activities which make up the educational sector. Many groups — politicians, bureaucrats, trustees, administrators, teachers, students, parents, lobby groups, professors of education, journalists, taxpayers, and "concerned citizens" among others — engage in school politics.

IDEOLOGIES

"Myths" and "trust" play important roles in social and political life. Before people can change their political order, they must imagine a new order worth working for (Rumantsev and Rubenchik, 1990). They must have faith in that vision and in the leaders they expect to carry out that vision. This means that, in changing a society, people must create and accept *ideologies.*

Ideologies are important for social change because they motivate and control people. In this way, they influence the distribution of power. Sometimes, they prevent social protest and social change; at other times, they make change easier.

Ideologies are beliefs that "explain" how society is, or should be, organized. In North America, we are used to ideological debates on political and economic topics. Recall from earlier chapters that ideologies contain ideas of right and wrong, good and bad, desirable and undesirable. People use them to interpret and react to events in the real world.

Ideological debates arise in widely varying areas of life; for example, in debates about whether Canada should admit more refugees, whether marijuana use should be decriminalized, and whether a foetus is a person, entitled to legal rights like other people.

Such debates are hard to resolve. That is because most people are sure they are right and equally sure that people on the other side are wrong. Usually, both sides fail to see that their opinion is just a belief, not the absolute truth. In fact, ideologies can never be proven or falsified by scientific means. And when people adopt these ideas, they usually don't know they are learning or believing in anything at all. They think they are discovering the "truth."

Over our lifetimes, we are exposed to beliefs and values in many subtle ways. We learn them as children, from our parents. This learning continues in youth and adulthood, when we interact with friends and workmates.

Even the educational system has an ideological content that sociologists call the "hidden curriculum." Year after year, students are taught a sense of the social structure and their place in it. For example, they learn to line up and wait their turn and to take notes and directions from teachers. As they do so, they learn to submit to authority in ways that employers will require in the workplace. They learn to work for grades, certificates, degrees and the approval of those in authority.

In so doing, they are being taught to work for extrinsic rewards, not intrinsic ones such as the joy of discovery (Bowles and Gintis, 1976). All of this learning helps to support the status quo. Sociologists call beliefs that support the status quo the "dominant ideology."

Ideology and control

There are two main types of ideology. On the one hand, *reformist* and radical ideologies rally the forces of change. We will say more about these in a little while. On the other hand, *dominant ideologies* support the "status quo" or existing power structure (Parkin, 1971; Abercrombie et al., 1980; Marchak, 1988). We call them "dominant" to point out their role in controlling people.

Whether an ideology is dominant is something we can learn only through empirical research. We consider it "dominant" if the most powerful (or socially dominant) groups in society sponsor it and if it also supports the interests of these groups.

The popular belief in "winners" and "losers" — in people getting what they deserve and deserving what they get — is an ideology that is "dominant" in this sense. In turn, the dominant ideology is an important part of popular culture and entertainment. In American culture, for example, a high value is placed on heroism and war. This makes it easy for American politicians to mobilize public sentiment behind activities like the Gulf War, and before that, the longstanding Cold War.

In the former Soviet Union, the dominant Communist ideology infused every aspect of social and political life, even sociology. By North American standards Soviet sociology was very biased, in that it denied legitimacy to a variety of opinions. Three sets of ideas dominated what sociologists could and could not say in public (Pankhurst, 1982). They were Marxist-Leninist theory (the vision of an ideal socialist society), Soviet ideology (which emphasized the goal of political order), and development ideology (which emphasized the goal of industrial productivity).

Everywhere, dominant ideologies influence political life by shaping *public opinion.* However, there is no single "public" in industrial societies. A wide range of social types — the result of a complex division of labour, large-scale immigration, and relatively easy social mobility — creates a variety of "publics." Each has its own opinions, values, and interests.

Any particular "public" is an unstructured set of people. Like the members of a "cohort" we discussed in the last chapter, the members of a "public" do not interact with one another and are rarely aware of belonging to the same group. All we really mean by a "public" is a set of people who hold certain interests in, views on, or concerns about a particular issue.

Often it is possible to reach the members of a public only through the mass media, since there are no other contacts between them. The media play a central role both in promoting the dominant ideology and shaping public opinion. Television shows, radio programs, magazines, newspapers, and advertising are all geared to reaching "the public". By varying their content, they can reach many different publics.Some media, however, choose to focus their energies on a very particular public.

Remember, the goal of the media is not only to reach and entertain the public; it is also to shape public opinion. The noted radical linguist, Noam Chomsky, argues in his book *Manufacturing Consent* (Herman and Chomsky, 1988), that the media are indeed trying consciously to shape our thinking. He reminds us that the media are big businesses, owned by very rich, powerful people. Their goal is to stay on the good side of the powerful, make a profit, and generally support the political and economic system that allows them to make a profit.

If, sometimes, the media elites seem uncoordinated or lacking in a clearly stated interest, this may be because we do not know all of their motivations. And, like other powerful organizations, media organizations may sometimes make mistakes — for example, back the "wrong" candidate or policy. In any event, we do not have to suppose there is a smoky backroom where everything gets planned once a week: manipulating public opinion does not require *that* kind of organization.

In principle, public opinion should be central to any democracy since what we mean by a "democracy" is "government by the people." A Latin proverb says *vox populi, vox dei*, meaning "the voice of the people is the voice of God." In a democratic society, this proverb should be the guiding principle. No wonder, then, that public opinion polls are so common: they are the best way to listen to the voice of democracy's God.

Polls measure public opinion quite accurately. They also manipulate or shape public opinion. As well, they impute certainty or "facticity" to opinions that (often) are in flux, creating something out of nothing.

The bandwagon effect shows how opinion polls influence public opinion. People like being part of a group that has succeeded; they want to "get on the bandwagon." The bandwagon effect shows up in post election polls, when a much larger number of voters claim to have voted for the winning candidate than did so. After the fact, people adopt opinions that are popular *because* they are popular. They may even support a politician who seems likely to win (i.e., according to the pre-election polls) just because they want to back a winner.

Political and other public opinion polls contribute to this illusion-making, but journalists play a far larger role when they report propaganda under the guise of news. **Propaganda** is any idea or doctrine that is spread for the purpose of influencing people's opinions and actions. It includes all attempts to influence other people's thoughts and opinions.

In this sense, Sunday-school lessons, advertising, and election campaigns are all propaganda. In fact, propaganda is any information that represents itself as pure, unquestionable truth.

So, for example, newspapers are sources of propaganda in our society. Though they are often owned by enormously wealthy individuals, they pretend to tell us the truth about events of the day. Often, we do not have to dig too deep to find an anti-labour bias in the reporting of strikes, or a particular slant on business, politics and crime.Consider the one-sided way in which some Canadian newspapers reported on the advantages and disadvantages of the Free Trade Agreement (FTA) and North American Free Trade Agreement (NAFTA). Though the information was there, one had to dig deep for the data that showed hundreds of thousands of jobs were being lost.

Not surprisingly, people are becoming more skeptical about the information they receive and the people who control government. Survey data show that Canadians distrust politicians more than almost anyone else (including advertising executives, who have never been famous for their honesty). The best way to protect against a blind acceptance of propaganda is education, an openness to new information, and a tolerance for ambiguity. It is particularly important to be willing to consider different views of a single issue.

Ideology and protest

Ideologies can dominate us, but they can also be liberating. Often, they increase the chance that people will protest against their life chances. Ideologies that advocate change are either radical or reformist. Those who support *reformist ideologies* call for changes without challenging the basic ground rules. In Canada, the provision of medicare, welfare and unemployment insurance are reforms that were based on this kind of ideology. These programs were intended as "safety nets" to help people who got into trouble.

Unemployment insurance, however, does not prevent unemployment. It does not create jobs. It makes unemployment less harmful without changing the factors that create unemployment.

Radical ideologies, on the other hand, call for a complete re-shaping of society. This is what the Co-operative Commonwealth Federation (CCF) — parent of today's reformist New Democratic Party — did at its founding in 1933, when it adopted the Regina Manifesto. This manifesto declared, "No CCF government will rest content until it has eradicated capitalism and put into oper ation the full programme of socialized planning which will lead to the establishment in Canada of the co-operative commonwealth."

The reform and radical ideologies we find in any society are what sociologists call *counter ideologies.* They are "counter" in the sense that they challenge the bases of the dominant ideologies. They also expose the interests that dominant ideologies serve and offer people a different vision of society.

Often, counter ideologies develop out of people's responses to experiences of unequal treatment. Counter ideologies call the status quo to account and deny legitimacy to customary ways of treating people. So, for example, feminism is a counter ideology that undermines sexism and traditional ways of treating people. Feminism as a *counter culture*, to which it is closely tied, promotes ideas and behaviours which are less immediately political. (For example, feminist academic and artistic works interpret women's experience.)

Groups which promote counter ideologies get their message out to people in many ways, particularly through public meetings and the media. Intellectuals and other highly educated people (called the "intelligentsia") often play an important part in promoting counter ideologies.

The Polish intelligentsia, for example, played a major part in the Solidarity movement during the early 1980s. And in both Poland and Hungary, the intelligentsia has helped to create a civil society since the collapse of communism (Kennedy, 1992).

SOCIAL MOVEMENTS

Often, social change results from the success of social protest movements (or "social movements"). The term "social movement" refers to any form of collective act that promotes or resists change in a society. Such movements usually engage in both political acts and media campaigns to get their views across and ensure that they achieve their goals. English-rights political groups in Quebec and western-rights political groups in Alberta are two social movements that have engaged in political action.

Some social movements are more visible than others. For example, the struggle of environmentalists against clear-cut logging in Clayoquot (British Columbia) made maximum use of the mass media to gain a lot of visibility. On the other hand, social movements supporting minority rights have, in the past, lobbied behind the scenes to get laws enacted that punished discrimination based on gender or race. For them, public visibility would not have contributed to ultimate legislative success.

Whether hidden or open, social movements are not the only groups that influence law-making. For example, powerful business leaders were heavily involved in negotiations over the North American Free Trade Agreement (NAFTA). Well organized and funded, they worked privately to make sure the law they wanted was passed in Parliament.

However, we do not consider such actions by people who already have power or influence to be part of a social movement. We reserve the term "social movement" for people who are seeking power or change, and who mobilize in large numbers. These are *not* defining features of the Canadian business elite.

Social movements are the result of a conscious reaction to social changes, or a conscious effort to bring about social changes. They may support any one of many social issues: abortion on demand, an end to storing toxic waste in a community, a nuclear-weapon-free Canada, an end to seal hunting, opposition to free trade, and so on. Whatever its specific concern, every social movement is guided by a particular ideology and generates propaganda that explains its cause to the public.

Usually, movements form along lines of social conflict or "cleavage." For example in Norway, people split politically along "cleavage lines" that include:

(a) conflicts between regional groups, cultural groups, religious groups, sexes and age groups;
(b) conflicts in the commodity market (i.e., owner versus renter, buyer versus seller) and in the labour market (i.e., employer versus employee); and
(c) conflicts between debtors and creditors, people who hold different views about new technologies, and people who disagree about relations with other countries (Nilson, 1987).

In Norway, social movements can form around any of these conflicts, or around several at a time. Whatever the issue, a movement will have a membership profile defined by many or all of the social cleavages noted above.

Generally, social movements arise out of a feeling that society is not working properly and needs changing. So, for example, in sub-Saharan Africa we find poor-quality schools and student protest aimed at improving the schools. Government responds by reducing spending and closing schools, in the hope of punishing the protesters. The result is a vicious circle of growing violence and rapidly worsening conditions (Nkinyangi, 1991).

In China, an alliance between students and workers led to the Tiananmen Square protests and subsequent massacre. Some say this protest resulted from a lack of Western-style democracy, but Ashley (1991) argues it resulted from the entry of Western and Asian capital into China. The entry of capital raised living standards but also led to massive corruption, new (and less secure) employment practices and a wider gap between the richest and the poorest.

Relative deprivation

One important theory — *relative deprivation theory* — argues that movements arise when large numbers of people feel deprived in comparison with other people. They feel there is a gap between the social rewards they are getting and those they are entitled to get. Or they feel cheated when they compare their own lives with those of others. Such people have a strong desire to join a social movement whose goal is to change the distribution of social rewards.

Relative deprivation is largely subjective and even temporary, compared to *absolute* deprivation — a serious, visible, and enduring lack of social rewards. Yet social scientists agree that *relative deprivation* is more likely to cause social movements to form than absolute deprivation. Indeed, social movements gain the strongest support when there is a "revolution of rising expectations" (Runciman, 1966).

People protest under improving conditions, not grinding, desperate poverty. For one thing, improvement makes it easier for people to protest, because they are not so fully preoccupied with the struggle to survive. When people's lives improve, their expectations for change often grow faster than the rate at which change can take place.

Feelings of frustration and discontent are caused by a sense of deprivation. They are *necessary* for a social movement to emerge; a movement will not form without them. Still, they are not enough by themselves to get a movement going. Many discontented people never join, let alone form, social movements. Another condition — the possibility of resource mobilization — must be met before a movement forms.

Resource mobilization

A second approach to analyzing social movements, *resource mobilization theory*, addresses the methods people use to put forward their views. This theory does not look at *why* people want to promote or resist social change, but at *how* they launch social movements. It sees social movements in terms of the ability of discontented people to organize.

Without discontent, there would be no social movements. Yet discontent is a constant of human life: it is always lurking in the background, waiting to express itself. Without the movement of resources, discontent can never express itself as a social force. It remains hidden or comes out in non political, personal pathologies: random violence, mental illness, heavy drinking, and so on.

No wonder data from the United States, the Netherlands and Germany show that group mobilization and the availability of resources are better predictors of political activism than personal values and dissatisfaction (Heunks, 1991).

Important elements in "getting organized" include using resources such as effective leadership, public support, money, legal aid, ties with influential officials and public personalities, and access to the mass media. Occasionally, organizing also means acquiring, and learning to use, weapons.

Without access to key resources, discontented people cannot change society or resist the powerful, and they rarely attempt it. Thus, the successes and failures of social movements indicate a change in access to key resources, and not necessarily a change in levels of contentment. Likewise, an absence of protest movements does not prove that people are contented. More often, it proves the state can suppress protest when it wishes and discontented people lack the resources they need to form a movement.

Generally, (the strength of earlier political protests will influence how a state acts in the face of new protests. We also know that leadership is an important resource in social movements. Elites play an important leadership role, and so do intellectuals, as we noted earlier. As a result, political conflicts vary according to whether the elites are united or not. When elites are not united, movements are less likely to succeed. Also, the (class) background of the leadership has an important effect. Often, it will determine whether a social movement has reformist, radical or revolutionary goals (Mars, 1985).

Occasionally, as in 1993 Somalia (see Exhibit 11.3), leadership and resources are all it takes to gain control of a society. Somalia is so poor and disorganized that the groups which are *least* disorganized and poor become powerful. As well, in Somalia kin groups and clans lend legitimacy to a leader's claims to control. But a far more important part was played by outside powers, such as the United States, that wanted a stable leadership they could work with.

Unlike deprivation theory, mobilization theory draws our attention toward objective or material factors in movement formation. This focus on practical issues is the greatest strength of the theory.

Charisma in social movements

As we have seen, social movements usually form around a set of common interests or grievances. In some cases, however, the goals of a social movement may become secondary to its leadership. In such cases the followers will develop a commitment to their leader which may become more important to them than their particular grievances.

Max Weber identified such a movement as one centred on a "charismatic," inspiring leader. The history of such a social movement is, largely, the history of its

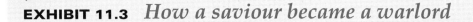

EXHIBIT 11.3   *How a saviour became a warlord*

Propaganda machines can play cruel tricks with the reputations of African leaders, inflating them one day into philanthropic visionaries, deflating them the next into ruthless despots. . . .

A few months ago, [Somalia's] General Aidid happily played the part of father of his nation, champion of the poor, promoter of democracy. Now, Central Casting has him on America's Most Wanted and the elite U.S. Rangers are turning Mogadishu inside out in an effort to capture him.

Not that he himself has changed. Just about everyone working in Somalia considered him a ruthless brute last year, and the year before that, but they tolerated him, even dressed him up in emperor's clothes. . . .

In a chaotic country, the Americans needed the support of local leaders. . . .

In private, Robert Oakley, the former U.S. special envoy to Somalia, made no secret of his distaste for [Aidid]. He considered him a bellicose, self-serving and perhaps mentally unstable thug. But war had created the necessity.

To promote peace, Mr. Oakley prevailed upon Gen. Aidid and Mr. Ali Mahdi [the interim president] to hide their bitter rivalry and parade together through the streets of Mogadishu. It played well on TV.

At the UN-sponsored peace talks that followed, Gen. Aidid was portrayed as de facto leader. It must have been heady for the former shepherd boy, who had served as a lieutenant in the Italian army. When Somalia gained independence from Italy in 1960, he became a captain in the new national army, although clan politics left him an outsider to real power.

Sensing a threat, the president, Maj. Gen. Siad Barre (a Darod from the Marehan subclan) imprisoned him, then sent him to India as ambassador.

Upon returning to Somalia in 1989, Gen. Aidid saw a new order in the making. The United States was fast withdrawing support for Gen. Siad Barre, who was unleashing attacks on opposition clans in the north. And so, he took up arms as leader of the rebel United Somali Congress.

With the world transfixed by Operation Desert Storm, Gen. Aidid led a fierce tank assault on Mogadishu in late 1990. The next 18 months were horrific. Gen. Siad Barre's clansmen were chased across the border, or massacred, while subclans turned on one another and on almost every aid agency in the country. The Aidid forces relentlessly shelled northern Mogadishu, killing thousands of civilians.

The UN relief team left in disgust and were succeeded by the Americans, whose strategy was not only to disarm but to "disempower" the warlords. And none more than the man they had once touted as Somalia's next president.

Source: John Stackhouse, "How a saviour became a warlord," *The Globe and Mail*, Fri. Sept. 3, 1993, p. A11.

leader and the successes or failures of that leader. That is not to say that each movement is just the unique product of a unique person. Nevertheless, the leader of a movement is charismatic when he or she inspires loyalty and enthusiasm among followers, despite the cost or danger this affiliation poses to these followers. So, for example, Mahatma Gandhi and Martin Luther King Jr. were **charismatic leaders** who were able to create movements based on non violence, despite the fact that violence was directed at their followers and at themselves. Other recent charismatic leaders include Jim Jones, who led his followers to mass suicide in Guyana, and David Koresh of the Branch Davidians, who perished in Waco, Texas in 1993.

Charismatic leaders hold unshakeable beliefs about the rightness of their cause and they exert a powerful hold on their followers. Followers believe their

Spontaneous expressions of public sentiment are often associated with a particular secular or religious leader. This is one way of measuring the leader's charisma.

qualities of personality are supernatural, superhuman or inaccessible to common people (Weber, 1964). Such powers, which often include the gift of prophecy, make it easier for leaders to control the masses — particularly in new or developing societies (Shpakova, 1988).

As well, charismatic leaders have abundant political skills. Often, their program includes many sound and acceptable policies. Most important, they have a willing audience. The distressed state of the followers helps them to believe in what the leader has to say.

Leaders may appeal to their followers' better instincts, or offer them higher self-esteem. For this reason, entry into the movement is an important step in the lives of those joining such a movement. Induction of the new member (or "neophyte") also includes conversion, testimony, identifying the leader as a "prophet," and accepting a belief in the prophecy (Tedeschi, 1988). In the end, some leaders abuse their followers and commit grave misdeeds in the name of a higher calling. When leaders consider themselves godlike, the charismatic movements they lead often turn into tyrannies. Happily this was not the case in the movements led by Gandhi or Martin Luther King.

However, charismatic social movements are also self-limiting. Attachment to the leader is intensely emotional, so these social movements are unpredictable and operate at a fever pitch. They can be loving one minute and violent the next. Paradoxically, the movement becomes more stable and predictable after the leader dies or retires.

Then, the movement enters a process of **routinization**. A bureaucratic structure emerges, patterns of authority develop, and day-to-day duties replace spontaneous acts. The group relies less on inspiration and more on tradition than it once did. Routinization creates institutions — for example, churches and trained clergy — that draw on people's deepest faith in the movement. Rational and well-organized, these institutions are strong enough to stand up against the tests of faith people suffer in everyday life. Through routinization, the movement achieves a measure of permanence. Movements that routinize charisma provide their members with friendship and help, maintaining their involvement with the group. Failure to routinize almost ensures the movement will die out.

OTHER SOURCES OF SOCIAL CHANGE

Political and social movements are only two sources of social change in the world today. We discussed the significance of another source — population pressure — in the last chapter. Other important sources of social change include new ideas, new technology, and the globalization of world markets. We will discuss each of these briefly, in turn.

New ideas and inventions

New ideas can be a powerful force for social change. Consider the importance of the following ideas in world history: *Liberty, Equality, Justice, Nation, God, Truth.* At one time or another, people have shed blood, even died, to defend these ideas. People are still doing so in many parts of the world.

Karl Marx viewed ideas as the *result* and reflection of social forces — not their cause. That is, he thought ideas grew out of people's life conditions; but this is only half of the story. Marx himself must have thought that ideas also affected people's life conditions. Otherwise he would not have spent his own life writing down ideas about class relations and capitalism. He must have known that *without* these ideas and the class awareness they would provoke, the chances of revolution and communism were slight.

Yet ideas are neither necessary nor sufficient for social change to occur. Consider the case of AIDS: significant numbers of AIDS patients were first noted in 1983. Since then, we have seen changes in sexual behaviours, medical treatments, civil liberties — even in people's faith in science. In this case, new ideas are a result; they were not *necessary* to initiate social change.

Nor are ideas *sufficient* for social change. Throughout history, many ideas — both beliefs and discoveries — have been lost or forgotten. For ideas to spread and take root they must gain the support of people in power. Ideas spread fastest when they arise among, or gain acceptance from, the powerful; this happened with the rise of Christianity, for example. Equally, the powerful ignore or suppress ideas that oppose ruling ideologies. People who support ideas that oppose the dominant ideology must be willing to fight for them. And, as we noted earlier, throughout history people have been willing to do so.

Technology and economics also have an effect. Generally, ideas that people cannot use are lost or ignored. Like popular movements, new ideas depend on resources for their survival. To survive and spread, new ideas must have a social movement or institution that adopts them. In that sense, they are then the few ideas (of many) whose "time has come."

Still, technology and economics are not sufficient either. Consider the matter of utopia: thinkers as far back as Sir Thomas More, four centuries ago, were able to imagine a "utopia" in which people would enjoy much leisure and good health. There, people would have the time to write poetry, sing songs and join in spirited debate about current affairs. In this imagined utopia, life would be civilized and fulfilling.

Four centuries ago, few people had a chance to lead such lives. By contrast, today we people in industrialized Western nations *do* have the chance, for we have much more leisure, greater longevity and better health. We also have more education and more knowledge about the arts and current affairs. So it would seem that the utopian idea is an idea whose "time has come." Strange to say, we do not yet live in a utopia. (What's your explanation?)

Innovations are new material objects or ways of doing things that become part of a culture. There are two forms of innovation: *discovery* and *invention*. A *discovery* involves finding out about and making known the existence of something that was always there, whose existence was unknown before.

Like ideas, discoveries have social origins. Usually they are the result of patient research, which often requires a societal commitment to finding out and using new knowledge. In turn, a commitment to scientific research has particular cultural roots. In the Western world, this commitment has flowered only in the last 300 years, alongside Protestantism and capitalism. The growth of science has required funding and also a cultural commitment to ideas like "truth," "progress," "efficiency," and "productivity."

Invention also has a cultural and social basis. It is the creation or design of something that did not exist before — for example, the bow and arrow, automobile, television, or Nintendo game. Many innovations – whether ideas, inventions or discoveries — spread from one place to another through a process called *diffusion.* They spread from group to group within a society and from one society to another. Usually the diffusion of an invention or idea starts slowly, picks up steam, then levels off when a large part of society has been exposed to it.

"Spreading the word" about one's findings is an important scientific norm and, in science, secrecy is considered almost as improper as plagiarism or falsified results.Diffusion also increases as the means for diffusing ideas improve. Here, the media have been very important. Improvements in communication technology since Gutenberg invented the printing press have all increased the cultural and scientific diffusion of ideas.

Sociologists have studied a variety of diffusion processes. One famous study by Coleman, Katz, and Menzel (1966) examined the diffusion of knowledge among physicians about a new pharmaceutical drug. Another examined Noah Webster's invention of American spelling practices (e.g., "center" for "centre," "labor" for "labour"). Webster purposely diffused these American spellings by using them in his dictionaries and in primary school readers of the day (Weinstein, 1982). His goal was to draw a cultural boundary between the United States and Great Britain; as you can see, he succeeded.

New technology

Today, much social change results from new technology. Genetic engineering and informatics — the combination of computing and communication technologies — are two of the newest major influences on our society. However, in discussing new technology we must be careful to avoid the dangers of technological determinism.

Technological determinism holds that social and cultural change are usually the result of changes in technology. Like other single-minded theories, this theory assumes that one particular factor — in this case, technology — always has the same effects. Technological determinists propose that technology has the same social effects, whatever the culture, society, or socio-historical setting in which it is being used.

A prime example of this view is Marshall McLuhan's famous slogan, "The medium is the message." By this, McLuhan meant that television influences us all by the way it conveys information, *not* because of the information it conveys. He believed that changes in communication technology would change the world's culture.

And, in fact, it has. Still, it is easy to overstate this view — to believe that technology does, or can do, more than is really possible. Without denying technology's importance, we cannot agree that all of social and cultural life are *determined* by technology. Like ideas, new technologies are neither sufficient nor necessary for social change to occur. Societies are too complex for that.

The evidence shows people use the same technology differently in different organizations, societies, or cultures. The precise effect of a new technology depends on the context into which it is introduced. The motives and attitudes of people who control the technology, and the prevailing culture — the beliefs, cultural practices, and existing technology — all make a difference.

This is why many inventions and technologies of the past are lost and forgotten today. Much of Alexandrian science, Greek philosophy, and folk med-

The microchip circuit can sit on your fingertip and replace 100s of larger components in a "thinking" machine.

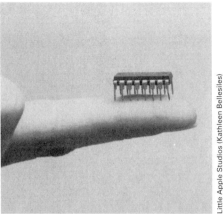

Little Apple Studios (Kathleen Bellesiles)

The microcomputer can sit on your desk and replace dozens of clerical workers in an office.

Dick Hemingway

This robotic factory can sit on the outskirts of your city and replace 1000s of manual workers.

General Motors of Canada

icine from around the world, is lost to us because no social institutions preserved, developed and spread this knowledge. Science and technology could not, and cannot, ensure their own survival.

Even today, we see a vast number of different uses made of computing technology. Computer use varies from one society to another and from one organization to another within the same society. People determine computer use, not *vice versa*. Computers and other new technologies have the most impact where they are dealing with problems that are readily "technifiable." These are problems that have a few very important features:

(a) the problems are specific and practical — for example, how to get money out of your bank account on a weekend or at 3 a.m.;

(b) ordinary people are hoping for new technology in that area — for example, cheaper, more reliable cars that do not pollute the air;

(c) the technology is powerful, meaning that it requires little instruction and can do a great deal for the user. A microwave oven, computerized chess game or reference library on CD-ROM are examples of this.

Often, making a technological change is too complicated and costly to be worthwhile. Things remain the same, even though better solutions are possible. Nonetheless, we are in the midst of a microelectronics revolution which is transforming many aspects of our society. With proper use, computers can become instruments of human betterment. With wrong use, they can become instruments of domination. In the 20th century we have seen that this is true of *all* technology.

Technology has even more impact under adverse conditions than otherwise. For example, countries that undergo the worst forms of civil war or foreign occupation are most likely to be changed by technology. In fact, they most often achieve rapid economic growth and a fair distribution of income and social welfare. Traditional groupings *would have* blocked these changes but war and/or occupation destroyed these groupings (Chan, 1987).

GLOBALIZATION

Many believe we have now entered a new stage of history. Throughout the world we find uneven development and conflict. World System theory explains the uneven pace of development in the world by looking at the unequal relations among different countries. It insists that we must study the world as a unit, and not study arbitrarily selected chunks of the world.

If we look at the history of selected societies (for example, Germany or India) over a long period, their boundaries change frequently. National boundaries offer no solid basis for the analysis of social change. In recent times, the only "society" with a clear boundary is the world-system itself (Wallerstein, 1986).

Since the world's states are all integrated into a world system, changes in one will provoke changes in the others. This integration of states into a world economic system began in the 15th century, with capitalism's expansion in western Europe. This process of integration is far from over.

Though states are all connected, they do not relate to one another as equals. Politically and economically, some dominate others. Dominant states form the *core* and subordinate states, the *periphery*.

Industrial core states take much of the raw materials and cheap labour they need from peripheral states. It is because they are economically and politically dominant that core states have the power to extract an economic surplus from the periphery. This helps them develop at an ever faster rate and prosper. Meanwhile, the periphery — ever more depleted of materials, labour, and capital — becomes increasingly dependent on the core region for manufactured goods. The gap between core and periphery widens.

Investors from the core states control the economies of peripheral states. As a result, profits made in the periphery drain out of the local economy and flow back to the core. Moreover, foreigners decide what kinds of businesses to operate and what resources to exploit in the periphery. They make these decisions with their own interests in mind and it is in their interest to keep the periphery dependent on the core. Dependence ensures they will have a continued source of cheap raw materials and labour, and a market for their manufactured goods.

Core states engage in *imperialism* — the exercise of political and economic control by one state over the territory of another, often by military means. Its purpose is to exploit the indigenous population and extract economic and political advantages.

Early European imperialism occurred through colonization — the settlement and administration of foreign lands. However, domination of a foreign land does not always require colonization. In fact, *economic* domination is far safer, less costly and (usually) more stable. By gaining control of a nation's economy — whether through ownership of lands or industries, the purchase of stocks and bonds, or monopolistic control of key resources (e.g., a long term contract to buy all its oil, or cars, or wheat, or water at a certain price) — it is possible to control the political and social life of the country very effectively. This is precisely how, first Britain and then the United States, have controlled Canadian society. Colonial rule has not been needed for the last 130 years.

Conversely, when colonization (or military intervention) is needed to control a foreign country, it is because normal economic controls are not working. Between 1415 and 1967, European colonization of Asia, Africa and the Americas diminished during long periods of economic expansion (Boswell, 1989). Similarly, world *de*colonization increased during the period of American world-dominance. It was rapid in the period after 1960, when imperialism lost its legitimacy around the world, and it was most rapid in societies where large numbers had the vote. As well, there is evidence that the process of decolonization accelerates over time (Strang, 1990). And as colonialism has declined, a more subtle form of imperialism — neocolonialism — has become common. Under neocolonialism, core states exercise economic control over countries that are (formally) politically independent.

Underdevelopment is the effect on the periphery of unequal exchanges with the core. An underdeveloped society is one that has lost its capacity to take care of its own needs. Signs of underdevelopment include:

- a dependence on the export of raw materials,
- the import of manufactured goods,
- little domestic control over the economy,
- a small industrial base,
- little economic diversity,
- settlement of most of the population in rural areas,
- high rates of unemployment,
- a lack of social programs such as health care,
- a high illiteracy rate, and
- a low standard of living.

Underdeveloped societies vary in the number and combination of typical characteristics they display. However, they are similar in that their condition is always a result of international differences in wealth and power, which permit other states to exploit them. The underdevelopment of the periphery is *not* due to a lack of resources, illiteracy, or a traditional or backward mentality. It results from domination by the core.

We see these signs of underdevelopment in much of sub-Saharan Africa. Prospects for growth are uncertain because the factors that produced these economic ills are still present (Amegbe, 1990). They include political upheaval, dependence on other economies, and the destabilizing effects of rigid, long-term planning. Some believe deteriorating social and economic conditions in Africa are leading to widespread corruption and underground economies. Successful development will require more flexibility, democratic reform and lots of foreign aid (Ergas, 1986).

Often, unsuccessful development occurs because of foreign meddling in local affairs — whether economically, politically, culturally or otherwise. Sometimes, as in Taiwan and South Korea, foreign "meddling" is beneficial. In still other countries like Argentina, foreigners have played little part in the economic failure.

Typically, we find an interaction between local conditions and the goals of imperial powers. So, for example, the North American Free Trade Agreement furthers the interests of rich and powerful Americans and Canadians. But, as the evidence in Exhibit 11.4 suggests, it also serves the interests of rich and powerful Mexicans.

Even semi-peripheral countries like Canada show some of the same signs of dependence. However, these countries are different in one main respect. Social movements are more important in semi-peripheral societies and, sometimes, they challenge existing social, political and economic relations. That is because people in semi-peripheral regions have the motivation and the opportunity to make major changes. These societies are fertile grounds for protest (Chase-Dunn, 1990).

EXHIBIT 11.4   *Mexico's elite like ruling party's agenda*

Anyone wanting to examine the close links between Mexico's ruling political elite and its wealthy private-sector upper crust need look no further than a dinner meeting held last year.

The meeting, at the mansion of a former secretary of finance, brought together 25 of Mexico's richest men, each willing to pony up $25-million (U.S.) to ensure that the Institutional Revolutionary Party (PRI) had the cash to maintain electoral domination into the next century.

But even in that high-powered crowd, Mexico's richest businessman couldn't resist a bit of one-upmanship. Emilio Azcarraga Milmo, the owner of the world's largest Spanish-language media conglomerate, suggested $50-million or even $75-million might be a more appropriate sum.

With a net worth of more than $5-billion, either amount would be petty cash to Mr. Azcarraga.

Similarly, a cheque that size wouldn't have caused financial difficulty for Carlos Slim Helu. Mexico's second-richest man, who was seated across the table from Mr. Azcarraga, has a net worth of between $3-billion and $4-billion. . . .

No segment of Mexican society has benefited as much from the neo-conservative, free-trade policies of President Carlos Salinas de Gortari as the tightly knit strata of financiers, entrepreneurs and old-money families who run much of the country's economy. . . .

Since 1988, when Mr. Salinas took power, the number of Mexican billionaires as tabulated by Forbes magazine has risen to 13 from one.

That's more than any country except the United States, Germany and Japan. Canada, with an economy about twice as large as Mexico's, has five individuals or families who can call themselves billionaires.

In many cases, the Mexican billionaires enjoy a virtual monopoly in their home market. . . .

But their influence doesn't come close to that exercised by Mr. Azcarraga and Mr. Slim.

Mr. Azcarraga is known nationwide as El Tigre, an apt nickname. An authoritarian who inherited a television station, he is probably Mexico's most feared businessman.

Televisa had sales of $60-million in 1972 when Mr. Azcarraga's father died and his children inherited the business. In 1993, Grupo Televisa SA is thought to have had revenue of about $1.6-billion.

About 90 per cent of Mexico's 15 million televisions are regularly tuned to Televisa's four TV networks. (A shopping channel is also being started.)

Mr. Azcarraga's control of television advertising is so complete that companies must pay for their spots in the calendar year before they run. . . .

. . . Televisa's evening news program, which is Mexico's dominant source of information, reflects Mr. Azcarraga's politics. . . .

Source: Drew Fagan, "Mexico's elite like ruling party's agenda," *The Globe and Mail*, Mon. Jan. 24, 1994, p. B1, B9.

For example, the 1993 federal election in Canada did more to challenge the *status quo* than the 1992 federal election in the United States, a core society. Protest movements, like those which gave rise to the Reform Party and Bloc Quebecois, are much more common in Canadian politics than they are in American politics.

In the core societies, imperialists try to avoid domestic problems by making wars abroad, focusing people's attention on foreign policy, or exporting problems (like unsafe working conditions) to the Third World (Block, Gardner and Walker, 1989). In the long run, the domestic problems explode: witness the problems of urban crime, violence, unemployment and drug use in America's inner cities.

Alongside economic and political imperialism is cultural imperialism — the mental colonization of developing societies with Western ideas. This process is subtle. Over time, exposure to Western media gradually alters cultural values, causes conflicts, and changes perceptions of local and world events (Salwen, 1991). Powerful (mainly American) media organizations are responsible for the worldwide distribution of a total cultural package that includes television, film, sports and consumer items (Schiller, 1991).

Even the worldwide flow of "news" is shaped by the imperial connection. Galtung (1971; also Galtung and Vincent, 1992) points to four main characteristics of news flow within a colonial system, where a core nation dominates peripheral nations. First, news about the core is more common than news about the periphery (e.g., people in countries that are politically or economically dominated by the United States hear more about the United States than they do about Canada). Second, news about the colonial core is more common than news about *other* colonial cores (e.g., in Canada, there is more news about the United States than about Japan).

Third, news about the core is dominant even in broadcasts that originate in the periphery (e.g., Canadians hear more about the United States than they hear about other parts of Canada). And fourth, there is little if any flow of information between peripheral countries, unless it is provided by the centre (e.g., there is little direct news flow between Canada and Mexico).

In Canada, the Americanization of culture by prime-time television is a matter of concern to many. In the Philippines, such Americanization has even led many Filipino intellectuals to stop writing literature in their native language (San Juan, Jr., 1988).

World system theory has its weaknesses. They include a failure to explain or predict the varied pathways of change in Third World countries. For example, the theory cannot explain why East Asia is getting richer and richer while Africa is getting poorer and poorer. Critics claim that world system theory fails to consider influences on social change that are internal to the state. For example, it says little about the role of social classes within the respective core and peripheral nations.

As a result, it cannot explain why Canada, a former colony and major exporter of raw materials, is not underdeveloped today to the same degree as Argentina, another former colony. In 1900, Canada and Argentina had equal levels of economic development (that is, gross national product) and today Argentina is far less economically developed than Canada. The theory cannot interpret this fact.

Still, world system theory reminds us that all significant social change produces conflict. No change, even change that evolves out of an earlier stage of development, can escape conflict. And no theory of exploitation makes much sense if it fails to take the global dimension into account (Bowles, 1988).

It is only in the last few years that foreigners have come in any number to marvel at China's ancient, highly developed and distinctive culture. Here, North Americans rub shoulders with local sightseers.

Lorne Tepperman

THE END OF HISTORY?

Predicting the future in a time of such momentous changes as we are experiencing now is a difficult task. Perhaps for this reason, some have proclaimed "the end of history."

There can be little doubt that we have entered a new phase of history with the fall of communism. Industrial bourgeois civilization seems to have won the day. But, according to Lash and Urry (1987), "modern" or "organized" capitalism has given way to "late capitalism," an unpredictable form with a few main properties.

First, late capitalism is *decentralized*. Increasingly, industrial, commercial and banking enterprises are multinational and oriented to a world market. Manufacturing is decentralized, with work sites spread around the world. Proletarian jobs are exported from the old industrial world to the Third World. Decentralization also means a decline in the size and importance of industrial cities. Work itself decentralizes, with average plant sizes becoming smaller. One consequence is a decline in the importance of national unions. Collective bargaining declines at the national level and increases at the company and plant levels. In general, nations and nation-level groupings (e.g., national elites) lose importance.

Second, traditional beliefs in science, modernity and nationalism come increasingly under attack. This skepticism about reason and progress often goes under the name of "post-modernity." In the past, most left-wing movements were based on a world-view (historical or scientific materialism, and a belief in progress and human betterment) that is collapsing all around us. Today the Left is changing its focus from economic to ethical (or human rights) concerns, from a belief in revolution to a belief in democracy, from involvement in the state to involvement in social movements, and from "vanguard" to grass-roots movements (Touraine and McDonald, 1991).

Throughout Europe, the past 30 years have seen a flowering of social movements. They include counterculture, antiwar, student, feminist, environmental, antinuclear and peace movements among others. At the same time, social-ist movements have lost their former power to win people's support.

The new movements rely on decentralized and grass-roots support and focus on ecological issues and (individual) empowerment, not economic issues (Brandt, 1986). Often, they express new social values and demand new social and cultural rights for minority groups. No longer is the character of a movement decided by its relationship to the state or political parties (Touraine, 1992).

"Real socialism" as it existed in Eastern Europe, included one-party rule, state domination and a culture based on an official ideology. Some (for exam-ple, Markovic, 1990) believe that real socialism has little in common with Karl Marx's theoretical ideas. As a result, they believe the failure of real socialism does not necessarily herald the end of Marx's vision.

Maybe so, but it is not clear what the next step ought to be. Aronowitz (1990), for one, sees radical democracy and a critique of bourgeois ideology ("work as ethics") as the key to a socialist reform of democratic Eastern European societies.

In the West, our whole conception of "modernity", and with that our idea of forward movement, is in confusion. What we have traditionally meant by the term "modern" is a social order characterized by capitalism, industrialism and democracy (Feher and Heller, 1983). With the collapse of communism, it has become evident that there is a wide variation among "modern" societies and among societies that are *not* modern.

Finally, many herald the growth of ecological consciousness. Increasingly, the future of human history depends on the ecological future of the planet. We are reminded time and again of the social and environmental costs of economic growth. We cannot continue to ignore the ecologically destructive effects of business (Leipert, 1986). Nor can people go much farther without resolving the built-in conflict between (disposable) consumer culture and traditional values, arts and ways of life (Chakrabarty, 1992).

In the end, humanity will need to evolve into a race of "sustainable people." These are people who can keep the planet alive because they possess the ability to renounce present gains in favour of people who are yet unborn. "Sustainable people" also have adequate and relevant knowledge about the problems nearby, feel a moral and aesthetic commitment to humanity and the earth, and believe that humanity must take control over its own future (Doob, 1991).

To survive, humanity will also have to turn its back on the mass-produced brutality that has characterized social and political conflict in the 20th century (see Exhibit 11.5.)

THE MACRO/MICRO CONNECTION

We have just noted some of the many concerns people have about the future. They include macro-level concerns about global conflict, technological dis-placement, imperialism and environmental destruction. Indeed, much of this chapter has been about macro-level conflicts and changes, and we should not lose sight of the corresponding micro-processes. By way of an example, consider the social role of optimism and courage (versus pessimism and fear). Both are causes and consequences of social change.

Optimism varies from one country to another for reasons that we do not yet fully understand. By international standards, Canadians are fairly op-timistic: they want and expect to be happy, and they expect their lives to go smoothly.

EXHIBIT 11.5   *Victims give testimony from the grave*

In 1982, two U.S. journalists reported that more than 800 civilians, most of them children, had been brutally killed by the Salvadorean army in a remote corner of El Salvador. The massacre was denied by the Salvadorean government and their U.S. military backers, and until last year few people believed the journalists.

Then a team of young Argentine forensic experts unearthed the horrible truth about what has become known as the El Mozote massacre. Skeletons and crushed bones found centimetres below the surface of the ground indicated the village had suffered the bloodiest and most savage attack in El Salvador's 12-year civil war. The forensic findings formed the basis of the 1993 United Nations-sponsored Truth Commission Report, which outlines in scientific detail El Salvador's nightmarish past.

The UN response marked a triumph for the Argentine Forensic Anthropology Team, the group responsible for the Mozote exhumation. . . .

Using techniques originally developed for excavating and analyzing ancient burial sites, the group formed to find and identify the victims of Argentina's 1976-'83 Dirty War against leftists. During the late seventies, Argentina's military regime "disappeared" some 9,000 people. When democracy returned to the country in 1983, skeletons of the victims had to be exhumed for evidence in trials against high-ranking members of the military junta who ordered the killings. . . .

The federal government set up a National Commission on the Disappeared in 1983. But much of the work on the skeletal remains by Argentine specialists was lacking because forensic experts usually had experience dealing only with cadavers and didn't know how to analyze bones. . . .

Identifying the remains of victims of violence is painstaking work. The team is still exhuming 348 bodies found in a mass grave in the Avallenada Cemetery on the outskirts of Buenos Aires. In the last decade, only the remains of 60 people from this site have been identified. . .

The restoration of a skull is particularly important. According to military documents, most of the disappeared leftists in Argentina were shot in "armed struggle." However, the team's findings indicate that most were executed with a bullet to the back of the head. . . .

. . . [A]n amnesty for crimes committed during the military period prevents former junta members from being prosecuted. Immunity for military crimes exists in just about every Latin American country where the military abused human rights.

Despite the impossibility of seeing the guilty punished, [anthropologist Luis] Fondebrider and his team are undaunted. "There is no official justice in Argentina," he says. "So why do we continue working? We have a responsibility to the families of the disappeared. It's torture for them not to know how their loved ones died."

Source: "Victims give testimony from the grave," *The Globe and Mail*, Sat., Feb. 12, 1994, p. D8.

Some people are even more optimistic than Canadians. Gallup polls conducted in 30 countries during the 1980s (Michalos, 1988) asked people "So far as you are concerned, do you think that [next year] will be better or worse than [the year just ending]?". By this measure, the world's greatest optimists turn out to live in Argentina, Greece, Korea, and the United States, where more than half the respondents expect that the next year would be better.

Along with Chileans and South African whites, Canadians rank just above the world's average on optimism, with 35 to 39 percent saying that next year would be better. On the other hand Canadians are twice as likely to express optimism as Germans, Austrians, and Belgians, for example.

Optimism is much influenced by changes in the economy and society. For this reason, with the weakening of Canada's economy, Canadian optimism has slipped in the last few years. Between 1984 and 1993, annual Decima/Maclean's opinion polls saw the percentage of Canadians saying they were optimistic about their economic future drop from 79% to 71% (Maclean's, January 3, 1994: 24), for example.

The same poll (Macleans, January 4, 1993: 42) found just over a quarter of Canadian adults saying they were pessimistic or very pessimistic about their personal economic situation. As well, over half believed the generation of Canadians being born now will be worse off than their parents. Fewer than one respondent in five believed the new generation would be better off (*op. cit.*: 44).

A recent poll on this topic (*Maclean's*, January 3, 1994: 32) finds 51% of respondents saying they are more pessimistic about the future than they were a decade ago, compared with only 32% who say they are more optimistic.

This change shows how macro-sociological events — for example, the continuing recession and fear of unemployment — produce micro-sociological results. These results include a drop in people's confidence in themselves, their lives and even the future of the country. Micro-events, such as a loss of optimism and confidence, also translate into macro-processes. For example, people who lack optimism and confidence are less likely to spend their money. This has the effect of *worsening* the economic recession and the problem of unemployment.

Pessimistic people are also more fearful that immigration will take away their jobs. As a result, there is a widespread desire to limit immigration, and this desire helped the election of Reform Party candidates in the 1993 federal election. At the same time, fears about unemployment strain ethnic and racial relations.

In general then, a worsening of the economy (a macro-event) reduces optimism and confidence (a micro-event in millions of homes and offices). This, in turn, worsens the economy still more and may also have political, legal and social effects on immigration and group relations (all macro-events). As you can see, it is impossible to understand politics, protest and change without understanding how the macro- and micro- levels of these processes influence one another.

CLOSING REMARKS

The sociological study of politics, protest and change offers yet another prime illustration of the connection between macro- and micro- perspectives.

As a macro- phenomenon, politics exists outside and "above" individual people; in their laws, political institutions and traditional voting practices. In this sense, the political structure of a society is very slow changing. Political parties last for generations. Rules of order, constitutions, and administrative procedures can last for centuries. The main elements of a polity outlast individuals and even generations of individuals.

On the other hand, politics is the pursuit of individual or collective goals. We all participate in one or another kind of politics, and many of us are active in electoral politics, as campaigners, contributors and informed voters. As such we can sometimes effect rapid and significant changes. Who would have bet on the immense electoral success of the Reform Party and the Bloc Quebecois in the federal elections of 1993. Or of the Ontario NDP in 1991?

Politics is something we all change or reproduce every day. Often we cannot even see the immense changes we are about to create, because they are occurring so quietly, so subtly, so gradually in millions of homes, then thousands of polling booths.

How do we know about these subtle, gradual and (often) *private* changes that culminate in momentous *public* changes? We know about them through social research, the topic of the next chapter. Finally, then, it is time to discuss the ways sociologists make and test their theories.

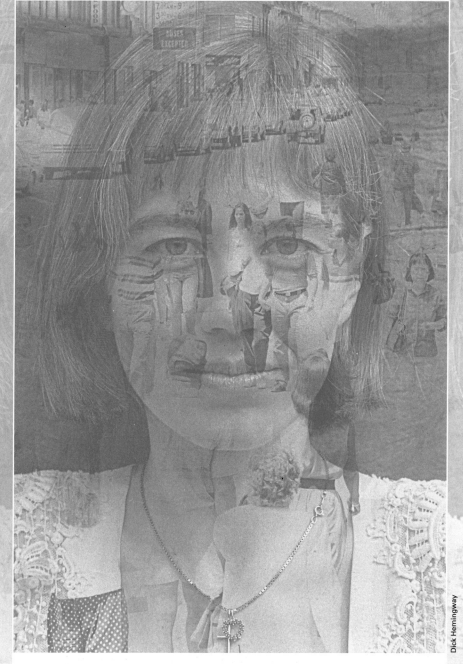

Dick Hemingway

Ultimately, all science is about causes and effects.

METHODS OF RESEARCH

SCIENTIFIC RESEARCH IS RIGOROUS AND OBJECTIVE

We began this book by noting that everyone is a sociologist of a kind. All of us use common sense to understand the social world in which we live, the behaviour of other people, and the events taking place around us. For this reason, much of what we have discussed in this book may have seemed familiar to you.

Almost certainly, you will have discovered for yourself some of what we have said about family life, culture, conformity, work, inequality, and so on. Often, you will have made your "discoveries" when experiencing personal troubles. You may have even found out for yourself that personal troubles are the other side of public issues — just as we have been saying throughout the book.

Personal experiences help to persuade us of the truth of many sociological findings; but they are no substitute for research. We cannot create sociology simply by living. That is because much of what goes on around us is neither obvious nor easily explained. What's more, personal experiences and emotions hide as much from us as they reveal, because we are so wrapped up in certain ways of seeing things.

So, understanding social life requires more than experience in living. It requires careful research; and fortunately, everyone is used to doing research in their own lives. For example, think about how we go about finding the lowest price on a new car: we do research. Research is nothing more than carefully and systematically asking and answering questions. Because of this, a lot of what we shall discuss in this chapter of the book will be familiar to you from your own experience. But be warned, much of it will not.

Scientific research differs in many ways from the everyday research with which we are all familiar, and one particularly important difference has to do with standards. In scientific research, other people — the scientific community — set the standards. This means that either we must make use of accepted and tested methods or we must make a convincing argument why we should not. It also means that our research will have to be as objective and rigorous as possible if others are to accept its findings as valid.

BASIC IDEAS OF SOCIAL RESEARCH

Most social research tries to answer the question "Why?". Why are some people poorer than others? Why do racial groups come into conflict? Why do so many people from small towns move to large cities? Why has the Canadian divorce rate risen in the last 25 years? Why are some societies more democratic than others?

Cause and effect

To answer the question "Why?" is to find the cause of an effect. We can restate the first question above as follows: What causes some people to be poorer than others? Restated this way, each question asks about an "effect" — poverty, racial conflict, migration, divorce, and democracy, respectively. An *effect* is something brought about by a cause.

Explanation and prediction

In trying to find the causes of observed effects, social research aims at explanation. Formally defined, an explanation is something that gives reasons for or interprets something else. Take the question about poverty: Why are some people poorer than other people? In the process of looking for an explanation we make informed guesses or suggest probable explanations, called hypotheses, which we then test with data. (You will recall from Chapter 1 that a hypothesis is a proposition or tentative statement about the relationship between a specific cause X and its effect Y that we can test through research.)

Many sociological researchers have shown that some people are poorer than others because they have not received enough formal education to get a well-paying job (Blau and Duncan, 1967; Boyd et al., 1985). It may be that they failed to learn crucial facts and skills, or perhaps they have learned these but lack the necessary piece of paper, or "credential."

Our operational definition of education is the number of years spent in the school system. X is the level of education a person has received and Y is that person's income. If our hypothesis is correct, the higher the level of education a person gets, the higher his or her income should be. We can now examine the data to verify the hypothesis — that is, test it with facts. If the data show that people with more education always earn a higher income than people with less education, then we have come part of the way towards an explanation.

However, explanation does not end when we show a connection between X and Y. We must also understand the reasons for that connection: *why* more education leads to higher earnings. Without understanding the process, we have only gained an ability to predict Y from X. **Prediction** is the act of forecasting an outcome. In predicting, we infer the outcome of an event or series of events from scientific — especially statistical — analyses of known events.

For example, you ask me to guess whether Frank earns more money than Alexander. I ask how much education each has completed. You tell me Frank completed Grade 12 and Alexander only completed Grade 9. Remembering my hypothesis that higher education usually means higher earnings, I predict that Frank earns more. If the hypothesis is valid, other things being equal, my prediction will be right.

Unfortunately for sociologists, the real world is more complicated than that. In social research, we almost never find an X that always causes Y or a Y that always results from X. Most of the processes sociologists study are multi-causal and conditional. By *multi-causal*, we mean that many Xs combine in complicated ways to produce a single Y. By *conditional*, we mean that a particular X will cause Y under some conditions but not others.

The relationship between education and earning power is a case in point. Education is not the only factor to influence earnings. Many others — gender, race, region of the country, even physical appearance — also affect how much money a person makes.

As well, education has more influence on earnings in some kinds of work than others. Consider two people making hamburgers at a fast food outlet. One has a grade 9 education, the other a grade 12 education. They are doing the same job and earning exactly the same amount of money, so education has no effect on earnings in this case. The effect of higher education is greatest when it allows a person to enter a restricted line of work — such as a skilled trade, a profession, or a managerial position — that pays higher-than-average wages. The "returns to education," or the amount of income an additional year's education will bring, vary from one sector of the economy to another.

For these reasons, it is not easy to predict something as simple as how much money a person will earn. It is even harder to *explain* an observed result. To explain something well means understanding the entire process that ties X and Y together.

Social scientific versus other explanations

Social scientists go about answering the question "why" differently from other people. Take the topic of suicide. Most of you are probably familiar with Shakespeare's play, *Hamlet*. In that play, one character — Ophelia — kills herself, and another character — Hamlet, Prince of Denmark — thinks about killing himself. In fact, Hamlet's famous soliloquy (see Exhibit 12.1) is about what goes on inside the mind of a person who is thinking of committing suicide. This soliloquy contains Shakespeare's "theory" about why people do, or do not, kill themselves.

It is not surprising that Shakespeare, a wise and eloquent poet, has a theory about suicide. In fact, every writer has theories about why people act the ways they do. But it's hard to tell what Shakespeare's theory is, because his statement of the theory is not explicit. What's more, Shakespeare makes no effort to test whether the theory is valid or not.

On the other hand, the sociologist Emile Durkheim, a much less skilful writer, makes every effort to state *his theory* about suicide in a way that is explicit, clear and testable. Then, he tests his theory with data. And unlike Shakespeare, Durkheim pays no attention at all to what is in people's minds when they kill themselves: he doesn't think he can get good data on that matter. So Durkheim's book, *Suicide*, is about the conditions under which people generally do, or do not, kill themselves.

In his study of suicide, Durkheim theorizes that two factors — social isolation and a breakdown of social norms — increase the chance of a person killing him- or herself. Using data, he sets out to explain variations in recorded suicide rates in a variety of countries.

To test his theory, Durkheim has to construct "operational definitions" for his concepts of cause and effect. Specifically, he must measure "suicide", "so-

EXHIBIT 12.1 *Shakespeare's Theory of Suicide*

Ham. To be, or not to be: that is the question:
Whether 'tis nobler in the mind to suffer
The slings and arrows of outrageous fortune,
Or to take arms against a sea of troubles,
And by opposing end them? To die; to sleep:
No more; and by a sleep to say we end
The heart-ache and the thousand natural shocks
That flesh is heir to, 'tis a consummation
Devoutly to be wish'd. To die, to sleep;
To sleep; perchance to dream; ay, there's the rub;
For in that sleep of death what dreams may come
When we have shuffled off this mortal coil,
Must give us pause: there's the respect
That makes calamity of so long life;
For who would bear the whips and scorns of time,
The oppressor's wrong, the proud man's contumely,
The pangs of despised love, the law's delay,
The insolence of office and the spurns

That patient merit of the unworthy takes,
When he himself might his quietus make
With a bare bodkin? who would fardels bear,
To grunt and sweat under a weary life,
But that the dread of something after death,
The undiscover'd country from whose bourn
No traveller returns, puzzles the will
And makes us rather bear those ills we have
Than fly to others that we know not of?
Thus conscience does make cowards of us all;
And thus the native hue of resolution
Is sicklied o'er with the pale cast of thought,
And enterprises of great pith and moment
With this regard their currents turn awry,
And lose the name of action.

Source: The Complete Works of William Shakespeare, vol. 3, Toronto: Leland Publishing, 1950, pp. 98-100.

cial isolation" and "social regulation" in each of these countries. Among other things, he uses marital status to measure social isolation. Married people are considered "socially connected" while single, divorced or widowed people are considered "socially isolated." Thus, Durkheim hypothesizes that people who are single, widowed or divorced are more likely to commit suicide than married people — especially, married people with children.

He then examines data to verify his hypothesis, or test it with facts. If the data show that people with a spouse and children run a lower than average risk of suicide, Durkheim can conclude that the hypothesis is valid and the theory which produced that hypothesis is also valid. He will have come part of the way towards explaining suicide.

As you can see from this brief comparison, Shakespeare and Durkheim have very different ideas of what it means to "explain" something and, further, what use one might make of "evidence" in seeking an explanation. In short, Shakespeare is an artist and Durkheim is a scientist.

Variables and units of analysis

Researchers speak about Xs and Ys in a particular way, so it is worthwhile defining our terms before going further. Xs and Ys are variables. A **variable** is any trait, quality, or social characteristic that can vary in size or amount over time, across individual cases, or among different groups. Sociologists typically measure the variation in terms of *deviation*, a statistical measure of the degree to which a score varies from the mean, or group average.

Frank, Alexander, Sarah, and Monica — the people we study — are *units of analysis*: the units under investigation in a given piece of research.

The Y variable we are trying to explain and predict is the dependent variable. A *dependent variable*, such as income in the example above, is influenced, changed, or caused by the effect of other variables. An X variable, or *independent variable*, causes a change or variation in the dependent variable. The independent variable is the causal or explanatory variable. As already noted, a dependent variable can be influenced by many independent variables. As well, any independent variable can influence many dependent variables. So when we come to research a particular relationship—the relationship between education and earnings, for example — we are isolating one particular relationship in a vast network of possible Xs and Ys.

Qualitative and quantitative data

Data on amount of education and earnings are examples of quantitative data. They are based on precise measurements in recognizable units. We can say exactly, in dollars and cents, how much a person earns. We can say exactly, in years, grades, or degrees and diplomas, how much education a person has completed. What is more, everyone knows what dollars and grades are, so we can easily share and discuss our findings. With such quantitative data, it is easy to *replicate* a study another researcher has done — that is, do it the same way, in order to see if we get the same results. We know exactly what the earlier researcher was measuring, and how.

What's more, such precise and clearcut measures allow us to evaluate the results with powerful statistical methods. They permit us to judge whether our finding could have occurred by chance alone. Quantitative measures also let us compare the importance of different Xs which have an effect on Y. Finally, they let researchers create mathematical models for their theory. In short, quantitative measures allow sociology to do research that is like research in economics and the physical sciences.

However, much of what sociologists study cannot be easily quantified. For example, attempts to measure how happy people are show little variation in degree of happiness between men and women, and little variation from one part of the country to another. Is that uniformity a "real" social fact, or proof that we have not figured out how to measure happiness accurately?

Or take love, as another example. Consider how difficult it would be to measure precisely how much in love two people are. If we wanted to attach numbers to their "degree of loving," what questions should we ask? How can we operationally define "love?" How would we combine the answers to get an overall score? What are the measurement units? Unlike quantitative data, qualitative data do not easily lend themselves to precise measurement.

But they have other strengths. It would be easy to form a judgment about how much in love two people are. People typically display or indicate to one another — and to others — that they are in love. To do good qualitative research, what we need is a clear, detailed description of people's behaviour, including information from people about their own feelings. This usually involves observing people, talking to them, and trying to understand them.

Qualitative data are useful for exploring relationships and developing new theories. They certainly make for interesting accounts of everyday life. In short, we get a subtler, more complex picture of the relationship of the couple when we do *not* try to compress their feelings into a simple measurement. All research needs this sensitivity of understanding; some research cannot be done without it.

Good research, whether qualitative or quantitative, is persuasive and enlightening. But it is hard to do. It requires: careful planning; an ability to define a workable problem and to find a feasible approach that suits the problem; and systematic research.

DESIGNING A STUDY

Types of research design

Planning and carrying out research requires the preparation of a research design. A research design is an orderly plan for collecting, analyzing, and interpreting data. The design chosen will depend on the nature of the problem that is being studied. It will also depend on the time, money, and skill that are available.

We can do research on any question in a number of different ways; there is no one "right" way to do research. However, a good research design will match an interesting question with the skills and resources we actually have available.

Sometimes, we lack the resources to study what we want to study in an effective way. Consider the following example. Research has suggested that migrants are more dynamic and ambitious than the people they leave behind. This hypothesis makes sense: after all, emigration does carry risks, and taking risks required courage, energy, and ambition. So we have a theory that explains the hypothesis; now we need data to test whether the hypothesis is valid. How should we measure whether immigrants really are more ambitious and dynamic than average and whom should we measure? We shall consider questions of measurement a little later. For now, let us consider the second question: *whom* to measure.

The researcher realizes that in the time available it will be impossible to study all immigrants. She decides to study immigrants from Portugal who live in Montreal. She makes her decision on the grounds of convenience: it happens that she speaks Portuguese and lives in Montreal. That's fine for her, but do *we* have any reason to suppose that Portuguese immigrants in Montreal represent all immigrants living everywhere? Unless she can give us a satisfactory answer to that question, or define the question more narrowly, the researcher should not go any further with this project.

Suppose the researcher does go on. She has a test that measures, on a scale from 1 to 10, how dynamic and ambitious a person is. She tests 50 Portuguese immigrants in Montreal and finds they score an average 6.5 out of 10. Is this score high or low? Does it prove her hypothesis right or not? To answer this, she must compare their score with another group's. But which group is appropriate: (a) Canadian-born people of non-Portuguese ancestry; (b) Canadian-born people of Portuguese ancestry; or (c) people born and continuing to live in Portugal?

The answer is (c). The researcher needs to compare these Portuguese non-immigrants — the people who stayed behind — with Portuguese immigrants, to see whether they differ in their dynamism and ambition. If the immigrants score significantly higher, she has validated her hypothesis. If they score the same or lower than the non-immigrants, the data have defeated her hypothesis. The important point to note is that any data she collected from groups (a) and (b) are irrelevant. They cannot answer the question the researcher has posed.

In short, we should not try to answer this particular question unless we can go to Portugal to collect the data we need. If we cannot go to Portugal, we should answer another question or study another topic. There is no way to complete *this* project with data collected only in Canada. This is the kind of problem a researcher can, and should, anticipate when designing research.

Correlation is not causation. Indeed, sociologists often wonder about the connection between them. For example, should insurance companies deny driver's insurance to people attitudinal data reveal to be accident-prone?

Canapress Photo Service/Bill Herriot

Experiments and quasi-experiments

Most scientists mean something more specific by the term "research design." Typically, they mean the decision to test a hypothesis with an experiment, quasi-experiment, correlational analysis, or single-case analysis. We shall consider each of these designs in turn, and show that each can bring particular insights to our research.

An **experiment** is a research method designed to investigate the effect of one variable on another. The experiment takes place under well-controlled, carefully regulated conditions, in an artificial setting, usually a laboratory. In brief, the experimenter introduces the independent variable, then observes and measures its effect on the dependent variable.

The experimental method allows the researcher to control any factors that might influence the phenomenon under study. One of the ways of controlling variables is by assigning each subject to one of two groups — an experimental group and a control group — in an unbiased way: either by random assignment or careful matching. The *experimental* group is exposed to the effects of the independent variable introduced by the researcher. The *control group* may be closely matched to the experimental group, and contains the same mix of ages, genders, educational levels, and so on. The experimenter does not expose control subjects to the independent variable whose effects he or she is studying.

Often sociologists argue that the experimental method is artificial: it is hard to imagine a real-life situation similar to the experimental ones research subjects usually find themselves in. For this reason, they prefer a research design that is more natural: for example, a quasi-experiment. A *quasi-experiment* modifies the experimental design, to study a problem that does not lend itself readily or naturally to an experiment.

Like an experiment, the quasi-experiment uses experimental and control groups, and compares people's behaviours before and after the experimental group receives their special treatment. However, the quasi-experiment does not randomly select or match experimental and control group subjects. Nor can it control other changes in the environment.

Consider the following example. Research has shown that delinquent behaviour often accompanies stress within a child's family. This has led to a number of quasi-experiments — sometimes called demonstration projects — that test the effects of direct state intervention on the families of juvenile delinquents. The experimental treatment is family-focused and the counselling programs are designed to treat youngsters as parts of their family units, rather than as isolated individuals. Services provided usually include family therapy, crisis intervention, and intensive counselling for the young offender and the family.

The results of these studies vary. For example, Baron and Feeney (1977) examined a Court Diversion Program in Sacramento (California) and reported that the program did help to reduce rates of recidivism. On the other hand, Urban and Rural Systems Associates (1975) found that the family-oriented program they studied reduced the number of minor offences (for example, curfew and liquor-law violations), but did not reduce the number of more serious offences (for example, running away from home and drug offences).

Substitutes for experiments

Neither the experiment nor the quasi-experiment is common in sociological research. Far more common is *correlational analysis*, a type of research design that measures the association between two phenomena — cross-sectional analysis — or associated changes in two phenomena — longitudinal analysis.

Consider the following example of a longitudinal analysis. A recent federal survey (whose results are described in *The Globe and Mail*, Wed. March 2, 1994, p. A1) "found no significant difference in the smoking rates of adolescents who had seen the Break Free television commercials and those who had not seen them." On the basis of these data, the federal government intends to discontinue its $8 million antismoking ad campaign, since it appears to have had no effect. There is no observed correlation between showing the ad, seeing the ad, and changing one's behaviour. Had there been a correlation, the government would have assumed the advertisements did reduce smoking and would have continued to show them.

In general, a *longitudinal study* involves gathering data from the same sample at intervals over time. It is a useful method for studying trends and the effects of particular changes. One form of longitudinal analysis, called a *panel study*, is the basis for Statistics Canada's monthly Labour Force Survey. Each month, Statistics Canada surveys a new batch of respondents and, also, some of the respondents it had surveyed the month before. In this way it can keep a running record of employment changes over time.

However, even panel studies are rare in sociology. There are problems with the initial selection of people, because most people do not want to commit themselves to repeated study. The group, or panel, may undergo changes as a result of being on the panel, and therefore becomes less representative of the general population. Most important, it costs a great deal of money to re-interview people after a lapse of time, especially if many of the original sample have died, moved away, or lost interest in the project, and must be tracked down.

More common is the *retrospective survey*, where respondents are asked to report what has happened to them in the last month, year, or other period. This method is used to collect valuable data about family life — as, for example, in the Family History Survey — and about work life — as in the Annual Work Pattern Survey.

Such research has produced interesting results that could not have been gained in another way. For example:

(1) At any given moment, the proportion of people who are cohabiting, or are single parents, is small. However, over a lifetime, a large proportion of the adult population passes through these statuses. Cohabitation and single parenthood prove to be brief but common experiences, not — as many believed — rare and semi-permanent ones. (See Burch, 1985; Moore, 1989).

(2) At any given moment, the proportion of people who are unemployed is large. However, until recently, unemployment was a brief and common experience for most. For a minority — the chronically unemployed — frequent and long-term unemployment occurs whenever the economy worsens. It is they who are pushed into poverty when jobs become scarce. What's more, we can identify who these high-risk people are (Shaw, 1985).

The most common research design in sociology is cross-sectional analysis. A *cross-sectional* study gathers evidence on subjects at just one point in time. The researcher tries to discover and explain the pattern of associations among variables. So, for example, the people in charge of Ontario's Lotto 6/49 lottery decided to do research to find out what lottery winners do with their winnings. (Presumably, knowing the answer would help the lottery organizers attract more ticket buyers.) As Exhibit 12.2 shows, the survey found most people don't let their new-found fortune change their lives: probably not what we would have guessed!

EXHIBIT 12.2 *Lotto winners lack imagination*

...A new study of lottery winners in Ontario shows that money doesn't necessarily change everything. In fact, many are afraid of what their instant riches might bring.

Only 9 per cent of those who have won at least $10,000 in Ontario's lotteries and the interprovincial 6/49 since January of 1991 say they have made any particular changes in their way of life. Even among winners of $500,000 or more, only 34 per cent used the windfall to change their careers or retire.

Surprisingly, only 32 per cent of all winners say they even took a vacation after collecting their cash. The study found that 87 per cent immediately put their loot into a bank, and 46 per cent shared it among family or friends.

Winners generally don't find fame or even publicity — only 28 per cent were even contacted by the media. But everybody loves a winner, and the survey found that 95 per cent of those who did speak to the press enjoyed "fair and courteous" treatment....

The bigger the prize, the more winners are tempted to "imagine the freedom," as the ads for Lotto 6/49 go.

Winners of prizes over $1-million do some dramatic things, said Melanie Kurzuk, spokeswoman for the Ontario Lottery Corp. One instant millionaire bought a resort on a remote Caribbean island. Another rushed off with his cheque and invested half of the $1-million in new equipment for his Ontario logging business....

About 82 per cent of Ontarians have played one of the province's nine lotteries or 6/49, and about 50 per cent buy in at least once a week. Just as many women buy tickets as men....

Source: Wallace Immen, "Money doesn't change everything," *The Globe and Mail*, Sun. Oct. 23, 1993, pp. A1, A6.

The problem with this kind of research is that it is difficult to sort out causes from effects, because the data give no clue about the time sequence. The researcher cannot know which variable changed first — presumably, it is the cause — and which changed next (and is therefore the effect). For example, did people *become* cautious with their money after winning the lottery, or do lotteries attract people who are (except for their tendency to buy lottery tickets) cautious with their money?

A related problem of "spuriousness" may arise: in cross-sectional analysis, it is more difficult to determine whether both the (supposed) cause and effect are, in fact, the result of a third factor researchers are failing to measure.

Despite these problems, cross-sectional analysis remains attractive because of its low cost and easy execution. The researcher has to collect data only once, which means he or she can afford to collect a lot of data at one time, instead of "thinner" data on several occasions. Consider the following example of a cross-sectional survey.

Common sense says that it is better to be rich than poor, famous than unknown, and powerful than powerless. But are high-income people really more satisfied with life, as lay-wisdom tells us? Research (Lane, 1993; Campbell, 1980; Atkinson, 1980) says "No; your income makes only a small difference in overall life satisfaction." Income does influence people's satisfaction with their financial situation. Not surprisingly, people with high incomes are more satisfied financially (with income, standard of living, and savings). However, it does not make people happier in other areas such as interpersonal relation-ships and self-development.

Most surveys find only a modest relationship between levels of income and overall life satisfaction. The belief that money can buy you happiness is, for the most part, a myth. After reviewing hundreds of cross-sectional surveys from around the world, Dutch sociologist Ruut Veenhoven (1984: 397) reports that "current beliefs on happiness are based on presupposition rather than on accumulated experience."

Veenhoven's efforts remind us that no single cross-sectional study can be conclusive. Testing a theory with cross-sectional data means finding support in many bodies of data and many past studies. Some of these studies may use other types of research design that will elicit other types of insights into the question. One such approach is the single case analysis.

Single case analysis

The study of a single case — whether a single person, a group or a society — has a great deal of appeal. *Single case analysis* is a type of research design that involves a detailed, in-depth examination of a single example of a class of phenomena. By getting to know a lot about that single case, we learn not only about the "why" of something, but also about the "how." That is, we learn more about the process by which a cause creates an effect.

Single case analysis is reasonably common in sociology, although less com-mon than in certain applied fields like clinical psychology, social work, and management studies. The reason sociologists shy away from it is because you cannot be certain that the case you have studied truly represents all of the cases you might have studied. So you run a great risk when you try to generalize from these findings to other cases.

The problem is simple to understand. Suppose you are a visitor from outer space. Your spacecraft crashes just outside 243 Fourteenth Avenue in Sometown, Canada and while you wait for the repair ship to arrive, you decide to study earthlings. Disguising yourself as a retired gentleman, you spend the day watch-ing and talking to the first human being you meet. You learn a lot about that per-son; but are you justified in telling your fellow space-creatures about humans in general? Not really. No one person you could have studied could stand in for the whole human race, because people vary in a great many ways.

One solution is to make a smaller claim for the truth value of what you have discovered. Instead of calling your work an explanatory, or theory-testing, project, you might be wiser to call it an exploratory, or theory-building, project.

Another solution is to see if the observed data conform to an already exist-ing theory. Take the case of Canadian smoking behaviour. In February 1994, Canada's federal government and Quebec's provincial government slashed the taxes on cigarettes, to combat cigarette smuggling. Shortly afterward, Ontario's government did the same. Statistics Canada reports that, the next month — March 1994 — there was a 62% increase in cigarette sales in Canada (*The Globe and Mail*, Wed. April 27, 1994, p. A1). Conversely, cigarette exports — the source of most smuggled cigarettes — fell 83% in the same month. However, Statistics Canada calculates that only about 30%, or half of the 62% rise in cigarette sales, was due to a switchover from smuggled to legal cigarettes.

What this suggests is that the tax cut on cigarettes had the expected effect of putting smugglers out of business. It may also have the *un*expected effect

of encouraging many more people to smoke, or smokers to each smoke more cigarettes. This finding — though tentative — is precisely what an economist
would have predicted: lower the price and you sell more cigarettes.

Yet another solution is to test the observed data — especially data as they
vary over time — against two or more competing theories. Robert Yin (1984) calls
this process "pattern matching." One theory will predict a certain sequence of
changes over time; another theory, a different sequence. The theory that matches
the observed sequence best is the (more) valid explanation. Yin (1984: 111) cites
research by Donald Campbell (1969) as one example of this strategy.

Campbell examined the effect of the 1955 reduction in Connecticut's speed
limit. There were claims that the reduction had led to a decline in the number
of fatalities and, in fact, there was a decline in the year following the change
in speed limit. But Campbell's research showed that over a ten-year period,
this decline was within the range of normal fluctuations in fatalities.

If the theory that a lowered speed limit lowered fatalities was valid, it
would have produced a large, one-time only decline immediately after the
speed limit came into effect. This did not happen: therefore, the theory was not
supported *by this single case*. However, we have no licence to generalize from
Connecticut to all jurisdictions, or from speed limits to other kinds of legislation
(for example, seat-belt or gun laws).

We are in a slightly stronger position if we conduct a type of single case analysis called deviant case analysis. *Deviant case analysis* is a research design that studies a single case that fails to conform to an expected pattern. By failing to support a
given hypothesis, the case forces us to revise and enrich the original hypothesis.

We start a deviant case analysis by conceding that there is truth to the theory we are testing. For example, recall our findings about the non-relationship
between income and happiness. For reasons already stated, we feel we need
more insight into this finding: particularly, to determine sequence, eliminate
spuriousness, and understand its human meaning. By "understanding its human
meaning," we mean that sociologists must practise *verstehen*, which we discussed in Chapter 1. That is, sociologists must put themselves in the shoes of the
people they are studying and try to see the world — make sense of the world
— just as they do. To do this, we select a deviant case for study.

We could start with a study that focused on a particular subpopulation,
such as the very rich or the very poor. For example, Diener, Horowitz, and
Emmons (1985) sampled people from *Forbes* business magazine's list of the
wealthiest Americans, and compared them with people selected randomly
from telephone directories. Those agreeing to participate completed a questionnaire about life concerns and life satisfaction.

In this survey, wealthy respondents prove to be happy a higher percentage
of the time, score significantly higher on two different life-satisfaction scales, and
report significantly lower levels of "negative affect" — that is, unhappiness.
Not all the wealthy are happy, of course; some are just as unhappy as the un-
happiest ordinary person sampled. Further, few respondents, whether wealthy
or ordinary, believe that money is a major source of happiness.

This research found that wealthy and ordinary people also differ in what sat-
isfies them. Wealthy respondents more often mention self-esteem and self-
actualization as sources of their satisfaction, while ordinary people more often
mention food, shelter, and other basic human needs and safety concerns as
sources of satisfaction.

In sum, this research challenges the conventional wisdom and shows that very rich people really are happier than everyone else. Perhaps that is because they never have to worry about the things the rest of us worry most about. Maybe it is because they can afford to concentrate their attentions on self-esteem and self-actualization much more than the rest of us. Still, we have little sense of the process of becoming and being happy: why the relationship between income and happiness that applies to 99 per cent of the population does not apply to the fabulously rich.

Here, the single case method of study would help. It encourages closely detailed work and a deep understanding. Consider, for example, historian Michael Bliss' long biography of Canada's first millionaire, Sir Joseph Wesley Flavelle (Bliss, 1985). Flavelle rose from humble origins to become exceptionally rich and powerful. What we learn from his biography is the great importance of Methodist religion in his life. Flavelle was actively involved with his church and carried his religious beliefs into all his secular activities. His religion not only encouraged him to participate in social and political activity, it gave him recognition for his good works and success.

Armed with this insight, we can consider a new theory for testing. The theory might run as follows: for most people, income has little effect on happiness. For people with a high income, money has a positive effect on happiness if they (a) see their income as a heavenly reward or proof of their merit, and (b) use their income to engage in socially gratifying (and religiously meaningful) activities. Stated otherwise, Scrooge was miserable not because he was rich but because he was socially isolated and irreligious (just as Dickens suggested!).

Note how much richer our understanding of the relationship between income and happiness becomes when we move from multiple case to single case analysis. People are no longer treated as "units of analysis" whose "variables" are manipulated: instead, they are complex systems of thought and action. Having said that, we have no more right to generalize our results from data on Flavelle than does the space creature we mentioned earlier. With deviant case analysis, we have enriched our theory and found new variables. We must

There are many sources of information, or data, about popular values and sentiments that permit sociologists to study causes and effects unobtrusively.

Dick Hemingway

study them more systematically with experimental, quasi-experimental, or correlational methods. With single case analysis we have only explored, not explained, happiness in a general sense.

MEASUREMENT

Good measurement is one of the most important — if not *the* most important — indicators of a mature science. If you cannot measure a variable well, you cannot hope to explain it, predict it, or make accurate theories about it. Therefore, it is critically important to know what distinguishes good measurement from bad measurement.

Measurement scales

Measurement is a process of finding the extent, size, or degree of something. Quantitative sociological research depends on its ability to measure things: the rate of suicide, the degree of integration of people into society, the level of satisfaction with life, and so on. Unfortunately, measurement is often difficult, especially when the variables to be measured are abstract concepts such as satisfaction, alienation, segregation, and inequality.

Measuring concepts well means, first, developing an operational definition of those concepts. An *operational definition* links the meaning of a concept to procedures for measuring it. An operational definition of intelligence, for example, would be the score obtained on a set of specific questions answered in specific ways. The IQ score reflects the method used to measure intelligence. There may be something else we mean by intelligence that is independent of the means we use to measure it but, without a specific measure, the concept cannot be used for quantitative research.

In order to measure particular traits and characteristics, we need to identify variables which can be scaled. **Scales** are systems of units arranged in steps or degrees, allowing the researcher to assign numbers to observed events or responses. After reducing them to number scores, the researcher can analyze response patterns to bring out whatever relationships exist among them. There are a number of ways in which this can be done.

One of the most common types of scales used by sociologists is a *nominal* or *categorical scale*. A nominal scale contains a set of categories that we cannot order from high to low, large to small. For example, to the question "What language do you speak at home?", people may answer English, French, German, Polish, Italian, Greek, and so on. A score on a nominal scale indicates the category into which a person falls. We would not say that speaking English gives one a higher or lower score than speaking Greek. The numbers we would assign to these scores would simply identify them and allow us to correlate language spoken with other social characteristics.

An *ordinal scale* contains categories that do range from high to low, so that movement along the scale indicates an increasing or decreasing size on some dimension. For example, eligible answers to the question "How often do you telephone your grandmother?" may include "very often," "occasionally," and "rarely." We know that "very often" is more than "occasionally" and that "occasionally" is more often than "rarely." This ordering, from high to low, is what characterizes an ordinal scale.

Like an ordinal scale, an *interval scale* contains categories that range from high to low. In the ordinal scale we cannot be certain of the distance between categories. We do not know if the person phoning his grandmother "very often" does so eight times as often as the person who phones his grandmother "occasionally," or if the person phoning his grandmother "occasionally" does so only twice as often as the person who phones "rarely." However, in an interval scale, the distances or intervals between neighbouring categories are the same.

Finally, a *ratio scale* has both characteristics of an interval scale — hierarchical ordering and equal distances between categories — and one more as well: an absolute zero point.

On an interval scale, respondents cannot indicate a complete absence of something: of work satisfaction or telephone calls to grandmother, for example. For some variables, no absolute zero exists. For example, no one has absolutely no intelligence, energy, or physical attractiveness. Judgments on these issues are always bound to be relative. However, in a great many cases, absolute zero does exist. You may have earned absolutely no dollars last month and telephoned your grandmother zero times last week. Maybe no one among the people you know will name you as their "best friend." Where an absolute zero does exist, it is better to use a ratio scale than any other.

Unobtrusive measures

Remember that research is a social enterprise. Even physicists, who study inanimate objects, realize that the act of measurement itself can disturb the thing being measured. As a result, researchers may never be able to get a truly accurate measure of something in its natural state. If this is true of atoms and molecules, imagine how serious the problem is when studying people. For this reason, it is often important that the measurement process itself be unobtrusive. An *unobtrusive measure* is one in which there is no interaction between the investigator and the people being studied. Because it does not require interaction, the responses of the people studied are not "reactive."

People are not only objects of sociological study, they are students of their own lives. People usually know when researchers are studying them. They judge the purpose and meaning of questions they are asked, and answer in ways that relate to the researcher's goals. In short, people play a role when they are aware of being studied. Occasionally, they give the researcher answers they think the researcher is looking for; or, they give the researcher the exact opposite, to shake the researcher up a bit. Often they think about things they have never considered before, and are transformed by the research process. In none of these cases is the respondent a passive object of study.

It is difficult for researchers to avoid or minimize such reactions from the people they study. It is far better to avoid the problem than to have to remedy it. That is where unobtrusive measures come in. Sociologists look for unobtrusive measures and often find them. They already exist in nature, if we are willing to look.

In their classic work on the topic, *Unobtrusive Measures*, Webb et al. (1966) discuss the strengths and weaknesses of several types of unobtrusive measure. One type is the "physical trace," the proof of erosion or accretion. A pathway worn through grass, over a carpet, or even on wood or stone shows where a great many people have been heading. By definition, the best-worn path is most popular; sociologists might want to find out why. Likewise, the largest line-up, the most graffiti on a wall, or pennies in a wishing well — these accretions show where the most people (or the most active people) are spending their time. Again, sociologists might want to find out why.

A second type of unobtrusive measure is the archival record, particularly any running record officially collected for public use. This includes records of births, deaths, and marriages; tax records, Census forms, court records, and records of Parliamentary debate. It also includes the mass media — television, newspapers, and books — and the arts. The problem with such data is that they were created for a reason other than research, at another time: their meaning is by no means always clear.

A third type of unobtrusive measure is offered by data that are usually kept private, such as sales records, institutional records, and personal documents (such as diaries, letters sent and received). Such data have often been used in inventive ways. However, they provide only partial evidence and need to be pieced together with a critical eye, if used at all. For example, it is not certain that what a person says in a suicide note really explains the suicide. Similarly, it is not certain that a rise in the sale of weight-reducing products or products to end smoking proves a growing popular concern with health, or with physical appearance in an aging population.

Other forms of unobtrusive research include the observation of external physical signs (beards, tattoos, clothing, expressive movements), physical locations (for example, clustering *versus* segregation), and the sampling of overheard conversation.

A recent piece of unobtrusive research examined garbage to find out the relationship between what people *said* they ate and what they *actually* ate. As Exhibit 12.3 shows, if you ask people what they eat, they tend to report healthy eating practices — for example, a lot of cottage cheese and not a lot of chips and candy. But if you check their garbage, you find there's a gap between what people say and what they do. The moral of this story: Be prepared to check the quality of your data in as many ways as you can afford to. (Also, wear a gas mask to the research site.)

Knowing if a measure is "good"

The first thing we must be concerned about when we measure something is to make sure that our procedures are appropriate for the question we are asking. Suppose we want to measure change in the number of "common law" marriages over time. Well, first of all, we have to be certain *we* know what we mean by "common law" marriage, then that our *respondents* know what we mean. Otherwise, an apparent change in the numbers may just show a change in what (1) we meant or (2) other people meant by the term — not a useful finding. To ensure we find out what we need to know, we need clear definitions and good measures based on these definitions.

For good research, a measure must be as complex as the idea, or concept, it is attempting to translate into practice. Unfortunately, there are many examples of research where the underlying concept is simple but the measurement is complex, or where the underlying concept is complex but the measurement is simple. Let's start with a case where we have simple ideas and simple measurements.

Simple concepts, simple measures

We can see this kind of match-up between simple concepts and simple measurements in the field of *demography*, or population studies. As we saw in Chapter 10, demography is concerned with three main things: births, deaths

EXHIBIT 12.3 *The Lean Cuisine Syndrome*

A phenomenon related to the Lean Cuisine Syndrome is the Surrogate Syndrome: People may provide inaccurate consumption reports about themselves, but if you ask them to describe the behavior of a family member or even a neighbor, they tend to squeal with chilling accuracy — especially when the behavior involved has a negative image. With respect to alcohol intake, for example, most people underreport their drinking by 40 to 60 percent; a surrogate in the same household who does not drink alcoholic beverages and who is asked to report on the habits of members of his family will get intake levels right to an accuracy of about 10 percent.

The Lean Cuisine Syndrome

	% Underreported		% Overreported
Sugar	94	Cottage Cheese	311
Chips/popcorn	81	Liver	200
Candy	80	Tuna	184
Bacon	80	Vegetable soup	94
Ice cream	63	Corn bread	72
Ham/lunch meats	57	Skim milk	57
Sausage	56	High-fibre cereal	55

Source: William Rathje and Cullen Murphy (1993) *Rubbish: The Archaeology of Garbage.* New York: Harper Collins Perennial, p. 71.

and migrations. In order to collect the basic data of demography, we only need a few simple facts about a person or group of people:

(1) in a particular period, were they alive or dead?
(2) if they were alive, where were they? That is, in what geographic location (for example, city, province, country).
(3) were they male or female?
(4) how old were they?

Often demographers will look at other variables that are a little bit harder to measure: for example, a person's educational level, ethnic group affiliation, or labour force participation. But by and large, the basic data of demography are age, sex, and location.

Still, there may be *some* difficulties in measuring these variables. For example, some people don't know how old they are, or they lie about their age. Other people are transsexual. Some people have no fixed address. But these people are the exceptions. Most of the time, we can ascertain a person's age, sex and location accurately.

What this means is that demographic data are much more accurate than most of the data we deal with in social science. And, because the concepts are simple and the measures are also simple and precise, we can easily test theories about births, deaths and migrations.

In fact, demography is one of the most scientific, and mathematical of the social sciences, in large part because it suffers from few measurement problems. That's because, when you can take the quality of your measurements for granted, you can devote all your time and effort to making and testing theories. Most social scientists can't do this. On the other hand, as we saw in Chapter

10, some demographic theories are overly simple. Largely, that is because they avoid using hard-to-measure variables like "family power."

Complex concepts, simple measures

Demography is exceptional, in that it has simple concepts and simple measures. Now let's look at another type of social science, which attempts to reduce complex concepts to simple measures. This is a common practice in political polling, where researchers are often trying to get a fix on "the mood of the public" or "the public's attitude toward government."

Now "public mood" and "public attitude" are vague, complex things and political pollsters know that. But they often measure things which appear clear, because the measure itself is simple, but which are actually unclear, because the underlying concept is complex.

Here's an example (Toronto Star, January 7, 1993: A9). The Gallup pollsters asked people the following question: "Out of every tax dollar that goes to the federal government in Ottawa, how many cents of each dollar would you say are wasted?" The average respondent said about 47 cents in every dollar were being wasted. The result has a certain obvious meaning: people are ticked off with the government. But when you start to analyze the responses, you see the problems. As one might expect, supporters of the Conservative Party — the party that was then in power — estimated the least amount of waste (about 37 cents per dollar, on average). Supporters of the Reform Party estimated the largest amount of waste (about 52 cents per dollar). But supporters of the Liberal, NDP and Bloc Quebecois parties fell in between at different amounts (46, 41 and 38 cents respectively). Why were their averages different from those of the Reform Party and different from one another?

We could continue picking this finding apart and identifying all sorts of variations in people's answers. But what this suggests is that a simple measurement often hides more than it reveals. Instead of directly measuring political values, attitudes and behaviours, it gives us a mysterious "fact" to decode. We do not even know what it is that people are reacting against; whether it is federal patronage, the civil service, the Prime Minister, or the general economic condition of Canada.

In short, we are stuck with a measure which is far too simple for the phenomenon we are trying to understand. We cannot make and test good theories so long as our measurements are too simple for the concepts they are representing.

Simple concepts, complex measures

Now consider the opposite situation: the concept is simple but the measurements are complex. We find this in marketing research, where investigators want to get a precise measure of people's attitudes towards certain products. They want precision because hundreds of millions of dollars are riding on the development and marketing of these products, so errors are costly.

Consider two marketing research studies that were done to compare different ways of measuring the same, simple concept; namely, how much do you like a certain product? In a study by Haley and Case (1979), respondents were asked to rate six leading brands in each of six categories of product — toothpaste, cola, analgesics (pain killers), toilet soap, coffee, and detergent — using *13* different methods of rating.

For example, they were asked to rate (1) how acceptable the product was; (2) whether they would, or did, buy it; (3) how good they thought it was; (4) how the product compared with each of the other products in the category; (5) whether it would be rated as first choice, second choice, third choice, and so on.

Haley and Case showed that certain groups of measures produce similar results, while other measures do not. Some measures are better than others at revealing people's willingness to distinguish between brands of pain-killer, or brands of toothpaste, for example. On the other hand, some measures make it seem that people have much stronger brand preferences than they really do.

In another study, Axelrod (1968; reprinted, 1982), tested ten different methods of measuring people's liking for a product; many of these methods overlapped with the methods Haley and Case used. Axelrod found that some measures of product acceptance are much better at predicting whether a person will actually buy the product than are other measures. For example, suppose you say this to the respondent:

 If you were to go out shopping right now for [product class, for example, tooth paste], what brand do you think you would buy? If that were not available, what brand would you be most likely to consider as a substitute for the one you wanted?

Brands that are mentioned first as choices turn out to be, more often than not, the brands people will actually buy. But for the degree of benefit obtained, this is precision overkill.

Market research shows, as clearly as any work organization, the degree to which all of our commercial activities have been influenced by science and the industrial revolution. All industries must *appear* to be scientific and effective, especially if there is no way of being sure that the strategies they are using are actually the best for selling a product.

Complex concepts, complex measures

Now, let's consider the most usual case in sociology. We can find a prime example in research on "marital adjustment." As Miller says in his book on measurement (1991), marital adjustment is "a process, the outcome of which is determined by the degree of: (a) troublesome marital differences; (b) interspousal tensions and personal anxiety; (c) marital satisfaction; (d) dyadic cohesion; and (e) consensus on matters of importance to marital functioning."

One commonly used measure in marital research is the "dyadic adjustment scale," or DAS, developed by Spanier and Filsinger. It contains 37 questions, which tap all five of the dimensions of marital adjustment we mentioned above. To develop this scale, the researchers tested 300 questions, or "items," on hundreds of respondents, then threw away the questions that were redundant or did not work.

Since it was developed, the DAS has been used in a variety of studies, with generally good results. But, as in most sociological research, we are still at the stage of perfecting our measurements. We are far from having powerful and consistent theories about why some marriages "succeed" and other marriages fail. In large part, that's because we are still developing complex measures that are suited to complex concepts.

To reiterate, measuring well is difficult yet crucially important. In the end, you have to be able to trust the data. As Exhibit 12.4 shows, people's careers — even their lives — may hang on meeting their (measured) quotas.

SAMPLING

Surveys and sampling

Accurate data are the essence of good social science. To get them we need appropriate measures; we also need good trustworthy samples. As we have seen, there are many ways to measure things in sociological research, yet no matter how you choose to measure something, you cannot expect to measure it for everyone. The population of Canada, let alone the population of the world, is too large. This is why researchers study samples of people, not entire populations.

A **population** is the set of all people who share a specific characteristic of interest to the researcher; for example, they may all be Canadians or they may be Canadians who are over 45, speak Chinese at home, play bridge for recreation, or drive sports cars. We define a population in relation to the specific research question we want to answer. Every research project may imply a different population.

A sample is a relatively small number of people drawn from the population of interest. Almost all research studies samples, not total populations. Pure research by academic sociologists, market research, political polls, labour market surveys by government — all use samples which may represent one percent of the population under study, or even less.

Even with a sample that comprises only a small percentage of the total population, great accuracy is possible. Estimates of the total population characteristics based on a small sample are no more than a few percentage points off in 19 times out of 20, if the sample is drawn correctly. Thus, samples are accurate enough for most purposes, as well as being convenient and cheap.

The only time that sampling is *not* used in social research is when complete enumeration is necessary and cost is no consideration. In practice, this occurs in only one case: a national Census of Canada, carried out on the total population once every ten years. However, for reasons of cost, the Census asks each household member only a few questions. A 20% sample of the population that is questioned in more detail at the same time yields more complete and sociologically interesting information.

Yet even when Statistics Canada tries to survey the whole population of Canada, as in the Census, many people are missed: possibly five or ten percent of the population. The Census most often misses fugitives, transients, illiterates, and people living in other people's households. In short, a Census misses the poorest, youngest, and least educated part of the Canadian population.

Another reason to sample instead of studying an entire population is to avoid "contaminating" the pool of respondents. Every time we study a person, we risk changing his or her thoughts and behaviour. For many reasons, it is better to study people who have not been studied previously. However, the more surveys researchers conduct, and the more people they study, the harder it becomes to find people to study who have been untouched by research.

EXHIBIT 12.4 *In China, central planners decide just about everything!*

. . . Beijing may be completing 15 years of capitalist-style reforms, but it hasn't given up the ghost of central planning. Stalinist-style quota fever has infected virtually every aspect of life here, the result of a cultural obsession with numbers, a bureaucratic urge to quantify and a Communist desire to control every aspect of life.

What other system has at least three words for quota? Or a vice-mayor in a city of 11 million in charge of quotas for six kinds of unnatural deaths?...

Each year the vice-mayor in charge of drownings issues a quota, said Mr. Sun, who is the head of the Beijing office of swimming safety. The number is then divided among Beijing's 18 districts and counties, depending on their population and number of swimming pools, canals and lakes.

There were too many drownings this year, he said, because officials were preoccupied with staging the Seventh National Games. To meet next year's quota, Mr. Sun said, new safety rules have been approved. District and county chiefs who exceeded their quotas face reduced bonuses and public criticism sessions. And starting Jan. 1, Mr. Sun will levy a fine for each drowning on the administrators of the swimming pool or lake where it occurred.

While Canadian institutions have affirmative-action quotas for minorities, women and disabled people, there are quotas here for drug dealers, Communist Party members and rightists. During the 1957 anti-rightist movement, Mao estimated that China had 4,000 "bourgeois rightists." But enthusiasm for fulfilling the quota for reducing that number sent more than 500,000 people to labour camps and jail, some for as long as 20 years....

Quotas can be a matter of life and death. In 1988, Deng ordered a nation-wide crackdown during an anti-crime campaign. To meet their quota, police in Changping county, just north of Beijing, summarily tried and executed several dozen people. The condemned were given three days to appeal. The normal appeal time is at least two weeks. . . .

Quotas also can be mundane. The number of people who move to Beijing is set by quota. So is the number of cars a Chinese organization can have. (One for every three senior government officials at the bureau level or higher.) Quotas also limit the number of college students sent abroad, and the number of primary students flunked each year. Anhui province recently set its failure quota at zero — no child can repeat a grade next year, apparently for budget reasons....

Source: Jan Wong, "What's a man to do when drownings exceed quotas?" *The Globe and Mail*, Thurs. Dec. 16, 1993, pp. A1, A10.

Types of samples

Of the many ways to draw a sample of the population, some are better than others. The question to be answered will determine the best sample type. The cost and time available determine the feasibility of using one sampling method instead of another.

The simplest type of sample is a *convenience (or availability) sample*. People who are accessible or willing to participate in the survey make up the sample. Interviewers station themselves in a public place — a busy street-corner, an airport waiting room, a museum lobby or large shopping centre, for example — and ask everyone who passes to answer a few questions. A convenience sample may fairly well represent the population that passes through that public place. For this reason, a convenience sample is good for generating new ideas, trying out measurements, and getting preliminary research findings: for exploring the problem. But this kind of sample is never good enough to test a theory.

Another easy but imperfect method is to use a snowball sample. A **snowball sample** is made up of people referred to the researcher by others already in the sample. Think of a snowball rolling downhill, getting bigger as it goes; that is how a snowball sample grows.

The obvious advantage of a snowball sample is its ease and low cost. A less obvious advantage is its usefulness in finding rare or hidden subjects. Imagine trying to put together a sample of cocaine users, chess players, Gypsies, or parents of children with leukemia. It would be much easier to sample them through networks of similar people than by advertising in the newspaper, stopping people on a street corner, or telephoning names drawn at random from a phone book. Where researchers are studying illegal or deviant behaviour, an introduction to the potential subject by an existing subject may make all the difference between cooperation and a refusal.

However, as with the convenience sample, we cannot be sure a snowball sample really represents all members of the population. Sociologists will use a snowball sample cautiously and for purposes of exploration, not explanation.

A third type of sample is the quota sample. A *quota sample* begins by defining categories that are in the same proportion as one finds in the population, then draws a certain number of respondents within each category. Suppose we want to study attitudes toward a more traditional school curriculum. We know that the population of the school district is 51% male, 49% female; 25% Catholic and 75% Protestant; 90% native-born and 10% immigrant; and so on. To get our sample of 100 adult respondents, we will continue selecting available people until we have 100 with the same "statistical profile" as the population.

In some ways, this sampling method is much better than the pure convenience sample. For example, it is more likely than the convenience sample to yield a variety of characteristics and opinions. However, we have no guarantee that people sampled in this way accurately represent the opinions of the whole population.

To avoid unwanted biases, good surveys use randomly selected samples. Researchers draw *random samples* from the population so that every member has an equal chance of being selected for the survey. To draw a simple *random sample* at your college, we would start with a complete list of all the students. Blindfolded, we would draw names out of a hat until we had the number of names we needed. Or we would assign an identification number to every name and use a table of random numbers, or a computerized random number generator, to select the sample.

A *systematic sample* is just as good. If we need a sample of 100 people and there are 5000 students at your college, we would select our first respondent on the list randomly, then select every 50th name after that. Like the simple random sample, the systematic sample avoids introducing a bias into the selection process. Everyone has the same chance for an interview. However, in both cases, pure chance may fail to give us enough cases of a kind we need: enough graduating students, handicapped students, or students in a particular field of study, for example. To prevent this from happening, we would use a stratified sample procedure.

Stratified sampling divides the population into categories (or strata) according to a characteristic of interest — in this case, let's say field of study. In general, the stratifying variable should be a major independent variable in the study. Then the researcher samples randomly within each category, using either the simple random or systematic sampling method. Doing this ensures the researcher will get no fewer (or more) respondents in a given category than are to be found in the population; and these will have been chosen without bias. In effect, a stratified sample is an unbiased version of the quota sample we discussed earlier.

Finally, there is the *cluster sample*, which divides the population into geographic locales, then samples randomly within each locale. The cluster sample is like a stratified sample in which the stratifying characteristic is location. Like the stratified sample, it is relatively unbiased. However, once a researcher chooses locales for sampling, people outside those locales have no chance of being studied. Like the convenience sample, the cluster sample reduces the costs associated with distance and travel. It is particularly useful, then, if distances are large, as in a national survey. Smaller distances do not require cluster sampling or justify it.

DATA COLLECTION STRATEGIES

Have you considered just how difficult it is to collect reliable data? Without such data, you have no hope of testing your theories. And you have no hope of developing good social policies and programs, since these rest on good theories. Just think of the practical consequences.

For example, the data in Exhibit 12.5 illustrate the magnitude of this problem in relation to the "black market" — a growing concern of all governments. Our best estimate is that just under $700 million worth of jewellery in Canada is sold "under the table," to avoid taxation. If only we could find out if this is an *accurate* estimate; and determine who is doing this buying and selling and, from a theoretical perspective, "why." These sorts of issues are what we want to examine now.

Sociologists collect many different kinds of data and collect them in a variety of different ways. This section will briefly touch on five particular data collection strategies: secondary data analysis, participant observation, content analysis, interviewing, and questionnaires.

Secondary data analysis

Sociologists often collect data first-hand to answer a question they are posing. However, they often also use data other researchers have collected to answer other questions. *Secondary data analysis* examines and interprets data that have been gathered by another researcher or by the federal government. For a small cost, researchers can buy computer-readable tapes of data from the 1991 Census or the monthly Labour Force Survey, for example. Statistics Canada currently makes available hundreds of high quality data sets for both academic research and market research. Indeed, scholars outside government probably analyze government-collected data more thoroughly than does anyone else.

Secondary analysis of data collected by other academics is also common. Archives such as the one at York University (Toronto) enable scholars to share with one another the data they have collected. Given the enormous costs of collecting survey data, occasionally in the millions of dollars, such data sharing is sensible and desirable.

EXHIBIT 12.5 *Tax man faces tough task mining the underground*

Jewelry and home renovations are notorious for untaxed dealings among the businesses that Revenue Canada plans to attack in the $100-billion-a-year underground economy....

Yesterday, Revenue Canada said it plans to identify "non-filers and non-registrants" and take a number of steps to collect taxes from them, including working more closely with the provinces and industry groups.

Among the types of businesses singled out were: construction, jewelry, hospitality, home renovations, car repairs and other service sectors.

In jewelry, black market sales have reached near epidemic proportions. Of the $2-billion Canadians spend annually on gold, diamonds and the like, about one-third — nearly $700-million — is paid under the table to avoid taxes, according to the Canadian Jewellers Association. . . .

Jewelry trade is a problem because, while it is relatively easy to convince some retailers to accept cash in return for waiving taxes, it is also increasingly common for jewelry to enter the country illegally, Mr. Biss said. "We have a serious smuggling problem."

He believes cracking down on the underground bauble trade is a wrong-headed strategy. The association has been urging Ottawa to lift the 10-per-cent excise tax on jewelry that was imposed after the First World War, a move it argues would remove some of the incentive for black market purchases.

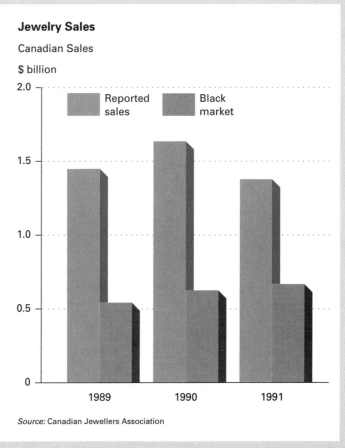

Jewelry Sales

Canadian Sales

$ billion

Source: Canadian Jewellers Association

The government might also benefit, he said, because excise tax revenue has been eroding steadily from a peak of $61-million in 1986-87 as more business has been forced underground. In 1991, the take was about $46-million. . . .

Source: John Heinzl, Patricia Lush and Timothy Pritchard, "Tax man faces tough task mining the underground," *The Globe and Mail*, Thurs. Nov. 25, 1993, pp. B1, B9.

The disadvantage of secondary data analysis is that these data were not collected with the researcher's goals in mind. For example, government-collected data rarely contain many of the variables that interest sociologists. Government data usually measure economic and demographic variables but shy away from data on people's feelings and attitudes. Government researchers avoid asking sensitive or intimate questions that might embarrass the Government if a Member of Parliament attacked a Statistics Canada survey in Parliament.

Participant observation

Observation has a longer history than any other form of social research. Since all of us can observe, it is also the easiest and least expensive form of research. But observation by itself can and usually does lead to distortions. We "read into" a situation more than might be there, or we fail to note subtle cues, gestures, or meanings we do not know enough to catch.

Because observation has so many limitations, sociologists make use of a particular variation known as participant observation to gain first-hand information on forms of social interaction and social processes. Participant observation is a method of gathering data that requires the sociologist to become a participant in the social group being studied. Because the researcher takes part in the activities of the group, he or she gains an insight into the subjective understandings of the group members.

The people being studied are usually unaware of being studied, and so they will behave in a typical, non-reactive manner. The participant observer might hang out with hustlers in bars (Prus and Sharper, 1977), go to synagogue with orthodox Jews (Shaffir, 1974), smoke marijuana with jazz musicians (Becker, 1963), befriend slum kids (Whyte, 1961), or work in a mental hospital (Goffman, 1961).

This research method assumes that researchers cannot understand a topic fully without intimately experiencing it first-hand. The method relies heavily on the skills, feelings, insights, and intuition of the researcher. Since his or her subjective understanding of the situation is critical, one cannot easily generalize the findings to other groups or to the population at large. Still, participant observation provides a useful alternative or supplement to survey research — which rarely includes observation of actual behaviour — and to experimental research — which observes behaviour in an artificial setting.

In participant observation, the sociologist acts as both object (i.e., participant) and subject (i.e., observer) of the research process. This double role causes conflict and confusion for the new researcher. It also runs a double risk of distorting the research. On one hand, by participating in the group, a researcher risks taking on the world-view of that group and losing an objective sense of what the group is doing. On the other hand, by observing the group while participating in it, the researcher risks changing the processes he or she has set out to study.

Like all activities — law, medicine, social work, journalism, and the ministry, for example — that require an intimate knowledge of people's lives, participant observation raises many ethical questions. How should the sociologist treat illegal behaviour, whether confessed or observed? How should the sociologist respond to vicious and immoral behaviour? How should the researcher deal with conflicts and coalitions within the group, and whose side should he or she take? There are no simple answers to these questions. That is why participant observation is much harder to learn and teach than any other type of research method.

Nevertheless, while participant observation is difficult, it has produced a significant legacy of excellent research. This particular research style was popularized among sociologists at the University of Chicago in the 1920s and came to be the method of choice for microsociologists such as symbolic interactionists. One microsociologist, Erving Goffman, produced such provocative and insightful research reports from his observations that his books remain among the best-selling sociology books to date (see, for example, Goffman 1959, 1961).

Content analysis

Content analysis involves analyzing the content of communications. They include private letters, books, speeches and conversations, scripts of TV shows, comic books, magazine articles, and popular songs. The researcher picks out the main themes and classifies them according to a predetermined set of categories.

Particular categories for classifying the data are chosen to illuminate the issues under study. For example, a researcher (Wilson, 1977) may study how women are stereotyped in magazine articles. Are they portrayed as less intelligent and more vain than men, or as sexual toys "created" for the pleasure of men? Answering these questions will mean classifying and analyzing the content of many articles in a consistent, systematic way.

Content analysis forces researchers to make judgments, both when drawing up lists of categories and when classifying the data according to those categories. Occasionally people classifying or *coding* the content will judge the material differently. For example, in analyzing the content of children's television programs, different coders may want to use different criteria for deciding what constitutes a "display of violence or aggression." The ways around this problem are, as always, preventive and remedial. To prevent the problem, the researcher must train the data coders thoroughly in how to use the coding scheme that has been devised. To remedy the problem, the researcher will check the consistency of the coded material: whether it shifts over time, and whether some coders are providing results that vary a great deal from the other coders' results. Badly flawed codework will have to be redone.

Interviews

The interview is another important method of gathering data in sociology. In an *interview*, an interviewer asks subjects questions in a face-to-face encounter or over the telephone. An interview may collect qualitative or quantitative data, and it may ask structured or unstructured questions.

A *structured interview* asks each respondent a standard set of questions in the same form and the same order. This type of interview often forces the respondent to choose from among predetermined choices. Questions may also be open-ended, allowing the respondent to answer in his or her own preferred way. An *unstructured interview* is more flexible than that. There are more open-ended questions the interviewee can answer freely. The interviewer often follows up on answers, to gain more insight into the interviewee's views and feelings.

Structured interviews permit the researcher to easily tabulate and analyze responses on a computer. Unstructured interviews provide data that are harder to compare across respondents. As well, unstructured interviews are particularly liable to errors resulting from poor interviewing skills. As with content analysis, these problems are more easily prevented than remedied afterwards. To prevent them, researchers must carefully select and train their interviewers and evaluate the material they are collecting as the research goes on.

Interviewing is a common and effective way of getting social information. Here a woman is collecting data from a convenience or availability sample.

Dick Hemingway

Questionnaires

Researchers often use *questionnaires* in surveys, too. They are sets of questions given to respondents and designed to provide answers to the central research question. Usually, questionnaires are sent by mail and filled out by the respondent without the assistance of an interviewer.

A questionnaire can be short — a few questions — or long — running to dozens or even hundreds of questions. The longer a questionnaire is, the less willing a respondent is to complete it or even begin filling it out. This fact encourages the researcher to make a questionnaire as short and appealing as possible, and to offer the respondent incentives for completing the questionnaire.

The researcher must avoid asking questions that are ambiguous or offensive, or that fail to permit a wide variety of responses. Ambiguous questions on a political attitude questionnaire might include "How much do you prefer Bouchard over Chretien because he is more charismatic?", or "Would you vote for the Reform Party if it supported free trade but opposed an increase in immigration?" Unambiguous questions will use familiar words and ask the respondent to make only one judgment at a time.

Even if great care is taken, questionnaires can offend respondents easily. Since getting and keeping cooperation is always a problem, the researcher must avoid offending respondents at all costs. Questions about personal income, intimate behaviour, religious beliefs, and relations with close relatives run the greatest risk of offending respondents.

Questions offering too narrow a range of answers are hard to avoid, since it is difficult to anticipate how widely people's views will vary. One way around this is by using open-ended questions. However, the answers to these questions must then be coded for analysis — a costly and error-prone procedure. Open-ended questions also slow down the rate at which respondents can answer, and therefore reduce their willingness to cooperate. The best way to prevent such problems is by pre-testing the questionnaire on people who are not part of the sample, and re-writing poor questions.

Some people are less willing to fill out a questionnaire than others. Even in a well-planned questionnaire survey, the response rate may fall well below 50%, meaning that half of the people that have been approached are refusing to participate. This forces us to ask whether the non-response is random or systematic. Response bias can seriously mar a study's validity.

The great advantage of collecting data by questionnaire is the low cost. In this way, a careful researcher can collect a lot of good-quality information for much less money than an interview study would cost. It is for this reason that sociologists have thought, learned, and written a great deal about questionnaire construction.

NON-SEXIST (NON-RACIST, NON-CLASSIST) RESEARCH

It is worthwhile, now that we are near the end of the book, to return to a theme that we stated at the very beginning. It is the importance but enormous difficulty of doing sociological research that is unbiased and value-free.

Bias in sociology is rarely the result of intentional falsehood or even sloppy work. More often than not, the problem derives from the peculiarity of sociologists. Most people in the world *are not* white, middle-class, middle-aged men with PhDs and secure, well-paying jobs. On the other hand, most sociologists still *are*. The typical academic sociologist who writes books and articles is an "insider" in the sense that he has a lot of insight into, and skill in the sociological analysis of, white, middle-class, Canadian society. In particular, he is interested in and good at studying how large public organizations (like colleges) work since, typically, he works in one. However, he is not quite so good at studying how households, small businesses, communities, intimate relations or informal groups work.

Now contrast this "insider" with someone we could call an "outsider." There are many kinds of outsiders and they are not all the same; in fact what they mainly have in common is that they are *not* insiders.

"Outsiders" include people who are non-white, non-male, non-middle-class, non-middle-aged, non-Canadian. Probably none of these outsiders has the same experience with, and perspective on, large public organizations as the typical male sociologist. But each is likely to have a variety of other valuable insights into such organizations. What's more, each is likely to have a better knowledge and understanding of private spaces, including households and small businesses, and of social inequality.

Each of these outsiders is a vulnerable member of Canadian society: in one way or another, a victim or potential victim of the way society is organized. In fact, "life on the outside" is characterized by uncertainty, dependency, prejudice, unfairness: it's not an Ivory Tower kind of existence. What this means is that people on the outside are bound to be critical of people who are on the inside, and sceptical of the ways they view and explain everyday life. They are likely to have very different views and explanations of everyday life.

Whether outsiders' views and explanations of "life on the inside" are more or less valid than the accounts provided by white, male professors may be debatable. What is much less debatable is their expertise about "life on the outside": for example, their understanding of sexual harassment, racial discrimination, living on welfare, going to prison, being unemployed, and so on. In short, outsiders are much more likely than insiders to have a good, intuitive sense of what the "outside experience" is all about.

Now consider where these ideas take us. The discrepancy between the characteristics, and everyday lives, of typical people and typical sociologists leads to three particular problems in the majority of sociological studies:

(1) an overemphasis on the sociology of "life on the inside," the conventional wisdom of sociology, or what we could call "insider views",

(2) a lack of scepticism about "life on the inside." Such research would benefit from what we might call "second opinions," critiques of insider views and/or outsiders writing about "the inside". For example, second opinions might include women analysing men's institutions (i.e., attitudes, behaviour, organizations), blacks analysing white people's institutions, poor people analysing middle-class institutions, and so on;

(3) a lack of understanding of "life on the outside." This problem would benefit from what we might call "social outsights," views provided by outsiders writing about the outside. For example, social outsights would include women analysing housework, black people analysing racial identity or black community organization, poor people analysing unemployment or "making ends meet."

From a research standpoint, making these changes would result in better, less biased and more revealing research. From a teaching standpoint, these changes would (1) undermine the idea that any single sociologist, especially an "insider", could possibly give the entire, true story of everyday life in Canada; (2) make clear that sociology is a discipline which struggles to explain everyday life *despite* competing versions of reality; and (3) show the student that he/she, as an outsider, can make a contribution to the debate.

If we are to do good research in sociology, it will have to be non-sexist, non-racist and non-classist, and the reason is simple: One-sided, biased research is bad research.

CLOSING REMARKS

Why do research at all? Because, as the data in Exhibit 12.6 show, reality is more complicated, more interesting and more surprising than we might imagine. For example, data show us that people experience more racism *indirectly* through their TV set, than they do in person! Other data show us that 70% Canadians have constructed their *own* religion, and church attendance is irrelevant! If we hadn't done the research, we wouldn't have found this out. There are millions of things we don't really know about the world until we do the research.

Here's another set of findings you may want to play with. See if you get the same results from an informal survey in your *own* college. In September 1993, incoming students at the University of Toronto were asked a number of questions. About 60% (nearly 4 000 students) responded. One question asked whether they rated themselves in "the highest ten percent" on academic ability; another, whether they rated themselves in "the highest ten percent" on mathematical ability; another, on writing ability; another still, on intellectual self-confidence; and finally, on the "drive to achieve." Here are some of the results:

◆ roughly one-quarter of the incoming University of Toronto men rated themselves in the top ten percent on academic ability, mathematical ability, intellectual self-confidence and drive to achieve.

- incoming men were twice as likely as incoming women to rate themselves in the top ten percent on academic ability, mathematical ability and intellectual confidence. Men and women rated themselves more similarly on writing ability and the drive to achieve.
- incoming men at (upper-middle-class) Trinity College were nearly twice as likely as incoming men in Engineering to rate themselves in the top ten percent in academic ability, writing ability, intellectual self-confidence, and drive to achieve. Only in mathematical ability were the Engineering students likely to rate themselves as highly as the Trinity students (from John Kirkness,"Gathering evidence," *The Bulletin*, University of Toronto, Mon. April 11, 1994, p. 16).

Now that you have studied sociology, you may be able to explain some of these findings; maybe, even to predict what will happen when these students find out that only ten percent can fit into "the highest ten percent" category.

In this chapter, we have only scratched the surface as far as sociological research methods are concerned. Even so, we have presented what seems to be a bewildering number of methods for doing research and a large inventory of issues to keep in mind in order to assure that it is good research. Why this largesse? Why do sociologists not agree on a common set of methods they can apply to all research problems?

The reason is that sociologists study such a wide variety of social phenomena that no single set of methods and no simple set of guidelines are ap-

EXHIBIT 12.6A *Canadians want mosaic to melt*

Most Canadians believe the multicultural mosaic isn't working and should be replaced by a cultural melting pot, says a survey released yesterday. . . .

The survey was designed to gauge the perception of racist activity in Canada.

It encompassed definitions of racism that ranged from "overt" acts to "socially unacceptable views on the part of Canadians."

It found that while Canadians generally regard themselves as tolerant of other cultures and races they are also growing more concerned about an apparent rise in racist activity.

The survey found that:

- 86 per cent of Canadians believe there is at least "some racism" in Canada;
- Three-quarters believe racism is a serious problem;
- More than half of Canadians believe the level of racism has increased over the past five years;
- About 41 per cent feel that the current immigration policy allows "too many people of different races and cultures coming into Canada;"
- On the other hand, 54 per cent of Canadians believe the current immigration policy "provides for a good balance of people."

The survey concludes that "much of the concern about racism. . . stems from exposure to the media rather than direct exposure to or experience of racism on a personal level." Television was cited as the major source for racial impressions.

Decima Research also concludes that, although the number of Canadians who believe racist incidents are high, "Canadians do not currently feel threatened [italics used in survey] by racism or the effects of racism, as their experience of it is currently indirect.". . .

Source: Jack Kapica, "Canadians want mosaic to melt, survey finds," *The Globe and Mail*, Tues. Dec. 14, 1993, pp. A1, A2.

EXHIBIT 12.6B *Belief in personal spirituality rising*

Canadians are rejecting traditional forms of religious worship, such as church attendance and prayer, in favour of a new definition of spirituality, says a study of Canadian religious attitudes. . . .

The study, called *A Survey Regarding the Spiritual Dimension in the Canadian Public*, found that:

◆ 46 per cent of Canadians do not believe in traditional religions;
◆ 83 per cent say a belief in God is a personal matter and church attendance is not necessary to prove one's faith;
◆ 70 per cent have constructed their "own personal religion."

The study discovered that the younger and more affluent Canadians are, the less interested they become in organized religion. Moreover, a large number — 60 per cent — believe that "all religions are equally valid."

The results suggest that Canadians are moving away from religions based on theology and denominational identification, and toward a view of religion as an inspiration for moral and ethical behaviour.

But the move is not motivated by disbelief in religion. The study discovered that an overwhelming number of respondents — 84 per cent — agreed that "there are many things in life that cannot be explained by science.". . .

Source: Jack Kapica, "Religious worship changing, study finds," *The Globe and Mail*, Tues. Dec. 7, 1993, p. A11.

propriate for all of them. As you have already seen in earlier chapters, sociology's field is extraordinarily wide and the issues with which it deals are both diverse and complex. Sociologists have made good use of all these methods to uncover a wide variety of facts about social life.

Few of you reading this book will become practising sociologists. But, as we noted at the beginning of this book, you are all sociologists of a kind.

We hope we stretched your sociological imagination. Remember, that's your ability to see connections between large and small, changing and unchanging, portions of social life. It requires an awareness of the relation between individuals and the wider society. It helps us to look at our own personal experiences in a different, more objective way. It forces us to ask how our lives are shaped by the larger social context in which we live. Finally, the sociological imagination helps us to see society as the result of millions of people working out their own personal lives and making a connection between the MACRO and the MICRO levels of society.

We've told you what we know. The rest is up to you.

A P P E N D I X

HOW TO WRITE AN ESSAY IN SOCIOLOGY

What we have to tell you now will be immediately useful in this course. What's more, it will be useful in writing essays for other courses, this year and in the future. And it will also be useful in writing good examination answers for this and other courses. In fact, it will be useful in whatever writing you do in your future life — business reports, letters to the editor, and so on. The problems of writing well and clearly are common across different writing assignments, however long or short they may be, however much or little time you may have.

Writing — actually facing a blank piece of paper, then filling it up with intelligent words and ideas — is *hard* work. In a way, it's like magic. You are making something new — perhaps something quite unique and terrific — out of a few simple materials — a pen and paper, say, and some serious effort. That is exciting stuff — real magic. Still, doing magic is hard work. That's why you need to know some ways to make it easier.

The first thing you have to know is that you can't write something good if you don't have anything to say. So thinking has to come before writing; the better the thinking, the better the written product will be. Don't do your best thinking while, or even worse, *after* you have written your essay. Do it beforehand. Give yourself enough time to think. A paper written in one evening, without any good thinking in advance, looks like what it is: poor work.

The key to good thinking about a writing assignment is that you have to know very clearly (1) what the question is you are trying to answer, and (2) what you think the answer is. That may sound obvious and silly to you, but we guarantee we have read hundreds of essays, and books, where it is difficult to know what question is being answered and what answer is being offered. That kind of writing is a recipe for disaster. Do not set pen to paper before you are absolutely certain you know what the question is, and what the answer is.

Another thing we have learned from many years of reading and writing is that *any* question can be answered in *any* amount of time: in three minutes, three hours, three days, three months, or three years. There is no such thing as a question that *must* take a week, or six months, or ten years. Any question can be answered in the time you have available.

Obviously, an intelligent answer that took three hours to complete will be better — more insightful, more thought-provoking, more complete — than an intelligent answer which took only three minutes. If you have only three minutes to answer, do the best you can in the time available and you will be respected for the result. But if you have three hours to answer, by all means use that three hours to its fullest. Your instructor will be expecting more from a three-hour answer than from a three-minute answer.

Here's something that's much less obvious: when you are writing something — whatever it is, exam answer, essay, report or book — always follow the "Rule of Equal Thirds." Always spend about one-third of your time thinking, reading and preparing to answer; another one-third of your time actually answering in first draft; and a final third of your time cleaning up and revising.

So, if you are writing a three month essay, spend one month thinking about the problem, collecting information at the library, and collecting whatever other data you may need. Spend your second month writing a first draft of the essay. And spend your final month of the essay reorganizing, revising, re-reading and checking your essay for errors and typos. And, incidentally, every essay should be submitted in typed form.

Let's spend a little time thinking about each of these thirds.

THE FIRST THIRD

In the first third of your available time, you should put to work all the things you know about sociological methods of research. This is the time for background reading, designing your research, measuring your variables, collecting your data, and analysing the data in a preliminary way.

A lot of post-secondary students do not know how to use a library. Before you get started on this essay, you need to know how to find out what you do not know. You also have to develop strategies for limiting what you need to know. If, for example, you decide you want to write something on modern family life, you will find hundreds of books and thousands of articles on that topic at the library. Obviously, you cannot read all of that material; you need a strategy to narrow down the question you are going to answer, and a way to decide which things you have to read and which things you can ignore.

You may have a chance to do additional reading, data collection or data analysis at the next stage, but at least two-thirds of all that kind of work should be done in the first third of your available time. Ideally, you should complete your research in the first third of the writing process.

THE SECOND THIRD

Once you have narrowed your question down and read and thought about your topic, you are ready to start writing your three month essay.

No, let's put that point more strongly: If you look at your calendar and it tells you that today is the first day of month number two, then you *must* lay down your books and start writing. Force yourself to obey the "equal thirds" rule. Eventually, when you have a lot of experience writing, you will know how and when to relax that rule. But at the beginning, follow the rule mechanically. If it is the start of month number two, start writing.

Some people insist on making a detailed plan of their essay before they start to write anything at all. That works for some people; and when they are ready to write, everything just flows into the appropriate boxes. However, by far a more common problem is getting the stuff to start flowing at all. Lots of people — all the way from beginning writers up to professionals — suffer anxiety about starting to fill up the blank page in front of them. That is the biggest problem you are going to have to face.

So we are going to urge you *not* to worry about making a highly detailed outline before you start to write. After all, you have thought and read about your problem for a month; it is time to start writing. In the second third of your time available, sit down and start filling up pages. But when you do so, follow certain rules that will make the actual writing process much easier and more systematic.

What distinguishes a good three-hour answer from a good three-minute answer, or a good three-month answer from a good three-week answer is *not* whether the answer is "right". It is how thoroughly you explore your reasons for giving the answer you do. That is the most important thing you are going to take care of during this second third of your work on an essay, report, book or whatever. In fact, learning to make good arguments is what post-secondary education is all about.

There's an excellent book called *Writing Under Pressure*, by Sanford Kaye, a fellow who has been teaching writing to students, professors and executives for many years; and we agree with everything he has to say. In fact, we have stolen lots of our essay-writing ideas from him.

One thing he discusses is the importance of "because clauses" in writing. To his mind, and ours as well, "because clauses" should make up at least two-thirds of anything you write. So any good written answer will have:

(1) a beginning — what is the question to be answered? What does it mean? What do I have to show? What is my tentative answer to the question?
(2) a middle — many because-clauses arguing on one side of the question; many because-clauses arguing on the other side.
(3) an end — what is the final answer to the question? What are the implications of the answer, if any, for theory? for social policy? for everyday life?

As a rough estimate, in a ten-page, 2500-word essay, no more than two pages (or 500 words) should be spent on the beginning and no more than two pages should be spent on the ending. All the rest — six pages or more — should be spent on the middle part: the "because clauses".

What are these "because-clauses" we keep talking about? They are the reasons why you are about to answer the question in one way, rather than another. "I think this is happening because ..... and because ..... and because ...." Those are the because clauses in support of your position. Let's call them "supporting because clauses."

Also, you are going to supply lots of "opposing because clauses" that say "Other people argue the opposite view because .... and because ..... and because ....." You will review opposing positions, and discuss them fairly and thoroughly in your essay, because your instructor expects it of you. If you do *not* do so, your work will appear one-sided, shallow and laughable, and you will get a rotten mark in the course. (That's our "because clause" explaining why you should take this advice.)

But after reviewing all those "opposing because clauses," you get your revenge: a chance to rebut the opposing views to show why you do not find them persuasive — why they do not lead you to support their position, rather than the one you declared at the outset of the essay.

People differ in the way they do things. Usually we prefer to give the opposing argument first, then shoot it down, then give the argument that supports our side. That strategy is like ripping down an old building and clearing the land, before you start putting up your own new house. So, our hypothetical ten-page essay might look like this:

Beginning (one to two pages)
(1) What is the question, and what is our rough answer to that question? — one to two pages

Middle (six to eight pages)
(2) Arguments against our answer — one to two pages
(3) Arguments against those arguments — one to two pages
(4) Arguments in favour of our answer — two to four pages

End (one to two pages)
(5) What is our final answer (this includes refinements, modifications, implications).

You should proportion your time to this use of space. Remember, the middle or "because" part, should receive at least 60% of your writing time (as well as space). And this rule applies whether we are talking about 60% of one minute, one week or one year; or 10 pages, 100 pages or 1000 pages.

The nature of "becauses"	What is the nature of this important "because part" of the essay, exam question, or book? Obviously, it has something to do with the presentation of evidence. It can be logical evidence, but mainly it is empirical evidence — data specifically collected to support your argument or destroy your opponent's argument.

You can gather a lot of interesting information if you have a month to collect it and two months to write it up.

What happens when you have more *time* to write an answer is that you can collect better *quality* data to support your argument: you can review more books and journals, maybe even collect some new data of your own through interviews or questionnaires or first-hand observation.

Remember that an essay or written answer that takes 100 pages should differ from one that takes 10 pages only in terms of *quantity*, not quality. You can simply display more because-information in 100 pages than you can in 10 pages. A typical undergraduate course essay should be high on quality (after all, you have three months to write it) but low on quantity (you may have only 10 pages to write it on). Whatever you do, don't give your teacher a lot of quantity but not much quality.

As you go along giving your because clauses, you may find that there is reading you should have done, data you should have collected, or data you have collected and now have to analyse. Go ahead: make these final adjustments to your data base. But remember, this stage of work — the middle third of your time — is primarily a writing stage. If you find you are spending a lot of time doing additional reading or data collection, you have organized your time poorly. Most of that work should have been done in the first third of your time.

THE THIRD THIRD

Some people may wonder why we have allotted as much as a third of our writing time to the cleaning up stage. It is because this is an important stage, and many students overlook it or give it short shrift.

We know they have done this, because many essays come to us that are messy, full of grammatical errors and spelling errors, and lacking a well chosen bibliography. And, once we start reading for content, we often find glaring holes in the logic and large gaps in the evidence presented. This makes us think that the student wrote the entire essay in a single evening — something instructors find very irritating — when, in some cases, the student may simply have failed to do a clean-up on the essay and may have devoted all his or her time to reading, then writing a first draft.

Never hand in a first draft of an essay. Teachers were not put on earth to correct, or even read, your typos and spelling mistakes. Making us read such incomplete work is disrespectful; worse still, it makes us readers angry and disinclined to believe what you are arguing. It makes us graders believe you are a sloppy thinker — a C student at best. So, after you have written your draft of the essay, there are several things you should be sure to do:

Submit your essay to the laugh test. This is important and can be done in a number of ways. Imagine reading your essay out loud to your parents, your friends or, even, to a public audience. If the thought of this makes you cringe in horror, or feel terrible embarrassment, that may be because you have written a silly essay — one that does not truly express thoughts you are willing to take responsibility for. If you are afraid to take responsibility for these thoughts, you should not be turning them in for a grade.

Think of your essay as a conversation with the grader and rewrite your essay so that no part of it is embarrassing, no matter who might read it. After re-writing, the thoughts you express should not be embarrassing. To help achieve this, the language you use in your essay should be your own language, not puffed up and fancy talk full of ten-dollar words.

Read the revised essay out loud to your family or friends, or give it to a friend you respect, and ask him or her to read it and criticize it.

Of course, nobody likes criticism. Everyone feels bad when they are criticised and happy when they are praised. However, when you are submitting something for criticism by a stranger — as you are doing with the essay you are writing — you may prefer to get criticism from a friend first. The criticism you get from a friend will not only be more friendly, it may save you from losing marks. So tell your friendly reader that you want criticism: it will help you out.

Some people — friends included — just love criticizing other people. Some even enjoy humiliating their friends. Too bad if this is the only kind of friend you have! But whatever your friend's motives and personality flaws, you should be able to deal with criticism. If your friend says, "Here are eight things that are wrong with your essay" you should deal with every one of these eight things before you turn in the essay for grading.

You will probably find that you can easily agree with *some* of your friend's points. If your friend is right, you need to re-think, or research further, some particular issues. Go do it! And, some of the points your friend makes may simply require clarification — you did not express your views clearly enough. Fine; re-write the confusing passages so that your friend (and other people) can understand them.

Finally, some of the points your friend makes may seem just plain wrong to you: he or she is misinformed, or suffering from a defect in logic. Nonetheless, go and re-write the passages in question — or add new information — so that even an average or stupid reader (like your friend) will go along with your argument.

You see, when you are writing something, you cannot control who is going to read the piece, or what ideas they bring to the reading. Even though you may be writing your essay for a professor with a background in the area, you should clearly develop your terms and ideas. Writers are *always* at the mercy of their readers, and you must prepare for the worst.

In our time, we authors have received some glowing reviews of our work and some absolutely damning, humiliating reviews, and everything in between. But we have to deal with all criticisms. What's more, as writers you (and we) must always anticipate what readers may say, and deal with their possible criticisms before they have a chance to make them.

So submit your work to the laugh test; undergo friendly criticism; re-write and re-think as much as you have time for in that final one-third of your time. Then take care of cosmetic details.

A lot of you probably use word-processors, and if you do, you should run your essay through a spelling checker to eliminate spelling errors in your written work. If you have serious trouble with speaking or writing English, you must seek out help; probably, there are courses to help you with this. If you are an English speaker but do not understand how to write two logical sentences in a row, there are writing labs to help you, and you should take advantage of them.

Finally, and remember this, your instructor wants to see no typos or scratchouts or things taped together. The essay should look like you spent a month cleaning it up, because (according to the rule of equal thirds) you did!

THE ESSAY YOU ARE GOING TO WRITE

Suppose the essay you are going to write is worth 20% of your final mark in the course. If so, you should spend about 20% of your time in this course writing it. If you are spending about eight or nine hours a week on *each* of your courses, you should spend about 220 hours on a full-year course, and, therefore, about 44 hours on an essay for that course. Let's make this 45 hours, to keep the calculations simple. (Cut these numbers in half if you are taking a half-year (or 1-semester) course.)

When you write your essay, keep a log of the hours you are spending and force yourself to follow the time budget we have laid out. Following what we have said above, it should look like this:

First stage: 15 hours. Thinking, reading, making notes, preparing to answer

Second stage: 15 hours. Writing the first draft of your essay. This comprises the following:

  The beginning. Stating the question and approximate answer your essay will give: 2.5 hours

The middle. Writing the "because clauses" portion. A total of 10 hours, comprising

2.5 hours to state the case against your answer

2.5 hours to rebut the case against your answer

5.0 hours to support your own case

The end. Refining and modifying your opening position. Stating the implications of your conclusion. 2.5 hours

Third stage: 15 hours. Doing the laugh test. Cleaning up and revising your essay. Adding new evidence, where needed. Fixing spelling and typing errors, making accurate footnotes and references.

WRITING AN EXAM ANSWER

When you are answering an exam question, things are slightly different, but not much. You still have an opportunity to prepare, to write, and to clean-up; and you should still follow the equal thirds rule when you do this.

Suppose you are writing an essay-type test. You read through the test paper completely, to get your brain cells fired up. You find you have to answer two half-hour questions and you decide which question you are going to answer first. This is what you should do next:

Prepare. Spend ten minutes just thinking about the question and making little notes to yourself on the backs of pages, or on scratch paper. Make sure you understand the question, and make sure you have decided on an answer by the end of the first ten-minute period.

Write. Spend ten minutes writing an answer: about one or two minutes to open the discussion; six to eight minutes for because-clauses; another one or two minutes for closing statements.

Clean-up. Spend ten minutes reading through your answer, checking for errors, things you have left out, spelling mistakes, and so on. Make the appropriate corrections.

You will find it is easier doing a clean-up if, when you answer the exam question, you leave two or three lines between each line you write. This allows you to add stuff in a neat way, if you have to. If you have prepared well, argued your "becauses" well, and cleaned up well, you should impress your reader and get a good grade.

An Example

So far we have been somewhat abstract, and now it is time to give an example. Here's what goes through the mind of one student — Jennifer — as she answers an examination question.

She has to write an answer to the following question: "Does Canada have a race problem?" Time available is 30 minutes. Maximum space available is 10 pages. There's no time to do background reading or collect data. She has to go with what she has in her head right now.

Prepare. Jennifer takes 10 minutes to get ready and spends a few minutes asking herself "What do I think about this question? Does Canada have a race problem? She starts to brainstorm, free associate and jot down ideas. Yes, Canada does have a race problem.

Write

Beginning: Time to write a two-page introduction. Yes, I think Canada has a race problem. Before I explain why I think so, I will explain what I think this question is about: namely, how people of African or Asian origins, or native peoples, get along in Canadian society.

I think Canada's visible minorities definitely have a problem. But is there a problem for the white majority? And is there a problem for Canadian society as a whole? I'm not sure. I'll come back to that issue — the issue of what kind of problem it is — at the end of the essay.

In the body of my essay, I am going to show that, by many different standards — jobs, health, living conditions, self-image, life chances — non-whites have a real problem in Canada.

Middle: I have about six or seven minutes to write this part. First, I will spend two minutes putting forward opposing arguments: the reasons why someone else might think Canada does not have a race problem.

(1)   There are no lynchings or race riots.
(2)   Most Canadians seem pretty tolerant towards racial minorities.
(3)   Canada has a long history of racial tolerance; no history of slavery like the United States, for example.
(4)   Canada has no laws that make racism officially okay, as South Africa did for a long time.
(5)   If Canadians were racists, they wouldn't let so many non-whites come into the country.
(6)   If there was a race problem in Canada, you would hear a lot about it on the news.

That's all I can come up with off the top of my head in two minutes. Now I have to destroy these points in two more minutes. Here goes:

(1)   The fact that there are no lynchings or race riots may simply mean that the conflict has taken on more polite forms.
(2)   The personal tolerance of Canadians may be irrelevant. After all, it is possible to be nice and tolerant but still ignore or exploit poor racial minorities.
(3)   Canadians don't want anyone to be slaves. But that doesn't mean we want to have much to do with visible minorities, especially if they are poor.
(4)   Canada does not have apartheid laws like South Africa, but many native people think Canada's Indian Act is discriminatory. And don't forget "systemic discrimination": many laws discriminate without necessarily intending to.
(5)   Open immigration only proves that Canadians need cheap, highly educated labour from the Third World.
(6)   The mass media are part business, part fantasy. You cannot rely on them to tell you if there is *really* a race problem.

Now I have two minutes to put forward my preferred position: namely, there *is* a race problem in Canada.

(1)   Economic inequality. There is lots of evidence of high unemployment, poverty and demoralization among the non-white communities. Often, it

shows up as bad health, poor nutrition, poor school attendance, high suicide rates.

(2) Job discrimination. The evidence provided by Henry and Ginzberg shows that Toronto whites do discriminate against blacks in hiring. The evidence of Peter Li shows that this results in lower than average incomes for blacks and Asians.

(3) Perceived racism. Many non-whites — especially blacks and native peoples — *believe* there is a race problem; and they see signs of it in the behaviour of the police towards blacks and native people, in job discrimination, and in the disputes over land claims.

End: Now, I have a minute or two to finish off. "I have shown that, while there is some merit to the opposing arguments, on balance I am persuaded by evidence of economic inequality, job discrimination, and white reactions to non-white concerns, that there is a race problem in Canada. Only time will tell whether the problem will get much worse before we take serious action to improve it. We would do well to see what has worked in other countries facing similar problems at earlier times in history."

Clean-up: Now I have ten minutes to read my answer through, correct errors, add any new ideas I may have, and take out stuff that is truly dumb.

I am also doing my own laugh test: what would my mother or my best friend say about this exam answer, I ask myself. Well, she might say that she didn't agree with my last point — just because people *think* there is a race problem doesn't make it so.

For example, most Quebecers think there is a problem with French-English relations in Canada, but most non-Quebecers do not think so, except that the Quebecers keep making such a fuss about things and want to destroy the country. Or take any two groups that are fighting — Israeli Jews and Palestinians, Irish Protestants and Catholics, Shiite and Sunni Moslems, and so on. They are always fighting and blaming each other for problems.

But mom, that is exactly the point I am making. I don't have to decide whether I agree more with the whites or the non-whites. The point is, the two groups are not equal and they probably don't agree on the reasons why. That's a race problem and some day it may grow into a race war.

I wish I had a chance to think about this some more, because it seems like a good issue to explore. It makes me remember what the sociologist W.I. Thomas said, "Things that are defined as real have real consequences." If non-whites think all whites are racists, and behave as though this is true, whites will be forced into behaving like racists. And if whites think all non-whites are trying to threaten them, or shame them, into sharing the wealth, and behave as though this is true, non-whites will harden their position and become more confrontational. Funny, isn't it, that we become what people think we are.

Now I have just a minute or two to write a few lines on this theme. If it doesn't fit on the page, I'll write it on the facing page and, with clear arrows, indicate where this new piece fits in. As I re-read, fix spelling and grammar and so on, I get some more ideas — good ones, I think. I put in a few words here and there.

My thoughts are getting really interesting, but I have to stop now. I am out of time. I have to go on to the next question. I don't want to use up any more of my precious time on the first answer. I can only hope that I did a good enough job on it in the time available.

CLOSING REMARKS

What have you learned from Jennifer's experience? Have you learned that writing an answer can be exciting and also frustrating, because of all those great ideas you start to get just when it is time to stop?

Don't be frightened when all your ideas start tumbling out — all those different because-clauses, arguments and counter-arguments. Most sociology instructors *love* seeing alternative interpretations, competing theories and important facts in search of a theoretical home. So let it all hang out but be sure to tie everything together in a sensible way by the time you are finished.

Remember, you have to discipline yourself, and that is true whether you have 30 minutes or three years to answer a question. You have to get the work out and then, go on to the next assignment. That is the secret of success in writing. Try to follow the rules we have given you and you will find that exams and essays go very smoothly indeed.

Glossary

agents of socialization   institutions and other structured relationships within which socialization takes place

alienation   estrangement of workers from the product of their work, from the work process, from themselves and other workers

anomie   according to Durkheim, it is a lack of regulation, or a lack of norms; anomie increases the likelihood of suicide and other "pathological" behaviours.

anomie theory   as developed by Robert Merton, this theory argues that inequality causes deviance by creating a gap between culturally defined goals and socially approved means for attaining those goals.

anticipatory socialization   socialization that prepares a person for roles they may eventually have to perform

assimilation   the process by which members of a minority group abandon their own cultural traits and adopt those of the dominant culture

authority   the ability of an individual or group to issue commands and have them obeyed because their control is perceived as legitimate

baby boom   a sudden and considerable rise in the birth rate occurring in the 1950s and early 1960s. It was a response to economic prosperity, and the end of restraints on marriage and childbearing caused by the Depression and the Second World War.

band   a grouping the government has created to administer status Indians, who are typically native people under the jurisdiction of the Indian Act

biological determinism   the view that differences among individuals or cultures exist because nature has selected for them; any genetic explanation of behaviour.

bourgeoisie   in Marxist terminology, the group of people who own the means of production (capitalists). Sometimes also used to refer to the middle class in a capitalist society. The bourgeoisie employ the proletariat (*see also* proletariat).

bureaucracy   a hierarchically organized formal organization found throughout industrial societies

bureaucratic control   a way of controlling workers which relies on a large number of written rules and the promise of career rewards for conformity and effective performance.

carrying capacity   the number of people a geographic area can support, given the current level of available resources and technology

caste system   a hierarchy of groups separated from each other by rules of ritual purity and prevented from intermarrying, changing castes through mobility, or carrying out inappropriate jobs

charismatic leader   a leader who has an exceptional capacity to inspire devotion and enthusiasm among followers

Charter Groups   Canadians of British and French ancestry, so named because settlers from England and France first came to Canada with royal permission to trade and settle (royal charters)

class   inequality based on the distribution of material resources

class system   a hierarchy of groups with different market conditions, work situations, and life chances. In Marxist theory, classes stand in different relations to the means of production

cognitive development   the development of abilities to think, believe, remember, perceive, and reason

cohabitation   a sexual union in which two people live together without marrying

cohort a group of people who share similar life experiences as the result of a major common experience (such as birth, marriage, graduation or migration in the same year or decade)

comprador an elite made up of the people who run corporations located in Canada but owned or controlled by foreign concerns.

conflict theory a theoretical paradigm that emphasizes conflict and change as the regular and permanent features of society, because society is made up of various groups who wield varying amounts of power

corporate capitalism an economic system in which the key players are corporate groups and their directors. Under corporate capitalism, monopolies and oligopolies also become common (*see also* laissez-faire capitalism).

counterculture a subculture that rejects conventionally accepted norms and values in favour of alternative ones

crime any act formally prohibited by criminal law

cultural capital a set of beliefs and skills that help people get ahead in an unequal society

cultural literacy a solid knowledge of our traditional culture; the ability to learn and communicate in our society

culture the objects, artifacts, institutions, organizations, ideas and beliefs that make up the symbolic and learned aspects of human society

demographic transition a fall in birth and death rates that accompanies industrialization, with the death rates falling first

demography the scientific study of the size, composition (structure), distribution, and patterns of change in a human population

dependency ratio the ratio of economically dependent people (aged 17 and under and 65 and over) to people of working age (ages 18 through 64)

deviance behaviour that leads to a negative reaction or response from a community or group

deviant subculture a subculture whose members conform to norms, values, and beliefs that the larger society considers deviant

differentiation the process whereby various sets of activities are divided up and performed by a number of separate institutions (*see also* integration below).

discrimination the denial of access to opportunities that would be available to equally qualified members of the dominant group

division of labour the breaking up of a job into a number of smaller jobs which are done by separate individuals

divorce the legal and formal dissolution of a legal marriage

domination the exercise of control over an individual or group who must submit to that person's power. It can be seen as inequality based on the distribution of authoritative resources.

double standard the application of different rules, or standards of behaviour, to men and women

dyad a two person group

economic order the institutionalized system which produces, distributes, and consumes material resources

elite a small group that has power or influence over others and that is regarded as being superior in some way.

endogamy the tendency for people to marry partners within their own kin group, clan, race, ethnic group or class

endogenous causes of death that are internal to the organism, not a result of externally induced trauma or infection

equalitarian (or egalitarian) family a family in which the husband and wife jointly make all the important decisions

equality of condition equality in the distribution of goods such as food, housing, health, wealth, respect, authority, power, and so on

equality of opportunity equality of access to that which society values; a situation in which all people may compete equally for all positions in society

ethnicity an ethnic group's distinctive cultural features, such as language, religion, sense of collective existence, and shared historical heritage

ethnocentrism   a tendency to view life from the point of view of one's own culture. Ethnocentrism enters into both common thought and social research

exogamy   (reverse of endogamy)   i.e., the tendency for people to marry partners from outside their own kin group, clan, race, ethnic group or class

experiment   a research method designed to investigate the effect of one variable on another under well-controlled and regulated conditions. A control and experimental group are compared before and after the experimental treatment.

explanation   something that gives the meaning of, gives reasons for, accounts for, or interprets, something else

family   traditionally, a group of people who are related to one another through marriage, descent, or legal adoption; increasingly, any group of people who, over a long period, depend on one another for emotional and material support.

femininity   that package of traits people expect to find in a typical woman (*see also* masculinity)

feminism   an ideology which supports equality of the sexes and opposes patriarchy and sexism

feminization of poverty   the growing tendency of poor people to be women, due to lone parenthood or impoverished old age

folkways   norms whose violation are punished informally, if at all

formal social control   an authorized procedure that defines how specific people (such as police officers) will enforce the rules and laws of a society (*see also* informal social control)

gendered division of labour   the cultural separation of work (whether inside the home or in public) into "men's work" and "women's work"

gender identity   the ways males and females learn to think of themselves; the learned part of the self that results from a person's recognition that he or she is a man or woman, boy or girl

gender   human traits that are linked by culture to each sex; the social, cultural and psychological aspects of masculinity and femininity

gender roles (or sex roles)   attitudes and activities that a culture links to each sex, or are typically expected of members of a particular sex

gender socialization (or sex role socialization)   the process of learning "appropriate" sex specific behaviour

generation gap   a difference in world views between parents and their children, or between the older and younger generations

generalized other   a person's general idea of how the society, or surrounding group, expects him or her to behave

genocide   the state-planned and systematic murder of people who belong to a particular ethnic, racial or religious group

goal displacement   in bureaucracies, the substitution of concerns about the survival of the organization for concerns about the goals for which the organization was created

groups   on a micro level, a group is a collection of people who interact regularly face-to-face. On a macro level, a group is a category of people who share some important trait in common.

growth rate   the (annual) rate at which the number of people in a population increases. Negative growth rate is the (annual) rate at which population size declines.

heterogamy   a pattern of mating between people who differ in important respects, especially in their social characteristics

high culture   the set of tastes, values, and norms that are characteristic of high status groups in society. They include the fine arts, classical music, ballet, and other "highbrow" concerns.

homogamy   a pattern of mating between people who are like each other, especially in their social characteristics (*see also* heterogamy).

human capital   the level of people's wellbeing, as influenced by their health, education and welfare, which affects their value as members of the work force

hypothesis   a proposition or tentative statement about the relationship between two or more variables that we can test through research

ideal culture the set of values people claim to believe in, as expressed in holy books, laws, institutions, novels, and mass media presentations

ideology an emotionally charged belief that either explains and justifies existing arrangements, or in the case of a counter ideology, calls for and justifies alternative ways of doing things

I and Me according to Mead, "I" is the part of the self that is not socialized; "me" is the part that is.

impression management the use of wealth, power, authority and cultural capital to appear virtuous and normal. According to labelling theory, this influences the way deviant behaviour will be handled.

Industrial Revolution a system of production that began around 1775 in England; it uses machinery and inanimate forms of energy (such as electric power) to mass produce goods, often in large factories

industrial society a society characterized by large-scale mechanized production and an extensive division of labour

informal social control the maintenance of order through gossip, praise or blame (*see also* formal social control).

institutional completeness a measure of the degree to which an ethnic group provides its members with all the services they require through their own institutions separate from those of the larger society

integration the complement to differentiation, whereby various elements of a society are combined to form a unified whole (*see also* differentiation)

internalization the process by which a person learns and accepts as binding the norms and values of a group or society

labelling theory a theory that assumes everyone behaves in a deviant manner occasionally, and labelling people "deviant" locks them into repeated norm violation

laissez-faire capitalism an economic system, dominant in 19th century England and America, that claimed government avoided interfering in the economy (*see also* corporate capitalism)

life cycle a recognized, predictable sequence of stages through which individuals pass in the course of their lives

looking-glass self a sense of ourselves formed through interaction with others, by assessing how they view us

macrosociology the study of large groups, processes that characterize whole societies, and the system of arrangements that exists in a given society

marriage an acknowledged sexual and economic union between two or more people

masculinity the package of traits that people in our society expect to find in a typical man (*see also* femininity)

mass production the production of goods in large quantities, by means of division of labour, mechanization, and large productive units (factories or offices)

material culture the artifacts and physical objects created or used by members of a culture, to be distinguished from what goes on in the minds of the people (**non-material culture**)

matriarchal family a structure in which the mother is the formal head of the household

matrilocal a residence pattern whereby married couples reside with, or very near the bride's parents

microsociology the study of small groups, and of the processes and patterns of face-to-face interactions that take place within these groups in everyday life

migration (internal) the movement of people from one part of a country to another

monopoly one group's exclusive control over the production and sales of a commodity or service. Both monopolies and cartels are limits to free competition

mores norms that carry moral significance, and are therefore cause for severe punishment when violated (*see also* folkways)

multiculturalism a philosophy of ethnic and race relations that promote the development of distinct cultural communities. It sees each person as the member of an ethnic or racial group and undertakes to protect the group, not the individual.

natural increase the excess of births over deaths in a population

neolocal residence   a family household that is set up separate from the households of the spouses' parents

net migration rate   the number of immigrants to a certain area, minus the number of emigrants from that area, per year per thousand inhabitants

norm   an expectation about correct or proper behaviour in a particular situation, which serves as a guideline for individuals' action

nuclear family   a family household consisting of two spouses (with or without children) or a parent and his/her children

organic solidarity   community cohesion that is based on the interdependence between people who are socially different

organized crime   a centralized and formal structure within which individuals devote themselves to the pursuit of goals by illegal means; centrally organized, professional crime

paradigm   a general way of seeing the world that embodies broad assumptions about the nature of society and people's behaviour. It suggests which questions sociologists should ask and how they should interpret the answers.

participant observation   a research technique in which the sociologist becomes a member of a group in order to observe and study it first-hand

patriarchal family   a family structure in which the father is the formal head of the household

patriarchy   a form of organization in which men dominate women

patrilocal   describes a residence pattern whereby married couples reside with, or very near the grooms' family

peer group   a group of companions with whom one interacts, particularly from late childhood through adolescence into early adulthood, and who relate to one another as equals

pluralism   a philosophy of ethnic and race relations that urges tolerance for group differences and protects the rights of minority individuals through provincial human rights codes and other legislation

polyandry   the marriage of one woman to more than one man

polygamy   the union of a spouse to two or more spouses at the same time. Conversely, monogamy is marriage between only one woman and one man.

polygyny   the marriage of more than one woman to one man

popular (or mass) culture   the culture of average people; it includes those preferences and tastes that are widespread in a society

population   in research, the set of all individuals who share some specific characteristic of interest to the researcher (*see also* sample)

positive checks   occurrences (such as war, famine, pestilence, and disease) which have the effect of reducing the population or limiting its growth (*see also* preventive checks)

poverty (absolute)   a condition that occurs when people have too little of the basic necessities (food, shelter and medicine, for example) for physical survival (*see also* relative poverty)

poverty (relative)   a condition defined by the general living standards of the society or group; a low standard of living compared to most (*see also* absolute poverty)

power   the capacity to exercise one's will despite resistance. In Marxist theory, power is the capacity of one class to realize its interests in opposition to other classes.

prediction   the process of forecasting by inference from scientific, especially statistical, analysis of past events

prejudice   a negative or hostile attitude towards members of a particular group simply because they belong to that group, based on untested assumptions about their characteristics

prestige   honour and respect, a type of stratification that is separate from income, authority, or class position

preventive checks   in Malthusian theory, processes (like late marriage, abstinence or abortion) which reduce population growth by limiting the number of live births (*see also* positive checks)

price-fixing   a secret (and usually illegal) agreement between producers to charge the same price for a product or service they all offer, in order to keep the prices high

primary labour market that set of jobs which offer high wages, good opportunities for advancement, and job security (*see also* secondary labour market)

primary socialization the early socialization of children, much of which takes place in a family setting

professionalization the conversion of jobs to professions, through group mobilization and the raising of educational requirements. As a result, the group gains income, respectability and the right to regulate itself

proletariat in Marx's theory, the working class who must sell their labour for wages. They own none of the means of production but their own labour power (*see also* bourgeoisie).

propaganda information, ideas, or doctrines disseminated for the purpose of influencing the opinions and actions of others

pull factors those factors that encourage people to move to a particular area. They include better job opportunities, more tolerance for ethnic or religious minorities, and greater freedom.

push factors those factors that encourage people to leave an area. They include famine, a lack of job opportunities, discrimination, and fear of oppression.

qualitative data data that do not require, or do not lend themselves to, precise measurement

quantitative data data that are based on precise measurement and to which rigorous statistical methods can be applied (*see also* qualitative data)

race a group whose members are defined as sharing the same physical characteristics. The term is used as a biological concept, not a cultural one.

racism the belief that one's own race is superior to all others

rationalization the process by which all human action, especially decision-making, becomes subject to calculation, measurement, and control

real culture the ways people actually dress, talk, act, relate, and think, which may differ markedly from the values and norms they claim to believe in (*see also* ideal culture)

recidivism a repeated lapse into crime and delinquency

reconstituted family a family to which one or both spouses bring children from a former union

research design an orderly plan for collecting, analyzing, and interpreting data

reserve where a band of status Indians live ("reservation" is the American term), under the terms of a treaty with the Federal or Provincial government

resocialization a learning process that reshapes the individual's personality by teaching radically different values, norms, and role expectations, often within a total institution

resource mobilization the ability of a group to gather, organize, and use necessary resources (such as money, leadership, support, and connections) to promote its views

routinization a process by which a bureaucratic structure emerges in a (formerly) charismatic movement, to better administer the day-to-day goals of the movement

sample a relatively small number of people drawn from the population of interest

scale a system of units arranged in steps or degrees. Measurement scales include nominal, ordinal, interval, and ratio

scientific method a systematic series of steps in research that ensures maximum objectivity. It involves collecting evidence, making theories, and testing predictions against careful observations.

secondary deviation deviance by a person who perceives him- or herself as deviant, because of reactions to **primary deviation**, the initial deviant behaviour

secondary (or marginal) labour market contains all the jobs that are characterized by low wages, few opportunities for advancement, and little job security (*see also* primary labour market)

secondary socialization the ongoing and lifelong process of socialization, including accumulated learning in adolescence and adulthood.

segregation the act or process of setting apart two or more groups of people within the same territory

serial (sequential) monogamy the union of a person to two or more spouses in a lifetime, one after another

sex   the division of humanity into biological categories of male and female; the biological and anatomical differences that distinguish males from females

sexism   the ideology or belief that people of one sex are naturally superior to people of the other, including beliefs that attribute certain characteristics to one or the other sex, thereby justifying inequality

sexual harassment   any unwanted behaviour, especially at work or school, which calls attention to a person's sexuality, thereby creating discomfort; or demands sexual favours in return for some work-related benefit (e.g., a promotion)

sign   a gesture, artifact, or word that meaningfully represents something else

simple control   a kind of control that relies on the close supervision of workers; it is often found in small workplaces with a simple division of labour

single-parent family   a family containing one parent (typically a mother) and his or her children (typically young and dependent)

snowball sample   a sample of individuals, most of whom have been referred to the researcher by others in the sample

social (or cultural) determinism   a theoretical approach that denies human free will and assumes that society causes people to act the way they do (*see also* biological determinism)

social distance   reserve in interactions between people who belong to groups ranked as superior and inferior in status

social mobility   the movement of individuals among different levels of the occupational hierarchy. Movement may be vertical or horizontal, across generations or within a generation.

social movements   forms of collective action that are aimed at promoting or resisting change in a given society

social statics   processes that keep societies stable or which develop and spread the culture of a society

social structure   any enduring, predictable pattern of relations; the participants may be people, roles, groups, or institutions

socialization   the learning process through which an individual becomes a capable member of society

socio-economic status (SES)   a method of ranking people which combines measures of wealth, authority (or power), and prestige

sociological imagination   an awareness of how individual experiences, values, beliefs, attitudes, and aspirations influence and are influenced by society

specialization   expertise in doing one particular job which has previously been part of a larger job category

(social) status   people's standing in the community, as measured by the amount of respect, deference or prestige they are granted; status differences create inequality based on the unequal distribution of symbolic resources.

stereotype   a fixed mental image embracing all that is believed to be typical of members of a given group

stratification system   a system of inequality that integrates class, status, and domination with other forms of differentiation, such as gender, race, ethnicity

structural functionalism, or functionalism   a theoretical paradigm that emphasizes the way each part of a society functions to fulfil the needs of society as a whole

subculture   a group in society that shares some of the cultural traits of the larger society but also has its own distinctive values, beliefs, norms, style of dress and behaviour

submission   subjection to control by another group or individual whose power is based on a higher class position or higher status position

symbol   a sign that generates some emotion (*see also* sign)

symbolic interactionism   a theoretical paradigm that studies the process by which individuals interpret and respond to the actions of others, and that conceives of society as the product of this continuous face-to-face interaction

systemic discrimination   the unintended denial of opportunities to members of particular groups because of certain physical or cultural characteristics

taboo   the powerful belief that a particular act, food, place (and so on) is totally repulsive. Violation is supposed to result in immediate punishment by the group or even by God.

technical control   a kind of worker control that relies on the productive technology to maintain the pace of work; it is often found where there is an assembly line

total fertility rate   an estimate of the average number of live children a woman will bear as she passes through the age-specific fertility rates of a society

underdevelopment   the effect on the periphery of unequal exchanges with the core. An underdeveloped society is one that has lost the capacity to take care of its own needs.

underemployment   employment in a job which requires far less expertise, skill or ability than the jobholder typically has.

values   shared conceptions of what is considered good, right, and desirable, which influence people's behaviour and serve as standards for evaluating the actions of others

variable   any trait, quality, or characteristic which can vary in size over time or across individuals or groups

vertical mosaic   a society in which ethnic group membership overlaps with class or socio-economic status, such that we can predict a person's position in society from his or her ethnic origins

victimless crime   a category of crime from which no one suffers directly except perhaps the persons engaging in the behaviour

white collar crimes   crimes committed by high-status people, often in the course of their work; they include fraud, forgery, tax evasion, price-fixing, work safety violations, and embezzlement

World System theory   a theory that analyses the change of societies by reference to their relation with other societies

zero population growth   this occurs when the factors leading to population growth are exactly balanced by the factors leading to population decline. It is also known as replacement, as the population size remains constant.

Review Exercises

CHAPTER ONE

Review Questions

1. How do microsociology and macrosociology differ?

2. What is a science?

3. What problems face sociology as a science?

4. What is meant by the terms "social structure" and "social relationships"?

5. What four sociological paradigms are discussed in the chapter?

6. How do the sociological perspectives of Karl Marx, Emile Durkheim and Max Weber differ?

7. What are the main assumptions of functionalism?

8. What is the basic sociological question asked by conflict theory?

9. What are the main assumptions of symbolic interactionism?

10. In what ways is feminism both an academic perspective and a form of political activism?

11. What is an ideology?

Discussion Questions

1. Have people write anonymous messages on slips of paper which, in a sentence or two, explain a personal problem they are having right now. Select one or more out of a hat, and discuss. Is this personal trouble the flip-side of a public issue? If so, what kind of issue?

2. Does sociology study different things than do other disciplines, or does it simply study the same things in different ways? Support each side of this argument with examples.

3. Is it really possible for sociology to be value free, and should it be value free? Why, when people in the physical sciences (for example, physicists, biologists) are becoming increasingly concerned about the ethics of their research and its consequences, should sociology be striving for value freedom?

4. Conflict theorists believe that most of us suffer from "false consciousness." What do they mean? Why do structural functionalists and symbolic interactionists not agree with this belief? What is your position on this?

5. If people really have "free will," as sociology seems to assume, does this mean they choose the lives they lead? Are they personally responsible for being poor, for example?

6. What are some of the main differences between pure research and applied research in sociology? Which kind of research do you consider more important to society; why? Should sociologists be prevented from doing certain kinds of pure or applied research?

Data Collection Exercises

1. Collect some data on rates of teenage suicide in Canada and other countries. Which countries rate high; which rate low? In which countries are the rates rising or falling? How might you begin to explain these differences? What additional data would you need to test your explanation?

2. How do people manage to "navigate" through crowds? Go to a crowded place (e.g., a shopping mall or busy street). Watch and record how people use their eyes, faces, and bodies to signal where they intend to walk, so as to clear a right-of-way. How do you suppose people learn to do this kind of signalling? Why does automobile traffic require other kinds of regulation?

3. Watch and record an interaction between two of your friends (or family members) as they try to resolve a disagreement. Did they reach an agreement? If so, what was the turning point in the negotiation — the point at which they began to close in on a resolution? Now that you have a hypothesis about conflict resolution, record a second interaction (observe different people, please!) and see if the same thing happens again.

4. Collect information about the way a public figure changed his or her "image" over the course of time. Can you show that the image changed in response to public opinion polls? Can you show that the changes made the public figure more popular?

CHAPTER TWO

Review Questions

1. What is culture?

2. What are some examples of cultural universals?

3. What are the differences between ideal culture and real culture; between material and non-material culture; and between high and popular culture?

4. What are "signs" and "symbols"?

5. What values are prominent among Canadian teenagers?

6. What are the different types of norms?

7. In what ways is language a system of signs and symbols?

8. How is cultural integration promoted?

9. What is ethnocentrism?

10. How do subcultures and countercultures differ?

11. How are cultural capital and cultural literacy unevenly distributed in society?

12. Is there a distinctive Canadian culture?

Discussion Questions

1. Self-destruction in various forms — for example, setting oneself on fire, or self-imposed starvation — is a common way of dramatizing political frustration. Are all self-destructive acts symbolic? That is, are they likely to have different meanings in different cultures?

2. Are people using less sexist language in the media today? What about in private conversation? Have changes in the use of language changed people's behaviour toward women?

3. Is multiculturalism a good thing for Canada, a waste of the government's money, or positively harmful to the country?

4. What conditions are likely to produce a subculture? For example, are you likely to find subcultures formed by drug addicts? antique collectors? people who love pizza?

5. How does the widespread belief that "winning is everything" support the ruling class? Is it possible for Canadians to compete economically and politically with other nations if we reject that belief?

6. Given the ways our technology and population are changing today, what changes in cultural values do you think will occur before the year 2010? What do you think it would take to cause a major cultural change?

Data Collection Exercises

1. What are the folkways and mores of your own friendship group? Try breaking one of the rules — for example, make a date and don't show up; borrow money and refuse to pay it back; or continue talking about something

long after everyone is bored stiff by it. How do you think they will react? How *do* they react? What have you learned from the discrepancy between the two?

2. Give five of your friends (who are not members of this sociology class) the "I AM…" test. Ask each one to print the numbers 1 through 10 down the left hand side of a page. Then, beside each number, have them write a word or phrase that (they feel) describes who they are. When you have all the data, analyze these responses to determine which of your friends are ethnocentric.

3. Look though three kinds of magazines: *True Romance* (or *Soap Opera Digest*), *Life* (or *Maclean's*), and *The New Yorker* (or *Harper's*). Describe the elements of high and popular culture you find in each one. What differences do you see in the physical appearance of each: the print size, layout, number and type of pictures, and so on? How about the content: how do they differ in what they talk about?

4. Pretend you are a participant observer. View a video on street gangs (e.g., *Boyz N the hood*) and record the evidence that these young people are part of a counterculture.

CHAPTER THREE

1. What is socialization?

2. Why is primary socialization considered so important by all of the sociological paradigms?

3. What is cultural determinism?

4. What do feral children teach us about the importance of primary socialization?

5. In what way is learning a natural human process.

6. What is cognitive development?

7. What is the self?

8. What did Cooley mean by the "looking glass self"?

9. Why did Mead consider "taking the role of the other" to be so important when interacting with others?

10. What are the stages in Mead's theory of internalization?

11. In what ways is socialization an active process?

12. How does gender socialization differ for boys and girls?

13. What are the different agents of socialization?

1. Everyone pays the cost of having people in society who have been inadequately or harmfully socialized, if they end up criminals or mentally ill as adults. Should this give society the right to direct the ways parents socialize their children?

2. What is the strongest evidence that people really have an untamed nature that is struggling to overcome reason and order? What would you offer as an alternative explanation for the same evidence?

3. "If the school exposes a child to rules that apply equally to everyone and rewards for merit, is this doing the child a disservice? After all, it is preparing the child for a world that does not exist outside the school." Discuss this statement.

4. Currently, childhood is a time of play and freedom from responsibility, while adulthood is a time of little play and a lot of responsibility. How might lives be organized in future to mix play and responsibility throughout the life cycle? How would childhood gain from this? How would adulthood gain?

5. Old people seem more satisfied with life than younger people, though they may have less money and poorer health. How do they learn this approach to life, and could younger people learn it too?

6. Is there any change people cannot make through resocialization? Give examples of where this change is limited or impossible.

**Data Collection
Exercises**

1. Try a small experiment on one of your friends and report the results to the class. Think of a thing he or she really does not want to do, then see if — through casual conversation and bargaining — you can get that person to do it for a certain reward. What does the outcome of this experiment teach you about the interactionist approach to socialization?

2. Try another small experiment on one of your friends and report the results to class. If the theory of the looking-glass self is valid, you should be able to change your friend's behaviour by changing the way you reflect his or her behaviour. Try persuading your friend that he/she is acting really strangely today and ask if anything is the matter. What does the outcome teach you about the looking-glass self theory?

3. Interview six mature adults you know, to find out what are their main goals in life. Did they always want these things, or did they change their goals from earlier ones? If so, when and why? What evidence can you collect that they are likely to change again?

4. Study advertisements in magazines and newspapers to see what proportion contain a blurring of gender roles. In which types of advertisements (i.e., for what kinds of products) is gender blurring more or less likely? How would you explain this relationship?

CHAPTER FOUR

Review Questions

1. What is deviance?

2. What are "formal" and "informal" social control?

3. What is meant by a "social pathology" perspective on deviance?

4. Why did Durkheim believe deviance could benefit society?

5. What are the flaws in Durkheim's approach?

6. What does Merton mean by anomie?

7. What are the adaptations to anomie Merton discusses?

8. What is the labelling approach to deviance?

9. How does the conflict perspective on deviance differ from the other perspectives?

10. What issues are of greatest concern to feminist criminologists?

11. What are "crimes," "norm violations" and "social diversions"?

12. Who is most likely to commit serious crimes?

Discussion Questions

1. *Grokking* is a form of deviant behaviour that was unknown 20 years ago, was barely mentioned 10 years ago, yet today is as widespread as the common cold. We have limited funds to study this change. To understand most about the rise of this new behaviour to prominence, should we spend our money studying Grokkers or the Grok-police?

2. Some believe sociology took a great stride forward when it rejected the social — and personal — pathology explanations of deviance in favour of subcultural theories. Others believe it was a step backward. What do you think?

3. How might different theorists we have discussed go about explaining the observed differences in consensus-crime rates between Canada and the United States? What evidence would we need to test which one was right?

4. Many kinds of crime and deviance are apparently more common in the lower classes than in the higher ones. Given what we know about the reasons for this, for which kinds of crime and deviance would class differences be *least*?

5. The debate over how to reduce crime and delinquency keeps polarizing people. One group says punish the criminal, the other group says treat the criminal. Where do you stand on this issue? Now, organize the most persuasive argument you can for the *opposite* position.

6. Why don't we put organized crime out of business by decriminalizing all the goods and services they offer?

Data Collection Exercises

1. Pairs of students should go to a busy public place (say, a park, shopping centre, subway station) and station themselves six to fifteen metres from each other. They should observe and record all deviant activities there for a period of one hour. Then they should report on their findings and the reasons why their findings are not identical.

2. Design a small questionnaire or interview schedule to measure the attitudes of fellow students to various types of sexual behaviour. Then analyze the data, looking for patterns: specifically, (a) what kinds of people have the greatest tolerance for sexual deviation, and (b) what kinds of attitudes group with which other attitudes.

3. Some have argued that law-abiding people are not criminal because they lack association with criminal skills, attitudes, and values — in short, with criminals. Casually interview your family and friends to determine whether they know any criminals and, if so, which kinds. Would they know how to fence stolen property? Get illegal drugs? Rob a bank?

4. Try a simple, harmless experiment on a friend to see if you can change his or her behaviour by labelling him or her differently. Can you get your friend to behave more politely by praising his politeness? Can you get him to behave more rudely by commenting repeatedly on his rudeness? (Be sure you brief your friend on the reasons for your experiment, and your findings, when you are finished.)

CHAPTER FIVE

**Review
Questions**

1. What is meant by social inequality?

2. In what ways is social inequality social in origin?

3. Define "domination" and "submission."

4. What are some of the symbols of domination we are likely to see in everyday life?

5. How do functionalists explain social inequality?

6. What is the role of class in Marx's theory of stratification?

7. What factors did Weber consider important in understanding inequality?

8. How have Marx's and Weber's theories been combined by more recent sociologists?

9. What issues have feminists raised about the relationship between gender and inequality?

10. What issues have interactionists addressed in looking at inequality?

11. How do equality of condition and equality of opportunity differ?

12. What is social mobility and what factors lead to upward social mobility?

13. What is an elite and how does it differ from a class?

14. What is the difference between absolute poverty and relative poverty?

15. Who tends to be poor in Canadian society?

**Discussion
Questions**

1. Research shows that people who are physically attractive enjoy better opportunities than people who are less physically attractive. Why is that? Is this a "social inequality," as we have defined the term?

2. Who has control over *your* access to the necessities of life — your food, shelter, and clothing? Who has control over that person's access? Are you in the same relation to the means of production as the person who controls your access to necessities?

3. How might one argue that the failure to eliminate inequality in the former Soviet Union does *not* prove Marx's theory wrong? Make the strongest case you can for that view. Then consider what evidence would be needed to prove Marx's theory wrong.

4. Ignoring gender and education, would you rate your chances of entering the Canadian elite as closest to one in (a) 1000, (b) 10,000, or (c) 100,000? (Here are two hints. (1) In 1965, Porter estimated that the corporate elite consisted of just under 1,000 white men. (2) The most recent edition of the *Canadian Who's Who* contained biographies on about 12,000 prominent people from all walks of life.) Give the reasoning behind your estimate.

5. Are the connections between Canada's ruling class and foreign ruling classes likely to become stronger or weaker in the next 50 years? What influences are likely to strengthen or weaken these connections?

6. Is there anything you can do to reduce the risk you will fall into poverty? If so, will you blame yourself if you fall into poverty nonetheless? Which poor people do you *not* blame for their poverty?

Data Collection Exercises

1. Select two or three job categories from the following: used car salesman, hockey player, secretary, dentist, garbage collector, plumber. Design a method for measuring the functional importance of each job, or contribution each one makes to society. Then, using published statistics, measure the average income earned in each category. How well does income correlate with a job's social importance?

2. Collect data on income inequalities in Russia and compare them with income inequalities in Canada. (For example, you might try to find out whether the income gap between hockey players, dentists, and secretaries is wider or narrower in the Soviet Union than it is in Canada.) Report on any data collection and measurement problems you encounter in making this comparison.

3. Using the Canadian Encyclopedia and other biographical sources, randomly select a dozen elite Canadians born since 1900, and collect data on their personal histories. With these data, determine what proportion were born into non-elite families. Of those born into non-elite families, how important was higher education in helping them enter the elite?

4. What are the major industries, or major employers, in your city of residence? Identify the two or three wealthiest companies and find out who owns them. Do the owners live elsewhere and, if so, where? Do these companies have branches in other cities or towns and, if so, where? Other than common ownership, what structures connect the branch in your town with branches elsewhere?

CHAPTER SIX

Review Questions

1. What is ethnicity?

2. What is race?

3. In what sense is Canada an ethnically "pluralistic" society?

4. Why do Canada's native peoples today demand some degree of self-government?

5. What is a "visible minority"?

6. What is assimilation?

7. What different forms can assimilation take?

8. What is the connection between residential segregation and ethnic identity?

9. What is institutional completeness?

10. Why did Porter describe Canada as a "vertical mosaic"?

11. Is Canada still a vertical mosaic?

12. What factors contribute to ethnic group cohesion?

13. What is the difference between "prejudice" and "discrimination"?

14. What is meant by "social distance"?

15. What is racism?

Discussion Questions

1. How are Canada's native peoples like, and how are they unlike, colonized Third World peoples?

2. Given Canada's history of immigration, what kinds of people — and how many — are likely to immigrate in the year 2000?

3. How might you test whether language loss within an ethnic minority leads to a decline in ethnic group cohesion?

4. Racism is only one possible response to economic difficulty. Other historical examples have been crime, political protest, escape into drugs and alcohol, and strengthened religious belief. What determines whether racism will be the response chosen at a particular time and place?

5. Worldwide, has there been more ethnic and racial conflict in the second half of the 20th century than in first half? If so, how do you account for this upsurge?

6. Is the amount of intermarriage between two groups a good measure of the prejudice one group feels for another? If not, why not? Would more intermarriage cause prejudice to decline?

Data Collection Exercises

1. Collect published statistics to show how the pattern of ethnic and racial migration to your home town has changed in the last 100 years.

2. Select any ethnic or racial community — for example, Winnipeg Greeks, Calgary Chinese, Montreal Algerians—and measure its community completeness. (Hint: You should see how Jeffrey Reitz did this in his book *The Survival of Ethnic Groups*. That is one approach to consider.)

3. Study changes in the residential segregation of one particular ethnic group between 1941 and 1991, using published Census statistics.

4. Canadian culture was, historically, founded on a notion of being "the true North, strong and free." Has "northern" meant the same in other cultures as it has in Canada? Study its meaning in one other northern country (for example, Sweden, Russia) and one southern country (for example, Argentina, India).

CHAPTER SEVEN

**Review
Questions**

1. Define sex and gender.

2. How do these two concepts differ?

3. What is meant by patriarchy?

4. What are the consequences of gender socialization?

5. Why did most sociologists in the past not pay much attention to gender issues?

6. Which sociological paradigm has paid the most attention to gender issues?

7. In what ways does gender inequality disadvantage most women?

8. In what ways is gender inequality present in family relations?

9. Are changes in the family structure altering the patterns of domestic gender inequality?

10. In what ways is gender inequality present in the workplace?

11. Is increased participation by women in the labour force altering the patterns of workplace gender inequality?

12. What is a "double standard"?

13. How are prejudice and discrimination against women interconnected with racial and ethnic discrimination?

14. What effects does the fear of violence have upon women's experiences?

15. What does the incidence of date rape tell us about sexual inequality?

16. How are traditional gender roles changing?

17. Has feminism had an effect on traditional gender roles?

**Discussion
Questions**

1. Why do you suppose North Americans are shifting away from preferring sons to preferring one son and one daughter ?

2. What evidence would prove that capitalism is responsible for the growth of inequality between men and women? What does the *actual* evidence indicate?

3. What social changes led to the elimination of a sexual "double standard" in North America? Do you think the change was a good one? Why or why not?

4. To what degree is discrimination responsible for the earnings gap between men and women?

5. Name several other male/female pairings in the workplace that illustrate, as well as doctors and nurses, the structure of gender inequality in our society.

6. Do you agree that "the battle of the sexes" is both more violent and more important than class or racial conflict in our society today?

Data Collection Exercises

1. Find out what are Canada's 10 lowest-paying jobs, as of the 1991 Census. Then using published data from the same Census, find out what proportion of workers in each of these 10 lowest-paying jobs is *female*.

2. In one national survey of attitudes, men and women were asked whether they thought "a proportion of top government jobs should be set aside for women." The answer people gave depended on who was interviewing them: a man or a woman (see Table). Try replicating this study: In cooperation with a person of the opposite sex, carry out interviews on gender-relevant topics and see whether you and your partner get different results.

Gender of Interviewer Effect:
Percent Agreeing with Statement*

Sex of respondent	Sex of interviewer	
	Male	Female
Male	37	58
Female	48	58

* Percent agreeing that "a proportion of top government jobs should be set aside for women."
Source: Institute for Social Research (York University) Newsletter, Spring 1992, Vol. 7, No. 2, Table D.2.

3. Collect data from two or more countries outside Europe and North America to find out whether the "feminization of poverty" is taking place there too.

4. Collect published data on (1) violence against women or (2) income discrimination or (3) domestic work-sharing in a country that is outside North America. What trends are visible in the last ten years or so? Are there the same uncertainties about identifying these trends as we find in North America?

CHAPTER EIGHT

1. Why is the family such an important social institution?

2. How do sociologists define the family?

3. What role does the functionalist perspective assign to the family?

4. What aspects of the family are the focus of the conflict perspective?

5. Why do feminists consider the family to be a "political" institution?

6. What are "polygamy," "polygyny," "polyandry," and "monogamy"?

7. What is the ideal of romantic love?

8. What are "endogamy," "exogamy," "homogamy," and "heterogamy"?

9. Why has marriage been described as a system of "erotic property"?

10. What are the advantages and disadvantages of an "extended" family and of a "nuclear" family?

11. What are some of the problems parenthood poses for husbands and wives?

12. What problems does prolonged dependency pose for family members?

13. What are current trends in family life?

14. What do we know about the causes and consequences of family violence?

1. No one knows precisely why early societies in history, before industrialization, had patriarchal families. What explanation would you offer? What evidence might historians gather to test the validity of your theory?

2. Does a division of labour between spouses have to lead to spousal inequality? Discuss how spousal inequalities might be avoided or reduced in modern marriages.

3. Has the mechanization of housework improved family relations? If so, how? What other kinds of mechanization might solve problems that remain today?

4. Under what conditions might the "flight from marriage and parenthood" stop or even reverse itself? What government policies, if any, might contribute to such a change?

5. What are the ways a two-income family might re-organize its use of time to reduce the tension and conflict parents (especially wives and mothers) commonly feel due to lack of time?

6. Imagine you are a marriage counsellor who has completed an evaluation of a couple. You have to determine whether that couple should stay together or divorce. What factors would your sociological training lead you to take into account?

Data Collection Exercises

1. Conduct confidential interviews with at least six friends and acquaintances to measure their first-hand knowledge of, and thinking about, the sexual abuse of children: how it happens, why it happens, how common it is.

2. Collect historical data on one community or society to measure the proportion of women who worked for pay, the kinds of jobs they did, and the ways they integrated work and family responsibilities.

3. Make a time budget to measure how much time your father and mother spend doing different kinds of tasks — working for pay, domestic chores, child care, relaxing, and so on — on an average working day and on a Saturday or Sunday. (Normally, time budget researchers check people's activities — or ask them to record their own activities — every fifteen minutes from waking up until going to sleep for the night.)

4. Collect data from two couples you know who are roughly the same age, where one is married and the other is cohabiting. What differences can you find in their satisfaction with the relationship, the ways they spend their time and money, and their feelings of commitment to their partner?

CHAPTER NINE

1. What is the "economic order"?

2. How have the four major paradigms approached the issue of work?

3. What was the "Industrial Revolution"?

4. What was the new perspective on society that developed during the Industrial Revolution?

5. What is liberal democracy?

6. What is corporate capitalism?

7. What are the characteristics of an industrial society?

8. What is meant by the convergence thesis?

9. What are the characteristics of Japanese industrial organization?

10. How does specialization produce anomie?

11. What are "mechanical" and "organic" solidarity?

12. What are the characteristics of a bureaucracy?

13. How do simple control and professionalization differ from bureaucratic control?

14. What are the "primary" and "secondary" labour markets?

15. What impact are the new technologies having on work?

16. What effect does alienation have upon work satisfaction?

1. Weber argues that the elimination of tradition, intuition, and superstition from decision-making played an important part in the rise of modern economic and political life. On balance, did social life improve?

2. Durkheim recognized that anomie is a problem of modern societies that will not go away easily. New ways of attaching people to one another, and to new rules, are needed. Is the problem of anomie getting better or worse in Canada?

3. Would people be alienated from their work in a non-capitalist society? Suppose you were studying a non-capitalist society—past, present, or future. What evidence would you look for to determine whether alienation was stronger or weaker than it is in Canada today?

4. Does the laissez-faire (or liberal) ideology increase or decrease people's sense of alienation from their work? From society as a whole?

5. Why would workers with the same amount of education who work equally hard make less money in the secondary labour market (for example, as waiters or taxi drivers) than in the primary labour market (as plumbers or lawyers)? And why would a well-educated, hard-working person be working in the secondary labour market?

6. Is it still appropriate for men and women to make different kinds of educational and occupational (or career) plans in our society?

Data Collection Exercises

1. Collect statistical data on at least three countries that have industrialized or are industrializing right now. With these data, show that as industrial production (for example, the proportion of people working in factories) increases, so does (1) the average person's annual income, (2) the percentage of people who can read and write, and (3) the percentage who live in cities.

2. Collect data from at least six working people to measure their jobs' objective characteristics *and* their degree of job satisfaction. Is there a close connection between the two? If not, why not?

3. Collect data from at least six recent graduates of the educational program you are currently enrolled in. What proportion is unemployed (or has been recently)? What proportion is *underemployed* (see definition in glossary)?

4. Select a particular job that interests you. Find out what new technologies have been adopted for widespread use in that job in the last 20 years. Has their adoption resulted in people losing their jobs?

CHAPTER TEN

Review Questions

1. What is demography?

2. What are some feminist concerns about demography?

3. What is the "Malthusian dilemma"?

4. What is overpopulation?

5. What are positive and preventive checks?

6. What is demographic transition theory?

7. What is meant by a population's fertility rate?

8. What is meant by a population's mortality rate?

9. How did population growth change after industrialization?

10. Why is there doubt about the validity of demographic transition theory?

11. How is fertility measured?

12. What role has migration played in Canadian society?

13. Why has migration become a political issue in Canada?

14. What impact does population change have upon the environment?

Discussion Questions

1. If the world's population is doubling every 40 years and the population today is about five billion people, what will be the population of the world in 200 years? What will be the population density of the world? Will that be too many people? Why or why not?

2. What are some of the reasons that some countries pass through the entire demographic transition process quickly and others take a much longer time?

3. Will future resource discoveries have as great an impact on the Canadian population as past ones have? Why or why not?

4. Mortality rates are an indication of social (class) inequalities, and we are all in favour of people living, not dying. Why, then, is little action taken to eliminate these social inequalities in risks of death?

5. How will the changing age composition of Canada's population change the industry that you are training to enter?

6. The graphs that end this chapter tell a more optomistic story than most of the evidence we have considered. Where do you stand in this debate about the future of the population and the environment? What evidence presented in this chapter has changed your mind?

Data Collection Exercises

1. Examine a Census of Canada that is at least 50 years old. How do the questions it asks about a particular topic (for example, household composition, employment status, ethnic origin) and the ways it categorizes the answers differ from the most recent Census?

2. Collect data from published Canadian sources on the fertility (childbearing behaviour) of women 20-24 years and 30-34 years old from 60 years ago, from 30 years ago, and for today. What has changed?

3. Use published statistics to determine what proportion of people in your town or city have changed their residence in the last five years. Does this proportion seem high or low, compared with your own experiences (for example, the mobility of the people you know)?

4. Collect statistics on the ages at which people typically leave (that is, die or retire from) the occupation you are training to enter. (If they are not available, what do you imagine they look like?) How would your career be affected if no one currently in the occupation was forced to retire at age 65?

CHAPTER ELEVEN

Review Questions

1. What is meant by an evolutionary theory of change?

2. What role do the concepts of "differentiation" and "integration" play in evolutionary theories?

3. What is meant by a revolutionary theory of change?

4. What is the "state"?

5. What are the characteristics of the authoritarian state?

6. What is the difference between the state and "civil society"?

7. What role do ideologies play in social change?

8. How do radical and reformist ideologies differ?

9. What is meant by a "social movement"?

10. What is relative deprivation theory?

11. What is resource mobilization theory?

12. What role does "charisma" play in social movements?

13. How does new technology result in social change?

14. What are the signs of underdevelopment?

15. What is cultural imperialism?

Discussion Questions

1. Why do you suppose Canada has never had authoritarian political rule and many countries have never had anything *but* authoritarian rule?

2. Where progressive thought is concerned, is public opinion usually ahead of, or behind, the views of political leaders? An example of where it is behind leaders' opinions is on the reinstatement of capital punishment. Most of the public want it; the leaders do not. Can you think of an example where public opinion is ahead of leaders' opinion?

3. Why are charismatic leaders more likely to emerge in some periods of history than in others?

4. Ideas are powerful forces for social change, but they must come from somewhere. Why are certain kinds of ideas — for example, gender equality — more likely to arise and find acceptance in some times and places and not others?

5. Computers can do great good or great harm. What factors will decide which use people make of them in your lifetime?

6. Why does the idea that we are at "the end of history" appeal to many people? Do you suppose people are always imagining that they are at a turning point in history? If so, why?

Data Collection Exercises

1. Collect some information about crowd behaviour at sporting events in the 19th and 20th centuries. How has this behaviour changed (e.g., is it more or less polite, more or less violent, and so on)? How do you account for the changes?

2. Select a particular social movement for closer study. Find out what resources members needed to become an effective voice of protest.

3. Study the science or technology of an ancient or medieval society to find out what discoveries that society had made in a particular area — for example, in medicine, sanitation, bridge building, or weaponry. Were their discoveries built upon by later civilizations, or lost and "rediscovered?"

4. Study a small group you know well — your family, for example — to find out whether contradiction and conflict mark change within a group. Is change discontinuous and marked by "leaps" from one stage to another?

CHAPTER TWELVE

Review Questions

1. What is the basic question asked by social research?
2. What is meant by "cause" and "effect"?
3. What is an explanation?
4. What is a hypothesis?
5. What is prediction?
6. What are "dependent" and "independent variables"?
7. What are "quantitative" and "qualitative data"?
8. What is a research design?
9. What are the different types of research design?
10. What are the different types of measurement scales?
11. How do we know when a measure is "good"?
12. How do concepts match-up with measurements?
13. What are the different types of samples used in research?
14. What are the different research strategies used by sociologists?
15. What are some common forms of bias sociologists should try to avoid when engaging in research?

Discussion Questions

1. You will learn more by studying a small problem in depth than a large problem superficially. Show this in respect to a particular example: for example, how the presence of a child with leukemia affects relations between family members *versus* the social effects of illness in Canadian society.

2. Discuss the arguments for and against experimenting on human beings. What useful information can we gain about social relationships only by experimenting? To what practical uses could we put this information?

3. Discuss how you might measure students' satisfaction with a college course they are taking. Should this measure be used to award promotions and cash bonuses for good teaching?

4. How would you select a sample of AIDS victims for study? That is, what type of sampling method would produce the required number of cases? Then, what would be your preferred method of collecting data? Why?

5. (This one assumes fluency in English.) What difficulty would an extraterrestrial have analysing the content of this year's best-selling books and most watched television programs? What would the being find out about North Americans by doing this?

6. Suppose a researcher has found that many juvenile delinquents have a low opinion of themselves: especially their intelligence and appearance. Give two

interpretations of this finding and devise research that would prove only one was right.

Data Collection Exercises

1. Collect published statistics on the average income and average education of people in (at least) ten different occupations. Which occupations most closely follow the rule that education and income vary together? Which occupations deviate most from that rule? Can you explain your findings?

2. Think of a sociological generalization — e.g., high education and high income go together — that you feel fairly certain is valid. After you figure out what the two deviant cases would be, select one for study. Find and interview a "deviant case" and come back prepared to explain your results.

3. Toronto has a new NBA basketball team, and the owners surveyed public opinion to help them choose a name for the team. A telephone survey of 302 Torontonians found support for the following names, in descending order of preference: Beavers, Bobcats, T-Rex, Grizzlies, Scorpions, Raptors, Terriers, Dragons, Hogs, Tarantulas. Only 10% of those surveyed had no opinion. The name "Beavers" proved to be particularly appealing to women and people over age 50 (*The Globe and Mail*, Wed. Apr. 20, 1994, p. C). Devise a theory to explain the responses to the survey, and design a research project that would test your theory. (Be sure to specify your hypotheses and what data you would collect; you don't actually have to collect them.)

4. By observing your classmates, figure out which pairs of students are best friends, which are mere acquaintances, and which ones are enemies. Are your classmates generally friends of their friends' friends and enemies of their enemies' friends? Check your conclusions three months later. Has anything changed?

Suggested Readings

CHAPTER ONE

Archer, M. (1991) "Sociology for one world: Unity and diversity" *International Sociology*, 6 (2), June, 131-147. An interesting essay on the challenges and problems of creating a world sociology. In particular, Archer warns us away from the notion of "modernization," because of its hidden assumptions.

Collins, R. and M. Mayakowsky (1989) *The Discovery of Society*. New York: Random House. A brilliant short history of the development of sociology, set against the backdrop of 19th- and 20th-century social and political change.

Giddens, A. (1987) *Sociology: A Brief but Critical Introduction*. San Diego: Harcourt Brace Jovanovich. A short, interesting book on one central debate in sociology: whether contemporary social problems are due to capitalism (as Marx would say), industrialism (as Durkheim would say), or bureaucracy (as Weber would say).

Mills, C. Wright (1967) *The Sociological Imagination*. New York: Oxford University Press. This classic work in sociology is written from the conflict perspective. It emphasizes the close connection between personal troubles (private experience) and public issues (the wider social context).

Nisbet, R. A. (1966) *The Sociological Tradition*. New York: Basic Books. Wonderfully written, this long book organizes much of the history of sociology around the "unit-ideas of sociology," or its founders' key concerns: community, authority, status, the sacred, and alienation.

Tepperman, L., J. Curtis, S. J. Wilson and A. Wain (eds.) (1994) *Small World: International Readings in Sociology*. Scarborough: Prentice-Hall Canada. This collection of 48 readings provides interesting case studies that illustrate many of the points made in this book. Despite the differences among people of different cultures, what are most impressive are the similarities of the problems people face and the solutions they use to solve these problems.

CHAPTER TWO

Brand, S. (1987) *The Media Lab: Inventing the Future at MIT*. New York: Viking Penguin. This book, about major advances in information technology, storage and communication, will specially appeal to "techies" who feel that cultural change is driven by technological change. A strong point of this book is the sense it gives of how people work to develop new communication technologies, media, and networks.

Burke, J. (1985) *The Day the Universe Changed*. Boston: Little, Brown. A fascinating and popular account of major changes in the cultural history of the world (an ambitious goal!) that was the basis of a PBS television series a few years back. This book gives you a different slant on the issue of "globalization" and global culture by reminding you just how tightly tied together people have been for centuries, if not millennia.

Buss, A. (1989) "The economic ethics of Russian-Orthodox Christianity," Parts I and II, *International Sociology*, 4 (3), September, and 4 (4), December, 447-472 respectively. An extended essay that follows in the tradition of Max Weber's attempt to explain social and economic change in terms of religious beliefs that help and hinder such change.

Fussell, P. (1983) *Class*. New York: Ballantine Books. A witty book on culture in general, and upper-class culture in particular, this book shows — among other things — how you can judge a person's class from his or her living-room decoration.

Jianxiong, P. (1989) "Duality in Chinese culture and its influence on Chinese society," *International Sociology*, 5(1), March, 75-88. Another attempt to apply Weber's cultural analysis to the explanation of economic and political change. This article finds the Chinese traditionally caught in a bind between religiosity and secularism, collectivism and individualism.

Willis, P. (1977) *Learning to Labor: How Working Class Kids get Working Class Jobs*. New York: Columbia University Press. This ethnography brilliantly describes the school subculture (or is it a counterculture?) of working class children. Its purpose is to explain how and why these young people reject the school's demands and, accordingly, reject the opportunities that conformity would bring them.

CHAPTER THREE

Elkin, F. and G. Handel (1989) *The Child and Society: The Process of Socialization*, fifth edition. New York: Random House. This is a classic reference work for anyone interested in knowing more about the topic of socialization.

Ellis, D. and L. Sayer (1986) *When I Grow Up: Expectations and Aspirations of Canadian Schoolchildren*. Ottawa: Labour Canada. This study of over 700 Canadian school children examines their opinions (stereotypes) of various occupational choices and their future plans. The authors find that children seem to understand that both boys and girls can work in non-stereotyped fields, but their own job choices do not reflect this diversity.

Handel, G. (1988) *Childhood Socialization*. New York: Adeline de Gruyter. This is a collection of 19 articles dealing with such topics as the family, schools, peer groups, and television as agents of gender and class socialization. Several of these articles look beyond the North American context.

Kostash, M. (1987) *No Kidding: Inside the World of Teenage Girls*. Toronto: McClelland and Stewart. This Canadian study is a rich analysis of the teen years, based on lengthy interviews with teenage girls who talk candidly about boys, friends, family and sex.

Shattuck, R. (1980) *The Forbidden Experiment: The Story of the Wild Boy of Aveyron*. New York: Pocket Books, Washington Square Press. Critic and poet Shattuck makes this case history into a general enquiry on the meaning of civilized life: what it gains us, and what it loses.

Tepperman, L. (1994) *Choices and Chances*, second edition. Toronto: Holt HBJ. This book of "sociology for everyday life" explains why people want what they want out of life and get what they get. It also suggests how the reader might close the gap between what he or she wants and gets in an unequal society.

CHAPTER FOUR

Becker, H. S. (1963) *Outsiders*. New York: Free Press. In this widely read classic, Becker spells out the labelling theory of deviance, then applies the theory to a variety of outsiders including jazz musicians and marijuana smokers.

Erikson, K. T. (1966) *Wayward Puritans*. New York: Wiley. The early Puritans in Massachusetts "created" deviants where none really existed. As Erikson shows, this strengthened their solidarity and sense of normality.

Goffman, E. (1961) *Asylums*. Garden City, New York: Doubleday. Through the eyes of participant-observers and inmates, we learn about life in "total institutions" which dramatize the boundary between insiders and outsiders.

Gullestad, M. (1984) *Kitchen-Table Society*. Oslo: Universitetsforlaget. This book on domestic life in Norway illustrates the fact that all social arrangements, from the smallest (two-person couples) up to the largest (total societies), are systems of rules and expectations that are constantly being negotiated, revised, enforced, destroyed, and recreated.

Levinson, D. (1989) *Family Violence in Cross-Cultural Perspective*. Frontiers of Anthropology, Vol. 1. Newbury Park: Sage Publications. This essay uses the Human Relations Area Files to find out typical characteristics of societies in which family violence is common, and why domestic violence is justified in different ways in different societies.

Williams, H. A. (1990) "Families in refugee camps," *Human Organization*, Vol. 49, No. 2, 100-109. As civil wars rage around the world, families are forced from their home communities into refugee camps and other temporary shelters. This article explores what happens to family members when they become refugees. In short, there is a breakdown of traditional social controls and an increase in deviance, even violence.

CHAPTER FIVE

Abercrombie, N., S. Hill, and B. S. Turner (1980) *The Dominant Ideology Thesis*. London: Allen and Unwin. A detailed analysis of theories on the role of ideology in supporting social inequalities, and in promoting social change.

Curtis, J., E. Grabb and N. Guppy, eds. (1993) *Social Inequality in Canada: Patterns, Problems and Policies*, second edition. Scarborough: Prentice-Hall. Contains a series of articles that show how patterns of social inequality are rooted in ideological supports (including the law), and that changes in an egalitarian direction have usually required political struggles between have-nots and haves.

Lewis, O. (1961) *The Children of Sanchez: Autobiography of a Mexican Family*. New York: Vintage. A poignant story of a poor Mexican family, told in the family members' own words. This book illustrates the experience of a culture of poverty.

Marchak, P. M. (1988) *Ideological Perspectives on Canada*, third ed. Toronto: McGraw-Hill Ryerson. Provides discussions of various ideologies in Canada, and their interpretations of relations to elites, class protests and nationalism.

Rossi, P. H. (1989) *Down and Out in America: The Origins of Homelessness*. Chicago: University of Chicago Press. A penetrating analysis of why, in North America, homelessness and extreme economic hardship increased markedly in the last decade. The author puts forward policy suggestions based on the analysis.

Tepperman, L. and J. Curtis, eds. (1994) *Haves and Have-Nots: International Readings on Social Inequality*. Englewood Cliffs, NJ: Prentice-Hall. A selection of edited readings from around the world that focusses on class, ethnic, racial and gender-based inequalities. Of particular interest are the different ways people resist, and protest against, their conditions.

CHAPTER SIX

Bienvenue, R. M. and J. E. Goldstein (1985) *Ethnicity and Ethnic Relations in Canada*, second edition. Toronto: Butterworths. An outstanding collection of readings that are historical and contemporary, descriptive and theoretical, about the experiences of different groups in Canada and, especially, about inequality and conflict in Canadian society.

Breton, R. et al. (1990) *National Survival in Dependent Societies: Social Change in Canada and Poland*. Ottawa: Carleton University Press. This volume focuses on policy directions around ethnicity and "multiculturalism" in the two countries. Canada has become more multicultural, while Poland has changed in the opposite direction.

Flere, S. (1991) "Explaining ethnic antagonism in Yugoslavia," *European Sociological Review*, 7(3), December, 183-193. This article is about the conflict between ethnic groups that results from regional disparities in the former Yugoslavia. The precipitating factor is the loss of people's confidence in the legitimacy of the state's way of regulating ethnic conflict.

Howitt, D. and J. Owusu-Bempah (1990) "The pragmatics of institutional racism: Beyond words," *Human Relations*, 43(9), 885-89   9. This study illustrates that white Britons are more willing to encourage white initiative than black initiative. Such unequal treatment demonstrates and maintains racial inequality just as well as the old-fashioned, more blatantly racist methods.

Porter, J. (1965) *The Vertical Mosaic*. Toronto: University of Toronto Press. In the most widely celebrated work in Canadian sociology, John Porter shows the connections between social class and ethnic status. He explains why ethnic groups have had trouble improving their standing in the society.

Telles, E. E. (1992) "Residential segregation by skin color in Brazil," *American Sociological Review*, 57, April, 186-197. Brazil has high levels of racial interaction, at least among the poor (who intermarry and form friendships across colour lines). And the "official" ideology of Brazil's government says that there is little or no racism. Yet residential segregation does exist in Brazil and whites are more segregated from blacks than from mulattoes.

CHAPTER SEVEN

Armstrong, P. and H. Armstrong (1993) *The Double Ghetto*. third edition. Toronto: McClelland and Stewart. Married women inhabit a "double ghetto" which means that, unlike their husbands, they work a double day. Their freedom to work for pay, pursue a career, and be economically independent does not mean freedom from domestic work. Instead it means a double burden.

Brownmiller, S. (1986) *Femininity*. London: Paladin Books. A witty survey of what we mean by the term "femininity" in our culture, and how (historically) the term came to take on that meaning. Includes sections on body, skin, hair, clothes, voice, movement, emotion and ambition.

DeKeseredy, W.S. and R. Hinch (1991) *Woman Abuse: Sociological Perspectives*. Toronto: Thompson Educational Publishing. An excellent review of the literature on wife abuse, dating abuse, rape and sexual assault by two Canadian sociologists, one of whom (DeKeseredy) is a co-researcher on the dating violence study cited in this chapter.

Hochschild, A. (1989) *The Second Shift*. New York: Avon Books. Here, the author thoroughly and eloquently explains the important relationship between domestic equality and marital satisfaction. She concludes that the happiest two-job marriages are between men and women who do not load housework onto the woman, nor devalue that work: they share the burden.

Kanter, R.M. (1977) *Men and Women of the Corporation*. New York: Basic Books. The first of Kanter's books to explore the reciprocal benefits between organizational openness (e.g., gender equality) and collective well-being. In short, everyone's happier and more productive, and the organization also does better, when women are numerous and included at all levels.

Weiss, D. (1991) *The Great Divide: How Males and Females Really Differ*. New York: Poseidon Press. A collection of undigested statistical facts about men and women divided into the following categories: marriage and home life, crime and drugs, romance and sex, work and money, school, social and political issues, sports and leisure, bodies and beauty, and so on. No doubt about it: men and women *really* are different. The question is, Why?

CHAPTER EIGHT

Arendell, T. J. (1987) "Women and the economics of divorce in the contemporary United States," *Signs*, 13,1, 121-135. This article documents the different costs of divorce for women and men. Men's economic position typically improves with divorce, while most women are far worse off economically. Arendell discusses the reasons for this inequity and outlines policies needed to narrow the gap.

Baker, M. (1990) *Families: Changing Trends in Canada*. Toronto: McGraw-Hill Ryerson. This multi-authored text focuses on changing families in Canada. Topics covered include: the origins of the family, mate selection, economic conditions and family structures, alternatives to traditional marriage, marital dissolution, family law and patterns of family violence.

Bernard, J. (1973) *The Future of Marriage*. New York: Bantam Books. This provocative book shows how the traditional marriage — in reality, an uneasy mix of "*his* marriage and *her* marriage" — is giving way to new thinking and new practices.

Burch, T. K. and B. J. Matthews (1987) "Household formation in developed societies," *Population and Development Review*, 13,3, September, 495-511. The authors of this article discuss trends in family structure and household size over the last quarter century. From their analysis, one would be tempted to predict a continued trend to ever smaller households, although cost will be a limiting factor.

Mandell, N. and A. Duffy, eds. (1993) *Reconstructing the Canadian Family: Feminist Perspectives*. Toronto: Butterworths. An important collection of the work of feminist scholars, this book puts the modern family against a backdrop of women's "hidden history." The focus is on gender inequality in family life.

Tepperman, L. and S. J. Wilson, eds. (1993) *Next of Kin: International Readings on the Changing Family*. Englewood Cliffs, NJ: Prentice Hall. A collection of readings from all over the world, showing that many of the problems in family life we are grappling with have already been solved in some societies, or have yet to arise in others. Topics discussed include marriage, reproduction, conflict, policy, and future patterns of change.

CHAPTER NINE

Bell, D. (1973) *The Coming of Post-industrial Society*. New York: Basic Books. This key work on the future of economic organization pulls together a great deal of earlier writing; it is also full of interesting ideas. The major debate about work started by this book has never ended.

Edwards, R. (1979) *Contested Terrain: The Transformation of the Workplace in the Twentieth Century*. New York: Basic Books. This exciting book about the evolution of worker-employer relations in North America explains how our own ambitions keep us doing what the boss wants us to do.

Hamper, B. (1992) *Rivethead: Tales From the Assembly Line*. New York: Warner Books. This lively, gritty and often funny book is written by a man who spent several years working on a General Motors assembly line. He offers an insider's perspective on why this kind of work can be, at different times, boring, challenging, ridiculous and tragic.

Howard, R.(1985) *Brave New Workplace*. New York: Viking. In many countries, there has been a growing trend toward more employee participation in workplace decision-making. This volume critically analyzes that development. The author concludes that most cases of this approach are really managers manipulating their employees. Workers believe they have control and

autonomy, but the most important result is more managerial control over workers.

Krahn, H. J. and G. S. Lowe (1988) *Work, Industry and Canadian Society*. Toronto: Nelson. An excellent introduction to work and industry in Canada, which includes up-to-date discussions of labour markets, women's work, and industrial conflict.

Sennett, R. and J. Cobb(1973) *The Hidden Injuries of Class*. New York: Vintage. The psychological costs of having a low status, menial job in a class-conscious society are examined in this book. The authors interviewed blue collar workers to find out their feelings about their own work and work in general.

CHAPTER TEN

Chen, P. (1984) "China's other revolution: Findings from the one in 1,000 fertility survey," *International Family Planning Perspectives*, 10, 2, June, 48-57. This huge survey of Chinese women documents the amazing reductions in fertility that followed from official state policy to promote the idea of one child per woman.

Huth, M. J. (1986) "Population prospects for sub-Saharan Africa: Determinants, consequences and policy," *Journal of Contemporary African Studies*, Vol. 5, No. 1/2, (April/October), 167-181. A comprehensive report on the state of fertility planning and fertility behaviour in sub-Saharan Africa, where many women still desire (and achieve) the world's highest levels of recorded childbearing.

Knodel, J. and E. van de Walle (1979) "Lessons from the past: Policy implications of historical fertility studies," *Population and Development Review*, 5 (2), June, 217-245. A systematic attempt to use historical materials to understand why fertility fell in Europe when, where and how it did. In short, we still don't know the answer, but we *do* know that it's not what we used to think the answer was!

Laslett, P. (1979) *The World We Have Lost*. London: Methuen. This classic work weaves dry statistics and historical documents into a fascinating picture of Europe (especially England) before the coming of industrialization. It asks whether we have lost more than we have gained from the change.

McNeill, W.H. (1976) *Plagues and Peoples*. Garden City, New York: Anchor Books. Written by a prize-winning author, this book shows how human history has been shaped by shifting "disease balances" and "disease pools." It will make you wonder whether people make their own history.

Ukaegbu, A.O. (1977) "Socio-cultural determination of fertility: A case study of rural Eastern Nigeria," *Journal of Comparative Family Studies*, 8, 1, Spring, 99-115. Based on a survey of Nigerian peasant women, this study gives us an idea of the cultural roots of African fertility — particularly, the high value Africans place on children as "gifts from God."

CHAPTER ELEVEN

Chirot, D. (1979) *Social Change in the Twentieth Century*. New York: Harcourt Brace Jovanovich. A brilliant and ambitious attempt to understand all social change since 1913 in the context of the "world system." Read how Canada managed, in only 80 years, to move from the periphery to the semi-periphery of world events.

Lane, D. (1982) *The End of Social Inequality? Class, Status and Power Under State Socialism*. London: Allen and Unwin. A detailed analysis of the relationship of state power to patterns of inequality in socialist regimes.

Laxer, G. (1982) *Open for Business*. Toronto: Oxford University Press. In this outstanding book, the author uses a comparative approach to examine the role of the state in shaping historical patterns of foreign ownership in the Canadian economy.

Skocpol, T. (1979) *States and Social Revolutions*. Cambridge: Cambridge University Press. A masterful comparison of the revolutions that occurred in France, Russia, and China. It attempts to explain why revolutions occur when and where they do, and the reasons they turn out differently.

Weber, M. (1946). *From Max Weber: Essays in Sociology* (H. Gerth and C.W. Mills, eds. and trans.). New York: Oxford University Press. Also, Weber, Max (1947) *The Theory of Social and Economic Organization* (T. Parsons, ed. and trans.), New York: The Free Press. One gets the impression that Weber was not an elegant writer. But what he lacks in grace he more than makes up for with encyclopedic knowledge, unquenchable curiosity, and an amazing ability to find connections between political, legal, social, economic and religious changes.

Wolf, E. (1982) *Europe and the People Without History*. Berkeley: University of California Press. A sweeping world-wide perspective on the ways expanding European capitalism and colonialism affected pre-capitalist societies, including their structures of class and stratification.

CHAPTER TWELVE

Babbie, E. (1988) *Observing Ourselves*. Belmont, California: Wadsworth. This author has written a number of enjoyable textbooks on sociology and social research. This one focuses on the methods of qualitative research and does so very well.

Converse, J.M. and H. Schuman (1974) *Conversations at Random: Survey Research as Interviewers See It*. New York: John Wiley. In this witty and entertaining book, the vignettes, anecdotes, and reflections of interviewers point out the dangers and challenges of data collection by interviewing.

Hammond, P. (1964) *Sociologists at Work: Essays on the Craft of Social Research*. New York: Basic Books. This highly readable account of some important sociological research projects includes information that rarely comes to the attention of readers.

Majchrzak, A. (1984) *Methods of Policy Research*. Beverly Hills: Sage Publications, 1984. This easy-to-read book discusses the problems of doing social research for a client in an organizational setting. The author finds that identifying points of conflict and "stakeholders" is critical for the research to succeed.

Whyte, W. F. (1955) *Street Corner Society: The Social Structure of an Italian Slum*. Chicago: University of Chicago Press, 1955. Whyte studied youth in an Italian slum of Boston during the 1930s. This is a classic study using participant observation and shows the strength and weakness of the method.

Yin, R.K. (1984) *Case Study Research: Design and Methods*. Beverly Hills, California. This author develops the notion of "pattern-matching" to test competing theories on only one case — a single person or organization. The writing is energetic, the research advice offered is practical and thorough.

References

Abercrombie, N., S. Hill and B. S. Turner (1980) *The Dominant Ideology Thesis*. London: Allen and Unwin

Adamchak, D.J. (1989) "Population aging in sub-Saharan Africa: The effects of development on the elderly," *Population and Environment*, 10 (3), spring, 162-176

Adebayo, A. and D.J. Adamchak (1991) "Ethnic affiliation and fertility attitudes of Nigerian university students," *College Student Journal*, 25 (1), Mar, 470-477

Adler, F. (1975) *Sisters in Crime: The Rise of the New Female Criminal*. New York: McGraw-Hill

Aflatooni, A. and M.P. Allen (1991) "Government sanctions and collective political protest in periphery and semi-periphery states: A time-series analysis," *Journal of Political and Military Sociology*, 19 (1), summer, 29-45

Aghajanian, A. (1988) "Husband-wife conflict among two-worker families in Shiraz, Iran," *International Journal of Sociology of the Family*, 18 (1), spring, 15-19

—— (1991) "The impact of development on the status of women: A district level analysis in Iran," *Journal of Developing Societies*, 7 (2), July-Oct, 292-298

Ahmed, U.A. (1986) "Marriage and its transition in Bangladesh" *International Journal of Sociology of the Family*, 16 (1) spring, 49-59.

Akindutire, I.O. (1992) "Sport as a manifestation of cultural heritage in Nigeria," *International Review for the Sociology of Sport*, 27 (1), 27-36

Albrecht, H.J. (1987) "Foreign minorities and the criminal justice system in the Federal Republic of Germany," *Howard Journal of Criminal Justice*, 26 (4), Nov, 272-286

Alexander, J.C., M.A. Morrissey and S.M. Shortell (1986) "Effects of competition, regulation, and corporatization on hospital-physician relationships," *Journal of Health and Social Behaviour*, 27 (3), Sept, 220-235

Alexander, K.L., A. M. Pallas and S. Holupka (1987) "Consistency and change in educational stratification: Recent trends regarding social background and college access," *Research in Social Stratification and Mobility*, 6, 161-185

Almaguer, T. (1991) "Chicano men: A cartography of homosexual identity and behavior," *Differences*, 3 (2), summer, 75-100

Alo, O.I. (1985) "Indigenous conceptions, work attitudes and national development in Nigeria," *International Journal of Sociology and Social Policy*, 5 (3), 1-10

Alt, J. (1983) "Sport and cultural reification: From ritual to mass consumption," *Theory, Culture and Society*, 1 (3), 93-107

Altrocchi, J. (1988) "Happy traditional and companionship marriages," *Social Casework*, 69 (7), Sept, 434-442

Amato, P.R. and G. Ochiltree (1987) "Child and adolescent competence in intact, one-parent, and step-families: An Australian study," *Journal of Divorce*, 10 (3-4), spring-summer, 75-96

Amegbe, A. (1990) "Debt relief and growth prospects in sub-Saharan Africa," *Journal of Social, Political and Economic Studies*, 15 (2), summer, 225-234

Annis, R.C. and B. Corenblum (1986) "Effect of test language and experimenter race on Canadian Indian children's racial and self-identity," *Journal of Social Psychology*, 126 (6), Dec, 761-773

Aptekar, L. (1989a) "Colombian street children: Gamines and chupagruescos," *Adolescence*, 24 (96), winter, 783-794

—— (1989b) "Characteristics of the street children of Colombia," *Child Abuse and Neglect*, 13 (3), 427-437

—— (1990) "Family structure and adolescence: The case of the Colombian street children," *Journal of Adolescent Research*, 5 (1), Jan, 67-81

Arliss, L. (1989-90) "An integration of accounts and interaction analysis of communication in long-standing relationships," *Research on Language and Social Interaction*, 23, 41-64

Armand, Y. (1989) "Democracy in Haiti: The legacy of anti-democratic political and social traditions," *International Journal of Politics, Culture and Society*, 2 (4), summer, 537-562

Armstrong, P. and H. Armstrong (1978) *The Double Ghetto*. Toronto: McClelland and Stewart

Arnold, F. and L. Zhaoxiang (1986) "Sex preference, fertility, and family planning in China," *Population and Development Review*, 12 (2), June, 221-246

Arnoti, B. (1987) "Low educational attainment in Canada, 1975–1985," *Canadian Social Trends*, spring, pp. 28–32.

Aronowitz, S. (1990) "The future of socialism?" *Social Text*, 24, 85-116

Ashley, D. (1991) "Class struggle in the P.R.C. before and after 'Tienanmen Square'," *Humanity and Society*, 15 (2), May, 156-182

Atkinson, T.H. (1980) "Public perceptions on the quality of life" in *Statistics Canada Perspectives Canada III.* (Catalogue No. 11-511E) Ottawa: Supply and Services, 275-291

Aucoin, P.M. (1990) "Domestic violence and social relations of conflict in Fiji," *Pacific Studies*, 13 (3), July, 23-42

Axelrod, J.N. (1982 [1968]) "Attitude measures that predict purchase," *Journal of Advertising Research*, Classics, Volume 1, September, 15-29

Aytac, I. (1990) "Sharing household tasks in the United States and Sweden: A reassessment of Kohn's theory," *Sociological Spectrum*, 10 (3), 357-371

Baar, E. (1978) "Issei, Nisei and Sansei" in D. Glenday, H. Guindon, and A. Turowetz (eds.) *Modernization and the Canadian State.* Toronto: Macmillan of Canada

Badets, J. (1989) "Canada's immigrant population," *Canadian Social Trends*, autumn, 2-6

Baer, D., E. Grabb, and W. Johnston (1990) "Reassessing differences in Canadian and American values," pp. 86-97 in J. Curtis and L. Tepperman (eds.), *Images of Canada: The Sociological Tradition.* Scarborough: Prentice-Hall Canada

—— (1993) "National character, regional culture and the values of Canadians," *Canadian Review of Sociology and Anthropology*, 30 (1), February, 13-36

Balakrishnan, T.R. (1976) Ethnic residential segregation in the metropolitan areas of Canada," *Canadian Journal of Sociology*, 1(4), 481-498.

—— (1982) " Changing patterns in ethnic residential segregation in the metropolitan areas of Canada," *Canadian Review of Sociology and Anthropology*, 19(1), 92-110.

Baldus, B. and V. Tribe (1978) "Perceptions of social inequality among public school children" *Canadian Review of Sociology and Anthropology*, 15 (1), 50-60

Balkwell, J. W. (1990) "Ethnic inequality and the rate of homicide," *Social Forces*, 69 (1), Sept, 53-70

Bane, M.J. and D.T. Ellwood (1989) "One fifth of the nation's children: Why are they poor?" *Science*, 245, 4922, 8 Sept, 1047-1053

Bannai, H. and D.A. Cohen (1985) "The passive-methodical image of Asian American students in the school system," *Sociology and Social Research*, 70 (1), Oct, 79-81

Barnett, R.C. and G.K. Baruch (1987) "Determinants of fathers' participation in family work," *Journal of Marriage and the Family*, 49 (1), Feb, 29-40

Baron, R. and F. Feeney (1977) "Juvenile diversion through family counseling: A program for the diversion of status offenders in Sacramento County" unpublished

Barthelemy, M. (1990) "Patterns of political socialization in a social democratic culture: The case of Norway," *European Journal of Political Research*, 18 (4), July, 467-489

Basu, A. (1990) "India's youth," *Population Review*, 34 (1-2), Jan-Dec, 38-44

Bautista-Foley, M.L.F. (1988) "Historical influences on gender preference in the Philippines," *Journal of Comparative Family Studies*, 19 (1), spring, 143-153

Beaujot, R. (1988) "Canada's demographic profile," pp. 39-70 in J. Curtis and L. Tepperman (eds.), *Understanding Canadian Society.* Toronto: McGraw-Hill Ryerson

Becker, C.B. (1988) "Old and new: Japan's mechanisms for crime control and social justice," *Howard Journal of Criminal Justice*, 27 (4), Nov, 283-296

Becker, G.S. (1981) *A Treatise on the Family.* Cambridge, Massachusetts: Harvard University Press

Becker, H.S. (1963) *Outsiders: Studies in the Sociology of Deviance.* New York: Free Press

Bell, D. (1960) "Crime as an American way of life," Reprinted in *The End of Ideology.* New York: Free Press

—— (1973) *The Coming of Post-industrial Society.* New York: Basic Books.

Ben-Ezer, G. (1985) "Cross-cultural misunderstandings: The case of Ethiopian immigrant Jews in Israeli society," *Israel Social Science Research*, 3 (1-2), 63-73

Ben-Rafael, E., R. Herzlich and M. Freund (1990) "A symbol of identity or symbolic capital; The social path of the French language in Israel," *Revue francaise de sociologie*, 31 (2), Apr-June, 315-329

Benson, M.L. (1989) "The influence of class position on the formal and informal sanctioning of white-collar offenders," *Sociological Quarterly*, 30 (3), Sept, 465-479

Berger, J. (1972) *Ways of Seeing.* New York: Viking

Bernard, J. (1973) *The Future of Marriage.* New York: Bantam Books

Berry, J.W., R. Kalin, and D.M. Taylor (1977) *Multiculturalism and Ethnic Attitudes in Canada.* Ottawa: Supply and Services

Betcherman, G. (1990) "Computer technology, work and society," *Canadian Journal of Sociology*, 15 (2), spring, 195-201

Bharat, S. (1986) "Single-parent family in India: Issues and implications," *Indian Journal of Social Work*, 47 (1), Apr, 55-65

—— (1988) "Children of single parents in a slum community," *Indian Journal of Social Work*, 49 (4), Oct, 367-376

Bibby, R.W. (1992) *Fragmented Gods: The Poverty and Potential of Religion in Canada*. Toronto: Irwin

Bibby, R.W. and D.C. Posterski (1985) *The Emerging Generation: An Inside Look at Canada's Teenagers*. Toronto: Irwin

Bielby, W.T. and D.D. Bielby (1989) "Family ties: Balancing commitments to work and family in dual earner families," *American Sociological Review*, 54 (5), Oct, 776-789

—— (1992) "I will follow him: Family ties, gender-role beliefs, and reluctance to relocate for a better job," *American Journal of Sociology*, 97 (5), Mar, 1241-1267

Biggart, N.W. (1990) "Institutionalized patrimonialism in Korean business," *Comparative Social Research*, 12, 113-133

Black, R.B. (1991) "Women's voices after pregnancy loss: couples' patterns of communication and support," *Social Work in Health Care*, vol. 16, no. 2, 19-36

Blau, P.M., and Duncan, O.D. (1967) *The American Occupational Structure*. New York: Wiley.

Blishen, B.R. and T.H. Atkinson (1982) *Regional and Status Differences in Canadian Values*. Toronto: York University, Institute for Behavioural Research

Bliss, M. (1985) *Canada's First Millionaire*. Toronto: McClelland and Stewart

Block, F., L. Gardner and W. O. Walker, III (1989) "Empire and domestic reform," *Radical History Review*, 45, fall, 98-114

Bo, Z. and G. Wenxiu (1992) "Sexuality in urban China," *Australian Journal of Chinese Affairs*, 28, July, 1-20

Bock, G. and B. Duden (1984) "Labor of love — Love as labor: On the genesis of housework in the West," *Development*, 4, 6-14

Bogardus, E.S. (1959) *Social Distance*. Yellow Springs, Ohio: Antioch College Press

Boohene, E. and J. Tsodzai (1991) "Fertility and contraceptive use among young adults in Harare, Zimbabwe," *Studies in Family Planning*, 22 (4), July-Aug, 264-271

Booth, A. and D. Johnson (1988) "Premarital cohabitation and marital success," *Journal of Family Issues*, 9 (2), June, 255-272

Booth, A., D.R. Johnson, L.K. White and J.N. Edwards (1986) "Divorce and marital instability over the life course," *Journal of Family Issues*, 7 (4), Dec, 421-442

Booth-Butterfield, M. (1989) "Perception of harassing communication as a function of locus of control, work force participation, and gender," *Communication Quarterly*, 37 (4), fall, 262-275

Bornschier, V. (1986) "Social stratification in six Western countries: The general pattern and some differences," *Social Science Information*, 25 (4), Dec, 797-824

Boswell, T. (1989) "Colonial empires and the capitalist world-economy: A time series analysis of colonialization, 1640-1960," *American Sociological Review*, 54, 2, April, 180-196

Bourdieu, P. (1977) *Reproduction in Education, Society and Culture*. Beverly Hills: Sage

Bowles, S. (1988) "Class versus world-systems analysis? Epitaph for a false opposition," *Review*, 11, 4, fall, 433-451

Bowles, S. and H. Gintis (1976). *Schooling in Capitalist America*. New York: Basic Books.

Boyd, M., J. Goyder, F.E. Jones, H.A. McRoberts, P.C. Pineo, & J. Porter, eds. (1985), *Ascription and Achievement: Studies in Mobility and Status Attainment in Canada*. Ottawa: Carleton University Press.

Brandt, K.W. (1986) "New social movements as a metapolitical challenge: The social and political impact of a new historical type of protest," *Thesis Eleven*, 15, 60-68

Bratton, J. (1991) "Japanization at work: The case of engineering plants in Leeds," *Work, Employment and Society*, 5 (3), Sept, 377-395

Braverman, H. (1974) *Labor and Monopoly Capital*. New York: Monthly Review Press

Brenner, M.H. (1987) "Economic instability, unemployment rates, behavioral risks, and mortality rates in Scotland, 1952-1983," *International Journal of Health Services*, 17 (3), 475-487

Breton, R. (1964) "Institutional completeness of ethnic communities and personal relations of immigrants" *American Journal of Sociology*, vol. 70, 193-205.

Breton, R., W. Isajiw, W. Kalbach and J. Reitz (1990) *Ethnic Identity and Equality: Varieties of Experience in a Canadian City*. Toronto: University of Toronto Press

Briggs, J.L. (1991) "Expecting the unexpected: Canadian Inuit training for an experimental lifestyle," *Ethos*, 19 (3), Sept, 259- 287

Brownfield, D. (1987) "Father-son relationships and violent behavior," *Deviant Behavior*, 8 (1), 65-78

Burch T. (1985) *Family History Survey: Preliminary Findings*. (Statistics Canada, Catalogue No. 99-955) Ottawa: Supply and Services

Burns, A. and R. Homel (1989) "Gender division of tasks by parents and their children," *Psychology of Women Quarterly*, 13 (1), Mar, 113-125

Burns, L.S. (1988) "Hope for the homeless in the US: Lessons from the Third World," *Cities*, 5 (1), Feb, 33-40

Cahill, S.E. (1989) "Fashioning males and females: Appearance management and the social reproduction of gender," *Symbolic Interaction*, 12 (2), fall, 281-298

Cain, M. (1986) "The consequences of reproductive failure: Dependence, mobility and mortality among the elderly of rural South Asia," *Population Studies*, 40 (3), Nov, 375-388

Cain, M. S. (1988) "The charismatic leader," *Humanist*, 48, 6, Nov-Dec, 19-23, 36

Caldwell, J.C. (1986) "Routes to low mortality in poor countries," *Population and Development Review*, 12 (2), June, 171-220

Callaghan, T.J. and L. Tepperman (1993) *Sociology and Nursing Practice*. Scarborough: Prentice-Hall Canada

Camara, S. (1976) "Cultural differences and interactions," *Ethnopsychologie*, 31 (3-4), Dec, 285-300

Campbell, A. (1980) *The Sense of Well-being in America: Recent Patterns and Trends*. New York: McGraw-Hill Ryerson

Campbell, A. (1984) *The Girls in the Gang*. Oxford: Basil Blackwell

Campbell, D. (1969) "Reforms as experiments," *American Psychologist*, 24, 409-429

Canada, Government of (1969) *Report of the Royal Commission on Bilingualism and Biculturalism*. Ottawa: Supply and Services

—— (1984) *Sexual Offenses Against Children, Report of the Committee on Sexual Offenses Against Children and Youth*. Ottawa: Supply and Services

Canestrini, S. and P. Basso (1989) "Italy's ethnic minorities and the contradictions of self-determination," *Social Justice*, 16, 1 (35), spring, 99-102

Capozza, D. and A.C. Tajoli (1992) "Educational and occupational expectations of Italian adolescents," *Social Science Information*, 31 (1), Mar, 43-67

Caringella-MacDonald, S. (1990) "State crises and the crackdown on crime under Reagan," *Contemporary Crises*, 14 (2), June, 91-118

Carroll, L. and P.I. Jackson (1982) "Minority composition, inequality and the growth of municipal police forces, 1960-71," *Sociological Focus*, 15 (4), Oct, 327-346

Casale, A. and P. Lerman (1986) *USA Today: Tracking Tomorrow's Trends*. Kansas City: Andrews, McNeel and Parker

Cashmore, E.E. (1990) "The functions of racial conflict," *European Journal of Intercultural Studies*, 1 (1), June, 7-20

Cespedes, R. L. (1988) "Social demands, politics and authoritarianism in Paraguay (1986-1988)," *Revista Paraguaya de Sociologia*, 25, 73, Sept- Dec, 237-251

Chakrabarty, D. (1992) "The death of history? Historical consciousness and the culture of late capitalism," *Public Culture*, 4 (2), spring, 47-65

Chan, S. (1987) "Growth with equity: A test of Olson's theory for the Asian Pacific-Rim countries," *Journal of Peace Research*, 24 (2), June, 135-149

Chandler, W.U. (1986) "Child health, education, and development," *Prospects*, 16 (3), 285-299

Chappell, D.A. (1990) "The crisis of bipolar ethnicity on the Great Frontier: Nativist 'democracy' in Fiji, Malaysia, and New Caledonia," *Journal of World History*, 1 (2), fall, 171-198

Chase-Dunn, C. (1990) "Resistance to imperialism: Semi-peripheral actors," *Review*, 13, 1, winter, 1-31

Chen, J. and T.R. Balakrishnan (1990) "Do gender preferences affect fertility and family dissolution in Canada?" Discussion Paper no. 90-7, Population Studies Centre, University of Western Ontario.

Chesnais, J.C. (1992) "The history of violence: Homicide and suicide through the ages," *International Social Science Journal*, 44, 2 (132), May, 217-234

Chowdhry, K., L. C. Chen and J. Tendler "Poverty, environment, development," *Daedalus*, 1989, 118, 1, winter, 141-154

Christie, I. (1992) "Social and political aspects of global warming," *Futures*, 24 (1), Jan-Feb, 83-90

Chusmir, L.H. and J. Mills (1989) "Gender differences in conflict management styles of managers: At work and at home," *Sex Roles*, 20 (3-4), Feb, 149-163

Clark, T.N. and S.M. Lipset (1991) "Are social classes dying?" *International Sociology*, 6 (4), Dec, 397-410

Clark, T.N., S.M. Lipset and M. Rempel (1993) "The declining political significance of social class," *International Sociology*, 8 (3), Sept, 293-316

Clement, R. (1991) "Modes of acculturation and situation identity: The case of Haitian immigrants of Montreal," *Canadian Ethnic Studies*, 23 (2), 81-94

Clement, W. (1975) *The Canadian Corporate Elite: Economic Power in Canada*. Toronto: McClelland and Stewart.

—— (1977) *Continental Corporate Power: An Analysis of Economic Power*. Toronto: McClelland and Stewart.

Coale, A.J. and S.C. Watkins (eds.) (1987) *The Decline of Fertility in Europe*. Princeton, NJ: Princeton University Press

Cohen, A.K. (1966) *Deviance and Control*, Foundations of Modern Sociology Series. Englewood Cliffs, NJ: Prentice Hall.

Coleman, J.S., E. Katz and H. Menzel (1966) *Medical Innovation: A Diffusion Study*. Indianapolis: Bobbs Merrill

Collins, R. (1982) *Sociological Insight: An Introduction to Non-obvious Sociology*. New York: Oxford University Press.

—— (1986) *Weberian Sociological Theory*. Cambridge: Cambridge University Press, Part I: Economics

—— (1990) "The organizational politics of the ASA," *American Sociologist*, 21 (4), winter, 311-315

Combs-Orme, T., J.E. Herzer and R.H. Miller (1988) "The application of labelling theory to alcoholism," *Journal of Social Service Research*, 11 (2- 3), 73-91

Commoner, B. (1991) "Rapid population growth and environmental stress," *International Journal of Health Services*, 21, 2, 199-227

Conklin, G.H. and M.E. Simpson (1985) "A demographic approach to the cross-national study of homicide," *Comparative Social Research*, 8, 171-185

Cooley, C.H. (1902) *Human Nature and Social Order*. New York: Charles Scribners

Corsaro, W.A. and T.A. Rizzo (1988) "Discussione and friendship: Socialization processes in the peer culture of Italian nursery school children," *American Sociological Review*, 53 (6), Dec, 879-894

Cotton, J. (1989) "From authoritarianism to democracy in South Korea," *Political Studies*, 37, 2, June, 244-259

Couch, C. J. (1989) "From hell to utopia and back to hell: Charismatic relationships," *Symbolic Interaction*, 12, 2, fall, 265-279

Crispell, D. (1992) "Myths of the 1950s," *American Demographics*, August, 38-43

Curtis, R.F. (1986) "Household and family in theory on inequality," *American Sociological Review*, 51 (2), Apr, 168-183

Dai, K.(1991) "The life experience and status of Chinese rural women from observation of three age groups," *International Sociology*, 6 (1), Mar, 5-23

Daly, G. (1989) "Homelessness and health: A comparison of British, Canadian and US cities," *Cities*, 6 (1), Feb, 22-38

Darling, C.A., D.J. Kallen and J.E. VanDusen (1984) "Sex in transition, 1900-1980," *Journal of Youth and Adolescence*, 13, (5), 385-399

Das, V. (1989) "Voices of children," *Daedalus*, 118 (4), fall, 263-294

Davis, K. "The world demographic transition," *Annals of the American Academy of Political and Social Science*, 1945, 237, Jan, 1-11

Davis, K. and W.E. Moore (1945) "Some principles of stratification," *American Sociological Review*, 10 (April), 242-249

Davis, N. and R.V. Robinson (1991) "Men's and women's consciousness of gender inequality: Austria, West Germany, Great Britain, and the United States," *American Sociological Review*, 56 (1), Feb, 72-84

Derber, C. (1983) "Managing professionals: Ideological proletarianization and post-industrial labor," *Theory and Society*, 12 (3), May, 309-341

Deveraux, M.S. (1993) "Time use of Canadians," *Canadian Social Trends*, Autumn, 13-16

Devetak, S. (1991) "The nation-state, democracy, ethnic diversity, equality and progress," *Innovation*, 4 (1), 125-132

Diener, E., J. Horowitz, and R.A. Emmons (1985) "Happiness of the very wealthy," *Social Indicators Research*, 16, 263-274

DiMaggio, P. and J. Mohr (1985) "Cultural capital, educational attainment and mate selection," *American Journal of Sociology*, 90 (6), 1231- 1261

Doige, D. (1990) "Young offenders," *Canadian Social Trends*, #18, autumn, 11-14

Doob, L. W. (1991) "Sustainable people: Hypotheses and a call for publishable research," *Journal of Social Psychology*, 131 (5), Oct, 601-605

Dore, R. (1989) "Where are we now: Musings of an evolutionist," *Work, Employment and Society*, 3 (4), Dec, 425-446

Douthitt, R.A. (1989) "The division of labor within the home: Have gender roles changed?" *Sex Roles*, 20 (11-12), June, 693-704

Drake, M. (1989) "Fifteen years of homelessness in the UK," *Housing Studies*, 4 (2), Apr, 119-127

Driver, E.D. (1981) "Social class in South India: A cognitive approach," *Journal of Asian and African Studies*, 16 (3-4), July-Oct, 238-260

Dube, S.C. (1988) "Cultural dimensions of development," *International Social Science Journal*, 40, 4 (118), Nov, 505-511

Dudley, M.G. and F.A. Kosinski, Jr. (1990) "Religiosity and marital satisfaction: A research note," *Review of Religious Research*, 32 (1), Sept, 78-86

Dugger, W. M. (1988) "An institutional analysis of corporate power," *Journal of Economic Issues*, 22, 1, Mar, 79-111

Durkheim, E. (1938) *The Rules of Sociological Method*. Chicago: University of Chicago Press.

____(1951) *Suicide*. New York: Free Press.

____(1964) *The Division of Labor in Society*. New York: Free Press

Dychtwald, K. and J. Flower (1990) *Age Wave*. New York: Bantam Books

Eades, D. (1984) "Misunderstanding aboriginal English: The role of socio-cultural context," *Occasional Papers — Applied Linguistics Association of Australia*, 8, 24-33

Easterlin, R.A. (1980) *Birth and Fortune: The Impact of Numbers on Personal Welfare*. New York: Basic Books

Edwards, R. (1979) *Contested Terrain: The Transformation of the Workplace in the Twentieth Century*. New York: Basic Books

Eggebeen, D.J. and D.T. Lichter (1991) "Race, family structure, and changing poverty among American children," *American Sociological Review*, 56 (6), Dec, 801-817

Eichler, M. (1981) "The inadequacy of the monolithic model of the family," *Canadian Journal of Sociology*, 6 (3), 367-388

Eisenberg, N., R. Hertz-Lazarowitz and I. Fuchs (1990) "Prosocial moral judgement in Israeli kibbutz and city children: A longitudinal study," *Merrill Palmer Quarterly*, 36 (2), Apr, 273-285

Eisenbruch, M. (1988) "The mental health of refugee children and their cultural development," *International Migration Review*, 22, 2 (82), summer, 282-300

Ekblad, S. (1986) "Social determinants of aggression in a sample of Chinese primary school children," *Acta Psychiatrica Scandinavica*, 73 (5), May, 515-523

Ellis, G.J. and Petersen, L.R. (1992) "Socialization values and parental control techniques: A cross-cultural analysis of child rearing," *Journal of Comparative Family Studies*, 23 (1), spring, 39-54

Emmison, M. and M. Western (1990) "Social class and social identity: A comment on Marshall et al.," *Sociology*, 24 (2), May, 241-253

Epstein, C.F. (1986) "Symbolic segregation: Similarities and differences in the language and non-verbal communication of women and men," *Sociological Forum*, 1 (1), winter, 27-49

Ergas, Z. (1986) "In search of development: Some directions for further investigation," *Journal of Modern African Studies*, 24 (2), June, 303-333

Erickson, B. (1991) "What is good taste?" *Canadian Review of Sociology and Anthropology*, 28 (2), 255-278

Erickson, T.H. (1990) "Linguistic diversity and the quest for national identity: The case of Mauritius," *Ethnic and Racial Studies*, 13 (1), Jan, 1-24

Erikson, E.H. (1950) *Childhood and Society*. New York: W.W. Norton

Etzioni-Halevy, E. (1989) "Elite power, manipulation and corruption: A demo-elite perspective," *Government and Opposition*, 24, 2, spring, 215-231

Fagenson, E.A. (1989) "The mentor advantage: Perceived career/job experiences of proteges versus non-proteges," *Journal of Organizational Behavior*, 10 (4) Oct, 309-320

Farrell, J.P. and E. Schiefelbein (1985) "Education and status attainment in Chile: A comparative challenge to the Wisconsin model of status attainment," *Comparative Education Review*, 29 (4), Nov, 490-506

Feher, F. and A. Heller (1983) "Class, democracy, modernity," *Theory and Society*, 12 (2), Mar, 211-244

Ferrarotti, F. (1991) "Considerations on Lewis Mumford as a literary critic," *Critica Sociologica*, 96, Jan-Mar, 59-69

Ferree, M.M. (1991) "The gender division of labor in two-earner marriages: Dimensions of variability and change," *Journal of Family Issues*, 12 (2), June, 158-180

Fine, G.A. and N.L. Ross (1984) "Symbolic meaning and cultural organizations," *Research in the Sociology of Organizations*, 3, 237-256

Finlay, W. (1988) "Commitment and the company: Manager-worker relations in the absence of internal labor markets," *Research in Social Stratification and Mobility*, 7, 163-187

Finlay, W., E.J. Mutran, R.R. Zeitler and C.S. Randall (1990) "Queues and care: How medical residents organize their work in a busy clinic," *Journal of Health and Social Behavior*, 31 (3), Sept, 292-305

Fishbein, E.G. (1990) "Predicting paternal involvement with a newborn by attitude toward women's roles," *Health Care for Women International*, 11 (1), winter, 109-115

Fitzgerald, T.K. (1991) "Media and changing metaphors of ethnicity and identity," *Media, Culture and Society*, 13 (2), Apr, 193-214

Fitzpatrick, M.A. (1991) "Sex differences in marital conflict: Social psychological versus cognitive explanations," *Text*, 11 (3), 341-364

Foot, D.K. (1982) *Canada's Population Outlook: Demographic Futures and Economic Challenges*. The Canadian Institute for Economic Policy Series. Toronto: Lorimer

Fox, B. (1990) "Selling the mechanized household: 70 Years of ads in *Ladies Home Journal*," *Gender and Society*, 4 (1), Mar, 25-40

Frank, Andre Gunder (1966) "The development of underdevelopment," *Monthly Review*, 18, 4, Sept., 17-31.

Frankel, B. (1983) *Beyond the state*. London: Macmillan

Frideres, J. (1988) *Native People in Canada: Contemporary Conflicts*. Toronto: Prentice-Hall Canada

Friedman, J. (1989) "Culture, identity and world process," *Review*, 12 (1), winter, 51-69

____(1990) "Being in the world: Globalization and localization," *Theory, Culture and Society*, 7 (2-3), June, 311-328

Friedman, M. and R. Friedman (1981) *Free To Choose*. New York: Avon Books

Friedson, E. (1975) *Doctoring Together: A Study of Professional Social Control*. New York: Elsevier

Fuller, B., J.H.Y. Edwards and K. Gorman (1986) "When does education boost economic growth? School expansion and school quality in Mexico," *Sociology of Education*, 59 (3), July, 167-181

Fuller, B. and S.M. Dornbusch (1988) "Organizational construction of intrinsic motivation," *Sociological Forum*, 3 (1), winter, 1-24

Galloway, P.R. (1986) "Long-term fluctuations in climate and population in the preindustrial era," *Population and Development Review*, 12 (1), Mar, 1-24

Galtung, J. (1971) "A structural theory of imperialism," *Journal of Peace Research*, 8(2), 135-149

Galtung, J. and R. Vincent (1992) *Global Glasnost: Toward a New International Information/Communications Order?* Cresskill, N.J.: Hampton

Garcia-Menendez, J. R. (1987) "The debate over 'dependent fascism' in Latin America," *Revista Paraguaya de Sociologia*, 24, 68, Jan-Apr, 37-63

Garner, R. (1991) "Preparing for an uncertain future: Lessons from a Florentine classroom," *Urban Education*, 26 (3), 327-347

Garreau, J. (1981) *The Nine Nations of North America*. New York: Avon

Gartner, R. (1989) "Patterns of victimization," 138-147 in L. Tepperman and J. Curtis (eds.), *Everyday Life: A Reader*. Toronto: McGraw Hill Ryerson

Gerber, L. (1984) "Community characteristics and out-migration from Canadian Indian reserves: path analyses," *Canadian Review of Sociology and Anthropology*, 21(2) May, 145-165

Gerhart, B. (1990) "Gender differences in current and starting salaries: The role of performance, college major, and job title," *Industrial and Labor Relations Review*, 43 (4), Apr, 418-433

Gershuny, J.I. (1987) "Technology, social innovation, and the informal economy," *Annals of the American Academy of Political and Social Science*, 493, Sept, 47-63

Gershuny, J.I., I. Miles, S. Jones, C. Mullings, G. Thomas and S. Wyatt (1986) "Time budgets: Preliminary analyses of a national survey," *Quarterly Journal of Social Affairs*, 2 (1), 13-39

Giles, H. and P. Johnson (1987) "Ethnolinguistic identity theory: A social psychological approach to language maintenance," *International Journal of the Sociology of Language*, 68, 69-99

Gillis, A.R. and J. Hagan (1990) "Delinquent Samaritans: Network structure, social conflict, and the willingness to intervene," *Journal of Research in Crime and Delinquency*, 27 (1), Feb, 30-51

Ginn, J. and S. Arber (1991) "Gender, class and income inequalities in later life," *British Journal of Sociology*, 42 (3), Sept, 369-396

Glenn, N.D. (1989) "Duration of marriage, family composition, and marital happiness," *National Journal of Sociology*, 3 (1), spring, 3-24

Glucksmann, M.A. (1990) "Domestic and wage labour: Women's class relations in interwar Britain," *Rethinking Marxism*, 3 (2), summer, 161-172

Gobbi, I. (1988) "Cultural changes and urban integration in a favela in Rio de Janeiro," *Studi di sociologia*, 26 (2), Apr-July, 204-215

Goff, C.H. and C.H. Reasons (1978) *Corporate Crime in Canada*. Toronto: Prentice-Hall (Canada)

Goffman, E. (1959) *Presentation of Self in Everyday Life*. Garden City, NY: Doubleday

—— (1961) *Asylums: Essays on the Social Situation of Mental Patients and Other Inmates*. Garden City, New York: Anchor

____(1964) *Stigma: Notes on the Management of Spoiled Identity*. Englewood Cliffs, NJ: Prentice Hall

Gofman, A.B. (1990) "Dilemmas, real and seeming ones, about mass and elite culture," *Sotsiologicheskie-Issledovaniya*, 17 (8), 106-111

Goldberg, A.I. and A. Kirschenbaum (1989) "Black newcomers to Israel: Contact situations and social distance," *Sociology and Social Research*, 74 (1), Oct, 52-57

Goldstein, A. and S. Goldstein (1986) "The challenge of an aging population: The case of the People's Republic of China," *Research on Aging*, 8 (2), June, 179-199

Goode, E. (1978) *Deviant Behavior*. Englewood Cliffs, N. J.: Prentice-Hall

Goode, W.J. (1963) *World Revolution and Family Patterns*. New York: Free Press

Gottman, J.S. (1989) "Children of gay and lesbian parents," *Marriage and family review*, 14 (3-4), 177-196

Goudsblom, J. (1967) *Dutch Society*. New York: Random House

____(1987) "The domestication of fire as a civilizing process," *Theory, Culture and Society*, 4 (2-3), June, 457-476

Grabb, E.G. (1981) "The ranking of self-actualization values: The effects of class, stratification, and occupational experiences," *Sociological Quarterly*, 22 (3), summer, 373-383

Graham, L. and R. Hogan (1990) "Social class and tactics: Neighborhood opposition to group homes," *Sociological Quarterly*, 31 (4), winter, 513-529

Granovetter, M. (1990) "Symposium: Dispelling the Japanese mystique? Convergence stood on its head: A new look at Japanese and American work organization," *Contemporary Sociology*, 19 (6), Nov, 789-791

Grasmick, H.G. and R.J. Bursik, Jr. (1990) "Conscience, significant others, and rational choice: Extending the deterrence model," *Law and Society Review*, 24 (3), 837-861

Grasmick, H.G., L.P. Patterson and S.R. Bird (1990) "The effects of religious fundamentalism and religiosity on preference for traditional family norms," *Sociological Inquiry*, 60 (4), fall, 352-369

Greif, G.L. (1985) "Children and housework in the single father family," *Family Relations*, 34 (3), July, 353-357

Gudykunst, W.B. and T.S. Lim (1985) "Ethnicity, sex, and self perceptions of communicator style," *Communication Research Report*, 2 (1), Dec, 68-75

Guindon, H. (1968) "Two cultures: an essay on nationalism, class and ethnic tension" in R.H. Leach (ed.), *Contemporary Canada*. Toronto: Macmillan

Gunther, S. (1991) "'A language with taste': Uses of proverbial sayings in intercultural communication," *Text*, 11 (3), 399-418

Guralnik, J.M., K.C. Land, D. Blazer, G.G. Fillenbaum, and L.G. Branch (1993) "Educational status and active life expectancy among older blacks and whites," *New England Journal of Medicine*, 329 (2), July 8, 110-116

Gusfield, J. (1963) *Symbolic Crusade*. Urbana: University of Illinois Press

Gutknecht, D.B. (1982) "Conceptualizing culture in organizational theory," *California Sociologist*, 5 (1), winter, 68-87

Haas, J. and W. Shaffir (1977) "The professionalization of medical students," *Symbolic Interaction*, 1 (Fall), 77-88

Haddad, T. and L. Lam (1988) "Canadian families - men's involvement in family work: A case study of immigrant men in Toronto," *International Journal of Comparative Sociology*, 29 (3-4), Sept-Dec, 269-281

Hagan, J. (1984) *Disreputable Pleasures: Crime and Deviance in Canada*, 2nd edition. Toronto: McGraw-Hill Ryerson

_____(1994) *Crime and Disrepute*. Sociology for a new century series. Thousand Oaks, California: Pine Forge Press

Hagedoorn, L. and G. Kleinpenning (1991) "The contribution of domain-specific stereotypes to ethnic social distance," *British Journal of Social Psychology*, 30 (1), Mar, 63-78

Haley, R.I. and P.B. Case (1979) "Testing thirteen attitude scales for agreement and brand discrimination," *Journal of Marketing*, 43, Fall, 20-32

Hansen, K. T. (1986) "Household work as a man's job: Sex and gender in domestic service in Zambia," *Anthropology Today*, 2 (3), June, 18-23

Hansen, S.L. and C.A. Darling (1985) "Attitudes of adolescents toward division of labor in the home," *Adolescence*, 20 (77), spring, 61-72

Hardesty, C. and J. Bokemeier (1989) "Finding time and making do: Distribution of household labor in nonmetropolitan marriages," *Journal of Marriage and the Family*, 51 (1), Feb, 253-267

Hardoy, J.E. and D. Satterthwaite (1991) "Environmental problems of Third World cities: A global issue ignored?" *Public Administration and Development*, 11 (4), July-Aug, 341-361

Hargrove, B. (1988) "Religion, development, and changing paradigms," *Sociological Analysis*, 49, supplement, Dec, 33S-48S

Harrell, S. (1990) "Ethnicity, local interests, and the state: Yi communities in southwest China," *Comparative Studies in Society and History*, 32 (3), July, 515-548

Hartmann, P. (1979) "Popular culture and development: A case study," *Studies in Comparative International Development*, 14 (3-4), fall-winter, 84-103

Harvey, A.S., K. Marshall and J.A. Frederick (1991) *Where Does the Time Go?* General Social Survey Analysis Series, Catalogue 11-612E, No. 4. Ottawa: Statistics Canada

Hassall, G. (1991) "Nationalism and ethnic conflict in the Pacific islands," *Current World Leaders*, 34 (2), Apr, 283-296

Hayes, B.C. (1991) "Religious identification and marriage patterns in Australia," *Journal for the Scientific Study of Religion*, 30 (4), Dec, 469-478

Health and Welfare Canada (1989a) *Charting Canada's Future: A Report of the Demographic Review*. Ottawa: Supply and Services, pp. 6-8

—— (1989b) *Health and Welfare in Canada*. Ottawa: Supply and Services Canada

Healy, B., T. Turpin and M. Hamilton (1985) "Aboriginal drinking: A case study in inequality and disadvantage," *Australian Journal of Social Issues*, 20 (3), Aug, 191-208

Heath, A. (1981) *Social Mobility*. Glasgow: Fontana Books

Heaton, T.B. and E.L. Pratt (1990) "The effects of religious homogamy on marital satisfaction and stability," *Journal of Family Issues*, 11 (2), June, 191-207

Heilig, G.K. and A.E. Wills (1989) "AIDS costs more `years of potential life' before age 65 than diabetes, TBC, or viral hepatitis," *Population Network Newsletter* (IIASA), No. 15, February, 1-8

Hein, N. and R. Wodak (1987) "Medical interviews in internal medicine. Some results of an empirical investigation," *Text*, 7 (1), 37-65

Held, D. (1989) *Political Theory and the Modern State*. Stanford: Stanford University Press

Henry, F. and E. Ginzberg (1990) "Racial discrimination in employment", pp. 302-309 in J. Curtis and L. Tepperman (eds.) *Images of Canada: The Sociological Tradition*. Toronto: Prentice-Hall (Canada)

Herman, E.S. and N. Chomsky (1988) *Manufacturing Consent: The Political Economy of the Mass Media*. New York: Pantheon Books

Heunks, F.J. (1991) "Varieties of activism in three western democracies," *Nonprofit and Voluntary Sector Quarterly*, 20 (2), summer, 151-172

Higgins, R. (1980) *The Seventh Enemy: The Human Factor in the Global Crisis*. London: Pan Books.

Higgins, P.J. and P. Shoar-Ghaffari (1991) "Sex-role socialization in Iranian textbooks," *MWSA Journal*, 3 (2), spring, 213-232

Hill, S. (1988) "Technology and organization culture: The human imperative in integrating new technology into organization design," *Technology in Society*, 10 (2), 233-253

Hirdes, J.P. and W.F. Forbes (1989) "Estimates of the relative risk of mortality based on the Ontario Longitudinal Study of Aging," *Canadian Journal on Aging*, 8 (3), fall, 222-237

Hirsch, E.D., Jr. (1988) *Cultural Literacy*. New York: Vintage Books

Hodson, R. (1990) "Symposium: Dispelling the Japanese mystique? Quality Circles: Are they America's future?" *Contemporary Sociology*, 19 (6), Nov, 792-795

____(1991) "The active worker: Compliance and autonomy at the workplace," *Journal of Contemporary Ethnography*, 20 (1), Apr, 47-78

Hoecker-Drysdale, Susan (1992) *Harriet Martineau*. Oxford: Berg

Hogan, D. (1981) *Transitions and Social Change: The Early Lives of American Men*. New York: Academic Press

Hood, J.C. (1988) "From night to day: Timing and the management of custodial work," *Journal of Contemporary Ethnography*, 17 (1), Apr, 96-116

Horowitz, D.L. (1989) "Incentives and behaviour in the ethnic politics of Sri Lanka and Malaysia," *Third World Quarterly*, 11 (4), Oct, 18-35

Hsu, D.Y. and P.Y. Ching (1991) "The worker-peasant alliance as a strategy for rural development in China," *Monthly Review*, 42 (10),Mar, 27-43

Hu, Y.H. (1987) "Patterns of mortality differentials by marital status in low mortality countries," *Journal of Population Studies*, 10, June, 97-128

Hull, T.H. (1990) "Recent trends in sex ratios at birth in China," *Population and Development Review*, 16 (1), Mar, 63-83

Hunter, S.S. (1990) "Orphans as a window on the AIDS epidemic in sub-Saharan Africa: Initial results and implications of a study in Uganda," *Social Science and Medicine*, 31 (6), 681-690

Hutaserani, S. and J. Roumasset (1991) "Institutional change and the demographic transition in rural Thailand," *Economic Development and Cultural Change*, 40 (1), Oct, 75-100

Hyman, E.L. (1990) "An assessment of World Bank and AID activities and procedures affecting urban environmental quality," *Project Appraisal*, 5 (4), Dec, 198-212

Igbinovia, P. E. (1991) "Begging in Nigeria," *International Journal of Offender Therapy and Comparative Criminology*, 35 (1), 21-33

Infante, D.A., T.C. Sabourin, J.E. Rudd and E.A. Shannon (1990) "Verbal aggression in violent and nonviolent marital disputes," *Communication Quarterly*, 38 (4), fall, 361-371

Inglehart, R. and N. Garcia-Pardo (1988) "Political culture and a stable democracy," *Revista Espanola de Investigaciones Sociologicas*, 42, Apr-June, 45-65

Innis, H. (1972) *Empire and Communication*. Toronto: University of Toronto Press

Ishida, H. (1989) "Class structure and status hierarchies in contemporary Japan," *European Sociological Review*, 5 (1), May, 65-80

Ishida, H., J.H. Goldthorpe and R. Erikson (1991) "Intergenerational class mobility in postwar Japan," *American Journal of Sociology*, 96 (4), Jan, 954-992

Jagacinski, C.M. and W. K. LeBold (1987) "The relative career advancement of men and women engineers in the United States," *Work and Stress*, 1 (3), July-Sept, 235-247

Jarvis, G.K. and H.C. Northcott (1987) "Religion and differences in morbidity and mortality," *Social Science and Medicine*, 25 (7), 813-824

Jithoo, S. (1985) "Indian family businesses in Durban, South Africa," *Journal of Comparative Family Studies*, 16 (3), autumn, 365-376

Johnson, G.D. (1989) "Capitalism, Protestantism and the private family: Comparisons among early modern England, France, and the American colonies," *Sociological Inquiry*, 59 (2), spring, 144-164

Johnson, H. (1987) "Homicide in Canada," *Canadian Social Trends*, winter, 2-6

—— (1988) "Wife abuse" *Canadian Social Trends*, Spring, 17-20

Johnson, H. and P. Chisholm (1989) "Family Homicide," *Canadian Social Trends*, autumn, 17, 18

Johnson, S.D., J.B. Tamney and R. Burton (1989) "Pat Robertson: Who supported his candidacy for President?" *Journal for the Scientific Study of Religion*, 28 (4), Dec, 387-399

Johnson, T. (1972) *Professions and Power*. London: Macmillan

John-Steiner, V. (1984) "Learning styles among Pueblo children," *Quarterly Newsletter of the Laboratory of Comparative Human Cognition*, 6 (3), July, 57-62

Johnston, H. (1989) "Toward an explanation of church opposition to authoritarian regimes: Religio-oppositional subcultures in Poland and Catalonia," *Journal for the Scientific Study of Religion*, 28 (4), Dec, 493-508

Johnston, H. and J. Figa (1988) "The Church and political opposition: Comparative perspectives on mobilization against authoritarian regimes," *Journal for the Scientific Study of Religion*, 27, 1, Mar, 32-47

Jones, C.J., L. Marsden, and L. Tepperman (1990) *Lives of Their Own: The Individualization of Women's Lives*. Toronto: Oxford University Press

Jungbluth, P. (1984) "Covert sex-role socialization in Dutch education: A survey among teachers," *Netherlands Journal of Sociology*, 20 (1), Apr, 43-57

Kallan, J. (1985) "Evidence that rural in-migrants may not catch up: Occupational mobility in Bangkok and Bogota," *Sociology and Social Research*, 70 (1), Oct, 84-88

Kalmijn, M. (1991) "Status homogamy in the United States," *American Journal of Sociology*, 97 (2), Sept, 496-523

Kaneko, Y. and Y. Yamada (1990) "Wives and mothers-in-law: Potential for family conflict in post-war Japan," *Journal of Elder Abuse and Neglect*, 2 (1-2), 87-99

Kaufman, R.L., T.L. Parcel, M. Wallace and W. Form (1988) "Looking forward: Responses to organizational and technological change in an ultra-high-technology firm," *Research in the Sociology of Work*, 4, 31-67

Kavoossi, M. and J. Frank (1990) "The language-culture interface in Persian Gulf states' print advertisement: Implications for international marketing," *Journal of International Consumer Marketing*, 3 (1) 5-26

Kaye, S. (1989) *Writing Under Pressure: The Quick Writing Process*. New York: Oxford University Press

Keane, C., A.R. Gillis and J. Hagan (1989) "Deterrence and amplification of juvenile delinquency by police contact: The importance of gender and risk-orientation," *British Journal of Criminology*, 29 (4), autumn, 336-352

Keddie, V. (1980) "Class identification and party preference among manual workers: The influence of community, union membership and kinship," *Canadian Review of Sociology and Anthropology*, 17 (1), Feb, 24-36

Kemp, A.A. (1990) "Estimating sex discrimination in professional occupations with the dictionary of occupational titles," *Sociological Spectrum*, 10 (3), 387-411

Kennedy, M.D. (1992) "The intelligentsia in the constitution of civil societies and post-communist regimes in Hungary and Poland," *Theory and Society*, 21 (1), Feb, 29-76

Kenney, M. and R. Florida (1989) "Japan's role in a post-Fordist age," *Futures*, 21 (2), Apr, 136-151

Kerbo, H.R. and M. Inoue (1990) "Japanese social structure and white collar crime: Recruit cosmos and beyond," *Deviant Behavior*, 11 (2), Apr-June, 139-154

Kerr, J. and J. MacPhail (1991) *Canadian Nursing: Issues and Perspectives*. Ottawa: Canadian Nurses Association.

Kerridge, R. (1985) "The universal travellers," *New Society*, 72, 1173, 21 June, 427-430

Khullar, M. (1989) "Values in educational knowledge: A case study from rural Delhi," *Indian Journal of Social Science*, 2 (4), Oct-Dec, 545-569

Kim, K.C., S. Kim and W.M. Hurh (1991) "Filial piety and intergeneration relationship in Korean immigrant families," *International Journal of Aging and Human Development*, 33 (3), 233-245

Klein, I. (1988) "Plague, policy and popular unrest in British India," *Modern Asian Studies*, 22 (4), Oct, 723-755

Koenig, F., W. Swanson and C. Harter (1981) "Future time orientation, social class and anomia," *Social Behavior and Personality*, 9 (2), 123-127

Kolarska-Bobinska, L. (1990) "The changing face of civil society in Eastern Europe," *Praxis International*, 10 (3-4), Oct-Jan, 324-336

Kondos, A. (1992) "The politics of ethnic identity: 'Conspirators' against the state or institutional racism?" *Australian and New Zealand Journal of Sociology*, 28 (1), Mar, 5-28

Koopman-Boyden, P.G. and M. Abbott (1985) "Expectations for household task allocation and actual task allocation: A New Zealand study," *Journal of Marriage and the Family*, 47 (1), Feb, 211-219

Kraak, A. (1987) "Uneven capitalist development: A case study of deskilling and reskilling in South Africa's metal industry," *Social Dynamics*, 13 (2), Dec, 14-31

Kratke, S. and F. Schmoll (1991) "The local state and social restructuring," *International Journal of Urban and Regional Research*, 15 (4), Dec, 542-552

Kurian, G. (1986) "Intergeneration integration with special reference to Indian families," *Indian Journal of Social Work*, 47 (1), Apr, 39-49

Kurthen, H.M. (1991) "Ethnic and gender inequality in the labour market: The case of West Berlin and Germany," *Studi Emigrazione*, 28, 101, Mar, 82-111

Kyle, S. C. and A. S. Cunha "National factor markets and the macroeconomic context for environmental destruction in the Brazilian Amazon," *Development and Change*, 1992, 23, 1, Jan, 7-33

Lackey, P.N. (1989) "Adults attitudes about assignments of household chores to male and female children," *Sex Roles*, 20 (5-6), Mar, 271-281

Lane, C. (1993) "Gender and the labour market in Europe: Britain, Germany and France compared," *Sociological Review*, 41 (2), May, 274-301

Larzelere, R.E. (1986) "Moderate spanking: Model or deterrent of children's aggression in the family?" *Journal of Family Violence* 1 (1), Mar, 27-36

Lash, S. and J. Urry (1987) *The End of Organized Capitalism*. Madison, WI: University of Wisconsin Press.

Laslett, P. (1993) "The Emergence of the Third Age", Plenary Address to the International Union for the Scientific Study of Population (IUSSP) General Conference, Montreal. August.

Lau, S. (1990) "Crisis and vulnerabilty in adolescent development," *Journal of Youth and Adolescence*, 19 (2), Apr, 111-131

Lavoie, Y. and J. Oderkirk (1993) "Social consequences of demographic change," *Canadian Social Trends*, winter, 2-5

Leipert, C. (1986) "Social costs of economic growth," *Journal of Economic Issues*, 20 (1), Mar, 109-131

Leslie, G.R. and S.K. Korman (1985) *The Family in Social Context*, 6th edition. New York: Oxford University Press

Levin, P. E. (1990) "Culturally contextualized apprenticeship: Teaching and learning through helping in Hawaiian families," *Quarterly Newsletter of the Laboratory of Comparative Human Cognition*, 12 (2), Apr, 80-86

Levitt, M.J., Antonucci, T.C., Clark, M.C., Rotton, J., & Finley, G.E. (1985) "Social support and well-being: Preliminary indicators based on two samples of the elderly," *International Journal of Aging and Human Development*, 21, 1, 61-77

Lewis, O. (1961) *The Children of Sanchez: Autobiography of a Mexican Family*. New York: Vintage Books

Li, L., X. Yang and F. Wang (1991) "The structure of social stratification and the modernisation process in contemporary China," *International Sociology*, 6 (1), Mar, 25-36

Li, P. (1982) "Chinese immigrants on the Canadian prairie, 1910-47," *Canadian Review of Sociology and Anthropology*, 19 (4), 527-540

Lincoln, J.R., M. Hanada and J. Olson (1981) "Cultural orientations and individual reactions to organizations: A study of employees of Japanese-owned firms," *Administrative Science Quarterly*, 26 (1), Mar, 93-115

Ling, C. Y. (1989) "Women, environment and devlopment: The Malaysian experience," *Development*, 2-3, 88-91

Lipset, S.M. (1968) *Agrarian Socialism: The Cooperative Commonwealth Federation in Saskatchewan. A Study in Political Sociology*. Garden City, NY: Anchor

____(1990) *Continental Divide: The Values and Institutions of the United States and Canada*. New York: Routledge

Lipset, S.M. and Bendix R. (1959) *Social Mobility in Industrial Society*. Berkeley: U. of Calif. Press

Lipset, S.M., M.A. Trow and J.S. Coleman (1956) *Union Democracy: The Internal Politics of the International Typographical Union*. Garden City, NY: Anchor

Litovsky, V.G. and J.B. Dusek (1985) "Perceptions of child rearing and self-concept development during the early adolescent years," *Journal of Youth and Adolescence*, 14 (5), Oct, 373-387

Littek, W. and U. Heisig (1991) "Competence, control, and work redesign," *Work and Occupations*, 18 (1), Feb, 4-28

Locke, E.A. (1976) "The nature and causes of job satisfaction," pp. 1297-1349 in M.D. Dunnette (ed.), *Handbook of Industrial and Organizational Psychology*. Chicago: Rand McNally

Lotmar, G. (1987) "Pan in danger: The steeldrum music of the black Trinidadians and its misunderstood reception in Switzerland," *Curare*, 10 (2), 135-144

Lowe, G.S. (1986) "The administrative revolution in the Canadian office: An overview," in K.I. P. Lundy and B. Warme, (eds.), *Work in the Canadian Context: Continuity Despite Change*, second edition. Toronto: Butterworths, 100-120

Lowy, M. (1987) "The Romantic and the Marxist critique of modern civilization," *Theory and Society*, 16 (6), Nov, 891-904

Lundgren, N. (1988) "When I grow up I want a Trans Am: Children in Belize talk about themselves and the impact of the world capitalist system," *Dialectical Anthropology*, 13 (3), 269-276

Lupri, E. (1988) "Fathers in transition: The case of dual-earner families in Canada," *Zeitschrift fur Sozialisations- forschung und Erziehungssoziologizse (ZSE)*, 8 (4), 281-297

____(1989) "Male violence in the home" *Canadian Social Trends*, autumn, 19-21

____(1991). *Hidden in the home: wife abuse in Canada*. Selected findings from a 1987 national survey.

____(1993) "Spousal violence: wife abuse across the life course," *Zeitschrift fur Sozialisationforschung und Erziehungssoziologie (ZSE)*, 13 (3), 236-257

Lupri, E. and J. Frideres (1981) "The quality of marriage and the passage of time: Marital satisfaction over the family life cycle" *Canadian Journal of Sociology*, 6 (3), 283-305

Lupri, E., E. Grandin, M.B. Brinkerhoff (forthcoming) "Socio-economic status and wife abuse in Canada: A re-examination," *Canadian Journal of Sociology*

Lusk, M.W. (1989) "Street children programs in Latin America," *Journal of Sociology and Social Welfare*, 16 (1), Mar, 55-77

Luthra, N. (1983) "Socio-economic correlates of child growth," *Guru Nanak Journal of Sociology*, 4 (1), April, 76-84

Luxton, M. (1983) "Two hands for the clock: Changing patterns in the gendered division of labour in the home," *Studies in Political Economy*, 12, fall, 27-44

Mackie, M. (1974) "Ethnic stereotypes and prejudice: Alberta Indians, Hutterites, and Ukrainians," *Canadian Ethnic Studies* 10, 118-129

MacLeod, L. (1987) *Battered but not Beaten: Preventing Wife Battering in Canada*. Ottawa: Canadian Advisory Council on the Status of Women.

Macpherson, C.B. (1962) *The Political Theory of Possessive Individualism: Hobbes to Locke*. Oxford: Clarendon Press

Macy, M.W. (1989) "Classes of positions or classes of persons: A test of the 'Empty Places' hypothesis," *National Journal of Sociology*, 3 (2), fall, 159-198

Malthus, T.R. (1959 [1798]) *Population: The First Essay*. Ann Arbor: University of Michigan Press.

Mandell, N. (1987) "The family" pp. 145-196 in M.M. Rosenberg et al. (eds.), *An Introduction to Sociology*. Toronto: Methuen

Marchak, P. M. (1988) *Ideological Perceptions on Canada*, 3rd edition. Toronto: McGraw-Hill Ryerson.

Markovic, M. (1990) "The meaning of recent social changes in Eastern Europe," *Praxis International*, 10 (3-4), Oct-Jan, 213-223

Mars, P. (1985) "Political mobilization and class struggle in the English-speaking Caribbean," *Contemporary Marxism*, 10, 128-147

Marsh, P., E. Rosser, and R. Harre (1978) *The Rules of Disorder*. London: Routlegde and Kegan Paul

Marshall, C. and J.D. Scribner (1991) "'It's all political': Inquiry into the micropolitics of education," *Education and Urban Society*, 23 (4), Aug, 347-355

Marshall, K. (1987) "Women in male-dominated professions," *Canadian Social Trends*, winter, 7-11

—— (1993) "Dual earners: Who's responsible for housework?" *Canadian Social Trends*, winter, 11-14

Martin, W.B. (1984) "Student perceptions of teachers' pets and class victims," *Canadian Journal of Education*, 9 (1) Winter, 89-99

Marx, G.T. (1985) "I'll be watching you: Reflections of the new surveillance," *Dissent*, 32, 1 (138), winter, 26-34

Marx, K. (1936 [1867]) *Capital*. New York: Modern Library

____(1969) *The German Ideology*. New York: International Publishers

Marx, K. and F. Engels (1955) *The Communist Manifesto*, S.H. Beer (ed.) New York: Appleton Century Crofts

Mayhew, H. (1968 [1861]) *London Labour and the London Poor*. Four volumes. New York: Dover Publications.

McAllister, I. and R. Moore (1991) "Social distance among Australian ethnic groups," *Sociology and Social Research*, 75 (2), Jan, 95-100

McAuley, P. and J.M.D. Kremer (1990) "On the fringes of society: Adults and children in a West Belfast community," *New Community*, 16 (2), Jan, 247- 259

McCord, C. and H.P. Freeman (1990) "Excess mortality in Harlem," *New England Journal of Medicine*, 322 (3), 18 Jan, 173-177

McLaughlin, S.D., B,D. Melber, J.O.G. Billy, D.M. Zimmerle, L.D. Winges and T.R. Johnson (1988) *The Changing Lives of American Women*. Chapel Hill, NC: University of North Carolina Press.

McLloyd, V.C. (1990) "The impact of emotional hardship on black families and children: Psychological distress, parenting, and socioemotional development," *Child Development*, 61 (2), Apr, 311-346

McLuhan, M. (1965) *Understanding Media: The Extensions of Man*. New York: McGraw-Hill

Mead, G.H. (1934) *Mind, Self and Society*. Chicago: University of Chicago Press

Meadows, D.H. et al. (1972) *The Limits to Growth*. New York: Universe Books

Meleis, A.I., J. Kulig, E.N. Arruda and A. Beckman (1990) "Maternal role of women in clerical jobs in southern Brazil: Stress and satisfaction," *Health Care for Women International*, 11 (4), 369-382

Merton, R.K. (1957a) "Manifest and latent functions," chapter 1 in *Social Theory and Social Structure*, revised edition. New York: Free Press

____(1957b) "Social structure and anomie" chapter 4 in *Social Theory and Social Structure*, revised edition. New York: Free Press

Methot, S. (1987) "Low income in Canada," *Canadian Social Trends*, spring, 2-7

Michalos, A.C. (1988) "Optimism in thirty countries over a decade," *Social Indicators Research*, 20 (2), April, 177-180

Milkman, R. and C. Pullman (1991) "Technological change in an auto assembly plant: The impact on workers' tasks and skills," *Work and Occupations*, 18 (2), Mar, 123-147

Miller, D.C. (1991) *Handbook of Research Design and Social Measurement*, fifth ed. Newbury Park, CA: Sage.

Mills, C.W. (1959) *The Sociological Imagination*. New York: Oxford University Press

Milne, R.S. (1988) "Bicommunal systems: Guyana, Malaysia, Fiji," *Publius*, 18 (2), spring, 101-113

Mitchell, T. (1991) "America's Egypt: Discourse on the development industry," *Middle East Report*, 21, 2(169), Mar.-Apr., 18-34.

Mitford, J. (1963) *The American Way of Death*. New York: Fawcett, Crest Books

Moghadam, V.M. (1992) "Patriarchy and the politics of gender in modernising societies: Iran, Pakistan and Afghanistan," *International Sociology*, 7 (1), Mar, 35-53

Moore, B. (1969) *Social Origins of Dictatorship and Democracy: Lord and Peasant in the Making of the Modern World*. London: Peregrine.

Moore, M. (1989) "Female lone parenting over the life course," *Canadian Journal of Sociology*, 14 (3), 335-352

Moustafa, S.A. (1988) "Problematic population phenomena in Arab countries," *Free Inquiry in Creative Sociology*, 16 (1), May, 45-49

Mucha, J. (1987) "Ethnicity or class: Economic interpretations of ethnic relations in American society," *Europa Ethnica*, 44 (1), 9-16

Murdock, G.P. (1945) "The common denominator of cultures," pp. 123-142 in R. Linton (ed.), *The Science of Man in the World Crisis*. New York: Columbia University Press.

Murnan, S.K., A. Perot and D. Byrne (1989) "Coping with unwanted sexual activity: Normative responses, situational determinants, and individual differences," *Journal of Sex Research*, 26 (1), Feb, 85-106

Murray, C. (1990) "The British underclass," *Public Interest*, 99, spring, 4-28

Nagata, J. (1987) "Is multiculturalism sacred? The power behind the pulpit in the religious congregations of Southeast Asian Christians in Canada," *Canadian Ethnic Studies*, vol. 1, no. 2, 26-43

Najafizadeh, M. and L. Mennerick (1989) "The impact of science and technology on Third World development: Issues of social responsibility," *Social Development Issues*, 12, 2, winter, 1-10

Newman, F.M., R.A. Rutter, and M.S. Smith (1989) "Organizational factors that affect school sense of efficacy, community, and expectations," *Sociology of Education*, 62 (4), Oct, 221-238

Newman, P.C. (1981) The New Acquisitors, volume 2 of *The Canadian Establishment*. Toronto: McClelland and Stewart

Niemi, R.G., J. Mueller and Tom W. Smith (1989) *Trends in Public Opinion: A Compendium of Survey Data*. New York: Greenwood Press

Nilson, S. S. (1987) "Five plus five dimensions of conflict: The historical sociology of Stein Rokkan revisited," *Tidsskrift for Samfunnsforskning*, 28, 6, 519-542

Nkinyangi, J.A. (1991) "Student protests in sub-Saharan Africa," *Higher Education*, 22 (2), Sept, 157-173

Oakley, A. (1974) *The Sociology of Housework*. London: Martin Robertson.

O'Connor, J. (1989) "Uneven and combined development and ecological crisis: A theoretical introduction," *Race and Class*, 30, 3, Jan-Mar, 1-11

O'Donnell, G. (1987) "Democracy in Argentina: Micro and macro," *Revista Paraguaya de Sociologia*, 24, 68, Jan-Apr, 65-76

Ogunnika, O. (1988) "Inter-ethnic tension: Management and control in a Nigerian city," *International Journal of Politics, Culture and Society*, 1 (4), summer, 519-537

Ornstein, M. (1988) "Social class and economic inequality" chapter 7 in J. Curtis and L. Tepperman (eds.), *Understanding Canadian Society*. Toronto: McGraw-Hill Ryerson

Orubuloye, I.O. (1991) "The implications of the demographic transition theory for fertility change in Nigeria," *International Journal of Sociology of the Family*, 21 (2), autumn, 161-174

Ostby, L. (1989) "The diffusion of modern contraception in Norway and its consequences for the fertility pattern," *European Journal of Population*, 5 (1), 27-43

Pande, B.B. (1983) "The administration of beggary prevention laws in India: A legal aid view point," *International Journal of the Sociology of Law*, 11 (3), Aug, 291-304

Pande, S.V. (1982) "Social stratification, elites and Indian society," *Indian Journal of Social Research*, 23 (2), Aug, 170-176

Panitch, Leo, ed. (1977) *The Canadian State: Political Economy and Political Power*. Toronto: University of Toronto Press

Pankhurst, J.G. (1982) "Factors in the post-Stalin emergence of Soviet sociology," *Sociological Inquiry*, 52 (3), summer, 165-183

Pappas. G., S. Queen, W. Hadden and G. Fisher (1993) "The increasing disparity in mortality between socioeconomic groups in the United States, 1960 and 1986," *New England Journal of Medicine*, 329 (2), July 8, 103-109

Parker, M. and J. Slaughter (1990) "Management by stress: The team concept in the US auto industry," *Science as Culture*, 8, 27-58

Parker, T. (1983) *Rules of Thumb*. Boston: Houghton Mifflin

Parkin, F. (1971). *Class, Inequality and Political Order*. London, McGibbon and Kee

Parks, Y.Y. (1982) "Organizational development and culture contact: A case study of sokagakkai in America," *Journal of Ethnic Studies*, 10 (1), spring, 1-16

Parsons, T. (1951) "Social structure and dynamic process: the case of modern medical practice" chapter 10 in *The Social System*. New York: Free press

—— (1975) "Some theoretical considerations on the nature and trends of changes of ethnicity," pp. 53-85 in N. Glazer and D. Moynihan (eds.), *Ethnicity: Theory and Experience*. Cambridge, Mass.: Harvard University Press

Parsons, T. and R.F. Bales (1955) *Family Socialization and Interaction Process*. New York: Free Press

Parsonson, K. (1987) "Intermarriages: Effects on the ethnic identity of offspring," *Journal of Cross-cultural Psychology*, 18 (3), Sept, 363-371

Partida-Bush, V. (1990) "The volume, age structure, and rhythm of population growth in Mexico. Analysis of the effects of the demographic dynamic and consequences," *Revista Mexicana de Sociologia*, 52 (1), Jan-Mar, 223-246

Patterson, J. and P. Kim (1992) *The Day America Told the Truth*. New York: Plume, Penguin Books

Pearson, J.L., A.G. Hunter, M.E. Ensminger and S.G. Kellam (1990) "Black grandmothers in multigeneration households: Diversity in family structure and parenting involvement in the Woodlawn community," *Child Development*, 61 (2), Apr, 434-442

Peirce, K and E.D. Edwards (1988) "Children's construction of fantasy stories: Gender differences in conflict resolution strategies," *Sex Roles*, 18, 7-8, April, 393-404

Perera, J. (1990) "Sri Lanka: History of ethnic relations, formation of the Tamil national identity and demand for a separate state," *Scandinavian Journal of Development Alternatives*, 9 (2-3), June-Sept, 67-82

Peters, J.F. (1985) "Adolescents as socialization agents to parents," *Adolescence*, 20 (80), winter, 921-933

Pettifer, S. and J. Torge (1987) *A Book About Sexual Assault.* Montreal: Health Press

Piaget, J. (1932) *The Moral Judgement of the Child.* New York: Free Press

Polanyi, K. (1944) *The Great Transformation.* New York: Farrar and Rinehart

Pool, I. and M. Moore (1986) *Lone Parenthood: Characteristics and Determinants.* Results from the 1984 Family History Survey (Statistics Canada, Catalogue No. 99-961) Ottawa: Supply and Services

Porter, J. (1965) *The Vertical Mosaic.* Toronto: University of Toronto Press

Portes, A. and A. D. Kincaid (1988) "The crisis of authoritarianism: State and civil society in Argentina, Chile and Uruguay," *Research in Political Sociology*, 1, 49-77

Poston, D.L., Jr. and M.Y. Yu (1986) "The one-child family: International patterns and their implications for the People's Republic of China," *Journal of Biosocial Science*, 18 (3), July, 305-310

Poulantzas, N. (1973) *Political Power and Social Classes.* London: New Left Books.

Prus, R.C. and C.R.D. Sharper (1977) *Road Hustler.* Toronto: Gage

Quah, S.R. (1980), "Sex-role socialization in a transitional society," *International Journal of Sociology of the Family*, 10, 2, July-Dec, 213-231.

Rahav, G. (1981) "Culture conflict, urbanism, and delinquency," *Criminology*, 18 (4), Feb, 523-530

Rainville, R.E. and E. McCormick (1977) "Extent of covert racial prejudice in pro football announcers' speech," *Journalism Quarterly*, 54(1), 20-26

Ratcliffe, J. (1983) "Social justice and the demographic transition: Lessons from India's Kerala State," pp. 64-82 in D. Morley et al. (eds.) *Practising Health for All.* Oxford: Oxford University Press.

Reiter, E. (1986) "Life in a fast-food factory," pp. 309-326 in C. Heron and R. Storey (eds.), *On the Job: Confronting the Labour Process in Canada.* Kingston and Montreal: McGill-Queen's University Press.

Reitz, J. (1980) *The Survival of Ethnic Groups.* Toronto: McGraw-Hill Ryerson

____(1988) "Less racial discrimination in Canada or simply less racial conflict? Implications of comparisons with Britain," *Canadian Public Policy*, XIV (4), 424-441

Reitz, J. and R. Breton (1994) *The Illusion of Difference: Realities of Ethnicity in Canada and the United States.* Toronto: C.D. Howe Institute

Rinehart, J.W. (1987) *The Tyranny of Work: Alienation and the Labour Process*, second edition. Toronto: Harcourt Brace Jovanovich

Ritchey, P.N. and B. Dietz (1990) "Catholic/Protestant differences in marital status," *Review of Religious Research*, 32 (1), Sept, 65-77

Ritzer, G. (1988) "Sociological metatheory: A defense of a subfield by a delineation of its parameters," *Sociological Theory*, 6 (2), fall, 187-200

Robins, R. S. (1986) "Paranoid ideation and charismatic leadership," *Psychohistory Review*, 15, 1, fall, 15-55

Rofel, L. (1992) "Rethinking modernity: Space and factory discipline in China," *Cultural Anthropology*, 7 (1), Feb, 93-114

Rosner, M. (1991) "Worker ownership, ideology and social structure in 'third-way' work organizations," *Economic and Industrial Democracy*, 12 (3), Aug, 369-384

Ross, C. E. (1987) "The division of labor at home," *Social Forces*, 65 (3), Mar, 816-833

Roy, D.A. (1992) "Saudi Arabian education: Development policy," *Middle Eastern Studies*, 28 (3), July, 477-508

Royal Society of Canada (1988) *AIDS: A Perspective for Canadians, Summary Report and Recommendations.* Ottawa

Rubington, E. and M. Weinberg (1968) *Deviance: The Interactionist Perspective.* New York: Macmillan

Rumantsev, O. and O. Runbenchik (1990) "Authoritarian modernization and the social-democratic alternative," *Social Research*, 57, 2, summer, 493-529

Runciman, W.G. (1966) *Relative Deprivation and Social Justice.* London: Routledge and Kegan Paul

Sacco, V.F. and H. Johnson (1990) *Patterns of Criminal Victimization in Canada.* General Social Survey Analysis Series, Catalogue 11-612E, No. 2. Ottawa: Statistics Canada.

Sadeque, M. (1986), "The survival characteristics of the poor: A case study of a village in Bangladesh," *Social Development Issues*, 10(1), spring, 11-27

Sainsaulieu, R. (1983) "The cultural regulation of organizations," *Annee Sociologique*, 33, 195-217

Salwen, M. B. (1991) "Cultural imperialism: A media effects approach," *Critical Studies in Mass Communication*, 8, 1, Mar, 29-38

San Juan, E., Jr. (1988) "Pacifying the 'boondocks': US cultural imperialism in the Philippines," *Peripherie*, 8, 29, 24-44

Sanik, M.M. and K. Stafford (1985) "Adolescents' contribution to household production: Male and female differences," *Adolescence*, 20 (77), spring, 207-215

Sapir, E. (1929) "The status of linguistics as a science," *Language*, 5(4), 207-214

Sato, I. (1982) "Crime as play and excitement: A conceptual analysis of Japanese bosozoku (motorcycle gangs)," *Tohoku Psychologica Folia*, 41 (1-4), 64-84

Savona, E.U. (1981) "Economic crime and the legal system in Italy," *International Review of Sociology*, 17 (2-3), Aug-Dec, 241-275

Sawinski, Z. and H. Domanski (1991) "Stability of prestige hierarchies in the face of social changes: Poland, 1958-1987," *International Sociology*, 6 (2), 227-241.

Schein, E.H. (1984) "Coming to a new awareness of organizational culture," *Sloan Management Review*, 25 (2), winter, 3-16

Schiller, H. I. (1991) "Not yet the post-imperialist era," *Critical Studies in Mass Communication*, 8, 1, Mar, 13-28

Schlesinger, A., Jr. (1991) "A dissent on multicultural education," *Partisan Review*, 58 (4), fall, 630-634

Schlozman, K.L. and S. Verba (1979) *Injury to Insult: Unemployment, Class and Political Response.* Cambridge: Harvard University Press

Schmidt, E. (1990) "Negotiated spaces and contested terrain: Men, women, and the law in colonial Zimbabawe, 1890-1939," *Journal of Southern African Studies*, 16 (4), Dec, 622-648

Schneider, S.C. (1989) "Strategy formulation: The impact of national culture," *Organization Studies*, 10 (2), 149-168

Schooler, C. and A. Naoi (1988) "The psychological effects of traditional and of economically peripheral job settings in Japan," *American Journal of Sociology*, 94 (2), Sept, 335-355

Schur, Edward M. (1984) *Labeling Women Deviant.* New York: Random House

Scott, W.A., R. Scott, K. Boehnke, S.W. Cheng, L. Kwok and M. Sasaki (1991) "Children's personality as a function of family relations within and between cultures," *Journal of Cross-cultural Psychology*, 22 (2), June, 182-208

Seabrook, J. (1990) "House of the rising sun," *New Statesman and Society*, 3, 93, 23 Mar, 31-33

Seeman, M. (1959) "On the meaning of alienation," *American Sociological Review*, 24 (December), 783-791

Seipel, M.M.O. (1992) "Promoting maternal health in developing countries," *Health and Social Work*, 17 (3), Aug, 200-206

Sell, R.R. (1990) "Relative social distance: An example from Cairo," *Sociology and Social Research*, 74 (2), Jan, 80-84

Seltzer, J.A. and D. Kalmuss (1988) "Socialization and stress explanations for spouse abuse," *Social Forces*, 67 (2), Dec, 473-491

Selvaratnam, V. (1988) "Ethnicity, inequality, and higher education in Malaysia," *Comparative Education Review*, 32 (2), May, 173 196

Shaffir, W. (1974) *Life in a Religious Community: The Lubavitcher Chassidim in Montreal.* Toronto: Holt Rinehart Winston

Sharma, K.L. (1984) "Caste and class in India: Some conceptual problems," *Sociological Bulletin*, 33, 1-2, Mar-Sept, 1-28

Sharma, S.S. (1986) "Untouchability, a myth or a reality: A study of interaction between scheduled castes and Brahmins in a Western U.P. village," *Sociological Bulletin*, 35 (1), Mar, 68-79

Sharma, V. (1988) "Leisure in a traditional West African society as seen through a work of fiction, " *Africa Quarterly*, XXVIII (1-2), 67-74

Sharma, V. and A. Sharma (1991) "Is the female child being neglected? Immunization in India," *Health Policy and Planning*, 6 (3), Sept, 287-290

Shaw, R.P. (1985) "The burden of unemployment in Canada" *Canadian Public Policy* XI (2), 143-160

Sheth, D.L. (1989) "Nation-building in multi-ethnic societies: The experience of South Asia," *Alternatives*, 14 (4), Oct, 379-388

Shpakova, R. P. (1988) "The types of leadership in the sociology of Max Weber," *Sotsiologicheskie Issledovaniya*, 15, 5, Sept-Oct, 134-139

Shrivastava, P., D. Miller and A. Miglani (1991) "The evolution of crises: Crisis precursors," *International Journal of Mass Emergencies and Disasters*, 9, 3, Nov, 321-337

Shumann, T.M. (1988) "Hospital computerization and the politics of medical decision-making," *Research in the Sociology of Work*, 4, 261-287

Sidhu, H.S. (1989) "Impact of agricultural modernisation on employment prospects of wage labourer — Empirical evidence from Punjab," *Indian Journal of Social Science*, 2 (3), July-Sept, 345-361

Sieber, S. (1981) *Fatal Remedies: The Ironies of Social Intervention.* New York: Plenum

Simmel, G., M. Ritter and S. Whimster (1991) "Money in modern culture," *Theory, Culture and Society*, 8 (3), Aug, 17-31

Sinopoloulos, P.A. (1990) "Working women in Greece: Their social penalty and how it can be quantified," *Journal of Sociological Studies*, 9, Jan, 1-16

Skovron, S.E., J.E. Scott and P. Kamalakara Rao (1987), "Cross cultural perceptions of offense severity: The United States, India and Kuwait," *International Journal of Comparative and Applied Criminal Justice*, 11 (1), spring, 47-60

Small, S.A. (1988) "Parental self-esteem and its relationship to childrearing practices, parent-adolescent interaction, and adolescent behavior," *Journal of Marriage and the Family*, 50 (4), Nov, 1063-1072

Smart, C. (1977) "Criminological theory: Its ideology and implications concerning women," *British Journal of Sociology*, 28 (1), Mar, 89-100

Smelser, N.J. (1989) "External influences on sociology," *International Sociology*, 4 (4), Dec, 419-429

Smith, A.D. (1990) "Towards a global culture?" *Theory, Culture and Society*, 7 (2-3), June, 171-191

Smith, M.D. (1990) "Patriarchal ideology and wife beating: A test of a feminist hypothesis," *Violence and Victims*, 5 (4), winter, 257-273

Smith, R.W. (1986) "Legalized recreation as deviance," *Quarterly Journal of Ideology*, 10 (1), Jan, 37-42

Spade, J.Z. and C.A. Reese (1991) "We've come a long way, maybe: College students' plans for work and family," *Sex Roles*, 24 (5-6), Mar, 309-321

Spakes, P. (1992) "National family policy: Sweden versus the United States," *Affilia*, 7 (2), summer, 44-60

Srivastava, A.K. (1985) "Social class and parent-child relationship in urban setting," *Eastern Anthropologist*, 38 (1), Jan-Mar, 19-32

Stark, E. and A.H. Flitcraft (1988) "Women and children at risk: A feminist perspective on child abuse," *International Journal of Health Services*, 18 (1), 97-118

Stasiulis, D. (1988) "Capitalism, democracy and the Canadian state," pp. 223-26 in D. Forcese and S. Richer (eds.), *Social Issues: Sociological Views of Canada*. Scarborough: Prentice-Hall Canada.

____(1990) "Theorizing Connections: Gender, Race, Ethnicity, and Class," pp. 269-305 in P. Li (ed.), *Race and Ethnic Relations in Canada*. Toronto: Oxford University Press.

Statistics Canada (1985) *Canada, The Provinces and the Territories: A Statistical Profile, Small Area Data Program*. (Catalogue No. 17-x-501) Ottawa: Supply and Services

—— (1987) *Current Demographic Analysis: Report on the Demographic Situation in Canada, 1986* (Catalogue No. 91-209E) Ottawa: Supply and Services

Steffenmeier, D., E. Allan and C. Streifel (1989) "Development and female crime: A cross-national test of alternative explanations," *Social Forces*, 68 (1), Sept, 262-283

Steil, J.M. and K. Weltman (1991) "Marital inequality: The importance of resources, personal attributes, and social norms on career valuing and the allocation of domestic responsibilities," *Sex Roles*, 24 (3-4), Feb, 161-179

Stephens, G. (1991) "Rap music's double-voiced discourse: A cross-roads for interracial communication," *Journal of Communication Inquiry*, 15 (2), summer, 70-91

Stevens, F., H. Philipsen and J. Diederiks (1992) "Organizational and professional predictors of physician satisfaction," *Organization Studies*, 13 (1), 35-49

Stevens, G. and E. Hoisington (1987) "Occupational prestige and the 1980 US labor force," *Social Science Research*, 16 (1), Mar, 74-105

Stolnitz, G.J. (1945) "The demographic transition," *Annals of the American Academy of Political and Social Science*, 237, Jan, 1-11

Stone, G. (1970) "The circumstances and situation of social status" pp. 250-59 in G. Stone and H. Faberman (eds.), *Social Psychology Through Symbolic Interaction*. Waltham, Mass.: Xerox College Publishing

Strang, D. (1990) "From dependency to sovereignty: An event history analysis of decolonization, 1870-1987," *American Sociological Review*, 55 (6), Dec, 846-860

Streeck, W. (1989) "Skills and the limits of neo-liberalism: The enterprise of the future as a place of learning," *Work, Employment and Society*, 3 (1), Mar, 89-104

Stunkel, K.R. (1991) "Technology and values in traditional China and the West," *Comparative Civilizations Review*, 24, spring, 58-75

Subotic, M. (1989) "The crisis of the authority of power and the power of authority," *Socioloski Pregled*, 23, 1-2, 65-71

Sumner, W.G. (1906) *Folkways*. New York: Ginn

Swaan, A. de (1989) "Jealousy as a class phenomenon: The petite bourgeoisie and social security," *International Sociology*, 4 (3), 259-271

Sydie, R. (1987) "Sociology and Gender," in M. Rosenberg, W. Shaffir, A. Turowetz and M. Weinfeld (eds.), *An Introduction to Sociology*. Toronto: Methuen

Taplin, I.M. (1989) "Segmentation and the organization of work in the Italian apparel industry," *Social Science Quarterly*, 70 (2), June, 408-424

____(1992) "Rising from the ashes: The deskilling debate and tobacco manufacturing," *Social Science Journal*, 29 (1), Jan, 87-106

Tarver, J.D. and H.M. Miller (1986) "Patterns of population growth in Africa," *African Studies*, 45 (1), 43-60

Tedeschi, E. (1988) "Symbolic strategies in a religious group," *Studi di Sociologia*, 26, 3-4, July-Sept, 437-447

Tenbruck, F.H. (1990) "The dream of a secular ecumene: The meaning and limits of policies of development," *Theory, Culture and Society*, 7 (2-3), June, 193-206

Tepperman, L. (1994) *Choices and Chances*, second edition. Toronto: Harcourt Brace Jovanovich.

Thio, A. (1983) *Deviant Behaviour*. Boston: Houghton Mifflin

Thomas, W.I. and D.S. Thomas (1928) *The Child in America*. New York: Alfred A. Knopf

Thomas, W. I. (1967) *The Unadjusted Girl*. New York: Harper and Row

Thrasher, F.M. (1937) *The Gang*. Chicago: University of Chicago Press

Touraine, A. (1988) "Modernity and cultural specificities," *International Social Science Journal*, 40, 4 (118), Nov, 443-457

—— (1990a) "Does French society still exist? The end of a national society," *Tocqueville Review*, 11, 143-171

—— (1990b) "The idea of revolution," *Theory, Culture and Society*, 7 (2-3), June, 121-141

—— (1992) "Beyond social movements?" *Theory, Culture and Society*, 9 (1), Feb, 125-145

Touraine, A. and K. McDonald (1991) "Can one still be on the Left?" *Thesis Eleven*, 28, 100-104

Trovato, F. (1988) "Mortality differentials in Canada, 1951-1971: French, British, and Indians," *Culture, Medicine and Psychiatry*, 12 (4), Dec, 459-477

Trovato, F. and G. Lauris (1989) "Marital status and mortality in Canada: 1951-1981," *Journal of Marriage and the Family*, 51 (4), Nov, 907-922

Tudge, J. (1982) "Lack of control and the development of incompetence," *Cornell Journal of Social Relations*, 16 (2), spring, 84-97

Turcotte, P. (1990). "Common-law unions: Nearly half a million in 1986," in C. Mckie and K. Thompson (eds.), *Canadian Social Trends*. Toronto: Thompson Educational Publishing, Inc.

Turner, J. H. (1986) "Toward a unified theory of ethnic antagonism: A preliminary synthesis of three macro models," *Sociological Forum*, 1 (3), summer, 403-427

Turner, R. and L.M. Killian (1987) *Collective Behaviour*, third edition, Englewood Cliffs, NJ: Prentice Hall

Tyree, A., M. Semyonov and V. Kraus (1987) "Which worm does the early bird get? Ethnic stratification in Israel," *Research in Social Stratification and Mobility*, 6, 239-256

Ujimoto, K.V. (1983) "Institutional controls and their impact on Japanese Canadian social relations, 1877-1977" in P.S. Li and B.S. Bolaria (eds.), *Racial Minorities in Multicultural Canada*. Toronto: Garamond Press

United Nations (1991) *The World's Women, 1970-1990: Trends and Statistics*. New York: United Nations Publications.

Urban and Rural Systems Associates (1975) Juvenile Diversion Demonstration Program. Final Report Evaluation Comprehensive Offender Program Effort (COPE), n.p.

Vallas, S.P. (1988) "New technology, job content, and worker alienation: A test of two rival perspectives," *Work and Occupations*, 15 (2), May, 148-178

Vannoy, D. (1991) "Social differentiation, contemporary marriage, and human development," *Journal of Family Issues*, 12 (3), Sept, 251-267

Vasary, I. (1989) "'The sin of Transdanubia': The one-child system in rural Hungary," *Continuity and Change*, 4 (3), Dec, 429-468

Vaughan, D. (1987) *Uncoupling: How Relationships Come Apart*. New York: Vintage

Veenhoven, R. (1984) *Conditions of Happiness*. Dordrecht, Holland: Reidel Publishing

Veevers, J.E. and E.M. Gee (1986) "Playing it safe: Accident mortality and gender roles," *Sociological Focus*, 19 (4), Oct, 349-360

Verbrugge, L.M. (1986) "Role burdens and physical health of women and men," *Women and Health*, 11 (1), spring, 47-77

Vigil, J.D. (1988) "Group processes and street identity: Adolescent Chicano gang members," *Ethos*, 16 (4) Dec, 421-445

von Glinow, M. (1988) *The New Professionals: Managing Today's High-Tech Employees*. Cambridge, Mass.: Ballinger Publishing Company

von Simson, O.R. de M. (1983) "Cultural changes, popular creativity and mass communication: The Brazilian carnival over the past two centuries," *Leisure Studies*, 2 (3), Sept, 317-326

Wagner, W., E. Kirchler and F. Clack (1990) "Male dominance, role segregation, and spouses' interdependence in conflict: A cross-cultural study," *Journal of Cross-Cultural Psychology*, 21 (1), Mar, 48-70

Wallerstein, I. (1986) "Societal development, or development of the World-system?" *International Sociology*, 1 (1), Mar, 3-17

Warhola, J.W. (1991) "The religious dimension of ethnic conflict in the Soviet Union," *International Journal of Politics*, Culture and Society, 5 (2), winter, 249-270

Watkins, S.C. (1993) "If all we knew about women was what we read in *Demography*, what would we know?" *Demography*, 30, 4, Nov, 551-577

Watkins, S.C. and J. Menken (1985) "Famines in historical perspective," *Population and Development Review*, 11 (4), Dec, 647-675

Webb, E.J. et al. (1966) *Unobtrusive Measures: Nonreactive Research in the Social Sciences*. Chicago: Rand McNally

Weber, M. (1946), *From Max Weber: Essays in Sociology*, trans. and edited by H.H. Gerth and C.W. Mills. New York: Oxford University Press.

—— (1958a) Class, status, party chapter 7 in H. Gerth and C.W. Mills (eds.), *From Max Weber: Essays in Sociology*, New York: Oxford University Press

(1958b) "Science as a vocation," Chapter 5 in H. Gerth and C.W. Mills (eds.), *From Max Weber: Essays in Sociology*, New York: Oxford University Press

____(1958c) "Bureaucracy" section 8 in H. Gerth and C.W. Mills (eds.), *From Max Weber: Essays in Sociology*. New York: Oxford University Press

____(1961) *General Economic History*. New York: Collier Books

____(1964) "The types of authority and imperative coordination" section 3 in T. Parsons (ed.), *The Theory of Social and Economic Organization*. New York: Free Press

____ (1974) *The Protestant Ethic and the Spirit of Capitalism*. London: George Allen and Unwin

Webster, J. (1991) "Advanced manufacturing technologies: Work organisation and social relations crystallised," *Sociological Review Monograph*, 38, 192-222

Weikart, D.P. (1989) "Early childhood education and primary prevention," *Prevention in Human Services*, 6 (2), 285-306

Weinstein, B. (1982) "Noah Webster and the diffusion of linguistic innovations for political purposes," *International Journal of the Sociology of Language*, 38, 85-108

Wenestam, C. G. and H. Wass (1987) "Swedish and U.S. children's thinking about death: A qualitative study and cross-cultural comparison," *Death Studies*, 11 (2), 99-121

Wexler, M.N. (1992) "Psycho-social factors in shared family delusions ('folie a famille')," *International Journal of Sociology of the Family*, 22 (1), spring, 161-173

White, H.C. and C.A. White (1965) *Canvases and Careers: Institutional Change in the French Painting World*. New York: Wiley

Whyte, W.F. (1961) *Street Corner Society*. Chicago: University of Chicago Press

Willis, P. (1977) *Learning to Labour: How Working Class Kids Get Working Class Jobs*. London: Saxon House

Wilson, K.L. and J.P. Boldizar (1990) "Gender segregation in higher education: Effects of aspirations, mathematics achievement, and income," *Sociology of Education*, 63 (1), Jan, 62-74

Wilson, S.J. (1977) "The changing image of women in Canadian mass circulating magazines" *Atlantis* 2 (2), 33-44

—— *Women, Family and the Economy*, second ed. Toronto : McGraw-Hill Ryerson. 1988.

Wilson, W.J. (1984) "The black underclass," *Wilson Quarterly*, Spring, 88-99.

Wilson, W.J. (1987) *The Truly Disadvantaged: The Inner City, The Underclass and Public Policy*. Chicago: University of Chicago Press

Winkel, F.W. (1990) "Crime reporting in newspapers: An explanatory study of the effects of ethnic references in crime news," *Social Behaviour*, 5 (2), June, 87-101

Wolanski, N. (1989) "Human life and culture: Dynamic components of ecosystems," *Zygon*, 24 (4), Dec, 401-427

Wood, S. (1989) "The Japanese management model," *Work and Occupations*, 16 (4), Nov, 446-460

Woodcock, G. (1970) *Canada and the Canadians*. Toronto: Macmillan of Canada

Wotherspoon, T. (1991) "Indian control or controlling Indians? Barriers to the occupational and educational advancement of Canada's indigenous population," pp. 249-272 in T. Wotherspoon (ed.), *Hitting the Books: The Politics of Educational Retrenchment* Toronto: Garamond Press.

Wright, E.O. (1985) *Classes*. London: Verso

Wrong, D. (1961) "The oversocialized conception of man in modern sociology," *American Sociological Review*, 26 (April), 183-193

Yin, R.K. (1984) *Case Study Research: Design and Methods*. Beverly Hills, CA: Sage Publications

Young, L. W. (1988) "Economic development and employment: Agroindustrialization in Mexico's El Bajio," *Journal of Economic Issues*, 22 (2), June, 389-396

Zirker, D. (1986) "Civilianization and authoritarian nationalism in Brazil: Idological opposition within a military dictatorship," *Journal of Political and Military Sociology*, 14, 2, fall, 263-276

—— (1991) "The civil-military mediators in post-1985 Brazil," *Journal of Political and Military Sociology*, 19, 1, summer, 47-73

Index